Ocean
and
Coastal
Law

Richard G. Hildreth
*University
of Oregon*

Ralph W. Johnson
*University
of Washington*

PRENTICE-HALL, INC.,
Englewood Cliffs, New Jersey 07632

Library of Congress Cataloging in Publication Data

Main entry under title:
  Ocean and coastal law.

  Includes bibliographies and index.
    1.–Coastal zone management—Law and legislation—
United States. 2.–Territorial waters—United States.
3.–Marine mineral resources—Law and legislation—
United States. 4.–Fishery law and legislation—United
States. I.–Hildreth, Richard G. II.–Johnson, Ralph Whitney (date).
KF5627.027–1982   346.7304'691   82-10221
ISBN 0-13-629204-6   347.3064691   AACR2

Editorial/production supervision
by Ellen W. Caughey and Paula Martinac
Interior design by Ellen W. Caughey
Cover design by Ray Lundgren
Manufacturing buyer: John Hall

Printed in the United States of America

10 9 8 7 6 5 4 3 2 1

ISBN 0-13-629204-6

Prentice-Hall International, Inc., *London*
Prentice-Hall of Australia Pty. Limited, *Sydney*
Prentice-Hall Canada, *Toronto*
Prentice-Hall of India Private Limited, *New Delhi*
Prentice-Hall of Japan, Inc., *Tokyo*
Prentice-Hall of Southeast Asia Pte. Ltd., *Singapore*
Whitehall Books Limited, *Wellington, New Zealand*

To My Parents with Gratitude

R. G. H.

To Anne

R. W. J.

Summary
Contents

1
Introduction 1

2
Ownership and Boundaries
in the Coastal Zone 23

3
State Common Law and the Coastal Zone 51

Contents

3
State Common Law and the Coastal Zone 51

6
Nonliving Resource Management 240

7
Oil Spills 288

8
Disposal of Wastes in the Ocean   339

9
Comprehensive Ocean Management   353

Preface

In the past few years the nation's coastal zone has received major legislative and judicial attention at both the federal and state levels. Many coastal states now have management "programs" for their coastal areas. These programs, combined with the large and still expanding body of federal legislation and regulations, have created a new and dynamic field of law. The quantity and uniqueness of this new body of law reflects the increasing importance of the coastal zone for human habitation, transportation, industrial and energy facility siting, living and nonliving resource exploitation, and recreation. Ocean and coastal law is thus becoming a permanent fixture in the legal landscape.

The subject of ocean and coastal law is not presently covered by other standard law school courses; land use planning, water law, and public land law are usually offered. Land use planning courses are oriented typically toward urban land use management problems. Water law courses usually concentrate on the management of freshwater resources. Public land law is ordinarily concerned with federal management of the government's huge upland holdings throughout the West. None of these courses deals with the special resource management problems posed in the coastal zone.

Until recently the coastal zone and its special needs were largely overlooked. As a nation we tended to underestimate the importance of this area; our eyes, minds, and legal regimes were fixed either toward the landmass or the high seas. It was as if the legal and legislative professions stood on the coast with blinders on, looking either inland, or out to sea, never down the coastline. This two-dimensional view tended to ignore the intimate interrelationship of the land and the sea. Today this interrelationship is rapidly becoming the subject of an increasingly comprehensive legal regime.

One of the major problems confronted in examining the coastal zone is the conflicting and duplicative jurisdictional pattern. Agencies at many different levels of government claim authority to control activities in the coastal zone without any real understanding or concern of the impact of their actions on others, or on the overall use or management of the area. Thus, until recently, management was so piecemeal as to be almost the perfect antithesis of "coordinated" or "comprehensive." The end result often was nonmanagement and noncontrol of many important activities in the coastal zone.

Ocean and Coastal Law is concerned with three geographic areas: (1) uplands affected by the sea; (2) coastal waters and the seabed underlying the territorial sea (presently 3 miles); and (3) offshore waters and resources outside the territorial sea to the extent of national jurisdiction, e.g., to the edge of the continental shelf and the 200-mile exclusive fisheries zone. The text has pulled together a welter of new cases, statutes, and regulations governing resource ownership, management, and use in these three areas and constitutes the first attempt to organize this material into comprehensible form.

Several informal editions of the book have been used for the past 5 years for courses at the University of Washington, University of Oregon, and other law schools. Out of this teaching experience the organizational format used in the text has evolved. The book first discusses the problems posed by earlier nonmanagement and the gradual public awakening to the need for a comprehensive legal regime for the coastal zone. We then move to questions of ownership and boundaries of the coastal zone. The state common law of the coastal zone is then covered because this body of law immediately preceded and highlighted the need for more comprehensive management of the coastal zone. Chapters 4 through 10 direct attention to the seaward aspects of ocean and coastal law, dealing with state–federal relations in offshore waters, management of living and nonliving resources offshore, the special problems of oil spills and waste disposal in the ocean, and regulation of dredging and filling in coastal waterways and wetlands. Chapters 11 and 12 cover the Federal Coastal Zone Management Act and several illustrative state coastal zone management programs.

For brevity's sake, only those footnotes and citations deemed significant remain in the cases and materials quoted with permission. Omissions from the original source other than footnotes or citations are indicated by ellipses.

ACKNOWLEDGMENTS

This book was supported in part by grants from the National Oceanographic and Atmospheric Administration under Sea Grant No. 04-7-158-44021 and NA 79-AA-D-00-106.

The following dedicated research assistants contributed significantly to the creation of this book: Michele C. Coyle, Kevin Davis, Richard A. Du Bey, John Dunnigan, John Epting, Sid Farcy, Ken Johansen, Gary Kahn, Sandy Landress, Harry Latto, Susan Lupton, John W. Milne, Richard Parrish, John Penfield, Dave Peters, Warren Westfall, Mark Wilk, Wilmar Williamson, and Alex Wypyszinski.

Professor Jon Jacobson, co-director of the University of Oregon Ocean and Coastal Law Center, provided support in a variety of useful ways. Thanks also are due to Andrea Coffman, Ocean and Coastal Law Center librarian.

Charles Roe, assistant attorney general for the State of Washington, co-authored two earlier versions with Professor Johnson, and Richard J. Goldsmith, then assistant to the director of the Pacific Marine Fisheries Commission, co-authored *Coastal Zone Law and Policy* (University of Washington Press, 1977), which was typed by Joyce Weinberger.

The manuscript for this book was typed and retyped ad infinitum by Marilynn Howard of the University of Oregon Ocean and Coastal Law Center, without whose dedicated efforts the book would never have been produced.

RICHARD G. HILDRETH
RALPH W. JOHNSON

Table of Cases

The principal cases are set in boldface italic type. Cases cited or discussed are set in italic type. All references are to page numbers in the text.

Introduction

SECTION A: OVERVIEW

EPTING & LAIST, "PERSPECTIVES ON AN OCEAN MANAGEMENT SYSTEM," 7 Ocean Development and International Law Journal 257 (1979)

The past decade has seen a truly startling about-face in the nation's perceptions of and relationships with the ocean. All segments of our society—public and private alike—have begun to recognize the ocean's vast resource potential. Nowhere is this more evident than in recent governmental initiatives to utilize and protect the nation's public ocean resources which stretch from the shorelines out to and beyond the continental shelf. In the course of this rapid change in attitude, the federal government—and to a lesser degree, coastal states—have moved through two distinct phases in their approach to the oceans and are on the verge of a third.

The first phase, leading up to the late 1960s, was characterized by a growing national recognition of the significance of our ocean and nearshore resources. Principally an outgrowth of marine research and scientific investigations, this recognition culminated in a call for action to protect the public's interest in these resources. In the second phase, extending from 1969 through 1977, a governmental response to that call for action was initiated. Congress considered and passed a variety of laws which addressed the allocation of specific marine resources and control over specific marine uses. One of the most significant single actions during this phase was the federal government's unilateral extension of its authority over fishery resources from 12 to 200 miles.

From this initial surge of single resource- or use-based legislation, a third phase now appears to be slowly evolving: the development of a more cohesive and integrated approach to national ocean policies, and specifically to the allocation of ocean resources. Often referred to as "ocean management," this concept is now undergoing investigations to define both its scope and possible future form. While still very much in the drafting stages, this concept could have far-reaching implications for the government's role and organization in the marine environment, particularly in establishing policy direction toward rationalizing and making cohesive the rather distinctive marine regulatory system that has evolved in the past ten years.

. . . .

The large number of uses illustrated in Table 1-1 (pages 4–5) are in competition for the coastal ocean's finite space and resources. Since the conflicts vary in intensity and occur in different combinations, the development of an ocean management system must avoid establishing absolute parameters. Rather, the inherent variability in the ocean and its resources should be recognized.

. . . .

State Marine Management Programs

One area of concern to ocean management that has not received the attention it deserves is an assessment of the current and potential state roles in an ocean management system.

. . . .

LAIST & EPTING, "THE GROWING NEED FOR FEDERAL–STATE COOPERATION IN MANAGING THE SEA," 6 Coastal Zone Management Journal 1, 3–5 (1979)

. . . Emphasizing the importance of the state's role in marine management is particularly crucial . . . for several reasons. First, although the federal government has undisputed authority over resources beyond the state jurisdictional limit (3 miles seaward of the baseline of the territorial sea except for the Gulf coasts of Florida and Texas where the distance is approximately 10.5 miles), state authorities within this perimeter can exert a significant impact on overall ocean management objectives. The following factors underscore the need for federal programs to provide state entities with a vital role in any (including the present) national ocean management system:

1. The resources within three miles of the coast represent a major segment of the nation's overall ocean resources;

2. The nature of marine ecosystems inseparably links the values and conditions of estuarine and nearshore environments with those of offshore ocean environments. As a result, the condition and value of state waters can be adversely affected by impacts to ocean waters well beyond three miles (and vice versa);

3. The coastal zone, including state waters out to three miles, represents a conduit and departure point for man's offshore activities and pollution; and

4. The states have broad federal mandates under the Submerged Lands Act and the Coastal Zone Management Act and related statutes to plan for and manage ocean resources within state jurisdiction.

On the other side of the coin, there is also ample justification for state entities to actively push for a more substantial role in federal ocean programs. The most obvious and important reason is simply to provide state input into decisions that will affect the environmental quality and economy of coastal states. Nowhere has this need for state involvement in federal ocean management decisions been more clearly demonstrated than with OCS oil and gas leasing.

The short shrift given state interests in OCS leasing decisions in 1974–75 was abruptly and justifiably brought to federal government attention by coastal state officials. Here, as with other decisions such as those concerning ocean mining, fisheries, and construction of offshore facilities, the coastal states will most likely shoulder the brunt of adverse impacts related to the development of onshore staging and operations areas necessary to develop offshore resources. Similarly, although these resources should benefit the nation as a whole, the greatest economic and social benefits will probably pass to the coastal states where resources not only will be landed but also most likely processed and transported, and possibly consumed. The social, economic, and environmental effects of ocean resource decisions on coastal states thus strongly support a more aggressive yet also more organized coastal state posture with respect to federal ocean resource development/allocation decisions.

. . . .

As noted, another reason for increased state involvement is the opportunity to coordinate federal and state research activities, particularly in terms of data collection and assimilation, and the possible joint funding of demonstration projects. The federal marine management programs also represent a collective pool of experience in marine issues which can be transferred to the states, and vice versa.

. . . .

SECTION B: OCEAN AND COASTAL RESOURCES

Ecological Concepts

J. CLARK, COASTAL ECOSYSTEMS 1–4, 59–82 (1974)

The Physical Setting

Each coastal ecosystem operates within the confines of a particular basin (or basins) formed by the geologic structure of the coast—a straight shoreline, a deep rocky fiord, a tidal river, or a shallow marshy embayment. Similarly, the

Ocean Uses and Activities

Ocean Resources	Commercial Fishing	Sports Fishing	Marine Recreation/Boating	OCS Oil and Gas Development	Conservation/Protection	Deep Water Ports	Deep Draft Onshore Ports	Shipping/Marine Transport
Marine mammals	D/I		D	I	D	I		
Stocks of commercial fish	D/I	D		I	D			
Stocks of sports fish	I	D	D	I	D			
Oil and gas reserves				D				
Deposits of sand, gravel, and shell	I							
Aesthetic quality		D	D	I		I	I	
Clean water	D	D	D	I	D	I	I	I
Open space/space for development	D	D	D			D	D	D
Distance from human populations			D			D	D	
Space for and dispersal of human wastes								
Special geologic formations					D			
Heat sink/cooling water								
Freshwater aquifers				I	D			
Submerged human artifacts	I		D/I	I				
Marine habitats/ecosystems/communities	D	D	D	I	D	D	D	
Shipping lanes						D	D	D
Air quality	I		D	I			I	

D, Use/Activity is Dependent on Resource.
I, Use/Activity may Adversely Impact Resource.

Marine Cables	LNG Transport & Facilities	Deep Seabed Mining	Sand, Gravel, and Shell Mining	Offshore Power Plants	Industries Requiring Salt Water for Cooling	Artificial Islands and Reefs	Desalinization/Fresh Water	Ocean Thermal Energy Conversion/Other Energy Sources	Ocean Dumping/Waste Disposal	Ocean Discharges	Ocean Incineration	Dredging	Defense Operations	Research and Education	Mariculture	Marine Sanctuaries	Nuclear Waste Disposal
										I		I		D		D	
			I	I			I	I		I		I		D	D	D	
			I	I				I		I		I		D	D	D	
										D		D		D			
		D										D		D			I
			I	I	I			I		I	I	I	I	D		D	
	I	I	I	I			D	I		I	I	I		D	D	D	I
D	D		D								D		D			I	
			D						D	D	D		D				D
			D	D			D	D	D	D	D			D	D	I	
		D	D				D					I		D		D	D
			D	D			D							D	D		
							D					I		D			I
I		I	I			I		I		I		I		D		D	
I		I	I	I	I		D/I	I		I	I	I		D	I	D	I
	D							D				D	I				
	I		I	I							I			D			

shoreland section of the ecosystem operates within the topographic confines of the watershed. The characteristics of the emergent and submergent counterparts—shorelands and basin bottom—are geologically related, as fixed by the general shape, size and depth of coastal water bodies. The enduring geologic characteristics are themselves modified somewhat by the dynamic forces of water flow, waves and wind, erosion and sedimentation, and by the effects of vegetation.

A wide continental shelf is generally associated with extensive low-lying shorelands and a wide band of wetlands next to the coast, while a narrow shelf is associated with steep or mountainous shorelands. These associations and their characteristic estuarine systems differ greatly from one coastal region to another.

Northern shores once covered by ice—New England, Puget Sound, and southeast Alaska—are sharply sculptured with generally steep shorelines and have deep, heavily indented embayments, islands, steep rocky shores and irregular bottom topography. These characteristics generally extend to unglaciated parts of the Pacific Coast.

The parts of the Atlantic and Gulf coasts that were unaffected by glaciation consist of relatively flat terrain in which wide coastal embayments and marshes are the predominant features. These are coasts formed primarily of sediments eroded from ancient mountains, and along which embayments and marshes form traps for sediments the rivers bring down to the sea. Characterized by great expanses of shallow water and aquatic vegetation, these coasts have extensive sand dunes, sandy ocean beachfront, and well developed estuaries behind them.

The constant input of sediments from erosion tends to fill up the estuary basin. In time, deltas may be formed, stretching out into the sea. The highest concentrations of sediment carried by estuarine waters are found in the inner, low-salinity, portion. Here, salt water meets fresh, coalescing river-borne silts into larger, heavier, particles which settle out as the estuary broadens and the flow slackens. . . .

The geologic form of the water basin controls the coastal ecosystem largely through secondary effects; that is, by influencing such factors as currents, temperature, vegetation, and *flushing rate* (the rate of replacement of water in the basin). For example, the structure of a typical estuary sets up a pattern of currents which retains nutrients—a condition favorable to the development of a rich and varied community of life.

The effect on a coastal water ecosystem of any particular environmental stress depends partly, sometimes largely, on the geologic form of the ecosystem basin and the ecologic characteristics induced by that form. Furthermore, subsystems of each ecosystem may be expected to react differently to any particular disturbance. . . .

The coastal waters of the United States may be conveniently divided into large biogeographical regions. These regions vary in such factors as: climatic condition, the oceanographic characteristics of the seas that border them, and in the way they are influenced by the type of land mass that lies behind them. Of climatic variables, temperature is the primary determinant of the distribution of species of plants and animals throughout the coastal zone. Other significant climatic factors are the amount and pattern of precipitation, of wind, and of sunlight. Large-scale oceanic forces that influence coastal ecosystems are prevailing wind and waves, permanent coastal currents, persistent coastal upwellings, massive oceanic warm water currents, and other factors that vary from place to place along the coast. Most climatic and oceanic forces are beyond significant human control. But man can significantly control the ways in which land influences coastal ecosystems.

. . . .

The essential qualities of a coastal ecosystem can be segregated into three categories—features, processes and characteristics. The *features* are the fixed physical objects, such as coral reefs, mud flats or grass beds. *Processes* are the driving forces of the system; such as, sunlight, water flow or nutrient recycling. *Characteristics* are the variable qualities that give each ecosystem distinctiveness, such as the species mix, the temperature or chemical content of the water. Analysis of these factors is useful in evaluation of ecosystems providing the procedure is not so complex as to obstruct its basic purpose—the design and execution of an effective management program. A system of evaluation and classification is required that can simplify the nearly limitless complexities of nature.

Standard ecologic classification does not readily provide a useful management framework. One can, however, work with ecologic concepts and generally known relationships to devise a practicable system—one that recognizes differences in capability for use imposed by variations in landscape and waterscape and relates these to specific management options and actions.

. . . .

Vital Areas

There are many components of the coastal ecosystem that are of such importance to certain species or to the functioning of the entire ecosystem as to require that they be classified as *vital areas* and provided (1) immunity from virtually all types of use and (2) protection from pollution and other external sources of disturbance. The protective program will involve both control of water use within the boundaries and abatement of pollution of water that flows across the boundaries from outside.

A *vital area* most often would be a *fixed* ecosystem feature of tangible physical character, such as a submerged oyster bed or a cordgrass marsh. Fixed *vital areas* are readily located, surveyed and mapped, and remain constant in location. However, there are many *transient* features of the water mass which have specific attributes but not fixed boundaries that need a high degree of protection. An example of a transient *vital area* is the salinity controlled feeding area for young white perch, which may shift up or down the estuary 10 miles or more in response to river inflow (the zooplankton food of the perch lives within a restricted salinity).

Transient *vital areas* change location but their boundaries shift between known limits and therefore it is possible to map out bounds which normally will encompass the full area, say 95 percent of the time. Such limits will be suitable for management purposes.

Fixed *vital areas* are readily evaluated, surveyed and mapped, and will remain virtually constant in location. They should not be dug or dredged out, filled over, or otherwise obliterated or altered.

. . . .

Coral Reefs

Coral is a living organism. As coral colonies grow they build reefs which are not only uniquely rich and beautiful but also highly sensitive to environmental disturbances. A much higher degree of protection than has been practiced in the past is necessary to preserve these *vital areas*. Sediment discharge from erosion, sewage pollution, chemical pollution and urban runoff all must be strictly controlled where reefs are significantly influenced by land drainage. Dredging in the vicinity of reefs may be particularly harmful because of the high incidence of silt fallout and sunlight screening caused by turbidity.

. . . .

Kelpbeds

Kelpbeds are an especially important component of certain coastal ecosystems, especially those of the partially sheltered waters off rocky Pacific shores. Kelp grows best in relatively cool waters with rich bottoms and depths of less than 100 feet. Kelp provides food and favorable habitat for many fishes, as well as sheltered vital nursery areas for their young. Stands of kelp are a favored haunt of sea otters and other marine mammals. The kelpbed breaks the force of the sea and provides a strip of quieter water between it and the shore, an effect which benefits many additional forms of shorelife.

Management plans should include protection of kelp against significant environmental disturbances. Sewage discharges may be adverse to kelp because the water enrichment favors the food chain of sea urchins and they in turn eat the kelp. Other potential dangers are chemical and thermal pollution and damage from boat propellers. Whether the harvest of kelp to produce algin and other saleable compounds should be allowed is a matter of unsettled controversy in California.

Shellfish Beds

Clams, oysters, and other valuable shellfish are not spread evenly over the bottom of estuaries but rather they are to be found concentrated in certain flats, banks, bars or reefs. These shellfish beds are *vital areas* that are rather easily identified and delineated in planning surveys.

Shellfish are notorious for filtering out of the water such harmful substances as bacteria, pesticides and toxic metals and concentrating them in their tissues, thus exposing the animals or people that eat them to dangerous concentrations. For this reason, millions of acres of estuarine shellfish beds have been closed to harvesting. A better solution than closing beds is to control the sources of pollution. This will not only make the shellfish safe, but maintain the natural balance of the ecosystem.

. . . .

Grass Beds

Beds of submerged marine grasses are essential elements of the estuarine ecosystem, particularly in systems where marshes are reduced or absent. They often provide a substantial amount of the primary productivity and of nursery ground habitat available in estuarine waters.

. . . .

Drainageways

Drainageways throughout the shorelands and coastal watersheds deliver runoff waters directly to the coastal ecosystem and therefore are a vital component. It is essential that they remain unaltered and protected in order to: (1) properly regulate the rate of runoff flow, (2) cleanse the runoff water by settling out suspended matter and (3) enable vegetative takeup of dissolved contaminants. All floodways, sloughs, swales or other drainageways throughout the coastal watershed should be identified and designated for preservation as *vital areas*, since their disruption is inimical to the quality of the estuarine ecosystem.

. . . .

Breeding Areas

Many species which spread out for feeding concentrate in specifically defined estuarine areas for spawning. Often these areas are so limited in size that a major disturbance could lead to elimination of much of the spawning and to the virtual demise of the stock breeding there. It is necessary to conduct a specific survey to identify and locate spawning areas and to designate the critical ones as *vital areas*.

Breeding places vary from species to species. For example, salmon normally spawn only in specific shallow areas far up certain fresh water streams where the right gravels are present for the deposit of eggs. On the other hand, striped bass cast their eggs into the water of tidal rivers above the salt front so that the tiny hatchlings drift down into brackish estuarine areas. Winter flounder spawn mostly in deeper areas of the brackish upper ends of certain estuaries.

Some important species of waterfowl (e.g., mallards and wood duck) and most wading birds also breed in limited coastal locations. These areas are to be surveyed and set aside as *vital areas* with generous surrounding buffer strips to insulate them from the disturbances of human development and habitation.

Many seabird species breed in limited mainland *rookeries* or on isolated coastal islands. Seals also haul out for breeding at special coastal or island rookeries. All significant rookeries should be preserved intact and protected as *vital areas*.

It is common for young stages of coastal fish species to be planktonic; that is, to remain suspended and to drift with the currents for an extended period of time. In estuaries, this is a vulnerable stage of life and where there are special areas of concentrated drift of young, larval drift areas should be identified and provided status as *vital areas* so they may be protected.

. . . .

Nursery Areas

The young of many coastal species settle into special areas called *nursery areas* when they are several weeks old. These are areas where the young creatures prosper because the right food is available, where predators are in the least abundance and where other conditions are most suitable for their survival. These precious nurseries are to be identified and mapped out as *vital areas* requiring a maximum of protection from environmental disturbance. They may or may not include within them other types of *vital areas*, such as marshes or tide flats. They may overlap with transient *vital areas* such as breeding areas or migration pathways.

. . . .

Estuarine Systems

The term *estuary* has a variety of definitions but as we use it here: *An estuary is any confined coastal water body with an open connection to the sea and a measurable quantity of salt in its waters.* We use this definition of estuary in preference to one which includes only those enclosed water bodies that receive a *significant* fresh water input. This simpler definition includes all enclosed coastal waters and avoids the problem of setting lagoons aside from estuaries because of a particular rate of inflow from the land. Where it is necessary to make the distinction, lagoons can be separately considered as one of many types of estuary. Consequently, our definition agrees with that of E. P. Odum (as modified from D. W. Pritchard): ". . . a semi-enclosed coastal body of water which has a free connection to the sea; it is thus strongly affected by tidal action, and within it sea water is mixed (and usually measurably diluted) with fresh water from land drainage."

When we use the term "confined" to describe one property of the estuary we recognize that at some point even the most landlocked estuary has an opening and thus might be technically termed partially confined or semi-enclosed. Where, for management purposes, one might wish to use a rule of thumb to distinguish between estuarine and open ocean areas based upon the degree of confinement, we suggest the following: *A confined coastal waterbody, or estuary, is one that has a shoreline length in excess of three times the width of its outlet to the sea.*

The exceptional natural value of the estuarine type of ecosystem derives from a beneficial combination of physical properties that separately or in combination perform such functions as those listed below:

1. *Confinement:* Provides shelter which protects the estuary from wave action and allows plants to root, clams to set and permits retention of suspended life and nutrients.

2. *Depth:* Allows light to penetrate to plants on the bottom; fosters growth of marsh plants and tideflat biota; discourages oceanic predators which avoid shallow waters.

3. *Salinity:* Fresh water flow may create a distinct surface layer over a saltier, heavier, bottom layer, thus inducing beneficial stratified flow; fresh water dilution deters oceanic predators and encourages estuarine forms.

4. *Circulation:* Sets up a beneficial system of transport for suspended life, when stratified, such that the bottom layer flows in and the surface layer flows out; enhances flushing; retains organisms in favorable habitats through behavior adaptations.

5. *Tide:* Tidal energy provides an important driving force; tidal flow transports nutrients and suspended life, dilutes and flushes wastes; tidal rhythm acts as an important regulator of feeding, breeding, and other functions.

6. *Nutrient storage:* Trapping mechanisms store nutrients within estuary; marsh and grass beds store nutrients for slow release as detritus; richness induces high accumulation of available nutrients in animal tissue.

SECTION C: USE OF OCEAN AND COASTAL RESOURCES

J. CLARK, COASTAL ECOSYSTEMS 37, 96 (1974)

Development activity anywhere in coastal areas—watersheds, floodplains, wetlands, tidelands or water basins—is a potential source of ecologic damage to the coastal waters ecosystem. . . .

Often the same qualities that make a coastal ecosystem so valuable also make it vulnerable to damage from pollution and other environmental disturbance. This is particularly true for estuarine ecosystems. Estuaries, surrounded by land on all sides, are easily accessible for urban or industrial development and for water-related human uses. . . .

There are special risks attached to development in any shorelands within reach of coastal storm or flood tides. On the open coast, the risks are mostly involved with the direct onslaught of storm-driven waves. . . . In the estuaries, risks are involved with storm-induced high waters.

The ocean coast is in a dynamic equilibrium between two factors: (1) the erosive forces of storm winds and waves and (2) the restorative powers of prevailing geologic, oceanic, and meteorological actions. . . . In response to the interplay of these forces, the whole system of beaches, barrier islands and dunes shifts more or less continuously.

Clearly, this is a risky place to maintain habitation. The costs in loss of property and life have been high for many beachfronts. Furthermore, the enormous private and public investments to stabilize and safeguard these inhabited beaches with structures have not often been rewarded with success. High energy natural processes undermine the bulkheads, erode sand from behind the groins, and throw damaging breakers over the bulwarks.

A related function of dunes is to serve as a storage area for sand to replace that eroded by waves or torn away by storms and thus to provide long-term stability to the shorefront. . . . Because dune formations are fragile, activities of man that cause even slight alterations to them may lead to significant disruptions. Once the barrier dune is weakened, its valuable functions are impaired and it no longer serves its unique protective role.

Although estuarine areas do not receive the wave pounding that ocean beaches do, they often suffer persistent erosion, particularly those characterized by a soil-bank front. Eroding shores must be bulkheaded or else the buildings must be set back a considerable distance from the bank edge. A setback allows the area between the bank and the building to be left as a naturally vegetated *buffer area* for cleansing of runoff waters and for scenic purposes. Where bulkheads are required and feasible they should be built behind the tideland or wetland vegetation.

Recreation

NATURAL RESOURCES DEFENSE COUNCIL, WHO'S MINDING THE SHORE? 23–24 (1976)

Recreation is the most direct use that most of us make of the coastal zone. The average time spent per capita in recreation on the coast is 10 days per year. Much of this time is spent vacationing on the sandy beaches of Florida or southern California, or the coastal headlands of Oregon, as examples. Sport fishing, another major form of coastal recreation, attracts over 9.5 million salt water anglers annually, and amounts to a billion-dollar-a-year business. Hunting, surfing, boating, skindiving, and nature studies are other popular coastal activities.

But the alarming fact is that while the demand for public recreation has been increasing, the opportunities have been declining. Only two per cent of the coastline is now available for public recreation and many of the finest and most accessible areas are rapidly being walled off by private development. Recreational uses should be a high priority of concern in the planning process. States should be urged to consider the acquisition of property, developer exactions, and other techniques for protecting and enhancing public recreational opportunities.

At the same time, management programs should recognize that excessive recreational use may damage certain fragile coastal resources. The organisms in tidepools may be depleted by collectors, or fish and wildlife populations may suffer from excessive fishing and hunting. Marshes and dunes may be damaged by too much foot traffic. The management program should tailor recreational use to the carrying capacity of the area.

Finally, certain types of recreational uses may unduly limit the variety of recreational experiences or the people who can enjoy them. Large-scale beach front hotel or condominium developments may limit access to a privileged few in an area which should be available to all and for a variety of uses.

Commercial Fishing

NATURAL RESOURCES DEFENSE COUNCIL, WHO'S MINDING THE SHORE? 25 (1976)

Commercial fishing is a billion-dollar-a-year business. The harvesting, processing, and marketing of coastal fish is a major economic activity, particularly in certain regions of the country. The shrimp industry is a major component of the coastal economies of the South Atlantic and Gulf states; oysters and clams are important to the Chesapeake Bay region; and salmon is of critical importance to the Pacific Coast. The harvest of menhaden, a fish used extensively for animal feed and industrial purposes, has made major contributions to the Chesapeake Bay, Atlantic, and Gulf regions. All of these fish species are in some way linked to coastal waters.

Disruption of the natural ecosystems by the filling of wetlands or pollution of coastal waters can directly threaten fisheries. For example, clams and oysters feed by filtering water through their bodies. Bacteria, pesticides, and toxic metals present in coastal waters are trapped and concentrated in their tissues; and people or animals who eat them can be exposed to dangerous concentrations of harmful substances. Because of pollution, millions of acres of estuarine shellfish beds have been closed to harvesting. If management programs adequately control pollution discharges, protect vital areas like breeding and nursery grounds, and prevent over-fishing, this acreage can be returned to production, and many species now dwindling in numbers can rebound to their former abundance.

Aquaculture

NATIONAL RESEARCH COUNCIL, AQUACULTURE IN THE UNITED STATES: CONSTRAINTS AND OPPORTUNITIES 9–11 (1978)

Aquaculture in the United States began over one hundred years ago, with salmon release programs designed to enhance natural supplies. The present high level of enthusiasm for fish farming is more recent, having begun several decades ago. This interest was stimulated by a potential for increased food, income, and recreation. Although economic profit has been the strongest stimulus to date, the need for food may, in the future, become the principal motivation for development of aquaculture. In contrast with agriculture, aquaculture is based on limited and relatively recent efforts to apply science to increase production efficiency.

Total worldwide aquaculture production amounted to about 6 million metric tons (mmt) in 1975. Of this amount, finfish represented about 66 percent, shellfish represented about 16.5 percent, and aquatic plants about 17.5 percent. Aquaculture production amounted to about 10 percent of total world fish production.

In some parts of the world, aquaculture production contributes significantly to human protein consumption. The greatest growth of aquaculture has occurred in countries with high levels of technology and risk capital, rather than in poor and protein-short nations. In Japan, production increased from 110,000 metric tons (mt) in 1971 to 500,000 mt in 1975; Israel obtains just under half of her finfish from culture, an amount that totalled 10,330 mt in 1974. These foreign achievements, and a series of laboratory-level and field successes in U.S. government and academic institutions, have increased enthusiasm for commercial aquaculture. Ocean ranching has become an important industry in Japan and in the U.S.S.R., having grown at an average annual rate of 7.3 percent in the last 20 years. These two countries combined released approximately 2 billion juvenile Pacific salmon from hatcheries in 1976. This represents a fourfold increase in the number of juvenile salmon released over the last 20 years and a potential harvest of about 40 million adult salmon by 1980.

Of the total world aquaculture production of 6 mmt in 1975, U.S. production amounted to only 65,000 mt. We estimate that world aquaculture production may reach 50 mmt by the year 2000. U.S. production may be over 250,000 mt by 1985 and, with proper support, could reach 1 mmt by the year 2000. U.S. production has not increased in recent years. This rate of development is slower than had been generally expected and has led to disappointment in aquaculture's contribution to U.S. food production.

Non-scientific factors are generally more responsible for this slow development than a lack of technical information. Nonetheless, research has concentrated on solutions to scientific problems, to the neglect of what now appear to be the most immediate problems—institutional constraints.

Although aquaculture for most species within the United States has not developed beyond the research stages, substantial progress has been made in several important sectors of commercial aquaculture, including the development of profitable production systems for trout, catfish, crayfish, baitfish, salmon, oysters, and ornamental fish such as goldfish.

Warm-water finfish culture is a significant use of the land and water resources in Alabama, Arkansas, Florida, Georgia, Louisiana, Mississippi, North Carolina, Oklahoma, South Carolina, Tennessee, and Texas. Isolated water resources such as geothermals in Idaho and Colorado permit culture of warm-water species in zones traditionally growing only cold-water fish. Products from these areas are sold to truckers who transport them live to distant markets, local fishing lakes, and processors. Fish produced with public money at public or private facilities are used for research, for supplementing natural populations, and for stocking public sport fishing waters. Channel catfish and bait minnows are the principal crops, but buffalofish, carp, tilapia, and various kinds of sunfish are also grown.

Marinas and Piers

J. CLARK, COASTAL ECOSYSTEMS 114–115 (1974)

The growth of pleasure boating has accentuated construction of new marinas and related waterfront development. As environmental restrictions increase, the centralized marina becomes a solution to the greater problem of innumerable private docksites. Increases in size and range of services of the marina, however, present their own problems of environmental impact. The significant determinants of this impact include: the location of the marina, site preparation and construction, modifications required to make that site practicable and design of the facility.

Locating marinas as much as possible in places that provide natural protection and accessibility greatly minimizes environmental impact. Similarly, marinas must be designed for minimum interference with *vital areas* and adequate control of pollutants.

Marinas on estuaries with restricted flushing rates endanger aquatic biota because of the waterbody's inability to rid itself of marina-source contaminants. Extensive surfacing for parking lots and drives leads to rapid runoff of contaminated water unless controlled. Where there is an inadequate natural harbor, breakwaters required to protect the marina may interfere with tides and currents.

Agriculture

J. CLARK, COASTAL ECOSYSTEMS 115–118 (1974)

Ecologic disturbances resulting from agriculture in the coastal area of the United States include sedimentation, nutrient enrichment and toxicity—caused by soils, fertilizers, animal wastes and biocides carried into tidal waters with surface runoff and stream flow. . . . Also, disruption of the natural runoff pattern (quantity, quality and rate of flow), occurs by diking, drainage and irrigation works. Proximity to coastal waters (and to the feeder streams) is the major factor controlling the severity of the impacts.
. . . .

The success of some crops—salt hay, rice, artichokes—depends upon proximity to the coastal area for suitable soil, water and other conditions, and cultivation of these away from the coast may not be feasible. Also, agricultural land use preserves open space in coastal areas for its scenic and aesthetic values and if through proper management significant disturbances are eliminated, this use is most desirable. Another advantage in encouraging use of coastal floodplain areas for agriculture, providing proper controls and buffer strips are used, is the prevention of extensive property damage and loss of life from flooding that may occur in urbanized floodway areas.

Roadways

J. CLARK, COASTAL ECOSYSTEMS 127 (1974)

The disturbances from highway construction in wetlands have been serious. The removal of unsuitable marsh soils to reach a stable substrate has required extensive excavation and problems with disposal of the overburden, or spoil. If placed in wetlands areas, the soil pre-empts marsh habitat, releases toxic substances, and depletes oxygen in the water. Soil discharge into waterways causes turbidity which reduces biological productivity and causes siltation of water bodies. . . . Roads built on solid fill causeways become dams that block natural water flow and degrade wetlands. Important sections of estuarine environment can be converted to polluted impoundments as a result of being cut off from tidal water flow by highway fill. Essential feeder roadways that must cross wetlands should be elevated to eliminate these adverse effects. . . .

Electric Power Plants

J. CLARK, COASTAL ECOSYSTEMS 130–134 (1974)

In the construction phase, power plants have the potential for such environmental disturbances as soil discharge, disruption of marshes and tidal flats and disruption of water flow in tidelands. This potential for environmental disturbance is similar to many other large-scale industrial developments in coastal shorelands and all appropriate construction safeguards are required.

Broad estuarine marshscapes offer particularly attractive sites for nuclear plants, because the price of marshland is low, cooling water is available and a high degree of seclusion is possible. . . .
. . . .

In the operating phase, steam electric plants pose a special and unique set of continuing disturbances to coastal water environments whether they are fueled by oil, coal, or nuclear energy. With a typical modern nuclear plant of 1,000 megawatts capacity fitted with open cycle cooling, water goes through the plant in less than one minute and its temperature is raised by 10° to 34°F (6° to 19°C) before being discharged directly back to public waters. . . . The resulting thermal pollution has adverse effects on aquatic life. . . .

It must be made clear that thermal discharges are not usually the major source of disturbance caused by coastal steam plants. The major disturbance is associated with *entrainment*, whereby multitudes of aquatic forms are drawn in with the cooling water and killed within the plant by heat, turbulence, abrasion and shock. . . . The effects are especially direct and severe with plants located on estuarine spawning and nursery areas of fish and shellfish.

Residential Development

J. CLARK, COASTAL ECOSYSTEMS 161–162 (1974)

The process of residential development in coastal areas involves a complex of potential ecologic disturbances to coastal waters, both from construction activity and from human occupancy and activity. The degree of disturbance is heightened by: (1) increased density of development, (2) closer proximity to the water, (3) extensive alteration of the shorescape and (4) the ecologic sensitivity of the ecosystem. In general, constraints appropriate to residential development depend upon the elevation of the land to be developed.

The assessment of environmental impacts of residential development in coastal areas must include the full effect of all ancillary development. A coastal residential community requires roads, marinas, storm drain systems, parking lots, waste treatment facilities and so forth. Each of these has the potential for disturbance of coastal ecosystems.

There is no important difference between "primary home" and "second home" developments other than those accounted for by characteristics of design and location of the community and individual homes.

The major sources of disturbance of the coastal ecosystem are: (1) pollution of coastal waters, (2) interference with water flows in the watershed or in the coastal water basin and (3) preemption or degradation of *vital areas*.

Oil and Gas Exploration and Production

J. CLARK, COASTAL ECOSYSTEMS 155–157 (1974)

Oil and gas extraction, transport and refining have the potential for serious adverse effects on coastal ecosystems. Major disturbances are: (1) general disruption of the marine environment from dredging, barge traffic and so forth. . . , (2) pre-emption or degradation of environmental *vital areas* (e.g., wetlands) and (3) pollution by oil spills from blowouts, pipeline ruptures and ship collision and other transport accidents, which can seriously damage water quality, waterfowl, fish and coastal ecosystems.

Other sources contributing to coastal ecosystem degradation are vessel deballasting and bilge pumping, detergent and chemical clean-up techniques and general oil transfer operations including pipeline leakage. Nearshore and estuarine areas are vulnerable to offshore spills through wind, ocean current and tidal transport of oil shoreward. Efforts to clean up these pollutants with chemical techniques may also be detrimental to coastal plants and animals by placing additional stresses on the ecosystem.

The major deleterious effects of petroleum pollution are: (1) disruption of physiological and behavioral patterns of feeding and reproductive activities; (2) direct mortality from toxic ingredients; (3) changes in physical and chemical habitat, causing exclusion of species and reduction of populations; and (4) serious energy demands on the ecosystem from decomposition of refinery effluents resulting in altered productivity, metabolism, system structure and species diversity. . . .

All phases of production—extraction, transport and refining—have the potential for serious environmental impacts on coastal waters. Extraction in wetland areas and near-coastal waters is the most dangerous in terms of the risk to coastal ecosystems. Pipeline ruptures in wetlands could permanently damage a valuable coastal resource. . . .

Although offshore extraction technology is improving rapidly, environmental protection technology is lagging far behind. In a recent assessment, three areas of inadequacy in safety devices were found: "velocity-actuated down-hole safety devices, well control technologies, and oil containment and clean-up devices." Petroleum discharge from spills, seeps, blowouts, pipeline ruptures, etc., is acutely toxic to virtually all marine and coastal organisms. Immobile or passive forms such as aquatic plants, many shellfish and plankton may be especially susceptible because they cannot escape.

Pipeline construction requires dredging, often including wide barge canals for the laying of equipment. These canals, dredged to 40 or more feet in width, traverse and cut through marshlands and estuaries affecting natural drainage patterns, disrupting currents in bays and waterflow in marshlands, and reducing animal and plant populations from dredging, turbidity and sedimentation within the rights-of-way. . . .

Extraction from offshore areas of the Continental Shelf poses specific threats to coastal ecosystems by way of facilities for transfer, refining, storage and reshipment of petroleum products and crew and construction centers. . . .

Consequently, assessment of offshore oil activities is to include a searching review of impacts from onshore facilities. Much of the coastline is clearly unsuitable for onshore facilities. A smaller fraction will be capable of supporting some development with rigid environmental safeguards.

Onshore facilities involve construction of:

1. Transmission pipelines and onshore pumping stations.

2. Channels, docks, buildings and roadways to accommodate water and land traffic at transfer facilities.

3. Onshore crew facilities and construction bases.

4. Refineries and associated petrochemical industries at or near onshore receiving stations.

5. Induced secondary development; supporting commercial and industrial facilities.

6. Residential development and community support for people working in and living near these facilities. . . .

Deep Seabed Mining

FRANK, "DEEPSEA MINING AND THE ENVIRONMENT," in American Society of International Law, Studies in Transnational Legal Policy 11–20 (1976)

Nodule mining, like any activity of its kind and magnitude, will entail substantial disturbance to the environment. The precise nature and significance of that impact is at present unclear. Some commentators predict that the ecological effect of retrieval will be nominal or conceivably beneficial. Others point to a variety of probable or possible harmful consequences of retrieval and processing that will or could be significant. These effects conceivably could be so environmentally harmful that deepsea mining should not ultimately be undertaken. More likely, adverse impact can be sufficiently minimized to make deepsea mining environmentally acceptable, if adequate governmental standards and regulatory controls are established. Definitive conclusions cannot, in fact, now be reached because of the lack of detailed measurements relating to, and inadequate knowledge about, the environments being considered (such as nutrient chemistry, phytoplankton productivity and benthic ecology) and insufficient data and analysis of the effects on the environment of largescale mining operations.

The following is a description of the potential environmental impacts, for analytical purposes divided into three categories—impact on the ocean bottom, impact on the top and middle layers, and impact from processing, either at sea or on land.

The Ocean Bottom

The ocean bottom (or benthos) where nodules are formed houses a sparse deepsea fauna which lives on the sea floor or within the upper few centimeters of the sediment and a limited population of fish. Scarce information exists on these deepsea benthic communities in the areas of prospective deepsea mining sites. Their relationship with the upper ocean layers and hence man's primary environment is uncertain. None of these species is now economically exploitable; they are thought not to mingle with upper layers and therefore probably do not play a role in the major marine food chains. This benthic fauna is relevant to the study of evolution.

The process of picking nodules from the ocean floor, where the nodules may be buried at a depth of from one-third to one-half their diameter, will inevitably disturb the seabed.

   . . . .

The ultimate impact of such disturbance is only partly known. While no studies have shown the effect of turbidity on deep ocean fauna, studies on fresh water varieties conclude that turbidity inhibits feeding and kills eggs of some species. The scraping of nodules from the floor will inevitably destroy bottom-living organisms. Should a large portion of the ocean floor be intensively mined, the marine analogue to on-land clear cutting, the Department of Interior has concluded that "a serious concern may be found in the preservability of the deep-ocean fauna," and that some types of mining "could diminish the probability of some species reproducing themselves thus leading to a more rapid extinction rate of this unique fauna." This would be particularly true of organisms with slow reproductive cycles, *e.g.,* a benthic clam which reaches sexual maturity at 200 years.

   . . . .

The Water Column and the Surface

After manganese nodules have been collected from the seafloor, they are transported, with certain quantities of sediment and bottom water, through the water column to the mining vessel on the surface either in a continuous line of buckets or in an air or water stream in a pipeline. Some sediment may separate on the way to the surface if a continuous line of buckets is used.

. . . .

Aesthetic considerations aside, the disposal of deep ocean sediment and bottom water in the surface areas could result in several types of environmental impacts. The upper layers of the ocean, known as the euphotic zone, are where phytoplankton exist, where photosynthesis takes place, and where part of the earth's oxygen is produced. By depositing sediment on top of this zone some basic aspects of nature would be tinkered with; with light penetration limited, phytoplankton could be reduced or eliminated and photosynthesis and early stages of the food chain impaired. If certain ocean layers are rendered less hospitable, the vertical distribution of phytoplankton may be changed. As sediment sinks, bacteria attached to it may use oxygen in oxygen-scarce zones and adversely affect organisms there.

. . . .

Locations where mining is going to take place are also, in part, areas of intensive fishing for tuna and other species. Whether these two uses of the ocean—fishing and deepsea mining—are compatible is, at present, unclear; whether the sediment discharged from the surface will be detrimental to commercial fish stocks either directly or indirectly through their effect on the food chain is not known.

. . . .

Finally, sediment brought from the bottom may contain quiescent spores, bacteria, antibodies, or other dormant or active forms of micro-organisms which have existed on the bottom of the ocean for years or centuries but which have not had opportunity to mingle with the upper layers.

Processing

Processing of nodules could take place either at the mining site or elsewhere at sea or in a conveniently located land area. Land sites most discussed have been those closest to the Pacific mining sites, Hawaii or Southern California in the United States or Central America. Most, but not all, United States mining companies have stated they intend to process on land. Processing at sea, it is said, creates severe technical difficulties because of the need to develop a platform or vessel which could house processing equipment, sizeable energy needs which may be difficult to meet at sea using conventional energy sources, and transport to sea of materials, including reagents, required for processing. On the other hand, processing at sea avoids the necessity of developing a land complex; cuts down on the expense of delivering nodules in unrefined form to land; and permits economical disposal of waste overboard.

Either processing at sea or on land could result in harmful environmental impacts. The former has been characterized as potentially "dangerous." At sea, the energy source, whether fossil fuel or nuclear, or a new and innovative form such as ocean thermal energy conversion, could lead to physical disruption, air and water pollution and other risks; toxic reagents used in the refining process, unless self-contained and recycled, would be dumped into the ocean possibly harming fish and phytoplankton, or reagents might be discharged unintentionally due to accident; and high quantities of waste with metal tailings, the effects of which cannot be predicted on the basis of existing information, would also be dumped. Man could ultimately be harmed if the contaminants persist, bioaccumulate, and work their way upward through the food chain.

Approximately 96% of the nodule is waste if manganese is not extracted. This sludge either would be stored in ponds on land, and thereby require the allocation of large areas in or near coastal zones, the character of which would be transformed, or would be returned to the sea. The waste will contain, in addition to clay and water, manganese oxides which, if returned to the ocean, could create presently unevaluated environmental problems. Metal tailing can be toxic, and a very small excess can alter population balances.

NOTE

See also Frank, *Environmental Aspects of Deepsea Mining,* 15 Va. J. Int'l L. 815 (1975).

Waste Disposal

NATIONAL ADVISORY COMMITTEE ON OCEANS AND ATMOSPHERE, THE ROLE OF THE OCEAN IN A WASTE MANAGEMENT STRATEGY 43 (1981)

Ocean disposal of the waste products of civilization has been practiced for many hundreds, perhaps thousands, of years. Most of the disposal has historically taken place in rivers or estuaries that empty into the ocean. Today pipelines are used to discharge materials directly into the sea, and barges or ships carry and dump waste materials at sea.

The ocean has a large capacity to absorb, recycle, or dilute waste materials. However, this capacity is finite, and the disposal of wastes in the ocean can cause changes that adversely affect ocean use for commerce, recreation, and food. Ocean pollution has been directly or indirectly responsible for changes in marine ecosystems and for adverse impacts on human health. Shellfish beds have exhibited high levels of contamination by toxic metals, and suspected pathogens, at some ocean dumpsites for sewage sludge. For example, shellfishing has been banned for several years at the New York City and Philadelphia dumpsites. The possibility of disease transmission through the discharge to the environment of pathogenic organisms that are subsequently ingested, either through contact recreation or by eating contaminated seafood, is a potential impact on human health of waste disposal in the ocean. Poisoning has occurred because of seafood contaminated with toxic substances. The incident in Minamata, Japan, where a number of deaths occurred owing to ingestion of mercury-contaminated shellfish, is the principal example. Another adverse impact on man is the loss of recreational resources, where beaches or wetlands are fouled with floating waste materials or are closed for fishing and shellfishing because of sewage pollution.

Intense public interest has focused on these adverse impacts. Major incidents have occurred in many coastal locations throughout the world, although most have been caused by grossly mismanaged waste disposal and have generally been very localized. These incidents have led to the passage of laws and regulations intended to minimize the risk of such hazards and has aroused concern that other, more subtle, impacts of waste disposal may be occurring on a widespread basis throughout the coastal marine waters. These concerns have focused on the real and potential ecological effects of waste disposal. There is little doubt that ecological effects, such as changes in species composition and habitat destruction, have been caused by disposal of waste materials in localized areas of intensive waste inputs. Similar, but less drastic, changes in species composition and habitats, as well as fish diseases, have occurred in some coastal areas of the ocean.

2

Ownership and Boundaries in the Coastal Zone

SECTION A: TIDELANDS AND UPLANDS

The basic question of the ownership of the tidelands has run a long but relatively straight course. The seminal case in this country, *Martin v. The Lessee of Waddell*, 41 U.S. (16 Pet.) 367 (1842), construed a royal patent of the present states of New York and New Jersey as passing the incidents of sovereignty as well as the title to the lands conveyed by Charles II. Thus, "the land under the navigable waters passed to the grantee as one of the royalties incident to the powers of government and were to be held by him in the same manner and for the same purposes that the navigable waters of England, and the soils under them, are held by the crown." 41 U.S. at 413–414. In England, it had long been held that, "the title in the soil of the sea, or of the arms of the sea, below ordinary highwater mark, is in the King . . . and that this title, *jus privatum*, is held subject to the public right, *jus publicum*, of navigation and fishing." *Shively v. Bowlby*, 152 U.S. 1, 11 (1894).

The character of this public trust apparently changed upon Independence, for while the power of the King to make an exclusive grant of the soil underlying navigable waters was questionable, the *Martin* court said that "when the Revolution took place the people of each State became themselves sovereign; and in that character hold the absolute right to all their navigable waters and the soils under them for their own common use, subject only to the rights since surrendered by the Constitution to the general government." 41 U.S. at 410. Given this power, "each state has dealt with the lands under the tide waters within its borders according to its own views of justice and policy, reserving its own control over such lands, or granting rights therein to individuals or corporations . . . as it considered for the best interests of the public." *Shively v. Bowlby,* 152 U.S. at 26.

In 1845, *Pollard's Lessee v. Hagan,* 44 U.S. (3 How.) 212, 223 (1845), held that upon admission of the state of Alabama into the Union, the title in the lands below high-water mark of the navigable waters passed to the state and could not afterwards be granted away by the Congress. This concept, the equal footing doctrine, is succinctly stated at 224: "The right of Alabama and every other new State to exercise all the powers of government, which belong to and may be exercised by the original States of the Union, must be admitted, and remain unquestioned, except so far as they are, temporarily, deprived of control over the public lands."

There are two exceptions to the rule of *Pollard v. Hagan*: (1) Prior to statehood, the United States held lands beneath the navigable waters in trust for the future states. In the interim, Congress could create vested rights in those lands. However, as decided in *Shively,* 152 U.S. at 48, Congress never did so by general law such that a federal patent of uplands would also convey title to the associated tidelands; (2) A vested right created by a foreign country prior to ceding that territory to the United States is recognized in conformity with the treaties and statutes of the United States and the law of nations. An example of the application of this exception to a Mexican land grant is *Knight v. United States Land Association,* 142 U.S. 161 (1891), which held that the Mexican grant precluded the state from conveying the tidelands of San Francisco pueblo in derogation of the grantee's rights.

SHIVELY V. BOWLBY, 152 U.S. 1, 14 S. Ct. 548, 38 L. Ed. 331 (1894)

MR. JUSTICE GRAY, after stating the case, delivered the opinion of the court.

This case concerns the title in certain lands below high water mark in the Columbia River in the State of Oregon; the defendant below, now plaintiff in error, claiming under the United States, and the plaintiffs below, now defendants in error, claiming under the State of Oregon; and is in substance this: James M. Shively, being the owner, by title obtained by him from the United States under the act of Congress of September 27, 1850, c. 76, while Oregon was a Territory, of a tract of land in Astoria, bounded north by the Columbia River, made a plat of it, laying it out into blocks and streets, and including the adjoining lands below high water mark; and conveyed four of the blocks, one above and three below that mark, to persons who conveyed to the plaintiffs. The plaintiffs afterwards obtained from the State of Oregon deeds of conveyance of the tide lands in front of these blocks, and built and maintained a wharf upon part of them. The defendant, by counter-claim, asserted a title, under a subsequent conveyance from Shively, to some of the tide lands, not included in his former deeds, but included in the deeds from the State.

The counter-claim, therefore, depended upon the effect of the grant from the United States to Shively of land bounded by the Columbia River, and of the conveyance from Shively to the defendant, as against the deeds from the State to the plaintiffs. The Supreme Court of Oregon, affirming the judgment of a lower court of the State, held the counter-claim to be invalid, and thereupon, in accordance with the state practice, gave leave to the plaintiffs to dismiss their complaint, without prejudice. Hill's Code of Oregon, §§ 246, 393.

The only matter adjudged was upon the counter-claim. The judgment against its validity proceeded upon the ground that the grant from the United States upon which it was founded passed no title or right, as against the subsequent deeds from the State, in lands below high water mark. This is a direct adjudication against the validity of a right or privilege claimed under a law of the United States, and presents a Federal question within the appellate jurisdiction of this court. . . .

. . . .

At common law, the title and the dominion in lands flowed by the tide were in the King for the benefit of the nation. Upon the settlement of the Colonies, like rights passed to the grantees in the royal charters, in trust for the communities to be established. Upon the American Revolution, these rights, charged with a like trust, were vested in the original States within their respective borders, subject to the rights surrendered by the Constitution to the United States.

Upon the acquisition of a Territory by the United States, whether by cession from one of the States, or by treaty with a foreign country, or by discovery and settlement, the same title and dominion passed to the United States, for the benefit of the whole people, and in trust for the several States to be ultimately created out of the Territory.

The new States admitted into the Union since the adoption of the Constitution have the same rights as the original States in the tide waters, and in the lands under them, within their respective jurisdictions. The title and rights of riparian or littoral proprietors in the soil below high water mark, therefore, are governed by the laws of the several States, subject to the rights granted to the United States by the Constitution.

The United States, while they hold the country as a Territory, having all the powers both of national and of municipal government, may grant, for appropriate purposes, titles or rights in the soil below high water mark of tide waters. But they have never done so by general laws; and, unless in some case of international duty or public exigency, have acted upon the policy, as most in accordance with the interest of the people and with the object for which the Territories were acquired, of leaving the administration and disposition of the sovereign rights in navigable waters, and in the soil under them, to the control of the States, respectively, when organized and admitted into the Union.

Grants by Congress of portions of the public lands within a Territory to settlers thereon, though bordering on or bounded by navigable waters, convey, of their own force, no title or right below high water mark, and do not impair the title and dominion of the future State when created; but leave the question of the use of the shores by the owners of uplands to the sovereign control of each State, subject only to the rights vested by the Constitution in the United States.

The donation land claim, bounded by the Columbia River, upon which the plaintiff in error relies, includes no title or right in the land below high water mark; and the statutes of Oregon, under which the defendants in error hold, are a constitutional and legal exercise by the State of Oregon of its dominion over the lands under navigable waters.

Judgment affirmed.

NOTES

1. Oregon, like all western states, could not claim title to submerged lands by grant from the King of England; nevertheless, Oregon and her sister states received the same rights in submerged lands as did the original 13 colonies. What constitutional doctrine did the Court apply to achieve this result?

2. The Court in *Shively v. Bowlby* held that the donation land claim upon which *Shively* relied did not include title in the land beneath the high-water mark. If the federal grant purported to convey title to the submerged land, would the outcome of *Shively* be different?

3. The Court traced the descent of rights in submerged coastal lands from the English Crown to the original colonies. After the American Revolution, did these rights reside in the states or the federal government? According to *Shively*, does federal or state law govern coastal property ownership questions?

4. "The terms 'navigable' and 'navigability'. . . are used as concepts to decide a host of legal relationships covering titles, rights of use, powers to legislate and the like. Some of the relevant uses of the terms are:

    (1) The English test of navigability to determine title to beds
    (2) The federal test of navigability for determining title to beds
    (3) The various federal tests of navigability in statutes passed under the commerce clause of the federal constitution
    (4) The various state tests of navigability for determining title to beds
    (5) The various state tests to determine the extent of the public right of use of the surface for recreation where the bed is privately owned
    (6) The various state tests to determine the extent of the right of other riparians to use the surface for recreation where the bed is privately owned
    (7) The various state tests to determine the extent of the public right to float logs on waters where the bed is privately owned
    (8) The various state tests set forth in statutes for different purposes

    In many of the above examples the terms 'navigable' and 'navigability' are determined differently. To say the least, caution is required in the use of these concepts to avoid confusion." Johnson & Austin, *Recreational Rights and Titles to Beds on Western Lakes and Streams*, 7 Nat. Res. J. 1, 4–5 (1967).
    Which definition of navigability is used by the Court in *Shively*?

BORAX CONSOLIDATED, LTD. v. CITY OF LOS ANGELES
296 U.S. 10, 56 S. Ct. 23, 80 L. Ed. 9 (1935)

Mr. Chief Justice Hughes delivered the opinion of the Court.

The City of Los Angeles brought this suit to quiet title to land claimed to be tideland of Mormon Island situated in the inner bay of San Pedro now known as Los Angeles Harbor. The City asserted title under a legislative grant by the State. Cal. Stat. 13, 1911, p. 1256; 1917, p. 159. Petitioners claimed under a preemption patent issued by the United States on December 30, 1881, to one William Banning. The District Court entered a decree, upon findings, dismissing the complaint upon the merits and adjudging that petitioner, Borax Consolidated, Limited, was the owner in fee simple and entitled to the possession of the property. 5 F. Supp. 281. The Circuit Court of Appeals reversed the decree. 74 F.2d 901. Because of the importance of the questions presented, and of an asserted conflict with decisions of this Court, we granted certiorari, June 3, 1935.

In May 1880, one W.H. Norway, a Deputy Surveyor, acting under a contract with the Surveyor General of the United States for California, made a survey of Mormon Island. The surveyor's field notes and the corresponding plat of the island were approved by the Surveyor General and were returned to the Commissioner of the General Land Office. The latter, having found the survey to be correct, authorized the filing of the plat. The land which the patent of Banning purported to convey was described by reference to that plat as follows: "Lot numbered one, of section eight, in township five south, of range thirteen west of San Bernardino Meridian, in California, containing eighteen acres, and eighty-eight hundredths of an acre, according to the Official Plat of the Survey of the said Lands, returned to the General Land Office by the Surveyor General."

The District Court found that the boundaries of "lot one," as thus conveyed, were those shown by the plat and field notes of the survey; that all the lands described in the complaint were embraced within that lot; and that no portion of the lot was or had been tideland or situated below the line of mean high tide of the Pacific Ocean or of Los Angeles Harbor. The District Court held that the complaint was a collateral, and hence unwarranted, attack upon the survey, the plat and the patent; that the action of the General Land Office involved determinations of questions of fact which were within its jurisdiction and were specially committed to it by law for decision; and that its determinations, including that of the correctness of the survey, were final and were binding upon the State of California and the City of Los Angeles, as well as upon the United States.

The Circuit Court of Appeals disagreed with this view as to the conclusiveness of the survey and the patent. The court held that the Federal Government had neither the power nor the intention to convey tideland to Banning, and that his rights were limited to the upland. The court also regarded the lines shown on the plat as being meander lines and the boundary line of the land conveyed as the shore line of Mormon Island. The court declined to pass upon petitioners' claim of estoppel in pais and by judgment upon the ground that the question was not presented to or considered by the trial court, and was also of the opinion that the various questions raised as to the failure of the City to allege and prove the boundary line of the island were important only from the standpoint of the new trial which the court directed. 74 F.2d p. 904. For the guidance of the trial court the Court of Appeals laid down the following rule: The "mean high tide line" was to be taken as the boundary between the land conveyed and the tideland belonging to the State of California, and in the interest of certainty the court directed that "an average for 18.6 years should be determined as near as possible by observation or calculation." *Id.*, pp. 906, 907.

Petitioners contest these rulings of the Court of Appeals. With respect to the ascertainment of the shore line, they insist that the court erred in taking the "mean high tide line" and in rejecting "neap tides" as the criterion for ordinary high water mark.

. . . .

[The court, in grappling with the issue of the conclusiveness of the survey and patent, concluded that ". . . the State was not bound by the survey and patent, and that its grantee was entitled to show, if it could, that the land in question was tideland." The court also affirmed the Appellate Court's decision to remand the case for a new trial "in which the issues as to the boundary between upland and tideland, and as to the defense urged by petitioner, are to be determined."]

There remains for our consideration, however, the ruling of the Court of Appeals in instructing the District Court to ascertain as the boundary "the mean high tide line" and in thus rejecting the line of "neap tides."

Petitioners claim under a federal patent which, according to the plat, purported to convey land bordering on the Pacific Ocean. There is no question that the United States was free to convey the upland, and the patent affords no ground for holding that it did not convey all the title that the United States had in the premises. The question as to the extent of this federal grant, that is, as to the limit of the land conveyed, or the boundary between the upland and the tideland, is necessarily a federal question. It is a question which concerns the validity and effect of an act done by the United States; it involves the ascertainment of the essential basis of a right asserted under federal law. Rights and interests in the tideland, which is subject to the sovereignty of the State, are matters of local law.

The tideland extends to the high water mark. This does not mean, as petitioners contend, a physical mark made upon the ground by the waters; it means the line of high water as determined by the course of the tides. By the civil law, the shore extends as far as the highest waves reach in winter. But by the common law, the shore "is continued to the flux and reflux of the sea at ordinary tides." It is the land "between ordinary high and low water mark, the land over which the daily tides ebb and flow. When, therefore, the sea, or a bay, is named as a boundary, the line of ordinary high water mark is always intended where the common law prevails."

The range of the tide at any given place varies from day to day, and the question is, how is the line of "ordinary" high water to be determined. The range of the tide at times of new moon and full moon "is greater than the average," as "high water then rises higher and low water falls lower than usual." The tides at such times are called "spring tides." When the moon is in its first and third quarters, "the tide does not rise as high nor fall as low as on the average." At such times the tides are known as "neap tides." The view that "neap tides" should be taken as the ordinary tides had its origin in the statement of Lord Hale. De Jure Maris, cap. VI; Hall on the Sea Shore, p. 10, App. xxiii, xxiv. In his classification, there are "three sorts of shores or littora marina, according to the various tides" (1) "The high spring tides, which are the fluxes of the sea at those tides that happen at the two equinoxials;" (2) "The spring tides, which happen twice every month at full and change of the moon;" and (3) "Ordinary tides, on nepe (sic) tides, which happen between the full and change of the moon." The last kind of shore, said Lord Hale, "is that which is property littus maris." He thus excluded the "spring tides" of the month, assigning as the reason that "for the most part the lands covered with these fluxes are dry and maniorable," that is, not reached by the tides.

The subject was thoroughly considered in the case of *Atty. Gen. v. Chambers*, 4 De G. M. & G. 206, 43 Eng. Reprint, 486. In that case Lord Chancellor Cranworth invited Mr. Baron Alderson and Mr. Justice Maule to assist in the determination of the question as to "the extent of the right of the Crown to the seashore". Those judges gave as their opinion that the average of the "medium tides in each quarter of a lunar revolution during the year" fixed the limit of the shore. Adverting to the statement of Lord Hale, they thought that the reason he gave would be a guide to the proper determination. "What", they asked, are "the lands which for the most part of the year are reached and covered by the tides?" They found that the same reason that excluded the highest tides of the month, the spring tides, also excluded the lowest high tides, the neaps, for "the highest or spring tides and the lowest high tides (those at the neaps) happen as often as each other." Accordingly, the judges thought that "the medium tides of each quarter of the tidal period" afforded the best criterion. They said: "It is true of the limit of the shore reached by these tides that it is more frequently reached and covered by the tide than left uncovered by it. For about three days it is exceeded, and for about three days it is left short, and on one day it is reached. This point of the shore therefore is about four days in every week, i.e., for the most part of the year, reached and covered by the tides." *Id.*, p. 215.

Having received this opinion, the Lord Chancellor stated his own. He thought that the authorities had left the question "very much at large." Looking at "the principle of the rule which gives the shore to the Crown," and finding that principle to be that "it is land not capable of ordinary cultivation or occupation, and so is in the nature of unappropriated soil," the Lord Chancellor thus stated his conclusion: "Lord Hale gives as his reason for thinking that lands only covered by the high spring tides do not belong to the Crown, that such lands are for the most part dry and maniorable; and taking this passage as the only authority at all capable of guiding us, the reasonable conclusion is that the Crown's right is limited to land which is for the most part not dry or maniorable. The learned Judges whose assistance I had in this very obscure question point out that the limit indicating such land is the line of the medium high tide between the springs and the neaps. All land below that line is more often than not covered at high water, and so may justly be said, in the language of Lord

Hale, to be covered by the ordinary flux of the sea. This cannot be said of any land above that line." The Lord Chancellor therefore concurred with the opinion of the judges "in thinking that the medium line must be treated as bounding the right of the Crown." *Id.*, p. 217.

This conclusion appears to have been approved in Massachusetts.

In California, the Acts of 1911 and 1917, upon which the City of Los Angeles bases its claim, grant the "tidelands and submerged lands" situated "below the line of mean high tide of the Pacific Ocean." Petitioners urge that "ordinary high water mark" has been defined by the state court as referring to the line of the neap tides. We find it unnecessary to review the cases cited or to attempt to determine whether they record a final judgment as to the construction of the state statute, which, of course, is a question for the state courts.

In determining the limit of the federal grant, we perceive no justification for taking neap high tides, or the mean of those tides, as the boundary between upland and tideland, and for thus excluding from the shore the land which is actually covered by the tides most of the time. In order to include the land that is thus covered, it is necessary to take the mean high tide line which, as the Court of Appeals said, is neither the spring tide nor the neap tide, but a mean of all the high tides.

In view of the definition of the mean high tide, as given by the United States Coast and Geodetic Survey, that "Mean high water at any place is the average height of all the high waters at that place over a considerable period of time," and the further observation that "from theoretical considerations of an astronomical character" there should be "a periodic variation in the rise of water above sea level having a period of 18.6 years," the Court of Appeals directed that in order to ascertain the mean high tide line with requisite certainty in fixing the boundary of valuable tidelands, such as those here in question appear to be, "an average of 18.6 years should be determined as near as possible." We find no error in that instruction.

The decree of the Court of Appeals is affirmed.

Mr. Justice McReynolds is of opinion . . . that the decree of the District Court should be affirmed.

NOTES

1. On rehearing, the trial court fixed the elevation of mean high tide at 4.7 feet above the mean of the lower low tides, but held for Borax Consolidated, Ltd., on the basis of estoppel in pais, 20 F.Supp. 69 (1937). Having induced Borax to expend approximately $1.5 million on harbor improvements, Los Angeles was estopped from claiming that said property was part of the city's tidelands. The Ninth Circuit affirmed on appeal, 102 F.2d 69 (1939) and *cert. denied* 307 U.S. 644 (1939).

2. What was the dispute in *Borax*? Why was the definition of the line between tideland and upland important? According to the *Borax* court, are rights and interests in tidelands subject to state or federal law? If tidelands are subject to state law, why was *Borax* in the federal courts?

3. In *Borax*, the Court defined the term "high-water mark." Is the high-water mark a physical mark on the beach? If not, what is it? Consider the following:

When boundaries are set by the course of the tides, there is a further problem involved; although the height of the mean high tide may be relatively constant, the line it scribes on the shore may vary considerably from year to year. As one expert put it:

Boundaries determined by the course of the tides involve two engineering aspects: a vertical one, predicated on the height reached by the tide during its vertical rise and fall, and constituting a tidal plane or datum, such as mean high water, mean low water, etc., and a horizontal one, related to the line where the tidal plane intersects the shore to form the tidal boundary desired, for example, mean high-water mark, mean low-water mark. The first is derived from tidal observations alone, and once derived (on the basis of long-term observations), is for all practical purposes a permanent one. The second is dependent on the first, but is also affected by the natural processes of erosion and accretion, and the artifical changes made by man. . . . 1 Shalowitz, *Sea and Shore Boundaries* 89 (1962).

The *Borax* court further narrowed its boundary definition by referring to the high-water mark. Is the ordinary high-water mark synonymous with "mean high water"? What is the significance of the line of ordinary high water?

4. *Borax* overruled the older English doctrine that placed the line of ordinary high water at the line of the medium high tide between the springs and the neaps. The rationale behind the English rule was logical; the idea was to vest the littoral owner with the land that was usually dry and usable, and to leave to the Crown the land that was usually submerged. Unusually high and low tides (the springs and the neaps, respectively) were excluded. *See Atty. General v. Chambers,* 43 Eng. Rep. 486 (Ch. 1854). Why did the *Borax* Court reject the English method? The answer may have more to do with convenience than any substantive difference. *See* Maloney & Ausness, *The Use and Legal Significance of the Mean High Water Line,* 53 N.C. L. Rev. 185, 206 (1974).

5. The *Borax* rule remains the federal definition of "ordinary high tide." The rule, however, is difficult to apply, as are all rules concerned with the tides. Humbach & Gale, in *Tidal Title and the Boundaries of the Bay: The Case of the Submerged "High Water" Mark*, 4 Fordham Urb. L.J. 91, 102–104 (1975), offer this criticism:

In sum, the "high water" line, as a real estate boundary, is not a line at all but a linguistic formulation. And as such, it is scarcely more definite than the concept, "the edge of the sea," which it is supposed to define. About the only contribution that the "high water line" formulation makes to our understanding of the boundary location is to tell us that the division between upland and sea lies toward the landward, not the seaward, of the area of tidal wash.

The Borax Company argued for the lower neap tide line or, alternatively, a vegetation line that evidence placed below the mean high-tide line. *See* Corker, *Where Does the Beach Begin, and to What Extent Is This a Federal Question?*, 42 Wash. L. Rev. 33, 57–61 (1966). The U.S. Supreme Court rejected this argument. Some states have utilized alternatives to the federal definition of ordinary high tide.

The next case in this chapter, *Hughes v. Washington*, concerns the State of Washington's attempt to define ordinary high tide as the line of vegetation. *Hughes* also raises the critical issue of which law should define "ordinary high tide," state or federal.

6. For additional reading, *see* 1 R. Clark, *Waters & Water Rights* § 36.3(C) at 193–94 (1967); 2 H. Farnham, *The Law of Waters & Water Rights* §§ 414, 417–18 (1904); Note, *Florida Sovereignty Lands: What Are They, Who Owns Them and Where Is the Boundary?*, 1 Fla. St. L. Rev. 596 (1973).

SECTION B: AMBULATORY BOUNDARIES

MALONEY & AUSNESS, "THE USE AND LEGAL SIGNIFICANCE OF THE MEAN HIGH WATER LINE IN COASTAL BOUNDARY MAPPING," 53 North Carolina Law Review 185, 224–27 (1974)

In most coastal states, tidal boundaries are considered to be ambulatory; that is, the physical location of the mean high (or low) water line may shift because of natural or artificial changes in the location of the shoreline. Accordingly, littoral owners may gain or lose land by virtue of accretion, reliction, erosion, or avulsion.

Before discussing the problem of ambulatory versus fixed boundaries, it may be helpful to consider the meaning of a number of terms commonly used in legal discussions of this problem. Accretions or accreted lands consist of additions to the land resulting from the gradual deposit by water of sand, sediment or other material. The term applies to such lands produced along both navigable and non-navigable water. Alluvion is that increase of earth on a shore or bank of a stream or sea, by the force of the water, as by a current or by waves, which is so gradual that no one can judge how much is added at each moment of time. The term "alluvion" is applied to the deposit itself, while accretion denotes the act, but the terms are frequently used synonymously.

Reliction refers to land which formerly was covered by water, but which has become dry land by the imperceptible recession of the water. Although there is a distinction between accretion and reliction, one being the gradual building of the land, and the other the gradual recession of water, the terms are often used interchangeably. The term "accretion" in particular is often used to cover both processes, and generally the law relating to both is the same.

Erosion is the gradual and imperceptible wearing away of land bordering on a body of water by the natural action of the elements. Avulsion is either the sudden and perceptible alteration of the shoreline by action of the water, or a sudden change of the bed or course of a stream forming a boundary whereby it abandons its old bed for a new one.

As a general rule, where the shoreline is gradually and imperceptibly changed or shifted by accretion, reliction or erosion, the boundary line is extended or restricted in the same manner. The owner of the littoral property thus acquires title to all additions arising by accretion or reliction, and loses soil that is worn or washed away by erosion. However, any change in the shoreline that takes place suddenly and perceptibly does not result in a change of boundary or ownership. Normally a landowner may not intentionally increase his estate through accretion or reliction by artificial means. However, the littoral owner is usually entitled to additions that result from artificial conditions created by third persons without his consent.

HUGHES v. WASHINGTON 389 U.S. 290, 88 S. Ct. 438, 19 L. Ed.
2d 530 (1967)

Mr. Justice Black delivered the opinion of the Court.

The question for decision is whether federal or state law controls the ownership of land, called accretion, gradually deposited by the ocean on adjoining upland property conveyed by the United States prior to statehood. The circumstances that give rise to the question are these. Prior to 1889 all land in what is now the State of Washington was owned by the United States, except land that had been conveyed to private parties. At that time owners of property bordering the ocean, such as the predecessor in title of Mrs. Stella Hughes, the petitioner here, had under the common law a right to include within their lands any accretion gradually built up by the ocean. Washington became a State in 1889, and Article 17 of the State's new constitution, as interpreted by its Supreme Court, denied the owners of oceanfront property in the State any further rights in accretion that might in the future be formed between their property and the ocean. This is a suit brought by Mrs. Hughes, the successor in title to the original federal grantee, against the State of Washington as owner of the tidelands to determine whether the right to future accretions which existed under federal law in 1889 was abolished by that provision of the Washington Constitution. The trial court upheld Mrs. Hughes' contention that the right to accretions remained subject to federal law, and that she was the owner of the accreted lands. The State Supreme Court reversed, holding that state law controlled and that the State owned these lands. 67 Wash. 2d 799, 410 P.2d 20 (1966). We granted certiorari. 385 U.S. 1000, 17 L. Ed. 2d 540, 87 S. Ct. 700 (1967). We hold that this question is governed by federal, not state law and that under federal law Mrs. Hughes, who traces her title to a federal grant prior to statehood, is the owner of these accretions.

While the issue appears never to have been squarely presented to this Court before, we think the path to decision is indicated by our holding in *Borax, Ltd. v. Los Angeles*, 296 U.S. 10, 80 L. Ed. 9, 56 S. Ct. 23 (1935). In that case we dealt with the rights of a California property owner who held under a federal patent, and in that instance, unlike the present case, the patent was issued after statehood. We held that

> [t]he question as to the extent of this federal grant, that is, as to the limit of the land conveyed, or the boundary between the upland and the tideland, is necessarily a federal question. It is a question which concerns the validity and effect of an act done by the United States; it involves the ascertainment of the essential basis of a right asserted under federal law. 296 U.S. at 22, 80 L. Ed. at 17.

No subsequent case in this Court has cast doubt on the principle announced in *Borax*. The State argues, and the court below held, however, that the *Borax* case should not be applied here because that case involved no question as to accretions. While this is true, the case did involve the question as to what rights were conveyed by the federal grant and decided that the extent of ownership under the federal grant is governed by federal law. This is as true whether doubt as to any boundary is based on a broad question as to the general definition of the shoreline or on a particularized problem relating to the ownership of accretion. We therefore find no significant difference between *Borax* and the present case.

Recognizing the difficulty of distinguishing *Borax*, respondent urges us to reconsider it. *Borax* itself, as well as *United States v. Oregon*, [295 U.S. 1, 55 S. Ct. 610, 79 L. Ed. 1267 (1935)] and many other cases, makes clear that a dispute over title to lands owned by the Federal Government is governed by federal law, although of course the Federal Government may, if it desires, choose to select a state rule as the federal rule. *Borax* holds that there has been no such choice in this area, and we have no difficulty in concluding that *Borax* was correctly decided. The rule deals with waters that lap both the lands of the State and the boundaries of the international sea. This relationship, at this particular point of the marginal sea, is too close to the vital interest of the Nation in its own boundaries to allow it to be governed by any law but the "supreme Law of the Land."

This brings us to the question of what the federal rule is. The State has not attempted to argue that federal law gives it title to these accretions, and it seems clear to us that it could not. A long and unbroken line of decisions of this Court establishes that the grantee of land bounded by a body of navigable water acquires a right to any natural and gradual accretion formed along the shore. In *Jones v. Johnston*, 18 How. 150, 15 L. Ed. 320 (1856), a dispute between two parties owning land along Lake Michigan over the ownership of soil that had gradually been deposited along the shore, this Court held that "[l]and gained from the sea either by alluvion or dereliction, if the same be by little and little, by small and imperceptible degrees, belongs to the owner of the land adjoining." 18 How. at 156, 15 L. Ed. at 323. The Court has repeatedly reaffirmed this rule, *County of St. Clair v. Lovingston*, 23 Wall. 46, 23 L. Ed. 59 (1874); *Jefferis v. East Omaha Land Co.*, 134 U.S. 178, 33 L. Ed. 872, 10 S. Ct. 518 (1890), and the soundness of the principle is scarcely open to question. Any other rule would leave riparian owners continually in danger of losing the access to water which is often the most valuable feature of their property, and continually vulnerable to harassing litigation challenging the location of the original water lines. While it is true that these riparian rights are to some extent insecure in any event, since they are subject to considerable control by the neighboring owner of the tideland, this is insufficient reason to leave these valuable rights at the mercy of natural phenomena which may in no way affect the interests of the tideland owner. We therefore hold that petitioner is entitled to the accretion that has been gradually formed along her property by the ocean.

The judgment below is reversed, and the case is remanded to the Supreme Court of Washington for further proceedings not inconsistent with this opinion.

Reversed and remanded.

. . . .

Mr. Justice Stewart, concurring.

I fully agree that the extent of the 1866 federal grant to which Mrs. Hughes traces her ownership was originally measurable by federal common law, and that under the applicable federal rule her predecessor in title acquired the right to all accretions gradually built up by the sea. For me, however, that does not end the matter. For the Supreme Court of Washington decided in 1966, in the case now before us, that Washington terminated the right to oceanfront accretions when it became a State in 1889. The State concedes that the federal grant in question conferred such a right prior to 1889. But the State purports to have reserved all post-1889 accretions for the public domain. Mrs. Hughes is entitled to the beach she claims in this case only if the State failed in its effort to abolish all private rights to seashore accretions.

Surely it must be conceded as a general proposition that the law of real property is, under our Constitution, left to the individual States to develop and administer. And surely Washington or any other State is free to make changes, either legislative or judicial, in its general rules of real property law, including the rules governing the property rights of riparian owners. Nor are riparian owners who derive their title from the United States somehow immune from the changing impact of these general state rules. For if they were, then the property law of a State like Washington, carved entirely out of federal territory, would be forever frozen into the mold it occupies on the date of the State's admission to the Union. It follows that Mrs. Hughes cannot claim immunity from changes in the property law of Washington simply because her title derives from a federal grant. Like any other property owner, however, Mrs. Hughes may insist, quite apart from the federal origin of her title, that the State not take her land without just compensation.

Accordingly, if Article 17 of the Washington Constitution had unambiguously provided, in 1889, that all accretions along the Washington coast from that day forward would belong to the State rather than to private riparian owners, this case would present two questions not discussed by the Court, both of which I think exceedingly difficult. First: Does such a prospective change in state property law constitute a compensable taking? Second: If so, does the constitutional right to compensation run with the land, so as to give not only the 1889 owner, but also his successors—including Mrs. Hughes—a valid claim against the State?

The fact, however, is that Article 17 contained no such unambiguous provision. In that Article, the State simply asserted its ownership of "the beds and shores of all navigable waters in the state up to and including the line of ordinary high tide, in waters where the tide ebbs and flows, and up to and including the line of ordinary high water within the banks of all navigable rivers and lakes." In the present case the Supreme Court of Washington held that, by this 1889 language, "[l]ittoral rights of upland owners were terminated." 67 Wash. 2d 799, 816; 410 P.2d 20, 29. Such a conclusion by the State's highest court on a question of state law would ordinarily bind this court, but here the state and federal questions are inextricably intertwined. For if it cannot reasonably be said that the littoral rights of upland owners were terminated in 1889, then the effect of the decision now before us is to take from these owners, without compensation, land deposited by the Pacific Ocean from 1889 to 1966.

We cannot resolve the federal question whether there has been such a taking without first making a determination of our own as to who owned the seashore accretions between 1889 and 1966. To the extent that the decision of the Supreme Court of Washington on that issue arguably conforms to reasonable expectations, we must of course accept it as conclusive. But to the extent that it constitutes a sudden change in state law, unpredictable in terms of the relevant precedents, no such deference would be appropriate. For a State cannot be permitted to defeat the constitutional prohibition against taking property without due process of law by the simple device of asserting retroactively that the property it has taken never existed at all. Whether the decision here worked an unpredictable change in state law thus inevitably presents a federal question for the determination of this court. The Washington court insisted that its decision was "not startling." 67 Wash. 2d 799, 814, 410 P.2d 20, 28. What is at issue here is the accuracy of that characterization.

The state court rested its result upon *Eisenbach v. Hatfield,* 2 Wash. 236, 26 P. 539, but that decision involved only the relative rights of the State and the upland owner in the tidelands themselves. . . . I can only conclude, as did the dissenting judge below, that the state court's most recent construction of Article 17 effected an unforeseeable change in Washington property law as expounded by the State Supreme Court.

There can be little doubt about the impact of that change upon Mrs. Hughes: The beach she had every reason to regard as hers was declared by the state court to be in the public domain. Of course the court did not conceive of this action as a taking. As is so often the case when a State exercises its power to make law, or to regulate, or to pursue a public project, pre–existing property interests were impaired here without any calculated decision to deprive anyone of what he once owned. But the Constitution measures a taking of property not by what a State says, or by what it intends, but by what it *does*. Although the State in this case made no attempt to take the accreted lands by eminent domain, it achieved the same result by effecting a retroactive transformation of private into public property—without paying for the privilege of doing so. Because the Due Process Clause of the Fourteenth Amendment forbids such confiscation by a State, no less through its courts than through its legislature, and no less when a taking is unintended than when it is deliberate, I join in reversing the judgment.

NOTES

1. In *Hughes v. State,* 67 Wash. 2d 799, 410 P.2d 20 (1966), the Washington supreme court had used the same word definition of mean high tide as the U.S. Supreme Court in *Borax*; nevertheless, the boundary of Mrs. Hughes' property, under the prevailing federal test, would have been 130 feet seaward of the Washington court's line. This discrepancy was due to the U.S. Coast and Geodetic Survey's use of a fictional flat sea to determine coastal boundaries. In addition, the Washington court chose to trace a line not at its definition of mean high tide, but still higher—at the line the water impressed on the soil by covering it for sufficient periods to deprive the soil of vegetation, the vegetation line. As if this were not enough, the Washington court extended the line yet higher, to the vegetation line as it existed in 1889, the year Washington became a state. In other words, the Washington supreme court "fixed" that state's coastal boundaries as of the date of statehood. Any subsequent accretions belonged not to the upland owner, but to the state.

    Professor Corker, in *Where Does the Beach Begin, and to What Extent Is This a Federal Question?*, 42 Wash. L. Rev. 33, 46 (1966), exhaustively examined *Hughes v. State*. In this article, he wrote a brief but helpful explanation of the Washington court's boundary diagram (see Figure 2-1):

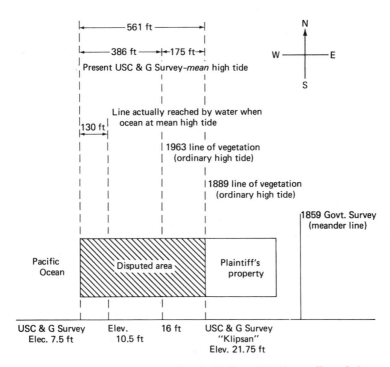

Figure 2-1 The alternative boundary lines in *Hughes v. Washington.* (From Corker, *Where Does the Beach Begin, and to What Extent Is This a Federal Question?* 42 Wash. L. Rev. 33, 46 (1966).)

The difference apparently consists of two components: (1) 130 feet is the difference between mean high tide, as defined in *Borax*, and the line actually reached by the water when the sea is at the mean high tide elevation. In other words, it is the difference between a line established at high tide by the plane surface of a waveless ocean, which does not exist in nature, and the line established by the waves which wash the shore at that elevation, where Mrs. Hughes' real estate is located. (2) The balance of 256 feet may be accounted for by a vegetation line determined by waves from tides which are higher than the 18.6 year average. This is not necessarily the average of the higher of the two daily high tides, but is fixed by the biological wisdom of plants which have not deposed to specify the precise frequency or intensity of sea water irrigation which makes the habitat unsatisfactory.

2. The Washington court in *Hughes v. State* had applied a rule derived from the prevailing practice of the Washington Commissioner of Public Lands. Seventy-three unreported superior court decisions had affirmed the validity of this practice. The source of the Commissioner's rule, a source concerned more with inland than coastal waters, reveals the basis of the Washington court's "vegetation line" definition of ordinary high water.

 Inland waters have no tidal flow and no mean high-water mark. In place of mean high tide, courts apply an "ordinary high-water line" to determine the boundary between public and private lands. One of the earliest expressions of the inland rule was *Howard v. Ingersoll*, 54 U.S. 381, 427 (1851):

This line is to be found by examining the bed and banks and ascertaining where the presence and action of waters are so common and usual and so long continued in all ordinary years, as to mark upon the soil of the bed a character distinct from that of the banks, in respect to vegetation, as well as in respect to the nature of the soil itself.

Professor Maloney, in *The Ordinary High Water Mark: Attempts at Settling an Unsettled Boundary Line*, 13 Land & Water L. Rev. 465, 467 (1978), warned that

The OHWL should be clearly distinguished from the mean high tide line of waters subject to tidal influence. The primary distinction is that the latter is determined through a statistical averaging technique while the former is generally ascertainable by reference to the physical characteristics of the banks and beds of the water body.

3. *Hughes* illustrates the difficulty of defining the ordinary high-water mark. In some situations the use of the ordinary high-water mark is not only difficult, it is impossible. Dense mangrove swamps, for example, cover parts of Florida's coast. Rather than apply a purely fictional tidal rule, Florida's courts sometimes use meander lines to define the boundary between public and private lands. *See Florida Bd., etc. v. Wakulla Silver Springs*, 362 So. 2d 706 (Fla. 3d Dist. Ct. App. 1978); *cf. Utah v. United States*, 425 U.S. 948 (1976) (involving title to lands exposed by the evaporation of Utah's Great Salt Lake). *But see St. Joseph Land, etc. v. Florida St. Bd.*, 365 So. 2d 1084 (Fla. 1st Dist. Ct. App. 1979).

    The meander line is a straight line or series of straight lines connecting points on the shore. The meander line is primarily for determining the quantity of public land in the subdivision being surveyed, and is not intended as an exact measurement. For a discussion of the problems of using meander lines as boundaries, *see* Maloney, *Ordinary High Water Mark, supra,* at 489–92.

4. Why would a state enact a statute or adopt a constitutional amendment providing that henceforth all coastal accretion belongs to the state? If the goal is greater public access along the coast, are there alternative means of achieving it? Does use of the vegetation line as the seaward limit of upland ownership promote public access? Are there any conceivable theories by which the public may have access up to the vegetation line where upland ownership extends down to the mean high tide line as defined in *Borax*? *See, e.g., State ex rel. Thornton v. Hay*, 254 Or. 584, 462 P.2d 671 (1969), *infra* at 251.

5. In *Bonelli Cattle Co. v. Arizona*, 414 U.S. 313, 94 S. Ct. 517, 38 L. Ed. 2d 526 (1973), the U.S. Supreme Court applied federal common law to resolve a dispute over inland navigable water boundaries. Four years later, however, in *Oregon ex rel. State Land Board v. Corvallis Sand & Gravel Co.,* the Supreme Court dramatically overruled *Bonelli*.

OREGON EX REL. STATE LAND BOARD v. CORVALLIS SAND AND GRAVEL COMPANY, 429 U.S. 363, 97 S. Ct. 582, 50 L. Ed. 2d 550 (1977)

MR. JUSTICE REHNQUIST delivered the opinion of the Court.

This lawsuit began when the State of Oregon sued Corvallis Sand and Gravel Company, an Oregon corporation, to settle the ownership of certain lands underlying the Willamette River. The Willamette is a navigable river, and this land is located near Corvallis, Oregon. The river is not an interstate boundary.

Corvallis Sand had been digging in the disputed part of the riverbed for 40 to 50 years without a lease from the State. The State brought an ejectment action against Corvallis Sand, seeking to recover 11 separate parcels of riverbed, as well as damages for the use of the parcels. The State's complaint alleged that by virtue of its sovereignty it was the owner in fee simple of the disputed portions of the riverbed, and that it was entitled to immediate possession and damages. Corvallis Sand denied the State's ownership of the bed.

Each party was partially successful in the Oregon courts, and we granted cross petitions for certiorari, 423 U.S. 1048. Those courts understandably felt that our recent decision in *Bonelli Cattle Co. v. Arizona*, 414 U.S. 313 [94 S. Ct. 517, 38 L. Ed. 2d 526] (1973), required that they ascertain and apply principles of federal common law to the controversy. Twenty-six states have joined in three *amicus* briefs urging that we reconsider *Bonelli* because of what they assert is its significant departure from long established precedent in this Court.

I

The nature of the case and the contentions of the parties may be briefly stated. Title to two distinct portions of land has been at issue throughout. The first of these portions has apparently been within the bed of the Willamette River since Oregon's admission into the Union.

The other portion of the land underlies the river in an area known as Fischer Cut, which was not a part of the riverbed at the time Oregon was admitted to the Union. The trial court found that prior to a flood which occurred in November 1909, the Willamette flowed around a peninsula–like formation known as Fischer Island, but that by 1890 a clearly discernible overflow channel across the neck of the peninsula developed. Before 1909 this channel carried the flow of the river only at its intermediate or high stages, and the main channel of the river continued to flow around Fischer Island. But in November 1909, a major flood, in the words of the Oregon trial court, "suddenly and with great force and violence converted Fischer Cut into the main channel of the river."

The trial court, sitting without a jury, awarded all parcels in dispute, except for the Fischer Cut lands, to the State. That court found that the State had acquired sovereign title to those lands upon admission into the Union, and that it had not conveyed that title. The State was also awarded damages to recompense it for Corvallis Sand's use of the lands.

With respect to the Fischer Cut lands, the trial court found that avulsion, rather than accretion, had caused the change in the channel of the river, and therefore the title to the lands remained in Corvallis Sand, the original owner of the land before it became riverbed.

The Oregon Court of Appeals affirmed. That court felt bound, under *Bonelli*, to apply federal common law to the resolution of this property dispute. In so doing, the court found that the trial court's award of Fischer Cut to

Corvallis Sand was correct either under the theory of avulsion, or under the so-called exception to the accretion rule, announced in *Commissioners v. United States*, 270 F. 10 (CA8 1920).[1] The court, finding that preservation of the State's interest in navigation, fishing and other related goals did not require that it acquire ownership of the new bed, rejected the argument that the State's sovereign title to a riverbed follows the course of the river as it moves.

II

In this Court, Oregon urges that we either modify *Bonelli* or expound "federal common law" in such a way that its title to all the land in question will be established. Corvallis Sand urges that we interpret "federal common law" in such a manner that it will prevail. *Amici* urge that we re-examine *Bonelli* because in their view that case represented a sharp break with well-established previous decisions of the Court.

The dispute in *Bonelli* was over the ownership of the former bed of the Colorado River, a bed which the river had abandoned because of a federal rechanneling project. The Bonelli land was part of the actual riverbed, however, neither at the time Arizona was admitted to the Union, nor at the time of suit. Before Arizona had been admitted as a State, Bonelli's predecessor in title had received a United States patent to the land. Over a period of years the Colorado River had migrated gradually eastward, eroding its east bank and depositing alluvion on its west bank in the process. In the course of this movement of the river the Bonelli land, which had at the time of patent been on the east bank, was submerged, and until the rechanneling project, most of it was under water. After the completion of the rechanneling project the bed of the Colorado River was substantially narrowed, and the Bonelli land re–emerged.

The Supreme Court of Arizona held that Arizona owned the title to the beds of navigable rivers within its borders, and that Arizona therefore acquired title to the Bonelli land when it became part of the riverbed as a result of the eastward migration of the Colorado. That court went on to hold that under state law the re-emergence of the land was an avulsive change, which did not divest

---

[1]The court quoted the following language from *Commissioners* in support of that rule:

". . . [The accretion rule] is applicable to and governs cases where the boundary line, the thread of the stream, by the slow and gradual processes of erosion and accretion creeps across the intervening space between its old and its new location. To this rule, however, there is a well-established and rational exception. It is that, where a river changes its main channel, not by excavating, passing over, and then filling the intervening place between its old and its new main channel, but by flowing around this intervening land, which never becomes in the meantime its main channel, and the change from the old to the new main channel is wrought during many years by the gradual or occasional increase from year to year of the proportion of its waters of the river passing over the course which eventually becomes the new main channel, and the decrease from year to year of the proportion of its waters passing through the old main channel until the greater part of its waters flow through the new main channel, the boundary line between the estates remains in the old channel subject to such changes in that channel as are wrought by erosion or accretion while the water in it remains a running stream. . . ."

the State of its title to the exposed land. This Court granted certiorari and reversed the Supreme Court of Arizona.

We phrased the critical inquiry in *Bonelli* in these words:

> The issue before us is not what rights the State has accorded private land owners in lands which the State holds as sovereign; but, rather *how far* the State's sovereign right extends under the equal-footing doctrine and the Submerged Lands Act— whether the State retains title to the lands *formerly* beneath the stream of the Colorado River *or whether that title is defeasible by the withdrawal of those waters.* 414 U.S., at 319–320 [94 S. Ct. at 523, 38 L. Ed. 2d at 535]. (Emphasis added.)

We held that federal common law should govern in deciding whether a State retained title to lands which had re-emerged from the bed of a navigable stream, relying in part on *Borax, Ltd. v. Los Angeles,* 296 U.S. 10 [56 S. Ct. 23, 80 L. Ed. 9] (1935). That case held that the extent and validity of a federal grant was a question to be resolved by federal law, and in *Bonelli* we decided that the nature of the title conferred by the equal-footing doctrine set forth in *Pollard's Lessee v. Hagan,* 3 How. 212 [11 L. Ed. 565] (1845), should likewise be governed by federal common law. Under the equal-footing doctrine "the new States since admitted have the same rights, sovereignty and jurisdiction . . . as the original States possess within their respective borders." *Mumford v. Wardwell,* 6 Wall. 423, 436 [18 L. Ed. 756, 761] (1867). *Pollard's Lessee* held that under the equal-footing doctrine new States, upon their admission to the Union, acquire title to the lands underlying navigable waters within their boundaries.

We went on to discuss the nature of the sovereign's interest in the riverbed, which we found to lie in the protection of navigation, fisheries, and similar purposes. We held that under federal common law, as we construed it in that case, Arizona's sovereign interest in the re-emerged land was not sufficient to enable it to retain title. We found that the principle governing title to lands which have been formed by accretion, rather than that which governs title where there has been an avulsive change in the channel of the river, to be applicable. We chose the former because it would both ensure the riparian owner access to the water's edge and prevent the State from receiving a windfall. We therefore decided that *Bonelli* as riparian owner, was entitled to the land in question.

Our analysis today leads us to conclude that our decision to apply federal common law in *Bonelli* was incorrect. . . .

The title to the land underlying the Colorado River at the time Arizona was admitted to the Union vested in the State as of that date under the rule of *Pollard's Lessee v. Hagan.* Although federal law may fix the initital boundary line between fast lands and the riverbeds at the time of a State's admission to the Union, the State's title to the riverbed vests absolutely as of the time of its admission and is not subject to later defeasance by operation of any doctrine of federal common law.

Bonelli's thesis that the equal-footing doctrine would require the effect of a movement of the river upon title to the riverbed to be resolved under federal common law was in error. Once the equal-footing doctrine had vested title to the riverbed in Arizona as of the time of its admission to the Union, the force of that doctrine was spent; it did not operate after that date to determine what effect on titles the movement of the river might have. Our error, as we now see it, was to view the equal-footing doctrine enunciated in *Pollard's Lessee v. Hagan* as a basis upon which federal common law could supersede state law in the determination of land titles. Precisely the contrary is true; in *Pollard's Lessee* itself the equal-footing doctrine resulted in the State's acquisition of title notwithstanding the efforts of the Federal Government to dispose of the lands in question in another way.

The equal-footing doctrine did not, therefore, provide a basis for federal law to supersede the State's application of its own law in deciding title to the *Bonelli* land, and state law should have been applied unless there were present some other principle of federal law requiring state law to be displaced. The only other basis[2] for a colorable claim of federal right in *Bonelli* was that the *Bonelli* land had originally been patented to its predecessor by the United States, just as had most other land in the western States. But that land had long been in private ownership and, hence, under the great weight of precedent from this Court, subject to the general body of state property law. Since the application of federal common law is required neither by the equal-footing doctrine nor by any other claim of federal right, we now believe that title to the *Bonelli* land should have been governed by Arizona law, and that the disputed ownership of the lands in the bed of the Willamette River in this case should be decided solely as a matter of Oregon law.

III

. . . .

[Mr. Justice Rehnquist expounds on both the rule laid down in *Pollard's Lessee v. Hagan* (establishing a new state's absolute title to lands underlying navigable waters within its boundaries) and the holding in *Borax, Ltd.* that the boundary between the upland and tideland was to be determined by federal law.]
. . . [But the Borax determination] . . . is solely for the purpose of fixing the boundaries of the riverbed acquired by the State at the time of its admission

---

[2]Arizona, in its brief, also relied upon The Submerged Lands Act of 1953, 43 U.S.C. §1301. However, as discussed in *Bonelli*, the Submerged Lands Act did not alter the scope or effect of the equal-footing doctrine, nor did it alter state property laws regarding riparian ownership. The effect of the Act was merely to confirm the States' title to the beds of navigable waters within their boundaries as against any claim of the United States Government. As merely a declaration of the States' pre-existing rights in the riverbeds, nothing in the Act in any way mandates, or even indicates, that federal common law should be used to resolve ownership of lands, which by the very terms of the Act, reside in the States. We recognized as much in *Bonelli* and our references to the Act in *Bonelli* in no way indicate that it was the Act, rather than the scope of equal-footing doctrine, which resulted in our application of federal common law:

> Since the Act does not extend to the States any interest beyond those afforded by the equal-footing doctrine, the state can no more base its claim to lands unnecessary to a navigational purpose on the Submerged Lands Act than on that doctrine. [*Bonelli Cattle Co. v. Arizona*, 414 U.S. 313, 324–325; 94 S.Ct. 517, 525; 38 L. Ed. 2d 526, 538].

to the Union; thereafter the role of the equal-footing doctrine is ended, and the land is subject to the laws of the State. The expressions in *Bonelli* suggesting a more expansive role for the equal-footing doctrine are contrary to the line of cases following *Pollard's Lessee*.[3]

For example, this Court has held that subsequent changes in the contour of the land, as well as subsequent transfers of the land, are governed by the state law. Indeed, the rule that lands once having passed from the Federal Government are subject to the laws of the State in which they lie antedates *Pollard's Lessee*. As long ago as 1839, the Court said:

> We hold the true principle to be this, that whenever the question in any Court, state or federal, is *whether* a title to land which had once been the property of the United States has passed, that question must be resolved by the laws of the United States; but that *whenever*, according to those laws, *the title shall have passed*, then that property, like all other property in the state, is *subject to state legislation*; so far as that legislation is consistent with the admission that the title passed and vested according to the laws of the United States. *Wilcox v. Jackson*, 13 Pet. 498, 517 [10 L. Ed. 264, 273] (1839). (Emphasis added.)

The contrary approach would result in a perverse application of the equal-footing doctrine. An original State would be free to choose its own legal principles to resolve property disputes relating to land under its riverbeds; a subsequently admitted State would be *constrained* by the equal-footing doctrine to apply the federal common law rule, which may result in property law determinations antithetical to the desires of that State.

Thus, if the lands at issue did pass under the equal-footing doctrine, state title is not subject to defeasance and state law governs subsequent dispositions.

IV

A similar result obtains in the case of riparian lands which did not pass under the equal-footing doctrine. This Court has consistently held that state law governs issues relating to this property, like other real property, unless some other principle of federal law requires a different result.

Under our federal system, property ownership is not governed by a general federal law, but rather by the laws of the several States. "The great body of law

---

[3]*Amici* Utah and New Mexico also urge us to reconsider our decision in *Hughes v. Washington*, 389 U.S. 290 [88 S. Ct. 438, 19 L. Ed. 2d 530] (1967). They advance the same reasons for such reconsideration as they do with respect to *Bonelli*. But *Hughes* was not cited by the Oregon courts below, and in *Bonelli* we expressly declined to rely upon it as a basis for our decision there. We therefore have no occasion to address the issue. We are aware of the fact that *Hughes* gave to *Borax*, the same sort of expansive construction as did *Bonelli*, but we are likewise aware that *Hughes* dealt with ocean-front property, a fact which the Court thought sufficiently different from the usual situation so as to justify a "federal common law" rule of riparian proprietorship:

> The rule deals with waters that lap both the lands of the State and the boundaries of the international sea. This relationship, at this particular point of the marginal sea, is too close to the vital interest of the Nation in its own boundaries to allow it to be governed by any law but the "supreme Law of the Land." *Id.*, at 293 [88 S. Ct. at 440, 19 L. Ed. 2d at 533].

in this country which controls acquisition, transmission, and transfer of property, and defines the rights of its owners in relation to the state or to private parties, is found in the statutes and decisions of the state." *Davies Warehouse v. Bowles,* 321 U.S. 144, 155 [64 S. Ct. 474, 480–481; 88 L. Ed. 635, 643] (1944). This is particularly true with respect to real property, for even when federal common law was in its heyday under the teachings of *Swift v. Tyson*, 16 Pet. 1 [10 L. Ed. 865] (1842), an exception was carved out for the local law of real property.

This principle applies to the banks and shores of waterways, and we have consistently so held. *Barney v. Keokuk* [94 U.S. 324, 24 L. Ed. 224 (1876)] involved an ejectment action by the plaintiff against the city involving certain land along the banks of the Mississippi River. After noting that the early state doctrines regarding the ownership of the soil of nontidal waters were based upon the then discarded English view that nontidal waters were presumed nonnavigable, the Court clearly articulated the rule that the States could formulate, and modify, rules of riparian ownership as they saw fit:

> Whether, as rules of property, it would now be safe to change these doctrines [arising out of the confusion of the original classification of nontidal waters as nonnavigable] where they have been applied, as before remarked, is for the several States themselves to determine. If they choose to resign to the riparian proprietor rights which properly belong to them in their sovereign capacity, it is not for others to raise objections. In our view of the subject the correct principles were laid down in *Martin v. Waddell*, 16 Pet. 367 [10 L. Ed. 997 (1842)], *Pollard's Lessee v. Hagan*, 3 How. 212 [11 L. Ed. 565 (1845)] and *Goodtitle v. Kibbe*, 9 *id.* 471 [13 L. Ed. 220 (1850)]. These cases related to tidewater, it is true; but they enunciate principles which are equally applicable to all navigable waters. [94 U.S.], at 338 [24 L. Ed. at 228].

In *Shively v. Bowlby*, [152 U.S. 1, 14 S. Ct. 548, 38 L. Ed 331 (1894)], the Court canvassed its previous decisions and emphasized that state law controls riparian ownership. The Court concluded that grants by Congress of land bordering navigable waters ". . . leave the question of the use of the shores by the owners of uplands to the sovereign control of each State, subject only to the rights vested by the Constitution in the United States," 152 U.S., at 58 [14 S. Ct. at 570, 38 L. Ed. at 352]. As the Court again emphasized in *Packer v. Bird*, 137 U.S. 661, 669 [11 S. Ct. 210, 212; 34 L. Ed. 819, 821] (1891):

> . . . [W]hatever incidents or rights attach to the ownership of property conveyed by the government will be determined by the States, subject to the condition that their rules do not impair the efficacy of the grants or the use and enjoyment of the property by the grantee.

This doctrine was squarely applied to the case of a riparian proprietor in *Joy v. City of St. Louis* [201 U.S. 332, 26 S. Ct. 478, 50 L. Ed. 776] (1906). The land at issue had originally been granted to the patentee's predecessor by Spain, and Congress had confirmed the grant and issued letters patent. This Court held that the fact that a plaintiff claimed accretions to land patented to his predecessor by the Federal Government did not confer federal question jurisdiction, and implicitly rejected any notion that "federal common law" had any application to the resolution. Central to this result was the holding that:

> As this land in controversy is not the land described in the letters patent or the Acts of Congress, but, as is stated in the petition, is formed by accretions or gradual deposits from the river, whether such land belongs to the plaintiff is, under the cases just cited, a matter of local or state law, and not one arising under the laws of the United States. [201 U.S.], at 343 [26 S. Ct. at 481, 50 L. Ed. at 782].

V

Upon full reconsideration of our decision in *Bonelli*, we conclude that it was wrong in treating the equal-footing doctrine as a source of federal common law after that doctrine had vested title to the riverbed in the State of Arizona as of the time of its admission to the Union. We also think there was no other basis in that case, nor is there any in this case, to support the application of federal common law to override state real property law. There are obviously institutional considerations which we must face in deciding whether for that reason to overrule *Bonelli* or to adhere to it, and those considerations cut both ways. Substantive rules governing the law of real property are peculiarly subject to the principle of *stare decisis*.

Here, however, we are not dealing with substantive property law as such, but rather with an issue substantially related to the constitutional sovereignty of the States. In cases such as this, considerations of *stare decisis* play a less important role than they do in cases involving substantive property law. Even if we were to focus on the effect of our decision upon rules of substantive property law, our concern for unsettling titles would lead us to overrule *Bonelli*, rather than to retain it. Since one system of resolution of property disputes has been adhered to from 1845 until 1973, and the other only for the past three years, a return to the former would more closely conform to the expectations of property owners than would adherence to the latter. We are also persuaded that, in large part because of the positions taken in the briefs presented to the Court in *Bonelli*, the *Bonelli* decision was not a deliberate repudiation of all the cases which had gone before. We there proceeded on the view, which we now think to have been mistaken, that *Borax* should be read so expansively as to in effect overrule *sub-silentio* the line of cases following *Pollard's Lessee*.

For all of these reasons, we have now decided that *Bonelli's* application of federal common law to cases such as this must be overruled.

The judgment under review is vacated, and the case remanded to the Supreme Court of Oregon for further proceedings not inconsistent with this opinion.

[The dissenting statement of MR. JUSTICE BRENNAN is omitted.]

MR. JUSTICE MARSHALL, with whom MR. JUSTICE WHITE joins, dissenting.

The Court today overrules a three–year–old decision, *Bonelli Cattle Co. v. Arizona*, 414 U.S. 313 [94 S. Ct. 517, 38 L. Ed. 2d 526] (1973), in which seven of the eight participating Justices joined. In addition, as the Court is certain to announce when the occasion arises, today's holding also overrules *Hughes v. Washington*, 389 U.S. 290 [88 S. Ct. 438, 19 L. Ed. 2d. 530] (1967), a nine-year-old decision also joined by all but one of the participating Justices.[4] It is surprising, to say the least, to find these nearly unanimous recent decisions swept away in the name of *stare decisis*.

The public, especially holders of riparian or littoral property whose titles derive from the United States, deserve some explanation for the Court's change of course. Yet today's majority does not contend either that circumstances have changed since 1973 or that experience has shown *Hughes* and *Bonelli* to be unworkable. Nor does the majority attempt to explain why a result it finds so clearly commanded by our earlier cases was almost unanimously rejected by this Court twice in the last decade. We are left, then, with a mystery.

I respectfully suggest that the solution to this puzzle is not hard to find. In contrast to the *Bonelli* and *Hughes* Courts, the Court today decides a question the parties did not present, brief, or argue. By so doing, the Court rules without the benefit of "that concrete adverseness which sharpens the presentation of issues upon which the court so largely depends for illumination of difficult constitutional questions." The lack of illumination has caused the Court to choose the wrong path.

I

The question the Court elects to decide in this case is whether a grant of riparian[5] land by the Federal Government is to be interpreted according to federal or state law. The Court holds that federal law governs only the determination of the initial boundaries of the grant; all other questions are to be determined under state law. This conclusion depends on an unjustifiably limited interpretation of the meaning of a riparian grant.

. . . .

There can be no doubt that the federal grantee's expectation that his grant would be interpreted according to federal law and his belief that federal law would recognize boundary shifts occasioned by changes in the course of the water bordering his land were well founded. . . .

Thus, the right to such additions[6] was part of the title which passed with the federal grant and was protected by federal law. By holding that state law

[4]Although the Court rejects the reasoning on which *Hughes* is based, it refrains from formally overruling *Hughes* on the ground that that case was not relied on in *Bonelli* and not cited by the Oregon courts below. . . .

Nevertheless, the majority suggest that *Hughes* might still control oceanfront property. It is difficult to take seriously the suggestion that the national interest in international relations justifies applying a different rule to oceanfront land grants than to other grants by the Federal Government. It is clear that the States have complete title to the lands below the line of mean high tide. These lands, of course, are the only place where the waters "lap both the lands of the State and the boundaries of the international sea." There are no international relations implications in the ownership of land above the line of mean high tide.

[5]For convenience, I will use "riparian" in place of "riparian or littoral" for the remainder of this opinion.

[6]In *Bonelli*, the question was ownership of relicted land, which is land exposed by the subsidence of the water. The law of reliction is identical to the law of accretion. In the present case,

now governs the impact of changes in the course of the bordering water on a federal riparian grant, the Court denies that "a question which concerns the validity and effect of an act done by the United States" is "necessarily a federal question." *Borax, Ltd. v. Los Angeles*, 296 U.S. 10, 22 [56 S. Ct. 23, 29; 80 L. Ed. 9, 17] (1935). As far as federal law is concerned, a federal riparian grant is now understood to have incorporated a fixed rather than ambulatory boundary. . . .

. . . .

Thus, the cases refute the majority's contention that the results in *Hughes* and *Bonelli* sharply departed from prior law. Today's holding cannot, therefore, be based on interpretation of the meaning of the prestatehood riparian grants under which Corvallis Sand and Gravel holds title, since the right to an ambulatory boundary was assumed to be part of the rights of a riparian grantee at the time the grants were made. Moreover, the cases also demonstrate that there is no constitutional basis for today's holding. The only constitutional question discussed in the majority opinion is the law governing the States' title to land beneath navigable waters, and the rights of the riparian holder are independent of that law.

II

Since today's ruling cannot be a matter either of constitutional law or of interpretation of the meaning of federal grants, it must be a choice-of-law decision. In deciding whether to formulate and apply a federal common law rule, "normally the guiding principle is that a significant conflict between some federal policy or interest and the use of state law in the premises must first be specifically shown." *Wallis v. Pan American Petroleum Corp.*, 384 U.S. 63, 68 [86 S. Ct. 1301, 1304; 16 L. Ed. 2d. 369, 373] (1966). In order to assure an informed presentation of federal policies and interests when faced with a choice between federal and state law, this Court in the past has invited the Solicitor General to file a brief *amicus curiae* expressing the views of the United States. We followed this practice in both *Bonelli* and *Hughes* and the Solicitor General participated as an *amicus* in both cases.

Today's majority has made no similar effort to inform itself about the impact of its ruling on the Federal Government. Indeed, the majority opinion does not even consider that issue, although it is normally central to a choice-of-law decision. As the opinion and result show, the only views the Court has received are those of the *amici* States, whose interests here are hostile to those of the United States.

I cannot, of course, know what the Solicitor General would have said had the Court indicated that it was considering a choice-of-law question and invited

---

the State claims title to land by virtue of the doctrine of erosion, the converse of accretion. Corvallis Sand and Gravel resists by arguing that the change in the river's course was not gradual, as erosion and accretion require, but sudden. A sudden, or avulsive, change does not effect a shift in boundaries. These doctrines form a coherent system. It would make no sense to hold that the federal doctrine of accretion must be applied to the benefit of a federal riparian grantee but that the federal doctrine of avulsion need not be applied.

him to present the views of the Government. In both *Bonelli* and *Hughes*, however, the submissions for the United States as *amicus curiae* strongly urged the Court to hold that federal rather than state law governed the case. In *Bonelli*, the Government noted that its quiet enjoyment of the more than 200 miles of Colorado River shoreline it owned in Arizona had been threatened by some interpretations of the state court's decision. The Government urged that the state court opinion be given a narrow interpretation and affirmed as consistent with the applicable federal law.

In *Hughes*, the Government urged that the decision of the State Supreme Court be reversed. The Solicitor General explained that the Government considered that decision a serious threat:

> The decision is of broad consequence. In trenches on a significant element of title to realty acquired from the United States in the past and it materially curtails the nature of the title that the United States may convey in the future. . . . Equally important, it affects the powers of the United States with respect to more than 200 miles of Washington's coastline owned today by the federal government. Moreover, the principle of a fixed tideland boundary may readily be brought to bear on the property of the United States and its patentees in other coastal States. . . . Nor is there any apparent reason why, in Washington or elsewhere, the principle should be limited to tidelands; it can be applied with consistency of logic to the shifting banks of rivers and lakes owned by a State. . . . An inducement for the adoption and expansion of this principle is not lacking, since it tends inevitably to bring land into State ownership, and the sale of land thus acquired has been recognized as an attractive source of State revenue. . . .
>
> To be sure, the court below stated that it did not 'question the federal government's right over its own property'. . . [But] the court below failed to recognize that 'the federal government's right over its own property' embraces the right effectively to dispose of such property. Memorandum for the United States as *Amicus Curiae* 3–5, *Hughes v. Washington*.

The Solicitor General explained that the decision in *Hughes* endangered the Government's ability to carry out congressional policy towards Indians, since the Government would no longer have been able to convey rights to a boundary adjacent to the sea if it turned over trust lands to the Indian beneficiaries. But the problem with the Indian trust lands was merely "exemplary" because the state decision in *Hughes*

> restrains the government from disposing of the full measure of its title in connection with any program or policy which it may wish to pursue in the future. In sum, we do not believe that it can be said here, as it could in *Wallis v. Pan American Petroleum Corp.*, 384 U.S. 63, 68 [86 S. Ct. 1301, 1304; 16 L. Ed. 2d. 369, 373], that there is 'no significant threat to any identifiable federal policy or interest'. Memorandum for the United States as *Amicus Curiae* 6, *Hughes v. Washington*.

Today's decision necessarily has an even greater impact on federal interests, since it casts doubt on the Government's continued ownership "of the full measure of its title."

III

One final word. *Stare decisis* should be more than a fine sounding phrase. This is especially true for us, because "unless we respect the . . . decisions of this Court, we can hardly expect that others will do so." *Mitchell v. W.T. Grant Co.,* 416 U.S. 600, 634 [94 S. Ct. 1895, 1913; 40 L. Ed. 2d. 406, 429] (1974) (STEWART, J., dissenting). Accordingly, "[a] substantial departure from precedent can only be justified . . . in the light of experience with the application of the rule to be abandoned or in the light of an altered historic environment." *Id.,* 416 U.S. at 634–635 [94 S. Ct. at 1913, 40 L. Ed. 2d at 429]. Such admonitions are even more salient where land titles are concerned. Yet the majority has advanced neither experience nor changed circumstances to justify its internment of a 7–1 decision of this Court issued barely three years ago.

I am convinced that if the Court had considered the cases on which it relies in the light of an adversary presentation and had invited the Government to explain its interest in the application of federal law, the result today would be different. I therefore respectfully dissent.

NOTES

1. After *Corvallis*, are the states free to adopt any boundary rules they please, even for inland navigable waters? *See State v. Florida Nat. Properties, Inc.,* 338 So. 2d 13 (Fla. 1976); Maloney, *The Ordinary High Water Mark: Attempts at Settling an Unsettled Boundary Line*, 13 Land & Water L. Rev. 465, 498 (1978).

   Limited by Const.

2. On remand, the Oregon Supreme Court held that long-standing principles of riparian water law, specifically the avulsion exception to the general accretion rule of shifting boundaries, gave title to the new bed of the Willamette River to the Corvallis Sand & Gravel Company. *See State v. Corvallis Sand & Gravel Co.,* 283 Or. 147, 582 P.2d 1352 (1978), criticized 60 Ore. L. Rev. No. 3 at 273 (1981). The state argued that such a decision would create a patchwork pattern of private ownership along the Willamette, make rules governing the leasing of rights in the riverbed difficult or impossible to enforce, and hamper state efforts to protect the environment. In holding against the state, the Oregon court cited *Hughes v. Washington* (concurring opinion by Stewart, J.) for the proposition that a drastic shift in Oregon law would result in a taking of property without compensation.

3. Subsequent to both *Hughes* and *Corvallis*, a unanimous Washington Supreme Court in *Columbia Rentals, Inc. v. State,* 89 Wash. 2d 819, 576 P.2d 62 (1978), reversed a summary judgment extending the western boundary of each respondents' oceanfront property to a line west of that established in 74 prior quiet-title actions, the last of which was resolved in 1961.

   The state contended the trial court was in error in its ruling for four reasons: (a) the actions were barred by the doctrine of *res judicata*; (b) the actions were barred by the statute of limitations; (c) the state had acquired title to the accretions by adverse possession; and (d) the owners were barred by the doctrine of laches.

   The Washington Supreme Court noted that *Corvallis* cast doubt on the continued viability of *Hughes*, and decided the case by application of the doctrine of *res judicata* (not reaching the other issues raised by the parties). The court found specifically that judgment in most of the earlier cases was entered by agreement of the parties, that each had been represented by attorneys, that none of the judgments had been appealed, and that "[i]f prior judgments could be modified to conform with subsequent changes in judicial interpretations, we might never see the end of litigation." 576 P.2d at 65. The effect of this decision and the *Hughes* decision has been the creation of a "checkerboard" pattern of ownership along the western boundaries of Washington's Pacific County.

4. *See also File v. State*, 593 P.2d 268 (Alaska 1979) (accreted land on Gustineau Channel awarded to state); *State by Kobayashi v. Zinsing*, 566 P.2d 725 (Hawaii 1977) (7.9 acres of volcanic lava flow added to the island of Hawaii awarded to the state); *U.S. v. Wilson*, 433 F. Supp. 57 (1977) (state law applies in allocating the burden of persuasion in an accretion–avulsion dispute).

5. For additional reading, see Comment, *Land Accretion and Avulsion: The Battle of Blackbird Bend*, 56 Neb. L. Rev. 814 (1977); Comment, *Mineral and Surface Rights Under the Doctrine of Accretion*, 20 Nat. Res. 199–203 (1980); Davis, *State Ownership of Beds of Inland Waters—A Summary and Reexamination*, 57 Neb. L. Rev. 665 (1978).

6. Supplement

3

State Common Law and the Coastal Zone

SECTION A: PRIVATE RIGHTS

The Wharf-Out Issue

**COMMISSION ON MARINE SCIENCE, ENGINEERING
AND RESOURCES, REPORT OF THE PANEL ON
MANAGEMENT AND DEVELOPMENT OF THE COASTAL ZONE**

Regulation of Wharves, Piers, and Other Structures

While in English common law the upland owner had no right to wharf out into the tidelands without a permit, early decisions in the United States encouraged the erection of wharves for the benefit of navigation and commerce. At present a majority of the coastal states allow the adjacent owner to wharf out in most cases without a permit, either as part of the state's common law or by statute. Of course, as we shall learn later, a federal permit from the Corps of Engineers is now required for all such structures in navigable waters.

However, probably all states exert some form of control over the construction of wharves, piers, and other structures, even where the state still recognizes the right of a riparian owner to wharf out over tidelands. Some states control construction of wharves, piers, and other structures through detailed legislation. Some exercise control through delegation to a state agency, or by delegation to a local agency.

Municipalities are normally granted powers by the state to regulate the construction of wharves and other structures in the waters within their boundaries, and to regulate the use of those structures, including regulation by zoning under the police power delegated to the municipalities.

BLOOM v. WATER RESOURCES COMMISSION
157 Conn. 528, 254 A.2d 884 (1969)

KING, Chief Justice

On October 9, 1967, the defendant Albert E. Vallerie filed with the named defendant, the state Water Resources Commission, hereinafter referred to as the commission, an application for a permit "to construct and maintain a travel lift well, ramps, floats, mooring piles and [to] dredge an area to 6' at mean low water in front of . . . [the Vallerie] property . . . [on the] Norwalk River. . . ." The application also stated that dredged material would be deposited in an approved spoil area in Long Island Sound and that a federal permit had been applied for from the army engineers.

In somewhat more detail, the application sought a permit (1) to construct a marina embracing three ramps, twenty-four feet by three feet, four lines of floats measuring from 120 feet by 5 feet to 200 feet by 5 feet with a total of twenty-one finger floats of from twenty feet by three feet to thirty feet by three feet, and sixty-eight mooring piles and then (2) to dredge approximately 5000 cubic yards of underwater material. The Norwalk River at the location in question is navigable, and, as shown on the plan accompanying the application, a United States Pier and Bulkhead line has been established.

. . . .

[An objection (by letter) to the issuance of a permit was filed with the commission by Norman and Hillard Bloom and Wallace H. Bell, Jr. (plaintiffs) who own and operate Bell's Boat Yard, which adjoins the Vallerie property on the north. The Blooms are also lessees and operators of the Tallmadge Brothers Oyster Company, which adjoins the Vallerie property on the south.

[The plaintiffs complained that the installation of piles and floats by Vallerie would prevent ingress or egress to the boat yard, except from the easterly side of the Bell property facing the channel. In addition, the proposed dredging would undermine a marine railway running along the southerly boundary of the Bell property.

[The plaintiffs also stated that some oyster boats, in entering or leaving the Tallmadge oyster pier, are often required by wind or tide conditions to swing as far north as the most northerly side of the Vallerie pier. Such actions might result in striking and damaging boats at the Vallerie marina and that efforts to avoid this risk might force the Tallmadge operation to close down.

[For these reasons, the plaintiffs asserted that the Vallerie proposal would be an impediment to navigation and an unwarranted interference with the proper development and use of adjoining uplands.

[The plaintiffs also offered to present evidence if the commission scheduled a hearing on the application.]

On December 27, 1967, the commission [without a hearing] issued a certificate or permit under General Statutes §§25–7b and 25–7d and sent a copy to the army engineers. The permit required that the work be completed on or before December 27, 1970, and that the commission be notified upon completion. It also contained a statement that the permit "is subject to and in no way derogates [sic] any present or future property or other rights or powers of the State of Connecticut, and conveys no property rights in real estate or material nor any exclusive privileges, and is further subject to any and all public and private rights and to any federal state or local laws or regulations pertinent to the property or activity affected hereby."

On January 8, 1968, the army engineers issued a federal permit for the work, conditioned and restricted in a manner similar to that set forth in the commission's permit.

From the commission's action in granting the permit, the plaintiffs, on December 29, 1967, appealed to the Superior Court, joining Vallerie as a party defendant. From an adverse decision of the Superior Court, the plaintiffs took this appeal.

The basic complaint is that the commission should have held a hearing before acting on the application for a permit, and this claim is based on two grounds: (1) Since the application seeks the dredging and removal of about 5000 cubic yards of underwater material, the application falls within the provisions of General Statutes §§25–10, 25–11 and 25–12, which require a public hearing before the issuance of a removal permit. (2) In any event the issuance of the permit was in essence an adjudicative proceeding directly affecting the rights of the plaintiffs, and thus due process required a hearing. . . .

At the outset, it is important to bear in mind certain of the common-law rights of Vallerie. The state, as the representative of the public, is the owner of the soil between high- and low-water mark upon navigable water where the tide ebbs and flows. But Vallerie's ownership of the adjoining upland gave him certain exclusive yet qualified rights and privileges in the waters and submerged land adjoining, and in front of, his upland. These rights included "the exclusive right to dig channels and build wharves from his land to reach deep water, so long as he does not interfere with free navigation."

It is apparent that the application for a permit sought nothing except "in front of" the Vallerie property. There is no claim, and nothing to indicate, that Vallerie seeks to place any installations on, or otherwise to interfere with any submerged land adjoining the plaintiffs' upland. There is nothing unreasonable or improper in digging the channel so as to have a minimum depth of six feet at mean low water. Indeed, anything much less in depth would obviously be inadequate safely to accommodate pleasure craft of the type the marina is intended to serve.

. . . .

It does not appear that any dredging was contemplated by Vallerie except, in the language of §25–7d, "incidental" to the erection of the marina in the manner described in the application and the provision for passage between the marina and the channel without which the marina would be unusable. There was no claim or justification for any claim that, as in *Shorehaven Golf Club, Inc. v. Water Resources Commission*, 146 Conn. 619, 625, 153 A.2d 444, the real purpose of Vallerie was to remove underwater material, and that the clearing of a channel was a subterfuge and a mere incident to an actual removal operation which would have required a permit under §25–11. It follows that §§25–7b and 25–7d were, as the commission and Vallerie claimed, the applicable sections and that there was no statutory requirement of a public hearing.

The second claim of the plaintiffs, and that most strongly stressed and relied upon by them, is that the commission's action was adjudicative and thus required a prior hearing regardless of the absence of any statutory requirement.

In the first place, as already pointed out, Vallerie sought nothing which he did not have at common law. The plaintiffs make no claim that Vallerie sought to erect any pile or structure on their property or on that in which they have littoral rights. Rather, the plaintiff's main claim really was that at times they could not maneuver their oyster boats up to their dock without swinging in front of the Vallerie pier and that in order that the plaintiffs might continue so to maneuver their oyster boats Vallerie would have to forgo the contemplated utilization of his own littoral rights. As to the marine railway, the plaintiffs seem to be claiming some right to its lateral support. If any such right exists, it would necessarily impair Vallerie's littoral rights.

But the most important factor is that it is clear from the limitations in the permit issued by the commission that it grants no rights to Vallerie as against the plaintiffs or anyone else. As pointed out in *Shorehaven Golf Club, Inc. v. Water Resources Commission, supra* 146 Conn. 624, 153 A.2d 444, the common-law riparian rights are subject to reasonable police [power] regulation in the interest of the public welfare and have been held subject to such regulation for many years. Such regulation is taking place here. In other words, Vallerie's common-law rights, if anyone's, are curtailed by the statutes in question. The plaintiffs' rights, such as they are, remain, by the express terms of the permit, unaffected by it.

The plaintiffs, when directly asked in oral argument, denied any claim that the failure of §25–7d to require a hearing was, in and of itself, a fatal constitutional defect. Rather, they claimed that in this particular case the issuance of the permit, without according the plaintiffs a hearing, was a denial of due process as to them and, so, rendered the issuance of the permit an unconstitutional act on the part of the commission.

More specifically, the plaintiffs' claim was that the proceeding was adjudicative and, so, required a hearing, and this claim, in turn, is based on the plaintiffs' contention that the commission, in issuing the permit, was engaging in a quasi-judicial determination of the respective littoral rights of Vallerie and the plaintiffs, stemming from their respective ownership of adjoining lands. For the reasons already pointed out, no such quasi-judicial determination took place or was attempted. The commission, like the army engineers, was determining to what, if any, extent, under the police power, there should be curtailment of Vallerie's common-law rights to wharf out and dredge to get access to the channel of the river. This was not, at least as to the plaintiffs, an adjudicative procedure and did not purport to, nor did it, curtail any rights the plaintiffs had. If the plaintiffs' rights were infringed, or threatened with infringement, by Vallerie, they can be protected, or damage to them redressed, in an appropriate action where, of course, the plaintiffs may be fully heard. To such an action the commission's permit to Vallerie, by its own terms, would not constitute an effective defense.

For the foregoing reasons we conclude that the issuance of the permit to Vallerie was not an adjudicative action as to the plaintiffs such as to entitle them, as a requirement of due process, to a hearing.

There is no error.

NOTES

1. The Commission in *Bloom* allowed Vallerie to build his marina despite its interference with the private use of the river by Bloom's oyster boats. Of what relevance in permit proceedings are conflicting uses by adjacent owners? *See Matter of Appeal from Denial of Permit to Dredge*, 261 S.E.2d 510 (N.C. App. 1980). Are the rights of adjacent owners different from the rights of the public? Would Vallerie's marina interfere with public use as well as private?

2. Vallerie did not have exclusive rights to use the submerged land adjacent to his property, but he had a qualified right to wharf out to deep water. Vallerie's common law rights were qualified by statutes and regulations. Statutory controls vary among the states. Recently, some states have enacted zoning laws forbidding any construction whatsoever along coastlines without special permission. *See* Maloney & O'Donnell, *Drawing the Line at the Oceanfront: The Role of Coastal Construction Setback Lines in Regulating Development of the Coastal Zone*, 30 U. Fla. L. Rev. 383 (1978).
   What happened to the common law right to wharf out?

3. Note the number of hoops a littoral landowner must jump through to exercise his common law rights. Vallerie had to comply with local, state, and federal regulations to build his marina. These regulations often overlap and cause confusion as to who has authority in a given situation. *See* Note, *The Wetlands Controversy: A Coastal Concern Washes Inland*, 52 Notre Dame Law. 1015 (1977).
   One thing, however, is clear. The Army Corps of Engineers, due to recent federal legislation, has gained increased power to regulate development of the coastal zone. For discussions of this expansion, *see* Note, *Federal Control over Wetland Areas: The Corps of Engineers Expands Its Jurisdiction*, 28 U. Fla. L. Rev. 787 (1976); and Power, *The Fox in the Chicken Coop: The Regulatory Program of the U.S. Army Corps of Engineers*, 63 Va. L. Rev. 503 (1977). For an example of the handling of a proposed coastal development project, *see* Power, *Watergate Village: A Case Study of a Permit Application for a Marina Submitted to the U.S. Army Corps of Engineers*, 2 Coastal Zone Mgmt. J. 103 (1975).

4. In *Lummis v. Lilly*, 429 N.E.2d 1146 (Mass. Sup. Ct. 1982), the court held that littoral owners exercising their littoral rights, e.g., by constructing a groin perpendicular to the beach pursuant to state and federal permits, must act reasonably with respect to neighboring littoral owners. Is *Lummis* consistent with *Bloom*?

SMITH TUG & BARGE CO. v. COLUMBIA-PACIFIC TOWING CORP., 250 Or. 612, 443 P.2d 205 (1968)

DENECKE, Justice.

The perplexing issue in this case is who has the right to moor logs and build facilities therefor in the Columbia River below the low-water mark.

The defendant, Columbia-Pacific Towing Corporation, purchased what is known as Sharkey or Sandy Island, which lies in the Columbia off Goble, on the Oregon side of the river. Its title goes to the island's high-water mark. The water around the island is a desirable log storage area.

The State of Oregon owns the area between the high- and low-water marks of the island. The State also has title to the bed of the river below the low-water mark.

The State advertised for bids for the lease of the land surrounding the island and lying between the low- and high-water marks. The defendant submitted the minimum bid and the plaintiffs submitted the bid of $15,000 per year. Pursuant to ORS 274.040, the defendant was given the opportunity to meet this highest bid of $15,000 and exercise its preference. It declined and the State leased such land to plaintiffs.

Plaintiffs brought this declaratory judgment proceeding and asked the trial court to declare that plaintiffs had the exclusive right to the use of all the land abutting upon or adjacent to the island below the low-water mark as well as land below the high-water mark. The State was named as a party but took no active part in the proceeding and is not a party to this appeal.

The trial court found in favor of plaintiffs, and the defendant appeals.

The river at this point is subject to the ocean tides. The logs would be moored below the low-water mark and the pilings and dolphins that must be driven into the land under water would be in the same area, with a few, perhaps, between the high- and low-water marks.

The land lying above the high-water mark is customarily called the upland. The land lying between the high-water mark and the low-water mark in tidal waters is described as tidelands. The Oregon statute, to describe the land between the high-water mark and the low-water mark in both tidal and nontidal waters, uses the phrase "submersible lands," and we shall likewise use such phrase to describe such lands. ORS 274.005(4). Oregon statutes use the phrase "submerged lands" to describe the land lying below the low-water mark whether in tidal or nontidal waters. ORS 274.705(8) and 274.005(5).

The parties claims are unique in property law in that they are both claiming the right to use the water below the low-water mark and the submerged land beneath this water, to which they claim no title or casement by grant. Their claim is grounded solely upon the proposition that their lease of the tidelands,— in the case of the plaintiffs,—and its ownership of the upland,—in the case of the defendant Columbia-Pacific Towing Corporation—carries with it the right to use the water and the submerged land below the water which is adjacent to the island.

This contention, although it is peculiar to rights in waters, is well accepted. The problem in this case is to determine what are the rights in the adjacent waters and submerged lands below concomitant to ownership of the upland and the tideland and, in the event of a conflict, which rights are paramount.

. . . .

The plaintiffs, the tideland lessees, primarily rely upon Bowlby v. Shively, 22 Or. 410, 30 P. 154, affm'd 152 U.S. 1, 14 S. Ct. 548, 38 L. Ed. 331 (1893). Shively platted certain Astoria property lying below the high-water mark and sold such property to Bowlby's predecessor in title. The conveyance made no mention of wharfage rights. Shively contended that such silence indicated a reservation to him of his right to wharf from the upland over the tidelands conveyed to Bowlby's predecessor out to navigable water. The State conveyed the tidelands to Bowlby. Bowlby built a wharf out into the Columbia River and Shively urged that such wharf was in violation of his riparian right of wharfage. The court held for Bowlby, the tidelands owner, and against Shively, the upland owner.

Mr. Justice Lord, writing for a unanimous court, declared that "'the opinion of some of our predecessors in adjudged cases'" was "that the state may sell and convey its tide lands, and that its grantees take them free from any right therein by the upland owner, and subject only to the paramount right of navigation inherent in the public. . . ." 22 Or. at 422–423, 30 P. at 158.

. . . .

This case was affirmed by the Supreme Court of the United States, which held:

" . . . The title and rights of riparian or littoral proprietors in the soil below high-water mark, therefore, are governed by the laws of the several States, subject to the rights granted to the United States by the Constitution." 152 U.S. at 57–58, 14 S. Ct. at 569.

. . . .

We have finally come to the conclusion that when the State has leased or conveyed the tidelands bordering on tidal waters the riparian rights are lodged in the tidelands owner or lessee. This includes the right to build structures on the bed below low-water mark and the right to moor logs on the water.

We believe such a decision is in accord with the tenor of most of our past decisions, particularly the cornerstone case of Bowlby v. Shively, supra, 22 Or. 423, 30 P. 154. Such disposition also appears to be the more realistic solution. If the ownership or possession of the tidelands were private at the time the upland was purchased, the purchaser should have been put on notice because of Bowlby v. Shively, supra, 22 Or. 410, 30 P. 154, and its successors, that at the very least it was questionable whether the upland had any rights across the privately-owned tidelands.

If ownership of the tidelands was in the State of Oregon at the time of the acquisition of the upland, the upland owner, pursuant to long-standing legislation, has a preference in leasing or purchasing the tidelands if the State decides to lease or convey the tidelands. As stated, the statutory preference is the right to lease or purchase by offering an amount equal to the highest price offered in good faith.

Usually, although not in the case of log storage, the upland owner's access to the interior makes the possession or ownership of the tidelands more valuable to the upland owner than to anyone else and he can, in the exercise of good business judgment, match the amount bid by anyone else.

It should be remembered that the public has certain rights in the tidelands, the submersible lands, and the land below the low-water mark; this element of the State's interest is referred to as jus publicum, i.e., the right of public use. It is not necessary in the instant case to specifically define these public rights. See Corvallis Sand & Gravel v. State Land Bd., 86 O.R.S. 469, 439 P.2d 575 (1968). In the newest treatise on the subject of water rights, 1 Clark (Editor-in-Chief), Waters and Water Rights, 247 (1967), the writer states: "jus publicum— i.e., the rights of the public to navigate, to fish, and to pass over the tidelands and submerged coastal lands, these being the principal public demands for the use of the seacoast."

As a consequence of our decision that the lessee of the tidelands has the right to moor logs below the low-water mark, we must consider the defendant's contention that the plaintiffs are not lessees because their bid and the lease made pursuant to such bid are invalid. Defendant charges that the bid and the lease are conditional, and, therefore, not in accord with the notice calling for bids.

. . . .

We find that the variation was substantial and rendered the bid and the consequent lease invalid.

NOTES

1. Oregon originally granted upland owners no riparian rights of access or wharfage over tidelands as against the state or its grantees. *Bowlby v. Shively*, 22 Or. 410, 30 P. 154 (1892), *aff'd Shively v. Bowlby*, 152 U.S. 1 (1894) *supra*. Later, the Oregon Supreme Court modified its position in *Bowlby*. The riparian owner on navigable water had, in the absence of any statute regulating or prohibiting such activity, the "right" to construct a log boom or other structure adjacent to his property. *Coquille M & M Co. v. Johnson*, 52 Or. 547, 98 P. 132 (1908).

2. So far we have mentioned only Columbia–Pacific's private rights to use the tidelands. The court in *Smith Tug & Barge* notes, almost as an aside, that "[i]t should be remembered that the public has certain rights in the tidelands." 350 Or. 612, 638; 443 P.2d 205 (1968). Here again, as in *Bloom*, the court tips its hat to the public trust doctrine. According to this doctrine, the state cannot convey unfettered ownership of submerged and tidal lands to private owners. The state may sell or lease certain proprietary rights which it owns, but the land remains subject to the *jus publicum*—the "nondelegable government obligation" to manage these lands in the public interest. *Brusco Towboat v. State Land Board*, 30 Or. App. 509, 567 P.2d 1037 (1977), *modified*, 31 Or. App. 491, *modified*, 284 Or. 627 (1978). The public interest is usually construed to include rights of free navigation, fishing, and recreation in the water overhead!

BRUSCO TOWBOAT v. STATE LAND BOARD, 30 Or. App. 509, 567 P.2d 1037, *rehearing denied*, 31 Or. App. 491, 570 P.2d 996 (1977), *aff'd as modified*, 284 Or. 627, 589 P.2d 712 (1978)

TANZER, J.

The basic issue in each of these three consolidated cases is the validity of rules promulgated by the State Land Board requiring users to enter into leases and to pay rent for the use of submerged and submersible lands underlying navigable waterways throughout the state.

The first case, an action in ejectment, was commenced by the Board against the Fort Vancouver Plywood Company to compel it either to enter into a lease for or to vacate submerged lands which it used for a log boom. It was treated below as a suit for declaratory judgment and it will be so treated here. The other two cases are suits for declaratory judgment commenced by various tugboat companies and by several port districts seeking to have the Board's leasing program declared invalid. Judgments in all three cases upheld the lease program and this appeal followed. For convenience, all parties challenging the leasing program will be referred to herein as plaintiffs.

I. The Rules

The rules in issue establish a program for leasing state-owned submerged and submersible lands:

"Any person engaged in a permanent or long-term use of state-owned submerged or submersible lands not exempted from leasing by statute or these regulations must obtain a lease from the Division. . . . " OAR 141–82–015(1).

Under the program, leases are required for most long-term uses of submerged and submersible lands which effectively preclude any other use and enjoyment of such lands and the overlying waters. Thus, leases are required for most industrial and commercial uses including log booms, aquatic cultivation facilities and marinas, as well as for private uses such as houseboat moorages and private docks.

All of the plaintiffs, in connection with the ordinary conduct of their business, maintain permanent facilities overlying submerged and submersible lands which are not exempted from the Board's leasing program. With minor exceptions, these facilities preclude the public's use and enjoyment of the lands and waters which overlie them. At least some of the plaintiffs are riparian landowners.

Plaintiffs challenge the validity of the Board's leasing program on several grounds. They contend that the state's proprietary interest in submerged and submersible lands underlying navigable waters does not empower it to convey leasehold interests in such land to private parties. The riparian landowner plaintiffs argue that they have the right to erect structures in aid of navigation on submerged and submersible land and that the charging of rent for the exercise of that riparian right is an unlawful taking of property without compensation. Plaintiffs also contend that the leasing program is beyond the statutory authority of the State Land Board and that the program violates various provisions of the Oregon and United States Constitutions.

Resolution of these challenges requires that we draw the line which separates the opposing property rights of the state and of the riparian owners. That in turn requires an understanding of the nature and extent of each.

II. The State's Ownership of Submerged and Submersible Lands

A. The Nature of the State's Interest

The sovereign interest of the State of Oregon in submerged and submersible lands underlying navigable waters is substantially the same as that enjoyed at common law by the English king. . . .

Under English common law, title to lands underlying tidal waters was held by the king as an element of sovereignty. After the American Revolution, each of the original colonies assumed its own sovereign powers, one aspect of which was ownership of all submerged and submersible lands underlying navigable waters. . . .

. . . Thus, upon its admission in 1859, title to submerged and submersible lands underlying navigable waters devolved upon the state as sovereign.

The state's ownership of submerged and submersible land is not, however, limited to the incidents of legal title. Rather, it is comprised of an interrelationship of two distinct aspects, each possessing its own characteristics.

As sovereign, the state holds full proprietary rights in such land; it is invested with a fee simple title. This first element of the state's interest is called the *jus privatum. See, Shively v. Bowlby,* 152 U.S. 1, 11, 14 S. Ct. 548, 38 L. Ed. 331 (1894).

Dominion, as opposed to title, over submerged and submersible lands, as a natural resource, is invested in the state in its capacity as the public's representative. The state holds such dominion in trust for the public. This second aspect of the state's ownership is called the *jus publicum. See, Shively v. Bowlby, supra,* 152 U.S. at 11.

The state's *jus privatum* interest is a construct of English common law. It is the traditional legal proprietary right of private ownership. It is axiomatic that within the common law property system all land must be owned by someone. Since submerged and submersible lands are incapable of ordinary private occupation and improvement and since their common uses are essentially public in nature, full legal ownership in fee simple devolved upon the sovereign. *See, Shively v. Bowlby, supra,* 152 U.S. at 11. Such ownership includes the most important aspect of the fee simple, the power of alienation. . . .

. . . .

The *jus publicum* aspect of the state's ownership is rooted in a philosophical conception of natural law. The principle that the public has an overriding interest in navigable waterways and lands underlying them is as old as the waterways themselves, traceable at least to the Code of Justinian in the Fifth Century A.D. *See,* Advisory Committee to the State Land Board, Oregon's Submerged and Submersible Lands 15 (1970). Navigable waterways are a valuable and essential natural resource and as such all people have an interest in maintaining them for commerce, fishing and recreation. The right of the public to use the waterways for these purposes has always been recognized at common law. . . .

. . . .

In essence, the *jus publicum* is a nondelegable government obligation. Regardless of how the state may choose to convey its private title to submerged and submersible lands, such title, even in the hands of a private party, remains subject to the paramount power of the state to intervene on behalf of the public interest.

This division of the state's interest into two parts, one alienable and one not, is consistent with English common law. . . .

. . . .

We hold, therefore, that the state has a proprietary interest sufficient to empower it to convey to private parties leasehold interests in submerged and submersible lands underlying navigable waters. The granting, withholding and management of such leaseholds, however, as exercises of the state's proprietary rights, remain subject to the public's paramount interest in such lands and the state, as trustee of that interest, must act accordingly.

B. Statutory Authority for the Lease Program

The next issue is whether the State Land Board is authorized to exercise the state's proprietary interest by leasing submerged and submersible lands pursuant to its rules. Plaintiffs contend that the constitutional and statutory provisions under which the Board acts do not provide such authority.

. . . .

In view of the broad constitutional and legislative delegation of power under which the Board operates, it could reasonably conclude that sound management with the object of obtaining the greatest benefit for the people dictates that persons, private businesses or public agencies which use state-owned lands to the exclusion of the public should compensate the state for such use. Indeed, the *jus publicum* to which the state's proprietary interest in submerged and submersible land is subject, implies an obligation for the Board to seek compensation for the exclusive private use of a public resource. The payment of compensation serves the public interest by increasing the common wealth. Thus, through such compensation, the public derives benefit from leased submerged and submersible lands although it gives away their direct use.

III. Riparian Rights

Our examination of the nature of the state's interest has led us to conclude that the state may exercise its rights. To determine whether that exercise is a taking for which compensation must be paid, requires a similar examination of the nature of the rights of the riparian owners.

A. The Nature and Type of Riparian Rights

At common law, riparian landowners, by reason of their adjacency to the waterway, were accorded certain rights additional to those of the public in general. The nature and extent of riparian rights is determined by state law, *Shively v. Bowlby*, 152 U.S. 1, 14 S. Ct. 548, 38 L. Ed. 331 (1894); *see also, Oregon v. Corvallis Sand and Gravel Co.*, 429 U.S. 263, 97 S. Ct. 582, 50 L. Ed. 2d 550 (1977), and although the states differ in their enumeration of these rights, it is generally agreed that they include access to the navigable portion of the stream. . . .

The Supreme Court has consistently recognized the right of riparian property owners to build certain structures other than wharves in aid of navigation in the waters bordering their land:[1] *Smith Tug v. Columbia-Pac. Towing,* 250 Or. 612, 637, 443 P.2d 205 (1967) ("This includes the right to build structures on the bed below the low-water mark and the right to moor logs on the water."). . . . This extended right to navigational structures is founded in the absence of statutes to the contrary, rather than in any statutory grant. It is thus a common law right subject to, but as yet unaffected by, legislation.

Although proprietary riparian rights may be regulated, they may not be eliminated without the payment of compensation. Such elimination would constitute a taking for which process is due. *See*, 5 Clark (ed), *Waters and Water Rights* 375 (1972); 1 Farnham, *Waters and Water Rights* 282 (1904); Note, *The Constitutional Sanctity of a Property Interest in a Riparian Right*, 1969 Wash. Univ. Law Q. 327 (1969). Plaintiffs, as riparian owners, argue that since the Board's lease program would require them to pay for or else lose the same privileges which they heretofore enjoyed as a matter of common law right, the program results in an uncompensated, and thus unconstitutional, taking of those riparian rights. This contention, however, is predicated upon a misperception of the nature of riparian rights and privileges to build structures on submerged and submersible land.

Although commonly viewed as a unitary collection of co-equal rights and privileges, riparian rights are actually a cluster of distinct prerogatives which are of two general types. For the most part, riparian rights arise naturally from the fact that one's land is adjacent to water. The benefit of having one's land washed by water is inherent in the ownership of the land itself. It does not depend on the acquiescence or goodwill of the state. These inherent benefits may be referred to as *proprietary rights*. They include the right to have the stream continue in place and the right to make proportionate use of it while the water flows past one's land. Such proprietary rights include, for example, access to navigable water and the owner's household use of water. These rights which inhere in the land cannot be taken away by the state without just compensation, 1 Farnham, *Waters and Water Rights* 281 (1904). The Board's rules do not require leases for such proprietary rights.

---

[1] Although early cases seemed to treat the riparian owner's right as being qualitatively different depending upon whether his land abutted tidal waters or fresh water, it appears that the rights of the riparian owner are the same so long as the abutting waterway is navigable. *See, Smith Tug v. Columbia-Pac. Towing*, 250 Or. 612, 443 P.2d 205 (1967).

We use the word "right" here in a general sense, rather than in distinction to "privilege." The Supreme Court cases upon which we rely do not require the making of a distinction between "right" and "privilege" and we infer that they also use "right" in its more inclusive sense. Hereinafter, we use "privilege" narrowly and "right" broadly or narrowly as the context requires.

The other "rights" accorded to riparian owners are not inherent in their ownership of the land. Rather, they are privileges which are extended or tolerated by the state because of the riparian owners' favorable situation of ready access to the water and because of a presumed benefit to the public arising from the private exercise of the rights. This class of riparian rights includes, for example, the privilege to build structures in aid of navigation, such as those here in issue, on submerged and submersible land. These privileges are not proprietary rights and they may not be insisted upon against the will of the state. 1 Farnham, *Waters and Water Rights* 281 (1904); 36 Op. Atty Gen. 150 (Or. 1972).

. . . .

The distinction between proprietary rights and nonproprietary riparian privileges, though not elsewhere articulated, has been implicit in the court's reasoning in decisions dealing with the right to erect structures on submerged and submersible land. In those cases, the court has consistently referred to the right to erect navigational structures as a passive or implied license which exists only so long as the state permits it. The court has emphasized that the right should be treated as a usufruct rather than as a property interest. In the leading case on this subject, *Coquille M. & M. Co. v. Johnson*, 52 Or. 547, 98 P. 132 (1908), the court held that riparian owners could construct wharves, piers, landings and booms, but made it clear that this right was subject to divestment, at least until it was exercised.

. . . .

Similarly, the Supreme Court has held that the statutory right to wharf out is only a license which may be revoked at any time until it is exercised. *Montgomery v. Shaver*, 40 Or. 244, 248, 66 P. 923 (1901); *Bowlby v. Shively*, 22 Or. 410, 30 P. 154 (1892).

The Supreme Court's analysis based on license is consistent with the longstanding common law rule. Access to the navigable portion of a waterway was deemed to be a proprietary riparian right analogous to that enjoyed by an abutter on a highway. It did not encompass the privilege to erect structures on submerged and submersible land. *Shively v. Bowlby*, 152 U.S. 1, 9–10, 14 S. Ct. 548, 38 L. Ed. 331 (1894). Every structure which was erected below the high-water mark without license was a mere purpresture which could, at the suit of the sovereign, be either removed or demolished. *See, Shively v. Bowlby, supra,* 152 U.S. at 9-10.

B. The Power to Revoke Exercised Licenses

Because the privilege to erect structures in aid of navigation is in the nature of a license rather than a proprietary interest, the elimination of that privilege without the payment of compensation is not an unconstitutional taking under either the United States or Oregon Constitution. We are therefore not concerned with the law of eminent domain. Rather, the power of the state to eliminate this nonproprietary riparian privilege and the limits upon that power must be determined according to general property law governing the revocability of licenses. Therefore, we look first to the general nature of licenses, and then to the interplay between the freedom of the licensor to revoke and the protection accorded to the licensee's investment.

A license is the authority to do without charge an otherwise wrongful act on another's land for the benefit of the licensee. The grant of a license does not convey any estate in land. *Forsyth v. Nathansohn*, 139 Or. 632, 636, 9 P.2d 1036, 11 P.2d 1065 (1932). Before it has been exercised, a license is revocable at the will of the licensor. *Rouse v. Roy L. Houck Sons'*, 249 Or. 655, 660, 439 P.2d 856 (1968); Restatement of Property § 519 (1944). Thus, a riparian landowner's license to wharf out and erect other navigational aids has been held "revocable at the pleasure of the legislature until acted upon." *Montgomery v. Shaver, supra* at 248; *Bowlby v. Shively*, 22 Or. 410, 30 P. 154 (1892).

The general law of licenses provides that a licensee who has expended labor and capital in the exercise of his license in reasonable reliance upon its continued availability, is privileged to continue the use permitted by the license to the extent reasonably necessary to realize upon his expenditures. Restatement of Property § 519(4) (1944). . . .

The riparian plaintiffs herein have made substantial investments in the exercise of their licenses and in reliance upon their continuing availability. Such reliance is reasonable in view of the fact that for nearly a hundred years the law of this state, as expressed by the Supreme Court, has affirmatively recognized the existence of a riparian right to erect navigational aids. The existence of this nonproprietary right must be regarded as affirmatively established at common law and the legislature has heretofore neither modified nor withdrawn it. Therefore, absent some reason for holding the general rule inapplicable in this context, the right of the state to revoke riparian licenses is limited by the right of the licensees to recover their as yet unrecouped investments.

The rule that a license is made irrevocable by reliant investment is essentially one of equitable estoppel. Generally, equitable estoppel principles are inapplicable against the state because it is thought that the improper acts of government officials should not prevent the government from subsequently correcting that impropriety. *See, Clackamas County v. Emmert,* 14 Or. App. 493, 513 P.2d 532, *rev. den.* (1973). However, where, as here, reasonable reliance arises from law rather than from improper government action, the state may be estopped. Thus, in *Savage v. City of Salem*, 23 Or. 381, 31 P. 832 (1893), the Supreme Court held that where a private party erected a water tank on a public street, at his own expense, pursuant to a properly granted license to do so from the city, the city could not thereafter revoke the license without compensating the licensee. *See also, Mead v. Portland*, 45 Or. 1, 76 P. 347 (1904).

Accordingly, we hold that riparian owners who exercised their right to erect navigational structures on state-owned submerged and submersible land prior to the effective date of the lease program, must be permitted to continue their use of such facilities, rent free, for a period of time reasonably necessary to recoup their expenditures, if they have not already done so. Because plaintiffs' entitlement to a remedy, if any, lies in estoppel rather than eminent domain, its quantification is based on investment cost rather than fair market value.

. . . .

In summary, we conclude that the Board is not precluded by existing riparian rights from requiring riparian landowners to lease submerged and submersible lands used for the construction of navigational aids other than wharves. As to all such structures erected after the effective date of the rules, the state may require the execution of leases and the payment of rent. As to such structures erected prior to the rules, riparian landowners must be given a reasonable time to recoup their investment, if that has not already occurred, before rents may be charged.

. . . .

Affirmed in part; reversed in part and remanded.

NOTES

1. On appeal, the Oregon supreme court modified *Brusco*. Concerning preexisting structures, and estoppel, the supreme court had this to say:

   A more difficult question concerns those structures for which the Board proposes to require leases and which were constructed prior to the institution of the state's leasing program. We are not concerned, in this case, with wharves which the legislature has expressly authorized by ORS 780.040 and its predecessors, and for which the Board does not require leases.
   . . . .
   The Court of Appeals held . . . riparian owners who had built structures on state-owned submerged and submersible land prior to the Board's institution of its leasing program had done so in reasonable reliance on the continuing availability of their license to occupy that land and were therefore entitled to maintain those structures rent free for whatever period of time was necessary to permit them to recoup their investments.
   The difficulty with applying the general rule in this case is that, as pointed out above, it has been held applicable only where the license to use the land was express. We have consistently described the riparian owner's license under consideration here as a "passive" or "implied" license. The Court of Appeals, mindful of this problem, found the necessary affirmative license or representation in the decisions of this court which recognized the riparian privilege to construct navigational structures on the state's land. That recognition, however, was of a revocable privilege or license, not of a perpetual license or one of any particular duration. We cannot agree with the Court of Appeals that the legislature is estopped to revoke the privilege by the decisions of this court which declare that only a revocable privilege exists. While application or pronouncement by this court of a rule of property law may create vested rights, our recognition that a privilege exists until prohibited by the legislature does not entitle those who choose to exercise that privilege to assume that the legislature will not act to limit or prohibit it in the future.
   In short, we find that the Board's requirement that riparian owners who have taken advantage of the legislature's past failure to prohibit their exclusive occupa-

tion of the state's submerged and submersible land pay rental for the privilege of continuing to do so in the future does not violate any right of property. Leases may, therefore, be required of those parties who claim riparian status and who have exercised in the past the privileges accompanying that status.

Brusco v. State Land Board, 284 Or. at 642–46. *See also Oglesby v. McCoy*, 255 S.E.2d 737 (Ct. App. N.C. 1979) (statute raising rent for river bottom oyster cultivation leases from $1 per acre to $5 per acre upheld); *Vujnovich v. Louisiana Wildlife & Fisheries Commission*, 376 So. 2d 330 (La. App. 1979) (commission decisions not to renew water bottom oyster cultivation leases and to designate the water bottoms as oyster seed reservations to be managed directly by commission upheld).

2. Recall that the Oregon court of appeals would have allowed a rent-free period to permit the owner to recoup his investment. Oregon is not the only state to have considered compensation for the private littoral landowner. In Louisiana, the state has the right to expropriate waterfront property. If structures were erected without prior permission from the authorities, expropriation is made without compensation; if, however, the riparian owner had permission to build, the owner has a claim for just compensation. *See* Yiannopoulos, *Public Use of the Banks of Navigable Rivers in Louisiana*, 31 La. L. Rev. 563 (1971).

   Would the court of appeals' estoppel reasoning, rejected by the Oregon supreme court, explain Louisiana's rule?

3. The cases thus far have dealt only obliquely with the rights of private owners of the banks or shores of navigable waters. What, exactly, *are* the rights of private owners? In light of the variations among the states, this is an impossible question to answer; however, some general idea is possible. The traditional, nineteenth-century common-law rights included:

   (1) the right to have the water remain in place and to retain its natural character;
   (2) the right to have contact with the water remain intact—the riparian owner's right of access to the water;
   (3) the right to erect wharves to reach the navigable portion of the stream;
   (4) the right of preference in case the land under water is sold;
   (5) the right to accretions;
   (6) the preferential right to fill out into the water, if such filling is permitted by the public;
   (7) the right to use the shore immediately adjacent to the land belonging to the public; and
   (8) the preferential right to service ferry franchises.

   1 H. Farnham, *The Law of Waters & Water Rights* § 62 at 279–80 (1904).

4. *Brusco* represents the modern trend to expand public rights at the expense of the private owner, yet it may also restrict public rights. Once public tidelands are leased to a private individual, it seems as if his right to use those lands would be exclusive. Judge Tanzer of the Oregon court of appeals apparently contemplated exclusion of the public when he said, "[t]hrough such compensation, the public derives benefit from leased submerged and submersible lands even though it gives away their direct use." *Brusco*, 30 Or. App. at 521, 567 P.2d at 1045. The Oregon supreme court affirmed this portion of the opinion, on the ground that the rules did not divest the legislature or the State Land Board of the state's power to protect the rights of the public in the state's navigable water. 284 Or. at 635.

   Nevertheless, individual members of the public may one day find themselves excluded because certain submerged and submersible lands have been leased to a private owner. Keep this in mind when you reach the public trust materials, and ask yourself whether *Brusco* is in perfect accord with the public trust doctrine in its classic form.

What are the advantages of a leasing program? What are the alternatives to a leasing program for managing state-owned tidelands and submerged lands?

5. Oregon has limited the riparian rights of private owners of the banks and shorelines of navigable waters, but it has not eliminated them. Oregon continues to recognize certain inherent benefits, the "proprietary rights" mentioned by Judge Tanzer, which cannot be taken without compensation. Washington State, in contrast, purports to have granted no rights whatsoever to the riparian or littoral landowner. *See Port of Seattle v. Oregon & W. R. Co.*, 255 U.S. 56 (1920).

6. For additional reading, *see* 1 R. Clark, *Waters & Water Rights* §§ 42–43 at 264–75 (1967); Nelson, *State Disposition of Submerged Lands Versus Public Rights in Navigable Waters*, 3 Nat. Res. Law. 491 (1970).

Right to Fill Wetlands: Herein of the Taking Issue

FIFTH AMENDMENT TO THE UNITED STATES CONSTITUTION

. . . nor shall private property be taken for public use, without just compensation.

4 R. CLARK, WATERS & WATER RIGHTS § 302, 53–54 (1970)

When private property is taken for a public use under the power of eminent domain, the owner is entitled to receive just compensation from the taker. Conversely, if a restriction upon the utilization of property is merely a proper exercise of the government's police power, no compensation is due.

COMMISSIONER OF NATURAL RESOURCES v. VOLPE & CO., 349 Mass. 104, 206 N.E.2d 666 (1965)

WILKINS, Chief Justice.

The Commissioner of Natural Resources and the Director of Marine Fisheries bring this bill in equity against S. Volpe & Co., Inc., a corporation of Massachusetts, to enjoin the defendant "from placing any further fill on Broad Marsh in the Town of Wareham" in violation of a condition imposed by the commissioner, and to order the defendant "to remove all fill placed on and in Broad Marsh" in violation of that condition. After a hearing a final decree was entered in which the defendant was enjoined and ordered accordingly. The defendant appealed. The judge made a report of the material facts found by him, from which, unless otherwise stated, are taken the facts in this opinion. G.L. c. 214, § 23 (as amended through St.1947, c. 365, § 2). The evidence is reported.

Broad Marsh is located westerly of Sunset Cove off Onset Bay in the coastal waters of Wareham. A tidal creek known as Broad Marsh Creek flows through the northerly portion of the marsh into Squaw's Hole, the northwestern end of Sunset Cove. The tide flows through mosquito control ditches in the marsh, at times flooding it.

In 1960 the defendant acquired a parcel of land containing 49.4 acres within Broad Marsh, which covers a total of 78 acres more or less. On October 3, 1963, as alleged in the bill, admitted in the answer, and found by the judge, the defendant gave written notice pursuant to G.L. c. 130, § 27A (inserted by St.1963, c. 426),[2] of "its intention to dredge a channel and basin into said Broad Marsh in connection with a marina to be constructed adjacent thereto at some future date." This finding is accurate as far as it goes, but, as we ourselves find, the channel, basin, and marina were incidental to the defendant's main project of filling the marsh for the construction of houses with water rights for boating.

On October 9, 1963, the board of selectmen of Wareham, pursuant to § 27A, conducted a hearing on the defendant's application. At the hearing the plaintiffs requested from the defendant a detailed plan of the proposed work. On October 21 this was furnished. Thereafter the director notified the defendant "that in the interest of protecting marine fisheries and maintaining the ecological components of this estuarine complex in their present protective form" "no fill of any type be placed upon that area known as Broad Marsh." The director did not, and does not now, object to the dredging of the channel and basin.

The defendant disputed that the condition contained in this notice was authorized by § 27A, and ignoring the director's notification, commenced filling Broad Marsh and continued doing so until temporarily enjoined on January 20, 1964. The local authorities, the State Department of Public Works, with reference to G.L. c. 91, § 30, § 30A (inserted by St.1950, c. 214), and the Secretary of the Army acting through the Corps of Engineers under 33 U.S.C. § 403 (1958) have all approved the project.

The trial judge concluded (A) that the restriction of "no fill" is a condition authorized by § 27A; (B) that Broad Marsh is a "saltmarsh" necessary to preserve and protect marine fisheries; (C) that § 27A is valid; and (D) that the "condition" imposed is not an unlawful taking entitling the defendant to compensation.

In support of his general findings (A) and (B) the judge found the following:

"The important biological significance of Broad Marsh is its nutrient contribution to the shellfish and other fishery resources of the Sunset Cove–Onset Bay area. The two most conspicuous plants of Broad Marsh are the cordgrasses, Spartina patens and Spartina Alterniflora. As these plants die and decay, large amounts of phos-

[2]Section 27A provides in part: "No person shall remove, fill or dredge any bank, flat, marsh, meadow or swamp bordering on coastal waters without written notice of his intention to so remove, fill or dredge to the board of selectmen in a town . . . , to the state department of public works, and to the director of marine fisheries. . . . The selectmen . . . shall hold a hearing on said proposal. . . . If the area on which the proposed work is to be done contains shellfish or is necessary to protect marine fisheries, the said director may impose such conditions on said proposed work as he may determine necessary to protect such shellfish or marine fisheries, and work shall be done subject thereto. . . . [T]he superior court shall have jurisdiction in equity to restrain a continuing violation of this section. . . . "

phates and nitrates are released into the adjacent waters. These nutrients are essential for the growth of microscopic plants and other micro-organisms, which in turn are the primary source of nutrition for shellfish as well as the young fish and crustaceans." "[T]he nutrients derived from Broad Marsh, and, in particular, the portion thereof intended to be filled by the . . . [defendant], play an important and integral part in sustaining the life of the shellfish and finfish in the areas adjacent thereto. . . . Without these nutrients untoward damage will result to the marine fisheries which depend on the productivity of the adjacent marsh for their sustenance."

We cannot pronounce these findings plainly wrong. Two experts for the plaintiff have provided supporting testimony.

As to the trial judge's finding (C), the protection of marine fisheries is undoubtedly a public purpose for which § 27A was properly enacted. The Legislature clearly has power to protect and preserve the fish and game of the Commonwealth.

. . . .

To this end, once a policy has been determined, its execution may be delegated to an appropriate public officer or board.

. . . .

This is not the whole matter, however. A crucial issue is whether, notwithstanding the meritorious character of the regulation, there has been such a deprivation of the practical uses of a landowner's property as to be the equivalent of a taking without compensation.

. . . .

The trial judge recognized the existence of this question, but the narrow finding of the scope of the project above referred to led to other findings which are inapplicable to the realities of the case and must be disregarded as lacking support in the evidence. Thus he found that the plaintiffs have not placed an absolute restraint on the defendant in imposing the condition prohibiting filling Broad Marsh; that the condition imposed relates only to the filling of Broad Marsh and does not completely restrain the defendant's commercial enterprise, which may be conducted and completed by alternative methods; that the defendant is not prevented from dredging and transporting the dredged material to any location other than Broad Marsh, thus causing no damage to marine fisheries; that the defendant may dredge a greater distance through Broad Marsh to upland property which it owns and where no significant nutrient values necessary to protect marine fisheries are extant; that the condition imposed by the director is reasonable; and that "[s]imply stated, he desires the . . . [defendant] to locate its proposed marina, yacht club and recreational center shoreward of Broad Marsh and to place no fill on the said marsh."

The question is analogous to that which arises when the validity of a zoning ordinance or by-law is considered. Whether there is a reasonable interference with a landowner's rights undertaken in the exercise of the police power for the public benefit or a deprivation of private property without compensation often depends upon the facts of the particular case. . . . This court has often held that on the facts presented in a given case a regulation achieves no valid public benefit and also so restricts the use of property as to constitute a taking without compensation.

. . . .

S. Volpe, the president, treasurer, and principal stockholder of the defendant, testified that the project he had in contemplation could not be carried out without filling the marsh as he proposed; that if the marsh were not to be filled no use, residential or commercial, could be made of the area owned by the defendant; that there was no point to the dredging if he could not fill the area; and that unless he could dredge the channel and fill the portion owned by the defendant on Broad Marsh the land was of no value to him.

While we find without hesitation that the project was as testified by him, we are in no position also to find whether there has been such a deprivation of the practical uses of the marsh as to be the equivalent of a taking without compensation. A finding one way or the other on this issue is essential to a proper disposition of the case.

The plaintiffs argue as though all that need be done is to demonstrate a public purpose and then no regulation in the interests of conservation can be too extreme. We quote an example from their brief: "if the decision of the trial judge is not upheld in this case, where the evidence is so overwhelming that the marsh . . . does contribute substantially to the ecological system necessary to the sustenance of shellfish and fin fish, the statute will be emasculated and our efforts to conserve our natural resources will have received a severe setback." An unrecognized taking in the guise of regulation is worse than confiscation. As the New York Court of Appeals said in the Arverne case, supra, 278 N.Y. 222, 232, 15 N.E.2d 587, 592: "An ordinance which *permanently* so restricts the use of property that it cannot be used for any reasonable purpose goes, it is plain, beyond regulation, and must be recognized as a taking of the property. The only substantial difference, in such case, between restriction and actual taking, is that the restriction leaves the owner subject to the burden of payment of taxation, while outright confiscation would relieve him of that burden."

In this conflict between the ecological and the constitutional, it is plain that neither is to be consumed by the other. It is the duty of the department of conservation to look after the interests of the former, and it is the duty of the courts to stand guard over constitutional rights.

In summary, our views are that the finding that Broad Marsh is a "salt-marsh" necessary to preserve and protect marine fisheries is not plainly wrong; that, considered apart from the taking issue, the rulings that the prohibition of filing the marsh is a condition authorized by § 27A, and that § 27A is valid, are correct as upholding a valid public purpose; and that whether the defendant is the uncompensated victim of a taking invalid without compensation depends upon further findings as to what uses the marshland may still be put and possibly upon other issues which have not been argued and which are enumerated below.

The final decree is reversed. The case is remanded for the following purposes:

First, for the taking of further evidence and for further findings on the following matters:

1. The portions, if any, of the 49.4 acres (the locus) which the owner desires to improve below the line of mean high water (see Commonwealth v. City of Roxbury, 9 Gray, 451, 483).

2. The uses which can be made of the locus in its natural state (a) independently of other land of the owner in the area; (b) in conjunction with other land of the owner.

3. The assessed value of the locus for each of the five years, 1960 to 1964, inclusive.

4. The cost of the locus to the defendant.

5. The present fair market value of the locus (a) subject to the limitations imposed by the Commissioner; (b) free of such limitations.

6. The estimated cost of the improvements proposed by the defendant.

7. Any relevant rules and regulations prescribed by the Director of Marine Fisheries.

8. Any relevant by-laws (including zoning provisions) or regulations of the town of Wareham.

Second, for further hearings to develop any relevant evidence on each of the following issues, none of which has been argued and as to which we express no opinion. Briefs and oral arguments should be directed at least to such issues upon any subsequent appeal to this court.

A. Would the Commonwealth, by the imposition of the proposed restriction, take property without just compensation, if there is no substantial possible use of the locus while subject to the proposed restriction which will yield to the owner of the locus a fair return (1) upon the amount of his investment in the locus, or (2) upon what would be the fair market value of the locus free of the restriction?

B. If it is contended that the land, if subject to the proposed restriction, may be profitably used in connection with other land, is this relevant, and, if so, to what extent?

C. Is it relevant to questions A or B that the locus is not suitable in its present state for residential or commercial use?

D. Is it relevant to questions A and B that the proposed filling, at least in part, will change coastal marshland, subject at times to tidal flow into upland?

E. What, if any, is the effect and relevance of the colonial ordinance on the case at bar and to what extent does the ordinance relate to matters other than navigation near and upon the locus?

So ordered.

1. The Massachusetts enabling statute at issue in *Volpe* conferred authority on the various local boards of selectmen to impose conditions on proposed marshland fill projects. What "condition" was imposed by the Board of Selectmen of Wareham in *Volpe*? What was the Board protecting? Did the Massachusetts legislature have the power to adopt such a policy? When a legislature adopts a policy to protect marine resources, what is really protected? Is the public trust involved?

2. From Ausness, *Water Use Permits in a Riparian State: Problems and Proposals*, 66 Ky. L.J. 191, 241–43 (1978):

   The police power has been defined as an exercise of the sovereign right of the state to enact laws for the protection of the lives, health, morals, comfort, and general welfare of the people. While property rights are subject to the police power, the concept of substantive due process limits the exercise of this power. . . .

   Substantive due process requires that police power regulations must have a rational relation to the safety, health, morals, or general welfare of the community. Substantive due process also requires regulation to be reasonable and not arbitrary or oppressive. An unreasonable exercise of the police power will be deemed a taking of property without due process of law.

   On remand, *Commissioner of Natural Resources v. Volpe* culminated in a decree invalidating the Board's fill prohibition. Despite this victory, Volpe & Co. did not build the proposed marina and housing project. Eleven years later, however, in *S. Volpe & Co. v. Board of Appeals of Wareham*, 4 Mass. App. 357, 348 N.E.2d 807 (1976), Volpe and Broad Marsh were back in the courts. This time, Volpe & Co. had applied for permission to fill the marsh for use as a commercial golf course. The zoning bylaws of Wareham would have allowed filling for residential development or recreational use provided the use was not "injurious, noxious or offensive," and only if authorized by the Board of Appeals subject to appropriate conditions where deemed necessary to protect the neighborhood and the town.

   As you might have guessed, the Board refused to authorize Volpe's commercial venture. Apparently, residential and noncommercial recreational use were fine; only commercial uses were prohibited. The grounds for the prohibition were the same as 10 years earlier—the fill would damage marine resources. Volpe & Co. did not argue, as they had before, that preservation of the marshland was not a legitimate purpose within the ambit of the Zoning Enabling Act, and they did not raise the taking issue. They argued instead that injury to the ecology resulting from the filling of the marsh for a nonprofit golf course would be just as severe as for a commercial one, and less than if filled for a residential development. What result in the courts? The court held that the Board's action was within its authority and not arbitrary or capricious. Volpe & Co. lost. Note the power of local governments over nearshore uses as illustrated by *Volpe*. Would you say that it is easy to overcome the presumption of validity accorded the actions of local governments?

3. The purpose of *Volpe* is to introduce the issue of the police power versus eminent domain as it affects regulation of the coastal zone. As you will discover in cases to come, the trend toward greater recognition of public rights in the coastal zone, and the consequent restrictions on traditional private rights, have altered concepts of property. Along with new ideas on the nature of property has come confusion as to exactly what is owned exclusively, what is owned subject

to public interests, and to what extent use of the coastal zone may be regulated. The distinction between a valid exercise of the police power and a taking of property under the right of eminent domain is critical, and difficult to define. *Volpe* introduced the problem, but provided few answers. Subsequent cases are in conflict.

State v. Johnson, 265 A.2d 711 (Sup. Ct. Me. 1970), struck down as an unreasonable exercise of the police power denial of a permit under the Maine Wetlands Act to a coastal saltmarsh owner who wanted to fill the saltmarsh for recreational housing development. *State v. Johnson* was the first case to arise under Maine's Wetlands Act, and was seen as a disaster by the state's environmentalists. The precedent created by *Johnson* was not as bad as feared, but the case remains a classic example of how *not* to handle a wetlands fill case—unless you are representing the landowner. Professor Halperin, in *Conservation, Policy, and the Role of Counsel*, 23 Me. L. Rev. 119 (1971), warned that the Wetlands Act should be approached in terms of the pattern of land ownership peculiar to Maine and Massachusetts. Contrary to English common law, the Colony of Massachusetts, which included Maine, gave the littoral landowner title to the intertidal zone from the high-tide line down to the low-tide line. Under Massachusetts and Maine case law, ownership of these tidal lands included the right to erect structures, such as wharves, and the right to fill. The Wetlands Act is, therefore, a limitation of a common law attribute of ownership. Furthermore, at the trial, according to Professor Halperin, the state's own expert witnesses testified that Dr. Johnson's property was useless without the fill, and then failed to link the proposed fill to any resulting damage to the marsh as a whole. The burden of proving these critical facts is normally on the landowner. In the words of Professor Halperin, "[g]iven the state of the trial record, it would have required incredible bungling by the landowner to have lost." Halperin, *Conservation, Policy, and the Role of Counsel, supra,* at 132.

4. Halperin, in *Conservation, Policy, and the Role of Counsel, supra,* at 134, distilled certain "common denominators" that often lead to a finding that property was taken without compensation. These common denominators are: "[a] dominant public purpose, the effort to require a de facto dedication of private property to an essentially public use, and the destruction of any significant utility or value of the property to the private owner."

A significant loss of value, one of Halperin's key factors, is nearly inescapable when coastal lands are subjected to government regulation. Wetlands are fragile. The restrictions necessary to save them often amount to virtual prohibition of development, and therefore near or total loss of all utility. If the Holmes diminution of value test is applied by the courts, the result in wetlands cases will nearly always be that a taking has occurred. Is there any way out of this dilemma?

5. In *Sibson v. State*, 115 N.H. 124, 336 A.2d 239 (1975), the court held that the denial of the permit to fill the saltmarsh was a valid exercise of the police power since its purpose was to proscribe future activities that would be harmful to the public. Which is the critical element of the holding, that a future use was involved, or that the future use would be harmful to the public? After *Sibson*, does a purchaser of wetlands acquire the right to develop his property as part of the fee simple? If he does not, can regulation of the future uses of wetlands *ever* be a taking? Has the *Sibson* court, as Justice Grimes argued in his dissenting opinion, destroyed private ownership in all undeveloped property in New Hampshire? Should the courts, no matter how good their intentions, have the power to redefine private property and defeat the expectations of landowners? Is this not precisely the kind of government interference that the fifth amendment was meant to prevent? How would you defend the *Sibson* court's holding?

6. Justice Grimes, in his dissenting opinion in *Sibson*, recognized along with the majority that the state could regulate that part of the marsh below the mean

high-tide line. Why did he distinguish tidal and submerged lands from neighboring upland? Recall *Brusco Towboat v. State Land Board*. If submerged and submersible lands are subject to the public trust, is regulation in fact an invasion of a protected private property right?

Most of the marsh in *Sibson* was apparently *above* the high-tide line and so supposedly free of the public trust.

7. The *Sibson* court applied a rule first stated in *Just v. Marinette County*, 56 Wis. 2d 7, 201 N.W.2d 761 (1972), noted, 59 Marq. L. Rev. 787 (1976). Consider the following excerpt from Large, *This Land Is Whose Land? Changing Concepts of Land as Property*, 1973 Wis. L. Rev. 1039, 1978:[3]

In addition to modifying the concept of taking, the court redefines property. In response to Just's argument that the ordinance constituted a constructive taking of his property, the court stated:

> The Justs argue their property has been severely depreciated in value. But this depreciation of value is not based on the use of the land in its natural state but on what the land would be worth if it could be filled and used for the location of a dwelling. While loss of value is to be considered in determining whether a restriction is a constructive taking, value based on changing the character of the land at the expense of harm to public rights is not an essential factor or controlling.

This brief language may radically revise generations of thinking on property valuation. Suppose I own a swamp, worth $1000 as is, but I have a plan to fill it, subdivide and construct vacation homes. If, as homesites, the land will be worth $50,000, what, then, is my land presently worth? Traditionally, property has always included the landowner's expectancy of gain, the land's speculation value. Yet the court now states that the only value that must be considered, for purposes of deciding whether or not there has been a taking of property, is value based on the use of the land in its natural state. Value based on changing the character of the land, while not entirely foreclosed or excluded from evidence, is no longer an "essential" factor to be considered.

Subsequent cases indicate that *Just* has been limited to public trust situations in Wisconsin. *See Omerick v. State*, 64 Wis. 2d 6, 218 N.W.2d 734 (1973); *State v. Deetz*, 66 Wis. 2d 1, 224 N.W.2d 407 (1974). The typical zoning case in Wisconsin has been decided based on the more traditional diminution-in-value test. *See, e.g., Kniec v. Town of Spider Lake*, 60 Wis. 2d 640, 211 N.W.2d 471 (1973).

The Justs paid dearly for their pursuit of principle. Professor Bryden in *A Phantom Doctrine: The Origins and Effects of Just v. Marinette County*, 1978 A.B.F. Res. J. 397, 443–45, provides a subsequent history of the Just property:

After losing on appeal, the Justs sold the land to Mrs. Just's sister and her husband (the Wiedemeiers) for $3,300. The Wiedemeiers applied for and received a conditional use permit to fill an area of 125 feet by 125 feet, which they planned to use for a cabin or at least a small building to store their recreational equipment when they visited the land. In the meantime, however, Congress—wishing to protect wetlands—had extended the power of the Corps of Engineers over navigable waters by enacting a law that required a permit from the corps before virtually any wetland could be filled. This law applies even to marshes that are not near a lake

[3]Copyrighted, University of Wisconsin, Wisconsin Law Review.

or stream. In the upper midwest the corps has granted a large majority of the applications for such permits, though sometimes after requiring modifications; and one supposes that, were it not for the *Just* decision, the Wiedemeier's application might have been routinely granted. In fact, the Chicago district office of the corps decided that, on balance, this fill project was in the public interest: the area was small; indigenous animals could move elsewhere; there was already some development nearby; this wetland was not ecologically or aesthetically "unique"; the applicant could not use the property if the permit were denied; and the U.S. Environmental Protection Agency and the county zoning office had approved the permit. The U.S. Fish and Wildlife Service, however, has expressed the view that, whereas the corps wishes to balance private benefit against public harm, the proper test is whether the *public* benefit from the project would exceed the harm to the public. Applying this standard, the service informed the corps that "we fail to see how a desire for the Wiedemeier's [*sic*] five daughters to go picnicing [*sic*] reflects a national concern." The letter further stated that inasmuch as 50 percent of the shoreline of Lake Noquebay was developed, a strong effort should be made to stop destruction of the remaining wetlands. Having determined that the area was frequented by deer and snowshoe hares, the service rejected the notion that these animals could go elsewhere; the nearby areas, it argued, were already occupied by other wildlife and should not be further crowded. Apparently, the service is also prepared to make other ecological arguments, the exact nature of which has not been disclosed. At last report, the corps had not yet finally decided whether to grant the permit.

8. For other recent wetlands and related cases, *see Askew v. Gables-By-The-Sea, Inc.,* 333 So. 2d 56 (Fla. Ct. App. 1976); *Brecciaroli v. Conn. Comm. of Environmental Protection,* 168 Conn. 349, 362 A.2d 948 (1975); *Graham v. Estuary Properties, Inc.,* 16 ERC 1767 (Fla. Sup. Ct. 1981); *Potomac Sand & Gravel Co. v. Governor of Maryland,* 266 Md. 358, 293 A.2d 241 (1972), *cert. denied,* 409 U.S. 1040 (1972); *Sands Point Harbor, Inc. v. Sullivan,* 136 N.J. Super. 436, 346 A.2d 612 (1975); *State v. Gagliano,* 384 A.2d 610 (R.I. 1978); *State Dept. of Ecology v. Pacesetter Const. Co.,* 89 Wash. 2d 203, 571 P.2d 196 (1977); *Zabel v. Pinellas County Water and Navigation Control Authority,* 171 So. 2d 376, 378 (Fla. Sup. Ct. 1965).

9. Related to wetlands protection laws is floodplain zoning. The constitutionality of floodplain zoning as a valid exercise of the police power was affirmed by the Massachusetts Supreme Judicial Court in *Turnpike Realty Co. v. Town of Dedham,* 72 Mass. 1303, 284 N.E.2d 891 (1972), *cert. denied,* 409 U.S. 1108 (1972). *Accord, Maple Leaf Investors, Inc. v. Dept. of Ecology,* 88 Wash. 2d 726, 565 P.2d 1162 (1977). Petitioner, who had purchased land in 1947, challenged a 1963 local ordinance which prohibited the residential use of land that was subject to seasonal or periodic flooding. Claiming that his land was worth $431,000 as an apartment building site, the petitioner asserted that the ordinance resulted in the property being valued at $53,000 as agricultural land. The court declared:

. . .we are unable to conclude even though the [trial] judge found that there was a substantial diminution in the value of the petitioner's land, that the decrease was such as to render it an unconstitutional deprivation of its property.

284 N.E.2d at 900.
Floodplain zoning ordinances have been struck down as unconstitutional takings in *Dooley v. Town Planning and Zoning Comm.,* 151 Conn. 304, 197 A.2d 770 (1964); and *Morris County Land Improvement Co. v. Parsippany Troy Hills Township,* 40 N.J. 539, 193 A.2d 232 (1963). *See also Bartlett v. Zoning Commission,* 161 Conn. 24, 282 A.2d 907 (1971).

10. For additional reading, *see* Binder, *Taking Versus Reasonable Regulation: A Reappraisal in Light of Regional Planning and Wetlands,* 25 Fla. L. Rev. 1 (1972); Dawson, *Protecting Massachusetts Wetlands* 12 Suffolk L. Rev. 755 (1978); Leschine and Cossella, *Wetlands Regulations and Public Perceptions in Massachusetts,* 3 Coastal Zone 1780 at 1789 (1980); Marsh, *Innovative Programs for the Reconciliation of Private and Public Interests in the California Coastal Zone,* 10 Nat. Res. Law. 257 (1977); Welsh, *The Wetlands Statutes: Regulation or Taking?,* 5 Conn. L. Rev. 64 (1972).

SECTION B: PUBLIC RIGHTS

The Public Trust Doctrine

ILLINOIS CENTRAL RAILROAD v. ILLINOIS 146 U.S. 387, 13 S. Ct. 110, 36 L. Ed. 1018 (1892)

. . . .

[The case grew out of a series of state and local land grants to the Illinois Central Railroad in the Chicago area. The original grants, by Chicago ordinance in 1853, was for tracks and other railroad facilities within the city and was expanded in later years in order to facilitate the use of the Randolph Street Station. In 1869 the state granted the railroad a fee title in a substantial portion of the harbor bed in exchange for annual rent. In 1873 the legislature repealed the earliest grant and the state brought an action to quiet title to the harbor bottom.

[In affirming te judgment in favor of the state, the Supreme Court (speaking through Mr. Justice Field) said:]

The question, therefore, to be considered is whether the legislature was competent to thus deprive the State of its ownership of the submerged lands in the harbor of Chicago, and of the consequent control of its waters; or, in other words, whether the ralroad corporation can hold the lands and control the waters by the grant against any future exercise of power over them by the State.

That the State holds the title to the lands under the navigable waters of Lake Michigan, within its limits, in the same manner that the State holds title to soils under tide water, by the common law, we have already shown, and that title necessarily carries with it control over the waters above them whenever the lands are subjected to use. But it is a title different in character from that which the State holds in lands intended for sale. It is different from the title which the United States hold in the public lands which are open to preemption and sale. It is a title held in trust for the people of the State that they may enjoy the navigation of the waters, carry on commerce over them, and have liberty of fishing therein freed from the obstruction or interference of private parties. The interest of the people in the navigation of the waters and in commerce over them may be improved in many instances by the erection of wharves, docks and piers therein, for which purpose the State may grant parcels of the submerged lands; and, so long as their disposition is made for such purpose, no valid objections can be made to the grants. It is grants of parcels of lands under navigable waters, that may afford foundation for wharves, piers, docks and other structures in aid of commerce, and grants of parcels which, being occupied, do not substantially impair the public interest in the lands and waters remaining, that are chiefly considered and sustained in the adjudged cases as a valid exercise of legislative power consistently with the trust to the public upon which such lands are held by the State. But that is a very different doctrine from the one which would sanction the abdication of the general control of the State over lands under the navigable waters of an entire harbor or bay, or of a sea or lake. Such abdication is not consistent with the exercise of that trust which requires the government of the State to preserve such waters for the use of the public.

The trust devolving upon the State for the public, and which can only be discharged by the management and control of property in which the public has an interest, cannot be relinquished by a transfer of the property. The control of the State for the purposes of the trust can never be lost, except as to such parcels as are used in promoting the interests of the public therein, or can be disposed of without any substantial impairment of the public interest in the lands and waters remaining.

It is only by observing the distinction between a grant of such parcels for the improvement of the public interest, or which when occupied do not substantially impair the public interest in the lands and waters remaining, and a grant of the whole property in which the public is interested, that the language of the adjudged cases can be reconciled. General language sometimes found in opinions of the courts, expressive of absolute ownership and control by the State of lands under navigable waters, irrespective of any trust as to their use and disposition, must be read and construed with reference to the special facts of the particular cases. A grant of all the lands under the navigable waters of a State has never been adjudged to be within the legislative power; and any attempted grant of the kind would be held, if not absolutely void on its face, as subject to revocation.

The State can no more abdicate its trust over property in which the whole people are interested, like navigable waters and soils under them, so as to leave them entirely under the use and control of private parties, except in the instance of parcels mentioned for the improvement of the navigation and use of the waters, or when parcels can be disposed of without impairment of the public interest in what remains, than it can abdicate its police powers in the administration of government and the preservation of the peace. In the administration of government the use of such powers may for a limited period be delegated to a municipality or other body, but there always remains with the State the right to revoke those powers and exercise them in a more direct manner, and one more conformable to its wishes. So with trusts connected with public property, or property of a special character, like lands under navigable waters, they cannot be placed entirely beyond the direction and control of the State.

The harbor of Chicago is of immense value to the people of the State of Illinois in the facilities it affords to its vast and constantly increasing commerce; and the idea that its legislature can deprive the State of control over its bed and waters and place the same in the hands of a private corporation created for a different purpose, one limited to transportation of passengers and freight between distant points and the city, is a proposition that cannot be defended.

. . . It is hardly conceivable that the legislature can divest the State of the control and management of this harbor and vest it absolutely in a private corporation. Surely an act of the legislature transferring the title to its submerged lands and the power claimed by the railroad company, to a foreign State or nation would be repudiated, without hesitation, as a gross perversion of the trust over the property under which it is held. So would a similar transfer to a corporation of another State. It would not be listened to that the control and management of the harbor of that great city—a subject of concern to the whole people of the State—should thus be placed elsewhere than in the State itself. All the objections which can be urged to such attempted transfer may be urged to a transfer to a private corporation like the railroad company in this case.

Any grant of the kind is necessarily revocable, and the exercise of the trust by which the property was held by the State can be resumed at any time. Undoubtedly there may be expenses incurred in improvements made under such a grant which the State ought to pay; but, be that as it may, the power to resume the trust whenever the State judges best is, we think, incontrovertible. The position advanced by the railroad company in support of its claim to the ownership of the submerged lands and the right to the erection of wharves, piers and docks at its pleasure, or for its business in the harbor of Chicago, would place every harbor in the country at the mercy of a majority of the legislature of the State in which the harbor is situated.

We cannot, it is true, cite any authority where a grant of this kind has been held invalid, for we believe that no instance exists where the harbor of a great city and its commerce have been allowed to pass into the control of any private corporation. But the decisions are numerous which declare that such property is held by the State, by virtue of its sovereignty, in trust for the public. The ownership of the navigable waters of the harbor and of the lands under them is a subject of public concern to the whole people of the State. The trust with which they are held, therefore, is governmental and cannot be alienated, except in those instances mentioned of parcels used in the improvement of the interest thus held, or when parcels can be disposed of without detriment to the public interest in the lands and waters remaining.

. . . .

In the case of *Stockton v. Baltimore and New York Railroad Company*, 32 Fed. Rep. 9, 19, 20, which involved a consideration by Mr. Justice Bradley, late of this court, of the nature of the ownership by the State of lands under the navigable waters of the United States, he said:

> It is insisted that the property of the State in lands under its navigable waters is private property, and comes strictly within the constitutional provision. It is significantly asked, can the United States take the state house at Trenton, and the surrounding grounds belonging to the State, and appropriate them to the purposes of a railroad depot, or to any other use of the general government, without compensation? We do not apprehend that the decision of the present case involves or requires a serious answer to this question. The cases are clearly not parallel. The character of the title or ownership by which the State holds the state house is quite different from that by which it holds the land under the navigable waters in and around its territory. The information rightly states that, prior to the Revolution, the shore and lands under water of the navigable streams and waters of the province of New Jersey belonged to the King of Great Britain as part of the *jura regalia* of the

crown, and devolved to the State by right of conquest. The information does not state, however, what is equally true, that, after the conquest, the said lands were held by the State, as they were by the king, *in trust* for the public uses of navigation and fishery, *and the erection* thereon of wharves, piers, light-houses, beacons and other facilities of navigation and commerce. Being subject to this trust, they were *publici juris*; in other words, they were held for the use of the people at large.

It is true that to utilize the fisheries, especially those of shell fish, it was necessary to parcel them out to particular operators, and employ the rent or consideration for the benefit of the whole people; but this did not alter the character of the title. The land remained subject to all other uses as before, especially to those of navigation and commerce, which are always paramount to those of public fisheries. It is also true that portions of the submerged shoals and flats, which really interfered with navigation, and could better subserve the purposes of commerce by being filled up and reclaimed, were disposed of to individuals for that purpose. But neither did these dispositions of useless parts affect the character of the title to the remainder.

. . . .

The soil under navigable waters being held by the people of the State in trust for the common use and as a portion of their inherent sovereignty, any act of legislation concerning their use affects the public welfare. It is, therefore, appropriately within the exercise of the police power of the State.

. . . .

. . .The legislature could not give away nor sell the discretion of its successors in respect to matters, the government of which, from the very nature of things, must vary with varying circumstances. The legislation which may be needed one day for the harbor may be different from the legislation that may be required at another day. Every legislature must, at the time of its existence, exercise the power of the State in the execution of the trust devolved upon it.

We hold, therefore, that any attempted cession of the ownership and control of the State in and over the submerged lands in Lake Michigan, by the act of April 16, 1869, was inoperative to affect, modify or in any respect to control the sovereignty and dominion of the State over the lands, or its ownership thereof, and that any such attempted operation of the act was annulled by the repealing act of April 15, 1873, which to that extent was valid and effective. There can be no irrepealable contract in a conveyance of property by a grantor in disregard of a public trust, under which he was bound to hold and manage it.

. . . .

It follows from the views expressed, and is so declared and adjudged, that the State of Illinois is the owner in fee of the submerged lands constituting the bed of Lake Michigan, which the third section of the act of April 16, 1869 purported to grant to the Illinois Central Railroad Company, and that the act of April 15, 1873 repealing the same is valid and effective for the purpose of restoring to the State the same control, dominion and ownership of said lands that it had prior to the passage of the act of April 16, 1869.

. . . .

[The dissent of Mr. Justice Shiras, joined by Mr. Justice Gray and Mr. Justice Brown, is omitted.]

1. Do you agree with the following comment about *Illinois Central* in Sax, *The Public Trust Doctrine in Natural Resources Law: Effective Judicial Intervention,* 68 Mich. L. Rev. 471, 490 (1970):

   [T]he Court articulated a principle that has become the central substantive thought in public trust litigation. When a state holds a resource which is available for the free use of the general public, a court will look with considerable skepticism upon *any* governmental conduct which is calculated *either* to reallocate that resource *or* to subject public uses to the self-interest of private parties.

2. The *Illinois Central* court observed that title to submerged and submersible lands was different from the title that the United States held in other public lands. Can a state *ever* grant trustlands to private parties? Under what circumstances? Is the size of the grant a factor in deciding its validity under the trust? *See Superior Public Rights, Inc. v. Dept. of Natural Resources,* 80 Mich. App. 72, 263 N.W.2d 290 (1977).

   Could the State of Illinois revoke its prior grant at any time it pleased? If the Illinois Central Railroad had improved the waterfront, would the state have to compensate the company for the improvements upon revocation of the grant? *Cf. Brusco Towboat, supra.* Could the railroad plead estoppel against the government? *Cf. Kaiser Aetna v. United States,* 100 S. Ct. 383 (1979), *infra.*

3. The Court cited *Stockton v. Baltimore & New York Railroad Co.,* in which Mr. Justice Bradley commented on leases of trust lands. Justice Bradley wrote:

   It is true that to utilize the fisheries, especially those of shell fish, it was necessary to parcel them out to particular operators, and employ the rent or consideration for the benefit of the whole people; but this did not alter the character of the title. The land remained subject to all other public uses as before, especially those of navigation and commerce, which are always paramount to those of public fisheries.

   32 Fed. Rep. at 20.

   Recall *Brusco Towboat v. State Land Board.* Judge Tanzer, as had Justice Bradley, wrote that leases of state trust lands would benefit the public through increased revenue. Tanzer, however, contemplated *exclusion* of the public from the leased trust land under some circumstances. Does the Oregon approach reflect traditional trust doctrine, or does it threaten the historic public right of navigation over leased trust lands?

4. The public trust doctrine is simple to state: The sovereign may dispose of its proprietary rights in trust lands, the *jus privatum,* but its obligation to manage trust lands in the public interest, the *jus publicum,* is inalienable. A private lessee or owner may have possession and the benefits of certain rights, but his interest is subject at all times to superior public interests.

   This simplicity, however, is deceptive. The next few cases will demonstrate the doctrine's complexity. But first, even to begin to understand the trust, you need some background.

   The public trust doctrine originated in Roman law. The Romans conceived of the air, water, sea, and seashore as *res communes,* as common to all the people and incapable of private ownership. The doctrine vanished during the Middle Ages, but returned in altered form in the reign of Elizabeth I of England. Lands under tide waters, according to the traditional American view of the English "doctrine," belonged to the King—and he held them in trust for the public. In fact, this was not the true English rule. The English public trust doctrine, like the navigability concept, was far more complex. Professor Wyche, in *Tidelands and the Public Trust: An Application for South Carolina*, 7 Ecology L.Q. 137, 141 (1978),[4] described the rebirth of the trust:

As grants from the Crown increased in number, most of the English coast eventually fell under private control—a situation that led to widespread public and commercial inconvenience. Concerned by this development, Elizabeth I, in 1569, commissioned Thomas Digges to devise a method whereby the Crown could regain control over the tidelands. Digges, an ingenious lawyer, responded with the so-called *prima facie* theory, under which it was presumed that grants of property abutting tidal waters did not operate to convey the tidelands unless there were specific words evincing such an intent in the deed. Because the early grants of coastal land generally were imprecise and incomplete, the theory, if accepted, would have returned most of the country's tidelands to the Crown. The Queen adopted Digges' proposal, but the English courts refused for some time to accept it. However, with the publication in 1787 of Lord Matthew Hale's treatise, *De Jure Maris*, the *prima facie* theory became a firmly established rule of the English common law.

The *prima facie* theory was not really a statement of the public trust doctrine, but it was a beginning. Lord Hale, in *De Jure Maris,* worked a subtle transformation of Digges' theory and brought English law a step closer to the modern trust doctrine. Lord Hale claimed that tidelands were burdened by the *jus publicum* despite private ownership. Under Digges' theory, tidelands could be owned in fee simple, including the right to obstruct navigation, as long as the tidelands had been clearly granted by the Crown. According to Hale, however, even a clear grant of tidelands did not convey the right to obstruct navigation.

Unfortunately, the English tidelands cases did not support Hale's position. Because of this conflict with the common law, English courts were slow to accept Hale's then revolutionary doctrine; American courts, however, were not so reluctant. In *Martin v. Waddell*, 41 U.S. (16 Pet.) 367, 410 (1842), Justice Roger Taney quoted Hale with approval as a matter of English law and stated:

[W]hen the revolution took place the people of each State became themselves sovereign; and in that character hold all the absolute right to all their navigable waters and the soils under them for their own common use, subject only to the rights since surrendered by the Constitution to the general government.

5. Despite the obscure origins of the public trust doctrine, it appears that the doctrine is here to stay. Professor Sax has written:

Of all the concepts known to American law, only the public trust doctrine seems to have the breadth and substantive content which might make it useful as a tool of general application for citizens seeking to develop a comprehensive legal approach to resource management problems. If that doctrine is to provide a satisfactory tool, it must meet three criteria. It must contain some concept of a legal right in the general public; it must be enforceable against the government; and it must be capable of an interpretation consistent with contemporary concerns for environmental quality.

Sax, *The Public Trust Doctrine in Natural Resources Law, supra,* at 474. Does the doctrine as set forth in *Illinois Central* meet Sax's three criteria?

How much freight should the public trust doctrine be expected to carry? Should all publicly owned lands, upland as well as tidelands and submerged lands, be subject to the doctrine? Several writers have urged courts to extend the doctrine to cover all public lands. Professor Large, in *This Land Is Whose*

---

[4]Copyrighted, Ecology Law Quarterly, footnotes omitted.

Land? Changing Concepts of Land as Property, 1973 Wis. L. Rev. 1039, 1069–70,[5] argued that:

[L]ogically, the public trust doctrine should also apply when a private interest pollutes a body of water and the state fails to curb the pollution. In theory, the state's inadequate regulation, which allows one person to destroy the river's purity, effectively diverts that river from a broad public use to one narrow private use— refuse disposal. Consequently, such a diversion should be subject to the public trust doctrine, since it achieves the same result as if the state had sold the river to the polluter. Although no case has expressly accepted this argument, the growing strength of the traditional public trust doctrine . . . indicates such an expansion may occur in the near future.

And Professor Sax in *The Public Trust Doctrine in Natural Resources Law: Effective Judicial Intervention*, 68 Mich. L. Rev. 471, 556–57 (1970), states:

It is clear that the historical scope of public trust law is quite narrow. Its coverage includes, with some variation among the states, that aspect of the public domain below the low-water mark on the margin of the sea and the great lakes, the waters over those lands, and the waters within rivers and streams of any consequence. Sometimes the coverage of the trust depends on a judicial definition of navigability, but that is a rather vague concept which may be so broad as to include all waters which are suitable for public recreation. Traditional public trust law also embraces parklands, especially if they have been donated to the public for specific purposes; and, as a minimum, it operates to require that such lands not be used for nonpark purposes. But except for a few cases . . . it is uncommon to find decisions that constrain public authorities in the specific uses to which they may put parklands, unless the lands are reallocated to a very different use, such as a highway.

If any of the analysis in this Article makes sense, it is clear that the judicial techniques developed in public trust cases need not be limited either to these few conventional interests or to questions of disposition of public properties. Public trust problems are found whenever governmental regulation comes into question, and they occur in a wide range of situations in which diffuse public interests need protection against tightly organized groups with clear and immediate goals. Thus, it seems that the delicate mixture of procedural and substantive protections which the courts have applied in conventional public trust cases would be equally applicable and equally appropriate in controversies involving air pollution, the dissemination of pesticides, the location of rights of way for utilities, and strip mining or wetland filling on private lands in a state where governmental permits are required.

Certainly the principle of the public trust is broader than its traditional application indicates. It may eventually be necessary to confront the question whether certain restrictions, imposed either by courts or by other governmental agencies, constitute a taking of private property; but a great deal of needed protection for the public can be provided long before that question is reached. Thus, for example, a private action seeking more effective governmental action on pesticide use or more extensive enforcement of air pollution laws would rarely be likely to reach constitutional limits. In any event, the courts can limit their intervention to regulation which stops short of a compensable taking.

Finally, it must be emphasized that the discussion contained in this Article applies with equal force to controversies over subjects other than natural resources. While resource controversies are often particularly dramatic examples of diffuse public interests and contain all their problems of equality in the political and

[5]Copyrighted, University of Wisconsin, Wisconsin Law Review.

administrative process, those problems frequently arise in issues affecting the poor and consumer groups. Only time will reveal the appropriate limits of the public trust doctrine as a useful judicial instrument.

For upland applications of public trust related concepts, *see,* e.g., *Michigan Oil Co. v. Natural Resource Comm.,* 71 Mich. App. 667, 249 N.W.2d 135 (1976) (denial of permit for oil drilling in unspoiled state forest upheld); *Gould v. Greylock Reservation Commission,* 350 Mass. 410, 215 N.E.2d 114 (1966) (4,000-acre lease for aerial tramway, ski lifts, and ski resort on Mount Greylock held to exceed agency's statutory authority); *Payne v. Kassab,* 312 A.2d 86 (1973) (criteria for judicial review of street-widening project encroaching upon public park); *Sacco v. Dept. of Public Works,* 352 Mass. 670, 227 N.E.2d 478 (1967) (filling of pond to widen highway); *San Diego County Archaeological v. Compadres,* 81 Cal. App. 3d 923, 146 Cal. Rptr. 786 (1978) (protection of "public interests" in historical artifacts). *See also Robbins v. Department of Public Works,* 355 Mass. 328, 244 N.E.2d 577 (1969); V. Yannacone, B. Cohen, & S. Davison, *Environmental Rights and Remedies* 12 (1972).

Expansion of the public trust doctrine also has occurred through legislative action, either by statutory enactment of the doctrine, or by constitutional provisions which incorporate the trust theory. Constitutional and statutory constraints have also been placed on disposition of trust properties. *See* Ariz. Rev. Stat. § 12–1112; Cal. Const. art. 10 §§ 3, 4; Conn. Gen. Stat. Ann. § 22a–1a to 1d; Hawaii Rev. Laws § 8–52; Idaho Code Ann. § 7–703; Mich. Const. art. 4, § 52; Mont. Rev. Codes Ann. § 93–9904; Nev. Rev. Stat. § 37–030; N.C. Gen. Stat. § 146–3; N.J. Stat. Ann. § 27, 7–36; Pa. Const. art. 1, § 27; S. C. Code Ann. § 1–793; S.D. Compiled Laws Ann. §§ 34A–10–1 to 15; Va. Const. art. XI, §§ 1–3; Vt. Stat. Ann. tit. 19, § 222; Wash. Const. art. 15.

Preservation and protection of state natural resources is the responsibility of trust commissions in at least two states, New York and Maryland. *See* N.Y. Envt'l Conserv. L. § 45–0101 (McKinney 1973); Md. Code Ann. § 3–201 (Cum. Supp. 1978).

Article 1, section 27, of the Pennsylvania constitution is particularly noteworthy for its expansive expression of the public trust doctrine. The provision enumerates specific interests in clean air and pure water and in the conservation and preservation of the natural, scenic, historic, and aesthetic values of the environment. *See Bucks County Bd. of Comm'r v. Commonwealth,* 11 Pa. Commw. Ct. 487, 313 A.2d 185 (1973); *Commonwealth v. Barnes,* 455 Pa. 392, 319 A.2d 871 (1974), *aff'd,* 371 A.2d 461 (Pa. 1977); *Commonwealth v. Nat. Gettysburg Battlefield Tower, Inc.,* 8 Pa. Commw. Ct. 231, 302 A.2d 886 (1973), *aff'd,* 454 Pa. 193, 311 A.2d 588 (1973); *Payne v. Kassab,* 11 Pa. Commw. Ct. 14, 312 A.2d 86 (1973).

See also Nanda & Ris, *The Public Trust Doctrine: A Viable Approach to International Environmental Protection,* 5 Ecology L.Q. 291 (1976).

6. In a subsequent case, *Appleby v. City of New York,* 271 U.S. 364, 46 S. Ct. 569, 70 L. Ed. 992 (1926), the Supreme Court seemed to retreat from its holding in *Illinois Central. See* Littman, *Tidelands: Trusts, Easements, Custom, and Implied Dedication,* 10 Nat. Res. Law. 279, 284–86 (1977). The Court held that a state could convey the *jus publicum* if the legislature decided that such a conveyance was in the public interest. The Court cited several New York cases for the proposition that sale of the *jus publicum* was possible provided the legislative intent to alienate public interests was clear.

7. The water-relatedness of the trust doctrine policy of protecting navigation and fishing is apparent—but what about the trust policy of promoting "commerce"? Are all improvements in furtherance of commerce a valid use of public trust lands? For an example, consider *People ex rel. Scott v. Chicago Park District,* 66 Ill. 2d 65, 360 N.E.2d 773 (1976). The Illinois legislature sold certain submerged

lands to the United States Steel Corporation. U.S. Steel planned to fill the site and construct a mill. The new mill, the company argued, would further commerce generally and provide jobs. The Illinois court, in rejecting U.S. Steel's argument, wrote:

In order to preserve the meaning and vitality of the public trust doctrine, when a grant of submerged land beneath waters is proposed under the circumstances here, the public purpose to be served cannot be only incidental and remote. The claimed benefit here to the public through additional employment and economic improvement is too indirect, intangible and elusive to satisfy the requirement of a public purpose. In almost every instance where submerged land would be reclaimed there would be employment provided and some economic benefit to the state.

Id. at 781.

In dicta, the court implied that if the private interest more directly served a public purpose, a conveyance of trust lands might be valid.

Instead of conveying the lands, could the Illinois legislature have authorized U.S. Steel to use the submerged lands by lease, license, or permit without violating the public trust doctrine? In answering, consider the next case, *Boone v. Kingsbury*.

BOONE v. KINGSBURY, 206 Cal. 148, 273 P. 797 (1928), *cert. denied*, 280 U.S. 517 (1929)

SEAWELL, J. Original applications for writs of mandamus by which the validity of chapter 303, Statutes and Amendments 1921, p. 404, and certain specific sections thereof, and also chapter 285, Statutes and Amendments 1923, p. 593, amendatory of said chapter 303, which provides for the granting of permits to residents of the state who are citizens of the United States, to enter and prospect upon tidal and submerged lands and to lease the same on a royalty basis, is assailed.

All of the petitioners herein are applicants for permits to enter and prospect for oil, oil shale, gas, phosphate, sodium, and other mineral deposits upon the several areas of public lands described in each respective application. Said lands are tidal and submerged lands situate in the vicinity of a small cove of the Pacific Ocean at Seacliff, county of Ventura, this state. Respondent, W. S. Kingsbury, surveyor general of the state of California and ex officio register of the state land office, has refused to grant the permits applied for, basing his refusal to do so upon the ground that the granting of the same would authorize the conduct of a business in and upon tidal and submerged lands which would interfere with and be destructive of navigation and the fisheries in the proximity of and within the areas described in said applications, and that the Legislature, in adopting the statute purporting to authorize the granting of said permits, exceeded its authority in attempting to provide a method by which tidal and submerged lands held by the state in trust for its inhabitants by virtue of its sovereign right and not by its proprietary right may be leased to residents of this state who are citizens of the United States or who had declared their intention to become citizens.

. . . .

We do not deem it necessary to pursue the question of the title to tide lands to the extent that the subject has been discussed by counsel, for the reason that the act does not purport to divest the state of its title to any part of its tide lands, but merely grants to its permittees a license or privilege of extracting minerals from the soil, the ownership of which is held in its proprietary right, for a term of years, upon an acreage and royalty basis. It is clear that one of the purposes of the Legislature by the enactment of said chapter 303, Statutes and Amendments 1921, p. 404, was to give to the citizens an opportunity to intercept the large volumes of oil gravitating seaward to inextricable depths, and to reduce to useful purposes oil, gas and mineral deposits reposing beneath the ocean's bed. The commercial value of these subterranean products is enormous. The contribution made to commerce and the varied industries of the world and to the comfort of the race by the modern intensive development of the oil and gas industry is not surpassed, if it is equaled, by any other of the natural agencies or physical forces which are contributing to the material welfare of mankind, including electrical energy. Gasoline is the power that largely moves the commerce of nations over lands and sea; it furnishes much of the power necessary to the manufacturer, agriculturist and miner, as well as power needful in the reclamation of swamp and overflowed land and in the irrigation of arid and waste land. It is the only power that is practical for aeroplane navigation. Gasoline is so closely allied with state and national welfare as to make its production a matter of state and national concern. If it can be said of any industry that its output is "in aid and furtherance of commerce and navigation," and its production "a public benefit," the production of gasoline, by reason of the motive elements that inhere in it and its universal use and adaptability to varied uses and the convenient and portable form in which it may be confined, would entitle it to a high classification in the scale of useful, natural products. . . .

The federal government from its earliest organization, has consistently adopted acts containing the most liberal terms as inducements to engage its citizens in the exploration and development of its mineral resources. . . .

. . . .

The license or privilege authorizing the permittee to prospect and mine tide lands is denominated by the act a lease, but in practical effect it strongly partakes of the character of a contract to prospect or mine said tide lands on a share or percentage basis. In no sense does the state part with title to its tide lands. More than this, it expressly "reserves from sale except upon a rental and royalty basis" all coal, oil, oil shale, phosphate, sodium and other mineral deposits in lands belonging to the state, and persons authorized by said act to prospect for, mine and remove such deposits are restricted to as small a portion of the surface area as may be reasonably required for mining and removing such deposits. In this respect the instant case is widely different from Illinois Central R. Co. v. People of the State of Illinois, 146 U.S. 452, 13 S. Ct. 118 (36 L. Ed. 1018), the case frequently cited by respondent, surveyor general, and the amici curiæ in sympathy with his position. . . .

. . . .

The surveyor general is constituted the agent of the state by the act under consideration, as he is made its agent in numerous acts providing for the sale of salt marsh, tide, and other public lands, to carry out and accomplish the purposes of the act and to that end he may make all rules and regulations not in conflict or inconsistent with the provisions of said act. His powers in the way of regulation and administration are many, and the legislation conferring them is to be given full force and effect when enacted according to the constitutional mandate and when not in conflict with the express provisions of said act. By chapter 227, Statutes and Amendments 1923, p. 452, the Attorney General, the chairman of the state board of control, and surveyor general are constituted a commission to lease to the highest responsible bidder any land belonging to the state of California and dedicated to a public use where such lands contain, in the judgment of said commission, oil, gas, and other hydro-carbons in commercial quantities. The act is but another illustration of the policy of the state with respect to the extraction of its minerals from state lands and was unquestionably passed to remove the obstacle pointed out in McNeil v. Kingsbury, 190 Cal. 406, 213 P. 50. In that case McNeil applied for a writ of mandate in this court to compel the surveyor general to issue to him a prospecting permit, under the provisions of the identical act attacked by respondent surveyor general, to prospect for oil upon the grounds of the Norwalk State Hospital for the Insane at Norwalk, Cal. The petition was denied on the grounds that it was not intended by the Legislature that said act should apply to lands already devoted to a public use.

A copy of a photograph taken January 23, 1928, twenty-four hours after high tide, showing the section of the ocean shore line upon which the tide lands in controversy abut, is appended to the briefs of Boone and Shudde. That the photograph is a true representation of the situation is admitted. It shows a precipitous, mountainous upland facing in crescent shape the open sea. A number of oil derricks are erected upon the highlands and several derricks and other structures appear to be erected upon the beach near the point where the surf extends its flow under normal conditions. The beach which skirts the shore is very narrow. The narrow shelf of the beach at the foot of the cliffs is occupied by the tracks of the Southern Pacific Railroad. Paralleling the railroad is the state highway, which for a considerable distance is built over tide lands upon a causeway. There is no wharf or landing structure of any kind erected in the vicinity. The court is invited to and will take judicial notice of the coast lines within the state and will also resort to publications issued by the department of commerce describing and delineating the United States coast and geodetic sur-veys. The coast in question is not a harbor, or haven, nor does it afford natural facilities for the landing of vessels. It is asserted, and not contradicted, that the record of the rise and fall of the tide at this point shows that the tide ebbs upon occasions a distance of seven hundred or eight hundred feet from the mean high-tide line and the sea is too heavy for small vessels to weather and too shallow to float large ones. It may be said of the situation that the coast line at the point in question is an unnavigable portion of a vast body of navigable water, and the use to which the state proposes to devote the soil, from a practical point of view, would not be incompatible with, or in "derogation of its governmental trust to preserve needed navigable waters for the benefit of its people." Bolsa Land Co. v. Burdick, 151 Cal. 254, 90 P. 532, 12 L. R. A. (N. S.) 275. No claim is made that the shallows, shoals or depths of the area in question are valuable for fishing purposes.

No uncertainty can exist as to the rights of the state to absolutely alienate its tide and submerged lands when they are unfit for navigation, are useless as aids of commerce and possess no substantial value as fishing grounds. The policy of this state is and has always been to encourage its citizens to devote waste and unused lands to some useful purpose. The power of the state to absolutely alienate lands perpetually covered by water has been upheld by all courts of the nation, state and federal, where the land so covered was severed from the main body by harbor and other improvements in such manner as to leave the remaining waters of no substantial use to navigation or commerce. It is only in those cases where the reduction of the water area amounts to a substantial interference with navigation and commerce or the fisheries that the absolute power of alienation by the sovereign and its control and dominion over said lands can be questioned.

. . . .

The state cannot abdicate its trust over property in which the whole people are interested, like navigable waters and soils under them, so as to leave them entirely under the use and control of private parties, except in the case of parcels used in promoting the interest of the public therein, or when parcels can be disposed of without impairment of the public interest in what remains.

Nothing is said in Illinois Central R. R. v. Illinois that would indicate that the uses to be made of the tide lands in the instant case by the agents or permittees of the state in extracting oil minerals from the ocean beds under its control and regulation would substantially impair the public interest in or use of the vast remaining area of the ocean.

The trust in which tide and submerged lands are held does not prevent the state from reclaiming tide and submerged lands from the sea where it can be done without prejudice to the public right of navigation and applying them to other purposes and uses. . . .

. . . .

The right of the state to alienate its tide and submerged lands by statute where the intent of the statute is clearly expressed or necessarily implied was again reaffirmed by this court in People v. California Fish Co., 166 Cal. 576, 597, 138 P. 79, 88. . . .

. . . .

In the instant case the state does not part with title to its lands, but withholds them from sale and also reserves an interest in said minerals mined on shares. No part of the lands from which said minerals are extracted is alienated into private ownership, nor is any legal right of the littoral owner invaded. No harm can come to fisheries under the protective provisions of the act, as it must be presumed that the provisions of the act will be observed, and, if not observed, the general laws enacted for the protection of fish and sea life against the pollution of waters by penalizing persons or corporations, who cause or are responsible for deleterious substances escaping into the public waters of the state, are amply sufficient to protect sea life against serious injury or destruction.

. . . .

We are satisfied that the state act under consideration is a valid exercise of a right which inheres in the state by virtue of its sovereign power. It does not impinge upon the state or federal Constitutions and is not in conflict with any act of Congress or the state of California.

. . . .

We concur: WASTE, C.J.; RICHARDS, J.; CURTIS, J.; PRESTON, J.; LANGDON, J.

What are the restrictions on governmental authority imposed in favor of the public through the public trust doctrine? Consider Sax, *The Public Trust Doctrine in Natural Resources Law: Effective Judicial Intervention,* 68 Mich. L. Rev. 471, 477 (1970):

> Three types of restrictions on governmental authority are often thought to be imposed by the public trust: first, the property subject to the trust must not only be used for a public purpose, but it must be held available for use by the general public; second, the property may not be sold, even for a fair cash equivalent; and third, the property must be maintained for particular types of uses. The last claim is expressed in two ways. Either it is urged that the resource must be held available for certain traditional uses, such as navigation, recreation, or fishery, or it is said that the uses which are made of the property must be in some sense related to the natural uses peculiar to that resource.

Were these restrictions enforced by the California Supreme Court in *Boone v. Kingsbury*?

MARKS v. WHITNEY, 6 Cal. 3d 251, 491 P.2d 374, 98 Cal. Rptr. 790 (1971)

McCOMB, Justice

This is a quiet title action to settle a boundary line dispute caused by overlapping and defective surveys and to enjoin defendants (herein "Whitney") from asserting any claim or right in or to the property of plaintiff Marks. The unique feature here is that a part of Marks' property is tidelands acquired under an 1874 patent issued pursuant to the Act of March 28, 1868 (Stats. 1867–1868, c. 415, p. 507); a small portion of these tidelands adjoins almost the entire shoreline of Whitney's upland property. Marks asserted complete ownership of the tidelands and the right to fill and develop them. Whitney opposed on the ground that this would cut off his rights as a littoral owner and as a member of the public in these tidelands and the navigable waters covering them. He requested a declaration in the decree that Marks' title was burdened with a public trust easement; also that it was burdened with certain prescriptive rights claimed by Whitney.

The trial court settled the common boundary line to the satisfaction of the parties. However, it held that Whitney had no "standing" to raise the public trust issue and it refused to make a finding as to whether the tidelands are so burdened. It did find in Whitney's favor as to a prescriptive easement across the tidelands to maintain and use an existing seven-foot wide wharf but with the limitation that "Such rights shall be subject to the right of Marks to use, to fill and to develop" the tidelands and the seven-foot wide easement area so long as the Whitney "rights of access and ingress and egress to and from the deep waters of the Bay shall be preserved" over this strip.

. . . .

Questions: First. *Are these tidelands subject to the public trust; if so, should the judgment so declare?*

Yes. Regardless of the issue of Whitney's standing to raise this issue the court may take judicial notice of public trust burdens in quieting title to tidelands. This matter is of great public importance, particularly in view of population pressures, demands for recreational property, and the increasing development of seashore and waterfront property. A present declaration that the title of Marks in these tidelands is burdened with a public easement may avoid needless future litigation.

Tidelands are properly those lands lying between the lines of mean high and low tide covered and uncovered successively by the ebb and flow thereof. The trial court found that the portion of Marks' lands here under consideration constitutes a part of the Tidelands of Tomales Bay, that at all times it has been, and now is, subject to the daily ebb and flow of the tides in Tomales Bay, that the ordinary high tides in the bay overflow and submerge this portion of his lands, and that Tomales Bay is a navigable body of water and an arm of the Pacific Ocean.

This land was patented *as tidelands* to Marks' predecessor in title. The patent of May 15, 1874, recites that it was issued by the Governor of California "by virtue of authority in me vested" pursuant to "Statutes enacted from time to time" for the "Sale and Conveyance of the *Tide Lands belonging to the State by virtue of her sovereignty."* [Emphasis added.]

The governing statute was the act of March 28, 1868, entitled "An Act to provide for the management and sale of the lands belonging to the State." By its terms it repealed all other laws relating to the sale of swamp and overflowed, salt-marsh and tidelands. These laws, including the Act of March 28, 1868, were codified in former Political Code sections 3440–3493½.

They were explicitly and expansively considered by this court entirely separate from the restrictions contained in Article 15, sections two and three, of the State Constitution (enacted in 1879) — In *Forestier v. Johnson*, 164 Cal. 24, 127 P. 156 (1912) and *People v. California Fish Co.*, 166 Cal. 576, 589–598, 138 P. 79 (1913). . . .

. . . .

Public trust easements are traditionally defined in terms of navigation, commerce and fisheries. They have been held to include the right to fish, hunt, bathe, swim, to use for boating and general recreation purposes the navigable waters of the state, and to use the bottom of the navigable waters for anchoring, standing, or other purposes. . . . The public has the same rights in and to tidelands.

The public uses to which tidelands are subject are sufficiently flexible to encompass changing public needs. In administering the trust the state is not burdened with an outmoded classification favoring one mode of utilization over another. There is a growing public recognition that one of the most important public uses of the tidelands—a use encompassed within the tidelands trust—is the preservation of those lands in their natural state, so that they may serve as ecological units for scientific study, as open space, and as environments which provide food and habitat for birds and marine life, and which favorably affect the scenery and climate of the area. It is not necessary to here define precisely all the public uses which encumber tidelands.

. . . .

We are confronted with the issue, however, whether the trial court may restrain or bar a private party, namely, Whitney, "from claiming or asserting any estate, right, title, interest in or claim or lien upon" the tidelands quieted in Marks. The injunction so made, without any limitation expressing the public servitude, is broad enough to prohibit Whitney from asserting or in any way exercising public trust uses in these tidelands and the navigable waters covering them in his capacity as a member of the public. This is beyond the jurisdiction of the court. It is within the province of the trier of fact to determine whether any particular use made or asserted by Whitney in or over these tidelands would constitute an infringement either upon the *jus privatum* of Marks or upon the *jus publicum* of the people. It is also within the province of the trier of fact to determine whether any particular use to which Marks wishes to devote his tidelands constitutes an unlawful infringement upon the *jus publicum* therein. It is a political question, within the wisdom and power of the Legislature, acting within the scope of its duties as trustee, to determine whether public trust uses should be modified or extinguished and to take the necessary steps to free them from such burden. In the absence of state or federal action the court may not bar members of the public from lawfully asserting or exercising public trust rights on this privately owned tidelands.

There is absolutely no merit in Marks' contention that as the owner of the *jus privatum* under this patent he may fill and develop his property, whether for navigational purposes or not; nor in his contention that his past and present plan for development of these tidelands as a marina have caused the extinguishment of the public easement. Reclamation with or without prior authorization from the state does not *ipso facto* terminate the public trust nor render the issue moot.

A proper judgment for a patentee of tidelands was determined by this court in *People v. California Fish Co., supra,* 166 Cal. at pp. 598–599, 138 P. at p. 88, to be that he owns "the soil, subject to the easement of the public for the public uses of navigation and commerce, and to the right of the state, as administrator and controller of these public uses and the public trust therefor, to enter upon and possess the same for the preservation and advancement of the public uses, and to make such changes and improvements as may be deemed advisable for those purposes."

Second: *Does Whitney have "standing" to request the court to recognize and declare the public trust easement on Marks' tidelands?*

Yes. The relief sought by Marks resulted in taking away from Whitney rights to which he is entitled as a member of the general public. It is immaterial that Marks asserted he was not seeking to enjoin the public. The decree as rendered does enjoin a member of the public.

. . . .

Whitney had standing to raise this issue. The court could have raised this issue on its own. "It is now well settled that the court may finally determine as between the parties in a quiet title action all of the conflicting claims regarding any estate or interest in the property." Where the interest concerned is one that, as here, constitutes a public burden upon land to which title is quieted, and affects the defendant as a member of the public, that servitude should be explicitly declared.

Third: *Does Whitney have rights as a littoral owner which are improperly enjoined by the judgment appealed from?*

Yes. In its memorandum opinion the trial court expressed its views as to the private rights between these parties. It stated that it would find and adjudge that the littoral owner does not own a private right of access or fishery across all of the tidelands adjoining his property; that, however, he may own a reasonable right to access; that here it would be found that he had exercised such right and his right of access is therefore confined to the wharf area; and that as between Marks and Whitney this has ripened into an easement in that specific area only. The judgment quieted an easement by prescription in Whitney as against Marks "for access and ingress and egress to and from the deep waters of Tomales Bay for pedestrians, fisheries, navigation and other purposes. Such right shall be subject to the right of MARKS to use, to fill and to develop . . . (including those within the above defined area seven feet in width), so long as such rights of access . . . shall be preserved over and across said area seven feet in width and MARKS may use and convey the same for use, for all purposes which do not defeat or substantially interfere with use by WHITNEY of such area for the above stated purposes."

A littoral owner has a right in the foreshore adjacent to his property separate and distinct from that of the general public (Gould on Waters, 3d ed., § 149). This is a property right and is valuable, and although it must be enjoyed in due subjection to the rights of the public, it cannot be arbitrarily or capriciously destroyed. (Yates v. Milwaukee (1870) 77 U.S. 497, 504, 10 Wall. 497, 504, 19 L.Ed. 984.) A littoral owner can enjoin as a nuisance interference by a private person with this right. (San Francisco Sav. Union v. R. G. R. Petroleum & Mining Co. (1904) 144 Cal. 134, 135–139, 77 P. 823.) A littoral owner has been held to have the right to build a pier out to the line of navigability; a right to accretion;[6] a right to navigation (the latter right being held in common with the general public) (see 65 C.J.S. Navigable Waters §§ 61–69; 56 Am.Jur. Waters, § 233); and a right of access from every part of his frontage across the foreshore (see Coulson & Forbes on Waters (6th ed. 1952) pp. 69–70). This right of access extends to ordinary low tide both when the tide is in and when the tide is out. (San Francisco Sav. Union v. R. G. R. Petroleum & Mining Co., supra, 144 Cal. 134, 77 P. 823.)

This littoral right is of course burdened with a servitude in favor of the state in the exercise of its trust powers over navigable waters (Colberg, Inc. v. State, supra, 67 Cal.2d 408, 420, 62 Cal. Rptr. 401, 432 P.2d 3: City of Newport Beach v. Fager (1940) 39 Cal.App.2d 23, 102 P.2d 438). The state has

---

[6]The judgment herein does not affect Whitney's right to accretion.

not exercised its power in this instance. The effect of this judgment is to limit Whitney's right to bathe, sunbathe, fish, etc. to the pier area of the tidelands, to restrict his *lateral* use of the pier for boating, etc., and to debar him from the use of any part of his 344 foot frontage along these tidelands except for the seven-foot wide pier area.

The quieting of a prescriptive easement in Whitney without a determination in the decree as to the effect thereof on the public rights in these tidelands, creates further confusion both as to the nature of Whitney's rights as littoral owner, apart from prescription, and as to the rights of the public.

While the authority given Marks "to use, to fill and to develop" the tidelands, except as limited by the wharf easement, was not intended by the trial court to place any limitation upon the state or federal government, in the absence of a declaration of the rights of the public or of the state as trustee it is subject to misinterpretation, i.e., as giving a blanket and otherwise unqualified authorization to Marks to fill and develop.

. . . .

Judgment is reversed and remanded for proceedings not inconsistent with this opinion.

NOTES

1. Do you agree with this assessment of *Marks v. Whitney* from Comment, *The Tideland Trust: Economic Currents in a Traditional Legal Doctrine*, 21 U.C.L.A. L. Rev. 826, 867 (1974):[7]

    For the first time the court explicitly stated that it would use the trust principle to take account of changing public needs, and that the tidelands were susceptible to an undefined number of encumbrances which the court saw fit to impose to promote the public welfare.

    Part of the difficulty in understanding the modern public trust doctrine is that it is not in fact a single, coherent legal doctrine; the trust is a mixture of several related concepts. Recall that in Roman law, the trust was simply communal ownership; submerged and submersible lands could not be privately owned. In modern American law, the trust is different. Trust lands are not communally owned, but may be privately owned subject to certain "necessary easements."

    The American necessary easement approach evolved from English common law, not from the Roman codes. The Roman communal concept may be the ultimate goal of some trust proponents, but for a number of reasons the easement approach is most often applied by the courts. In Comment, *The Public Trust in Tidal Areas: A Sometimes Submerged Traditional Doctrine*, 79 Yale L.J. 762, 770 (1970),[8] the author explained the dominance of the necessary easement approach in English and American law:

    Because large portions of the tidal areas and navigable rivers had already become private property in Britain, it would have been difficult or impossible for the courts to expropriate them. . . . Easements also proved a much more flexible tool than fee

---

[7]Copyrighted, U.C.L.A. Law Review.

[8]Reprinted by permission of The Yale Law Journal Company and Fred B. Rothman & Company from *The Yale Law Journal*, Vol. 79, p. 762, 770.

interests because they are defined in terms of activities, not land. An acre is an acre, but "navigation" or "commerce" can be defined in various ways. Such flexibility, even if purchased at the cost of some certainty, better enables judges to match law and justice, case by case.

2. *Marks v. Whitney* is important for at least two reasons. First, the California court's definition of the trust was open ended. The court did not embrace the Roman concept of communal ownership, the ultimate form of the public trust, but it did greatly expand the "necessary easements." If such expansion continues, how much will be left of the distinction between communal ownership and the easement theory? Second, the court conclusively established the rights of the public to bring suit to enforce the trust in California. In *The Tideland Trust: Economic Currents in a Traditional Legal Doctrine*,[9] *supra*, at 868, the author discussed the effect of the court's holding that members of the public had standing to sue:

Because this principle provides a means for public involvement in the trust decisions, it helps to bring further input into tideland cases . . . . By giving standing to members of the public, the holding could have a profound impact on tideland trust litigation by simply increasing the volume of cases in this area.

However, other state courts may restrict standing to enforce the public trust. *See, e.g., Save Our Wetlands, Inc. v. Werner Bros., Inc.,* 372 So. 2d 231 (La. Ct. App. 1979) (environmental organization did not have standing to sue for removal of alleged illegal pilings).

3. Beginning around 1950, land title insurance companies noted the growing shortage of open space, reviewed the nature of title to lands burdened by the public trust, and began making specific exceptions in their policies as to the public interests protected by the trust. Because of these exceptions, lending institutions grew reluctant to make loans for tideland development. After the court's broad definition of the trust in *Marks v. Whitney*, title companies refused to ensure *any* new improvements on relatively undeveloped tidelands without the prior approval of the governmental agency in charge of trustlands. *See* Taylor, *Patented Tidelands: A Naked Fee?, supra.* The mere existence of the public trust, even without its actual enforcement, clearly inhibits private development of submerged and submersible lands.

4. In *Morse v. Oregon Div. of State Lands*, 30 Or. App. 516, 581 P.2d 520 (1978), the City of North Bend applied for and was granted a state permit to fill 32 acres of a tidal estuary for the purpose of extending a city airport runway. The appeals court invalidated the permit, holding that under the public trust doctrine, submerged and tidelands could only be filled for water-related purposes, and that the Oregon dredge-and-fill law codified the public trust doctrine. Thus the court found that a nonwater-related use such as an airport runway extension was impermissible under the state dredge-and-fill law.

The Oregon Supreme Court affirmed, but on different grounds, stating that the public trust doctrine does not prohibit all nonwater-related fills. According to the supreme court, under the dredge-and-fill statute a fill permit for a nonwater-related use could be issued where it was shown the public need for the fill outweighed the detriment to the use of the waters in question for navigation, fishing, and recreational purposes. *Morse v. Oregon Div. of States Lands*, 285 Or. 197, 590 P.2d 709, 711, 714 (1979); *see* 35 Op. Ore. Atty Gen. 844 (1971); *cf. Appeal of Dept. of Natural Resources*, 401 A.2d 93 (Del. Super. 1978) (blanket restrictions on fills beyond legislative intent); *Shablowski v. State*, 370 So. 2d 50 (Fla. Ct. App. 1979) (dredging allowed only where public interest would be served by the

[9]Copyrighted, U.C.L.A. Law Review.

project, whereas filling is allowed unless the project would be contrary to the public interest). Should the public trust doctrine be interpreted to limit filling in coastal waters to water-related purposes? In *Morse* both the appeals court and the supreme court left open the question of whether the state legislature has the authority to modify the public trust doctrine. Does the state legislature have such authority under *Illinois Central* and *Shively v. Bowlby*? See *International Paper Co. v. Mississippi St. Hwy. Dept.*, 271 So. 2d 395 (Miss. Sup. Ct. 1973).

5. Preserving public recreational access rights in navigable waters has become one of the principal uses of the public trust doctrine. This is true for inland streams and lakes as well as coastal waters. *See State v. Superior Court of Lake County*, 29 Cal. 3d 210, 615 P.2d 239, 179 Cal. Rptr. 696 (1981); Commentary, *The Public Trust Doctrine and Ownership of Florida's Navigable Lakes*, 29 U. Fla. L. Rev. 730, 732 (1977); Johnson, *Public Trust Protection for Stream Flows and Lake Levels*, 14 U.C. Davis L. Rev. 233 (1981). Regarding the definition of navigability for public recreational access purposes, see *Hitchings v. Del Rio Woods Recreation and Park District*, 55 Cal. App. 3d 560, 127 Cal. Rptr. 830 (1976). *See also People v. Emmert*, 597 P.2d 1025 (Colo. 1979) (floating on nonnavigable stream held a trespass).

For the relationship between the public trust doctrine and public access to dry lands such as beach areas above the mean high-tide line, *see Neptune City v. Avon-By-The-Sea, infra.*

6. Under what circumstances, if any, can the state restrict public access to public trust lands and the waters overhead? *See People v. Deacon*, 87 C.A. 2d Supp. 29, 151 Cal. Rptr. 277 (1978) (county ordinance prohibiting motorcycle use for tidelands access upheld); *State v. San Luis Obispo Sportsman's Ass'n*, 22 C.A. 3d 440, 584 P.2d 1088, 149 Cal. Rptr. 482 (1978) (public right to fish extends to all state-owned land not being used for a special purpose incompatible with public use).

Where a state permits a private individual or entity to use and occupy state-owned tidelands, what is the liability, if any, of the occupier to members of the public injured on the occupied premises? *See Smith v. Scrap Disposal Corp.*, 158 Cal. Rptr. 134 (Cal. Ct. App. 1979).

CITY OF BERKELEY v. SUPERIOR COURT, 26 Cal. 3d 515, 606 P.2d 362, 162 Cal. Rptr. 327 (1980), *cert. denied*, 101 S. Ct. 119 (1980)

MOSK, Justice

We are concerned in this case with whether tidelands[10] in San Francisco Bay granted to private parties by the state Board of Tide Land Commissioners (board) in the latter part of the 19th century, pursuant to a legislative act passed in 1870, conveyed title to the purchasers free of the public trust for commerce, navigation, fishing, and related uses. *Knudson v. Kearney* (1915) 171 Cal. 250, and *Alameda Conservation Association v. City of Alameda* (1968) 264 Cal. App. 2d 284, held that these grants were in fee simple and not subject to the rights of the public. We conclude that these decisions were erroneous and must be

---

[10]The term "tidelands," properly speaking, are lands between the lines of mean high tide and mean low tide, whereas "submerged lands" are those seaward of mean low tide and not uncovered in the ordinary ebb and flow of the tide. (*City of Long Beach v. Mansell* (1970) 3 Cal. 3d 462, 478, fn. 13.) For literary convenience, the term "tidelands" will refer to both types of property in this opinion, unless otherwise noted.

overturned, but that tracts of land granted by the board that have been improved or filled are, to the degree hereinafter described, free of the public trust.

Santa Fe Land Improvement Company, a corporation, and George W. Murphy (plaintiffs) each brought an action against the City of Berkeley and the State of California (defendants) to quiet title to 79 acres of land located in the City of Berkeley adjacent to the Berkeley Marina, for declaratory relief, and inverse condemnation. Plaintiffs' predecessors in interest had acquired the parcels from the board by deeds issued pursuant to the 1870 act. At the time of acquisition the property was tideland, but all except a small portion has been filled.[11] Plaintiffs alleged that they owned these parcels free of any trust on behalf of the public for commerce, navigation and fishing.

Defendants denied that plaintiffs own the 79 acres in question, and the state filed a cross-complaint,[12] claiming that Berkeley owns the property in fee under a grant from the state,[13] or, in the alternative, that plaintiffs' title is subject to the public trust. The cross-complaint alleged also that Santa Fe claims 608 acres and Murphy 48 acres of Berkeley's tidelands, comprising 77 percent of that city's entire waterfront, that this additional acreage was, like the 79 acres involved in plaintiffs' complaint, acquired by deeds issued pursuant to the 1870 act, and that Santa Fe asserts that the additional property is also free of the public trust. The cross-complaint sought to include the additional acreage in the action.

. . . .

The doctrine that the public owns the right to tidelands for purposes such as commerce, navigation and fishing originated in Roman law, which held the public's right to such lands to be "illimitable and unrestrainable" and incapable of individual exclusive appropriation. (See Note, *The Public Trust in Tidal Areas* (1970) 79 Yale L.J. 762, 763, fn. 7.) The English common law developed similar limitations upon private authority over such property: the rights of the public prevailed over the rights of private persons claiming under tideland grants made by the crown. (See Note, *California's Tideland Trust* (1971) 22 Hastings L.J. 759, 761–762.) After the American Revolution, the federal government acquired "absolute right to all . . . navigable waters, and the soils under them, for [its] own common use . . . ." *(Martin v. Waddell* (1842) 41 U.S. 367, 410.)

When California was admitted to statehood in 1850, it succeeded to title in the tidelands within its borders not in its proprietary capacity but as trustee for the public. *(City of Long Beach v. Mansell, supra,* 3 Cal.3d 462, 482; *People v.*

[11]According to defendants, the fill was placed there by Berkeley some time before 1965 under a garbage disposal program.

[12]The cross-complaint was filed by the State Lands Commission, which has jurisdiction over submerged lands owned by the state as well as residual jurisdiction of tidelands granted by the state. (See, e.g., Pub. Res. Code, §§ 6216, 6301.) Section 6308 requires that the state be joined as a party in any action involving title to tidelands granted by the state to a local entity.

[13]Berkeley's claim of title stems from statutes enacted in 1913 and thereafter, which granted the state's right to the tidelands within Berkeley's boundaries to the city. (Stats. 1913, ch. 347, § 1, pp. 705–706; Stats. 1915, ch. 534, § 1, pp. 902–903; Stats. 1917, ch. 596, § 1, p. 915; Stats. 1919, ch. 517, § 1, pp. 1089–1091; Stats. 1961, ch. 2180, § 1, pp. 4516–4518; Stats. 1963, First Ex. Sess. 1962, ch. 55, § 1, pp. 343–345.) The city's claim depends upon the extent of the state's interest at the time the grants were made. Our references to the interests of the state or the public in this property apply also to the city's rights.

Kerber (1908) 152 Cal. 731, 733; *Ward v. Mulford* (1867) 32 Cal. 365, 372.) Although early cases expressed the scope of the public's right in tidelands as encompassing navigation, commerce and fishing, the permissible range of public uses is far broader, including the right to hunt, bathe or swim, and the right to preserve the tidelands in their natural state as ecological units for scientific study. (*Marks v. Whitney* (1971) 6 Cal. 3d 251, 259–260.)

There were limitations imposed by this ancient doctrine upon the alienation of tidelands to private parties. *Illinois Central Railroad Company v. Illinois* (1892) 146 U.S. 387, was the seminal case on the scope of the public trust doctrine and remains the primary authority even today, almost nine decades after it was decided. The decision established the principle that a state, as administrator of the trust in tidelands on behalf of the public, does not have the power to abdicate its role as trustee in favor of private parties.

. . . .

. . . The decision recognized that parcels of land under navigable waters conveyed to private parties for wharves or docks and other structures in aid of commerce may be granted free of the public trust because such uses are consistent with trust purposes.[14] But it determined that the Legislature did not have the power to convey the entire waterfront of the city to a private party free of the trust. The court declared that one legislature does not have the power to "give away nor sell the discretion of its successors" to "exercise the powers of the State" in the execution of the trust and that legislation "which may be needed one day for the harbor may be different from the legislation that may be required at another day." (See also *Mallon v. City of Long Beach* (1955) 44 Cal. 2d 199, 207; *People v. California Fish Co.* (1913) 166 Cal. 576, 593.)

The principles of *Illinois Central* have suffered a checkered history in California. Soon after statehood, the Legislature began to sell into private ownership vast tracts of tidelands, often at public auction. In San Francisco Bay, large parcels were sold by deeds purporting the transfer title in fee simple absolute. Many of these transfers were fraudulently made. . . .

The widespread abuses in the disposition of tidelands led to the adoption in 1879 of article XV, sections 2 and 3 of the Constitution (now art. X, §§ 3 & 4). These provisions prohibit the sale to private persons of tidelands within two miles of an incorporated city, and state that no individual may obstruct the free navigation of tidelands on navigable waters nor the right of way to such waters, when required for a public purpose. In the debate that preceded adoption of the measure, one legislator observed that in the preceding 25 years the grants by the state had nearly resulted in "the monopolizing of every frontage upon navigable waters in this state . . . by private individuals . . . ." (Debates and Proceedings, Cal. Const. Convention 1878–1879, *op. cit.*, at p. 1481.)

---

[14]The court stated also that "grants of parcels which, being occupied, do not substantially impair the public interest in the lands and waters remaining" may also be conveyed free of the trust. (146 U.S. at p. 452.) The meaning of the term "lands and waters remaining" is not clear. The court may have had in mind either former navigable waters which had been filled and were thus no longer useful for navigation, or shoals and swamp lands. In one portion of its opinion, the court quotes from a case in which submerged shoals and flats are characterized as "useless parts" which "really interfered with navigation" and did not "affect the character of the title to the remainder." (*Id.* at p. 457.)

As a result of these open-handed policies, today almost one-quarter of the Bay is claimed by private persons. Of the remainder, approximately one-quarter has been granted by the state to cities and counties, the state owns about one-half, and the federal government 5 percent. (S.F. Bay Plan Supp., Bay Cons. & Dev. Com., p. 447.)

. . . . Much of San Francisco's downtown business district is situated on land filled in connection with the development of the harbor created pursuant to these acts. From the early days of statehood, it was held that conveyances made pursuant to such a program passed title free of the public trust. (*See*, e.g., *Eldridge v. Cowell*, *supra*, 4 Cal. 80, 87; *Ward v. Mulford*, *supra*, 32 Cal. 365, 372–373; *Oakland v. Oakland Water Front Co.* (1897) 118 Cal. 160, 184–185; see *People v. California Fish Co.*, *supra*, 166 Cal. 576, 585.)

But conveyances of tidelands to private parties not made for the furtherance of navigation or commerce did not pass title free of the trust. The acts authorizing such conveyances are sometimes referred to as "general acts." *California Fish*, which contains a comprehensive analysis of the public trust doctrine, recognized this distinction. The effect of the decision was to retain the public's right in vast grants of tidelands purportedly conveyed in fee between 1855 and 1872 to private parties by legislative authorization.[15]

. . . .

The first focus of our inquiry, therefore, is whether the act of 1870, which authorized the sale of tidelands to plaintiffs' predecessors in interest, had as its purpose the promotion of navigation, commerce or fisheries.

. . . .

The total acreage placed under the board's jurisdiction under the 2 acts was 56,400 acres of tideland or 88 square miles of the Bay. Of this, the board conveyed 22,299 acres. The area sold pursuant to the 1870 act exceeded many times that conveyed in the City of San Francisco under the 1868 act. Roughly 14,447 acres, or 24 square miles, constituting 64.8 percent of the area under the board's jurisdiction, is still tideland. About 4,186 acres of the subdivided tidelands (18.8 percent) have been filled but not improved, and 3,666 acres (16.4 percent) are both filled and improved with structures. These conveyances extend from Hamilton Air Force Base and Richmond in the northern part of the Bay to San Bruno and San Leandro in the south. In Berkeley, the board sold all the lots extending to 12 feet at ordinary high tide from the shore, granting to the purchasers the entire 2½ miles of the city's waterfront, without any provision for public access. Most of the tidelands in Berkeley are now owned by plaintiff Santa Fe. Of the 854 acres in Berkeley sold under the act, 525 are still under water. In other areas, such as Sausalito, canals providing public access to the Bay were reserved from sale. Over the years, most of the lots sold by the board have been acquired by a relatively small number of corporations that own

---

[15] . . . The tidelands conveyed pursuant to the statutes involved in *California Fish* included "the entire sea beach from the Oregon line to Mexico and the shores of every . . . inlet, estuary, and navigable stream as far up as tide water goes and until it meets the lands made swampy by the overflow and seepage of fresh water streams." (166 Cal. at p. 591.) Perhaps 80,000 acres of tidelands (as distinguished from submerged lands) were conveyed to private parties before *California Fish* was decided. (See Taylor, *Patented Tidelands: A Naked Fee?* (1972) 47 State Bar J. 420, 421.)

substantial parcels purchased from the original grantees or their successors. (Scott, Future of S.F. Bay, *op. cit.*, p. 7.)

. . . .

. . . [W]e proceed on the basis of the principles expressed in *California Fish*: statutes purporting to abandon the public trust are to be strictly construed; the intent to abandon must be clearly expressed or necessarily implied; and if any interpretation of the statute is reasonably possible which would retain the public's interest in tidelands, the court must give the statute such an interpretation.

. . . .

. . . The [1870] statute makes no reference to a specific public improvement to promote navigation, and does not state the improvement of navigation as its purpose. The fact that the word "navigation" is used in the act and that some of the lands within the board's jurisdiction could be withheld from sale for canals and basins needed for navigation is clearly insufficient to justify the conclusion reached by the court. What is required and is missing from the act is a clear intent expressed or necessarily implied that the purpose of the act was to further navigation or some other trust use. In *Illinois Central* the fact that the grant to the railroad prohibited it from impairing the right of navigation did not prevent the United States Supreme Court from holding that the conveyance violated the trust.

Confirmation that the grants were not intended to be free of the public trust is provided by legislative history. The Attorney General advised the Legislature prior to the enactment of the 1868 statute that the public would retain its right to the tidelands conveyed under the act. In a letter of advice attached to the report of the committee appointed to study the measure, the Attorney General wrote:

> "The State, in making this disposition [of tidelands], passes the title with the same disability which obtains with the State. Her purchaser can acquire from the State no such title as will enable the owner or holder of them to use them to the detriment, destruction or prejudice of commerce or navigation. For such uses the public have an easement, and the Government retains and has the authority to enforce the right." (Rep. Assem. Special Com. in Relation to S.F. Tide Lands, 2 Appendix to Sen. and Assem. J. (1866–1867) p. 6.)[16]

Moreover, there is evidence that the Legislature may have been primarily motivated by a desire to raise revenue rather than to improve navigation. The committee's report to the Legislature before the 1868 act was passed, as well as reports by the Governor to the Legislature and by the Attorney General to the Governor regarding the progress of the disposition program, refer only to the funds that would be or had been realized from the sales authorized by the act; they are devoid of any reference to the improvement of navigation. Presumably,

[16]Plaintiffs argue that the use of the word "Government" in the Attorney General's advice letter indicates that he was referring to the federal government's right to regulate obstructions to navigation rather than the state's power to alienate tidelands free of the public trust. We doubt the correctness of this argument in view of the language quoted above. In any event, it cannot be said that the construction urged by plaintiffs is compelled by the language of the Attorney General. In view of the rules of construction referred to above, we must adopt the interpretation that favors retention of the public trust.

this evidence of legislative intent is not determinative, at the very least it reinforces our conclusion that the 1870 statute may and should be interpreted to preserve the public's rights in the tidelands that it authorized the board to convey to private parties.[17]

. . . [E]ven if the court had been justified in concluding that the purpose of the 1870 act was to promote navigation . . . , *Illinois Central* holds that a state may not grant to private persons tidelands as vast in area as the board was authorized to sell by the 1870 act. Such action amounts to an improper abdication by the state of its role as trustee on behalf of the people.

Moreover, . . . the plan for improving navigation, which was the purported purpose of the 1870 statute . . . [has] not been fulfilled. (See Comment, *The Tideland Trust* (1974) 21 UCLA L.Rev. 826, 844–847, fn. 90, 93.) As to the status of these tidelands at the present time, the McAteer–Petris Act, passed in 1965 (Gov. Code, § 66600 et seq.), a statute enacted in the state's capacity as trustee of the tidelands (see *People ex. rel. S.F. Bay etc. Com. v. Town of Emeryville* (1968) 69 Cal.2d 533, 544–549), demonstrates that the Legislature's current policy regarding these lands is different from that expressed by the 1870 act.

Finally, a number of cases had held or stated . . . that a grant of tidelands, even if made for the improvement of navigation, does not vest absolute title in a private party until the improvements are actually made. (*See*, e.g., *People v. Williams* (1884) 64 Cal. 498, 499; *People v. Kerber, supra,* 152 Cal. at pp. 736–737; *California Fish, supra,* 166 Cal. at pp. 599–600; *see also* Comment, *supra*, 21 UCLA L.Rev. 826, 844–847, fn. 90, 93.) . . . .

Our conclusion is made with due recognition of the special role of the "rule of property" in the application of the doctrine of stare decisis. As explained in *Abbott v. City of Los Angeles* (1958) 50 Cal. 2d 438, 456–457, the doctrine relates to a

> "settled rule or principle, resting usually on precedents or a course of decisions, regulating the ownership or devolution of property . . . . [D]ecisions long acquiesced in, which constitute rules of property or trade or upon which important rights are based, should not be disturbed, even though a different conclusion might have been reached if the question presented were an open one, inasmuch as uniformity and certainty in rules of property are often more important and desirable than technical correctness. Thus, judicial decisions affecting the business interests of the country should not be disturbed except for the most cogent reasons, as where the evils of the principle laid down will be more injurious to the community than can possibly result from a change, or upon the clearest grounds of error." (*See also County of L.A. v. Southern Cal. Tel. Co.* (1948) 32 Cal. 2d 378, 392–393.)

There are "most cogent reasons" in the present case for our determination to overturn *Knudson* and *Alameda Conservation*. We do not divest anyone of title to property; the consequence of our decision will be only that some

---

[17]The matters set forth above regarding the Legislature's intent apply to both the 1868 and 1870 enactments. Nevertheless, there can be no doubt that the promotion of harbor development may be more readily inferred from the language of the earlier statute. We are directly concerned in the present case only with the meaning of the 1870 act, and our holding applies only to it.

landowners whose predecessors in interest acquired property under the 1870 act will, like the grantees in *California Fish*, hold it subject to the public trust. The *Knudson* decision in 1915 and *Alameda Conservation* 53 years later were the only cases holding that the grants in issue were free of the public trust, and it was apparent from the face of the *Knudson* opinion that although the public's right to large tracts of tidelands in the Bay was at stake, the state as trustee of those rights was not a party to the action. The summary and conclusory nature of the decision of the issues in *Knudson*, virtually devoid of reasoning, undermines its status as substantial authority. Finally, these decisions have not been overturned on some minor technicality: to the contrary, our conclusion is based on a studied analysis revealing that they are wholly in error, failed to follow prior law on the subject, and misinterpreted the Legislature's intention. . . .

. . . .

The consequences of allowing the patently erroneous decisions to stand in the present case would be to deprive the people of the state of full control over many thousand acres of tidelands acquired by them at the time of statehood. In these circumstances, and with the limitations upon reassertion of the public's trust rights which we outline below, we do not doubt that it would be more injurious to the public interest to perpetuate the error of *Knudson* and *Alameda Conservation* than to overturn those decisions.

Finally, we reach a crucial question: whether to give our determination full retroactive effect. We note in this connection that *California Fish*, decided in 1913, involved grants of tidelands purportedly in fee to private parties, authorized by almost a dozen different statutes enacted between 1861 and 1872. The extent of the lands involved in that case was far greater than those authorized for sale by the 1870 act (*see* fn. 9, *ante*), and presumably the improvements made by the grantees were substantial. Yet in that case our court did not hesitate to hold the conveyances were subject to the public trust. Of course, any improvements made on such lands could not be appropriated by the state without compensation. (*Illinois Central*, 146 U.S. at p. 455; Pub. Resources Code, § 6312.)

We could, like the court in *California Fish*, declare that all grants made under the 1870 act are subject to the public trust, or we could hold that our decision is prospective only. We reject both these alternatives. The first would reduce the value of investments that may have been made in reliance on the decisions we overturn, without necessarily promoting the purposes of the trust; while the second would render our holding in this case an academic exercise, because the grants were made more than a century ago.

We choose, instead, an intermediate course: the appropriate resolution is to balance the interests of the public in tidelands conveyed pursuant to the 1870 act against those of the landowners who hold property under these conveyances. In the harmonizing of these claims, the principle we apply is that the interests of the public are paramount in property that is still physically adaptable for trust uses, whereas the interests of the grantees and their successors should prevail insofar as the tidelands have been rendered substantially valueless for those purposes.

In keeping with this principle, we hold that submerged lands as well as lands subject to tidal action that were conveyed by board deeds under the 1870 act are subject to the public trust. Properties that have been filled, whether or not they have been substantially improved, are free of the trust to the extent the areas of such parcels are not subject to tidal action, provided that the fill and improvements were made in accordance with applicable land use regulations.[18] Tidelands that have been neither filled nor improved are not only the most suitable for the continued exercise of trust uses, but because there is only a remote likelihood that these parcels may be filled (see 33 U.S.C. § 401 et seq.; Gov. Code § 6600 et seq.; Candlestick Properties, Inc. v. San Francisco Bay Conservation etc. Com. (1970) 11 Cal.App.3d 557, 570–573) the economic loss to the grantees of such lots is speculative at best and is clearly outweighed by the interests of the public.[19]

An obvious illustration of absolute title is a parcel that no longer has Bay frontage. Such property is valueless in its present state for trust uses. Defendants urge us, however, to include reclaimed but unimproved land with Bay frontage in the areas subject to the trust on the ground that such property may still be useful for the exercise of the public trust. To the contrary, we believe that in balancing the interests at stake, the public right in such parcels may be adequately protected by our holding that only the tidal portions thereof are subject to the trust, coupled with the requirement of section 66602 of the Government Code that maximum feasible public access, consistent with a proposed project, must be provided to the shoreline of the Bay.[20]

We are not unaware that the implementation of our holding in the manner set forth above makes assumptions which are not valid in every case. Thus, for example, some reclaimed land might be eminently useful for trust purposes, and numerous persons who reclaimed or improved tidelands purchased under the 1870 act may not in fact have relied on either Knudson or Alameda Conservation. Indeed, many parcels affected by our decision may have been improved before Knudson was decided in 1915. Nevertheless, our broad assumptions are justified by the need to avoid the enormous burden of individual adjudications of

[18]Defendants' pleadings alleged that plaintiffs acquired no title whatever by the board deeds and that Berkeley owns the tidelands conveyed by those deeds in fee. Acceptance of this claim would return us to the law as it existed prior to California Fish. Before that case was decided, grants of tidelands conveyed in violation of the trust were held to be either void or voidable. (Kimball v. Macpherson (1873) 46 Cal. 103, 107; Taylor v. Underhill (1870) 40 Cal. 471, 473.) These determinations were modified in California Fish, which held that lands conveyed in violation of the trust were subject thereto. The suggestion of defendants that no title passed by the board deeds is unnecessarily draconian in its effect. As we point out above, there are means to achieve a substantial part of the objectives of the public trust by means which do not eliminate all the property rights of landowners whose predecessors in interest acquired title under the 1870 act.

[19]Appleby v. City of New York (1926) 271 U.S. 364, relied upon by defendants, is distinguishable. There, the city had conveyed lots below tidewater to the plaintiffs for the specific purpose of developing a harbor. Later, the city built piers adjacent to the lots, and its tenants used the lots for mooring. It was held that under the laws of New York, the plaintiffs had received fee title to the lots, and they were thus entitled to an injunction to prevent the city from using the property for mooring. Since the grants made to plaintiffs in the present case were not to promote navigation, their titles, unlike that of the plaintiffs in Appleby, are subject to the public trust.

[20]A number of cases hold or state that the reclamation of tidelands subject to the public trust does not, without more, terminate the trust. (E.g., Marks v. Whitney, supra, 6 Cal. 3d 251, 261; Atwood v. Hammond (1935) 4 Cal. 2d 31, 40.) But these cases did not involve the interests of landowners who had reclaimed tidelands in reliance upon decisions that were subsequently overruled.

such questions and to preclude clouding the titles of landowners around the Bay who own filled or improved properties conveyed under the 1870 act.

We appreciate also that there may be some improvements upon tideland areas, such as docks, in which a landowner's reliance interest should be recognized to some degree. It is impossible to anticipate in this opinion every conceivable nuance in the application of the basic principle set forth above. Individual variations may be revealed subsequently, requiring further explication of the principles declared herein through future adjudication.

CLARK, Justice, dissenting.

Thousands of pleasure boats, freighters, docks, and harbor areas frame San Francisco Bay as testimonials to the wisdom of the Legislature in creating, and this court in upholding, a "public trust for commerce, navigation, fishing and related uses."

Principal trust purposes are promotion of commerce, navigation and fishing, and not maintenance and protection of tidelands as some would have us believe.

For over 100 years California citizens have progressively improved the bay edges, demonstrating their reliance on the legislative acts before us today as having conveyed trust-free title. Likewise, state and local governments and the public at large have acquiesced in and endorsed those activities, revealing they too recognize the law as authorizing trust-free conveyances. Given the contemporaneous and longstanding construction of the law by public authority, private individuals and our courts, it is presumptuous for the majority of this court to now tell us the Legislature never intended to permit such progress.

. . . .

Because the trust purposes have been fulfilled by termination of the trust—particularly through the Legislature's policy encouraging dredging and filling tidelands for public and private harbors—it is unnecessary to guess whether those purposes would have been fulfilled had the trust not been terminated.

. . . .

It is urged that even if conveyances pursuant to the 1868 and 1870 acts passed trust-free title, grantees and their successors were required to reclaim their land within a reasonable time or suffer reinstatement of the trust. Nothing in the deed or statute warrants implication of such a condition subsequent. Moreover, conditions subsequent are disfavored because they may result in forfeiture. (*MacDonald Properties, Inc. v. Bel-Air Country Club* (1977) 72 Cal. App. 3d 693, 699.) The condition subsequent would cause manifest injustice to those who—relying on *Knudson*—filled land and built upon it, and those who paid real property taxes over the past 100 years.

. . . .

Rather than condemning the Legislature's fundamental policy encouraging private parties to dredge and fill tidelands to permit public and private harbor development, we should recognize the determination greatly furthered the purposes of the trust. The bay has been developed permitting widespread public access according to long settled rules. We should not now attempt to impeach those rules, the legislative determination establishing them, or this court's affirmance of them. We should embrace our heritage and be thankful for it.

Public policy as to development of San Francisco Bay may have changed as the majority suggest, but this furnishes no basis for impeaching the legislative determinations of 1868 and 1870 to terminate the trust as to portions of the tidelands and submerged lands in furtherance of trust purposes. The program has been too successful to be condemned by judicial fiat, and the need to promote commerce and harbor development is as great now as ever.

. . . .

NOTES

1. In *People v. California Fish Co.*, 166 Cal. 576, 138 P. 79 (1913), the California Supreme Court first faced the choice of allowing private ownership to continue at the expense of public rights, or voiding the titles granted earlier by the state itself. Since much of the tidal land had been improved between the grants and *California Fish*, the case raised difficult issues of estoppel against the government and taking without compensation. The California court, by the masterful use of the public trust doctrine, found a middle ground between the extremes. The public right, the court held, had never been conveyed. Private owners possessed tidal lands subject to the public right of navigation, and subordinate to the right of the state to retake possession in the public interest. If the private owners had never owned the *jus publicum*, there could, of course, be no grounds for the argument that the state had taken property without compensation.

   Estoppel against the state, unlike the taking issue, cannot be so easily dismissed. Although the state was held not to be estopped from reasserting public rights in tidal lands in *California Fish*, in the subsequent case of *City of Long Beach v. Mansell*, 6 Cal. 3d 462, 476 P.2d 423, 91 Cal. Rptr. 23 (1970), the California Supreme Court held that a previous legislative grant of tidelands *did* estop California from asserting the trust doctrine. The state, according to the *Mansell* court, could free certain lands from the trust forever—provided the land involved was (a) part of a highly beneficial program of harbor development, and (b) a relatively small area in comparison to the total acreage improved. *See* Taylor, *Patented Tidelands: A Naked Fee? Marks v. Whitney and the Public Trust Easement*, 47 Cal. St. B.J. 420, 487 (1972).

   How could a legislative grant convey both the *jus privatum* and the *jus publicum* in *Mansell*, while similar grants conveyed only the *jus privatum* in *California Fish*? The answer may have more to do with economics than legal doctrine:

   The court's use of the estoppel concept for weighing the costs and benefits in [*Mansell*] demonstrates the economic nature of the public trust doctrine. Pure application of trust principles would have yielded an opposite result. Since it found itself unable to achieve the desired result under trust principles, the court, instead of applying that doctrine and accepting an economically unjustifiable result or expanding the trust to the point of making bad precedent, utilized an alternative doctrine under which it could take into account features beyond those within the sweep of the trust doctrine. The case may stand for the general principle that the public trust doctrine will only be used to the extent that it will operate to achieve the appropriate economic result, and that in the case where it will not achieve such result it will not be applied.

Comment, *The Tideland Trust: Economic Currents in a Traditional Legal Doctrine, supra,* at 863.[21] *See also* Littman, *Tidelands: Trusts, Easements, Custom and Implied Dedication,* 10 Nat. Res. Law. 279, 289 (1977); Parker, *History, Politics and the Law of the California Tidelands Trust,* 4 W. St. U. L. Rev. 149 (1977).

In *California Fish,* the public trust doctrine had the positive economic effect of restoring public rights in valuable tidelands. *Mansell* involved a proposed trade of 5 acres of public tidelands, which had previously been filled, for 8.5 acres of privately owned land. The traditional trust doctrine would have prevented the trade of filled trust lands for potentially useful private property.

As *Mansell* illustrates, the California State Lands Commission is authorized to exchange state-owned tidelands for private lands of equal value when "in the best interests of the State" and where the exchange "will not substantially interfere with the right of *navigation* and *fishing* in the waters involved." Cal. Pub. Res. Code § 6307 (West 1977) (emphasis added). The validity of section 6307 has not been challenged in court to date, but it has come under some criticism. *See The Loss of Public Tidelands to Private Parties Through Unconstitutional Land Trades,* 13 U. S. F. L. Rev. 39 (1978). *See also County of Orange v. Heim,* 30 Cal. App. 3d 694, 106 Cal. Rptr. 825 (1973).

2. The state courts differ in their methods of judicial review of legislative grants of trust lands. Many courts are reluctant to invalidate acts of the legislature, but want some control over the conveyance of trust lands. In *Gould v. Greylock Reservation Commission,* 350 Mass. 410, 215 N.E.2d 114 (1966), the Massachusetts Supreme Court created a presumption that the state does not ordinarily intend to divert trust properties in such a way as to lessen public uses. *See Boston Waterfront Development Corp. v. Commonwealth,* 378 Mass. 623, 393 N.E.2d 356 (1979), *aff'g,* 6 Mass. App. 214, 374 N.E.2d 598 (1978); *Opinion of the Justices,* 424 N.E.2d 1092(1981). In other words, the court will if at all possible construe the grant as a partial conveyance only; the "necessary easements" remain in the public absent clear legislative intent to convey the *jus publicum* along with the state's proprietary interest. *See Bryant v. Lovett,* 201 So. 2d 720 (Fla. 1967) (claim of exclusive right to plant and harvest oysters rejected); Sax, *The Public Trust Doctrine in Natural Resources Law, supra,* at 494–95.

Can private ownership of tidal and submerged lands ever be established without express language in a conveyance from the state purporting to convey them as tidelands and submerged lands? *Cf. Parmele v. Eaton,* 83 S.E.2d 93 (N.C. Sup. Ct. 1954); *State v. Fain,* 259 S.E.2d 606 (S.C. Sup. Ct. 1979). Do not some grantees of California tidelands at least have a claim to absolute title free of the public trust based on long-held occupancy and use? *Cf. State v. Hanson Properties, Inc.,* 371 So. 2d 871 (Miss. Sup. Ct. 1979).

An alternative to the Massachusetts and California approaches is Wisconsin's "active trust" concept. In Wisconsin the *jus publicum* is inalienable; nevertheless, development of trust land is permitted if certain conditions are met. In *State v. Public Service Commission,* 275 Wis. 112, 118, 81 N.W.2d 71, 73 (1957), the Wisconsin Supreme Court held that a legislative grant of trust lands underlying inland lakes was valid if:

1. Public bodies would control use of the area;
2. The area would be devoted to public purposes and open to the public;
3. The diminution of the lake area would be small;
4. No one of the public uses would be destroyed or greatly impaired;
5. And if the disappointment of those members of the public who desired to boat, fish, or swim in the area to be filled was negligible when compared with the benefits to the general public.

[21]Copyrighted, U.C.L.A. Law Review.

Do the California, Massachusetts, and Wisconsin approaches fit within the public trust constraints upon the states described by Sax in *The Public Trust Doctrine in Natural Resources Law: Effective Judicial Intervention, supra,* at 488–89: "These traditional cases suggest the extremes of the legal constraints upon the states: No grant may be made to a private party if that grant is of such amplitude that the state will effectively have given up its authority to govern, but a grant is not illegal solely because it diminishes in some degree the quantum of traditional public uses"? Or is the Comment, *The Public Trust Doctrine,* 59 Marq. L. Rev. 787, 801 (1976), more accurate: "The public trust was an active trust; it did not instruct the legislature to leave the shores . . . in the same condition they had been in prior to settlement"? Which state's approach best satisfies the policies underlying the modern public trust doctrine? What are those policies?

3. Regarding the evolution of the public trust doctrine in California, *see* Eikel & Williams, *The Public Trust Doctrine and the California Coastline,* 6 Urb. Law. 519 (1974); Note, *California's Tideland Trust: Shoring It Up,* 22 Hastings L.J. 759 (1971); Note, *The Extent of State Ownership of Submerged Lands in California,* 31 Hastings L.J. 329 (1979). However, in some states the status of the public trust doctrine as a matter of state law is not clear. For a discussion of the uncertain situation in South Carolina, *see* Wyche, *Tidelands and the Public Trust: An Application for South Carolina,* 7 Ecology L.Q. 137 (1978). *See also* C. Leawell, *Legal Aspects of Ownership and Use of Estuarine Areas in Georgia and South Carolina* (1971); Smith & Sammons, *Public Rights in Georgia's Tidelands,* 9 Ga. L. Rev. 79 (1974).

The State of Washington lags behind other states in recognition and use of the public trust. *See* Johnson & Cooney, *Harbor Lines and the Public Trust Doctrine in Washington Navigable Waters,* 54 Wash. L. Rev. 275 (1979); Nelson, *State Disposition of Submerged Lands Versus Public Rights in Navigable Waters,* 3 Nat. Res. Law. 491, 500 (1970). *See also* Berland, *Toward the True Meaning of the Public Trust,* 1 Sea Grant L.J. 83 (1976); Comment, *The Public Trust in Tidal Areas: A Sometimes Submerged Traditional Doctrine,* 79 Yale L.J. 762 (1970); and Deveney, *Title, Jus Publicum, and the Public Trust: An Historical Analysis,* 1 Sea Grant L.J. 13 (1976).

All aspects of the public trust doctrine are thoroughly reviewed in *The Public Trust Doctrine in Natural Resources Law and Management,* 14 U.C. Davis L. Rev. 181 (1980).

Federal and State Navigation Servitudes

MORRIS, "THE FEDERAL NAVIGATION SERVITUDE: IMPEDIMENT TO THE DEVELOPMENT OF THE WATERFRONT," 45 St. John's Law Review 189, 189 (1970)

The navigation servitude is the paramount right of the federal government, under the commerce clause of the United States Constitution, to compel the removal of any obstruction to navigation, without the necessity of paying "just compensation" ordinarily required by the fifth amendment of the Constitution. It has been held to apply to all waters up to the high-water mark which are "navigable in fact," whether tidal or non-tidal, and even to nonnavigable tributaries of navigable waters.

KAISER-AETNA v. UNITED STATES, 100 S. Ct. 383 (1979)

Mr. Justice REHNQUIST delivered the opinion of the Court.

The Hawaii Kai Marina was developed by the dredging and filling of Kuapa Pond, which was a shallow lagoon separated from Maunalua Bay and the Pacific Ocean by a barrier beach. Although under Hawaii law Kuapa Pond was private property, the Court of Appeals for the Ninth Circuit held that when petitioners converted the pond into a marina and thereby connected it to the bay, it became subject to the "navigational servitude" of the Federal Government. Thus, the public acquired a right of access to what was once petitioners' private pond. We granted certiorari because of the importance of the issue and a conflict concerning the scope and nature of the servitude.

I

Kuapa Pond was apparently created in the late Pleistocene Period, near the end of the ice age, when the rising sea level caused the shoreline to retreat, and partial erosion of the headlands adjacent to the bay formed sediment that accreted to form a barrier beach at the mouth of the pond, creating a lagoon. It covered 523 acres on the island of Oahu, Haw., and extended approximately two miles inland from Maunalua Bay and the Pacific Ocean. The pond was contiguous to the bay, which is a navigable waterway of the United States, but was separated from it by the barrier beach.

Early Hawaiians used the lagoon as a fishpond and reinforced the natural sand bar with stone walls. Prior to the annexation of Hawaii, there were two openings from the pond to Maunalua Bay. The fishpond's managers placed removable sluice gates in the stone walls across these openings. Water from the bay and ocean entered the pond through the gates during high tide, and during low tide the current flow reversed toward the ocean. The Hawaiians used the tidal action to raise and catch fish such as mullet.

Kuapa Pond, and other Hawaiian fishponds, have always been considered to be private property by landowners and by the Hawaiian government. Such ponds were once an integral part of the Hawaiian feudal system. And in 1848 they were allotted as parts of large land units, known as "Ahupuaas," by King Kamehameha III during the Great Mahele or royal land division. Titles to the fishponds were recognized to the same extent and in the same manner as rights in more orthodox fast land. Kuapa Pond was part of an ahupuaa that eventually vested in Bernice Pauahi Bishop and on her death formed a part of the trust corpus of petitioner Bishop Estate, the present owner.

In 1961, Bishop Estate leased a 6,000 acre area, which included Kuapa Pond, to petitioner Kaiser Aetna for subdivision development. The development is now known as "Hawaii Kai." Kaiser Aetna dredged and filled parts of Kuapa Pond, erected retaining walls and built bridges within the development to create the Hawaii Kai Marina. Kaiser Aetna increased the average depth of the channel from two to six feet. It also created accommodations for pleasure boats and eliminated the sluice gates.

When petitioners notified the Corps of Engineers of their plans in 1961, the

Corps advised them they were not required to obtain permits for the development of and operations in Kuapa Pond. Kaiser Aetna subsequently informed the Corps that it planned to dredge an 8-foot deep channel connecting Kuapa Pond to Maunalua Bay and the Pacific Ocean, and to increase the clearance of a bridge of the Kalanianaole Highway—which had been constructed during the early 1900's along the barrier beach separating Kuapa Pond from the bay and ocean—to a maximum of 13.5 feet over the mean sea level. These improvements were made in order to allow boats from the marina to enter into and return from the bay, as well as to provide better waters. The Corps acquiesced in the proposals, its chief of construction commenting only that the "deepening of the channel may cause erosion of the beach."

At the time of trial, a marina-style community of approximately 22,000 persons surrounded Kuapa Pond. It included approximately 1500 marina waterfront lot lessees. The waterfront lot lessees, along with at least 86 nonmarina lot lessees from Hawaii Kai and 56 boat owners who are not residents of Hawaii Kai, pay fees for maintenance of the pond and for patrol boats that remove floating debris, enforce boating regulations and maintain the privacy and security of the pond. Kaiser Aetna controls access to and use of the marina. It has generally not permitted commercial use, except for a small vessel, the Marina Queen, which could carry 25 passengers and was used for about five years to promote sales of marina lots and for a brief period by marina shopping center merchants to attract people to their shopping facilities.

In 1972, a dispute arose between petitioners and the Corps concerning whether (1) petitioners were required to obtain authorization from the Corps, in accordance with § 10 of the Rivers and Harbors Act, 33 U.S.C. § 403 (1970), for future construction, excavation or filling in the marina, and (2) petitioners were precluded from denying the public access to the pond because, as a result of the improvements, it had become a navigable water of the United States. The dispute foreseeably ripened into a lawsuit by the United States Government against petitioners in the United States District Court for the District of Hawaii. In examining the scope of Congress' regulatory authority under the Commerce Clause, the District Court held that the pond was "navigable water of the United States" and thus subject to regulation by the Corps under § 10 of the Rivers and Harbors Act. 408 F.Supp. 42, 53 (D.Haw.1976). It further held, however, that the government lacked the authority to open the now dredged pond to the public without payment of compensation to the owner. *Id.*,54. In reaching this holding, the District Court reasoned that although the pond was navigable for the purpose of delimiting Congress' regulatory power, it was not navigable for the purpose of defining the scope of the federal "navigational servitude" imposed by the Commerce Clause. *Ibid.* Thus, the District Court denied the Corps' request for an injunction to require petitioners to allow public access and to notify the public of the fact of the pond's accessibility.

The Court of Appeals agreed with the District Court's conclusion that the pond fell within the scope of Congress' regulatory authority, but reversed the District Court's holding that the navigational servitude did not require petitioners to grant the public access to the pond. 584 F.2d 378 (CA9 1978). The Court of Appeals reasoned that the "federal regulatory authority over navigable waters

. . . and the right of public use cannot consistently be separated. It is the public right of navigational use that renders regulatory control necessary in the public interest." *Id.*, 383. The question before us is whether the Court of Appeals erred in holding that petitioners' improvements to Kuapa Pond caused its original character to be so altered that it became subject to an overriding federal navigational servitude, thus converting into a public aquatic park that which petitioners had invested millions of dollars in improving on the assumption that it was a privately owned pond leased to them.

II

The Government contends that petitioners may not exclude members of the public from the Hawaii Kai Marina because "The public enjoys a federally protected right of navigation over the navigable waters of the United States." Brief of the United States, p. 13. It claims the issue in dispute is whether Kuapa Pond is presently a "navigable water of the United States." *Ibid.* When petitioners dredged and improved Kuapa Pond, the government continues, the pond—although it may once have qualified as fast land—became navigable water of the United States. The public thereby acquired a right to use Kuapa Pond as a continuous highway for navigation, and the Corps of Engineers may consequently obtain an injunction to prevent petitioners from attempting to reserve the waterway to themselves.

The position advanced by the Government, and adopted by the Court of Appeals below, presumes that the concept of "navigable waters of the United States" has a fixed meaning that remains unchanged in whatever context it is being applied.

. . . .

It is true that Kuapa Pond may fit within definitions of "navigability" articulated in past decisions of this Court. But it must be recognized that the concept of navigability in these decisions was used for purposes other than to delimit the boundaries of the navigational servitude: for example, to define the scope of Congress' regulatory authority under the Interstate Commerce Clause, see, *e. g., United States v. Appalachian Power Co.*, 311 U.S. 377, 61 S.Ct. 291, 85 L.Ed. 243 (1940), *South Carolina v. Georgia,* 93 U.S. (3 Otto) 4, 23 L.Ed. 782 (1876), *The Montello,* 87 U.S. (20 Wall.) 430, 22 L.Ed. 391 (1874), *The Daniel Ball,* 77 U.S. (10 Wall.) 557, 19 L.Ed. 999 (1870), to determine the extent of the authority of the Corps of Engineers under the Rivers and Harbors Act of 1899, and to establish the limits of the jurisdiction of federal courts, conferred by Art. III, § 2, of the United States Constitution, over admiralty and maritime cases. Although the Government is clearly correct in maintaining that the now dredged Kuapa Pond falls within the definition of "navigable waters" as this Court has used that term in delimiting the boundaries of Congress' regulatory authority under the Commerce Clause, . . . this Court has never held that the navigational servitude creates a blanket exception to the Takings Clause whenever Congress exercises its Commerce Clause authority to promote navigation. Thus, while Kuapa Pond may be subject to regulation by the Corps of Engineers, acting under the authority delegated it by Congress in the Rivers and

Harbors Act, it does not follow that the pond is also subject to a public right of access.

A

Reference to the navigability of a waterway adds little if anything to the breadth of Congress' regulatory power over interstate commerce. It has long been settled that Congress has extensive authority over this Nation's waters under the Commerce Clause. Early in our history this Court held that the power to regulate commerce necessarily includes power over navigation. *Gibbons v. Ogden*, 22 U.S. (9 Wheat.) 1, 189, 6 L.Ed. 23 (1824). As stated in *Gilman v. Philadelphia*, 70 U.S. (3 Wall.) 713, 724–725, 18 L.Ed. 96:

> "Commerce includes navigation. The power to regulate Commerce comprehends the control for that purpose, and to the extent necessary, of all the navigable waters of the United States which are accessible from a state other than those in which they lie. For this purpose, they are the public property of the nation, and subject to all the requisite legislation by Congress."

The pervasive nature of Congress' regulatory authority over national waters was more fully described in *United States v. Appalachian Power Co., supra,* 311 U.S., at 426–427, 61 S.Ct., at 308:

> "[I]t cannot properly be said that the constitutional power of the United States over its waters is limited to control for navigation. . . . In truth the authority of the United States is the regulation of commerce on its waters. Navigability . . . is but a part of this whole. Flood protection, watershed development, recovery of the cost of improvements through utilization of power are likewise parts of commerce control. . . . [The] authority is as broad as the needs of commerce. . . . The point is that navigable waters are subject to national planning and control in the broad regulation of commerce granted the Federal Government."

Appalachian Power Co. indicates that congressional authority over the waters of this Nation does not depend on a stream's "navigability."

. . . .

B

In light of its expansive authority under the Commerce Clause, there is no question but that Congress could assure the public a free right of access to the Hawaii Kai Marina if it so chose. Whether a statute or regulation that went so far amounted to a "taking," however, is an entirely separate question. *Pennsylvania Coal Co. v. Mahon,* 260 U.S. 393, 415, 43 S.Ct. 158, 160, 67 L.Ed. 322 (1922). As was recently pointed out in *Penn. Central Transportation Co. v. City of New York,* 46 U.S.L.W. 4856 (1978), this Court has generally "been unable to develop any 'set formula' for determining when 'justice and fairness' require that economic injuries caused by public action be compensated by the Government, rather than remain disproportionately concentrated on a few persons." *Id.,* at 124, 98 S.Ct., at 2659, 438 U.S. 104, 98 S.Ct. 2646, 57 L.Ed.2d 631. Rather, it has examined the "taking" question by engaging in essentially ad hoc, factual inquiries that have identified several factors—such as the economic impact of the regulation, its interference with reasonable investment backed expectations, and the character of the governmental action—that have particular significance. *Ibid.* When the "taking" question has involved the exercise of the public right of navigation over interstate waters that constitute highways for commerce, however, this Court has held in many cases that compensation may not be required as a result of the federal navigational servitude. See, *e. g., United States v. Chandler-Dunbar*, 229 U.S. 53, 33 S.Ct. 667, 57 L.Ed. 1063 (1913).

C

The navigational servitude is an expression of the notion that the determination whether a taking has occurred must take into consideration the important public interest in the flow of interstate waters that in their natural condition are in fact capable of supporting public navigation. See *United States v. Cress*, 243 U.S. 316, 37 S.Ct. 380, 61 L.Ed. 746 (1917). Thus, in *United States v. Chandler-Dunbar Co., supra*, 229 U.S., at 69, 33 S.Ct., at 674, this Court stated "that the running water in a great navigable stream is [in]capable of private ownership . . . . " And, in holding that a riparian landowner was not entitled to compensation when the construction of a pier cut off his access to navigable water, this Court observed:

> "The primary use of the waters and the lands under them is for purposes of navigation, and the erection of the piers in them to improve navigation for the public is entirely consistent with such use, and infringes no right of the riparian owner. Whatever the nature of the interest of a riparian owner in the submerged lands in front of his upland bordering on a public navigable water, his title is not as full and complete as his title to fast land which has no direct connection with the navigation of such water. It is a qualified title, a bare technical title, not at his absolute disposal, as is his upland, but to be held at all times subordinate to such use of the submerged lands and of the waters flowing over them as may be consistent with or demanded by the public right of navigation." *Scranton v. Wheeler*, 179 U.S. 141, 163, 21 S.Ct. 48, 57, 45 L.Ed. 126 (1900).

For over a century, a long line of cases decided by this Court involving government condemnation of "fast lands" delineated the elements of compensable damages that the government was required to pay because the lands were riparian to navigable streams. The Court was often deeply divided, and the results frequently turned on what could fairly be described as quite narrow distinctions. But this is not a case in which the government recognizes any obligation whatever to condemn "fast lands" and pay just compensation under the Eminent Domain Clause of the Fifth Amendment to the Bill of Rights of the United States Constitution. It is instead a case in which the owner of what was once a private pond, separated from concededly navigable water by a barrier beach and used for aquatic agriculture, has invested substantial amounts of money in making improvements. The government contends that as a result of one of these improvements, the pond's connection to the navigable water in a manner approved by the Corps of Engineers, the owner has somehow lost one of the most essential sticks in the bundle of rights that are commonly characterized as property—the right to exclude others.

. . . .

. . . The navigational servitude, which exists by virtue of the Commerce Clause in navigable streams, gives rise to an authority in the Government to assure that such streams retain their capacity to serve as continuous highways for the purpose of navigation in interstate commerce. Thus, when the Government acquires fast lands to improve navigation, it is not required under the Eminent Domain Clause to compensate landowners for certain elements of damage attributable to riparian location, such as the land's value as a hydro-electric site, *Twin City Power Co., supra*, or a port site, *United States v. Rands, supra*. But none of these cases ever doubted that when the Government wished to acquire fast lands, it was required by the Eminent Domain Clause of the Fifth Amendment to condemn and pay fair value for that interest. See *United States v. Kansas City Life Insurance Co., supra*, 339 U.S., at 800, 70 S.Ct., at 886 (1950); *United States v. Virginia Electric & Power Co.*, 365 U.S., at 628, 81 S.Ct., at 788 (1961); *United States v. Rands*, 389 U.S., at 123, 88 S.Ct., at 266 (1967). The nature of the navigational servitude when invoked by the Government in condemnation cases is summarized as well as anywhere in *United States v. Willow River Co.*, 324 U.S. 499, 502, 65 S.Ct. 761, 764, 89 L.Ed. 1101:

> "It is clear, of course, that a head of water has value and that the Company has an economic interest in keeping the St. Croix at the lower level. But not all economic interest [sic] are 'property rights'; only those economic advantages are 'rights' which have the law back of them, and only when they are so recognized may courts compel others to forbear from interfering with them or to compensate for their invasion."

We think, however, that when the Government makes the naked assertion it does here, that assertion collides with not merely an "economic advantage" but an "economic advantage" that has the law back of it to such an extent that courts may "compel others to forbear from interfering with [it] or to compensate for [its] invasion." *United States v. Willow River Co., supra*, 502, 65 S.Ct., at 764.

Here the Government's attempt to create a public right of access to the improved pond goes so far beyond ordinary regulation or improvement for navigation as to amount to a taking under the logic of *Pennsylvania Coal Co. v. Mahon, supra*. More than one factor contributes to this result. It is clear that prior to its improvement, Kuapa Pond was incapable of being used as a continuous highway for the purpose of navigation in interstate commerce. Its maximum depth at high tide was a mere two feet, it was separated from the adjacent bay and ocean by a natural barrier beach, and its principal commercial value was limited to fishing. It consequently is not the sort of "great navigable stream" that this Court has previously recognized as being "[in]capable of private ownership." See, *e. g., United States v. Chandler-Dunbar, supra*, 389 U.S., at 66, 33 S.Ct., at 673; *United States v. Twin City Power Co., supra*, 350 U.S., at 228, 76 S.Ct., at 262. And, as previously noted, Kuapa Pond has always been considered to be private property under Hawaiian law. Thus, the interest of petitioners in the now dredged marina is strikingly similar to that of owners of fast land adjacent to navigable water.

We have not the slightest doubt that the Government could have refused to allow such dredging on the ground that it would have impaired navigation in the bay, or could have conditioned its approval of the dredging on petitioners' agreement to comply with various measures that it deemed appropriate for the promotion of navigation. But what petitioners now have is a body of water that was private property under Hawaiian law, linked to navigable water by a channel dredged by them with the consent of the respondent. While the consent of individual officials representing the United States cannot "estop" the United States, see *Montana v. Kennedy,* 366 U.S. 308, 314–315, 81 S.Ct. 1336, 1340–1341, 6 L.Ed.2d 313 (1968); *INS v. Hibi,* 414 U.S. 5, 94 S.Ct. 19, 38 L.Ed.2d 7 (1973), it can lead to the fruition of a number of expectancies embodied in the concept of "property,"—expectancies that, if sufficiently important, the Government must condemn and pay for before it takes over the management of the landowner's property. In this case, we hold that the "right to exclude," so universally held to be a fundamental element of the property right, falls within this category of interests that the Government cannot take without compensation. This is not a case in which the Government is exercising its regulatory power in a manner that will cause an insubstantial devaluation of petitioners' private property; rather, the imposition of the navigational servitude in this context will result in an actual physical invasion of the privately owned marina.

. . . the Government wishes to make what was formerly Kuapa Pond into a public aquatic park after petitioners have proceeded as far as they have here, it may not, without invoking its eminent domain power and paying just compensation, require them to allow free access to the dredged pond while petitioners' agreement with their customers calls for an annual $72 regular fee.

Accordingly the judgment of the Court of Appeals is

Reversed.

Mr. Justice BLACKMUN, with whom Mr. Justice BRENNAN and Mr. Justice MARSHALL join, dissenting.

The Court holds today that, absent compensation, the public may be denied a right of access to "navigable waters of the United States" that have been created or enhanced by private means. I find that conclusion neither supported in precedent nor wise in judicial policy, and I dissent.

My disagreement with the Court lies in four areas. First, I believe the Court errs by implicitly rejecting the old and long established "ebb and flow" test of navigability as a source for the navigational servitude the Government claims. Second, I cannot accept the notion, which I believe to be without foundation in precedent, that the federal "navigational servitude" does not extend to all "navigable waters of the United States." Third, I reach a different balance of interests on the question whether the exercise of the servitude in favor of public access requires compensation to private interests where private efforts are responsible for creating "navigability in fact." And finally, I differ on the bearing that state property law has on the questions before us today.

I

The first issue, in my view, is whether Kuapa Pond is "navigable water of the United States," and if so, why. The Court begins by asking "whether . . . petitioners' improvements to Kuapa Pond caused its original character to be so altered that it became subject to an overriding federal navigational servitude." *Ante,* at 387. It thus assumes that the only basis for extension of federal authority must have arisen *after* the Pond was "developed" and transformed into a marina. This choice of starting point overlooks the Government's contention, advanced throughout this litigation, that Kuapa Pond was navigable water in its natural state, long prior to petitioners' improvements, by virtue of its susceptibility to the ebb and flow of the tide.

The Court concedes that precedent does not disclose a single criterion for identifying "navigable waters." I read our prior cases to establish three distinct tests: "navigability in fact," "navigable capacity," and "ebb and flow" of the tide. Navigability in fact has been used as a test for the scope of the dominant federal interest in navigation since *The Propeller Genesee Chief v. Fitzhugh,* 12 How. 443, 457, 13 L.Ed. 1058 (1852), and *The Daniel Ball,* 10 Wall. 557, 563, 19 L.Ed. 999 (1871). The test of navigable capacity is of more recent origin; it hails from *United States v. Appalachian Power Co.,* 311 U.S. 377, 407–408, 61 S.Ct. 291, 299–300, 85 L.Ed. 243 (1940), where it was used to support assertion of the federal navigational interest over a river nonnavigable in its natural state but capable of being rendered fit for navigation by "reasonable improvements." Ebb and flow is the oldest test of the three. It was inherited from England, where under common law it was used to define ownership of navigable waters by the Crown. In the early days of the Republic, it was regarded as the exclusive test of federal jurisdiction over the waterways of this country. See *The Thomas Jefferson,* 10 Wheat. 428, 429, 6 L.Ed. 358 (1825); *Waring v. Clarke,* 5 How. 441, 463–464, 12 L.Ed. 226 (1847).

. . . .

The ebb and flow test is neither arbitrary nor unsuitable when applied in a coastwise setting. The ebb and flow of the tide define the geographical, chemical, and environmental limits of the three Oceans and the Gulf that wash our shores. Since those bodies of water in the main are navigable, they should be treated as navigable to the inner reach of their natural limits. Those natural limits encompass a water body such as Kuapa Pond, which is contiguous to Maunalua Bay, and which in its natural state must be regarded as an arm of the sea, subject to its tides and currents as much as the Bay itself.

I take it the Court must concede that, at least for regulatory purposes, the Pond in its current condition is "navigable water" because it is now "navigable in fact." . . . I would add that the Pond was "navigable water" prior to development of the present marina because it was subject to the ebb and flow of the tide. . . . [T]his alternative basis for navigability carries significant implications.

II

A more serious parting of ways attends the question whether the navigational servitude extends to all "navigable waters of the United States," however the latter may be established. The Court holds that it does not, at least where navigability is in whole or in part the work of private hands. I disagree.

. . . .

Federal authority over Kuapa Pond does not stem solely from an effect on navigable water elsewhere, although this might be a sound alternative basis for regulatory jurisdiction. Instead, the authority arises because the Pond itself is navigable water.

. . . .

The Court holds, in essence, that the extent of the servitude does not depend on whether a waterway is navigable under any of the tests, but on whether the navigable waterway is "natural" or privately developed. In view of the fact that Kuapa Pond originally was created by natural forces, and that its separation from the Bay has been maintained by the interaction of natural forces and human effort, neither characterization seems particularly apt in this case. One could accept the Court's approach, however, and still find that the servitude extends to Kuapa Pond, by virtue of its status prior to development under the ebb and flow test. Nevertheless, I think the Court's reasoning on this point is flawed. In my view, the power we describe by the term "navigational servitude" extends to the limits of interstate commerce by water; accordingly, I would hold that it is coextensive with the "navigable waters of the United States."

As the Court recognizes, *ante*, at 390, the navigational servitude symbolizes the dominant federal interest in navigation implanted in the Commerce Clause.

. . . .

. . . The National Government is guardian of a public right of access to navigable waters of the United States. The navigational servitude is the legal formula by which we recognize the paramount nature of this governmental responsibility.

The Court often has observed the breadth of federal power in this context. In *United States v. Twin City Power Co.*, 350 U.S. 222, 76 S.Ct. 259, 100 L.Ed. 240 (1956), for example, it stated:

> "The interest of the United States in the flow of a navigable stream originates in the Commerce Clause. That Clause speaks in terms of power, not of property. But the power is a dominant one which can be asserted to the exclusion of any competing or conflicting one. The power is a privilege which we have called 'a dominant servitude' . . . or 'a superior navigation easement.'" (Citations omitted.) *Id.*, at 224–225, 76 S.Ct., at 261.

. . . .

The Court in *Twin City Power Co.* recognized that what is at issue is a matter of power, not of property. The servitude, in order to safeguard the Federal Government's paramount control over waters used in interstate commerce, limits the power of the States to create conflicting interests based on local law. That control does not depend on the form of the water body or the manner in which it was created, but on the fact of navigability and the corresponding commercial significance the waterway attains. Wherever that commerce can occur, be it Kuapa Pond or Honolulu Harbor, the navigational servitude must extend.

III

The conclusion that the navigational servitude extends to privately created or enhanced waters does not entirely dispose of this case. There remains the question whether the Government's resort to the servitude requires compensation for private investment instrumental in effecting or improving navigability. The Court, of course, concludes that there is no navigational servitude and, accordingly, that assertion of public access constitutes a compensable taking. Because I do not agree with the premise, I cannot conclude that the right to compensation for opening the Pond to the public is a necessary result. Nevertheless, I think this question requires a balancing of private and public interests.

Ordinarily, "[w]hen the Government exercises [the navigational] servitude, it is exercising its paramount power in the interest of navigation, rather than taking the private property of anyone." What is distinction

. . . .

The Court's prior cases usually have involved riparian owners along navigable rivers who claim losses resulting from the raising or lowering of water levels in the navigable stream, or from the construction of artificial aids to navigation, such as dams or locks. In these cases the Court has held that no compensation is required for loss in water power due to impairment of the navigable water's flow, e. g., *United States v. Twin City Power Co.*, 350 U.S., at 226–227, 76 S.Ct., at 261–262; *United States v. Chandler-Dunbar Co.*, 229 U.S., at 65–66, 33 S.Ct., at 672–673; for loss in "head" resulting from raising the stream, *United States v. Willow River Co.*, 324 U.S., at 507–511, 65 S.Ct., at 766–768; for damage to structures erected between low and high water marks, *United States v. Chicago, M., St. P. & P. R. Co.*, 312 U.S. 592, 595–597, 61 S.Ct. 772, 774–776, 85 L.Ed. 1064; for loss of access to navigable water caused by necessary improvements, *United States v. Commodore Park, Inc.*, 324 U.S. 386, 390–391, 65 S.Ct. 803, 805–806, 89 L.Ed. 1017 (1945); *Scranton v. Wheeler*, 179 U.S., at 163, 21 S.Ct., at 57; or for loss of value to adjoining land based on potential use in navigational commerce, *United States v. Rands*, 389 U.S. 121, 124–125, 88 S.Ct. 265, 267–268, 19 L.Ed.2d 329 (1967). The Court also has held that no compensation is required when "obstructions," such as bridges or wharves, are removed or altered to improve navigation, despite their obvious commercial value to those who erected them, and despite the Federal Government's original willingness to have them built.

. . . .

These cases establish a key principle that points the way for decision in the present context. In most of them, the noncompensable loss was related, either directly or indirectly, to the riparian owner's "access to, and use of, navigable waters." *United States v. Rands*, 389 U.S., at 124–125, 88 S.Ct., at 268. However that access or use may have been turned to account for personal gain, and no matter how much the riparian owner had invested to enhance the value, the Court held that these rights were shared with the public at large. Actions taken to improve their value for the many caused no reimbursable damage to the few who, by the accident of owning contiguous "fast land," previously enjoyed the blessings of the common right in greater measure. See, *e. g., United States v. Commodore Park, Inc.,* 324 U.S., at 390–391, 88 S.Ct., at 805–806. The Court recognized that encroachment on rights inhering separately in the adjoining "fast land," *United States v. Virginia Electric Co.,* 365 U.S. 624, 628, 81 S.Ct. 784, 788, 5 L.Ed.2d 838 (1961), or resulting from access to *nonnavigable* tributaries, see *United States v. Cress,* 243 U.S. 316, 37 S.Ct. 380, 61 L.Ed. 746 (1917), might form the basis for a valid compensation claim. But the principal distinction was that these compensable values had nothing to do with use of the navigable water.

Application of this principle to the present case should lead to the conclusion that the developers of Kuapa Pond have acted at their own risk and are not entitled to compensation for the public access the Government now asserts.

. . .[T]he Government's interest in vindicating a public right of access to the Pond is substantial. It is the very interest in maintaining "common highways, . . . forever free." After today's decision, it is open to any developer to claim that private improvements to a waterway navigable in interstate commerce have transformed "navigable water of the United States" into private property, at least to the extent that he may charge for access to the portion improved. Such appropriation of navigable waters for private use directly injures the freedom of commerce that the navigational servitude is intended to safeguard. In future cases, of course, the Army Corps of Engineers may alleviate this danger by conditioning permission for connection with other waterways on a right of free public access. But it seems to me that the inevitable result of today's decision is the introduction of new legal uncertainty in a field where I had thought the "battles long ago," *ante,* at 391, had achieved some settled doctrine.

IV

I come, finally, to the question whether Kuapa Pond's status under state law ought to alter this conclusion drawn from federal law.

. . . I think it clear that local law concerns rights of title and use between citizen and citizen, or between citizen and state, but does not affect the scope or effect of the federal navigational servitude.

. . . .

. . . I do not think Hawaii or any other State is at liberty through local law to defeat the navigational servitude by transforming navigable water into "fast land." Instead, state-created interests in the waters or beds of such navigable water are secondary to the navigational servitude. Thus, I believe this case should be decided purely as a matter of federal law, in which state law cannot control the scope of federal prerogatives.

For all of the foregoing reasons, the judgment of the Court of Appeals was correct. I therefore dissent.

1. Before reacting to *Kaiser-Aetna*, some background on the navigation servitude is helpful. Professor Morris, in *The Federal Navigation Servitude: Impediment to the Development of the Waterfront, supra,* defined the navigation servitude as the right of the federal government, under the commerce clause, to compel the removal of obstructions to navigation without having to pay. The right of the federal government to regulate and control navigable waters is paramount; all private and state projects must comply with federal regulations; all state leases to private parties are made subject to the superior federal rights; and all interests in navigable waters may be taken without compensation under the federal navigation servitude.

   Professor Eva Morreale, in *Federal Power in Western Waters: The Navigation Power and Rule of No Compensation*, 3 Nat. Res. J. 1, 2 (1963), wrote:

   > It is important to note at the very outset that the terms "navigation *power*" and "navigation *servitude*" describe two related but nevertheless distinct phenomena. Navigation *power* designates the regulatory power which Congress, under the commerce clause and since *Gibbons v. Ogden*, exercises over navigable waters. Navigation *servitude* designates the rule that *certain* private property may be taken in the exercise of the navigation power without the payment of compensation.

   Many writers and courts have attempted to justify the "no compensation" rule. The dominant explanation is the notice theory. The courts simply presume that landowners are aware that any rights in navigable waters are subject to destruction without compensation (as if the federal government had a recorded easement for navigation); any investments made in light of this risk were made at the landowner's own risk and are noncompensable.

   Professor Morreale, in *Federal Power in Western Waters: The Navigation Power and Rule of No Compensation, supra,* at 24–25, criticized the notice theory on several grounds. First, she made the usual objections to the obviously fictional basis of the notice theory. Second, she observed that even though the landowner knows that his or her property is subject to the superior power of Congress, it is not unreasonable for him or her to expect compensation for improvements made prior to the exercise of that power.

   > Finally, the notice theory fails to take account of two pertinent developments. One is the constitutionally sanctioned increase in federal activity under the navigation power from its humble beginnings in *Gibbons v. Ogden*. The other is the expansion of the word "navigable." Today that expansion subjects streams to federal control which not long ago would have been treated as nonnavigable and thus immune from the dominant federal power. To justify the no compensation rule by the idea of notice of a paramount federal right in navigable streams would require that navigability be defined as of the time the private right in question was acquired. The cases make no such distinction.

   Id.

   For an interesting attack on the notice theory as applied to Indian rights in navigable waters, see Ericsson, *The Navigation Servitude and Reserved Indian Property: Does the Rule of No Compensation Apply to Indian Interests in Navigable Waters?*, 1979 Utah L. Rev. 57. *U.S. v. 5,677.94 Acres of Land*, 162 F. Supp. 108 (D. Mont. 1957) also addresses the question and awards compensation.

   If the notice theory does not explain the no-compensation rule, what does?

The answer to this question not only explains the unique treatment of lands below the high-water mark, but reveals the source of the navigation power of Congress as well.

Recall that in England, according to Lord Hale, title to submerged and submersible lands was held by the King in *jus publicum* for the protection of transport and fishing. The protection, however, was limited to a guarantee of free passage. Navigability was maintained through summary abatement of obstructions. Chief Justice Marshall, in *Gibbons*, based his decision not merely on the right of the public to free passage, but rather on the power of Congress to regulate and protect interstate commerce on navigable waterways. The navigation power is, therefore, an expanded, "active" trust. *See* Allen, *Federal Evaluation of Riparian Property: Section III of the Rivers and Harbors Act of 1970*, 24 Me. L. Rev. 175, 179 (1972); Johnson, *Public Trust Protection for Stream Flows and Lake Levels*, 14 U.C. Davis L. Rev. 233 (1981). In at least one writer's opinion, this transformation of the public trust doctrine into the navigation servitude was the result of a mistaken interpretation of English law by American courts. *See* Stoebuck, *Condemnation of Riparian Rights: A Species of Taking Without Touching*, 30 La. L. Rev. 394, 436–37 (1970).

Now that the navigation servitude has been linked to the public trust, it should be easy for you to reason out why Congress can take a private landowner's "property" under the servitude without compensation. The answer is simply that the *jus publicum*, the public right of navigation in the water, cannot be conveyed to a private owner. Therefore, the right to impair navigation was never conveyed and never a part of the bundle of sticks that made up the riparian's "property." *See* Morreale, *Federal Power in Western Waters, supra,* at 30.

The servitude, in its traditional form, could only be enforced to improve navigation. The transformation of the navigation servitude was gradual. In 1931, Justice Brandeis, the first proponent of the multipurpose application, wrote: "That purposes other than navigation will *also* be served could not invalidate the exercise of the authority conferred, even if those other purposes would not alone have justified an exercise of Congressional power." *Arizona v. California*, 283 U.S. 423, 456 (1931). Brandeis implied, however, that navigation had to be the primary purpose. Ten years later, in *Oklahoma v. Atkinson*, 313 U.S. 508, 534 (1941), the Court noted: "That ends other than flood control will also be served, or that flood control may be relatively of lesser importance, does not invalidate the exercise of the authority conferred on Congress." The requirement that navigation be the primary purpose had vanished. Professor Morreale, in *Federal Power in Western Waters, supra,* at 10–12, summarized the present status of the navigation servitude:

In the conflict between "primary" and "other" purposes the balance thus had been shifted in favor of "other" purposes. In *United States v. Twin City Power Co.* [350 U.S. 222] finally, the Court sanctioned a project which at best benefited navigation incidentally. That at least was the manner in which the House Report accompanying the Savannah River Clark Hill Project described the navigational aspects of the project.

For the time being, this is where the matter rests. The rule that evolves from these cases supports federal projects in the name of the navigation power for non-navigation purposes. The origin of the power still demands that *one* purpose be the protection or the improvement of navigation. But once that requirement has been complied with, Congress may in effect use the waters of both navigable and non-navigable streams for whatever purposes it wishes.

The *Twin City* case also defined "compensable" property rights. The Twin City Power Company argued that the value of its upland, for which the Government *did* have to pay, should be its value as a hydroelectric site. The Government argued that the increased value derived from the flow of the stream itself, and offered a much lower sum than Twin City Power was willing to accept. The Court held for the Government. The ordinary high-water mark remained the upper reach of the servitude, and land above that mark still had to be paid for, but no value derived from the flow of the stream was compensable. *See* Morreale, *Federal Power in Western Waters, supra*, at 53–54.

Twin City was followed in 1967 by *United States v. Rands*, 389 U.S. 121 (1967), which held that the compensable value of certain riparian land on the Columbia River, taken from the condemnees by the United States as part of a comprehensive development plan, did not include the land's special value as a port site. In response, Congress enacted section III of the Rivers and Harbors Act of 1970, 33 U.S.C. § 595a (1976). Section III requires that:

In all cases where real property shall be taken by the United States for the public use in connection with any improvement of rivers, harbors, canals, or waterways of the United States, and in all condemnation proceedings by the United States to acquire lands or easements for such improvements, the compensation to be paid for real property taken by the United States above the normal high water mark of navigable waters of the United States shall be the fair market value of such real property based upon all uses to which such real property may reasonably be put, including its highest and best use, any of which uses may be dependent upon access to or utilization of such navigable waters. In cases of partial takings of real property, no depreciation in the value of any remaining real property shall be recognized and no compensation shall be paid for any damages to such remaining real property which result from loss of or reduction of access from such remaining real property to such navigable waters because of the taking of real property or the purposes for which such real property is taken. The compensation defined herein shall apply to all acquisitions of real property after December 31, 1970, and to the determination of just compensation in any condemnation suit pending on December 31, 1970.

Pub. L. 91–611, title I, § III, Dec. 31, 1970, 84 Stat. 1821.

Although it is clear that section III overrules cases such as *Rands* (where the contested value lay in the location of the fast lands), it has been suggested that it might not overrule *Twin City* (where the value was not so much the land but the flow of the river). Most commentators, however, feel that section III overrules *Twin City* as well as *Rands*. Section III illustrates that Congress can choose to compensate the upland owner regardless of the navigation servitude:

[T]he federal government is not constitutionally compelled to take private property without compensation by reliance on the rule of no compensation. It can instead, and often does, pay for the interests destroyed, by proceeding with a project under authority other than the navigation power, despite precedent which would have allowed it to invoke the servitude, or by providing for compensation in spite of prior interpretations which would not have required it to do so.

Ericsson, *The Navigation Servitude and Reserved Indian Property, supra*, at 62–63.

Now that you have some idea of what the federal navigation power is, what practical effect do you think it has on the management and development of the coastal zone? The Rivers and Harbors Act, specifically 33 U.S.C. § 403 (1976), prohibits any obstruction of navigable waters unless it is approved by the Secretary of the Army, subject to the recommendations of the Chief of the U.S. Army Corps of Engineers. Federal approval is required for *any* project that would obstruct navigation—including interferences with nonnavigable streams that might ultimately hinder navigation.

If the Secretary denies a fill permit below OHM to a riparian owner, has the government taken a valuable aspect of the owner's property without compensation? Why or why not? What if the denial was based on a predicted adverse environmental impact rather than interference with navigation? *See* Power, *The Fox in the Chicken Coop: The Regulatory Program of the U.S. Army Corps of Engineers*, 63 Va. L. Rev. 503, 541–43 (1977).

Is it possible for the federal government to grant the states the ownership of the first 3 miles of seabed while retaining paramount control over navigation? *See* 43 U.S.C. § 1314a (1976); *Zabel v. Tabb*, 430 F.2d 199, 206 (5th Cir. 1970).

For additional reading on the navigation servitude, *see* 2 R. Clark, *Waters & Water Rights*, ch. 7 (1967); Munro, *The Navigation Servitude and the Severance Doctrine*, 6 Land & Water L. Rev. 491 (1971). For a discussion of the use of the navigation servitude in *Wilbour v. Gallagher, State v. Johnson, Commissioner of Natural Resources v. Volpe & Co.,* and *Sibson v. State, supra,* see Comment, *The Navigation Servitude as a Method of Ecological Protection*, 75 Dick. L. Rev. 256 (1970).

2. Does *Kaiser-Aetna* hold that the navigation servitude is merely an incident of the federal commerce clause power over navigation? If so, does it not follow that use of the servitude has always been subject to the limitations of the fifth amendment? Does it seem plausible, as Justice Rehnquist writing for the majority suggests, that until *Kaiser-Aetna* the public interest in freely navigable waterways always outweighed the individual interest injured by assertion of the servitude? For arguments that navigation servitude cases should be decided under the property clause, *see* Bartke, *The Navigation Servitude and Just Compensation–Struggle for a Doctrine*, 48 Or. L. Rev. 1 (1968).

3. The majority opinion states: "The navigational servitude is an expression of the notion that the determination whether a taking has occurred must take into consideration the important public interest in the flow of interstate waters that in their natural condition are in fact capable of supporting public navigation." 100 S. Ct. at 391. How is the public's interest in improved waterways less compelling than in naturally navigable waters? What about major intrastate bodies of waters?

4. Does the majority opinion imply that the amount of private investment is a factor to be considered in determining whether compensation is required? Was the amount invested a factor in previous takings cases? How should the amount of compensation be determined? The value to the public of free access? The value of the pond as a private marina versus its value as a public marina? Is the burden of public access adequately compensated by allowing the developer access to navigable waters? What property right of *Kaiser-Aetna* was taken by the Corps of Engineers?

5. Justice Rehnquist writes: "*Appalachian Power Co.* indicates that congressional authority over the waters of this nation does not depend on a stream's 'navigability'." What does such congressional authority depend on? What is the purpose of the "navigability" test? Has *Kaiser-Aetna* redefined what U.S. waters are covered by the navigation servitude?

6. What result if this case was decided under the law of California as set forth in *Colberg infra*? Does it matter whether the state or the federal navigational

servitude is applicable? Should it? How do you determine which applies in a given case? What is the relationship between the federal navigation servitude and the state public trust doctrine?

7. With respect to future waterfront developments requiring a Corps permit, how may the Corps preserve public access without running afoul of *Kaiser-Aetna*?

8. In *Vaughn v. Vermilion Corporation*, 100 S. Ct. 399 (1979), decided together with *Kaiser-Aetna*, petitioners asserted public access rights to canals constructed by respondents which were both subject to tidal fluctuations and navigable in fact. The Court in a per curiam opinion refused to apply *Kaiser-Aetna*, instead remanding for resolution of a factual dispute as to whether respondents' canal construction activities had diverted and destroyed preexisting natural navigable waterways. What difference, if any, should such diversion and destruction make with respect to public access rights?

9. In *United States v. Kane*, 602 F.2d 490 (2d Cir. 1979), *rev'g,* 461 F. Supp. 554 (E.D.N.Y. 1978), the Corps of Engineers sought removal of two fences extending 40 feet below the mean high-tide line into a navigable waterway which were constructed by the upland owner without a Corps permit. The Corps wanted the fences removed to promote public use of the bay. The Second Circuit Court of Appeals remanded to the Corps with instructions to reconsider issuing an "after-the-fact" permit to the upland owner. If the Corps' removal order had been upheld, would the owner have been entitled to compensation under *Kaiser-Aetna*? Should it make any difference that the upland owner was also the lessee at $300 per year of the 300 feet of bay bottom adjacent to her property under a 5–year renewable lease which granted her the right to "peaceably hold and occupy" the bay bottom "without molestation or disturbance"? Is the lease valid?

STOEBUCK, "CONDEMNATION OF RIPARIAN RIGHTS: A SPECIES OF TAKING WITHOUT TOUCHING," 30 Louisiana Law Review 394, 432–35 (1970)

Under the commerce clause, the power of Congress to control navigation is superior to any such power in the states. However, it has long been established that if Congress has not seen fit to exercise its power over a particular navigable waterway, the state may regulate navigation there. . . .

COLBERG, INC. v. STATE, 67 Cal. 2d 408, 432 P.2d 3, 62 Cal. Rptr. 401 (1967), *cert. denied*, 390 U.S. 949 (1968)

SULLIVAN, Justice

These consolidated actions for declaratory relief present the common issue whether plaintiff shipyard owners will have any causes of action for damages under the law of eminent domain arising out of the impairment of their access to the Stockton Deep Water Ship Channel as a result of the construction of two proposed fixed low level parallel bridges spanning a connecting navigable waterway to which their properties are riparian. Separate judgments on the pleadings in favor of defendant State of California were entered below and all plaintiffs have appealed.

. . . .

The Stockton Deep Water Ship Channel is a navigable tidal waterway extending from the mouth of the San Joaquin River to the Port of Stockton. From the turning basin adjoining the port, the channel continues easterly for about 5,000 feet and comes to a dead end within the confines of the city. This portion of the waterway is known as the Upper Stockton Channel. Plaintiffs Colberg and Stephens Marine, Inc. (Stephens), own real property in the City of Stockton riparian to the Upper Stockton Channel upon which for more than sixty years they have conducted shipyards for the construction and repair of yachts and ocean-going vessels. Both yards are improved with marineways, buildings, docks and allied facilities. Colberg's property consists of approximately eight acres; Stephens' of approximately six. Ships and other craft now using the Upper Stockton Channel can proceed to the turning basin and the Stockton Deep Water Ship Channel and thereupon navigate to the open sea by way of the Carquinez Straits and San Francisco Bay.

The state proposes to construct twin stationary freeway bridges across the Upper Stockton Channel between plaintiffs' properties and the turning basin. The vertical clearance of these bridges is to be, generally speaking, 45 feet above the water line. Pursuant to federal law the state applied to the Secretary of the Army and the Chief of Engineers for a permit to build such bridges. After a public hearing, consideration of the views of various interested persons including these plaintiffs, and an extensive economic survey, approval of the location and plans of the bridges was granted by federal authorities in February 1964, subject to conditions not here necessary to be detailed.

Colberg alleges that 81 percent of its current business involves ships standing more than 45 feet above the water line. Plaintiff Stephens alleges that 35 percent of its current business involves such ships. The present minimum clearance between plaintiffs' yards and the Pacific Ocean is 135 feet, established by the Antioch Bridge. Plaintiffs allege in substance that after the construction of the proposed bridges, no vessel with fixed structure in excess of 45 feet above the water line will be able to enter their respective shipyards; that there is no other access by water to the yards from the San Joaquin River, San Francisco Bay and the oceans of the world; and that plaintiffs, their properties and their businesses will suffer loss and damages because of the impairment of access resulting from the construction of the bridges. . . .

Counsel for the state pointed out to us at oral argument that a bridge or vertical clearance sufficient to accommodate plaintiffs' shipyard traffic would involve greatly increased construction costs because it would entail extended approaches; that the added height of such approaches would have an adverse effect upon intangible community values; and that a draw or swing bridge would be unsuitable for freeway purposes.

The trial court granted the state's motion for judgment on the pleadings in both cases and entered judgments accordingly. In its memorandum opinion it held that diminution of the scope of plaintiffs' access from their respective properties to the Stockton Deep Water Ship Channel as a result of the state's proposed action relative to its navigable waters would not constitute a taking or damaging of private property for which just compensation would be required.

. . . .

The sole question in this case is whether the alleged impairment of plaintiffs' access to the Stockton Deep Water Ship Channel constitutes a taking or damaging of private property within the meaning of article 1, section 14 of the California Constitution. In order to answer this question we are led to an examination of the interest of the state in its navigable waters; in the course of this examination we explain the relationship between the state's power to deal with its navigable waters and the extent of its constitutional duty to make compensation for damage caused by the exercise of that power.

In order to put the controversy into proper focus, we must first make some preliminary observations concerning plaintiffs' position and the nature and extent of their claim. First, it is clear that plaintiffs must assert the taking or damaging of a *private* right in order to bring themselves within the protective embrace of article I, section 14. Thus, they cannot ground their claim in the right of navigation, for this is a public right from the abridgment of which plaintiffs will suffer no damage different in character from that to be suffered by the general public. Instead, they must have recourse to the private right of an owner riparian to a navigable waterway to have access to the channel. However, it appears that the access from plaintiffs' property to the navigable portion of the waterway to which they are riparian, to wit, the Upper Stockton Channel, will not be impaired by the proposed project, so that their private right of access, if limited to its traditional scope, will not be "taken or damaged" and no claim for compensation can arise. It is therefore plaintiffs' position that the private right of access must be expanded. They assert that the construction of the bridge in question will render their private right of access useless insofar as it pertains to vessels with a fixed structure more than 45 feet above the waterline; that after such construction they "can launch ships, but they can go nowhere." Action which renders a right valueless, they urge, effectively "takes or damages" that right.

We deem it unnecessary to decide this question, for we have determined that, whatever the scope of plaintiffs' right of riparian access *as against other private persons,* that right must yield without compensation to a proper exercise of the power *of the state* over its navigable waters. It is to a discussion of this latter power that we now turn.

The State of California holds all of its navigable waterways and the lands lying beneath them "as trustee of a public trust for the benefit of the people." Its power to control, regulate and utilize such waters within the terms of the trust is absolute except as limited by the paramount supervisory power of the federal government over navigable waters. The nature and extent of the trust under which the state holds its navigable waterways has never been defined with precision but it has been stated generally that acts of the state with regard to its navigable waters are within trust purposes when they are done "for purposes of commerce, navigation, and fisheries for the benefit of all the people of the state."

The courts have construed the purposes of the trust with liberality to the end of benefiting all the people of the state. In the early case of *People v. Potretro & B.V.R.R. Co.* (1885) 67 Cal. 166, 7 P.445 defendant, under authority of a franchise granted by the Legislature, constructed a railroad bridge across Islais Creek, a navigable waterway. The bridge was an obstruction to navigation, and the Board of State Harbor Commissioners sought to have it abated as a nuisance. It was contended that the legislative act granting the right to build the bridge was in conflict with the act of Congress admitting California into the Union, which act provided that "'all the navigable waters within the state shall be common highways, and forever free, as well to the inhabitants of said state as to the citizens of the United States, without any tax, impost, or duty therefor.'" This court rejected this contention, holding *inter alia* that "while the power of the state with respect to the construction, regulation, and control of bridges . . . is subordinate to that of congress, still until congress acts on the subject, the power of the state is plenary." (67 Cal. at p. 168, 7 P. at p. 447.) Though we there made no explicit reference to the extent of the trust relating to navigable waters, we impliedly held that the spanning of navigable waters by a railroad bridge was an act within the trust purposes of "commerce, navigation, and fisheries."

In *Boone v. Kingsbury* (1928) 206 Cal. 148, 273 P.797 the state surveyor-general had refused to issue to plaintiffs permits to prospect for oil and gas upon tidal lands covered by navigable sea waters upon the ground, *inter alia*, that the granting of such permits would constitute an act without the scope of the trust because such prospecting would not be "in aid and furtherance of commerce and navigation." We rejected that contention, holding that the relationship of gasoline to commerce was manifest. . . .

Finally, in the case of *Gray v. Reclamation District No. 1500*, [1977] 174 Cal. 622, 163 P. 1024, plaintiffs sought to enjoin the operations of defendant district, which was engaged in efforts to reclaim land and prevent flooding, with incidental benefits to navigation, near the confluence of the Sacramento and Feather Rivers. We there rejected plaintiffs' contention that the state had no power to deal with its navigable waters unless its dominant purpose was to improve navigation.

> "The supreme control of the state over its navigable waters was early declared in *Eldridge v. Cowell*, 4 Cal. 80, approved in *United States v. Mission Rock Co.*, 189 U.S. 391, 23 S. Ct. 606, 47 L. Ed. 865. This right of control embraces within it not alone the power to destroy the navigability of certain waters for the benefit of others, but extends in the case of streams to the power to regulate and control the navigable or nonnavigable tributaries, as in the debris cases, *to the erection of structures along or across the stream,* to deepening or changing the channel, to diverting or arresting tributaries; *in short, to do anything subserving the great purpose,* . . . ." (Emphasis added.) (174 Cal. at p. 636, 163 P. at p. 1030.)

We deem it too clear to warrant the citation of further authority that the state, as trustee for the benefit of the people, has power to deal with its navigable waters in any manner consistent with the improvement of commercial intercourse, whether navigational or otherwise. It is equally clear, however, that the question of governmental *power* is quite different from that of *compensation* for damage caused by the exercise of such power. It is to the latter question that we now turn.

We have referred above to the paramount supervisory power of the federal government over navigable waters. This power, though superior to that of the state, is not grounded in ownership of the navigable waterways upon which it operates, but rather derives from the commerce clause of the United States Constitution, and it has been stated that it may properly be exercised *only* in order to aid navigation. The Fifth Amendment to the United States Constitution is of course applicable to the exercise of the federal navigational power within its proper scope, just as article I, section 14 of the state Constitution is applicable to the exercise of state power over navigable waters, but in many cases compensation for "damage" caused by exercise of the federal power is denied because the rights and values affected are deemed to be burdened with the so-called federal "navigation servitude." Among the rights so burdened is that of the access from riparian land to the affected navigable waterway. The limits of the servitude are reached, however, and just compensation must be paid in spite of the fact that the power has been exercised within its scope, when permanent physical encroachment upon or invasion of land riparian to the navigable waterway but above the ordinary high-water mark results.

As we have shown above, the power of the State of California to deal with its navigable waters, though subject to the superior federal power, is considerably wider in scope than that paramount power. The state, as owner of its navigable waterways subject to a trust for the benefit of the people, may act relative to those waterways in any manner consistent with the improvement of commercial traffic and intercourse. We are of the further view that the law of California burdens property riparian or littoral to navigable waters with a servitude commensurate with the power of the state over such navigable waters, and that "when the act [of the state] is done, if it does not embrace the actual taking of property, but results merely in some injurious effect upon the property, the property owner must, for the sake of the general welfare, yield uncompensated obedience."

We have arrived at this conclusion after an examination of cases from other jurisdictions. It appears that in some states the servitude operates only when the state acts upon its navigable waters for the purpose of improving navigation, and that private rights "damaged" by acts not in aid of navigation are therefore compensable. (*Beidler v. Sanitary District* (1904) 211 Ill. 628, 637, 71 N.E. 1118, 67 L.R.A. 820; *Natcher v. City of Bowling Green* (1936) 264 Ky. 584, 592–593, 95 S.W.2d 25; *State ex rel. Andersons v. Masheter* (1964) 1 Ohio St. 2d 11, 12–13, 203 N.E.2d 325; *In re Construction of Walnut Street Bridge* (1899) 191 Pa. 153, 43 A. 88; *Conger v. Pierce County* (1921) 116 Wash. 27, 31, 198 P.377, 18 A.L.R. 393; cf. *Green Bay & Mississippi Canal Co. v. Kaukauna Water Power Co.* (1895) 90 Wis. 370, 398, 60 N.W. 1121, 63 N.W. 1019, 28 L.R.A. 443; *Michaelson v. Silver Beach Improvement Association, Inc.* (1961) 342 Mass. 251, 173 N.E.2d 273, 91 A.L.R.2d 846.) This appears to be the law of the State of New York. (*Marine Air Ways v. State of New York* (1951) 201 Misc. 349, 350, 104 N.Y.S.2d 964; *Crance v. State of New York* (1954) 205

Misc. 590, 593, 128 N.Y.S.2d 479, modified 284 App.Div. 750, 136 N.Y.S.2d 156, reinstated 309 N.Y. 680, 128 N.E.2d 324.) Other jurisdictions hold as we do in the instant case, that the state's servitude operates upon certain private rights, including those of access, whenever the state deals with its navigable waters in a manner consistent with the public trust under which they are held. (*Lovejoy v. City of Norwalk* (1930) 112 Conn. 199, 152 A. 210; *Frost v. Railroad Co.*, 96 Me. 76, 51 A. 806, 59 L.R.A. 68; *Nelson v. DeLong* (1942) 213 Minn. 425; 7 N.W.2d 342; *Crary et ux. v. State Highway Comm.* (1953) 219 Miss. 284, 293–296, 68 So.2d 468; *Darling v. City of Newport News* (1918) 123 Va. 14, 96 S.E. 307, 3 A.L.R. 748, *aff'd* 249 U.S. 540, 39 S.Ct. 371, 63 L.Ed. 759; *Milwaukee-Western Fuel Co. v. Milwaukee* (1913) 152 Wis. 247, 139 N.W. 540.) We are of the opinion that this view is supported not only by the present law of California, but also by considerations of sound public policy.

The limitation of the servitude to cases involving a strict navigational purpose stems from a time when the sole use of navigable waterways for purposes of commerce was that of surface water transport. That time is no longer with us. The demands of modern commerce, the concentration of population in urban centers fronting on navigable waterways, the achievements of science in devising new methods of commercial intercourse—all of these factors require that the state, in determining the means by which the general welfare is best to be served through the utilization of navigable waters held in trust for the public, should not be burdened with an outmoded classification favoring one mode of utilization over another.

It is clear that the conclusions above expressed dispose of plaintiffs' contention that their right of access to the navigable waters fronting on their respective properties must, in order to be of utility, include the right to navigate freely to the sea. Whatever the scope and character of their right to have access to those navigable waters, we hold that such right is burdened with a servitude in favor of the state which comes into operation when the state properly exercises its power to control, regulate, and utilize such waters.

. . . We are neither advised of, nor can conceive of, any reason why rules relating to one kind of navigable waters, to wit, tidewaters, should not be applied with equal reason to similar situations involving other kinds of navigable waters. In any event, we take judicial notice of the fact that tidal influence extends some distance up the San Joaquin River past the Port of Stockton.

We also reject plaintiffs' contention that our highway access cases require that compensation be paid for any substantial impairment of plaintiffs' right of access. We are not persuaded that the analogy between highway access and navigational access will bear close scrutiny. The right of access to a land highway derives from the "land service road" concept, whereby roads are conceived of as arteries constructed through condemnation of private land for the purpose of serving other land abutting on them, rather than for the purpose of serving public traffic passing over them. Principles applicable to such a right cannot reasonably be extended to the case of navigable waterways, which constitute a natural resource retained within the public domain for the purpose of serving public traffic in accordance with the greatest common benefit.

Finally, we emphasize that the state servitude upon lands riparian or littoral to navigable waters, like the federal servitude burdening such lands, does not extend to cases wherein the proper exercise of state power results in actual physical invasion of or encroachment upon fast lands. In the case of *Miramar Co. v. City of Santa Barbara*, 23 Cal. 2d 170, 143 P.2d 1, plaintiff was the owner of lands littoral to a navigable bay and defendant, a political subdivision of the state, constructed a permanent breakwater in the bay about three miles to the west of plaintiff's property. The effect of this breakwater upon natural drifts and currents operated in the course of time to denude plaintiff's property of sandy beach, rendering the property valueless as a beach resort.

It was alleged that defendant, before it built its breakwater, knew that the effect complained of would occur. Plaintiff sued in inverse condemnation, and the trial court entered a judgment of dismissal after sustaining defendants' demurrer without leave to amend. Upon affirmance of the judgment by this court it was said:

> "Plaintiff's littoral right to sandy water [which provided the accretion necessary to offset tidal washing], like its littoral right to access to the ocean, was derived entirely from the proximity of plaintiff's land to the ocean. It gave to plaintiff's land the advantage of sandy accretions. Nevertheless, the enjoyment of that advantage did not constitute a right to its perpetuation, for plaintiff's littoral rights were always subordinate to the state's right to improve navigation. The duration of the sandy accretions depended entirely upon the continuation of the littoral right, which from the beginning was subject to termination by the state. The withdrawal of the sandy accretions, constituting the damage to plaintiff's land, was an incidental consequence of the state's use of the public domain for a public interest that was at all times superior to private littoral rights. There has therefore been no taking or damaging of private property for public use within the meaning of article I, section 14, of the California Constitution." (23 Cal. 2d at 176, 143 P.2d at 4.)

In a separate concurring opinion, it was said that direct physical encroachment or invasion upon plaintiff's lands was required in order that there be "a taking within the meaning of the constitutional provision." (23 Cal. 2d at 178, 143 P.2d at 5.)

After reference to certain cases of the United States Supreme Court . . . (*e.g. Pumpelly v. Green Bay Company*, 80 U.S. (13 Wall.) 166, 20 L. Ed. 557) the concurring opinion concluded that "The doctrine of taking under the Fifth Amendment has never been extended beyond the rule stated, and certainly there is no necessity for doing so under a constitutional provision which provides compensation for both taking and damaging." (23 Cal. 2d at 178–179, 143 P.2d at 5.)

Three justices of the court dissented upon the basis that under the facts a physical taking of the plaintiff's land *was* involved.

It therefore appears that this court in the *Miramar* case, though divided as to the proper result under the facts there at issue, reached fundamental agreement on the extent to which the state, through the proper exercise of its trust power to deal with navigable waters, may impair without compensation rights appurtenant to property riparian or littoral to such waters. The servitude with which such property is burdened precludes compensation for impairment or curtailment of all rights not damaged by permanent physical invasion of or encroachment upon fast lands; when the exercise of the power does cause such physical invasion or encroachment, the servitude is inapplicable and rights damaged as a result are compensable in accordance with article I, section 14, of the state Constitution.

We hold that plaintiffs' right of access from their respective riparian properties to the waters of the channel, whatever its scope as against private parties, is burdened with a servitude in favor of the state and that, since there is here no direct physical invasion of, or encroachment upon, said properties by the state, plaintiffs are not entitled to compensation for the abridgment or diminution, if any, of such right of access as a result of the lawful exercise of the state's power to regulate, control and deal with its navigable waters.

The judgments are, and each of them is affirmed.

TRAYNOR, C. J., and McCOMB, TOBRINER, and BURKE, JJ., concur.

Dissenting Opinion [in which MOSK, J. concurs]

PETERS, Justice

I dissent.

I cannot agree that because the state wants to build two low level highway bridges across the mouth of an inlet where plaintiffs' shipyards are located, plaintiffs must suffer the complete loss caused by the impairment of their right of one-way water access to deep water. Principles of fairness, logic and public policy suggest that this loss is part of the cost of the freeway that should not be borne by plaintiffs but should be borne by the public. Compensation should therefore be allowed.

The access impaired here is one-way access to the oceans of the world. Such access is indispensable to the operation of plaintiffs' businesses. So, the impairment is not technical. It is substantial and different in nature and degree from the impairment suffered by the general public. There is not involved the mere hypothetical damage to vacant land, nor are we dealing with speculators, nor with newly created businesses. Both plaintiffs have been operating bona fide shipyards in the inlet for over 60 years. Thus, we are not involved with a mere incidental impairment of the right of access but are dealing with a very substantial impairment. The impairment is not caused by a construction strictly in aid of navigation but the bridges are part of a state freeway. If the freeway impaired land access to the same degree such impairment would be compensable. These facts are indisputable.

The majority hold that, under these facts, case law and public policy dictate the conclusion that compensation should not be allowed. So far as case law is concerned the majority have done a commendable job in collecting the cases discussing the nature of the rights involved. But all that this exhaustive analysis proves is that there are no definitive cases in California, and that the decisions of other states reach conflicting results. A decision either way is permissible under the cases. Thus, the decision in this case is really a public policy one, and the majority, recognizing this, claim that public policy supports their conclusion. How can there be a public policy to cut off plaintiffs' only access to deep water and so put well established businesses out of operation without compensation? The answer is obvious. There can be and is no such public policy. The question is not an open one. It has been decided that, as a matter of public policy, impairment of land access under such circumstances requires compensation. The majority fly in the face of that determination.

Today government is big and complex and constantly growing bigger. The legitimate need of government for property is constantly expanding. Thus, more and more frequently, the rights of individuals and the government come into conflict. When this occurs then this court must referee the conflict and try to protect the rights of the state and the rights of the individual. In doing so we must keep in mind the admonition of our Constitution that property "shall not be taken or damaged for public use without just compensation."

. . . .

NOTES

1. Did the court in *Colberg* extend the state navigation servitude beyond the reach of the federal servitude? Did the U.S. Supreme Court in *Kaiser-Aetna* authorize the injury to property above the high-water mark without compensation? The California court admitted that the federal servitude was "paramount." Does the paramount position of the federal servitude imply that state servitudes cannot be more extensive? The U.S. Supreme Court denied certiorari in *Colberg*.

2. What is the relationship between the state navigation servitude and the public trust doctrine? *Colberg* appears to go beyond the traditional navigation servitude. Does the public trust doctrine support the new, expansive *Colberg* servitude? Consider the following:

   The *Colberg* doctrine resulted from a combination of traditional navigation servitude theory with a specific grant of power over navigable waterways . . . . The California Constitution contains an independent grant of broad proprietary authority to the state, as trustee for the people, over all navigable waters in the state. In *Colberg*, the California Supreme Court combined the navigation servitude with this constitutional grant to find an extended "servitude" allowing a non-compensable, non-trespassory taking of private property rights in aid of any beneficial public project.

   Wernberg v. State, 519 P.2d 801, 802–03 (Alaska 1974).

   Did the court, by combining the public trust doctrine and the navigation servitude, expand public rights over private property beyond what *either* concept alone would have allowed? Are uplands within the reach of the traditional public trust doctrine? *See Neptune City, infra.* Professor Johnson, in *Public Trust Protection for Stream Flows and Lake Levels*, 14 U.C.D. L. Rev. 233 (1981), argues that the state navigation servitude is simply a special application of the public trust doctrine.

3. Part of the problem in *Colberg* is the nature of the property right that was supposedly taken. The shipyard owners claimed a right of access to the ocean, nearly 100 miles away. Rights of access have been held to be compensable property rights in many states. *See Dept. of Highways v. Thomas,* 427 S.W.2d 213 (1967); *St. Lawrence Shores, Inc. v. State*, 60 Misc. 2d 74, 302 N.Y.S.2d 606 (Ct. Cl. 1969); *Wernberg v. State*, 516 P.2d 1191 (Alaska 1974). *But cf. Marine Airways, Inc. v. State*, 116 N.Y.S.2d 778 (1952). Most states, however, have held that the private right of access extends only to the channel of the watercourse; the right of access does *not* extend to the navigation of the watercourse itself.

Courts usually reason that since the right of access does not include navigation, bridges built up or downstream take no compensable property right. *See* Comment, *The State Navigation Servitude*, 4 Land & Water L. Rev. 521 (1969). The *Colberg* court mentioned the distinction between private rights of access and public rights of navigation, but decided the case on other grounds. Why did the *Colberg* court not take this easy way out? One writer observed that a limitation on the right of access in California would have (1) left the riparian owners without rights against other private individuals, and (2) gone against precedent hailing the value of the right. *See* Note, *Colberg, Inc. v. State: Riparian Landowner's Right to Eminent Domain Relief for State Impairment of Access to a Navigable Waterway*, 72 Dick. L. Rev. 375 (1968).

4. According to the *Colberg* court, what is the limit of the state navigation servitude? Does the servitude extend to cases where the exercise of state power results in actual physical invasion of uplands? How valid is the physical invasion test in light of modern concepts of property as a bundle of rights, rather than a specific, tangible thing?

5. Most commentators have been critical of the *Colberg* decision. Some writers, not content with merely criticizing *Colberg*, have attacked the basic premises of the navigation servitude itself:

Underlying the navigation servitude, there is the policy argument that (a) governmental power to control navigation is supreme—especially sacred in some way—and (b) that to grant compensation would cripple the power. Consider first the second part of this supposed reason. Assuredly, the state and federal governments may take riparian property rights. They may take any property rights in any thing real or personal if necessary to achieve some governmental object, be it the building of roads, post offices, school, parks, fortifications, lighthouses, dams, and so on. All these objects are in furtherance of some power of government; yet compensation must generally be paid. Does anyone argue that having to pay for land for a highway or post office "cripples" the power to build these things? Is compensation denied for the takings? Of course not. Why? Because the constitutional clauses requiring compensation coexist with the powers granted or reserved to the governments. We say to our governments, "Yes, of course you may do these things, but if you do them you must pay for them." And so with the navigation power. Of course the federal and state governments may, within their respective spheres, regulate and improve navigation, but they should pay compensation for property, including riparian rights, taken in the process.

Consider now the argument that the navigation power has some special sacredness about it. Of course it is "supreme" in the sense that no citizen may block its exercise. So are all the powers of government, including the powers to build roads and post offices, to defend the nation—to do everything government may do. What is so special about the power to regulate and control navigation? Who will contend that the navigation power is of a higher order than the war power, in the exercise of which the Government must compensate for riparian rights? Even if there is utility in pigeonholing and labeling the powers of government, there is no logic to setting apart the navigation power as more sacrosanct than the others.

An alternative choice would be to say the other powers are as sacred as the navigation power. The implications of this choice boggle the mind, for this would mean to extend to the exercise of every power an immunity from compensation. Land for roads, post offices, and all the rest would be taken without compensation, so that the compensation clause of the fifth amendment and of every state constitution would become a nullity. The possibility is not pure fantasy, for it was precisely this kind of extension that occurred in the *Colberg* case, which created a servitude for every state activity "dealing with" navigable waters. And whether or not the navigation servitude is extended, to the degree it exists at all, it is by just that much a negation of the constitutional guarantee of compensation.

Finally, the navigation servitude is an atavism. The doctrine runs counter to the historical process by which eminent domain law has increasingly come to recognize and protect intangible property, including riparian rights. It is as though the courts wished to retain a string onto the past.

Born out of a mistake in reading English law, nourished by a misconception of the powers of government, sustained by misunderstanding of the relationship between powers and the principle of compensation, the navigation servitude is an anachronism. If it is too much to hope that the courts will abandon the servitude doctrine, could it not at least be limited? Jurisdictions that do not have it should not adopt it. Those that have it should limit it. Statutes authorizing navigation projects should expressly allow compensation for riparian rights. Certainly the doctrine should be among the most disfavored in the law.

Stoebuck, *Condemnation of Riparian Rights: A Species of Taking Without Touching*, 30 La. L. Rev. 394, 437–39 (1970).

Do you agree with Professor Stoebuck?

SECTION C: BEACH ACCESS

D. BROWER, ACCESS TO THE NATION'S BEACHES: LEGAL AND PLANNING PERSPECTIVES, 19–20 (1978)

Can coastal motels fence off their beach area for the exclusive use of motel guests? Can members of the public fish from the surf anywhere they want? Or use any beach for swimming, sunbathing, or picnicking? To what extent can owners of beach cottages prohibit anyone else from sitting on "their" beach or walking across their property to get to the beach?

These questions raise the issue of who owns the beach, and to what extent the public has a legal right to use the beach, and to gain access to it. The answers to the questions are based on sometimes complex legal issues and doctrines.

. . . .

Before examining these cases it is important to clarify terminology on two points—what is "ownership" and what is the "beach". . . .

. . . .

The prevalent pattern of beach ownership involves public ownership of the wet-sand or foreshore and private ownership of the dry sand and uplands. The access problem can be defined by reference to this ownership pattern, using the example of a public highway running parallel to the ocean. The road itself is publicly owned. Accordingly, the public has the right to use the road, though such use does not necessarily include the right to park along it. The land on the ocean side of the road, the upland area, is privately owned, and may or may not be developed. The land to the ocean side of the uplands is the dry-sand, again in

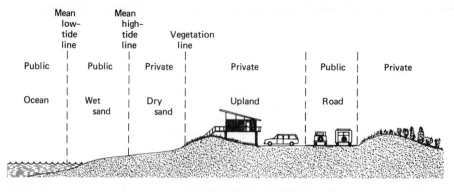

Figure 3-1 Typical pattern of beach ownership. Note that in Delaware, Maine, Massachusetts, New Hampshire, Pennsylvania, and Virginia, private ownership extends to the mean low-tide line. (Adapted from D. Brower, *Access to the Nation's Beaches: Legal and Planning Perspectives*, 19–20, 60–61 (1978).

private ownership and usually belonging to the owners of the adjoining upland. Seaward of both the upland and the dry-sand is the wet-sand or foreshore, which the public owns and has the right to use. Thus the public has the right to use the road and the wet-sand. However, the public has no right, either of ownership or use, in the lands in between—the upland and the dry-sand. The access problem by and large concerns the way in which the public obtains the right to proceed from the road down to the foreshore.

   . . . .

   . . . On the second point, what is the "beach", for the purposes of this discussion the "beach" is divided into four parts: the sea, the wet-sand, the dry-sand, and the upland.

First, that area seaward of the mean low tide line is termed the sea, or sea bed (lake or lake bed in non-oceanic situations). Second, the area between the mean low tide and mean high tide lines, which is covered by the usual flow of tides, is termed the wet-sand. "Foreshore" and "tideland" are generally synonymous with this term. Third, the area between the mean high tide line and the line of vegetation, or dune line, an area inundated only during severe storms, is termed the dry-sand. Fourth, that area landward of the vegetation line is termed the upland.

The Public Trust and the Uplands

NEPTUNE CITY v. AVON-BY-THE-SEA, 61 N.J. 296, 294 A.2d 47 (1972)

HALL, J.

The question presented by this case is whether an oceanfront municipality may charge non-residents higher fees than residents for the use of its beach area. The Law Division sustained an amendatory ordinance of defendant Borough of

Avon-By-The-Sea (Avon) so providing. 114 N.J. Super. 115, 274 A.2d 860 (1971). The challenge came from plaintiffs Borough of Neptune City, an adjacent inland municipality, and two of its residents. We granted plaintiffs' motion to certify their appeal to the Appellate Division before argument in that tribunal. R.2:12–2. The question posed is of ever increasing importance in our metropolitan area. We believe that the answer to it should turn on the application of what has become known as the public trust doctrine.

. . . .

Years ago Avon's beach, like the rest of the New Jersey shore, was free to all comers. As the trial court pointed out, "with the advent of automobile traffic and the ever-increasing number of vacationers, the beaches and bathing facilities became overcrowded and the beachfront municipalities began to take steps to limit the congestion by regulating the use of the beach facilities and by charging fees." 114 N.J. Super. at 117, 274 A.2d at 861. . . .

Legislative authority to municipalities to charge beach user fees, for revenue purposes, was granted by two identical statutes—the first, L.1950, c. 324, p. 1083, N.J.S.A. 40:92-7.1, applicable only to boroughs, and the second, L.1955, c. 49, p. 165, N.J.S.A. 40:61-22.20, applicable to all municipalities. . . .

. . .[W]e see no legislative intent . . . [in the second statute] to authorize discrimination in municipal beach fees between residents and non-residents. The statute amounts to a delegation to a municipality having a dedicated beach (dry sand area) of the state's police power over that area and the tide-flowed land seaward of the mean high water mark; the proviso indicates an affirmation of the state's paramount interest and inherent obligation in insuring that such seaward land be equally available for the use of all citizens.

. . . .

The distinction between residents and non-residents was made by an amendment to the ordinance in 1970, the enactment which is attacked in this case. It was accomplished by making the rate for a monthly badge the same as that charged for a full season's badge ($10.00), by restricting the sale of season badges to residents and taxpayers of Avon and the members of their immediate families, and also apparently by substantially increasing the rates for daily badges (from $1.00 and $1.25 to $1.50 and $2.25). . . .

Plaintiffs attacked the ordinance on several grounds, including the claim of a common law right of access to the ocean in all citizens of the state. This in essence amounts to reliance upon the public trust doctrine, although not denominated by plaintiffs as such. . . .

. . . .

That broad doctrine derives from the ancient principle of English law that land covered by tidal waters belonged to the sovereign, but for the common use of all the people. Such lands passed to the respective states as a result of the American Revolution. . . .

. . . .

The original purpose of the doctrine was to preserve for the use of all the public natural water resources for navigation and commerce, waterways being the principal transportation arteries of early days, and for fishing, an important source of food. . . .

There is not the slightest doubt that New Jersey has always recognized the trust doctrine.[22] . . .

. . . .

It is safe to say, however, that the scope and limitations of the doctrine in this state have never been defined with any great degree of precision. That it represents a deeply inherent right of the citizenry cannot be disputed. Two aspects should be particularly mentioned, one only tangentially involved in this case and the latter directly pertinent. The former relates to the lawful extent of the power of the legislature to alienate trust lands to private parties; the latter to the inclusion within the doctrine of public accessibility to and use of such lands for recreation and health, including bathing, boating and associated activities. Both are of prime importance in this day and age. Remaining tidal water resources still in the ownership of the State are becoming very scarce, demands upon them by reason of increased population, industrial development and their popularity for recreational uses and open space are much heavier, and their importance to the public welfare has become much more apparent. All of these factors mandate more precise attention to the doctrine.

Here we are not directly concerned with the extent of legislative power to alienate tidal lands because the lands seaward of the mean high water line remain in state ownership, the municipality owns the bordering land, which is dedicated to park and beach purposes, and no problem of physical access by the public to the ocean exists. The matter of legislative alienation in this state should, nonetheless, be briefly adverted to since it has a tangential bearing. . . . [I]t has always been assumed that the State may convey or grant rights in some tidal lands to private persons where the use to be made thereof is consistent with and in furtherance of the purposes of the doctrine, *e.g.*, the improvement of commerce and navigation redounding to the benefit of the public. However, our cases rather early began to broadly say that the State's power to vacate or abridge public rights in tidal lands is absolute and unlimited, and our statutes dealing with state conveyances of such lands contain few, if any, limitations thereon. . . .

. . . This case does not require resolution of such issues and we express no opinion on them. We mention this alienation aspect to indicate that, at least where the upland sand area is owned by a municipality—a political subdivision and creature of the state—and dedicated to public beach purposes, a modern court must take the view that the public trust doctrine dictates that the beach and the ocean waters must be open to all on equal terms and without preference and that any contrary state or municipal action is impermissible.

We have no difficulty in finding that, in this latter half of the twentieth century, the public rights in tidal lands are not limited to the ancient prerogatives of navigation and fishing, but extend as well to recreational uses, including bathing, swimming and other shore activities. The public trust doctrine, like all

[22]In probably most states the doctrine covers all navigable waters, non-tidal as well as tidal. New Jersey early limited it to tidal waters and does not apply the navigability test. *Cobb v. Davenport*, 32 N.J.L. 369 (S. Ct. 1867).

common law principles, should not be considered fixed or static, but should be molded and extended to meet changing conditions and needs of the public it was created to benefit. The legislature appears to have had such an extension in mind in enacting N.J.S.A. 12:3–33,34. Those sections, generally speaking, authorize grants to governmental bodies of tide-flowed lands which front upon a public park extending to such lands, but only upon condition that any land so granted shall be maintained as a public park for public use, resort and recreation.

Other states have readily extended the doctrine, beyond the original purposes of navigation and fishing, to cover other public uses, and especially recreational uses. . . . Courts in several other states have recently recognized the vital public interest in the use of the sea shore for recreational purposes and have, under various theories consistent with their own law, asserted the public rights in such land to be superior to private or municipal interests. Modern text writers and commentators assert that the trend of the law is, or should be, in the same direction.

We are convinced it has to follow that, while municipalities may validly charge reasonable fees for the use of their beaches, they may not discriminate in any respect between their residents and non-residents. The Avon amendatory ordinance of 1970 clearly does so by restricting the sale of season badges to residents, as defined in the ordinance, resulting in a lower fee to them. . . .

. . . .

We ought also to say that we fully appreciate the burdens, financial and otherwise, resting upon our oceanfront municipalities by reason of the attraction of the sea and their beaches in the summer season to large numbers of people not permanently resident in the community. The rationale behind N.J.S.A. 40:61–22.20 certainly is that such municipalities may properly pass on some or all of the financial burden, as they decide, by imposing reasonable beach user fees, which we have held here must be uniform for all. . . . They may also, we think, very properly regulate and limit, on a first come, first served basis, the number of persons allowed on the beach at any one time in the interest of safety.

The judgment of the Law Division is reversed and the cause is remanded to that tribunal for the entry of a judgment consistent with this opinion.

FRANCIS, J. (dissenting).

I cannot agree with the result reached by the majority.

. . . .

. . . The basic question may be couched in these terms: Since the people generally have the common right to use and enjoy the ocean and the portion of the beach below the mean high water mark, of what utility is that right if access from the upland does not exist or is refused by the upland owner? Although the majority opinion disclaims any positive ruling on the subject, it seems to imply that exercise of the common right carries with it by way of implementation, the right to use and enjoy *any* beach upland for purposes of recreation and access to the ocean.

In my view, the common right is not so pervasive. Of course, generally speaking reasonable access to the ocean and to the land strip which is in the public domain cannot be denied, but the law does not require that such access be without limitation or qualification. . . .

. . . .

Communities like Avon which have only a few blocks of ocean front are aware that their publicly owned and maintained beaches risk overcrowding to the detriment of local residents and taxpayers unless some reasonable limitations are imposed on use by non-residents. In my view it is neither arbitrary nor invidiously discriminatory for the local governing body which owns, operates and maintains a public beach in the interest of its residents to charge a higher daily, weekly or monthly fee to non-residents who seek the privilege of using the beach.

. . . .

For the reasons stated, I would affirm the judgment of the trial court. Justice MOUNTAIN joins in this dissent.

NOTES

1. The beach access cases are somewhat similar to the cases on the rights of private owners of uplands to wharf out, fill, and dredge in navigable waters. Once again, public use rights are in conflict with traditional concepts of exclusive, private ownership. As in the wharf-out cases, an understanding of the various zones involved is critical. Review the diagram adapted from Brower, *supra*.

2. Did the public have physical access to *Avon's* beach? If they did, why is *Neptune City v. Avon-By-The-Sea* an "access" case? The New Jersey court held that "while municipalities may validly charge reasonable fees for the use of their beaches, they may not discriminate in any respect between their residents and non-residents." Would discrimination against non-residents violate the Equal Protection Clause of the fourteenth amendment to the U.S. Constitution? Did the New Jersey court apply constitutional rationales in reaching its holding?

   In *County Board of Arlington County v. Richards*, 434 U.S. 5, 98 S. Ct. 24 (1977), the U.S. Supreme Court held that a municipal parking ordinance that discriminated against non-residents was not a violation of the fourteenth amendment. Such discrimination is constitutional, as long as it furthers a legitimate legislative purpose. Did the ordinance in *Neptune City* have a legitimate purpose? If so, why was the ordinance invalid?

3. Recall the materials on the public trust doctrine. The *Neptune City* court reviewed public rights in submerged and tidal lands, then applied the doctrine to conclude that *Avon's* beach was burdened with the "necessary easement" of public enjoyment. How does *Neptune City* differ from *Illinois Central R.R. v. Illinois* and *Marks v. Whitney, supra*? The traditional public trust doctrine protected rights of navigation, fishing, and commerce; the New Jersey court expanded the doctrine to protect "public enjoyment" as well. In what other way did the court expand the trust?

   In *Neptune City* the municipality owned the beach. Would the outcome have differed if the beach had been privately owned? Could an owner of upland, dry sand beach assert that the *Neptune City* holding changed prior law, and that the newly created right of public enjoyment of his land amounted to a taking of property without compensation? In light of this, do you think the New Jersey court intended *Neptune City* to apply in cases involving publicly owned beaches only? If it did intend such a limitation, is the public trust doctrine an effective tool to guarantee public access to beaches?

4. In *Van Ness v. Borough of Deal*, 78 N.J. 174, 393 A.2d 571, 573 (1978), the New Jersey court confirmed the implication that *Neptune City v. Avon-By-The-Sea* was limited to its facts. "Our ruling here," the court wrote, "as in *Avon*, is concerned with municipality owned open beaches. We are not called upon to deal with beaches on which permanent improvements may have been built, or beaches as to which a claim of private ownership is asserted." Under *Avon* and *Van Ness*, may a publicly owned beach club consisting of changing rooms and other facilities and located on upland adjacent to a public beach charge higher fees to non-residents? Does the public trust doctrine as interpreted in *Avon* only apply to natural resources or to human-made structures as well? *See Hyland v. Borough of Allenhurst*, 148 N.J. Super. 437, 373 A.2d 1133 (1977). *See also Brindley v. Borough of Lavallette*, 33 N.J. Super. 344, 110 A.2d 157 (L. Div. 1954) (the borough, by maintaining a boardwalk, pavilions, and bathing facilities, had acquired a public easement for recreational purposes).

5. Under the principles of *Neptune City*, may city charter provisions declaring a city-owned beach to be a public park be amended to limit use to city residents and their invited guests? *See Gewirtz v. City of Long Beach*, 69 Misc. 2d 763, 330 N.Y.S.2d 495 (Sup. Ct. 1972); Note, *Non-Resident Restrictions in Municipally Owned Beaches: Approaches to the Problem*, 10 Colum. J. L. & Soc. Prob. 177 (1973–74). For an application of the public trust doctrine to inland parks, *see Gould v. Greylock Reservation Commission*, 350 Mass. 410, 214 N.E.2d 114 (1966).

6. In 1977, the Texas legislature repealed the Texas Open Beaches Law. *See* Acts 1977, 65th Leg., p. 2689, ch. 871, art. I, § 2(a)(1). This repeal, however, was merely a part of a general recodification of Texas law. The provisions of the Open Beaches Law, Tex. Stat. Ann. tit. 86, art. 5415d (Vernon 1962), are substantially mirrored by the new code. *See* Tex. Nat. Res. Code tit. 2, §§ 61.001–.024 (Vernon 1978). Former article 5416d provided that the public should have access to state-owned beaches and other beaches where the public had acquired access rights by prescription, dedication, "or has retained a right by virtue of continued right in the public." Would a repeal of the Open Beaches Law without substantial recodification have been valid under the principles of *Neptune City* and *Illinois Central Railroad v. Illinois*, 146 U.S. 387 (1892), Chapter 3, Section B, *supra*?

In *Seaway Company v. Attorney General*, 375 S.W.2d 923 (Tex. Cir. App. 1964), the court found that Texas had validly conveyed its fee ownership of a dry sand beach to a private buyer. Therefore, under article 5415d, section 1, the Attorney General was forced to prove that the public had regained an interest in Seaway's beach through either prescription, dedication, or by virtue of a "continuous right in the public." What if Texas had never conveyed the beach? Does the first clause of article 5415d, section 1, create public trustlike rights in the dry sand area? If it does, is the state now prohibited from conveying beach lands free of the public rights of use and access?

Given this legislative approval of at least public trustlike rights in the dry sand beach, could the *Seaway* court have reasoned that the early Texas grant had conveyed only the state's proprietary interest, and therefore the beach had always been subject to a "continuous right in the public"?

Do the provisions of article 5415d allow Texas to take privately owned property without compensation? Why not?

Prior to the 1960s, many courts presumed that as to "open lands," in contrast to "roadways," public use was under a revocable license from the owner. *See* Note, *Public Beaches: A Reevaluation*, 15 San Diego L. Rev. 1241, 1254 (1978); Note, *Public Access to Beaches*, 22 Stan. L. Rev. 564, 574–75 (1970).

The *Seaway* court avoided this rule by finding the use of the beach in question analogous to use as a "roadway."

Implied Dedication and Prescription

GION v. CITY OF SANTA CRUZ, 2 Cal. 3d 29, 465 P.2d 50, 84 Cal. Rptr. 162 (1970)

PER CURIAM

We consider these two cases [*Gion v. City of Santa Cruz* and *Dietz v. King*] together because both raise the question of determining when an implied dedication of land has been made.

Gion v. City of Santa Cruz concerns three parcels of land on the southern or seaward side of West Cliff Drive, between Woodrow and Columbia Streets in Santa Cruz. The three lots contain a shoreline of approximately 480 feet and extend from the road into the sea a distance varying from approximately 70 feet to approximately 160 feet. Two of the three lots are contiguous; the third is separated from the first two by approximately 50 feet. Each lot has some area adjoining and level with the road (30 to 40 feet above the sea level) on which vehicles have parked for the last 60 years. This parking area extends as far as 60 feet from the road on one parcel, but on all three parcels there is a sharp cliff-like drop beyond the level area onto a shelf area and then another drop into the sea. The land is subject to continuous, severe erosion. Two roads previously built by the city have been slowly eroded by the sea. To prevent future erosion the city has filled in small amounts of the land and placed supporting riprap in weak areas. The city also put an emergency alarm system on the land and in the early 1960's paved the parking area. No other permanent structures have ever been built on this land.

Since 1880, the City of Santa Cruz has had fee title to a road at some location near the present road. Also since 1880, there has been an area south or seaward of the road area that has been in private hands. As the area south of the road eroded, the city moved its road a short distance to the north. In 1932, after moving the road to its present location, the city gave a quitclaim deed for the land previously covered by the road, but no longer used as a road, to G. H. Normand, the owner and developer of the surrounding property. The area presently under dispute, therefore, includes an old roadbed. Most of the area, however, has never been used for anything but the pleasure of the public.

Since at least 1900 various members of the public have parked vehicles on the level area, and proceeded toward the sea to fish, swim, picnic, and view the ocean. Such activities have proceeded without any significant objection by the fee owners of the property. M. P. Bettencourt, who acquired most of the property in dispute in 1941 and sold it to Gion in 1958 and 1961, testified that during his 20 years of ownership he had occasionally posted signs that the property was privately owned. He conceded, however, that the signs quickly blew away or were torn down, that he never told anyone to leave the property, and that he always granted permission on the few occasions when visitors requested permission to go on it. In 1957 he asked a neighbor to refrain from dumping refuse on the land. The persons who owned the land prior to Bettencourt paid even less attention to it than did Bettencourt. Every witness who testified about the use of the land before 1941 stated that the public went upon the land freely without any thought as to whether it was public or privately owned. In fact, counsel for Gion offered to stipulate at trial that since 1900 the public has fished on the property and that no one ever asked or told anyone to leave it.

The City of Santa Cruz has taken a growing interest in this property over the years and has acted to facilitate the public's use of the land. In the early 1900's, for instance, the Santa Cruz school system sent all the grammar and high school students to this area to plant ice plant, to beautify the area and keep it from eroding. In the 1920's, the city posted signs to warn fishermen of the dangers from eroding cliffs. In the 1940's the city filled in holes and built an embankment on the top level area to prevent cars from driving into the sea. At that time, the city also installed an emergency alarm system that connected a switch near the cliff to an alarm in the firehouse and police station. The city replaced a washed out guardrail and oiled the parking area in the 1950's, and in 1960–61, the city spent $500,000 to prevent erosion in the general area. On the specific property now in dispute, the city filled in collapsing tunnels and placed boulders in weak areas to counter the eroding action of the waves. In 1963, the city paved all of the level area on the property, and in recent years the sanitation department has maintained trash receptacles thereon and cleaned it after weekends of heavy use.

The superior court for the county of Santa Cruz concluded that the Gions were the fee owners of the property in dispute but that their fee title was "subject to an easement in defendant, City of Santa Cruz, a Municipal corporation, for itself and on behalf of the public, in, on, over and across said property for public recreation purposes, and uses incidental thereto, including, but not limited to, parking, fishing, picnicking, general viewing, public protection and policing, and erosion control, but not including the right of the City or the public to build any permanent structures thereon." This conclusion was based on the following findings of fact:

> The public, without having asked or received permission, has made continuous and uninterrupted use of the said property for a period of time in excess of five (5) years preceding the commencement of this action, for public recreation purposes.
>
> The City of Santa Cruz, through its agents and employees, has continously for a period in excess of five (5) years preceding the commencement of this action, exercised continuous and uninterrupted dominion and control over the said property, by performing thereon, grading and paving work, clean-up work, erosion control work, and by maintaining a planting program, and by placing and maintaining safety devices and barriers for the protection of the public using said property.
>
> Plaintiffs and plaintiffs' predecessors in title had full knowledge of the dominion and control exercised over said property by the City of Santa Cruz, and of the public user of said property throughout the period of said public user, for a period of time in excess of five (5) years preceding the commencement of this action.

In *Dietz v. King*, plaintiffs, as representatives of the public, asked the court to enjoin defendants from interfering with the public's use of Navarro Beach in Mendocino County and an unimproved dirt road, called the Navarro Beach Road, leading to that beach. The beach is a small sandy peninsula jutting into the Pacific Ocean. It is surrounded by cliffs at the south and east, and is bounded by the Navarro River and the Navarro Beach Road (the only convenient access to the beach by land) on the north. The Navarro Beach Road branches from a county road that parallels State Highway One. The road runs in a southwesterly direction along the Navarro River for 1,500 feet and then turns for the final 1,500 feet due south to the beach. The road first crosses for a short distance land owned by the Carlyles, who maintain a residence adjacent to the road. It then crosses land owned by Mae Crider and Jack W. Sparkman, proprietors of an ancient structure called the Navarro-by-the-Sea Hotel, and, for the final 2,200 feet, land now owned by defendants.

The public has used the beach and the road for at least 100 years. Five cottages were built on the high ground of the ocean beach about 100 years ago. A small cemetery plot containing the remains of shipwrecked sailors and natives of the area existed there. Elderly witnesses testified that persons traveled over the road during the closing years of the last century. They came in substantial numbers to camp, picnic, collect and cut driftwood for fuel, and fish for abalone, crabs, and finned fish. Others came to the beach to decorate the graves, which had wooden crosses upon them. Indians, in groups of 50 to 75 came from as far away as Ukiah during the summer months. They camped on the beach for weeks at a time, drying kelp and catching and drying abalone and other fish. In decreasing numbers they continued to use the road and the beach until about 1950.

In more recent years the public use of Navarro Beach has expanded. The trial court found on substantial evidence that "For many years members of the public have used and enjoyed the said beach for various kinds of recreational activities, including picnicking, hiking, swimming, fishing, skin diving, camping, driftwood collecting, firewood collecting, and related activities." At times as many as 100 persons have been on the beach. They have come in automobiles, trucks, campers, and trailers. The beach has been used for commercial fishing, and during good weather a school for retarded children has brought its students to the beach once every week or two.

None of the previous owners of the King property ever objected to public use of Navarro Beach Road. The land was originally owned by a succession of lumber and railroad companies, which did not interfere with the public's free use of the road and beach. The Southern Pacific Land Company sold the land in 1942 to Mr. and Mrs. Oscar J. Haub who in turn sold it to the Kings in 1959. Mrs. Haub testified by deposition that she and her husband encouraged the public to use the beach. "We intended," she said, "that the public would go through and enjoy that beach without any charge and just for the fun of being out there." She also said that it "was a free beach for anyone to go down there," "you could go in and out as you pleased," and "[w]e intended that the beach be free for anybody to go down there and have a good time." Only during World War II, when the U.S. Coast Guard took over the beach as a base from which to patrol the coast, was the public barred from the beach.

In 1960, a year after the Kings acquired the land, they placed a large timber across the road at the entrance to their land. Within two hours it was removed by persons wishing to use the beach. Mr. King occasionally put up No Trespassing signs, but they were always removed by the time he returned to the land, and the public continued to use the beach until August 1966. During that month, Mr. King had another large log placed across the road at the entrance to his property. That barrier was, however, also quickly removed. He then sent in a caterpillar crew to permanently block the road. That operation was stopped by the issuance of a temporary restraining order.

The various owners of the Navarro-by-the-Sea property have at times placed an unlocked chain across the Navarro Beach Road on that property. One witness said she saw a chain between 1911 and 1920. Another witness said the chain was put up to discourage cows from straying and eating poisonous weeds. The chain was occasionally hooked to an upright spike, but was never locked in place and could be easily removed. Its purpose apparently was to restrict cows, not people, from the beach. In fact, the chain was almost always unhooked and lying on the ground.

From about 1949 on, a proprietor of the Navarro-by-the-Sea Hotel maintained a sign at the posts saying, "Private Road—Admission 50¢—please pay at hotel." With moderate success, the proprietor collected tolls for a relatively short period of time. Some years later another proprietor resumed the practice. Most persons ignored the sign, however, and went to the beach without paying. The hotel operators never applied any sanctions to those who declined to pay. In a recorded instrument the present owners of the Navarro-by-the-Sea property acknowledged that "for over one hundred years there has existed a public easement and right of way" in the road as it crosses their property. The Carlyles and the previous owners of the first stretch of the Navarro Beach Road never objected to its use over their property and do not now object.

The Mendocino county superior court ruled in favor of defendants, concluding that there had been no dedication of the beach or the road and in particular that widespread public use does not lead to an implied dedication.

. . . .

Three problems of interpretation have concerned the lower courts with respect to proof of dedication by adverse use: (1) When is a public use deemed to be adverse? (2) Must a litigant representing the public prove that the owner did not grant a license to the public? (3) Is there any difference between dedication of shoreline property and other property?

In determining the adverse use necessary to raise a conclusive presumption of dedication, analogies from the law of adverse possession and easement by prescriptive rights can be misleading. An adverse possessor or a person gaining a personal easement by prescription is acting to gain a property right in himself and the test in those situations is whether the person acted as if he actually claimed a personal legal right in the property. Such a personal claim of right need not be shown to establish a dedication because it is a public right that is being claimed. What must be shown is that persons used the property believing the public had a right to such use. This public use may not be "adverse" to the interests of the owner in the sense that the word is used in adverse possession cases. If a trial court finds that the public has used land without objection or interference for more than five years, it need not make a separate finding of "adversity" to support a decision of implied dedication.

Litigants, therefore, seeking to show that land has been dedicated to the public need only produce evidence that persons have used the land as they would have used public land. If the land involved is a beach or shoreline area, they should show that the land was used as if it were a public recreation area. If a road is involved, the litigants must show that it was used as if it were a public road. Evidence that the users looked to a governmental agency for maintenance of the land is significant in establishing an implied dedication to the public.

Litigants seeking to establish dedication to the public must also show that various groups of persons have used the land. If only a limited and definable number of persons have used the land, those persons may be able to claim a personal easement but not dedication to the public. An owner may well tolerate use by some persons but object vigorously to use by others. If the fee owner proves that use of the land fluctuated seasonally, on the other hand, such a showing does not negate evidence of adverse user. "[T]he thing of significance is that whoever wanted to use [the land] did so . . . when they wished to do so without asking permission and without protest from the land owners." (*Seaway Company v. Attorney General* (Tex. Civ. App. 1964), 375 S.W.2d 923, 936.)

The second problem that has concerned lower courts is whether there is a presumption that use by the public is under a license by the fee owner, a presumption that must be overcome by the public with evidence to the contrary. . . .

    . . . .

No reason appears for distinguishing proof of implied dedication by invoking a presumption of permissive use. The question whether public use of privately owned lands is under a license of the owner is ordinarily one of fact. We will not presume that owners of property today knowingly permit the general public to use their lands and grant a license to the public to do so. For a fee owner to negate a finding of intent to dedicate based on uninterrupted public use for more than five years, therefore, he must either affirmatively prove that he has granted the public a license to use his property or demonstrate that he has made a bona fide attempt to prevent public use. Whether an owner's efforts to halt public use are adequate in a particular case will turn on the means the owner uses in relation to the character of the property and the extent of public use. Although "No Trespassing" signs may be sufficient when only an occasional hiker traverses an isolated property, the same action cannot reasonably be expected to halt a continuous influx of beach users to an attractive seashore property. If the fee owner proves that he has made more than minimal and ineffectual efforts to exclude the public, then the trier of fact must decide whether the owner's activities have been adequate. If the owner has not attempted to halt public use in any significant way, however, it will be held as a matter of law that he intended to dedicate the property or an easement therein to the public, and evidence that the public used the property for the prescriptive period is sufficient to establish dedication.

A final question that has concerned lower courts is whether the rules governing shoreline property differ from those governing other types of property, particularly roads. Most of the case law involving dedication in this state has concerned roads and land bordering roads. This emphasis on roadways arises from the ease with which one can define a road, the frequent need for roadways through private property, and perhaps also the relative frequency with which express dedications of roadways are made. The rules governing implied dedication apply with equal force, however, to land used by the public for purposes other than as a roadway. In this state, for instance, the public has gained rights, through dedication, in park land, in athletic fields and in beaches.

Even if we were reluctant to apply the rules of common-law dedication to open recreational areas, we must observe the strong policy expressed in the constitution and statutes of this state of encouraging public use of shoreline recreational areas.

Among the statutory provisions favoring public ownership of shoreline areas is Civil Code, section 830. That section states that absent specific language to the contrary, private ownership of uplands ends at the high-water mark. The decisions of this court have interpreted this provision to create a presumption in favor of public ownership of land between high and low tide.

There is also a clearly enunciated public policy in the California Constitution in favor of allowing the public access to shoreline areas. . . .

Recreational purposes are among the "public purposes" mentioned by this constitutional provision. (*Bohn v. Albertson* (1951) 107 Cal. App. 2d 738, 744, 238 P.2d 128 . . .) Although article XV section 2 may be limited to some extent by the United States Constitution it clearly indicates that we should encourage public use of shoreline areas whenever that can be done consistently with the federal constitution.

Other legislative enactments . . . indicate the strong public policy in favor of according public access to the coast. . . .

This court has in the past been less receptive to arguments of implied dedication when open beach lands were involved than it has when well-defined roadways are at issue. With the increased urbanization of this state, however, beach areas are now as well-defined as roadways. This intensification of land use combined with the clear public policy in favor of encouraging and expanding public access to and use of shoreline areas leads us to the conclusion that the courts of this state must be as receptive to a finding of implied dedication of shoreline areas as they are to a finding of implied dedication of roadways.

We conclude that there was an implied dedication of property rights in both cases. In both cases the public used the land "for a period of more than five years with full knowledge of the owner, without asking or receiving permission to do so and without objection being made by any one." (*Union Transp. Co. v. Sacramento County*, 42 Cal. 2d 235, 240, 267 P.2d 10, 13 quoting from *Hare v. Craig*, 206 Cal. 753, 757, 276 P.336.) In both cases the public used the land in public ways, as if the land was owned by a government, as if the land were a public park. (For a similar result see *State ex rel. Thornton v. Hay* (1969) Or., 462 P.2d 271.)

In *Gion v. City of Santa Cruz*, the public use of the land is accentuated by the active participation of the city in maintaining the land and helping the public to enjoy it. The variety and long duration of these activities indicate conclusively that the public looked to the city for maintenance and care of the land and that the city came to view the land as public land.

No governmental agency took an active part in maintaining the beach and road involved in *Dietz v. King*, but the public nonetheless treated the land as land they were free to use as they pleased. The evidence indicates that for over a hundred years persons used the beach without regard to who owned it. A few persons may have believed that the proprietors of the Navarro-by-the-Sea Hotel owned or supervised the beach, but no one paid any attention to any claim of the true owners. The activities of the Navarro-by-the-Sea proprietors in occasionally collecting tolls has no effect on the public's rights in the property because the question is whether the public's use was free from interference or objection by the fee owner or persons acting under his direction and authority.

The rare occasions when the fee owners came onto the property in question and casually granted permission to those already there have, likewise, no effect on the adverse user of the public. By giving permission to a few, an owner cannot deprive the many, whose rights are claimed totally independent of any permission asked or received of their interest in the land. If a constantly changing group of persons use land in a public way without knowing or caring whether the owner permits their presence, it makes no difference that the owner has informed a few persons that their use of the land is permissive only.

The present fee owners of the lands in question have of course made it clear that they do not approve of the public use of the property. Previous owners, however, by ignoring the wide-spread public use of the land for more than five years have impliedly dedicated the property to the public. Nothing can be done by the present owners to take back that which was previously given away. In each case the trial court found the elements necessary to implied dedication were present—use by the public for the prescriptive period without asking or receiving permission from the fee owner. There is no evidence that the respective fee owners attempted to prevent or halt this use. It follows as a matter of law that a dedication to the public took place. The judgment in *Gion* is affirmed. The judgment in *Dietz* is reversed with directions that judgment be entered in favor of plaintiffs.

NOTES

1. According to the *Gion* court, a common law dedication of property to the public could be proved by (a) showing acquiescence of the owner to the public use under circumstances negating a finding of a license, or (b) by showing "open and continuous use by the public for the prescriptive period." Which method did the *Gion* court apply? How did the court distinguish the second test from classic prescription theory?

    Prescription is, of course, similar to adverse possession. The distinction between the two theories turns on the type of property interest that may be acquired. Easements, such as a public right of access to beaches, may be gained by prescription. Where possessory interests are involved, however, the rules of adverse possession apply.

    The *Gion* court noted that a person seeking a personal easement by prescription must actually claim a legal right in the property. Did members of the public, in *Gion*, actually claim a legal right of access? If they did not, how did the court conclude that public rights of access had been created? Does the case hold that "mere" public use is sufficient for establishing a presumption of "adverse" use? Is the case retroactive so that it affects many areas where the public has been using private land over the years? Consider the following passage from the case:

What must be shown is that persons used the property believing the public had a right to such use. This public use may not be "adverse" to the interests of the owner in the sense that the word is used in adverse possession cases. If a trial court finds that the public has used the land without objection or interference for more than five years, it need not make a separate finding of "adversity" to support a decision of implied dedication.

Gion v. City of Santa Cruz, 2 Cal. 3d at 39, 465 P.2d at 56 (1970).

2. Consider the following from Berger, *Nice Guys Finish Last—At Least They Lose Their Property: Gion v. City of Santa Cruz*, 8 Cal. W. L. Rev. 75, 76 (1971):

On the Palos Verdes peninsula in Los Angeles County, major landowners have recently erected a 7-foot high fence topped by three strands of barbed wire in order to keep the public from reaching the beach by crossing their property. It is believed that other owners in that area have dynamited paths leading to the water. In Orange County, one land owner has erected a large fence with cactus planted at its base to discourage barefoot access to the beach over his property. Land formerly used for parking and beach access in San Mateo County is being vigorously plowed to deter unauthorized users. Parts of Sonoma County are beginning to look like the beaches of Normandy in 1944, complete with tank traps: automobile transmissions have been planted in the ground to stop vehicular access.

On the other hand, governmental authorities from one end of the state to the other have been rubbing their hands at the possibility of obtaining control over vast beach acreages without cost. Lawsuits have been filed state-wide in an attempt to have what were formerly thought to be private lands declared public, or at least subject to a massive easement in favor of "the public."

What has prompted all of this frenetic action and reaction is a year-old, eleven-page, anonymous and essentially uncontested decision of the Supreme Court of California in two consolidated cases: *Gion v. City of Santa Cruz* and *Dietz v. King*.

. . . .

In a nutshell, *Gion–Dietz* says that where, for a period of five years, members of the public have used a private beach or access to a beach over private land under the belief that they had a right to do so, the use is presumed to be adverse to the owner's interest, the owner is presumed to have intended to dedicate the beach or access thereto to the public, and "the public" has acquired at least an easement for recreational purposes on the land used.

Have the property owners (and their attorneys) described by Berger overreacted to *Gion*? Is Berger correct in his assessment of *Gion*?

3. In its rush to further the policy of encouraging public use of the beaches, the California court ignored a number of questions on the nature of property ownership after a finding of implied dedication. For example, what attributes of ownership are left to the former fee holder after the recreational easement has been established? *See* O'Flaherty, *This Land is My Land: The Doctrine of Implied Dedication and Its Application to California Beaches*, 44 S. Cal. L. Rev. 1092 (1971). What uses can the fee holder thereafter make of his property? Could an

owner build a hotel on pilings over the beach, leaving a space underneath for public access to the shore? Is a right to light and air implicit in the court's holding?

Also, when does the 5-year public use period begin to run? What if the public used the area for 6 years between 1910 and 1916—is the land still subject to the easement today? See O'Flaherty, *supra*, at 1094.

4. The California legislature responded to *Gion* by enacting two laws. They have been described as follows:

First, the California Civil Code now contains amended section 813. This section, in effect, states that a fee owner, the holder of record title, may record an instrument which declares that any use by the public of his land is permissive and with license. Such recording is conclusive evidence of consent to use (any use) and such use will not ripen into a dedication to the public or into a prescriptive right in an individual.

. . . .

Second, the legislature added section 1009 to the California Civil Code, which makes a legislative declaration covering essentially the following points:

1. The best interests of the state encourage private landowners to allow public use for recreational purposes.
2. Private real property owners are threatened in their rights when they allow such use.
3. Stability of titles and freedom of alienation is thereby clouded.
4. Notwithstanding private land-owner compliance with section 813 or section 1008 [which prevents the ripening of use into an easement by prescription if the owner posts signs on his property in a certain manner], no use by the public will ripen into a dedication unless such dedication was made by an express irrevocable offer from the land owner.
5. Where public funds are expended in improving property, however, and the owner has actual or constructive knowledge of the improvement, and does not object or take reasonable steps to interrupt, the public right to use vests in five years.
6. The area of land generally between the mean high tide line and 1000 yards inland is not affected by item (4) above.
7. If the owner complies with section 1008 or section 813, or enters into a written agreement with a governmental body providing for public use, no public use of land as mentioned in (6) above will be admissible as evidence of rights acquired by implied dedication. However, if the owner takes action as described, he may not prevent public use during the pendency of his actions.
8. Use of land under (7) above can be reasonably restricted by the landowner, but use in violation of those restrictions shall not be considered for an implied dedication.

Gallagher, Juke & Agnew, *Implied Dedication: The Imaginary Waves of Gion--Dietz*, 5 Sw. U. L. Rev. 48, 79–80 (1973).

What is the effect of these statutes? Are they retroactive?

As a result of section 813 and section 1009, it is hard to see any new effect on the law of implied dedication except as to *future* public use. Rights that may have vested prior to the effective dates of the legislation or prior to the landowner's implementation of the statutory procedures can only be contested in the manner previously available to the landowner.

Id.

5. In a recent case, *County of Los Angeles v. Berk*, 161 Cal. Rptr. 742 (1980), the California Supreme Court reaffirmed the *Gion–Dietz* decision.

6. For a case involving express dedication of a city-owned beach to public use, *see Gewirtz v. City of Long Beach*, 69 Misc. 2d 763, 330 N.Y.S.2d 495 (Sup. Ct. 1972).

The Doctrine of Custom

STATE EX REL. THORNTON v. HAY, 254 Or. 584, 462 P.2d 671 (1969)

GOODWIN, Justice

William and Georgianna Hay, the owners of a tourist facility at Cannon Beach, appeal from a decree which enjoins them from constructing fences or other improvements in the dry-sand area between the sixteen-foot elevation contour line and the ordinary high-tide line of the Pacific Ocean.

The issue is whether the state has the power to prevent the defendant landowners from enclosing the dry-sand area contained within the legal description of their oceanfront property.

The state asserts two theories: (1) the landowners' record title to the disputed area is encumbered by a superior right in the public to go upon and enjoy the land for recreational purposes; and (2) if the disputed area is not encumbered by the asserted public easement, then the state has power to prevent construction under zoning regulations made pursuant to ORS 390.640.

The defendant landowners concede that the State Highway Commission has standing to represent the rights of the public in this litigation, ORS 390.620, and that all tideland lying seaward of the ordinary, or mean high-tide line is a state recreation area as defined in ORS 390.720.[23]

From the trial record, applicable statutes, and court decisions, certain terms and definitions have been extracted and will appear in this opinion. A short glossary follows:

ORS 390.720 refers to the "ordinary" high-tide line, while other sources refer to the "mean" high-tide line. For the purposes of this case the two lines will be considered to be the same. The mean high-tide line in Oregon is fixed by the 1947 Supplement to the 1929 United States Coast and Geodetic Survey data.

---

[23]ORS 390.720 provides:

Ownership of the shore of the Pacific Ocean between ordinary high tide and extreme low tide, and from the Oregon and Washington state line on the north to the Oregon and California state line on the south, excepting such portions as may have been disposed of by the state prior to July 5, 1947, is vested in the State of Oregon, and is declared to be a state recreation area. No portion of such ocean shore shall be alienated by any of the agencies of the state except as provided by law.

The land area in dispute will be called the dry-sand area. This will be assumed to be the land lying between the line of mean high tide and the visible line of vegetation.

. . . .

The only issue in this case, as noted, is the power of the state to limit the record owner's use and enjoyment of the dry-sand area, by whatever boundaries the area may be described.

The trial court found that the public had acquired, over the years, an easement for recreational purposes to go upon and enjoy the dry-sand area, and that this easement was appurtenant to the wet-sand portion of the beach which is admittedly owned by the state and designated as a "state recreation area."

Because we hold that the trial court correctly found in favor of the state on the rights of the public in the dry-sand area, it follows that the state has an equitable right to protect the public in the enjoyment of those rights by causing the removal of fences and other obstacles.

. . . .

In order to explain our reasons for affirming the trial court's decree, it is necessary to set out in some detail the historical facts which lead to our conclusion.

The dry-sand area in Oregon has been enjoyed by the general public as a recreational adjunct of the wet-sand or foreshore area since the beginning of the state's political history. The first European settlers on these shores found the aboriginal inhabitants using the foreshore for clam-digging and the dry-sand area for their cooking fires. The newcomers continued these customs after statehood. Thus, from the time of the earliest settlement to the present day, the general public has assumed that the dry-sand area was a part of the public beach, and the public has used the dry-sand area for picnics, gathering wood, building warming fires, and generally as a headquarters from which to supervise children or to range out over the foreshore as the tides advance and recede. In the Cannon Beach vicinity, state and local officers have policed the dry sand, and municipal sanitary crews have attempted to keep the area reasonably free from man-made litter.

Perhaps one explanation for the evolution of the custom of the public to use the dry-sand area for recreational purposes is that the area could not be used conveniently by its owners for any other purpose. The dry-sand area is unstable in its seaward boundaries, unsafe during winter storms, and for the most part unfit for the construction of permanent structures. While the vegetation line remains relatively fixed, the western edge of the dry-sand area is subject to dramatic moves eastward or westward in response to erosion and accretion. For example, evidence in the trial below indicated that between April 1966 and August 1967 the seaward edge of the dry-sand area involved in this litigation moved westward 180 feet. At other points along the shore, the evidence showed, the seaward edge of the dry-sand area could move an equal distance to the east in a similar period of time.

Until very recently, no question concerning the right of the public to enjoy the dry-sand area appears to have been brought before the courts of this state. The public's assumption that the dry sand as well as the foreshore was "public property" had been reinforced by early judicial decisions. See *Shively v. Bowlby*, 152 U.S. 1, 14 S. Ct. 548, 38 L. Ed. 331 (1894), which affirmed *Bowlby v. Shively*, 22 Or. 410, 30 P. 154 (1892). These cases held that landowners claiming under federal patents owned seaward only to the "high-water" line, a line that was then assumed to be the vegetation line.

. . . .

Recently, however, the scarcity of oceanfront building sites has attracted substantial private investments in resort facilities. Resort owners like these defendants now desire to reserve for their paying guests the recreational advantages that accrue to the dry-sand portions of their deeded property. Consequently, in 1967, public debate and political activity resulted in legislative attempts to resolve conflicts between public and private interests in the dry-sand area:

ORS 390.610 (1) The Legislative Assembly hereby declares it is the public policy of the State of Oregon to forever preserve and maintain the sovereignty of the state heretofore existing over the seashore and ocean beaches of the state from the Columbia River on the North to the Oregon-California line on the South so that the public may have the free and uninterrupted use thereof.

. . . .

(3) Accordingly, the Legislative Assembly hereby declares that all public rights and easements in those lands described in subsection (2) of this section are confirmed and declared vested exclusively in the State of Oregon and shall be held and administered in the same manner as those lands described in ORS 390.720.

. . . .

The state concedes that such legislation cannot divest a person of his rights in land, *Hughes v. Washington*, 389 U.S. 290, 88 S.Ct. 438, 19 L.Ed.2d 530 (1967), and that the defendants' record title, which includes the dry-sand area, extends seaward to the ordinary or mean high-tide line. *Borax Consolidated Ltd. v. Los Angeles, supra*.

The landowners likewise concede that since 1899 the public's rights in the foreshore have been confirmed by law as well as by custom and usage. Oregon Laws 1899, p. 3, provided:

That the shore of the Pacific ocean, between ordinary high and extreme low tides, and from the Columbia river on the north to the south boundary line of Clatsop county on the south, is hereby declared a public highway, and shall forever remain open as such to the public.

The disputed area is *sui generis*. While the foreshore is "owned" by the state, and the upland is "owned" by the patentee or record-title holder, neither can be said to "own" the full bundle of rights normally connoted by the term "estate in fee simple."

. . . .

Because many elements of prescription are present in this case, the state has relied upon the doctrine in support of the decree below. We believe, however, that there is a better legal basis for affirming the decree. The most cogent basis for the decision in this case is the English doctrine of custom. Strictly construed, prescription applies only to the specific tract of land before the court, and doubtful prescription cases could fill the courts for years with tract-by-tract litigation. An established custom, on the other hand, can be proven with reference to a larger region. Ocean-front lands from the northern to the southern border of the state ought to be treated uniformly.

The other reason which commends the doctrine of custom over that of prescription as the principal basis for the decision in this case is the unique nature of the lands in question. This case deals solely with the dry-sand area along the Pacific shore, and this land has been used by the public as public recreational land according to an unbroken custom running back in time as long as the land has been inhabited.

A custom is defined in 1 Bouv. Law Dict., Rawle's Third Revision, p. 742 as "such a usage as by common consent and uniform practice has become the law of the place, or of the subject matter to which it relates."

In 1 Blackstone, Commentaries *75–*78, Sir William Blackstone set out the requisites of a particular custom.

Paraphrasing Blackstone, the first requirement of a custom, to be recognized as law, is that it must be ancient. It must have been used so long "that the memory of man runneth not to the contrary." Professor Cooley footnotes his edition of Blackstone with the comment that "long and general" usage is sufficient. In any event, the record in the case at bar satisfies the requirement of antiquity. So long as there has been an institutionalized system of land tenure in Oregon, the public has freely exercised the right to use the dry-sand area up and down the Oregon coast for the recreational purposes noted earlier in this opinion.

The second requirement is that the right be exercised without interruption. A customary right need not be exercised continuously, but it must be exercised without an interruption caused by anyone possessing a paramount right. In the case at bar, there was evidence that the public's use and enjoyment of the dry-sand area had never been interrupted by private landowners.

Blackstone's third requirement, that the customary use be peaceable and free from dispute, is satisfied by the evidence which related to the second requirement.

The fourth requirement, that of reasonableness, is satisfied by the evidence that the public has always made use of the land in a manner appropriate to the land and to the usages of the community. There is evidence in the record that when inappropriate uses have been detected, municipal police officers have intervened to preserve order.

The fifth requirement, certainty, is satisfied by the visible boundaries of the dry-sand area and by the character of the land, which limits the use thereof to recreational uses connected with the foreshore.

The sixth requirement is that a custom must be obligatory; that is, in the case at bar, not left to the option of each landowner whether or not he will recognize the public's right to go upon the dry-sand area for recreational purposes. The record shows that the dry-sand area in question has been used, as of right, uniformly with similarly situated lands elsewhere, and that the public's use has never been questioned by an upland owner so long as the public remained on the dry sand and refrained from trespassing upon the lands above the vegetation line.

Finally, a custom must not be repugnant, or inconsistent, with other customs or with other law. The custom under consideration violates no law, and is not repugnant.

Two arguments have been arrayed against the doctrine of custom as a basis for decision in Oregon. The first argument is that custom is unprecedented in this state, and has only scant adherence elsewhere in the United States. The second argument is that because of the relative brevity of our political history it is inappropriate to rely upon an English doctrine that requires greater antiquity than a newly-settled land can muster. Neither of these arguments is persuasive.

The custom of the people of Oregon to use the dry-sand area of the beaches for public recreational purposes meets every one of Blackstone's requisites. While it is not necessary to rely upon precedent from other states, we are not the first state to recognize custom as a source of law.

On the score of the brevity of our political history, it is true that the Anglo-American legal system on this continent is relatively new. Its newness has made it possible for government to provide for many of our institutions by written law rather than by customary law. This truism does not, however, militate against the validity of a custom when the custom does in fact exist. If antiquity were the sole test of validity of a custom, Oregonians could satisfy that requirement by recalling that the European settlers were not the first people to use the dry-sand areas as public land.

Finally, in support of custom, the record shows that the custom of the inhabitants of Oregon and of visitors in the state to use the dry sand as a public recreation area is so notorious that notice of the custom on the part of persons buying land along the shore must be presumed. In the case at bar, the landowners conceded their actual knowledge of the public's long-standing use of the dry-sand area, and argued that the elements of consent present in the relationship between the landowners and the public precluded the application of the law of prescription. As noted, we are not resting this decision on prescription, and we leave open the effect upon prescription of the type of consent that may have been present in this case. Such elements of consent are, however, wholly consistent with the recognition of public rights derived from custom.

Because so much of our law is the product of legislation, we sometimes lose sight of the importance of custom as a source of law in our society. It seems particularly appropriate in the case at bar to look to an ancient and accepted custom in this state as the source of a rule of law. The rule in this case, based upon custom, is salutary in confirming a public right, and at the same time it takes from no man anything which he has had a legitimate reason to regard as exclusively his.

For the foregoing reasons, the decree of the trial court is affirmed.

DENECKE, Justice (specially concurring).

I agree with the decision of the majority; however, I disagree with basing the decision upon the English doctrine of "customary rights." In my opinion the facts in this case cannot be fitted into the outlines of that ancient doctrine.

In my opinion the doctrine of "customary rights" is useful but only as an analogy. I am further of the opinion that "custom," as distinguished from "customary rights," is an important ingredient in establishing the rights of the public to the use of the dry sands.

I base the public's right upon the following factors: (1) long usage by the public of the dry sands area, not necessarily on all the Oregon beaches, but wherever the public uses the beach; (2) a universal and long held belief by the public in the public's right to such use; (3) long and universal acquiescence by the upland owners in such public use; and (4) the extreme desirability to the public of the right to the use of the dry sands. When this combination exists, as it does here, I conclude that the public has the right to use the dry sands.

NOTES

1. *Gion* cites *State ex rel. Thornton* as a "case reaching a similar conclusion." How similar are implied dedication and the custom doctrine? The *Thornton* court listed seven elements necessary to establish a custom. How do these differ from the elements needed to prove a dedication? What element of dedication did the court find lacking in *Thornton*?

2. The *State ex rel. Thornton* decision was cited with approval in *County of Hawaii v. Sotomura*, 55 Hawaii 176, 517 P.2d 57 (1973), *cert. denied*, 419 U.S. 872 (1974), in which the Hawaii Supreme Court decreed that all property seaward of the vegetation line belonged to the public. However, a federal district court found that the previous line, consistent with accepted practice, common law, and relevant precedent, was the mean high-water line (MHW) or the seaweed line (limu line in Hawaii). It found the action of the Hawaii Supreme Court deprived property owners of procedural due process since the state and county had not made claim to such land and there was no hearing regarding title before the boundary was relocated, and also that the decree was so radical a departure from prior state law as to constitute a taking without just compensation. *Sotomura v. County of Hawaii*, 460 F. Supp. 473 (1978). *See also In re Ashford*, 50 Hawaii 314, 440 P.2d 76 (1968).

    Was the decision in *Thornton* an unconstitutional taking of Oregon beach-front owners' private property? In *Hay v. Bruno*, 344 F. Supp. 286 (D. Or. 1972), a three-judge panel held that the Oregon statutes confirming public customary rights along the ocean shore (held and administered as state recreation areas) are constitutional and do not violate the rights of the owners of "dry sand areas." *See also State Highway Commission v. Bauman*, 16 Or. App. 275, 517 P.2d 1202 (1974) (customary right of access does not extend to sand dunes inland from the vegetation line); *State Highway Commission v. Fultz*, 261 Or. 289, 491 P.2d 1171 (1971) (denial of permit to build a road on an ocean beach upheld on the basis of interference with public use of the dry sand area).

3. A 1970 Washington Attorney General Opinion (1970 AGO No. 27) concluded that the custom doctrine would be applicable in the State of Washington to give the public a right to the free and unhindered use of the wet and dry sand areas of the Pacific Ocean beaches. The opinion also considered the application of the doctrine to those areas of the Pacific beaches which fall within the boundaries of the Quinault Indian Reservation; it concluded that the treaty establishing the reservation for the *exclusive use* of the Indians would bar a finding of a public easement in the beaches within the reservation. In addition, since the presidential executive order establishing the reservation used the low-water mark as the

boundary, the bar against public access would extend to both wet and dry sand areas.

4. In *United States v. St. Thomas Beach Resorts, Inc.*, 386 F. Supp. 769 (D. St. Thomas and St. John 1974), the federal court ordered the defendant to remove fences that were constructed along the sides of its property, across a beach and toward the low-tide line. The court held that the "custom" doctrine was part of the federal common law and denied the defendant the right to close off the beach. But *cf. City of Daytona Beach v. Tona Rama, Inc.,* 294 So. 2d 73 (Fla. Sup. Ct. 1974), *rev'g,* 271 So. 2d (1972) (construction of viewing tower held not to be inconsistent with public access rights).

5. Additional material dealing with the ownership and use of dry sand areas may be found in Degman, *Public Rights in Ocean Beaches: A Theory of Prescription,* 24 Syracuse L. Rev. 935 (1973); Maloney, Fernandez & Parrish, *Public Beach Access: A Guaranteed Place to Spread Your Towel,* 29 Fla. L. Rev. 853 (1977); National Association of Attorneys General, *Legal Issues in Beach Access* (1977); Nixon, *Public Access to the Shoreline: The Rhode Island Example,* 4 Coastal Zone Mgmt. J. 65 (1978); Note, *Open Beaches in Florida: Right or Rhetoric,* 6 U. Fla. L. Rev. 983 (1978); D. Owens & D. Brower, *Public Use of Coastal Beaches* (1976); Roberts, *Beaches: The Efficiency of the Common Law and Other Fairy Tales,* 28 U.C.L.A. L. Rev. 169 (1981); Symposium, *Beach Access,* 5 Coastal Zone Mgmt. J. No. 1/2 (1979).

Beach Access Taking Issues

IN RE OPINION OF THE JUSTICES, 313 N.E.2d. 561 (Mass. Sup. Ct. 1974)

To the Honorable the House of Representatives of the Commonwealth of Massachusetts:

The Justices of the Supreme Judicial Court respectfully submit this reply to the question set forth in an order adopted by the House on May 8, 1974, and transmitted to us on May 10, 1974. The order recites the pendency before the General Court of a bill, a copy of which has been transmitted to us with the order. The bill is entitled, "An Act authorizing public right-of-passage along certain coastline of the Commonwealth" (House No. 481).

The bill declares that the reserved interests of the public in the land along the coastline between the mean high water line and the extreme low water line include a "public on-foot free right-of-passage." This "right-of-passage" is only to be exercised after sunrise and before one-half hour after sunset and is not to be exercised in those areas designated by the Commissioner of the Department of Natural Resources as of critical ecological significance and so posted. It is not to be exercised where there exists a structure or enclosure authorized by law, or an agricultural fence enclosing livestock, if such areas are clearly posted. An attempt to prevent the exercise of this right of passage is made punishable by fine, and the burden of proof in any action concerning the exclusion of the exercise of the right is to be on the party seeking to exclude or limit it. Interference with or making unsafe such passage is made unlawful, and a civil remedy is provided to any person affected by such action. Littering while exercising the right of passage is prohibited. The limited tort liability of G.L. c. 21, § 17C, is extended to coastal owners with respect to persons exercising the "right-of-passage" except for injuries caused by a violation of the proposed act.

The bill further provides that it is not to be construed as altering existing statutory or common law property or personal rights or remedies. It then states that any person having a recorded interest in any land affected may "within two years from the effective date of this act" petition the Superior Court under G.L. c. 79 "to determine whether . . . the activities authorized herein constitute an injury for which the owner is entitled to compensation under said chapter 79." Finally, the bill requires the Commissioner of Public Works to record a notice of its adoption, prior to its effective date, in every county where coastline land is required to be recorded. He is also required to give such notice by publication within sixty days after its effective date for three consecutive weeks in newspapers in cities and towns containing affected coastal land.

The order asserts that grave doubt exists as to the constitutionality of the bill if enacted into law and propounds the following question:

> "Would the pending Bill if enacted into law violate Article X of the Bill of Rights of the Constitution of the Commonwealth or the Fourteenth Amendment to the Constitution of the United States?"

At common law, private ownership in coastal land extended only as far as mean high water line. Beyond that, ownership was in the Crown but subject to the rights of the public to use the coastal waters for fishing and navigation. Whittlesey, Law of the Seashore, Tidewaters and Great Ponds (1932) xxviii–xxix. Commonwealth v. Roxbury, 9 Gray 451, 482–483, (1857). When title was transferred to private persons it remained impressed with these public rights. Shively v. Bowlby, 152 U.S. 1, 13, 14 S.Ct. 548, 38 L.Ed. 331 (1893). The property inherent in the Crown in England was passed by charter to the Massachusetts Bay Colony and ultimately to the Commonwealth. Massachusetts Constitution, Part II, c. 6, art. 6. See Commonwealth v. Roxbury, *supra*, 9 Gray at 483–484. In the 1640's, in order to encourage littoral owners to build wharves, the colonial authorities took the extraordinary step of extending private titles to encompass land as far as mean low water line or 100 rods from the mean high water line, whichever was the lesser measure. Storer v. Freeman, 6 Mass. 435 (1810). This was accomplished by what has become known as the colonial ordinance of 1641–47, which is found in the 1649 codification, The Book of the General Lawes and Libertyes, at p. 50.

> "Every Inhabitant who is an housholder shall have free fishing and fowling in any great ponds, bayes, Coves and Rivers, so farr as the Sea ebbs and flowes, within the precincts of the towne where they dwell, unles the freemen of the same Town or the General Court have otherwise appropriated them. . . . The which clearly to determine, It is Declared, That in all *Creeks, Coves* and other places, about and upon *Salt-water*, where the Sea ebbs and flowes, the proprietor of the land adjoyning, shall have propriety to the low-water mark, where the Sea doth not ebb

above a hundred Rods, and not more wheresoever it ebbs further. Provided that such proprietor shall not by this liberty, have power to stop or hinder the passage of boates or other vessels, in or through any Sea, Creeks, or Coves, to other mens houses or lands."

Although strictly the ordinance was limited to the area of the Massachusetts Bay Colony, it has long been interpreted as effecting a grant of the tidal land to all coastal owners in the Commonwealth. Weston v. Sampson, 8 Cush. 347, 353–354 (1851), and cases cited. The language of the ordinance well illustrates the notion, previously alluded to, of reserved public right. It expressly specifies that the public is to retain the rights of fishing, fowling and navigation. Notwithstanding these limitations and the use of such ambiguous terms as "propriety" and "liberty," there is ample judicial authority to the effect that the ordinance is properly construed as granting the benefitted owners a fee in the seashore to the extent described and subject to the public rights reserved. It is unnecessary to cite more than a few of the many cases to that effect. In Commonwealth v. Alger, 7 Cush. 53 (1851), probably the leading case on the subject, Chief Justice Shaw wrote, "[The ordinance] imports not an easement, an incorporeal right, license, or privilege, but a *jus in re,* a real or proprietary title to, and interest in, the soil itself, in contradistinction to a usufruct, or an uncertain and precarious interest." *Id.* at 70. "[It created] a legal right and vested interest in the soil, and not a mere permissive indulgence, or gratuitous license, given without consideration, and to be revoked and annulled at the pleasure of those who gave it." *Id.* at 71. In Butler v. Attorney Gen., 195 Mass. 79, 83, 80 N.E. 688, 689 (1907), it was said, "Except as against public rights, which are protected for the benefit of the people, the private ownership is made perfect," and in Boston v. Boston Port Dev. Co., 308 Mass. 72, 78–79, 30 N.E.2d 896 (1941), this ownership in tidal land was deemed property of a "substantial nature." See, e.g., Walker v. Boston & Maine R. R., 3 Cush. 1, 21 (1849); Henry v. Newburyport, 149 Mass. 582, 584–585, 22 N.E. 75 (1889); Jubilee Yacht Club v. Gulf Ref. Co., 245 Mass. 60, 140 N.E. 280 (1923); Michaelson v. Silver Beach Improvement Assn. Inc., 342 Mass. 251, 257, 173 N.E.2d 273 (1961).

If, therefore, the right of passage authorized by the bill is, as it declares, merely an exercise of existing public rights, and not a taking of private property, it must be a natural derivative of the rights preserved by the colonial ordinance. It has been held proper to interfere with the private property rights of coastal owners in the tidal area for purposes reasonably related to the protection or promotion of fishing or navigation without paying compensation. Home for Aged Women v. Commonwealth, 202 Mass. 422, 89 N.E. 124 (1909). Crocker v. Champlin, 202 Mass. 437, 89 N.E. 129 (1909). An "on-foot right-of-passage" is not so related to these public rights. The cases interpreting the right of the public in navigation all deal with the use in boats or other vessels of the area below mean high water mark "when covered with tide water." Commonwealth v. Charlestown, 1 Pick. 180, 183–184 (1822). Commonwealth v. Alger, 7 Cush. 53, 97 (1851). Old Colony St. Ry. v. Phillips, 207 Mass. 174, 180–181, 93

N.E. 792 (1911). Thus the right of passage over dry land at periods of low tide cannot be reasonably included as one of the traditional rights of navigation.
. . . .

We are unable to find any authority that the rights of the public include a right to walk on the beach. . . .

We have considered an able argument made in the brief of one of the amici curiae that we should interpret the colonial ordinance as vesting in the Commonwealth the right to allow all significant public uses in the seashore. It is contended that while fishing, fowling and navigation may have exhausted these uses in 1647, these public uses change with time and now must be deemed to include the important public interest in recreation. Whatever may be the propriety of such an interpretation with respect to public rights in littoral land held by the State, compare Borough of Neptune City v. Borough of Avon-by-the-Sea, 61 N.J. 296, 308–309, 294 A.2d 47 (1972), we think the cases we have cited make clear that the grant to private parties effected by the colonial ordinance has never been interpreted to provide the littoral owners only such uncertain and ephemeral rights as would result from such an interpretation. The rights of the public though strictly protected have also been strictly confined to these well defined areas. . . .

It is next necessary to inquire whether the authorization of the right of passage provided by the bill, while not within the public rights reserved by the colonial ordinance, is nonetheless a proper exercise of the Commonwealth's police power and, as such, does not require that compensation be paid to the private owners. See, e.g., Massachusetts Commn. Against Discrimination v. Colangelo, 344 Mass. 387, 394–397, 182 N.E.2d 595 (1962). The elusive border between the police power of the State and the prohibition against taking of property without compensation has been the subject of extensive litigation and commentary. See Bosselman, Callies & Banta, The Taking Issue (1973). But these difficulties need not concern us here. The permanent physical intrusion into the property of private persons, which the bill would establish, is a taking of property within even the most narrow construction of that phrase possible under the Constitution of the Commonwealth and of the United States.

It is true that the bill does not completely deprive private owners of all use of their seashore property in the sense that a formal taking does. But the case is readily distinguishable from such regulation as merely prohibits some particular use or uses which are harmful to the public. See Commonwealth v. Alger, 7 Cush. 53, 86 (1851). The interference with private property here involves a wholesale denial of an owner's right to exclude the public. If a possessory interest in real property has any meaning at all it must include the general right to exclude others. Nichols, Eminent Domain (Rev. 3d ed.) § 5.1 [1] (1970).
. . . .

The bill, therefore, would effectively appropriate property of individuals to a public use and thus is controlled by the constitutional restriction of art. 10 of the Declaration of Rights of the Massachusetts Constitution, and the Fourteenth Amendment to the United States Constitution. These provisions require that such takings be for a public purpose and that reasonable compensation be paid. See

Caleb Pierce, Inc. v. Commonwealth, 354 Mass. 306, 308–309, 237 N.E.2d 63 (1968). We think it is evident that the creation of the proposed right of passage would serve the recognized public interest in the providing of recreational facilities. Salisbury Land & Improvement Co. v. Commonwealth, 215 Mass. 371, 374, 102 N.E. 619 (1913). Rindge Co. v. County of Los Angeles, 262 U.S. 700, 708, 43 S.Ct. 689, 67 L.Ed. 1186 (1923). There is considerable question, however, whether the bill as written makes adequate provision for the constitutional requirement of fair compensation.

[The portion of the opinion describing the substantive and procedural inadequacies of the bill's compensation provisions is omitted.]

NOTE

Barry v. Grela, 361 N.E.2d 1251 (Mass. Sup. Ct. 1977), held that the plaintiff did have a right to walk on defendant's land between the high- and low-water marks in order to fish from a jetty now owned by the defendant. In light of *In re the Opinion of the Justices*, how do you explain the result in *Barry v. Grela*? *Cf. Allen v. Allen*, 19 R.I. 114, 32 A. 166 (1895), holding that the public trust allows the taking of clams below the high-water mark even when grass or sedge is disturbed, as the public fishing right is paramount to the private right of the upland owner to cut the grass. *See also* Note, *Coastal Recreation: Legal Methods for Securing Rights in the Seashore*, 33 Me. L. Rev. 69 (1981).

4

State-Federal Relationships Offshore

SECTION A: CONTINENTAL SHELF
RESOURCES

Continental Shelf Ownership

HARDWICKE, ILLIG & PATTERSON, "THE CONSTITUTION AND THE CONTINENTAL SHELF," 26 TEXAS LAW REVIEW 304, 413–14 (1947)

By the Declaration of Independence, July 4, 1776, the several colonies, united for the purpose of common defense, asserted their new character as "free and independent states." As such states, they succeeded to all of the rights of the British Crown, including ownership of land within their original charter grants.[1] So in 1779, these states, through the Second Continental Congress, instructed the American Peace Commissioners to claim all of the territory granted by their original charters, since the states had separated from the Crown as original units and were entitled to such boundaries. And in 1782 when these instructions were revised for use in the Paris Congress of 1783, the Continental Congress, speaking of the *boundaries of the states,* said:

[1]This is held in a number of cases, including those cited in note 13 *supra*. The statement of the Court in Shively v. Bowlby, 152 U.S. 1 (1893) is typical: "And upon the American Revolution, all the rights of the Crown and of Parliament vested in the several states subject to the rights surrendered to the national government by the Constitution of the United States."

"On this occasion it is to be observed that our contest will be with his Britannic Majesty alone. Under his authority the limits of these states, while in the character of colonies, was established; to those limits the United States, considered as independent sovereignties, have succeeded. *Whatever territorial rights therefore, belonged to them before the revolution, were necessarily devolved upon them at the era of independence.*"

It is significant that the United States are "considered as independent sovereignties," and only the "boundaries of states" are mentioned. The boundaries of the United States are the "boundaries of the states" "considered as independent sovereignties." In other words, the American Commissioners were not to attempt to fix the boundaries of the United States as a national state or as a separate political entity, but of the states "considered as independent sovereignties." It is unmistakably clear that the boundary of the Union which was established by the states in 1781 and which was exclusively composed of states was fixed by the boundaries of the states composing the Union. The Union as such had nothing to do with the fixing of the boundary of a state when it entered the Union. Thus, in 1781, when Maryland joined the Union as the thirteenth state, the boundary of the Union automatically included Maryland. It made no difference whether Maryland claimed one mile or ten miles at sea or what any other state claimed—it was only a matter of boundaries of states "considered as independent sovereignties." There was no rule of uniformity or equality in this matter. The equality was that of sovereign states, regardless of size or boundaries.

So Article I of the Treaty of Paris, signed in 1783, enumerates the states and acknowledges them

"to be free, sovereign and independent states, that he [His Britannic Majesty] treats with them as such, and for himself, his heirs and successors, relinquishes all claims to the Government, Proprietary and territorial rights of the same, and every part thereof."

This important document repeatedly referred to the "said states" and unequivocally recognized that the territory ceded belonged to the states as separate sovereignties and that the boundaries fixed by the treaty were the boundaries of the United States "considered as separate sovereignties." Of special relevance in connection with the tidelands or the continental shelf, is the fact that by this document the states were allowed to include within their boundaries "all islands within twenty leagues of any part of the shores of the United States."

NOTE

Shively v. Bowlby, 152 U.S. 1 (1893), confirmed the traditional stance of the U.S. Supreme Court on ownership of the coastal zone: the states, not the federal government, owned and controlled submerged and submersible lands. *See Pollard's Lessee v.*

Hagan, 44 U.S. (3 How.) 212, 11 L. Ed. 565 (1845); *Martin v. Waddell,* 41 U.S. (16 Pet.) 367, 10 L. Ed. 997 (1842). This rule was based on a "states' rights" view of the American history popular in the nineteenth century. Professor Morris, in *The Forging of the Union Reconsidered: A Historical Refutation of State Sovereignty Over Seabeds,* 74 Colum. L. Rev. 1056, 1057 (1974), reviewed the historical basis of the states' claims to tidal and submerged lands:

> Critical to the states' claims is the contention that their existence as independent sovereignties preceded the formation of the national government. As they construe the history of the crucial years of independence, the Declaration of Independence created thirteen independent sovereign nations. Since there was no national government in existence, the states necessarily gained title to the submerged offshore lands as a result of the successful revolt from Great Britain. This transfer of title was confirmed by the Treaty of Paris entered into with Great Britain in 1783. They contend further that their existence as thirteen sovereign independent states enjoyed recognition under international law until their ratification of the Constitution. By the act of ratification, they parted only with the external aspects of their sovereignty, retaining proprietary rights to the adjacent seabed and subsoil.

This was the position favored by Hardwicke, Illig & Patterson in *The Constitution and the Continental Shelf, supra.* Morris, however, advocates the more recent, and dominant, view of the historical origins of rights in the marginal sea:

> The United States, on the other hand, while pointing out the dubious legal import of the colonial charters and grants, maintains that any rights to the seas, seabed and subsoil existed as an incident of external sovereignty, which it alone possessed as the sole sovereign entity to emerge upon the issuance of the Declaration of Independence, if not before. The federal Union not only preceded the states in time, but initiated their formation. Thus, any rights to the continental shelf passed directly from the Crown to the United States in Congress Assembled—a transfer formalized by the Treaty of 1783, which Congress, not the states, negotiated with Great Britain. Although the separate states possessed internal sovereignty, their authority did not encompass attributes of external sovereignty, such as dominion over the seas, seabed and subsoil.

Morris, *Forging of the Union Reconsidered, supra,* at 1057.

TAYLOR, "THE SETTLEMENT OF DISPUTES BETWEEN FEDERAL AND STATE GOVERNMENTS CONCERNING OFFSHORE PETROLEUM RESOURCES: ACCOMMODATION OR ADJUDICATION?," 11 Harvard International Law Journal 358, 361 (1970)

Letter dated December 22, 1933, from Julius Albert King, the then United States Secretary of the Interior, giving his interpretation of the federal government's policy:

> Title to the soil under the ocean within the 3-mile limit is in the State of California, and the land may not be appropriated except by authority of the state. . . . I find no authority of law under which any right can be granted . . . outside the 3-mile limit of the jurisdiction of the State of California.

E. BARTLEY, THE TIDELANDS OIL CONTROVERSY, 159 (Univ. of Texas Press, 1953) Copyright 1953 by Ernest R. Bartley

At 12:30 P.M., 29 May 1945, the Department of Justice issued a press release which stated that a suit to enjoin the Pacific Western Oil Company from "extracting additional oil in the rich submerged Elwood field near Santa Barbara" had been filed in the Federal District Court for the Southern District of California. As has been previously noted, the Pacific Western Company had been operating in this area under lease from the state of California. The action transferred the battle for the control of California offshore oil from the political branches to the judicial department of the national government.

UNITED STATES v. CALIFORNIA, 332 U.S. 19 (1947)

MR. JUSTICE BLACK delivered the opinion of the Court.

The United States by its Attorney General and Solicitor General brought this suit against the State of California invoking our original jurisdiction under Article III, § 2, of the Constitution which provides that "In all Cases . . . in which a State shall be Party, the supreme Court shall have original Jurisdiction." The complaint alleges that the United States "is the owner in fee simple of, or possessed of paramount rights in and powers over, the lands, minerals and other things of value underlying the Pacific Ocean, lying seaward of the ordinary low water mark on the coast of California and outside of the inland waters of the State, extending seaward three nautical miles and bounded on the north and south, respectively, by the northern and southern boundaries of the State of California." It is further alleged that California, acting pursuant to state statutes, but without authority from the United States, has negotiated and executed numerous leases with persons and corporations purporting to authorize them to enter upon the described ocean area to take petroleum, gas, and other mineral deposits, and that the lessees have done so, paying to California large sums of money in rents and royalties for the petroleum products taken. The prayer is for a decree declaring the rights of the United States in the area as against California and enjoining California and all persons claiming under it from continuing to trespass upon the area in violation of the rights of the United States.

California has filed an answer to the complaint. It admits that persons holding leases from California, or those claiming under it, have been extracting petroleum products from the land under the three-mile ocean belt immediately adjacent to California. The basis of California's asserted ownership is that a belt extending three English miles from low water mark lies within the original boundaries of the state, Cal. Const. Art. XII (1849);[2] that the original thirteen states acquired from the Crown of England title to all lands within their bound-

[2]The Government complaint claims an area extending three nautical miles from shore; the California boundary purports to extend three English miles. One nautical mile equals 1.15 English miles, so that there is a difference of .45 of an English mile between the boundary of the area claimed by the Government, and the boundary of California. See Cal. Const. Art. XXI, § 1 (1879).

aries under navigable waters, including a three-mile belt in adjacent seas; and that since California was admitted as a state on an "equal footing" with the original states, California at that time became vested with title to all such lands. The answer further sets up several "affirmative" defenses. Among these are that California should be adjudged to have title under a doctrine of prescription; because of an alleged long-existing Congressional policy of acquiescence in California's asserted ownership; because of estoppel or laches; and, finally, by application of the rule of res judicata.[3]

After California's answer was filed, the United States moved for judgment as prayed for in the complaint on the ground that the purported defenses were not sufficient in law. The legal issues thus raised have been exhaustively presented by counsel for the parties, both by brief and oral argument. Neither has suggested any necessity for the introduction of evidence, and we perceive no such necessity at this stage of the case. It is now ripe for determination of the basic legal issues presented by the motion. But before reaching the merits of these issues, we must first consider questions raised in California's brief and oral argument concerning the Government's right to an adjudication of its claim in this proceeding.

[The Court's discussion of the preliminary issues has been omitted.]

Third. The crucial question on the merits is not merely who owns the bare legal title to the lands under the marginal sea. The United States here asserts rights in two capacities transcending those of a mere property owner. In one capacity it asserts the right and responsibility to exercise whatever power and dominion are necessary to protect this country against dangers to the security and tranquility of its people incident to the fact that the United States is located immediately adjacent to the ocean. The Government also appears in its capacity as a member of the family of nations. In that capacity it is responsible for conducting United States relations with other nations. It asserts that proper exercise of these constitutional responsibilities requires that it have power, unencumbered by state commitments, always to determine what agreements will be made concerning the control and use of the marginal sea and the land under it. See McCulloch v. Maryland, 4 Wheat. 316, 403–408; United States v. Minnesota, 270 U. S. 181, 194. In the light of the foregoing, our question is whether the state or the Federal Government has the paramount right and power to determine in the first instance when, how, and by what agencies, foreign or domestic, the oil and other resources of the soil of the marginal sea, known or hereafter discovered, may be exploited.

California claims that it owns the resources of the soil under the three-mile marginal belt as an incident to those elements of sovereignty which it exercises in that water area. The state points out that its original Constitution, adopted in 1849 before that state was admitted to the Union, included within the state's

[3]The claim of res judicata rests on the following contention. The United States sued in ejectment for certain lands situated in San Francisco Bay. The defendant held the lands under a grant from California. This Court decided that the state grant was valid because the land under the Bay had passed to the state upon its admission to the Union. United States v. Mission Rock Co., 189 U. S. 391. There may be other reasons why the judgment in that case does not bar this litigation; but it is a sufficient reason that this case involves land under the open sea, and not land under the inland waters of San Francisco Bay.

boundary the water area extending three English miles from the shore, Cal. Const. (1849) Art. XII; that the Enabling Act which admitted California to the Union ratified the territorial boundary thus defined; and that California was admitted "on an equal footing with the original States in all respects whatever," 9 Stat. 452. With these premises admitted, California contends that its ownership follows from the rule originally announced in *Pollard's Lessee* v. *Hagan*, 3 How. 212; see also *Martin* v. *Waddell*, 16 Pet. 367, 410. In the *Pollard* case it was held, in effect, that the original states owned in trust for their people the navigable tidewaters between high and low water mark within each state's boundaries, and the soil under them, as an inseparable attribute of state sovereignty. Consequently, it was decided that Alabama, because admitted into the Union on "an equal footing" with the other states, had thereby become the owner of the tidelands within its boundaries. Thus the title of Alabama's tidelands grantee was sustained as valid against that of a claimant holding under a United States grant made subsequent to Alabama's admission as a state.

The Government does not deny that under the *Pollard* rule, as explained in later cases, California has a qualified ownership of lands under inland navigable waters such as rivers, harbors, and even tidelands down to the low water mark. It does question the validity of the rationale in the *Pollard* case that ownership of such water areas, any more than ownership of uplands, is a necessary incident of the state sovereignty contemplated by the "equal footing" clause. *Cf. United States* v. *Oregon*, 295 U.S. 1, 14. For this reason, among others, it argues that the *Pollard* rule should not be extended so as to apply to lands under the ocean. It stresses that the thirteen original colonies did not own the marginal belt; that the Federal Government did not seriously assert its increasingly greater rights in this area until after the formation of the Union; that it has not bestowed any of these rights upon the states, but has retained them as appurtenances of national sovereignty. And the Government insists that no previous case in this Court has involved or decided conflicting claims of a state and the Federal Government to the three-mile belt in a way which requires our extension of the *Pollard* inland water rule to the ocean area.

It would unduly prolong our opinion to discuss in detail the multitude of references to which the able briefs of the parties have cited us with reference to the evolution of powers over marginal seas exercised by adjacent countries. From all the wealth of material supplied, however, we cannot say that the thirteen original colonies separately acquired ownership to the three-mile belt or the soil under it, even if they did acquire elements of the sovereignty of the English Crown by their revolution against it. *Cf. United States* v. *Curtiss-Wright Export Corp.*, 299 U.S. 304, 316.

At the time this country won its independence from England there was no settled international custom or understanding among nations that each nation owned a three-mile water belt along its borders. Some countries, notably England, Spain, and Portugal, had, from time to time, made sweeping claims to a right of dominion over wide expanses of ocean. And controversies had arisen among nations about rights to fish in prescribed areas.[4] But when this nation was formed, the idea of a three-mile belt over which a littoral nation could exercise

[4]See, *e. g.*, Fulton, *op. cit. supra*, 3–19, 144–145; Jessup, *op. cit. supra*, 4.

rights of ownership was but a nebulous suggestion.[5] Neither the English charters granted to this nation's settlers,[6] nor the treaty of peace with England,[7] nor any other document to which we have been referred, showed a purpose to set apart a three-mile ocean belt for colonial or state ownership.[8] Those who settled this country were interested in lands upon which to live, and waters upon which to fish and sail. There is no substantial support in history for the idea that they wanted or claimed a right to block off the ocean's bottom for private ownership and use in the extraction of its wealth.

It did happen that shortly after we became a nation our statesmen became interested in establishing national dominion over a definite marginal zone to protect our neutrality.[9] Largely as a result of their efforts, the idea of a definite three-mile belt in which an adjacent nation can, if it chooses, exercise broad, if not complete dominion, has apparently at last been generally accepted throughout the world,[10] although as late as 1876 there was still considerable doubt in England about its scope and even its existence. See *The Queen* v. *Keyn*, 2 Ex. D. 63. That the political agencies of this nation both claim and exercise broad dominion and control over our three-mile marginal belt is now a settled fact. *Cunard Steamship Co.* v. *Mellon*, 262 U.S. 100, 122–124.[11] And this assertion of national dominion over the three-mile belt is binding upon this Court. See

[5]Fulton, *op. cit. supra,* 21, says in fact that "mainly through the action and practice of the United States of America and Great Britain since the end of the eighteenth century, the distance of three miles from shore was more or less formally adopted by most maritime states as . . . more definitely fixing the limits of their jurisdiction and rights for various purposes, and, in particular, for exclusive fishery."

[6]Collected in Thorpe, Federal and State Constitutions (1909).

[7]Treaty of 1783, 8 Stat. 80.

[8]The Continental Congress did for example authorize capture of neutral and even American ships carrying British goods, "if found within three leagues [about nine miles] of the coasts." Journ. of Cong. 185, 186, 187 (1781). *Cf.* Declaration of Panama of 1939, 1 Dept. of State Bull. 321 (1939), claiming the right of the American Republics to be free from a hostile act in a zone 300 miles from the American coasts.

[9]Secretary of State Jefferson in a note to the British minister in 1793 pointed to the nebulous character of a nation's assertions of territorial rights in the marginal belt, and put forward the first official American claim for a three-mile zone which has since won general international acceptance. Reprinted in H. Ex. Doc. No. 324, 42d Cong., 2d Sess. (1872) 553–554. See also Secretary Jefferson's note to the French Minister, Genet, reprinted American State Papers, I Foreign Relations (1833), 183, 184; Act of June 5, 1794, 1 Stat. 381; 1 Kent, Commentaries, 14th Ed., 33–40.

[10]See Jessup, *op. cit. supra,* 66; *Research in International Law,* 23 A.J.I.L. 249, 250 (Spec. Supp. 1929).

[11]See also *Church* v. *Hubbart,* 2 Cranch 187, 234. Congressional assertion of a territorial zone in the sea appears in statutes regulating seals, fishing, pollution of waters, etc. 36 Stat. 326, 328; 43 Stat. 604, 605; 37 Stat. 499, 501. Under the National Prohibition Act, territory including "a marginal belt of the sea extending from low-water mark outward a marine league, or 3 geographical miles" constituting the "territorial waters of the United States" was regulated. U. S. Treas. Reg. 2, § 2201 (1927), reprinted in *Research in International Law, supra,* 250; 41 Stat. 305. Anti-smuggling treaties in which foreign nations agreed to permit the United States to pursue smugglers beyond the three-mile limit contained express stipulations that generally the three-mile limit constitutes "the proper limits of territorial waters." See *e. g.,* 43 Stat. 1761 (Pt. 2).

There are innumerable executive declarations to the world of our national claims to the three-mile belt, and more recently to the whole continental shelf. For references to diplomatic correspondence making these assertions, see 1 Moore, International Law Digest (1906) 705, 706, 707;

Jones v. *United States*, 137 U.S. 202, 212–214; *In re Cooper*, 143 U. S. 472, 502–503.

Not only has acquisition, as it were, of the three-mile belt been accomplished by the National Government, but protection and control of it has been and is a function of national external sovereignty. See *Jones* v. *United States*, 137 U.S. 202; *In re Cooper*, 143 U. S. 472, 502. The belief that local interests are so predominant as constitutionally to require state dominion over lands under its land-locked navigable waters finds some argument for its support. But such can hardly be said in favor of state control over any part of the ocean or the ocean's bottom. This country, throughout its existence has stood for freedom of the seas, a principle whose breach has precipitated wars among nations. The country's adoption of the three-mile belt is by no means incompatible with its traditional insistence upon freedom of the sea, at least so long as the national Government's power to exercise control consistently with whatever international undertakings or commitments it may see fit to assume in the national interest is unencumbered. See *Hines* v. *Davidowitz*, 312 U.S. 52, 62–64; *McCulloch* v. *Maryland, supra*. The three-mile rule is but a recognition of the necessity that a government next to the sea must be able to protect itself from dangers incident to its location. It must have powers of dominion and regulation in the interest of its revenues, its health, and the security of its people from wars waged on or too near its coasts. And insofar as the nation asserts its rights under international law, whatever of value may be discovered in the seas next to its shores and within its protective belt, will most naturally be appropriated for its use. But whatever any nation does in the open sea, which detracts from its common usefulness to nations, or which another nation may charge detracts from it,[12] is a question for consideration among nations as such, and not their separate governmental units. What this Government does, or even what the states do, anywhere in the ocean, is a subject upon which the nation may enter into and assume treaty or similiar international obligations. See *United States* v. *Belmont*, 301 U. S. 324, 331–332. The very oil about which the state and nation here contend might well become the subject of international dispute and settlement.

The ocean, even its three-mile belt, is thus of vital consequence to the nation in its desire to engage in commerce and to live in peace with the world; it also becomes of crucial importance should it ever again become impossible to preserve that peace. And as peace and world commerce are the paramount responsibilities of the nation, rather than an individual state, so, if wars come, they must be fought by the nation. See *Chy Lung* v. *Freeman*, 92 U.S. 275, 279. The state is not equipped in our constitutional system with the powers or the facilities for exercising the responsibilities which would be concomitant with the dominion which it seeks. Conceding that the state has been authorized to exercise local police power functions in the part of the marginal belt within its

---

1 Wharton, Digest of International Law (1886) 100. See also Hughes, *Recent Questions and Negotiations*, 18 A.J.I.L. 229 (1924).

The latest and broadest claim is President Truman's recent proclamation that the United States "regards the natural resources of the subsoil and sea bed of the continental shelf beneath the high seas but contiguous to the coasts of the United States as appertaining to the United States, subject to its jurisdiction and control. . . ." Exec. Proc. 2667, Sept. 28, 1945, 10 F. R. 12303.

[12]See *Lord* v. *Steamship Co.*, 102 U. S. 541, 544.

declared boundaries,[13] these do not detract from the Federal Government's paramount rights in and power over this area. Consequently, we are not persuaded to transplant the *Pollard* rule of ownership as an incident of state sovereignty in relation to inland waters out into the soil beneath the ocean, so much more a matter of national concern. If this rationale of the *Pollard* case is a valid basis for a conclusion that paramount rights run to the states in inland waters to the shoreward of the low water mark, the same rationale leads to the conclusion that national interests, responsibilities, and therefore national rights are paramount in waters lying to the seaward in the three-mile belt. *Cf. United States* v. *Curtiss-Wright Corp.*, 299 U. S. 304, 316; *United States* v. *Causby*, 328 U.S. 256.

As previously stated, this Court has followed and reasserted the basic doctrine of the *Pollard* case many times. And in doing so it has used language strong enough to indicate that the Court then believed that states not only owned tidelands and soil under navigable inland waters, but also owned soils under all navigable waters within their territorial jurisdiction, whether inland or not. All of these statements were, however, merely paraphrases or offshoots of the *Pollard* inland-water rule, and were used, not as enunciation of a new ocean rule, but in explanation of the old inland-water principle. Notwithstanding the fact that none of these cases either involved or decided the state-federal conflict presented here, we are urged to say that the language used and repeated in those cases forecloses the Government from the right to have this Court decide that question now that it is squarely presented for the first time.

. . . .

. . . The question of who owned the bed of the sea only became of great potential importance at the beginning of this century when oil was discovered there.[14] As a consequence of this discovery, California passed an Act in 1921 authorizing the granting of permits to California residents to prospect for oil and gas on blocks of land off its coast under the ocean. Cal. Stats. 1921, c. 303. This state statute, and others which followed it, together with the leasing practices under them, have precipitated this extremely important controversy, and pointedly raised this state-federal conflict for the first time. Now that the question is here, we decide for the reasons we have stated that California is not the owner of the three-mile marginal belt along its coast, and that the Federal Government rather than the state has paramount rights in and power over that belt, an incident to which is full dominion over the resources of the soil under that water area, including oil.

Fourth. Nor can we agree with California that the Federal Government's paramount rights have been lost by reason of the conduct of its agents. The state sets up such a defense, arguing that by this conduct the Government is barred from enforcing its rights by reason of principles similar to laches, estoppel or adverse possession. It would serve no useful purpose to recite the incidents in detail upon which the state relies for these defenses. Some of them are undoubt-

[13]See *Utah Power & Light Co.* v. *United States*, 243 U. S. 389, 404; *cf. The Abby Dodge*, 223 U. S. 166, with *Skiriotes* v. *Florida*, 313 U. S. 69, 74–75.

[14]Bull. No. 321, Dept. of Interior, Geological Survey.

edly consistent with a belief on the part of some Government agents at the time that California owned all, or at least a part of the three-mile belt. This belief was indicated in the substantial number of instances in which the Government acquired title from the states to lands located in the belt; some decisions of the Department of Interior have denied applications for federal oil and gas leases in the California coastal belt on the ground that California owned the lands. Outside of court decisions following the *Pollard* rule, the foregoing are the types of conduct most nearly indicative of waiver upon which the state relies to show that the Government has lost its paramount rights in the belt. Assuming that Government agents could by conduct, short of a congressional surrender of title or interest, preclude the Government from asserting its legal rights, we cannot say it has done so here. As a matter of fact, the record plainly demonstrates that until the California oil issue began to be pressed in the thirties, neither the states nor the Government had reason to focus attention on the question of which of them owned or had paramount rights in or power over the three-mile belt. And even assuming that Government agencies have been negligent in failing to recognize or assert the claims of the Government at an earlier date, the great interests of the Government in this ocean area are not to be forfeited as a result. The Government, which holds its interests here as elsewhere in trust for all the people, is not to be deprived of those interests by the ordinary court rules designed particularly for private disputes over individually owned pieces of property; and officers who have no authority at all to dispose of Government property cannot by their conduct cause the Government to lose its valuable rights by their acquiescence, laches, or failure to act.

We have not overlooked California's argument, buttressed by earnest briefs on behalf of other states, that improvements have been made along and near the shores at great expense to public and private agencies. And we note the Government's suggestion that the aggregate value of all these improvements are small in comparison with the tremendous value of the entire three-mile belt here in controversy. But however this may be, we are faced with the issue as to whether state or nation has paramount rights in and power over this ocean belt, and that great national question is not dependent upon what expenses may have been incurred upon mistaken assumptions. Furthermore, we cannot know how many of these improvements are within and how many without the boundary of the marginal sea which can later be accurately defined. But beyond all this we cannot and do not assume that Congress, which has constitutional control over Government property, will execute its powers in such way as to bring about injustices to states, their subdivisions, or persons acting pursuant to their permission. See *United States* v. *Texas*, 162 U.S. 1, 89, 90; *Lee Wilson & Co.* v. *United States*, 245 U.S. 24, 32.

We hold that the United States is entitled to the relief prayed for. The parties, or either of them, may, before September 15, 1947, submit the form of decree to carry this opinion into effect, failing which the Court will prepare and enter an appropriate decree at the next term of Court.

It is so ordered.

[Dissenting opinions by Justices Reed and Frankfurter have been omitted.]

1. *U.S. v. California* was decided on national security grounds. Justice Black, author of the majority opinion, wrote that "[t]he three-mile rule is but a recognition of the necessity that a government next to the sea must be able to protect itself from dangers incident to its location." 332 U.S. at 35. The United States has rarely been attacked by sea. Even conceding the possibility of attack, is it not feasible for the states to recognize the superior power of the federal government to deal with external threats, and yet control the marginal seas for domestic purposes?

   Did *U.S. v. California* overrule the old Alabama case, *Pollard v. Hagan,* 44 U.S. (3 How.) 212, 11 L. Ed. 565 (1844), which seemed to give the states control of the tidelands? If not, how was *Pollard* distinguished from *California?*

   What justification did the Court give for holding that the actions of federal officers could not cause the government to lose its rights?

2. *United States v. California* was a complex case, both in terms of the events leading up to it and its outcome. E. Bartley, in his book *The Tidelands Oil Controversy, supra,* explained the unexpected legal twist in the Supreme Court's holding:

   The California pleadings were stated almost entirely in terms of property concepts. Since the case of the United States was premised on that line of reasoning, there was no reason for California to do otherwise.

   These were lawyers arguing, on the legal bases with which they were familiar, a concept of title and all that title implies. It appears that they saw no reason to argue the larger but ephemeral concept of "paramount rights," a doctrine of far greater importance to the general theory of federalism than the more prosaic and legalistic concept of title. Whether the outcome could or would have been different if the State of California had chosen to devote the bulk of its pleadings to this more inclusive theory is a matter for pure conjecture. . . . The fact remains that the case was argued entirely on one basis and decided on another.

   Bartley, *The Tidelands Oil Controversy, supra,* at 166 (copyright 1953 by Ernest R. Bartley).

   The final outcome of *U.S. v. California* was ambiguous. At the following term, the government proposed a decree which would have given the United States proprietorship, as well as paramount rights, in the marginal sea. California objected, however, and the word "proprietorship" was deleted. Therefore, though neither California nor the United States had title to the area, the United States was entitled to an injunction to prevent further removal of oil under California leases. *See* Hardwicke, Illig & Patterson, *The Constitution and the Continental Shelf*, 26 Tex. L. Rev. 304, 405 (1947).

3. *United States v. California* dragged on for decades. The first decree, discussed in note 2, was entered at 332 U.S. 448 (1947). A supplemental decree dealing with the definition of "inland waters" was handed down at 382 U.S. 448 (1966). A second supplemental decree, applying the concept of ambulatory boundaries, was granted at 432 U.S. 40 (1977). Finally, a third supplemental decree, dealing with ownership of the marginal sea in a former federal marine reserve in the Santa Barbara Channel, affirmed state ownership at 436 U.S. 32 (1978).

4. The dispute which generated the litigation in *United States v. California* also resulted in a number of other Supreme Court decisions. In *United States v. Louisiana,* 339 U.S. 699, 70 S. Ct. 914, 94 L. Ed. 1216 (1950), the Court rejected claims by Louisiana which were similar to those made by California. In addition to the 3-mile belt, Louisiana also claimed the seabed to a distance of 24 additional marine miles on the basis of a 1938 state statute extending the states' seabed boundaries that distance. Following the reasoning of *California,* the Court

held that statute had no effect on the national government's paramount rights.

In *United States v. Texas*, 339 U.S. 707, 70 S. Ct. 918, 74 L. Ed. 1221 (1950), the issues were somewhat different, as Texas was never a territory but had been an independent nation prior to statehood. In spite of this difference in Texas history, the Court held that Texas, once it became a state, could have no greater rights of sovereignty than the other states. Texan claims to the bed of the marginal sea were also denied.

For discussions of *United States v. Louisiana* and *United States v. Texas*, see Morris, *The Forging of the Union Reconsidered: A Historical Refutation of State Sovereignty Over Seabeds, supra* at 1058–59; and C.E. Dinkins, *Texas Seashore Boundary Law: The Effect of Natural and Artificial Modifications*, 10 Hous. L. Rev. 43 (1972).

The latest in this series of cases is *United States v. Maine*, 420 U. S. 515, 95 S. Ct. 1155, 43 L. Ed. 2d 363 (1975), which involved various claims by the Atlantic coast states to the seabed beyond the 3-mile marginal sea. *Maine* is discussed in more detail later in this chapter.

5. The decision in *United States v. California* was not limited to oil. The doctrine of paramount rights applies to all resources in the marginal sea. *See* Bartley, *The Tidelands Oil Controversy, supra*, at 276.

The states, faced with this disastrous loss of resources, turned to their representatives in Congress to restore state ownership and control of the coastal zone. After *United States v. California* at least 29 bills restoring state control of the marginal seas were presented to the 80th Congress. *See* Taylor, *The Settlement of Disputes Between Federal and State Governments Concerning Offshore Oil Reserves: Accommodation or Adjudication?*, 11 Harv. Int'l L. J. 358, 365 n. 33 (1970); E. Bartley, *The Tidelands Oil Controversy, supra*, at 195. One bill was passed by both houses in 1952, but was vetoed by President Truman. After Eisenhower's election, however, a quitclaim bill was passed and enacted into law. This bill was entitled the Submerged Lands Act and was the second round of the great federal–state battle for ownership of the marginal sea.

6. *United States v. California* was a landmark case and prompted an extensive response among academic observers. *See, e.g.,* Hanna, *The Submerged Lands Cases*, 3 Stan. L. Rev. 193 (1950); Illig, *Offshore Lands and Paramount Rights*, 14 U. Pitt. L. Rev. 10 (1952); Metcalfe, *The Tidelands Controversy: A Study in Development of a Political–Legal Problem*, 4 Syracuse L. Rev. 39 (1952); Thomason, *United States v. California, Paramount Rights of the Federal Government in Submerged Coastal Lands*, 26 Tex. L. Rev. 304 (1947). For an historical perspective on ownership and control of the marginal sea before *United States v. California, see* Ireland, *Marginal Seas Around the States*, 2 La. L. Rev. 252 (1940); Fraser, *The Extent and Delimination of Territorial Waters*, 11 Cornell L.Q. 455 (1926). Cases discussing the issue of estoppel against the government are annotated at 27 A.L.R. Fed. 702 (1976).

The Submerged Lands Act

HARDWICKE, ILLIG & PATTERSON,
"THE CONSTITUTION AND THE CONTINENTAL SHELF,"
26 Texas Law Review 304, 439 (1947)

In view of our political history and organization, the exercise of control for more than a century by the littoral states, and the investment of millions of dollars under the belief, justified by many decisions of the Supreme Court, that the states had title and the right of control, the littoral states have substantial grounds for insisting upon a release of federal claims out to their territorial limits or, in the case of a state having no seaward claims, to three miles. Any realistic handling of the total problem therefore favors a release to the states of federal claims.

SUBMERGED LANDS ACT,
43 U.S.C. §§ 1311 & 1312

§ 1311. Rights of the States—Confirmation and establishment of title and ownership of lands and resources; management, administration, leasing, development, and use

(a) It is determined and declared to be in the public interest that (1) title to and ownership of the lands beneath navigable waters within the boundaries of the respective States, and the natural resources within such lands and waters, and (2) the right and power to manage, administer, lease, develop, and use the said lands and natural resources all in accordance with applicable State law be, and they are, subject to the provisions hereof, recognized, confirmed, established, and vested in and assigned to the respective States or the persons who were on June 5, 1950, entitled thereto under the law of the respective States in which the land is located, and the respective grantees, lessees, or successors in interest thereof;

Release and relinquishment of title and claims of the United States; payment to States of moneys paid under leases

(b) (1) The United States releases and relinquishes unto said States and persons aforesaid, except as otherwise reserved herein, all right, title, and interest of the United States, if any it has, in and to all said lands, improvements, and natural resources; (2) the United States releases and relinquishes all claims of the United States, if any it has, for money or damages arising out of any operations of said States or persons pursuant to State authority upon or within said lands and navigable waters; and (3) the Secretary of the Interior or the Secretary of the Navy or the Treasurer of the United States shall pay to the respective States or their grantees issuing leases covering such lands or natural resources all moneys paid thereunder to the Secretary of the Interior or to the Secretary of the Navy or to the Treasurer of the United States and subject to the control of any of them or to the control of the United States on May 22, 1953, except that portion of such moneys which (1) is required to be returned to a lessee; or (2) is deductible as provided by stipulation or agreement between the United States and any of said States;

§ 1312. Seaward boundaries of States

The seaward boundary of each original coastal State is approved and confirmed as a line three geographical miles distant from its coast line or, in the case of the Great Lakes, to the international boundary. Any State admitted subsequent to the formation of the Union which has not already done so may extend its seaward boundaries to a line three geographical miles distant from its coast line, or to the international boundaries of the United States in the Great Lakes or any other body of water traversed by such boundaries. Any claim heretofore or hereafter asserted either by constitutional provision, statute, or otherwise, indicating the intent of a State so to extend its boundaries is approved and confirmed, without prejudice to its claim, if any it has, that its boundaries extend beyond that line. Nothing in this section is to be construed as questioning or in any manner prejudicing the existence of any State's seaward boundary beyond three geographical miles if it was so provided by its constitution or laws prior to or at the time such State became a member of the Union, or if it has been heretofore approved by Congress. May 22, 1953, c. 65, Title II, § 4, 67 Stat. 31.

NOTES

1. Section 1301(b) of the Submerged Lands Act sets the seaward boundaries of the states at 3 geographical miles into the Atlantic and Pacific Oceans, and 3 marine leagues into the Gulf of Mexico. The Gulf states extend a greater distance seaward because of documented historical claims. Although of no great legal importance, the general acceptance of 3 miles, or 3 leagues, as the seaward boundary may have sparked your curiosity. Why always the magic number three? The alternative name for the 3-mile rule, the "cannonball" rule, gives a broad hint. The origin of the cannonball rule was discussed in Note, *Right, Title and Interest in the Territorial Sea: Federal and State Claims in the United States,* 4 Ga. J. Int'l & Comp. Law 463 (1974):

   One of the earliest assertions concerning the extent of a nation's control over the sea was made in 1702 by the Dutch judge, Judge Bynkershock, who stated that the best rule is that coastal state jurisdiction over the sea should extend as far as a cannon can fire. Control should extend to where the power of man's weapons end, since weapons are what guarantee possession. By the eighteenth century this test was accepted by both writers and national practices, equating the distance of a "cannon shot" with three nautical miles, or one marine league.

   How did the Gulf states acquire *three* marine leagues?

2. Section 1313 of the Submerged Lands Act led to the third supplemental decree granted in *United States v. California,* 436 U.S. 32 (1978). The last sentence of section 1313(a) exempted from the grant to the states "any rights the United States has in lands presently occupied by the United States under claim of right." The United States claimed dominion over the submerged lands and waters within the Channel Islands National Monument, situated inside the 3-mile marginal sea off the southern California mainland. The United States had maintained and controlled the monument for decades, and claimed that this was "actual occupation" under 1313(a).

   The U.S. Supreme Court held that the United States did *not* have dominion, and that title to the disputed area was in the State of California. The Court noted that the entire purpose of the Submerged Lands Act would have been nullified if the "claim of right" exemption saved claims based solely on paramount rights obtained in the 1947 *United States v. California* decision. Thus, the exception in 1313(a) applies only if the United States' claim rests on some basis other than paramount rights. The United States, in *California IV*, failed to show any other basis of ownership.

What "other basis" might the United States have for claiming ownership within the 3-mile marginal sea?

3. The Submerged Lands Act created a number of boundary problems, the most serious of which was the definition of "inland waters." Coastlines, unfortunately, are rarely straight. Bays, estuaries, and shallow indentions make straight boundary lines impossible. The act, in section 1301(c), mentioned "inland waters" but failed to provide a definition. At issue was whether the 3-mile marginal sea was to be measured from a line following the sinuosities of the coast, or a straight line drawn from headland to headland. The baseline method, following the coast, is illustrated in Figures 4-1 and 4-2.

States with deeply indented coastlines, however, favored the straight baseline method (Figure 4-3).

The United States, in 1963, filed an amended complaint against the State of California and sought a supplemental decree defining "inland waters." The U.S. Supreme Court granted the supplemental decree in *United States v. California* (California II), 381 U.S. 139 (1965).

California, using the straight baseline method, claimed a huge area as inland water, as illustrated in Figure 4-4.

The Supreme Court ruled that by eliminating the definition of inland waters from the bill, Congress intended to leave the meaning of the term to the courts. The Court then held that the definition should conform to the one adopted by the Convention on the Territorial Sea and the Contiguous Zone, an international treaty. The Convention adopted a 24-mile closing line rule for bays and a semicircle test for the sufficiency of water enclosed as the definition of

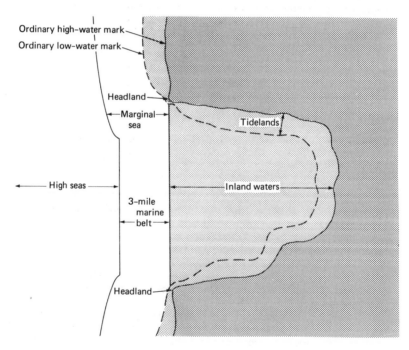

Figure 4-1 Terminology. (From Shalowitz, *Boundary Problems Raised by the Submerged Lands Act*, 54 Colum. L. Rev. 1021 [1954]).

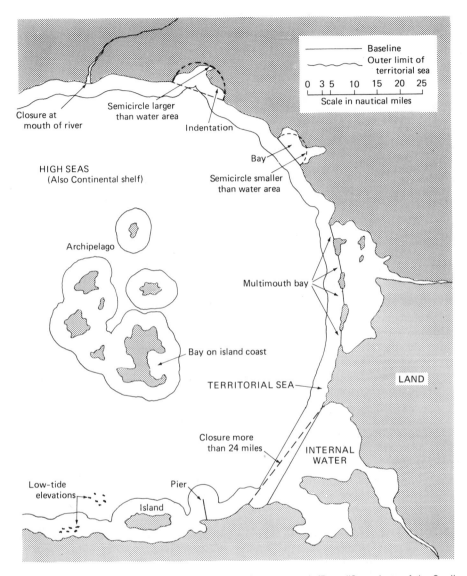

Figure 4-2 The baseline from which the territorial sea is measured. (From "Sovereignty of the Sea," U.S. Department of State Geographic Bulletin No. 3, April, 1965).

inland waters. Professor Shalowitz, in *Boundary Problems Raised by the Sub-merged Lands Act, supra,* at 1031–32, explained the test:

Since bays in nature are seldom exactly circular, recourse is had to the theory of equivalence and the rule adopted that if the area of a bay in nature is greater than the area of the semicircle formed with the distance between the headlands as a diameter, the bay is a closed bay, or intra-territorial, and the seaward boundary of inland waters is a headland-to-headland line. But if the area of the bay is less than the area of the semicircle, the bay is an open bay, or extra-territorial, and the boundary line of inland waters would be the ordinary low-water mark following the

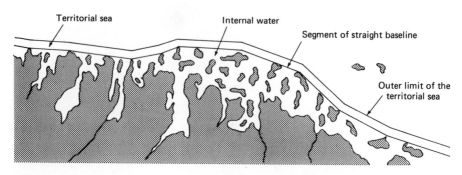

High seas
(Also Continental shelf)

Territorial sea

Internal water

Segment of straight baseline

Outer limit of the
territorial sea

Figure 4-3 The straight baseline along deeply indented coast or one fringed with islands. (From "Sovereignty of the Sea," U.S. Department of State Geographic Bulletin No. 3, April, 1965).

sinuosities of the coast. This is illustrated in Figure 4-5. Curve *A* is a true semicircle whose diameter is the line *DE* joining the two headlands of the indentation. If the shoreline of the indentation whose status is to be determined is curve *B*, it is readily apparent that area *DBE* is greater than area *DAE*. The indentation is therefore a closed bay and would be part of the inland waters of a country. But if the shoreline of the indentation is curve *C*, then area *DCE* is less than area *DAE* and the indentation is an open bay and outside of the inland waters, and the boundary line would be the ordinary low-water mark following the sinuosities of the coast. If the area is exactly equal to the semicircle, the indentation should be regarded as inland waters.

When the Court applied the Convention's test to the California coast it found that only Monterey Bay qualified as inland water. The remainder of the huge expanse of ocean claimed by California, the Court held, was open sea and therefore measured by the baseline method more favorable to the federal government.

5. One last boundary problem remains under the Submerged Lands Act—the problem of ambulatory boundaries. Not only are ocean coastlines irregular, they are subject to change. In *United States v. Louisiana*, 394 U.S. 11 (1969), the U.S. Supreme Court held that if erosion takes place so that the historic boundary is more than 3 marine leagues from the present coastline, the *present* 3-league line becomes the new boundary; in other words, the state loses territory. However, in places where accretion has extended the coastline, the seaward boundary of the state does not expand. The states can lose, but cannot gain, submerged lands through the action of natural forces.

What effect would these shifting territories have on state leases near the boundary line? Would the lessee have to renegotiate his lease with the federal government? See Swan, *Remembering Maine: Offshore Federalism in the United States and Canada*, 6 Calif. West. Int'l L.J. 296, 315 (1976).

Although natural accretions may not help the states, some (but not all) artificial coastline extensions, such as harbors and breakwaters, may. *See United States v. California*, 100 S. Ct. 1994 (1980). For qualifying artificial extensions, the marginal sea is measured from their farthest seaward extent—see the figures above illustrating the baseline method of measurement.

Krueger, in *The Background of the Continental Shelf and the Outer Continental Shelf Lands Act, supra*, at 463, criticized the concept of ambulatory boundaries:

The concept of an ambulatory boundary is a sound one from an international

[handwritten margin note: La. only has 3 miles]

standpoint. If the United States or any other country increases its land mass artificially, there are good reasons, such as national defense, for extending its territorial sea appropriately. It is not, however, a good rule of law with respect to federal-state relationships. It could lead to further federal-state litigation over boundaries and title and may have an inhibiting influence on beneficial coastal developments. It has been recommended that the federal government and the various states adopt appropriate legislation to fix their offshore boundaries.

6. In *Douglas v. Seacoast Products, Inc.,* 431 U.S. 265 (1977), Section B, *infra*, the U.S. Supreme Court defined "ownership" under the Submerged Lands Act. Ownership consists of the right to exploit offshore resources subject to encumbrances previously created by the exercise of the commerce, navigation,

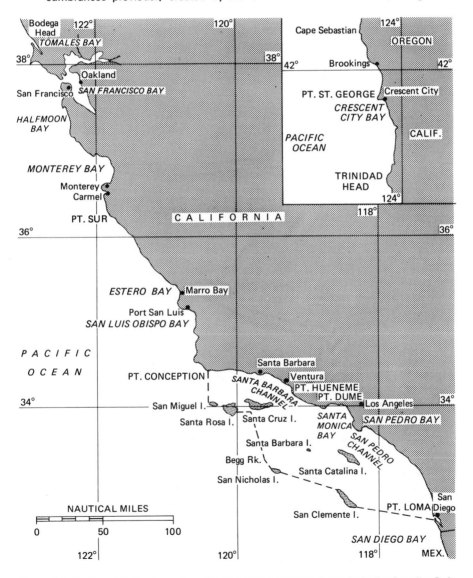

Figure 4-4 Section of California coast considered by Special Master. (From Shalowitz, *Boundary Problems Raised by the Submerged Lands Act,* 54 Colum. L. Rev. 1021, 1025 (1954).)

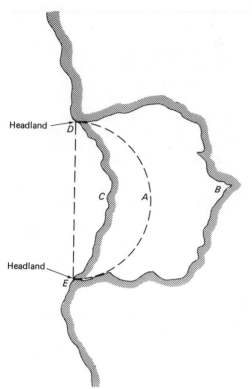

Headland

Headland

Figure 4-5 Alternative baselines. (From Shalowitz, *Boundary Problems Raised by the Submerged Lands Act,* 54 Colum. L. Rev. 1021, 1031–32 [1954]).

national defense, and international affairs powers of the federal government. Justice Rehnquist, dissenting, preferred an alternative reading of the act—that the reservation of powers clause only gives fair warning of the possibility that the government may, at some time in the future and in furtherance of the specifically enumerated powers, find it necessary to intrude upon state ownership and control of coastal submerged lands. *See* Schoenbaum & Parker, *Federalism in the Coastal Zone: Three Models of State Jurisdiction and Control,* 57 N.C. L. Rev. 231 (1979).

In *Zabel v. Tabb*, 430 F.2d 199 (5th Cir. 1970), *cert. denied*, 401 U.S. 910 (1971), the Court held that Congress has the power under the Commerce Clause to regulate submerged lands for conservation purposes, and that it had not given up this power in the Submerged Lands Act. *See* Annot., 25 A.L.R. Fed. 684 (1975).

7. The Submerged Lands Act, unfortunately, raised nearly as many questions as it answered. One of the most important unanswered questions was ownership of lands beyond the marginal sea:

Soon after the enactment of the Submerged Lands Act in 1953, Congress passed the Outer Continental Shelf Lands Act to deal with the submerged lands lying seaward of the 3-mile zone given to the states. This statute broadly states: "It is declared to be the policy of the United States that the subsoil and seabed of the outer Continental Shelf appertain to the United States and are subject to its jurisdiction, control, and power of disposition . . . . " The term "outer Continental Shelf" was defined as all submerged lands under American jurisdiction which lie seaward of the areas granted to the states in the Submerged Lands Act.

The Outer Continental Shelf Lands Act represented an extension of American national sovereignty or, more accurately, a congressional ratification of President Truman's territorial claim to the seabed and resources of the continental shelf. The statute purported to establish both jurisdiction and ownership in the Federal Government. The jurisdiction asserted in the statute was later confirmed by the Geneva Convention on the Continental Shelf, which officially recognized coastal nations' sovereignty over the seabed of the continental shelf in 1958. The Convention granted coastal nations jurisdiction over:

> The seabed and subsoil of the submarine areas adjacent to the coast but outside the area of the territorial sea, to a depth of 200 meters or, beyond that limit, to where the depth of the superjacent waters admits of the exploitation of the natural resources of the said area.

As a result of the Outer Continental Shelf Act and the Geneva Convention, the continental shelf lands, whatever their seaward extent, are now, in a limited sense, territory of the United States. The enormous tracts of submerged land beyond state offshore properties are consequently within national jurisdiction and owned outright by the Federal Government.

Breeden, *Federalism and the Development of Outer Continental Shelf Mineral Resources*,[15] 28 Stan. L. Rev. 1107, 1112–14 (1976).

8. In *United States v. California* and subsequent cases the Supreme Court held in favor of federal paramount rights within 3 geographical miles (or leagues) of the coastline. The basis of these paramount rights was, in large part, national security. Congress subsequently enacted the Submerged Lands Act and the Outer Continental Shelf Lands Act discussed above, the latter asserting federal jurisdiction over the outer continental shelf beyond the 3 miles of seabed returned to the states under the Submerged Lands Act. Why, then, did the 13 Atlantic states in *United States v. Maine*, 420 U.S. 515 (1975), unsuccessfully attempt to claim state ownership of the outer continental shelf? Is not the national security argument even stronger when applied to the outer continental shelf?

   The explanation of the Atlantic states' position is threefold. First, the 13 defendants in *Maine* were the original colonies, and felt they had stronger historical claims to offshore lands. *See* Flaherty, *Virginia and the Marginal Sea: An Example of History in the Law,* 58 Va. L. Rev. 694 (1972). Second, the paramount rights doctrine of *United States v. California* was and is suspect. Justice Frankfurter, in his *California* dissent, accused the majority of confusing the concepts of *dominium* and *imperium. Dominium* concerns ownership; *imperium* is the superior right of the federal government to act as sovereign in international affairs. *See* Note, *States' Rights in the Outer Continental Shelf Denied by the United States Supreme Court,* 30 U. Miami L. Rev. 203, 210 (1975). Third, the Submerged Lands Act was ambiguous on the question of more expansive state ownership based on historic claims. *See* Submerged Lands Act, 43 U.S.C. § 1312 (1976).

   The Submerged Lands Act was ambiguous not only in specific sections, but as a whole. The situation after passage of the act was reviewed in Note, *Right, Title and Interest in the Territorial Sea: Federal and State Claims in the United States*, 4 Ga. J. Int'l & Comp. Law 463, 469 (1974):

Both federal and state interests found support for their positions in the Act. States asserted that this Act was a congressional recognition that broad rights to these lands and waters had always existed in the states and that upon each states' entry into the Union the federal government had relinquished these broad rights to the states rather than retaining them in the federal government. The federal theory

[15]Copyright 1976 by the Board of Trustees of the Leland Stanford Junior University.

maintained that this Act merely granted limited authority over these lands back to the states, leaving most aspects of authority still vested in the hands of the federal government.

For additional reading, *see* Henri, *The Atlantic States' Claim to Offshore Oil Rights: U.S. v. Maine,* 2 Envt'l Affairs 827 (1973); Lewis, *A Capsule History and the Present Status of the Tidelands Controversy,* 3 Nat. Res. Law. 620 (1970); Swan, *Remembering Maine: Offshore Federalism in the United States and Canada,* 6 Cal. W. Int'l L.J. 296 (Spr. 1976); 1 *Water & Water Rights,* § 36.2(A)–37, 188–202 (R.E. Clark ed. 1967).

KRUEGER, "THE BACKGROUND OF THE CONTINENTAL SHELF AND THE OUTER CONTINENTAL SHELF LANDS ACT," 10 Natural Resources Journal 442, 445 (1970)

With due regard to the highly irregular coastline in portions of the Atlantic Coast . . . and in Alaska, a critical issue when these areas are under consideration will be what constitutes "inland waters" or bays. Even if standards set forth in the Convention on the Territorial Sea and Contiguous Zone are not met, an area may nevertheless be subject to claim by the coastal state if historically it was treated as inland waters or the United States applied a "straight baseline" form of measurement to it in determining its territorial sea. The convention makes an exception with respect to "historic" bays and the treatment of these areas by the United States and others of the community of nations would be relevant. In this regard it is clear that activities of the coastal states are to be considered as part of the treatment by the United States.

UNITED STATES v. ALASKA, 422 U.S. 184 (1975)

Mr. Justice Blackmun delivered the opinion of the Court.

The issue here is whether the body of water known as Cook Inlet is a historic bay.[16] The inlet extends northeastward well over 150 miles into the Alaskan land mass, with Kenai Peninsula to the southeast and the Chigmit Mountains to the northwest. The city of Anchorage is near the head of the inlet. The upper, or inner portion, of the inlet is not in dispute, for that part is conceded to be inland waters subject to Alaska's sovereignty.

If the inlet is an historic bay, the State of Alaska possesses sovereignty over the land beneath the waters of the lower, or seaward, portion of the inlet. If the inlet is not a historic bay, the United States, as against the State, has paramount rights to the subsurface lands in question.

I

In early 1967 the State of Alaska offered 2,500 acres of submerged lands in lower Cook Inlet for a competitive oil and gas lease sale. The tract in

---

[16]Cook Inlet is larger than Great Salt Lake and Lake Ontario. It is about the same size as Lake Erie. It dwarfs Chesapeake Bay, Delaware Bay, and Long Island Sound, all of which the United States has claimed as historic bays.

question is more than three geographical miles from the shore of the inlet and is seaward more than three miles from a line across the inlet at Kalgin Island, where the headlands are about 24 miles apart, as contrasted with 47 miles at the natural entrance at Cape Douglas. In the view of the United States, the Kalgin Island line marks the limit of the portion of the inlet that qualifies as inland waters. The United States, contending that the lower inlet constitutes high seas, brought suit in the United States District Court for the District of Alaska to quiet title and for injunctive relief against the State.[17] Alaska defended on the ground that the inlet, in its entirety, was within the accepted definition of a "historic bay" and thus constituted inland waters properly subject to state sovereignty. Alaska prevailed in the District Court. 352 F Supp 815 (1972). The United States Court of Appeals for the Ninth Circuit affirmed with a per curiam opinion. 497 F2d 1155 (1974). We granted certiorari because of the importance of the litigation and because the case presented a substantial question concerning the proof necessary to establish a body of water as a historic bay. 419 US 1045, 42 L Ed 2d 639, 95 S Ct 616 (1974).

II

State sovereignty over submerged lands rests on the Submerged Lands Act, 67 Stat 29 (1953), 43 USC §§ 1301–1315 [43 USCS §§ 1301–1315]. By this Act, Congress effectively confirmed to the States the ownership of submerged lands within three miles of their coastlines. See United States v Maine, 420 US 515, 43 L Ed 2d 363, 95 S Ct 1155 (1975). "Coast line" was defined in terms not only of land but, as well, of "the seaward limit of inland waters." The term "inland waters" was left undefined.

In United States v California, 381 US 139, 161–167, 14 L Ed 2d 296, 85 S Ct 1401 (1965), the Court concluded that the definitions provided in the Convention on the Territorial Sea and the Contiguous Zone, [1964] 2 UST 1606, TTAS No. 5639, should be adopted for purposes of the Submerged Lands Act. See also United States v Louisiana (Louisiana Boundary Case), 394 US 11, 35, 22 L Ed 2d 44, 89 S Ct 773 (1969). Under Art 7 of the Convention, and particularly ¶¶ 5 and 6 thereof, a bay with natural entrance points separated by more than 24 miles is considered as inland water only if it is a "historic" bay. Since the distance between the natural entrance points to Cook Inlet is greatly in excess of 24 miles, the parties agree that Alaska must demonstrate that the inlet is a historic bay in order successfully to claim sovereignty over its lower waters and the land beneath those waters.

The term "historic bay" is not defined in the Convention. The Court, however, has stated that in order to establish that a body of water is a historic bay, a coastal nation must have "traditionally asserted and maintained dominion with the acquiescence of foreign nations." United States v California, 381 US, at

---

[17]It would appear that the case qualifies, under Art III, § 2, cl 2, of the Constitution, for our original jurisdiction. United States v West Virginia, 295 US 463, 470, 79 L Ed 1546, 55 S Ct 789 (1935). We are not enlightened as to why the United States chose not to bring an original action in this Court.

172, 14 L Ed 2d 296, 85 S Ct 1401. Furthermore, the Court appears to have accepted the general view that at least three factors are significant in the determination of historic bay status: (1) the claiming nation must have exercised authority over the area; (2) that exercise must have been continuous; and (3) foreign states must have acquiesced in the exercise of authority. Louisiana Boundary Case, 394 US, at 75, 22 L Ed 2d 44, 89 S Ct 773 and 23–24, n 27, 22 L Ed 2d 44, 89 S Ct 773. These were the general guidelines for the District Court and for the Court of Appeals in the present case.

III

The District Court divided its findings on the exercise of authority over lower Cook Inlet into three time periods, namely, that of Russian sovereignty, that of United States sovereignty, and that of Alaskan statehood. We discuss these in turn.

[Sections A and B discussing Soviet and U.S. acts of sovereignty have been omitted.]

C

The District Court stressed two facts as evidence that Alaska had exercised sovereignty over all the waters of Cook Inlet in the recent period of Alaska statehood. First, the court found that since statehood Alaska had enforced fishing regulations in basically the same fashion as had the United States during the territorial period. Second, the court found that in 1962 Alaska had arrested two vessels of a Japanese fishing fleet in the Shelikof Strait. Since we have concluded that the general enforcement of fishing regulations by the United States in the territorial period was insufficient to demonstrate sovereignty over Cook Inlet as inland waters, we also must conclude that Alaska's following the same basic pattern of enforcement is insufficient to give rise to the historic title now claimed. The Shelikof Strait incident, however, deserves scrutiny because the seizure of a foreign vessel more than three miles from shore manifests an assertion of sovereignty to exclude foreign vessels altogether.

The facts of the incident, for the most part, are undisputed. In early 1962 a private commercial fishing enterprise in Japan, Eastern Pacific Fisheries Company, publicly announced its intention to send a fishing fleet into the waters of Cook Inlet and the Shelikof Strait. Alaska officials learned of the plan through newspaper accounts and requested action by the Federal Government to prevent entry of the fleet into the inlet and the strait. The Federal Government, although thus forewarned of the intrusion, significantly took no action. In March 1962, the mothership Banshu Maru 31 and five other vessels arrived at the Kodiak fishing grounds. On April 5, the six vessels sailed north of the Barren Islands into the lower portion of Cook Inlet. The vessels left the inlet the next day without incident and sailed southwest into the Shelikof Strait. The vessels fished in the strait for approximately 10 days undisturbed. Then, on April 15, Alaska law enforcement officials boarded two of the vessels in the Shelikof Strait. At the time, at least one of the ships was more than three miles from shore. The officials arrested three of the fleet's captains and charged them with violating the state fishing regulations applicable to the strait. On April 19, Eastern Pacific Fisheries Company and the State of Alaska entered into an agreement whereby the State released the company's employees and ships in return for a promise from the company that it would not fish in the inlet or in the strait pending judicial resolution of the State's jurisdiction to enforce fishing regulations therein. 2 App 1186–1188. The Japanese Government did not participate in, or approve of, the agreement between the company and Alaska. Instead, shortly after the agreement was executed, Japan formally protested to the United States Government. Our Government declined to take an official position on the matter pending completion of the judicial proceedings. Ultimately, the judicial proceedings were dismissed without reaching any conclusion on the extent of Alaskan jurisdiction over the strait. The Federal Government took no formal position on the issue after the dismissal of the proceedings.

To the extent that the Shelikof Strait incident reveals a determination on the part of Alaska to exclude all foreign vessels, it must be viewed, to be sure, as an exercise of authority over the waters in question as inland waters. Nevertheless, for several reasons, we find the incident inadequate to establish historic title to Cook Inlet as inland waters. First, the incident was an exercise of sovereignty, if at all, only over the waters of Shelikof Strait. The vessels were boarded in the strait, some 75 miles southwest from the nearest portion of the inlet. Although Alaska officials knew of the fleet's earlier entry into Cook Inlet, no action was taken to force the vessels to leave the inlet, and no charges were filed for the intrusion into those waters. Second, even if the events in Shelikof Strait could constitute an assertion of authority over the waters of Cook Inlet as well as those of the strait, we are not satisfied that the exercise of authority was sufficiently unambiguous to serve as the basis of historic title to inland waters. The adequacy of a claim to historic title, even in a dispute between a State and the United States, is measured primarily as an international, rather than a purely domestic, claim. See United States v California, 381 US, at 168, 14 L Ed 2d 296, 85 S Ct 1401; Louisiana Boundary Case, 394 US, at 77, 22 L Ed 2d 44, 89 S Ct 773. Viewed from the standpoint of the Japanese Government, the import of the incident in the strait is far from clear. Alaska clearly claimed the waters in question as inland waters, but the United States neither supported nor disclaimed the State's position. Given the ambiguity of the Federal Government's position, we cannot agree that the assertion of sovereignty possessed the clarity essential to a claim of historic title over inland waters. Finally, regardless of how one views the Shelikof Strait incident, it is impossible to conclude that the exercise of sovereignty was acquiesced in by the Japanese Government. Japan immediately protested the incident and has never acceded to the position taken by Alaska. Admittedly, the Eastern Pacific Fisheries Company formally and tentatively agreed to respect the jurisdiction claimed by Alaska but, as we have already noted, the acts of a private citizen cannot be considered representative of a government's position in the absence of some official license or other governmental authority.

In sum, we hold that the District Court's conclusion that Cook Inlet is a historic bay was based on an erroneous assessment of the legal significance of the facts it had found.[18] The judgment of the Court of Appeals, accordingly, is reversed and the case is remanded for further proceedings consistent with this opinion.

It is so ordered.

Mr. Justice Douglas took no part in the consideration or decision of this case.

Mr. Justice Stewart and Mr. Justice Rehnquist would affirm the judgment, believing that the findings of fact made by the District Court and adopted by the Court of Appeals were not clearly erroneous, and that both of those courts applied the correct legal criteria in ruling that Cook Inlet is a historic bay.

NOTES

1. In *United States v. Louisiana,* 394 U.S. 11, 89 S. Ct. 773, 22 L. Ed. 2d 44 (1969), the Supreme Court defined the prerequisites for a claim of historic bay status. These were:

   (a) The exercise of authority over the area by the state claiming the historical right
   (b) The continuity of this exercise of authority
   (c) The attitude of foreign states

   Which of these criteria did Alaska fail to meet in its claim of historic bay status for Cook Inlet?

2. In determining that the various federal assertions of fisheries jurisdiction in the Lower Cook Inlet were insufficient to establish a claim of exclusive dominion, the Court stated: "The assertion of national jurisdiction over coastal waters for purposes of fisheries management frequently differs in geographic extent from the boundaries claimed as inland or even territorial waters. *See, e.g.*, Presidential Proclamation No. 2668, 59 Stat. 885 (1945)." 442 U.S. at 198–99. On what possible basis in prestatehood international law—indeed in pre-1945 international law—could the federal government have asserted exclusive fisheries jurisdiction over the waters of Lower Cook Inlet beyond 3 miles from shore?

3. On the subject of bays, *see* Bouchez, *The Regime of Bays in International Law* (1964); Note, *International Law and the Delimitation of Bays,* 49 N.C. L. Rev. 943 (1971); Note, *Law of the Sea–Submerged Lands Act–A State Must Exercise Substantial, Continuous, and Recognized Authority to Establish a Body of Water as a Historic Bay,* 6 Ga. J. Int'l & Comp. L. 309 (1976); M. McDougal & W. Burke, *The Public Order of the Oceans* 358–68 (1962); 1 Shalowitz, *Shore and Sea Boundaries* 128–25 (1962); Strohl, *The International Law of Bays* (1963); Walz, *The United States Supreme Court and Article VII of the 1958 Convention on the Territorial Sea and Contiguous Zone,* 11 U.S.F. L. Rev. (1976).

[18]The United States has argued that historic title to Cook Inlet is defeated by several United States disclaimers of sovereignty over the waters of lower Cook Inlet. The Court previously has discussed the importance of governmental disclaimers in weighing claims to historic title in actions of this kind. Louisiana Boundary Case, 394 US, at 76–78, 22 L Ed 2d 44, 89 S Ct 773; United States v California, 381 US 139, 175, 14 L Ed 2d 296, 85 S Ct 1401 (1965). The District Court rejected the disclaimers on the grounds that they were ill-advised and, perhaps, self-serving. 352 F Supp, at 818–819. Inasmuch as we have concluded that none of the facts relied upon by the District Court suffice to establish historic title, we have no occasion to consider whether the disclaimers of the United States could have defeated otherwise sufficient facts.

4. With regard to nonpetroleum continental shelf resources, *see Treasure Salvors, Inc. v. Unidentified Wrecked and Abandoned Sailing Vessel,* 569 F.2d 330 (5th Cir. 1978) (rights to treasure salvage); *United States v. Alexander,* 602 F.2d 1228 (5th Cir. 1979) (defendant acquitted of committing criminal damage to a viable coral community); *United States v. Ray,* 423 F.2d 16 (5th Cir. 1970) (federal permit required for private construction of artificial island on submerged coral reefs 4½ miles off the Florida coast).

SECTION B: FISHERIES MANAGEMENT

DOUGLAS v. SEACOAST PRODUCTS, 431 U.S. 265 (1977)

Mr. Justice Marshall delivered the opinion of the Court.

The issue in this cast is the validity of two Virginia statutes that limit the right of nonresidents and aliens to catch fish in the territorial waters of the Commonwealth.

I

Persons or corporations wishing to fish commercially in Virginia must obtain licenses. Section 28.1–81.1 of the Virginia Code (§81.1) (Supp. 1976), enacted in 1975, limits the issuance of commercial fishing licenses to United States citizens. Under this law, participants in any licensed partnership, firm, or association must be citizens. A fishing business organized in corporate form may be licensed only if it is chartered in this country; American citizens own and control at least 75% of its stock; and its president, board chairman, and controlling board majority are citizens.

Section 28.1–60 of the Virginia Code (§ 60) (Supp. 1976) governs licensing of nonresidents of Virginia to fish for menhaden, an inedible but commercially valuable species of fin fish. Section 60 allows nonresidents who meet the citizenship requirements of § 81.1 to obtain licenses to fish for menhaden in the three-mile-wide belt of Virginia's territorial sea off the Commonwealth's eastern coastline. At the same time, however, § 60 prohibits nonresidents from catching menhaden in the Virginia portion of Chesapeake Bay.

Appellee Seacoast Products, Inc., is one of three companies that dominate the menhaden industry. . . . Seacoast was founded in New Jersey in 1911 and maintains its principal offices in that State; it is incorporated in Delaware and qualified to do business in Virginia. . . . In 1973, the family of Seacoast's founder sold the business to Hanson Trust, Ltd., a United Kingdom company almost entirely owned by alien stockholders. Seacoast continued its operations unchanged after the sale. All of its officers, directors, boat captains, and crews are American citizens, as are over 95% of its plant employees.

At the time of its sale, Seacoast's fishing vessels were enrolled and licensed American-flag ships. See *infra,* at 272–274. Under 46 U.S.C. §§ 808, 835, the transfer of these vessels to a foreign-controlled corporation required the approval of the Department of Commerce. This was granted unconditionally over the opposition of Seacoast's competitors after a full public hearing that considered the effect of the transfer on fish conservation and management, on American workers and consumers, and on competition and other social and economic concerns. See 38 Fed. Reg. 29239–29240 (1973); 39 Fed. Reg. 7819, 33812–33813 (1974); App. 29–32. Following this approval, appellees' fishing vessels were re-enrolled and relicensed pursuant to 46 U.S.C. §§ 251–252, 263. They remain subject to all United States laws governing maritime commerce.

In past decades, although not recently, Seacoast had operated processing plants in Virginia and was thereby entitled to fish in Chesapeake Bay as a resident. Tr. of Oral Arg. 28–29, 34. More recently, Seacoast obtained nonresident menhaden licenses as restricted by § 60 to waters outside Chesapeake Bay. In 1975, however, § 81.1 was passed by the Virginia Legislature, c. 338, 1975 Va. Acts, and appellant James E. Douglas, Jr., the Commissioner of Marine Resources for Virginia, denied appellees' license applications on the basis of the new law. Seacoast and its subsidiaries were thereby completely excluded from the Virginia menhaden fishery.

Appellees accordingly filed a complaint in the District Court for the Eastern District of Virginia, seeking to have §§ 60 and 81.1 declared unconstitutional and their enforcement enjoined. A three-judge court was convened and it struck down both statutes. It held that the citizenship requirement of § 81.1 was pre-empted by the Bartlett Act, 16 U. S. C. § 1081 *et seq.,* and that the residency restriction of § 60 violated the Equal Protection Clause of the Fourteenth Amendment. We noted probable jurisdiction of the Commissioner's appeal, 425 U.S. 949 (1976), and we affirm.

II

Seacoast advances a number of theories to support affirmance of the judgment below. See *Fusari v. Steinberg,* 419 U.S. 379, 387 n. 13 (1975); *Dandridge v. Williams,* 397 U.S. 471, 475 n. 6 (1970). Among these is the claim that the Virginia statutes are pre-empted by federal enrollment and licensing laws for fishing vessels. The United States has filed a brief as *amicus curiae* supporting this contention. Although the claim is basically constitutional in nature, deriving its force from the operation of the Supremacy Clause, Art. VI, cl. 2, it is treated as "statutory" for purposes of our practice of deciding statutory claims first to avoid unnecessary constitutional adjudications. See *Hagans v. Lavine,* 415 U.S. 528, 549 (1974). Since we decide the case on this ground, we do not reach the constitutional issues raised by the parties.

The well-known principles of pre-emption have been rehearsed only recently in our decisions. See, *e. g., Jones v. Rath Packing Co.,* 430 U.S. 519, 525–526 (1977); *De Canas v. Bica,* 424 U.S. 351 (1976). No purpose would be served by repeating them here. It is enough to note that we deal in this case with federal legislation arguably superseding state law in a "field which . . . has been traditionally occupied by the States." *Jones v. Rath Packing Co., supra,* at 525. Preemption accordingly will be found only if " 'that was the clear and manifest purpose of Congress.' *Rice v. Santa Fe Elevator Corp.,* 331 U.S. 218, 230 (1947)." *Ibid.* We turn our focus, then, to the congressional intent embodied in the enrollment and licensing laws.

A

The basic form for the comprehensive federal regulation of trading and fishing vessels was established in the earliest days of the Nation and has changed little since. Ships engaged in trade with foreign lands are "registered," a documentation procedure set up by the Second Congress in the Act of Dec. 31, 1792, 1 Stat. 287, and now codified in 46 U. S. C., c. 2. "The purpose of a register is to declare the nationality of a vessel . . . and to enable her to assert that nationality wherever found." *The Mohawk,* 3 Wall. 566, 571 (1866); *Anderson v. Pacific Coast S. S. Co.,* 225 U.S. 187, 199 (1912). Vessels engaged in domestic or coastwise trade or used for fishing are "enrolled" under procedures established by the Enrollment and Licensing Act of Feb. 18, 1793, 1 Stat. 305, codified in 46 U. S. C., c. 12. "The purpose of an enrollment is to evidence the national character of a vessel . . . and to enable such vessel to procure a . . . license." *The Mohawk, supra; Anderson v. Pacific Coast S. S. Co., supra.*

A "license," in turn, regulates the use to which a vessel may be put and is intended to prevent fraud on the revenue of the United States. See 46 U. S. C. §§ 262, 263, 319, 325; 46 CFR § 67.01–13 (1976). The form of a license is statutorily mandated: "license is hereby granted for the . . . [vessel] to be employed in carrying on the (. . . 'coasting trade,' 'whale fishery,' 'mackerel fishery,' or 'cod fishery,' as the case may be), for one year from the date hereof, and no longer." 46 U. S. C. § 263. The law also provides that properly enrolled and licensed vessels "and no others, shall be deemed vessels of the United States entitled to the privileges of vessels employed in the coasting trade or fisheries." § 251. Appellees' vessels were granted licenses for the "mackerel fishery" after their transfer was approved by the Department of Commerce.

The requirements for enrollment and registration are the same. 46 U. S. C. § 252; *The Mohawk, supra,* at 571–572. Insofar as pertinent here, enrolled and registered vessels must meet identification, measurement, and safety standards, generally must be built in the United States, and must be owned by citizens. An exception to the latter rule permits a corporation having alien stockholders to register or enroll ships if it is organized and chartered under the laws of the United States or of any State, if its president or chief executive officer and the chairman of its board of directors are American citizens, and if no more of its directors than a minority of the number necessary to constitute a quorum are noncitizens. 46 U. S. C. § 11; 46 CFR § 67.03–5 (a) (1976). The Shipping Act, 1916, further limits foreign ownership of American vessels by requiring the Secretary of Commerce to approve any transfer of an American-owned vessel to noncitizens. 46 U. S. C. § 808.

B

Deciphering the intent of Congress is often a difficult task, and to do so with a law the vintage of the Enrollment and Licensing Act verges on the impossible. There is virtually no surviving legislative history for the Act. What we do have, however, is the historic decision of Mr. Chief Justice John Marshall in *Gibbons v. Ogden,* 9 Wheat. 1 (1824), rendered only three decades after passage of the Act. *Gibbons* invalidated a discriminatory state regulation of shipping as applied to vessels federally licensed to engage in the coasting trade. Although its historic importance lies in its general discussion of the commerce power, *Gibbons* also provides substantial illumination on the narrower question of the intended meaning of the Licensing Act.

. . . .

Although *Gibbons* is written in broad language which might suggest that the sweep of the Enrollment and Licensing Act ousts all state regulatory power over federally licensed vessels, neither the facts before the Court nor later interpretations extended that far. *Gibbons* did not involve an absolute ban on steamboats in New York waters. Rather, the monopoly law allowed some steam vessels to ply their trade while excluding others that were federally licensed. The case struck down this discriminatory treatment. Subsequent decisions spelled out the negative implication of *Gibbons*: that States may impose upon federal licensees reasonable, nondiscriminatory conservation and environmental protection measures otherwise within their police power.

For example, in *Smith v. Maryland,* 18 How. 71 (1855), the Court upheld a conservation law which limited the fishing implements that could be used by a federally licensed vessel to take oysters from state waters. The Court held that an "enrolment and license confer no immunity from the operation of valid laws of a State," *id.,* at 74, and that the law was valid because the State "may forbid all such acts as would render the public right [of fishery] less valuable, or destroy it altogether," *id.,* at 75. At the same time, the Court explicitly reserved the question of the validity of a statute discriminating against nonresidents. *Ibid.* To the same effect is the holding in *Manchester v. Massachusetts,* 139 U.S. 240 (1891). There, state law prohibited the use by any person of certain types of fishing tackle in specified areas. Though Manchester was a Rhode Island resident basing a claim on his federal fisheries license, the Court held that the statute

> "was evidently passed for the preservation of the fish, and makes no discrimination in favor of citizens of Massachusetts and against citizens of other States. . . . [T]he statute may well be considered as an impartial and reasonable regulation . . . and the subject is one which a State may well be permitted to regulate within its territory, in the absence of any regulation by the United States. The preservation of fish . . . is for the common benefit; and we are of opinion that the statute is not repugnant to the Constitution and the laws of the United States." *Id.,* at 265.

More recently, the same principle was applied in *Huron Portland Cement Co. v. Detroit,* 362 U. S. 440 (1960), where we held that the city's Smoke Abatement Code was properly applicable to licensed vessels. Relying on earlier cases, we noted that "[t]he mere possession of a federal license . . . does not immunize a ship from the operation of the normal incidents of local police power." *Id.,* at 447. As an "[e]venhanded local regulation to effectuate a legitimate local public interest," *id.,* at 443, the ordinance was valid.

Although it is true that the Court's view in *Gibbons* of the intent of the Second Congress in passing the Enrollment and Licensing Act is considered incorrect by commentators, its provisions have been repeatedly re-enacted in substantially the same form. We can safely assume that Congress was aware of the holding, as well as the criticism, of a case so renowned as *Gibbons*. We have no doubt that Congress has ratified the statutory interpretation of *Gibbons* and its progeny. See *Albemarle Paper Co. v. Moody,* 422 U. S. 405, 414 n. 8 (1975); *Snyder v. Harris,* 394 U. S. 332, 339 (1969); *Francis v. Southern Pacific Co.,* 333 U. S. 445, 449–450 (1948). We consider, then, its impact on the Virginia statutes challenged in this case.

C

The federal licenses granted to Seacoast are, as noted above, identical in pertinent part to Gibbons' licenses except that they cover the "mackerel fishery" rather than the "coasting trade." Appellant contends that because of the difference this case is distinguishable from *Gibbons*. He argues that *Gibbons* upheld only the right of the federal licensee, as an American-flag vessel, to navigate freely in state territorial waters. He urges that Congress could not have intended to grant an additional right to take fish from the waters of an unconsenting State. Appellant points out that the challenged statutes in no way interfere with the navigation of Seacoast's fishing boats. They are free to cross the State's waters in search of fish in jurisdictions where they may lawfully catch them, and they may transport fish through the State's waters with equal impunity.

Appellant's reading of *Gibbons* is too narrow. *Gibbons* emphatically rejects the argument that the license merely establishes the nationality of the vessel. That function is performed by the enrollment. 9 Wheat., at 214. Rather, the license "implies, unequivocally, an authority to licensed vessels to carry on" the activity for which they are licensed. *Id.,* at 212. In *Gibbons*, the "authority . . . to carry on" the licensed activity included not only the right to navigate in, or to travel across, state waters, but also the right to land passengers in New York and thereby provide an economically valuable service. The right to perform that additional act of landing cargo in the State—which gave the license its real value—was part of the grant of the right to engage in the "coasting trade." See *Harman v. Chicago,* 147 U.S. 396, 405 (1893).

The same analysis applies to a license to engage in the mackerel fishery. Concededly, it implies a grant of the right to navigate in state waters. But, like the trading license, it must give something more. It must grant "authority . . . to carry on" the "mackerel *fishery*." And just as *Gibbons* and its progeny found a grant of the right to trade in a State without discrimination, we conclude that appellees have been granted the right to fish in Virginia waters on the same terms as Virginia residents.

Moreover, 46 U. S. C. § 251 states that properly documented vessels "and no others" are "entitled to the privileges of vessels employed in the coasting trade or fisheries." Referring to this section, *Gibbons* held: "[T]hese privileges . . . cannot be enjoyed, unless the trade may be prosecuted. The grant of the privilege . . . convey[s] the right [to carry on the licensed activity] to which the privilege is attached." 9 Wheat., at 213. Thus, under § 251 federal licensees are "entitled" to the same "privileges" of fishery access as a State affords to its residents or citizens.

Finally, our interpretation of the license is reaffirmed by the specific discussion in *Gibbons* of the section granting the license, now 46 U. S. C. § 263. The Court pointed out that "a license to do any particular thing, is a permission or authority to do that thing; and if granted by a person having power to grant it, transfers to the grantee the right to do whatever it purports to authorize. It certainly transfers to him all the right which the grantor can transfer, to do what is within the terms of the license." 9 Wheat., at 213–214. *Gibbons* recognized that the "grantor" was Congress. *Id.,* at 213. Thus *Gibbons* expressly holds that the words used by Congress in the vessel license transfer to the licensee "all the right" which Congress has the power to convey. While appellant may be correct in arguing that at earlier times in our history there was some doubt whether Congress had power under the Commerce Clause to regulate the taking of fish in state waters, there can be no question today that such power exists where there is some effect on interstate commerce. *Perez v. United States,* 402 U. S. 146 (1971); *Heart of Atlanta Motel v. United States,* 379 U. S. 241 (1964); *Wickard v. Filburn,* 317 U. S. 111 (1942). The movement of vessels from one State to another in search of fish, and back again to processing plants, is certainly activity which Congress could conclude affects interstate commerce. Cf. *Toomer v. Witsell,* 334 U. S. 385, 403–406 (1948). Accordingly, we hold that, at the least, when Congress re-enacted the license form in 1936, using language which, according to *Gibbons,* gave licensees "all the right which the grantor can transfer," it necessarily extended the license to cover the taking of fish in state waters, subject to valid state conservation regulations.

D

Application of the foregoing principles to the present case is straightforward. Section 60 prohibits federally licensed vessels owned by nonresidents of Virginia from fishing in the Chesapeake Bay. Licensed ships owned by noncitizens are prevented by § 81.1 from catching fish anywhere in the Commonwealth. On the other hand, Virginia residents are permitted to fish commercially for menhaden subject only to seasonal and other conservation restrictions not at issue here. The challenged statutes thus deny appellees their federally granted right to engage in fishing activities on the same terms as Virginia residents. They violate the "indisputable" precept that "no State may completely exclude federally licensed commerce." *Florida Lime & Avocado Growers v. Paul,* 373 U. S. 132, 142 (1963). They must fall under the Supremacy Clause.

Appellant seeks to escape this conclusion by arguing that the Submerged Lands Act, 67 Stat. 29, 43 U. S. C. §§ 1301–1315, and a number of this Court's decisions recognize that the States have a title or ownership interest in the fish swimming in their territorial waters. It is argued that because the States "own" the fish, they can exclude federal licensees. The contention is of no avail.

The Submerged Lands Act does give the States "title," "ownership," and "the right and power to manage, administer, lease, develop, and use" the lands beneath the oceans and natural resources in the waters within state territorial jurisdiction. 43 U. S. C. § 1311 (a). But when Congress made this grant pursuant to the Property Clause of the Constitution, see *Alabama v. Texas,* 347 U. S. 272 (1954), it expressly retained for the United States "all constitutional powers of regulation and control" over these lands and waters "for purposes of commerce, navigation, national defense, and international affairs." *United States v. Louisiana,* 363 U. S. 1, 10 (1960); see 43 U. S. C. § 1314 (a). Since the grant of the fisheries license is made pursuant to the commerce power, see *supra,* at 281–282; *Wiggins Ferry Co. v. East St. Louis,* 107 U. S. 365, 377 (1883), the Submerged Lands Act did not alter its pre-emptive effect. Certainly Congress did not repeal by implication, in the broad language of the Submerged Lands Act, the Licensing Act requirement of equal treatment for federal licensees.

In any event, "[t]o put the claim of the State upon title is," in Mr. Justice Holmes' words, "to lean upon a slender reed." *Missouri v. Holland,* 252 U. S. 416, 434 (1920). A state does not stand in the same position as the owner of a private game preserve and it is pure fantasy to talk of "owning" wild fish, birds, or animals. Neither the States nor the Federal Government, any more than a hopeful fisherman or hunter, has title to these creatures until they are reduced to possession by skillful capture. *Ibid.; Geer v. Connecticut,* 161 U. S. 519, 539–540 (1896) (Field, J., dissenting). The "ownership" language of cases such as those cited by appellant must be understood as no more than a 19th-century legal fiction expressing "the importance to its people that a State have power to preserve and regulate the exploitation of an important resource." *Toomer v. Witsell,* 334 U. S., at 402; see also *Takahashi v. Fish & Game Comm'n,* 334 U. S. 410, 420–421 (1948). Under modern analysis, the question is simply whether the State has exercised its police power in conformity with the federal laws and Constitution. As we have demonstrated above, Virginia has failed to do so here.

III

Our decision is very much in keeping with sound policy considerations of federalism. The business of commercial fishing must be conducted by peripatetic entrepreneurs moving, like their quarry, without regard for state boundary lines. Menhaden that spawn in the open ocean or in coastal waters of a Southern State may swim into Chesapeake Bay and live there for their first summer, migrate south for the following winter, and appear off the shores of New York or Massachusetts in succeeding years. A number of coastal States have discriminatory fisheries laws, and with all natural resources becoming increasingly scarce and more valuable, more such restrictions would be a likely prospect, as both protective and retaliatory measures. Each State's fishermen eventually might be effectively limited to working in the territorial waters of their residence, or in the federally controlled fishery beyond the three-mile limit. Such proliferation of residency requirements for commercial fishermen would create precisely the sort of Balkanization of interstate commercial activity that the Constitution was intended to prevent. See, *e. g., H. P. Hood & Sons, Inc. v. Du Mond,* 336 U. S. 525, 532–539 (1949); cf. *Allenberg Cotton Co. v. Pittman,* 419 U. S. 20 (1974). We cannot find that Congress intended to allow any such result given the well-known construction of federal vessel licenses in *Gibbons.*

For these reasons, we conclude that §§ 60 and 81.1 are pre-empted by the federal Enrollment and Licensing Act. Insofar as these state laws subject federally licensed vessels owned by nonresidents or aliens to restrictions different from those applicable to Virginia residents and American citizens, they must fall under the Supremacy Clause. As we have noted above, however, reasonable and evenhanded conservation measures, so essential to the preservation of our vital marine sources of food supply, stand unaffected by our decision.

The judgment of the District Court is

Affirmed.

[Mr. Justice Rehnquist filed an opinion omitted here, concurring in the judgment and concurring in part and dissenting in part, in which Mr. Justice Powell joined.]

NOTES

1. *Manchester v. Massachusetts,* 139 U. S. 240 (1891), cited with approval in *Douglas,* upheld enforcement of a Massachusetts statute prohibiting the use of certain types of fishing tackle in Buzzard's Bay against a Rhode Island resident. How can *Douglas* and *Manchester* be reconciled? Manchester statutes applied to both residents and nonresidents.

2. In rejecting the contention that the federal license merely establishes the nationality of the vessel, the Court cites language in the historic case of *Gibbons v. Ogden* that "the license 'implies, unequivocally, an authority to licensed vessels to carry on' the activity for which they are licensed." The Court goes further:

   Accordingly, we hold that, at the least, when Congress re-enacted the license form in 1936, using language which, according to *Gibbons,* gave licensees "all the right which the grantor can transfer," it necessarily extended the license to cover the taking of fish in state waters, subject to valid state conservation regulations.

   431 U. S. at 282. An issue not addressed by the Court was whether this right rose to the level of a property right protected by the fifth amendment prohibition against taking of private property for public use without just compensation. At what point do valid state conservation regulations so hinder or diminish the right to fish so as to constitute a taking? *See* G. Knight & J. Lambert, *Legal Aspects of Limited Entry for Commercial Marine Fisheries* 65–66 (National Marine Fisheries Service, 1975).

3. Another area of potential conflict between state and federal authority is that of Native American fishing rights. These rights have been established primarily by treaty, and the supremacy of federal law here generally seems clear. Controversy has arisen, however, in the allocation of fishing rights where local concerns for conservation and environmental protection have produced statutes restricting access or establishing quotas. At issue is whether these state laws may abrogate or even limit treaty rights. Of course, the initial determination is the nature of the rights themselves. The recent Supreme Court opinion in *Washington v. Fishing Vessel Ass'n,* 443 U. S. 658, 99 S. Ct. 3055, 3066, 3069, 3072, 3080 (1979), is instructive:

   Mr. Justice STEVENS delivered the opinion of the Court.

   To extinguish the last group of conflicting claims to lands lying west of the Cascade Mountains and north of the Columbia River in what is now the State of Washington, the United States entered into a series of treaties with Indian tribes in 1854 and 1855. The Indians relinquished their interest in most of the territory in exchange for monetary payments. In addition, certain relatively small parcels of land were reserved for their exclusive use, and they were afforded other guarantees, including protection of their "right of taking fish, at usual and accustomed grounds and stations . . . in common with all citizens of the Territory."

The principal question presented by this litigation concerns the character of that treaty right to take fish.

. . . .

In sum, it is fair to conclude that when the treaties were negotiated, neither party realized or intended that their agreement would determine whether, and if so how, a resource that had always been thought inexhaustible would be allocated between the native Indians and the incoming settlers when it later became scarce.

Unfortunately, that resource has now become scarce, and the meaning of the Indians' treaty right to take fish has accordingly become critical.

. . . .

The treaties secure a "right of taking fish." The pertinent articles provide:

"The right of taking fish, at all usual and accustomed grounds and stations, is further secured to said Indians, in common with all citizens of the Territory, and of erecting temporary houses for the purpose of curing, together with the privilege of hunting, gathering roots and berries, and pasturing their horses on open and unclaimed lands: *Provided, however,* That they shall not take shell fish from any beds staked or cultivated by citizens."

At the time the treaties were executed there was a great abundance of fish and a relative scarcity of people. No one had any doubt about the Indians' capacity to take as many fish as they might need. Their right to take fish could therefore be adequately protected by guaranteeing them access to usual and accustomed fishing sites which could be—and which for decades after the treaties were signed were— comfortably shared with the incoming settlers.

Because the sparse contemporaneous written materials refer primarily to assuring access to fishing sites "in common with citizens of the Territory," the State of Washington and the commercial fishing associations, having all adopted the Game Department's original position, argue that it was merely access that the negotiators guaranteed. It is equally plausible to conclude, however, that the specific provision for access was intended to secure a greater right—a right to harvest a share of the runs of anadromous fish that at the time the treaties were signed were so plentiful that no one could question the Indians' capacity to take whatever quantity they needed. Indeed, a fair appraisal of the purpose of the treaty negotiations, the language of the treaties, and this Court's prior construction of the treaties, mandates that conclusion.

. . . .

In the more recent litigation over this treaty language between the Puyallup Tribe and the Washington Department of Game, the Court in the context of a dispute over rights to the run of steelhead trout on the Puyallup River reaffirmed both of the holdings that may be drawn from *Winans*—the treaty guarantees the Indians more than simply the "equal opportunity" along with all of the citizens of the State to catch fish, and it in fact assures them some portion of each relevant run. But the three *Puyallup* cases are even more explicit; they clearly establish the principle that neither party to the treaties may rely on the State's regulatory powers or on property law concepts to defeat the other's right to a "fairly apportioned" share of each covered run of harvestable anadromous fish.

. . . .

Whether Game and Fisheries may be ordered actually to promulgate regulations having effect as a matter of state law may well be doubtful. But the District

Court may prescind that problem by assuming direct supervision of the fisheries if state recalcitrance or state-law barriers should be continued. It is therefore absurd to argue as do the fishing associations, both that the state agencies may not be ordered to implement the decree and also that the District Court may not itself issue detailed remedial orders as a substitute for state supervision. The federal court unquestionably has the power to enter the various orders that state official and private parties have chosen to ignore, and even to displace local enforcement of those orders if necessary to remedy the violations of federal law found by the court. *E. g., Hutto v. Finney,* 437 U.S. 678, 98 S.Ct. 2565, 57 L.Ed.2d 522; *Milliken v. Bradley,* 433 U.S. 267, 280–281, 290, 97 S.Ct. 2749, 53 L.Ed.2d 745; *Swann v. Charlotte-Mecklenburg Board of Education,* 402 U.S. 1, 14, 91 S.Ct. 1267, 1275, 28 L.Ed.2d 554.

. . . .

4. The next case involves the converse of the situation where a state has attempted to control nonresident fishing within its territorial waters. The question raised is the extent of state authority over its own citizens, even beyond territorial limits.

SKIRIOTES v. FLORIDA,
313 U.S. 69 (1941)

MR. CHIEF JUSTICE HUGHES delivered the opinion of the Court.

Appellant, Lambiris Skiriotes, was convicted in the county court of Pinellas County, Florida, of the use on March 8, 1938, of diving equipment in the taking of sponges from the Gulf of Mexico off the coast of Florida in violation of a state statute. Compiled General Laws of Florida (1927), § 8087. The conviction was affirmed by the Supreme Court of Florida (144 Fla. 220; 197 So. 736) and the case comes here on appeal.

The case was tried without a jury and the facts were stipulated. The statute, the text of which is set forth in the margin, forbids the use of diving suits, helmets or other apparatus used by deep-sea divers, for the purpose of taking commercial sponges from the Gulf of Mexico, or the Straits of Florida or other waters within the territorial limits of that State.

The charge was that appellant was using the forbidden apparatus "at a point approximately two marine leagues from mean low tide on the West shore line of the State of Florida and within the territorial limits of the County of Pinellas." The state court held that the western boundary of Florida was fixed by the state constitution of 1885 at three marine leagues (nine nautical miles) from the shore; that this was the same boundary which had been defined by the state constitution of 1868 to which the Act of Congress had referred in admitting the State of Florida to representation in Congress. Act of June 25, 1868, 15 Stat. 73. The state court sustained the right of the State to fix its marine boundary with the approval of Congress, and concluded that the statute was valid in its application to appellant's conduct.

By motions to quash the information and in arrest of judgment, appellant contended that the constitution of Florida fixing the boundary of the State and the statute under which he was prosecuted violated the Constitution and treaties of the United States; that the criminal jurisdiction of the courts of Florida could not extend beyond the international boundaries of the United States and hence could not extend "to a greater distance than one marine league from mean low tide" on the mainland of the State and adjacent islands included within its territory.

In support of this contention appellant invoked several provisions of the Constitution of the United States, to wit, Article I, § 10, Clauses 1 and 3, Article II, § 2, Clause 2, Article VI, and the Fourteenth Amendment. Appellant also relied upon numerous treaties of the United States, including the Treaty with Spain of February 22, 1919, and the treaties with several countries, signed between 1924 and 1930, inclusive, for the prevention of smuggling of intoxicating liquors. There were also introduced in evidence diplomatic correspondence and extracts from statements of our Secretaries of State with respect to the limits of the territorial waters of the United States. These contentions were presented to the highest court of the State and were overruled.

The first point of inquiry is with respect to the status of appellant. The stipulation of facts states that appellant "is by trade and occupation a deep-sea diver engaged in sponge fishery, his residence address being at Tarpon Springs, Pinellas County, Florida," and that he "has been engaged in this business for the past several years." Appellant has not asserted or attempted to show that he is not a citizen of the United States, or that he is a citizen of any State other than Florida, or that he is a national of any foreign country. It is also significant that in his brief in this Court, replying to the State's argument that as a citizen of Florida he is not in a position to question the boundaries of the State as defined by its constitution, appellant has not challenged the statement as to his citizenship, while he does contest the legal consequences which the State insists flow from that fact.

It further appears that upon appellant's arrest for violation of the statute, he sued out a writ of *habeas corpus* in the District Court of the United States and was released, but this decision was reversed by the Circuit Court of Appeals. *Cunningham v. Skiriotes*, 101 F. 2d 635. That court thought that the question of the statute's validity should be determined in orderly procedure by the state court subject to appropriate review by this Court, but the court expressed doubt as to the right of the appellant to raise the question, saying: "Skiriotes states he is a citizen of the United States resident in Florida, and therefore is a citizen of Florida. His boat, from which his diving operations were conducted, we may assume was a Florida vessel, carrying Florida law with her, but of course as modified by superior federal law." *Id.*, pp. 636, 637.

In the light of appellant's statements to the federal court, judicially recited, and upon the present record showing his long residence in Florida and the absence of a claim of any other domicile or of any foreign allegiance, we are justified in assuming that he is a citizen of the United States and of Florida. Certainly appellant has not shown himself entitled to any greater rights than those which a citizen of Florida possesses.

In these circumstances, no question of international law, or of the extent of the authority of the United States in its international relations, is presented. International law is a part of our law and as such is the law of all States of the Union (*The Paquete Habana*, 175 U. S. 677, 700), but it is a part of our law for the application of its own principles, and these are concerned with international rights and duties and not with domestic rights and duties. The argument based on the limits of the territorial waters of the United States, as these are described by this Court in *Cunard Steamship Co. v. Mellon,* 262 U. S. 100, 122, and in diplomatic correspondence and statements of the political department of our Government, is thus beside the point. For, aside from the question of the extent of control which the United States may exert in the interest of self-protection over waters near its borders, although beyond its territorial limits, the United States is not debarred by any rule of international law from governing the conduct of its own citizens upon the high seas or even in foreign countries when the rights of other nations or their nationals are not infringed. With respect to such an exercise of authority there is no question of international law, but solely of the purport of the municipal law which establishes the duty of the citizen in relation to his own government. *American Banana Co. v. United Fruit Co.,* 213 U. S. 347, 355, 356; *United States v. Bowman,* 260 U. S. 94; *Cook v. Tait,* 265 U. S. 47; *Blackmer v. United States,* 284 U. S. 421, 437.

. . . .

For the same reason, none of the treaties which appellant cites are applicable to his case. He is not in a position to invoke the rights of other governments or of the nationals of other countries. If a statute similar to the one in question had been enacted by the Congress for the protection of the sponge fishery off the coasts of the United States there would appear to be no ground upon which appellant could challenge its validity.

The question then is whether such an enactment, as applied to those who are subject to the jurisdiction of Florida, is beyond the competency of that State. We have not been referred to any legislation of Congress with which the state statute conflicts. By the Act of August 15, 1914 (38 Stat. 692, 16 U. S. C., § 781), Congress has prohibited "any citizen of the United States, or person owing duty of obedience to the laws of the United States" from taking "in the waters of the Gulf of Mexico or the Straits of Florida outside of state territorial limits" any commercial sponges which are less than a given size, or to possess such sponges or offer them for sale. But that Act is limited to the particular matter of size and does not deal with the divers' apparatus which is the particular subject of the Florida statute. According to familiar principles, Congress having occupied but a limited field, the authority of the State to protect its interests by additional or supplementary legislation otherwise valid is not impaired. *Reid v. Colorado,* 187 U. S. 137, 147, 150; *Savage v. Jones,* 225 U. S. 501, 533; *Mintz v. Baldwin,* 289 U. S. 346, 350; *Kelly v. Washington,* 302 U. S. 1, 10. It is also clear that Florida has an interest in the proper maintenance of the sponge fishery and that the statute so far as applied to conduct within the territorial waters of Florida, in the absence of conflicting federal legislation, is within the police power of the State. *Manchester v. Massachusetts,* 139 U. S. 240, 266. See, also, *Cooley v. Board of Port Wardens,* 12 How. 299; *Morgan's S.S. Co. v. Louisiana,* 118 U. S. 455; *Compagnie Francaise v. Board of Health,* 186 U. S. 380; *Minnesota Rate Cases,* 230 U. S. 352, 402–410; *California v. Thompson, post,* p. 109. Nor is there any repugnance in the provisions of the statute to the equal protection clause of the Fourteenth Amendment. The statute applies equally to all persons within the jurisdiction of the State.

Appellant's attack thus centers in the contention that the State has transcended its power simply because the statute has been applied to his operations inimical to its interests outside the territorial waters of Florida. The State denies this, pointing to its boundaries as defined by the state constitution of 1868, which the State insists had the approval of Congress and in which there has been acquiescence over a long period. See *Lipscomb v. Gialourakis,* 101 Fla. 1130, 1134, 1135; 133 So. 104; *Pope v. Blanton,* 10 F. Supp. 18, 22. Appellant argues that Congress by the Act of June 25, 1868, to which the state court refers, did not specifically accept or approve any boundaries as set up in the state constitution but merely admitted Florida and the other States mentioned to representation in Congress. And, further, that if Congress can be regarded as having approved the boundaries defined by the state constitution, these have been changed by the treaties with foreign countries relating to the smuggling of intoxicating liquors, in which the principle of the three-mile limit was declared.

But putting aside the treaties, which appellant has no standing to invoke, we do not find it necessary to resolve the contentions as to the interpretation and effect of the Act of Congress of 1868. Even if it were assumed that the *locus* of the offense was outside the territorial waters of Florida, it would not follow that the State could not prohibit its own citizens from the use of the described divers' equipment at that place. No question as to the authority of the United States over these waters, or over the sponge fishery, is here involved. No right of a citizen of any other State is here asserted. The question is solely between appellant and his own State. The present case thus differs from that of *Manchester v. Massachusetts, supra,* for there the regulation by Massachusetts of the menhaden fisheries in Buzzards Bay was sought to be enforced as against citizens of Rhode Island *(Id.,* p. 242) and it was in that relation that the question whether Buzzards Bay could be included within the territorial limits of Massachusetts was presented and was decided in favor of that Commonwealth. The question as to the extent of the authority of a State over its own citizens on the high seas was not involved.

If the United States may control the conduct of its citizens upon the high seas, we see no reason why the State of Florida may not likewise govern the conduct of its citizens upon the high seas with respect to matters in which the State has a legitimate interest and where there is no conflict with acts of Congress. Save for the powers committed by the Constitution to the Union, the State of Florida has retained the status of a sovereign. Florida was admitted to the Union "on equal footing with the original States, in all respects whatsoever." And the power given to Congress by § 3 of Article IV of the Constitution to admit new States relates only to such States as are equal to each other "in power, dignity and authority, each competent to exert that residuum of sovereignty not delegated to the United States by the Constitution itself." *Coyle v. Smith,* 221 U. S. 559, 567.

There is nothing novel in the doctrine that a State may exercise its authority over its citizens on the high seas. That doctrine was expounded in the case of *The Hamilton,* 207 U. S. 398.

. . . .

. . . . "[T]he same authority would exist as to citizens domiciled within the State, even when personally on the high seas, and not only could be enforced by the State in case of their return, which their domicil by its very meaning promised, but in proper cases would be recognized in other jurisdictions by the courts of other States." That is, "the bare fact of the parties being outside the territory in a place belonging to no other sovereign would not limit the authority of the State, as accepted by civilized theory." *The Hamilton, supra,* p. 403. When its action does not conflict with federal legislation, the sovereign authority of the State over the conduct of its citizens upon the high seas is analogous to the sovereign authority of the United States over its citizens in like circumstances.

We are not unmindful of the fact that the statutory prohibition refers to the "Gulf of Mexico, or the Straits of Florida or other waters within the territorial limits of the State of Florida." But we are dealing with the question of the validity of the statute as applied to appellant from the standpoint of state power. The State has applied it to appellant at the place of his operations and if the State had power to prohibit the described conduct of its citizen at that place we are not concerned from the standpoint of the Federal Constitution with the ruling of the state court as to the extent of territorial waters. The question before us must be considered in the light of the total power the State possesses *(Castillo v. McConnico,* 168 U. S. 674, 684; *Hebert v. Louisiana,* 272 U. S. 312, 316; *United Gas Co. v. Texas,* 303 U. S. 123, 142), and so considered we find no ground for holding that the action of the State with respect to appellant transcended the limits of that power.

The judgment of the Supreme Court of Florida is

Affirmed.

NOTES

1. By what authority did the Court find that Florida could properly assert jurisdiction beyond its territorial waters? Is it persuasive? Would the result be the same if Skiriotes had been a citizen of another state?

    The supreme court of Alaska addressed this issue in *State v. Bundrant,* 546 P.2d 530 (Alaska, 1976). After holding that the state police power could extend beyond territorial waters in order to protect resources within the state, the court elaborated on which persons could be legally controlled:

    Appellees urge a restrictive reading of *Skiriotes* to limit the extra-territorial control over fisheries solely to residents of the State of Alaska. The effect of such a result is obvious from both a conservation and a practical standpoint.

    If the state has no authority to regulate non-resident fishermen of a migratory fishery species it has no effective authority to regulate the fishery.

    . . . .

    Further, if a state is forced to distinguish between its own citizens and citizens of other states in giving extra-territorial effect to its laws, the state's own citizens can easily frustrate the legitimate objectives of these laws by simply transferring their citizenship to another state.

    . . . .

    In order that there is no confusion with regard to our holding, we reiterate that the difference in status between each offender does not affect Alaska's jurisdiction over him. Whether the appellee was an Alaska resident (as is Vinberg), was arrested within the three-mile limit (as was Bundrant), or was arrested on the high seas in the Bering Sea crab area (as was Uri), the State may proceed to enforce its crab regulations herein against said appellee.

546 P.2d at 554–56. Although the logic of the Alaska court's argument is persuasive, can it be reconciled with the apparent basis for jurisdiction so carefully enunciated in *Skiriotes*? What are the potential problems of allowing a state to assert extraterritorial jurisdiction over nonresidents for activities beyond that state's boundaries? Are there any international implications?

2. One obvious way that more effective management of fish could be achieved is through the cooperation of various adjacent states in whose waters a particular species might be found. This approach is not without its problems, however. In addition to absolutely prohibiting a state from entering into "a treaty, alliance, or confederation," Article I, Section 10 of the U. S. Constitution provides:

No State shall, without the consent of Congress . . . enter into any agreement or compact with another state, or with a foreign power . . . .

Although a number of compacts have been formed and a few have been successful, the constitutional burden and the natural competition between states have rendered interstate agreements ineffective in dealing with the complex problems of fishery management. For a detailed treatment of the legal aspects of fishery compacts, *see* G. Knight and T. Jackson, Legal Impediments to the Use of Interstate Agreements in Coordinated Fisheries Management Programs: States in N.M.F.S. Southeast Region, (Louisiana State University Office of Sea Grant Development, Sept. 28, 1973).

3. There has been a federal fisheries agency of one sort or another for some time. The first was called the Bureau of Fisheries and was in the Department of Commerce. In 1939 the Bureau was transferred to the Department of the Interior and in 1940 renamed the U.S. Fish and Wildlife Service. In 1956 the Fish and Wildlife Service was split in two; part became the Bureau of Commercial Fisheries and part the Bureau of Sport Fisheries and Wildlife.

The federal law concerning sponges mentioned in *Skiriotes* was, until 1976, one of the few entries into fisheries management made by the national government. Other than a series of international agreements, the federal government left fisheries management primarily up to the states. As the domestic and worldwide demand for fish increased, so did pressure on the states to manage a growing and more technologically competent fishing industry. These pressures and a growing interest by foreign fleets in fishing near our shores led to testing of the limits of state jurisdiction and power.

In the early 1960s the fishing pressure by foreign fleets off our shores reached a critical level and the Bureau of Commercial Fisheries finally entered marine fisheries regulation in a big way. Congress passed the Bartlett Act, 16 U.S.C. 1081 *et seq.* (1964), and charged the Bureau of Commercial Fisheries with its implementation. The Bureau's responsibilities expanded with the passage of amendments to the Bartlett Act in 1966, 1968, and 1970. For an analysis of the Bartlett Act, *see* Fidell, *Ten Years Under the Bartlett Act,* 54 Wash. L. Rev. 703 (1974).

In 1970, the Bureau of Commercial Fisheries was transferred back to the Department of Commerce as part of President Nixon's administrative reorganization plan. The Bureau became part of Commerce's new National Oceanic and Atmospheric Administration (NOAA) and was renamed the National Marine Fisheries Service (NMFS).

Neither the Bartlett Act, due to its limited scope, nor the plethora of international agreements, due to their lack of enforcement provisions, could cope with the increasing level of conflict between domestic and foreign fishers over offshore fisheries. The foreign fleets were technologically superior and were far outstripping the domestic fleets harvest on many stocks. The scramble led to serious overfishing by both foreigners and domestic fishers. Without a comprehensive national management program, some states felt compelled to take drastic action, including unprecedented jurisdictional claims.

Maine claimed general state jurisdiction over fishing for a distance of 200 miles from shore. Me. Rev. Stat. Ann. Ch. 1, § Z–A (Supp. 1973). Massachusetts claimed fishing jurisdiction out to 200 miles or the 100 fathom curve, whichever was farther. Mass. Ann. Laws ch. 130, § 17 (1965), as amended (Supp. 1971). Rhode Island made claims similar to Massachusetts. 20 R.I. Gen. Laws ch. 36, § 1 (Supp. 1972). New Hampshire claimed *title* for the state out to 200 nautical miles. N.H. Rev. Stat. Ann. ch. 1, §§ 14–19 (Supp. 1973).

Both houses of the Oregon legislature overrode Governor Tom McCall's veto and enacted the Fisheries Conservation Zone Act, ORS 506.750–.755 (1974), claiming jurisdiction out to sea 50 miles. For an analysis of the constitutional infirmities of Oregon's law, *see* Comment, *Constitutionality of State Fishing Zones in the High Seas: The Oregon Fisheries Conservation Zone,* 55 Or. L. Rev. 141 (1976). For a general commentary on extended state jurisdiction, *see* Comment, *Territorial Jurisdiction–Massachusetts Judicial Extension Act—State Legislature Extends Jurisdiction of State Courts to 200 Miles at Sea,* 5 Vand. J. Transnat'l L. 490 (1972).

4. One common state approach to fisheries management is the use of limited entry programs, which establish the optimal amount of fishing effort to be permitted. Various methods of limited entry include: restrictions on the number of participants, restrictions on the number of vessels, restrictions on gear and the methods used to fish, closed and open seasons, and licensing systems with fees calculated to produce a given number of entrants into the fishery. Determining the optimal amount of effort to be allowed is primarily a scientific and economic question. In recognizing the legitimacy of state fisheries regulation, the federal district court in *Corsa v. Tawes,* 149 F. Supp. 771, 774 (D.C. Md. 1957), stressed concerns for preventing depletion of a particular fishery:

[T]he State may conclude that the time for action is long before the destruction has gone that far. The state is interested not merely in the preservation of specimens for museums but in conserving and perpetuating a constant supply.

Serious constitutional issues are raised, however, in determining the method of allocating entry rights, particularly if a reduction in the amount of fishing effort is required. Unless special provisions are made, this generally necessitates eliminating some individuals or vessels that had previously engaged in the fishery. To avoid the serious legal and social problems associated with limited entry, most schemes include provisions for buy-back programs or include grandfather clauses. Simply put, a grandfather clause ensures that one already established in a fishery may continue until death or revocation or voluntary relinquishment of his or her permit. Ultimately, the number of outstanding permits is reduced to the desired level. Buy-back programs have the same effect but accomplish it by government purchases of outstanding permits and fishing gear. For accounts of these provisions in action, *see* B. Campbell, Limited Entry in the Salmon Fishery: The British Columbia Experience (PASGAP Paper No. 6 (May 1972)), and C. Newton, Experience with Limited Entry in Fisheries: British Columbia, available from the Economics and Statistical Services of the Department of Fisheries and the Environment, 1090 W. Tender St., Vancouver, B.C., Canada. But even these compensatory provisions are not necessarily enough to allow a limited entry program to pass constitutional muster.

In 1973, Alaska passed a comprehensive limited entry statute giving effect to a public referendum amending the state constitution to permit a limited entry program. This was held unconstitutional on equal-protection grounds by the Alaska Supreme Court in *Isakson v. Rickey*, 550 P.2d 359, 365 (Alaska 1976):

Thus the question presented to this court is: does holding a gear license before January 1, 1973, bear a fair and substantial relation to the purpose of the legislation, which is the segregation of hardship and non-hardship cases? In our opinion, it does not.

AS 16.43.260(a) precludes fishermen from applying for an entry permit unless they were gear license holders before January 1, 1973. As a result, many fishermen are automatically excluded from receiving entry permits, even though they might be able to demonstrate significant hardship by exclusion due to economic dependence upon the fishery. On the other hand, there is no requirement that persons applying for permits demonstrate that they were active fishermen dependent upon the fisheries, on or near the cut-off date. Hence, many people are allowed to apply for permits although they have long since sold their vessel and gear, retired from commercial fishing, and have no intention of fishing in the future.

Because persons such as appellants are automatically excluded from the class eligible to apply for permits, in spite of active participation and economic dependence upon the fishery, the January 1, 1973, classification is under-inclusive with respect to persons allowed to apply for permits. Because persons who have long since retired and have no economic dependence upon the fishery as of the cut-off date are allowed to apply for entry permits, the classification is overbroad with respect to those allowed to apply.

In essence, the January 1, 1973, cut-off date created an irrebuttable presumption that no one acquiring a license after that time could suffer the requisite hardship necessary for an entry permit. Yet a number of people in that class would be able to demonstrate substantial indicia of hardship as a result of their exclusion from commercial fishing. Appellants, for example, show both previous participation and objective manifestations of future intent to participate in the industry. Procedure by presumption is always easier than individualized determination. But when, as here, the procedure forecloses the determinative issue of hardship, it needlessly risks running roughshod over the important interests of the fisherman whose livelihood is at stake. This must not be allowed to happen; indeed, the equal protection clause was designed to protect the fragile values of a vulnerable citizenry from the overbearing concern for efficiency and efficacy that is often characterized in the most praiseworthy legislation.

See also *Bozanich v. Reetz*, 297 F. Supp. 300 (D. Alaska 1969), *vacated on procedural grounds sub. nom.; Reetz v. Bozanich*, 397 U.S. 82 (1970); *Dobard v. State*, 233 S.W.2d 435 (1950).

However, the Alaska experience is not typical of the fate of limited entry programs, which have generally been successful in withstanding constitutional attack. See G. Knight & J. Lambert, *Legal Aspects of Limited Entry for Commercial Marine Fisheries* 48 (National Marine Fisheries Service, 1975).

5. For further reading on the subject of limited entry in fisheries, *see* the following sources: A. Adasiak, *Experience with Limited Entry: Alaska,* Alaska Commercial Fisheries Entry Comm., Juneau, Alaska (1977); Cameron, *Constitutional Impediments to Limited Entry Fisheries Legislation,* U. of Rhode Island Marine Affairs Program (1973); F. Christy, *Limited Access Systems Under the Fishery Conservation and Management Act of 1976,* in *Economic Impacts of Extended Fisheries Jurisdiction* (L. Anderson, ed. 1977); Christy & Scott, *The Common Wealth in Ocean Fisheries* (1965); Gordon, *The Economic Theory of a Common Property Resources: The Fishery,* 62 J. Pol. Econ. 124 (1954); Gorelick, *Exploitation of the*

Alaska Salmon Fishery, 3 Ecology L.Q. 391 (1975); Hansen & Jaeger, *A Limited Entry Collage: Some Published Aspects 1974–1975,* N. Pacific Fishing Vessel Owners Assn., Seattle, Wash. (1975); Hardin, *The Tragedy of the Commons,* 162 Science 1243 (1968); *Legal Dimensions of Entry Fishery Management,* 17 William & Mary L. Rev. 757 (1976); *Limited Entry into the Commercial Fisheries,* Inst. for Marine Studies, Univ. of Wash. (Seattle 1975); Smith, *Fishing Success in a Regulated Commons,* 1 Ocean Dev. & Int'l L. 369, 369–81 (1974); Wilson & Gates, *The Pros & Cons of Limited Entry: A Synoptic Discussion Paper,* N.J.F.S. Office of Policy and Development and Long Range Planning, Discussion Paper Series No. 1 (1976).

6. What possible problems might arise in a limited entry program that favored citizens of the particular state? Of U.S. nationality? Of native American ancestry? These questions are addressed in the next case and the notes following.

TOOMER v. WITSELL, 334 U.S. 385 (1948)

Mr. Chief Justice Vinson delivered the opinion of the Court.

This is a suit to enjoin as unconstitutional the enforcement of several South Carolina statutes governing commercial shrimp fishing in the three-mile maritime belt off the coast of that State. Appellants, who initiated the action, are five individual fishermen, all citizens and residents of Georgia, and a non-profit fish dealers' organization incorporated in Florida. Appellees are South Carolina officials charged with enforcement of the statutes.

The three-judge Federal District Court which was convened to hear the case upheld the statutes, denied an injunction and dismissed the suit. On direct appeal from that judgment we noted probable jurisdiction.

The fishery which South Carolina attempts to regulate by the statutes in question is part of a larger shrimp fishery extending from North Carolina to Florida. Most of the shrimp in this area are of a migratory type, swimming south in the late summer and fall and returning northward in the spring. Since there is no federal regulation of the fishery, the four States most intimately concerned have gone their separate ways in devising conservation and other regulatory measures. While action by the States has followed somewhat parallel lines, efforts to secure uniformity throughout the fishery have by and large been fruitless. Because of the integral nature of the fishery, many commercial shrimpers, including the appellants, would like to start trawling off the Carolinas in the summer and then follow the shrimp down the coast to Florida. Each State has been desirous of securing for its residents the opportunity to shrimp in this way, but some have apparently been more concerned with channeling to their own residents the business derived from local waters. Restrictions on non-resident fishing in the marginal sea, and even prohibitions against it, have now invited retaliation to the point that the fishery is effectively partitioned at the state lines; bilateral bargaining on an official level has come to be the only method whereby any one of the States can obtain for its citizens the right to shrimp in waters adjacent to the other States.

. . . .

The statutes appellants challenge relate to shrimping during the open season in the three-mile belt: Section 3300 of the South Carolina Code provides that the waters in that area shall be "a common for the people of the State for the taking of fish." Section 3374 imposes a tax of 1/8¢ a pound on green, or raw, shrimp taken in those waters. Section 3379, as amended in 1947, requires payment of a license fee of $25 for each shrimp boat owned by a resident, and of $2,500 for each one owned by a non-resident. . . .

. . . .

Since the present case evinces no conflict between South Carolina's regulatory scheme and any assertion of federal power, the District Court properly concluded that the State has sufficient interests in the shrimp fishery within three miles of its coast so that it may exercise its police power to protect and regulate that fishery.

It does not follow from the existence of power to regulate, however, that such power need not be exercised within the confines of generally applicable Constitutional limitations. In the view we take, the heart of this case is whether South Carolina's admitted power has been so exercised. We now proceed to various aspects of that problem.

. . . Appellants contend that §3374, which imposes a tax of 1/8¢ a pound on green shrimp taken in the maritime belt, taxes imports and unduly burdens interstate commerce in violation of §§8 and 10 of Art. I of the Constitution. We agree with the court below that there is no merit in this position.

. . . .

. . . Appellants' most vigorous attack is directed at §3379 which, as amended in 1947, requires non-residents of South Carolina to pay license fees one hundred times as great as those which residents must pay. The purpose and effect of this statute, they contend, is not to conserve shrimp, but to exclude non-residents and thereby create a commercial monopoly for South Carolina residents. As such, the statute is said to violate the privileges and immunities clause of Art. IV, §2, of the Constitution and the equal protection clause of the Fourteenth Amendment.

Article IV, §2, so far as is relevant, reads as follows:

"The Citizens of each State shall be entitled to all Privileges and Immunities of Citizens in the several States."

The primary purpose of this clause, like the clauses between which it is located—those relating to full faith and credit and to interstate extradition of fugitives from justice—was to help fuse into one Nation a collection of independent, sovereign States. It was designed to insure to a citizen of State A who ventures into State B the same privileges which the citizens of State B enjoy. For protection of such equality the citizen of State A was not to be restricted to the uncertain remedies afforded by diplomatic processes and official retaliation. "Indeed, without some provision of the kind removing from the citizens of each State the disabilities of alienage in the other States, and giving them equality of privilege with citizens of those States, the Republic would have constituted little more than a league of States; it would not have constituted the Union which now exists."

In line with this underlying purpose, it was long ago decided that one of the privileges which the clause guarantees to citizens of State A is that of doing business in State B on terms of substantial equality with the citizens of that State.

Like many other constitutional provisions, the privileges and immunities clause is not an absolute. It does bar discrimination against citizens of other States where there is no substantial reason for the discrimination beyond the mere fact that they are citizens of other States. But it does not preclude disparity of treatment in the many situations where there are perfectly valid independent reasons for it. Thus the inquiry in each case must be concerned with whether such reasons do exist and whether the degree of discrimination bears a close relation to them. The inquiry must also, of course, be conducted with due regard for the principle that the States should have considerable leeway in analyzing local evils and in prescribing appropriate cures.

With these factors in mind, we turn to a consideration of the constitutionality of §3379.

By that statute South Carolina plainly and frankly discriminates against non-residents, and the record leaves little doubt but what the discrimination is so great that its practical effect is virtually exclusionary. This the appellees do not seriously dispute. Nor do they argue that since the statute is couched in terms of residence it is outside the scope of the privileges and immunities clause, which speaks of citizens. Such an argument, we agree, would be without force in this case.

As justification for the statute, appellees urge that the State's obvious purpose was to conserve its shrimp supply, and they suggest that it was designed to head off an impending threat of excessive trawling. The record casts some doubt on these statements. But in any event, appellees' argument assumes that any means adopted to attain valid objectives necessarily squares with the privileges and immunities clause. It overlooks the purpose of that clause, which, as indicated above, is to outlaw classifications based on the fact of non-citizenship unless there is something to indicate that non-citizens constitute a peculiar source of the evil at which the statute is aimed.

In this connection appellees mention, without further elucidation, the fishing methods used by non-residents, the size of their boats, and the allegedly greater cost of enforcing the laws against them. One statement in the appellees' brief might also be construed to mean that the State's conservation program for shrimp requires expenditure of funds beyond those collected in license fees— funds to which residents and not non-residents contribute. Nothing in the record indicates that non-residents use larger boats or different fishing methods than residents, that the cost of enforcing the laws against them is appreciably greater, or that any substantial amount of the State's general funds is devoted to shrimp conservation. But assuming such were the facts, they would not necessarily support a remedy so drastic as to be a near equivalent of total exclusion. The State is not without power, for example, to restrict the type of equipment used in its fisheries, to graduate license fees according to the size of the boats, or even to charge non-residents a differential which would merely compensate the State for any added enforcement burden they may impose or for any conservation expenditures from taxes which only residents pay. We would be closing our eyes to reality, we believe, if we concluded that there was a reasonable relationship between the danger represented by non-citizens, as a class, and the severe discrimination practiced upon them.

Thus, § 3379 must be held unconstitutional unless commercial shrimp fishing in the maritime belt falls within some unexpressed exception to the privileges and immunities clause.

Appellees strenuously urge that there is such an exception. Their argument runs as follows: Ever since Roman times, animals *ferae naturae*, not having been reduced to individual possession and ownership, have been considered as *res nullius* or part of the "negative community of interests" and hence subject to control by the sovereign or other governmental authority. More recently this thought has been expressed by saying that fish and game are the common property of all citizens of the governmental unit and that the government, as a sort of trustee, exercises this "ownership" for the benefit of its citizens. In the case of fish, it has also been considered that each government "owned" both the beds of its lakes, streams, and tidewaters and the waters themselves; hence it must also "own" the fish within those waters. Each government may, the argument continues, regulate the corpus of the trust in the way best suited to the interests of the beneficial owners, its citizens, and may discriminate as it sees fit against persons lacking any beneficial interest. Finally, it is said that this special property interest, which nations and similar governmental bodies have traditionally had, in this country vested in the colonial governments and passed to the individual States.

Language frequently repeated by this Court appears to lend some support to this analysis. But in only one case, *McCready v. Virginia,* 94 U.S. 391 (1876), has the Court actually upheld State action discriminating against commercial fishing or hunting by citizens of other States where there were advanced no persuasive independent reasons justifying the discrimination. In that case the Court sanctioned a Virginia statute applied so as to prohibit citizens of other States, but not Virginia citizens, from planting oysters in the tidal waters of the Ware River. The right of Virginians in Virginia waters, the Court said, was "a property right, and not a mere privilege or immunity of citizenship." And an analogy was drawn between planting oysters in a river bed and planting corn in state-owned land.

It will be noted that there are at least two factual distinctions between the present case and the *McCready* case. First, the *McCready* case related to fish which would remain in Virginia until removed by man. The present case, on the other hand, deals with free-swimming fish which migrate through the waters of several States and are off the coast of South Carolina only temporarily. Secondly, the *McCready* case involved regulation of fishing in inland waters, whereas the statute now questioned is directed at regulation of shrimping in the marginal sea.

Thus we have, on the one hand, a single precedent which might be taken as reading an exception into the privileges and immunities clause and, on the other, a case which does not fall directly within that exception. Viewed in this light, the question before us comes down to whether the reasons which evoked the exception call for its extension to a case involving the factual distinctions here presented.

However satisfactorily the ownership theory explains the *McCready* case, the very factors which make the present case distinguishable render that theory but a weak prop for the South Carolina statute. That the shrimp are migratory makes apposite Mr. Justice Holmes' statement in *Missouri v. Holland*, 252 U.S. 416, 434 (1920), that "To put the claim of the State upon title is to lean upon a slender reed. Wild birds are not in the possession of anyone; and possession is the beginning of ownership." Indeed, only fifteen years after the *McCready* decision, a unanimous Court indicated that the rule of that case might not apply to free-swimming fish. The fact that it is activity in the three-mile belt which the South Carolina statute regulates is of equal relevance in considering the applicability of the ownership doctrine. While *United States v. California*, 332 U.S. 19 (1947), does not preclude all State regulation of activity in the marginal sea, the case does hold that neither the thirteen original colonies nor their successor States separately acquired "ownership" of the three-mile belt.

The whole ownership theory, in fact, is now generally regarded as but a fiction expressive in legal shorthand of the importance to its people that a State have power to preserve and regulate the exploitation of an important resource. And there is no necessary conflict between that vital policy consideration and the constitutional command that the State exercise that power, like its other powers, so as not to discriminate without reason against citizens of other States.

These considerations lead us to the conclusion that the *McCready* exception to the privileges and immunities clause, if such it be, should not be expanded to cover this case.

Thus we hold that commercial shrimping in the marginal sea, like other common callings, is within the purview of the privileges and immunities clause. And since we have previously concluded that the reasons advanced in support of the statute do not bear a reasonable relationship to the high degree of discrimination practiced upon citizens of other States, it follows that §3379 violates Art. IV, §2, of the Constitution.

. . . .

[Section 3414 (which requires that all boats licensed to trawl for shrimp in South Carolina's waters dock at a State port and unload, pack, and tax stamp their catch before shipping or transporting the shrimp interstate) was determined by the court to be in violation of the commerce clause of Art. I, §8 of the Constitution.]

To sum up, we hold . . . that South Carolina has power, in the absence of a conflicting federal claim, to regulate fishing in the marginal sea; and that in §3374 of the South Carolina Code, though not in §§3379 and 3414, the State has exercised that power in a manner consistent with restraints which the Constitution imposed upon the States. The District Court's judgment refusing equitable relief is affirmed with respect to §3374 and reversed with respect to §§3379 and 3414.

Affirmed in part and reversed in part.

[The concurring opinions of Justices Black, Rutledge, and Frankfurter (in which Jackson, J. joined) are omitted.]

1. The initial hurdle the Court had to clear in *Toomer* was establishing South Carolina jurisdiction over fishing in coastal waters. In *United States v. California,* 332 U.S. 19 (1947), the U.S. Supreme Court decided the United States possessed paramount rights in the "lands, minerals, and other things underlying the Pacific Ocean lying seaward of the ordinary low-water mark on the coast of California . . . . " 332 U.S. at 804. Does the *Toomer* opinion make clear the basis for state fisheries jurisdiction beyond the low-water mark in light of *United States v. California?*

   The question of state jurisdiction, as it was affected by *United States v. California,* was essentially answered by passage of the Submerged Lands Act, 43 U.S.C. 1131–43 (1953). The act, *inter alia,* gave the states title to the lands and natural resources within their seaward boundaries, subject to certain limitations and exceptions discussed in Section B, *infra.*

2. The scope of the Privileges and Immunities Clause of article IV was first addressed in *Corfield v. Coryell,* 6 Fed. Cas. 546, 551–52 (No. 3230) (C.C.E.D. Pa. 1823):

   The inquiry is what are the privileges and immunities of citizens of the several states? We feel no hesitation in confining these expressions to those privileges and immunities which are *fundamental:* which belong of right to the citizens of all free governments, and which have at all times been enjoyed by citizens of the several states which compose this Union.

   Among these "fundamental" rights were included "the right of a citizen of one state to pass through or reside in any other state, for purposes of trade . . . or otherwise; to claim the benefit of habeus corpus; to institute and maintain actions of any kind in the courts of the state; to take, hold, and dispose of property; and to be exempt from higher taxes or impositions than are paid by other citizens of the state." Can fishing be considered such a "fundamental" right or privilege to deserve special protection? What if one's livelihood is dependent upon it?

3. *Toomer* was the first of several so-called "commercial livelihood" cases involving the Privileges and Immunities Clause. In *Mullaney v. Anderson,* 342 U.S. 415 (1952), the Court recognized the right of a state to "charge non-residents a differential which would merely compensate the State for any added enforcement burden they may impose or for any conservation expenditures from taxes which only residents pay." But it held that mere assertions of such justifications were insufficient to uphold a licensing scheme whereby resident commercial fishermen paid a $5 fee while nonresidents paid $50.00. *See also Takahashi v. Fish and Game Commission,* 334 U.S. 410 (1948) (California statute barring issuance of commercial fishing licenses to persons "ineligible for citizenship" struck down as violative of general policy embodied in U.S. law that all persons lawfully in this country shall abide "in any state on an equality of legal privileges with all citizens under non-discriminatory laws" (334 U.S. at 419–20)); *Hicklin v. Orbeck,* 437 U.S. 518 (1978) ("Alaska Hire" statute, requiring employers working on the Alaska pipeline to hire qualified Alaska residents in preference to nonresidents, struck down as violative of the Privileges and Immunities Clause).

4. Where the privilege asserted is less "fundamental" than, for example, the right to pursue a livelihood in a state other than one's own, the Privileges and Immunities Clause may be inapplicable. In *Baldwin v. Montana Fish and Game Comm'n.,* 436 U.S. 371 (1978), at issue was a licensing scheme whereby nonresi-

dents were charged 7½ times more for a Montana fish and game combination license than residents (25 times more if they wished to hunt only elk). The Supreme Court held that access by nonresidents to recreational big-game hunting in Montana is not a right protected by the Privileges and Immunities Clause:

Does the distinction made by Montana between residents and nonresidents in establishing access to elk hunting threaten a basic right in a way that offends the Privileges and Immunities Clause? Merely to ask the question seems to provide the answer. We repeat much of what already has been said above: Elk hunting by nonresidents in Montana is a recreation and a sport. In itself—wholly apart from license fees—it is costly and obviously available only to the wealthy nonresident or to the one so taken with the sport that he sacrifices other values in order to indulge in it and to enjoy what it offers. It is not a means to the nonresident's livelihood. The mastery of the animal and the trophy are the ends that are sought; appellants are not totally excluded from these. The elk supply, which has been entrusted to the care of the State by the people of Montana, is finite and must be carefully tended in order to be preserved.

Appellants' interest in sharing this limited resource on more equal terms with Montana residents simply does not fall within the purview of the Privileges and Immunities Clause. Equality in access to Montana elk is not basic to the maintenance or well-being of the Union. Appellants do not—and cannot—contend that they are deprived of a means of a livelihood by the system or of access to any part of the State to which they may seek to travel. We do not decide the full range of activities that are sufficiently basic to the livelihood of the Nation that the States may not interfere with a nonresident's participation therein without similarly interfering with a resident's participation. Whatever rights or activities may be "fundamental" under the Privileges and Immunities Clause, we are persuaded, and hold, that elk hunting by nonresidents in Montana is not one of them.

(436 U.S. at 388.)

Mr. Justice Brennan, joined by Mr. Justice White and Mr. Justice Marshall, wrote a dissenting opinion in which he analyzed the countervailing approaches to the issue.

I think the time has come to confirm explicitly that which has been implicit in our modern privileges and immunities decisions, namely that an inquiry into whether a given right is "fundamental" has no place in our analysis of whether a State's discrimination against nonresidents—who "are not represented in the [discriminating] State's legislative halls," . . . violates the Clause. Rather, our primary concern is the State's justification for its discrimination. Drawing from the principles announced in *Toomer* and *Mullaney,* a State's discrimination against nonresidents is permissible where (1) the presence or activity of nonresidents is the source or cause of the problem or effect with which the State seeks to deal, and (2) the discrimination practiced against nonresidents bears a substantial relation to the problem they present. Although a State has no burden to prove that its laws are not violative of the Privileges and Immunities Clause, its mere assertion that the discrimination practiced against nonresidents is justified by the peculiar problem nonresidents present will not prevail in the face of a prima facie showing that the discrimination is not supportable on the asserted grounds. This requirement that a State's unequal treatment of nonresidents be reasoned and suitably tailored furthers the federal interest in ensuring that "a norm of comity," . . . prevails throughout the Nation while simultaneously guaranteeing to the States the needed leeway to draw viable distinctions between their citizens and those of other States.

436 U.S. at 402.

5. The cases considered in this section illustrate well judicial concerns with the proper distribution of power between the federal and state governments. Underlying these decisions is the constitutional principle of federalism, embodied in the propositions that the federal government is one of limited, enumerated powers and that all legal authority without its scope is reserved to the states. Federalism values decentralized political decision making; supporters credit it with contributing to democracy and diversity in areas where uniform, national law is unnecessary.

Traditionally, the states have always exercised relatively broad regulatory power over fisheries management, with little federal interference. In marked contrast, the exploration and exploitation of the resources of the continental shelf have been subjected to national control. What are possible reasons for the differences in treatment between fisheries and continental shelf resources? Are the differences based primarily on economic, political, and social considerations or on legal doctrines? Consider the alternatives of national, state, or local control of ocean and coastal resources.

5

Living
Resource
Management

SECTION A: THE FISHERY CONSERVATION
AND MANAGEMENT ACT OF 1976

MAGNUSON, "THE FISHERY CONSERVATION AND
MANAGEMENT ACT OF 1976: FIRST STEP TOWARD IMPROVED
MANAGEMENT OF MARINE FISHERIES,"
52 Washington Law Review 427, 427–433 (1977)

After two years of active debate, the Congress of the United States enacted the Fishery Conservation and Management Act of 1976 (FCMA) to extend national fishery management jurisdiction to 200 nautical miles. During consideration of the bills that proposed this new limit, Congress conducted nearly three weeks of public hearings, involving five separate committees of the House and Senate. Despite strong opposition by the executive branch, led by the Law of the Sea Office of the National Security Council, President Ford signed the legislation into law on April 13, 1976. On March 1, 1977, fishery law enforcement officials began to enforce the provisions of the Act.

. . . .

A short description of the fisheries off the United States coast and the fishing industry is also necessary to permit a fuller understanding of the new legislation. Although the total annual world landings of fish (edible and nonedible) have tripled since 1938, from approximately 50 billion pounds to over 150 billion pounds, United States landings have increased only from 4.3 to 4.7 billion pounds from 1938 to 1973. But the volume of fish caught off the shores of the United States has also tripled—approximately 4.4 billion pounds were harvested in 1948, compared to 11.8 billion pounds in 1973. Because United States vessel landings remained relatively static during this twenty-five year period, the increase is attributable to the efforts of foreign fishing. Foreign vessels take nearly seventy percent of the commercial catch of United States coastal fisheries.

As has been the case with total landings, United States consumption has also increased during this period, although slightly less dramatically. The United States more than doubled its consumption of fish products from approximately 3.1 billion pounds in 1948 to 7 billion pounds in 1973. Yet the importance of these statistics lies in the fact that since the United States catch has remained relatively constant, the difference represents imported fish, much of which has been taken from waters adjacent to the United States. This has had a significant impact on the United States balance-of-trade deficit, not to mention the economic damage to United States fisheries.

The fact that almost seventy percent of the fish caught off the coasts of the United States is taken by foreign fishermen is not in and of itself the most disturbing factor. Rather, it is the fact that foreign fishermen are highly efficient and mobile and can move to other parts of the world if they overfish United States waters. With the use of huge factory vessels and large fleets of smaller fishing boats that deliver their catch to the processing vessels, the foreigners have been virtually vacuuming the seas of precious life and economic value. At the time of the congressional debate, sixteen species of fish were judged by United States scientists to be overfished off our shores. Although not all of the overfishing can be blamed on foreign efforts, the majority can be. If a coastal nation does not take action to protect the fishery resources near its shore, then no one will. And someone must, or the ramifications of such overfishing will have profound impacts on all of mankind and on our citizens whose livelihoods depend on fishing.

. . . .

The United States approach to marine fishery management in the past may be considered haphazard at best. Our federal fishery management legislation resembled a crazy patchwork quilt of pieced-together remnants. Generally its basis was not in resource information, landing statistics, and data, but in weak divided authority and inadequate enforcement among complex jurisdictions. The authorizing legislation itself was merely a collection of single purpose statutes and international agreements loosely coupled through the commonality of fisheries. In reality the states, by virtue of federal inaction and the authority given them by the Submerged Lands Act of 1953, were the only government units with comprehensive fishery management authority.

More than a decade prior to passage of the Submerged Lands Act, the United States Supreme Court in *Skiriotes v. Florida* made clear that a state may regulate activities of its own citizens with respect to a fishery on the high seas when the state has a legitimate interest in the fishery and there is no conflicting federal law. Until enactment of the 1976 Act, the federal government did no more than act as caretaker or custodian of the waters of the contiguous zone and as a research backup to state conservation efforts. At the same time, our international agreements were doing little to help conserve the fishery stocks on the high seas.

It was with this historical background and the realization that the Law of the Sea negotiations were inextricably bogged down in the debate over the future of seabed mining that the 94th Congress took action. Thirty-six bills were introduced for the purpose of conserving and managing fish stocks. These proposals can be classified into the following seven general approaches: (1) Single interim extension of jurisdiction to 200 miles with control over anadromous fish (H.R. 200); (2) extension of jurisdiction to 200 miles, control over anadromous species, regulation by regional councils, and federal support and final approval authority (S. 961); (3) extension of jurisdiction to 200 miles, control over anadromous species, regulation by regional councils, and federal management and enforcement (H.R. 9840); (4) establishment of a fishing zone to conform with article 7 of the Convention on Conservation of the Living Resources of the High Seas (H.R. 1070); (5) extension of fisheries jurisdiction to the edge of the Continental Shelf (H.R. 2173); (6) a fisheries management program regulated by regional councils without extension of jurisdiction (H.R. 8265); and (7) an embargo on fish imports from countries violating the waters of the contiguous zone (H.R. 80). The Fishery Conservation and Management Act of 1976 is an amalgam of several of the approaches suggested by the various bills.

Foreign Fishing

G. KNIGHT, MANAGING THE SEA'S LIVING RESOURCES, 83–85 (1977)[1]

Foreign Fishing and International Fishery Agreements.

Foreign fishing in the zone is prohibited unless it is authorized by an existing fishery treaty or agreement or by a "governing international fishery agreement" (a treaty or an executive agreement) negotiated pursuant to the Act. Each fishing vessel of a nation authorized to fish within the zone must have a valid permit and must fish in accordance with the conditions and restrictions of that permit.

Foreign fishing may continue pursuant to and in accordance with fishery treaties or agreements in effect on March 1, 1977, that have not been renegotiated or that have not otherwise ceased to be in effect with respect to the United States. The Secretary of State has a duty to renegotiate such treaties pertaining to fishing within the conservation zone (or anadromous or continental shelf species beyond such zones) that are in any manner inconsistent with the purposes, policy, or provisions of the Act. Agreements may not be renewed except as set forth in the Act, as described below.

"Governing international fishery agreements" (GIFA) are to be negotiated

---

[1]Reprinted by permission of the publisher (Lexington, Mass: D. C. Heath and Company, Copyright 1977, D. C. Heath and Company).

with any nations desiring access to the exclusive fishery zone (or to anadromous or sedentary species subject to United States jurisdiction) after the effective date of the Act or after the expiration of existing agreements. Permits for individual vessels will only be issued to vessels of nations that are parties to a GIFA with the United States. Such agreements must acknowledge the exclusive fishery management authority of the United States and must include a binding commitment on the part of the foreign nation and its fishing vessels to comply with a wide range of conditions including regulations promulgated by the Secretary of Commerce pursuant to the Act; provisions for boarding, searching, and inspecting the vessels engaged in fishing activities within the zone; compliance with allocations of allowable levels of foreign fishing; and assurances that the nation will take steps under its own law to assure that permit holders comply with applicable conditions and restrictions. Foreign fishing is not, however, to be authorized for vessels of any nation unless that nation satisfies the United States that it extends substantially the same fishing privileges to vessels of the United States as the United States extends to foreign fishing vessels.

GIFA's in the form of executive agreements (i.e., those not submitted to the Senate as treaties for its advice and consent pursuant to the Constitution) are made subject to review and disapproval by the Congress. Each such agreement must be forwarded to the Congress and may not become effective for sixty days after it is so transmitted. Congress may disapprove the agreement by passage of a joint resolution. Presumably Congress could make a GIFA effective prior to the expiration of the sixty-day period by taking affirmative action to that effect in the form of a joint resolution.

The total allowable level of foreign fishing is that portion of the optimum yield of the fishery that will not be harvested by vessels of the United States, as determined in accordance with the management plan in effect. Allocation of the allowable level of foreign fishing is to be made by the Secretary of State, in cooperation with the Secretary of Commerce, taking into consideration: (1) traditional fishing activities; (2) cooperation with the United States in fishery research, enforcement, conservation, and management of fishery resources; and (3) such other matters as the Secretary of State and Secretary of Commerce deem appropriate.

The act contains a "sense of the Congress" provisions that the United States government should not recognize the claim of foreign fishery conservation zones by nations that fail to take into account traditional fishing activities of fishing vessels of the United States, fail to recognize and accept that highly migratory species are to be managed by applicable international fishery agreements (whether or not such nation is a party to any such agreements), or impose on fishing vessels of the United States any conditions or restrictions that are unrelated to fishery conservation and management. This provision was designed to protect the tuna fishing industry by permitting the Fishermen's Protective Act to remain applicable to tunaboat seizures within 200 miles of a nation's coast. The United States could no longer take the position that 200-mile fishing zones were *per se* illegal, since it now claims one of its own. However, by excluding highly migratory species from coverage in the Act, the United States remains in a position to argue that such species are legally managed only by international agreements and may not be subject to the exclusive jurisdiction of a coastal state beyond a 12-mile limit.

Permits for foreign fishing are obtained by application of a foreign nation (with which the United States has entered into a GIFA) to the Secretary of State on an annual basis for each fishing vessel that wishes to engage in fishing within the zone (or for anadromous or continental shelf species beyond the zone). Applications must be stock specific and provide detailed information about the fishing effort to be undertaken as well as the area, season, or period during which the fishing will occur. The application must be published in the Federal Register, with copies provided to the Secretary of Commerce, the appropriate regional management councils, the Secretary of Transportation (for the Coast Guard), the House Committee on Merchant Marine and Fisheries, and the Senate Committees on Commerce and Foreign Relations. Approval of permit application is obtained through a process of consultation among all parties to whom copies are transmitted, and the Secretary of Commerce is authorized to establish the conditions and restrictions to be included in the permit. Disapprovals are to be communicated to foreign nations by the Secretary of State. Reasonable fees are to be paid to the Secretary of Commerce by the owner or operator of vessels to whom a permit is issued pursuant to the Act. Violations of the Act may subject the permit owner to permit revocation or suspension, or imposition of additional conditions and restrictions.

Finally, if a foreign nation (1) does not allow United States vessels access to its fishery conservation zone on the same terms and conditions as foreign vessels are admitted to the United States fishery conservation zone, (2) does not permit United States vessels to engage in fishing for highly migratory species in accordance with applicable international fishery agreements (whether or not such nation is a party to that agreement), (3) does not comply with obligations under existing fishery agreement, or (4) seizes a United States fishing vessel in violation of a treaty or international law, the Secretary of the Treasury is required to prohibit the importation of fish and fish products from the fishery involved and may prohibit the importation of other fish and fish products from the country involved.

NOTES

1. Prior to the FCMA most fisheries agreements with foreign nations were made without congressional participation. Under the FCMA foreign fishing is subject to congressional as well as executive approval. Given the history of failure in federal marine fisheries management, do the FCMA's provisions regarding GIFA's suggest anything about the relationship between the two branches of government with respect to fisheries management? Recall that congressional approval of a GIFA is in the form of nonexercise of the legislative veto. Do those provisions imply distrust by Congress of the executive branch?

2. Despite the ominous warnings of those opposed to the FCMA, the transition to a permit system for foreign fishers in the fishery conservation zone (FCZ) was relatively smooth. By March 1, 1977 (the FCMA's effective date), the Department of State had negotiated GIFA's with 12 nations interested in harvesting fishery resources subject to U.S. jurisdiction. A total of 1,472 fishing permits were

requested, 927 of which were finally issued. Permit requests were disapproved for the following reasons: (a) Requests were for fisheries for which there was no allocation to the requesting nation; (b) requests were for fisheries for which no preliminary management plan (PMP) or fishery management plan (FMP) had been implemented; and (c) requests were withdrawn prior to approval action. A number of permits initially approved were never issued because of the failure of GIFA nations to employ as many vessels as contemplated when applications were submitted. Of the permits issued, about 200 were for processing or support vessels. In 1978 the number of permits declined to about 740, 692 of which were for fishing vessels. This is down from the 1975 level of 2,700 foreign fishing vessels operating in the area of the FCZ. *See* National Oceanic and Atmospheric Administration, Resource Statistics Division, *Fisheries of the United States*, 1978 (Apr. 1979) *and* Hearings on Oversight of the FCMA and S. 3050 Before the Sen. Comm. on Commerce, Science, and Transportation, 95th Cong., 2d Sess. (1978).

3. The foreign catch in the FCZ has also shown a decline.

Year	Catch (million metric tons)
1974	3.1
1975	2.7
1976	2.6
1977	1.7 (out of allocation of 2.1)
1978	1.7 (out of allocation of 1.9)
1979	1.7 (allocation; final catch figures unavailable)

As a result of reduced foreign catches and increased domestic interest in underutilized species, the U.S. share of the total harvest in the FCZ rose from 48 percent in 1976 to 56 percent in 1977 and to 61 percent in 1978. *See* National Oceanic and Atmospheric Administration, Resource Statistics Division, *Fisheries of the United States*, 1978 (Apr. 1979) *and* Hearings on Oversight of the FCMA and S. 3050 Before the Sen. Comm. on Commerce, Science, and Transportation, 95th Cong., 2d Sess. (1978).

Foreign Processing

In 1977, applications were received from foreign fishing companies that proposed to use foreign vessels to purchase, process, and transport fish caught by U.S. fishers.

The major proposals for these "joint ventures" concerned the foreign purchase of pollock from Alaska fishers and hake from lower west coast fishers. Other species considered for joint venture operations included herring, salmon, black cod, and squid. Granting such permits could have (1) resulted in exceeding the optimum yield (OY) since regulations in place contemplated harvest levels without the product outlet provided by joint ventures, (2) decreased the catch available to domestic processors, and (3) expanded market opportunities for U.S. fishers. Because of the potential effects, the joint venture proposals generated considerable controversy and led to extensive public hearings.

. . . .

On August 28, 1978, the Processor Priority Amendment of 1978, Pub. L. No. 95–354, 92 Stat. 519–20, was enacted. The law amended certain sections of the FCMA to give processors an advantage similar to the advantages given catchers with the original FCMA. That is, Pub. L. No. 95–354 gives priority to U.S. processors to receive fish caught by U.S. fishers in the FCZ up to their full capacity and intent to process such fish. Only fish in excess of those which the U.S. industry can and will process can be allocated to foreign processors. *See* 18 U.S.C. § 1824, as amended by Processor Priority Amendment of 1978, Pub. L. No. 95–354 § 4(5)–(8), 92 Stat. 520.

NOTES

1. United States fishers cannot sell their FCZ-caught fish to foreign processors if U.S. processors have "adequate capacity" and intent to process such fish. § 204 (b) (6) (B) (i). Does this give U.S. processors an unfair advantage over fishers? Can domestic processors offer fishers low prices as a result of the elimination of the competitive foreign market?

2. Under the 1978 amendments a number of joint ventures were approved. Despite the safeguards provided by the Processor Priority Amendment, processors found reasons to challenge some of the permits issued to foreign processors. *See*, e.g., *New England Fish Co. et al. v. Kreps*, Civ. No. 79–1196 (D.D.C. dismissed Jan. 3, 1980).

3. During the last days of the 96th Congress several major pieces of fisheries legislation were passed on to President Carter as a single bill (S. 2163) which he signed on December 22, 1980—the last possible day before it would have died as a pocket veto. The legislation known as the American Fisheries Promotion Act, affects foreign fishing in the FCZ in two important ways. First, the legislation requires allocation of the Total Allowable Level of Foreign Fishing (TALFF) to foreign nations based on their beneficial treatment of the U.S. fishing industry, i.e., the reduction of trade barriers for seafood produced here. This part of the legislation should increase opportunities for the domestic industry in the international market—a triumph for the so-called "fish and chips" policy in meting out fishing privileges. Second, a number of provisions are designed to accelerate the phaseout of foreign fishing in the FCZ and the concurrent development of the U.S. industry in those fisheries. The development of the U.S. industry is to be aided by moneys received as a result of increased fees charged to those foreign fishers who remain in the FCZ.

   The legislation contained controversial provisions affecting a wide range of industry concerns, but one provision was generally agreeable to all. Out of respect to the retiring Senator Warren Magnuson (D. Washington), the FCMA was officially renamed the Magnuson Fisheries Conservation and Management Act of 1976.

Regional Council System

FISHERY CONSERVATION AND MANAGEMENT ACT OF 1976, § 302, 16 U.S.C. 1852 (1976), as amended by PROCESSOR PRIORITY AMENDMENT OF 1978, Pub. L. No. 95-354, § 5(1), 92 Stat. 521

Sec. 302. Regional fishery management councils

(a) ESTABLISHMENT.—There shall be established, within 120 days after the date of the enactment of this Act, eight Regional Fishery Management Councils, as follows:

(1) NEW ENGLAND COUNCIL . . . .
(2) MID-ATLANTIC COUNCIL . . . .
(3) SOUTH ATLANTIC COUNCIL . . . .
(4) CARIBBEAN COUNCIL . . . .
(5) GULF COUNCIL . . . .
(6) PACIFIC COUNCIL . . . .
(7) NORTH PACIFIC COUNCIL . . . .
(8) WESTERN PACIFIC COUNCIL . . . .

Each Council shall reflect the expertise and interest of the several constituent States in the ocean area over which such Council is granted authority.

(b) VOTING MEMBERS.—
  (1) The voting members of each Council shall be:
    (A) The principal State official with marine fishery management responsibility and expertise in each constituent State, who is designated as such by the Governor of the State . . . .
    (B) The regional director of the National Marine Fisheries Service for the geographic area concerned, or his designee . . . .
    (C) The members required to be appointed by the Secretary shall be appointed by the Secretary from a list of qualified individuals submitted by the Governor of each applicable constituent State . . . .
  (2) Each voting member appointed to a Council pursuant to paragraph (1)(C) shall serve for a term of 3 years; . . . .

(e) TRANSACTION OF BUSINESS.—

  (1) A majority of the voting members of any Council shall constitute a quorum, but one or more such members designated by the Council may hold hearings. All decisions of any Council shall be by majority vote of the voting members present and voting.
  (2) The voting members of each Council shall select a Chairman for such Council from among the voting members.
  (3) Each Council shall meet in the geographical area concerned at the call of the Chairman or upon the request of a majority of its voting members.
  . . . .
  (2) Each Council shall establish such other advisory panels as are necessary or appropriate to assist it in carrying out its functions under this Act.

(h) FUNCTIONS.—Each Council shall, in accordance with the provisions of this Act—

  (1) prepare and submit to the Secretary a fishery management plan with respect to each fishery within its geographical area of authority and, from time to time, such amendments to each such plan as are necessary;
  (2) prepare comments on any application for foreign fishing . . . .;
  (3) conduct public hearings at appropriate times and in appropriate locations in the geographical area concerned, . . .

(4) submit to the Secretary—

    (A) a report, before February 1 of each year, on the Council's activities during the immediately preceding calendar year,

    (B) such periodic reports as the Council deems appropriate, and

    (C) any other relevant report which may be requested by the Secretary;

. . . .

(6) conduct any other activities which are required by, or provided for in, this Act or which are necessary and appropriate to the foregoing functions.

NOTES

1. Councils must meet in the "geographical area of concern." Does this mean that councils must meet in the region adjacent to that council's fisheries management jurisdiction? The FCMA also encourages councils to work together. Where can two councils legally meet in a joint session?

2. Oregon and Washington are separated from Alaska by many hundreds of miles of Canadian-managed waters. Why does the North Pacific Council have members from those states and the Pacific Council a member from Alaska?

3. What conflicts of interest exist among the members of the regional councils? Consider the following excerpt from Pontecorvo, *Fishery Management and the General Welfare: Implications of the New Structure*, 52 Wash. L. Rev. 641, 650–51 (1977):

In analyzing the structure of these Councils, it is logical to assume that the fishery officer appointed by the governor is primarily concerned with state problems. The set of state problems includes the condition of the resource, and the welfare of the fishermen and the industry within a state. Further, the generation of income by fishermen and the level of unemployment in the industry is of particular importance to a state's political leaders. Because the primary interests and concerns of the states are reasonably apparent, each state's input to the eight Councils may be regarded as roughly similar on many issues. All states will have a similar set of immediate concerns and will act to protect their legitimate interests.

One substantial question raised by the composition of the Councils is whether the federal appointees will identify with state as well as personal interests. To the extent that state and personal interests coincide, they may create, particularly in the North Pacific Council, a state rather than a regional bias. In other Councils where no single state is dominant, there remains the possibility of coalitions among states. These coalitions may create particular advantages for one state's fishermen in the regulations proposed to implement a fishery management plan. Areas subject to coalition agreement might include seasonal opening or closing dates, geographical specification, and most importantly, the kind of "windows" that may be opened to foreign fleets.

What appears to be of consequence in this structure is that the combination of the governors' representatives plus the appointments by the Secretary of Commerce will function in an economic and political environment that will have a bias towards shortrun protection for state interests and local producers. The trade-offs are likely to be between states for different types of shortrun advantages. There does not seem to be any element in this state level mechanism which will force consideration of the general welfare or longrun bioeconomic policy objectives.

See also Note, *Judicial Review of Fishery Management Regulations Under the Fishery Conservation and Management Act of 1976*, 52 Wash. L. Rev. 599, 618–23 (1977) (judicial review of conflicts of interest).

The initial fears of balkanization of fisheries management have, for the most part, not materialized. The councils appear to have handled their responsibilities well. *See* New York Journal of Commerce, Feb. 15, 1978, at 1, col. 4. *See also* Hearings on Oversight of the FCMA and S. 3050 Before the Sen. Comm. on Commerce, Science, and Transportation, 95th Cong., 2d Sess. (1978); U.S. General Accounting Office, Progress and Problems of Fisheries Management Under the Fishery Conservation and Management Act (1979).

Management Plans

FISHERY CONSERVATION AND MANAGEMENT ACT OF 1976, § 301, 16 U.S.C. 1851 (1976)

Sec. 301. National standards for fishery conservation and management

(a) IN GENERAL.—Any fishery management plan prepared, and any regulation promulgated to implement any such plan, pursuant to this title shall be consistent with the following national standards for fishery conservation and management;

(1) Conservation and management measures shall prevent overfishing while achieving, on a continuing basis, the optimum yield from each fishery.

(2) Conservation and management measures shall be based upon the best scientific information available.

(3) To the extent practicable, an individual stock of fish shall be managed as a unit throughout its range, and interrelated stocks of fish shall be managed as a unit or in close coordination.

(4) Conservation and management measures shall not discriminate between residents of different States. If it becomes necessary to allocate or assign fishing privileges among various United States fishermen, such allocation shall be (A) fair and equitable to all such fishermen; (B) reasonably calculated to promote conservation; and (C) carried out in such manner that no particular individual, corporation, or other entity acquires an excessive share of such privileges.

(5) Conservation and management measures shall, where practicable, promote efficiency in the utilization of fishery resources; except that no such measure shall have economic allocation as its sole purpose.

(6) Conservation and management measures shall take into account and allow for variations among, and contingencies in, fisheries, fishery resources, and catches.

(7) Conservation and management measures shall, where practicable, minimize costs and avoid unnecessary duplication.

(b) GUIDELINES.—The Secretary shall establish guidelines, based on the national standards, to assist in the development of fishery management plans.

NOTES

1. It appears that one of the primary goals of the FCMA is to manage each fishery for a harvest level equivalent to the "optimum yield." With reference to the wording of the act, what are "relevant economic, social, or ecological factor(s)"? Is it relevant that some fishers feel they receive greater benefits from freedom from regulations than they would from regulations that would increase their earnings? Is it relevant that achieving the status of "high-liner" (a fisher who catches more fish than other fishers) is an important motivating factor in most fishing communities? How does a management council justify using traditional management techniques that reduce efficiency resulting in higher prices for the consumers of seafood? Is it relevant that some fisheries target on species from the middle of the food chain—i.e., those stocks that are food for other species? What if the species higher on the food chain is not one currently being utilized for human consumption?

2. A pair of goals of the FCMA is to promote commercial and recreational fishing. Are these goals mutually exclusive? How can the regional fishery management councils promote seemingly competing interests? With such vague goals the management councils have a great deal of discretion. It becomes clear that the makeup of the management councils will to a large extent determine the interpretation given to the various goals and guidelines provided by the act and its accompanying regulations.

3. The second national standard requires that management measures be based on the "best scientific information available." Who decides what is such information? What yardsticks should be used to measure how well such information is analyzed? *See* Alverson, *The Role of Conservation and Fishery Science Under the Fishery Conservation and Management Act of 1976*, 52 Wash. L. Rev. 723, 730–33 (1977).

State Jurisdiction

**FISHERY CONSERVATION AND MANAGEMENT ACT OF 1976,
§ 306, 16 U.S.C. 1856 (1976)**

Sec. 306. State jurisdiction

(a) IN GENERAL.—Except as provided in subsection (b), nothing in this Act shall be construed as extending or diminishing the jurisdiction or authority of any State within its boundaries. No State may directly or indirectly regulate any fishing which is engaged in by any fishing vessel outside its boundaries, unless such vessel is registered under the laws of such State.

(b) EXCEPTION.—(1) If the Secretary finds, after notice and an opportunity for a hearing in accordance with section 554 of title 5, United States Code, that—

(A) the fishing in a fishery, which is covered by a fishery management plan implemented under this Act, is engaged in predominately within the fishery conservation zone and beyond such zone; and

(B) any State has taken any action, or omitted to take any action, the results of which will substantially and adversely affect the carrying out of such fishery management plan;

the Secretary shall promptly notify such State and the appropriate Council of such finding and of his intention to regulate the applicable fishery within the boundaries of such State (other than its internal waters), pursuant to such fishery management plan and the regulations promulgated to implement such plan.

(2) If the Secretary, pursuant to this subsection, assumes responsibility for the regulation of any fishery, the State involved may at any time thereafter apply to the Secretary for reinstatement of its authority over such fishery. If the Secretary finds that the reasons for which he assumed such regulation no longer prevail, he shall promptly terminate such regulation.

EXPLANATORY STATEMENT OF THE COMMITTEE OF CONFERENCE H.R. REP. NO. 94-711, 94th CONG., 2d SESS. (1976), reprinted in A LEGISLATIVE HISTORY OF THE FISHERY CONSERVATION AND MANAGEMENT ACT OF 1976, at 91 (1976)

Section 306. State jurisdiction

The conference substitute follows the House bill in providing for a limited exception to the principle (contained in both the House bill and the Senate amendment) that nothing in this legislation shall extend or diminish the jurisdiction of any State. The conference substitute also specifies that no State may directly or indirectly regulate any fishing which is engaged in by any fishing vessel outside its boundaries, unless such vessel is registered under the laws of such State. The exception in section 306(b) would authorize the Federal Government to regulate a fishery (which is predominantly located in waters outside a State's boundaries but in which some fishing occurs within such boundaries) within a State's boundaries if (1) a hearing is held; and (2) the Secretary finds on the basis of the hearing record that any State has taken any action, or omitted to take any action, the results of which will substantially and adversely affect the carrying out of a fishery management plan covering such fishery. State regulation would be reinstated as soon as the Secretary finds that the reason for which Federal regulation was assumed no longer prevails.

There is little dispute over the meaning of section 306(b). It is clearly written and thoroughly dealt with in the legislative history. Comm. on Commerce, 94th Cong., 1st Sess., A Legislative History of the Fishery Conservation and Management Act of 1976, at 843–847 and 900–901 (1976) (hereinafter cited as Legislative History). There is also little doubt that the federal government may regulate fisheries in the territorial sea. *See Douglas v. Seacoast Products*, 431 U.S. 265, 281–282 (1977).

The first sentence of section 306(a) is likewise clearly written and is the subject of a clarifying colloquy between Senators Stevens and Gravel during Senate debates. Legislative History at 460–63.

The second sentence of section 306(a), "No state may directly or indirectly regulate any fishing which is engaged in by any fishing vessel outside its boundaries, unless such vessel is registered under the laws of such state," is the subject of some confusion. The question is whether Congress intended to preempt well-established bases of state extraterritorial jurisdiction.

NOTES

1. Most conflicts involving section 306 have occurred in or near California. After the close of the 1980 shrimp season in California, a number of Oregon-based shrimpers, who also held California commercial fishing licenses, sailed into the FCZ off California's north coast and made their best catches of the season. These catches were landed at Oregon ports, where the season was still open. Given that no federal Fishery Management Plan was in place, could California have prevented this fishing off its shores? How? *See People v. Weeren*, 163 Cal. Rptr. 255, 607 P.2d 1279 (1980), *cert. denied*, 101 S. Ct. 115 (1980).

2. Another potential trouble spot in section 306 is the wording that limits the regional councils' usurpation power to state waters "other than its internal waters." What divides "internal" from external waters? Neither the Act nor its legislative history helps define "internal waters." Is Cook Inlet in Alaska internal waters? *See United States v. Alaska*, 422 U.S. 184 (1975), Chapter 4, *supra*. Is Puget Sound?

3. For additional reading, *see* W. Andrews, North Carolina Fisheries Law: Its Relationship to International, Federal, and Sister State Law (1975); M. Ball, *Law of the Sea: Federal–State Relations* (Aug. 1978) (monograph of The Dean Rusk Center for International and Comparative Law, University of Georgia); and T. Schoenbaum and P. McDonald, *State Management of Fisheries* (Sept. 1977) (University of N. Carolina Sea Grant Publication).

Enforcement

FIDELL, "ENFORCEMENT OF THE FISHERY CONSERVATION AND MANAGEMENT ACT OF 1976: THE POLICEMAN'S LOT,"
52 Washington Law Review 513, 537–38 (1977)

The FCMA incorporates a complex web of sanctions that may be invoked in the event of violations by fishing vessels. Some, as will be seen, apply only to foreign fishing vessels, but most apply to both domestic and foreign craft. The sanctions may be divided into direct and indirect measures. The direct sanctions are those prescribed in sections 308, 309 and 310, calling respectively for civil penalties assessed by the Commerce Department; criminal prosecutions leading to fines, imprisonment, or both; and forfeitures of offenders' fishing vessels and illegal catch. Arguably, the direct sanctions category includes the citation procedure of section 311(c), which is an alternative to both the formal enforcement steps of arrest, boarding, search and seizure of section 311(b), and the forfeiture sanction set forth in section 310.

In addition to these direct sanctions, a variety of indirect sanctions may be invoked in response to offenses under the Act, regulations, GIFA's, or fishing permits. These indirect sanctions include criminal or administrative punishment by the flag state of a foreign vessel, which both the Act and GIFA's contemplate; reduction of the catch quota of the vessel's flag state; and the revocation, suspension, or further conditioning of a permit to fish. Although not specifically referred to in the Act, violations of applicable requirements would be an appropriate ground upon which to refuse renewal of a permit for a particular foreign fishing vessel, or to deny port call privileges to a particular vessel or to vessels of a particular country. The latter is a sanction of questionable utility where alternative provisioning or liberty arrangements may be made, or their need reduced through at-sea-fleet support and transfer activities. For masters of United States vessels who violate the Act, regulations, or a management plan, the possibility also exists that the Coast Guard will take administrative action affecting their federal licenses, as has occasionally been done with respect to violations of the Tuna Conventions Act of 1950.

. . . .

Lurking behind this catalog of enforcement powers is the question of probable cause, which is usually required for a constitutional search or arrest. The legislative history does not explain the relationship of the term "reasonable cause" to the constitutional standard, but at least as to United States vessels, broad powers of Coast Guard inspection have been recognized by some courts, and an analogy to border searches may provide some basis for random inspection of foreign vessels entering territorial waters. Certainly it is no more "practical to set up checkpoints at the outer perimeter" of the 200-mile fishery conservation zone than it is at the limit of territorial waters. Beyond the three-mile limit, however, and a fortiori in enforcement against foreign vessels fishing for anadromous species beyond the fishery conservation zone, this rationale would be unavailing. The Government will then have to rely, presumably, on an analogy to the warrantless administrative inspections upheld in *Colonnade Catering Corp. v. United States* and *United States v. Biswell*. Because it will never be feasible to obtain a warrant on the high seas, the exigencies of enforcement could be viewed as compelling a departure from shoreside practices.

Furthermore, with respect to foreign vessels the Act requires that GIFA's include an agreement to permit boarding, search, or inspection *"at any time,"* apparently without regard to the presence of probable or reasonable cause. The Polish GIFA does not include an explicit agreement to this effect; instead, a more general undertaking to "allow and assist the boarding and inspection" is stated. Assuming this portion of the GIFA meets the standards of section 201(c)(2) of the FCMA, and assuming further that the constitutional tests are applicable to FCMA searches, one may wonder whether a foreign government may, in this fashion, waive the rights of its citizens. This article does not debate the rights of nonresident aliens under the Constitution, but it is safe to say that issues of probable cause are quite likely to be litigated under the FCMA.

NOTES

1. Some fishing vessels are required to keep logbooks under regulations implementing the FCMA. The logs are to contain, *inter alia*, information on catch and effort and are subject to scrutiny by "any authorized officer at any time." *See* 16 U.S.C. § 1853(c); 50 C.F.R. 611.9 (1978). Do these regulations expose fishers to violations of their fifth amendment rights against self-incrimination? *See Ward v. Coleman,* 444 U.S. 939 (1980); *Massachusetts Inshore Draggermen's Association v. Hanks,* Civ. No. 79-1169 (D. Mass., filed June 13, 1979).

2. For violations of logbook regulations, the Japanese fishing vessel Kaiyo Maru # 53 lost her permit to fish in the FCZ. *See United States v. Kaiyo Maru # 53,* Civ. No. A79-160 (D. Alaska, July 13, 1979). The permit was revoked without a pretermination hearing. Since such permits are recognized as licenses (*see* 5 U.S.C. 551(8) (1970)), was this not a case of deprivation of property without due process of law? *See Board of Regents v. Roth,* 408 U.S. 564 (1972); *Bell v. Burson,* 402 U.S. 535 (1971); *In re Carter,* 177 F.2d 75 (D.C. Cir. 1949), *cert. denied,* 70 S. Ct. 250 (1949).

Indian Treaty Rights

The U.S. Supreme Court has held many times that treaties with Indian tribes are "treaties" under the U.S. Constitution. *See, e.g., United States v. Winans,* 198 U.S. 371 (1905). Under the Supremacy Clause of the Constitution such treaties are the "supreme law of the land," the same as federal statutes, and are controlling over inconsistent state laws whether those laws are enacted prior or subsequent in time. *Antoine v. Washington,* 420 U.S. 194 (1975). Treaties also supersede prior inconsistent federal laws, although subsequent federal laws can alter the rights and responsibilities of the parties under the treaty if Congress makes its intent to do so clear. *Menominee Tribe v. United States,* 391 U.S. 404 (1968).

The potential impact of Indian treaties on ocean and coastal resource management is best illustrated by a case arising out of the salmon fishing controversy of the Pacific Northwest. The Indians there claimed that under 1855 treaties they are entitled to a specific share of the salmon and steelhead runs that swim past their traditional, off-reservation fishing sites. The Supreme Court, in *Washington v. Fishing Vessel Ass'n,* 443 U.S. 658 (1979) (quoted pages 233–34, *supra*), confirmed that right, holding that treaty tribes were entitled to an opportunity to harvest up to 50 percent of the harvestable fish (total run less spawning escapement) passing their traditional off-reservation sites. The decision forced changes in the management plans for ocean salmon fishing developed under the FCMA. *See* Davis, *Supreme Court Ruling on Boldt Decision Used to Close Ocean Troll Fishery,* Ocean Law Memo Issue No. 15 (Ocean Resources Law Program, University of Oregon School of Law, Aug. 1969).

While *Fishing Vessel* is important to the management of the salmon runs and the coastal zone of the Pacific Northwest, a follow-up case, *U.S. v. Washington (Phase II)*, 506 F. Supp. 187 (W.D. Wash. 1980), raises issues that are probably even more significant to coastal resource management, both in the Pacific Northwest and elsewhere in the nation.

In *United States v. Washington* the Indian tribes claimed that their 50 percent entitlement also gives them a right to a healthy fishery environment. They pointed out that dams, pollution, logging, and similar activities tend to injure the fishery environment and to render their treaty rights meaningless. *See generally* A. Netboy, *The Salmon, Their Fight for Survival* (1974); Pacific Northwest Regional Commission, Columbia Basin Salmon and Steelhead Analysis 2–23 (1976). They argued that they had a right to stop, or at least significantly influence, all future decisions about activities affecting the fishery environment—*even though such activities might have been approved by an appropriate state or federal agency.* The federal district court upheld this claim in principle, leaving to a subsequent phase of the case just how this generalized right is to be implemented. In the same case the Indian tribes successfully claimed that their 50 percent entitlement includes hatchery runs of salmon and steelhead as well as natural runs.

NOTES

1. How should Indian treaty rights be accounted for in the FCMA process? *See* Note, *Indian Fishing Rights in the Pacific Northwest: Impact of Fishery Conservation and Management Act of 1976*, 8 Envt'l L. 101 (1977); U.S. General Accounting Office, The Pacific Fishery Management Council's Role in Salmon Fisheries (1978).

2. How should the treaty right to a quality environment be implemented? What if the fishery environment for one run is damaged by dams or pollution, can Indian tribes complain as long as they are compensated with fish from another run?

3. The court in *United States v. Washington* also noted that the federal government is under an obligation to refrain from degrading the fish habitat. Does this mean that the Department of Interior, as part of its function in carrying out U.S. trust-related obligations, must assure compliance with such a duty, or that each federal agency must individually comply with this requirement? How, if at all, is this duty to be reflected in relevant federal agency regulations? Does the decision provide the tribes with an expanded role in federal licensing and permitting procedures? Could the decision affect the process used by federal agencies in approving state water quality–related programs?

4. It was argued in *U.S. v. State of Michigan*, 471 F. Supp. 192, 274 (W.D. Mich. 1979), that the Submerged Lands Act, discussed in Chapter 4, *supra*, "subsilentio" abrogated the Indians' treaty fishing rights. Is there any reasonable basis for this argument?

5. The issues raised in *U.S. v. Washington* must be considered in conjunction with other developments. Recent legislation, such as the Northwest Power Bill (Pub. L. No. 96–501) and the Salmon Enhancement Act (Pub. L. No. 96–561), also may strongly affect salmon management.

6. Regarding the relationship of Indian treaty rights to the federal navigation servitude, *see U.S. v. 5,677.94 Acres of Land*, 162 F. Supp. 108 (D. Mont. 1957); Note,

The Navigation Servitude and Reserved Indian Property: Does the Rule of No Compensation Apply to Indian Interests in Navigable Waters?, 1979 Utah L. Rev. 57.

7. Regarding related issues in salmon management, *see Idaho v. Oregon and Washington*, 100 S. Ct. 616 (1980) (apportionment of salmon between states); *Tlingit and Haida Indians of Alaska v. U.S.*, 389 F.2d 778 (9th Cir. 1968) (commerce clause issues raised by state management); Copes, *Law and the Management of Anadromous Fish Stocks*, 4 Ocean Dev. & Int'l L. 233 (1977); D. Johnson, *The International Law of Fisheries* (1965); Johnson, *The Japan–United States Salmon Conflict*, 43 Wash. L. Rev. 1 (1967).

SECTION B: MARINE MAMMAL PROTECTION ACT[2]
16 U.S.C. §§ 1361–1407

Marine Mammal Protection and Commercial Fishing

COMMITTEE FOR HUMANE LEGISLATION, INC. v. RICHARDSON
540 F.2d 1141 (D.C. Cir. 1976)

PER CURIAM:

I. Introduction

In this appeal we are asked to review a judgment of the District Court[3] that the Secretary of Commerce, through the Director of the National Marine Fisheries Service (NMFS), has violated the provisions of the Marine Mammal Protection Act of 1972[4] by granting to the American Tunaboat Association a general permit for the practice of purse-seine fishing for yellowfin tuna "on porpoise." We concur with the conclusion of the District Court that the permit for fishing "on porpoise" was not issued in compliance with the requirements of the Act. Rather than order an immediate halt to operations of the tuna fleet, however, we have determined to stay the effect of the District Court order until January 1, 1977, for reasons stated hereinafter.

II. Background

A. Purse-Seine Fishing "on Porpoise"

Prior to 1960 the most common method of fishing for yellowfin tuna was use of pole, line, and live bait. In the eastern tropical Pacific yellowfin tuna fishery, fishermen observed in the late 1950's that yellowfin habitually associate with certain species of dolphin (commonly called porpoise), and began setting

---

[2]The materials in this chapter are in part derived with permission from 1 T. Schoenbaum, Ocean and Coastal Law Teaching Materials 247–89 (Univ. of N.C. 1977).

[3]*Committee for Humane Legislation, Inc. v. Richardson*, 414 F.Supp. 297 (D. D.C. 1976).

[4]16 U.S.C. § 1361 *et seq.* (Supp. IV 1974).

their nets "on porpoise." When porpoise are spotted at the ocean surface, speedboats are deployed to herd them to where the net will be set. The tuna follow below the porpoise. The porpoise then are encircled with a cup-like purse-seine net, the open bottom of which is then drawn closed in the manner of a drawstring purse,[5] trapping both the porpoise and the tuna beneath.

Although efforts are made to free the trapped porpoise,[6] purse-seine fishing has resulted in substantial incidental deaths of porpoise. Porpoise are air-breathing mammals, and may be suffocated if they become entangled in the net, or drowned as a result of shock or physical injury. The number of incidental porpoise deaths in recent years has been as follows:[7]

1971	312,400
1972	304,600
1973	175,000
1974	97,800
1975	130,000 (est.)

The average number of porpoise killed each time purse-seine nets are "set" was 70 in 1971, 43 in 1972, 19 in 1973, 12 in 1974, and 17 in 1975. SWFC Report at 87, Table 2.

The effectiveness of purse-seine fishing has led to dramatic increases in its use by the United States tuna fishing fleet. The catch of yellowfin tuna caught by United States purse-seiners on porpoise was 99,000 tons in 1974, or 60 percent of the total United States yellowfin catch (of 165,000 tons) and about 43 percent of the total United States tuna catch. For the period 1971–1974 purse-seiners fishing on porpoise accounted for 72 percent of the total catch of yellowfin. FEIS at 40.

[5]*See* 40 C.F.R. § 216.24(d)(2) (1975), *as amended*, 40 Fed.Reg. 56899 (Dec. 5, 1975).

[6]Speedboats are used to stretch the net in an open position to permit the porpoise to swim out of the net without becoming entangled. 40 C.F.R. § 216.24(d)(2)(vi). As the net is brought aboard the seining vessel, the porpoise tend to congregate at the extreme end of the net, while tuna swim back and forth between the porpoise and the seiner. The seiner then follows a "backdown" procedure whereby it is backed rapidly to cause the corkline of the net to submerge at the end where the porpoise are located. When tuna swim toward this escape route, the vessel slows and the corkline bobs to the surface. The "backdown" procedure allows a substantial number of porpoise to escape unharmed. *Progress of Research on Porpoise Mortality Incidental to Tuna Purse-Seine Fishing for FY 1975*, National Marine Fisheries Service, Southwest Fisheries Center (Aug. 8, 1975), at 54 (hereinafter SWFC Report); 40 C.F.R. § 216.24(d)(2)(vi).

The net itself is provided with a safety panel, known as a Medina panel, of very fine mesh net along the outer edge of the net. 40 C.F.R. § 216.24(d)(2)(iv). The fine mesh panel is intended to help prevent entanglement of porpoise in the net. SWFC Report at 58–59. Other devices are being studied, such as a "porpoise apron" to prevent entrapment of porpoise during the backdown procedure, SWFC Report at 54–55, improved net gear to prevent delays in a seining operation, *id*. at 60–61, and methods of removing porpoise from the net manually, *id*. at 61–62.

It is estimated that 98% of the netted porpoise are released, primarily through the backdown procedure, and that 2% die. SWFC Report at 51.

[7]Final Environmental Impact Statement on promulgation of rules and proposed issuance of permits to commercial fishermen allowing the taking of marine mammals in the course of normal commercial fishing operations, Office of Resource Management, NMFS (Nov. 18, 1975) (hereinafter FEIS); 1975 data is from 40 Fed.Reg. 56899, 56900 (Dec. 5, 1975) (promulgation of regulations dealing with incidental taking of marine mammals in the course of commercial fishing operations).

B. The Marine Mammal Protection Act of 1972

The Marine Mammal Protection Act of 1972 was addressed in part to the growing problem of porpoise deaths incidental to commercial fishing. The Act was founded on a concern that certain species of marine mammals were in danger of extinction or depletion as a result of man's activities,[8] and a concomitant belief that those species "should not be permitted to diminish below their optimum sustainable population."[9] A moratorium was imposed on taking and importation of all marine mammals, with a two-year exemption from the moratorium for taking of marine mammals incidental to the course of commercial fishing operations. Although the Secretary of Commerce was permitted to license incidental taking of marine mammals subsequent to the two-year exemption, the statute directs that "[i]n any event it shall be the immediate goal that the incidental kill or incidental serious injury of marine mammals permitted in the course of commercial fishing operations be reduced to insignificant levels approaching a zero mortality and serious injury rate."

The permits to be issued after the exemption period expired—on October 21, 1974—were authorized under 16 U.S.C. § 1374, which in turn required compliance with regulations issued under Section 1373. Section 1374 requires that the permit specify, *inter alia*, "the number and kind of animals which are authorized to be taken or imported," and the location, period, and method of the authorized taking. Section 1374(b)(2),(c). The applicant for a permit "must demonstrate to the Secretary that the taking or importation of any marine mammal under such permit *will be consistent with the purposes of this chapter and the applicable regulations established under section 1373 of this title.*" Section 1374(d)(3) (emphasis added).

Section 1373, in turn, authorizes the Secretary to promulgate regulations "on the basis of the best scientific evidence available" for permits for taking marine mammals, "as he deems necessary and appropriate to insure that such taking will not be to the disadvantage of those species and population stocks and will be consistent with the purposes and policies set forth in section 1361 of this title."[10] The Act requires that prior to promulgating any such regulations

---

[8]16 U.S.C. § 1361(1)

[9]16 U.S.C. § 1361(2). "The term 'optimum sustainable population' means, with respect to any population stock, the number of animals which will result in the maximum productivity of the population of the species, keeping in mind the optimum carrying capacity of the habitat and the health of the ecosystem of which they form a constituent element." 16 U.S.C. § 1362(9). The House report on the proposed legislation emphasized that the benefit of the marine mammals was to be the paramount consideration:

> [M]arine mammals are resources of great significance and . . . it is congressional policy that they should be protected and encouraged to develop consistent with sound policies of resource management. *The primary objective of this management must be to maintain the health and stability of the marine ecosystem; this in turn indicates that the animals must be managed for their benefit and not for the benefit of commercial exploitation.*

H.R.Rep.No.92–707, Committee on Merchant Marine and Fisheries, 92d Cong., 1st Sess. 22 (Dec. 4, 1971), U.S.Code Cong. & Admin.News 1972, pp. 4144, 4154 (emphasis added.)

[10]16 U.S.C. § 1373(a). The Secretary is directed to consider the following factors:

the Secretary shall publish and make available to the public either before or concurrent with the publication of notice in the Federal Register of his intention to prescribe regulations under this section—

(1) a statement of the estimated existing levels of the species and population stocks of the marine mammal concerned;

(2) a statement of the expected impact of the proposed regulations on the optimum sustainable population of such species or population stock;

(3) a statement describing the evidence before the Secretary upon which he proposes to base such regulations; and

(4) any studies made by or for the Secretary or any recommendations made by or for the Secretary or the Marine Mammal Commission which relate to the establishment of such regulations.

16 U.S.C. § 1373(d).

C. The Regulations

On March 13, 1974 NMFS published notice of its intent to prescribe regulations for taking porpoise incidental to commercial fishing. 39 Fed. Reg. 9685. It took this action despite its professed lack of knowledge as to the actual populations of porpoise, the optimum sustainable populations, or the effect of the takings on the optimum sustainable populations of porpoise. Final regulations were promulgated on September 5, 1974, 39 Fed. Reg. 32117, and the American Tunaboat Association was granted a general permit for the period October 21, 1974 to December 31, 1975 under which fishermen holding certificates of inclusion in the general permit were permitted to take an unlimited number of porpoise.

Despite subsequent warnings by the Marine Mammal Commission that the levels of incidental porpoise deaths would remain unacceptably high,[11] NMFS did not impose a quota, although it later amended its regulations to require improved gear and techniques. The number of porpoise killed by commercial fishermen increased from 97,800 in 1974 to about 130,000 in 1975.

The American Tunaboat Association's application for renewal of its permit was granted on December 19, 1975. Although NMFS published population estimates for two species of porpoise, it again stated that it could not make any statement as to the optimum sustainable populations or the effect of the proposed taking, and determined to set no quota as to incidental deaths unless it appeared that the total number of deaths would exceed 70 percent of the final 1975 estimate. Although the Marine Mammal Commission again warned that there

---

(1) existing and future levels of marine mammal species and population stocks;

(2) existing international treaty and agreement obligations of the United States;

(3) the marine ecosystem and related environmental considerations;

(4) the conservation, development, and utilization of fishery resources; and

(5) the economic and technological feasibility of implementation.

16 U.S.C. § 1373(b).

[11]Before final regulations were promulgated the Marine Mammal Commission concluded that even use of advanced fishing techniques would not bring incidental porpoise deaths down to an acceptable level; . . .

was no basis for assurance that porpoise stocks would not be harmed by the taking,[12] NMFS expressed its belief in proposing regulations that existing porpoise populations would neither increase nor decrease as a result of the taking.

Appellees, various environmental protection organizations, filed suit in 1974 and 1975 to challenge the legality of the permits issued the American Tunaboat Association. The suits were consolidated, and on May 11, 1976 the District Court entered summary judgment for plaintiffs. The court found that the overriding purpose of the Marine Mammal Protection Act was protection of the animals' interests, and held that the Act required (1) that NMFS find that the effect of any proposed taking on the optimum sustainable populations of the species involved not be to the disadvantage of the animals, (2) that the permit specify the number and kind of animals which may be taken, and (3) that the applicant for a permit demonstrate that the taking will serve the purposes of the Act. The court declared the American Tunaboat Association's general permit void and ordered that no further permit be issued until the Act has been complied with. The effect of the decision has been stayed pending further order of this court.

III. Argument

The first major issue presented by this appeal is whether NMFS has discretion under the Marine Mammal Protection Act of 1972 to issue permits for incidental taking of marine mammals in the course of commercial fishing when estimates of the optimum sustainable populations of the species involved and of the effect of that taking upon the optimum sustainable populations are not available.

As a preliminary matter, we may state our agreement with the District Court's conclusion that the Act was to be administered for the benefit of the protected species rather than for the benefit of commercial exploitation. That general legislative intent, however, is not dispositive of the instant question. Congress was confronted directly with the conflict between protection of the porpoise and protection of the American tuna fishing industry; one result of that conflict was the express two-year exemption granted commercial fishermen from the moratorium on taking marine mammals. More significantly for this case, the committee reports contain strong language indicating that the Act was not intended to force tuna fishermen to cease operations: . . .

It is clear that Congress did not intend that the Marine Mammal Protection Act would force American tuna fishermen to cease operations; the Act does not prohibit purse-seine fishing on porpoise.[13] It is equally clear, however, that

---

[12]40 Fed. Reg. at 56899 ("the Commission could not, on the basis of reliable scientific information, arrive at a figure of permissible incidental mortality which could with reasonable assurance enable the principal stocks of porpoise to increase in size"); *see Committee for Humane Legislation, Inc. v. Richardson, supra,* note 1, 414 F.Supp. at 305.

[13]The major concern at the time of enactment was that the Marine Mammal Protection Act not be read to prohibit many forms of commercial fishing solely because those methods result in incidental deaths of marine mammals. Rep. Goodling, the senior minority member of the conference committee, expressed that concern when the conference committee report came to the House floor:

Congress intended that the requirements of the Act be complied with. Perhaps most telling in this regard is the most recent oversight hearing of the Subcommittee on Fisheries and Wildlife Conservation and the Environment of the House Committee on Merchant Marine and Fisheries, held after entry of the District Court decision in the instant case. Congressman Robert L. Leggett, the present chairman of the Subcommittee, reiterated throughout the hearings that, although he did not wish to see the tuna fleet's permit cancelled, he also believed that the District Court had correctly interpreted the law as written.

. . . .

The specific requirements of the Act are indeed so clear as to require little discussion. 16 U.S.C. § 1373(d) requires that the Secretary publish, *inter alia*, a statement of "the estimated existing levels of the species and population stocks" of the marine mammals to be taken, and a statement of the expected impact of the takings on the optimum sustainable populations of the species. As the House committee report explained, the Act was deliberately designed to permit takings of marine mammals only when it was *known* that that taking would not be to the disadvantage of the species . . . . H.R. Rep. No. 92–707, *supra*, at 15, U.S. Code Cong. & Admin. News 1972, p. 4148. In promulgating the instant regulations in both 1974 and 1975, NMFS did not fulfill the requirement that it determine the impact of the takings on the optimum sustainable populations of the species of porpoise involved. The statement that "[t]here is no evidence that the porpoise populations would substantially increase or decrease as a result of the regulations and reissuance of the general permit" is not at all responsive; the fact that actual stocks may be stable may supply little or nothing to the determination of effect on optimum sustainable populations.[14] We therefore affirm the judgment of the District Court on this issue.

The second line of argument in this appeal concerns the requirement of 16 U.S.C. § 1374(b)(2)(A) that a permit "specify . . . the number and kind of animals which are authorized to be taken . . . . " The District Court held that

---

In regard to those marine mammals taken accidentally or incidentally to commercial fishing operations, the conferees adopted a general goal that such damage should be "reduced to insignificant levels approaching a zero mortality and serious injury rate." I wish to make it crystal clear that this language in no way will or should result in the closure or drastic curtailment of the Nation's commercial fishing industry simply because the biological fact exists that some species of fish and marine mammals cannot be separated from a commonly shared food source in order to permit commercial fishing operations without the taking of a single marine mammal.

118 Cong.Rec.—House 34642–34643 (Oct. 10, 1972). *See* Marine Mammal Protection Act of 1972, Conference Report, H.R.Rep.No.92–1488, 92d Cong., 2d Sess. 23 (Oct. 2, 1972), U.S.Code Cong. & Admin.News 1972, p. 4187.

We do not reach the question whether present levels of porpoise deaths incidental to commercial fishing constitute compliance with the requirement that deaths be reduced to insignificant levels.

[14]*See* comments at note 11 *supra*. The House committee report observed, with regard to the need for a sustainable population level, that certain whale stocks had not recovered in spite of a worldwide ban on their taking which had existed for several years. H.R.Rep.No.92–707, *supra* note 9, at 15.

NMFS had failed to satisfy this requirement inasmuch as no specified limit was placed on incidental takings. The Government has conceded on appeal that the Act requires that a permit contain a fixed number, and NMFS has amended 50 C.F.R. § 216.24(d)(2)(i)(A) to impose a limit of 78,000 on the total number of marine mammals which may be taken by those operating under the general permit. 41 Fed. Reg. 23680 (June 11, 1976).

Appellees contend, however, that the statute is not satisfied by aggregation of all marine mammals into one figure, relying on the express language of the Act that the permit specify both "number and kind." The determination whether the single quota established by NMFS is, in this case, in compliance with the Marine Mammal Protection Act may require development of evidence as to the suitability of aggregation in the context of purse-seine fishing on porpoise; it is a dispute which properly cannot be decided in the first instance by this court. We therefore remand the case to the District Court for prompt consideration and decision of this question.

The remaining statutory requirement relevant to this appeal is contained in 16 U.S.C. § 1374(d)(3): an applicant for a permit for taking marine mammals must demonstrate that the taking "will be consistent with the purposes of this chapter and the applicable regulations established under section 1373 of this title." Again, the purpose of the requirement was stated clearly in the legislative history:

> If that burden is not carried—and it is by no means a light burden—the permit may not be issued. The effect of this set of requirements is to insist that the management of the animal populations be carried out with the interests of the animals as the prime consideration.

H.R. Rep. No. 92–707, *supra*, at 18, U.S. Code Cong. & Admin. News 1972, p. 4151. The court has carefully examined the American Tunaboat Association's 1974 permit application and its 1975 renewal application. Neither contains any discussion of the predicted impact of the proposed takings on the optimum sustainable population of the porpoise species involved, or otherwise displays consistency with the purposes of the Marine Mammal Protection Act. We concur in the judgment of the District Court that the applications were deficient under the terms of the Act and should not have been granted. We therefore affirm the judgment of the District Court.

IV. Remedies

When this appeal was presented to the court on motions for stay pending review, it was represented by counsel for the Government that "[i]t is estimated that reasonably supportable scientific guesses at optimum sustainable populations of porpoise will not be available for 90 days." Motion of Federal Appellants for Stay Pending Appeal at 9. The request for stay was founded in part on the assertion that if ongoing research being conducted with the tuna fleet were permitted to continue figures could be obtained by autumn of this year. The court is now informed that "[i]t will take three to seven years for a scientifically valid figure." Brief for federal appellants at 21.

The court granted a stay pending appeal in the belief that compliance with the Act could be effected within a short time and invalidation of the American Tunaboat Association's general permit thereby averted. We cannot, however, approve the suggestion of NMFS that it might not be in compliance with the Act as much as a decade after enactment. Our obligation is to enforce the law as it is written; the court may not be turned from its course by a proffer of statements that Congress really did not mean what it said.[15]

The court is aware, however, that the immediate impact of this decision would be disastrous to the commercial fishermen operating under the general permit. In further consideration of the efforts by the Government to achieve good faith compliance with the requirements of the Act, and of the need to conduct ongoing gear studies throughout the entire fishing season,[16] we find it appropriate to continue our stay of the District Court order until January 1, 1977.

So ordered.

NOTES

1. After *Richardson*, the National Marine Fisheries Service amended the tuna–porpoise regulations on December 29, 1976, 2 days before the expiration of the stay. 42 Fed. Reg. 1034. The NMFS also extended to April 30, 1977, the general permit issued to the American Tunaboat Association (ATA) for commercial fishing, set a limit of 9,972 as the total number of porpoise and other marine mammals that could be taken pursuant to the permit, and set limits within the total for each kind of mammal. Citing the amendments, the Court of Appeals issued a second stay of the District Court order. The D.C. Circuit's brief per curiam order allowed ATA to fish for yellowfin tuna under the extended permit until April 30 or until a 1977 permit was issued, whichever came first, with any porpoise taken under the modified permit being counted toward the total permissible take for 1977. *Committee for Humane Legislation v. Kreps*, 9 E.R.C. 1880 (D.C. Cir., March 8, 1977). *See also Motor Vessel Theresa Ann v. Kreps*, 548 F.2d 1382 (9th Cir. 1977) (similar relief extended to non-ATA fishermen); *Save the Dolphins v. U.S. Dept. of Commerce*, 404 F. Supp. 407 (D. Cal. 1975) (suit under Freedom of Information Act to obtain research cruise film of release of marine mammals trapped during fishing operations).

   In December 1977 the National Marine Fisheries Service announced a 3-year program to reduce the incidental mortality of porpoises. For 1980 the quota was

[15]A major subject of controversy in the instant appeals has been the extent to which the American tuna fishing industry would be harmed by withdrawal of the general permit for purse-seine fishing on porpoise pending completion of the actions necessary to bring the parties into compliance with the Act. We accept as sufficiently demonstrated that the tuna fleet would be seriously harmed by such a ban. The arguments, however, properly should be addressed to Congress rather than to the courts. Balancing of interests between the commercial fishing fleet and the porpoise is entirely a legislative decision, dictated at present by the terms of the Act.

[16]Affidavit of Robert W. Schoning, Director, National Marine Fisheries Service, May 25, 1976. Appendix A to Motion of Federal Appellants for Stay Pending Appeal.

half the 62,429 allowed in 1977. Included in the program were an enforcement policy on accidental taking of prohibited species, additions to the previous gear and fishing procedure requirements, a strengthened on-board observer program, and improved enforcement of the prohibition on importing yellowfin tuna from countries that do not comply with U.S. requirements. U.S. Dept. of Commerce, The Marine Mammal Protection Act of 1972 Annual Report 4 (1978); see 50 C.F.R. § 215.24(d)(3) (1980) (regulations delimiting permitted take, encirclement, and mortality of each species as a stock-management unit).

In 1981, the Marine Mammal Protection Act was amended to provide that the zero mortality goal "shall be satisfied in the case of the incidental taking of marine mammals in the course of purse seine fishing for yellowfin tuna by . . . the application of the best marine mammal safety techniques and equipment that are economically and technologically practicable." 16 U.S.C. § 1371(a)(2). Based on the technological developments reflected in *Richardson* and this note, was the yellowfin tuna fleet meeting the zero mortality goal as revised in 1981?

2. Could U.S. tuna boat owners avoid the MMPA's restrictions by registering their boats under foreign flags and "exporting" their catch to the United States? *See* Armstrong, *The Porpoise–Tuna Controversy*, 4 Ocean Law Memo Issue No. 1 at 3 (University of Oregon Ocean and Coastal Law Center, June 1, 1977).

3. On what grounds did the court in *Richardson* reject the appellant's "congressional ratification" argument that Congress did not object when informed during the 1973, 1974, and 1975 oversight hearings that NMFS was issuing permits for taking porpoise without knowing the optimum sustainable species populations? Were there other grounds for rejecting the ratification argument?

4. The 1981 amendments to the Marine Mammal Protection Act also authorize the Secretary of Commerce to allow nontuna commercial fishers and U.S. citizens engaged in a nonfishing activity within a specified geographical region to take incidentally "small numbers" of undepleted marine mammal species or populations if such takings will have a "negligible impact." 16 U.S.C. §§1371(a)(4), (5). Authorized nonfishing activities also must have a negligible impact on habitat. What nontuna commercial fishers might be expected to seek authorization to take incidentally small numbers of marine mammals? What other activities might seek such authorization?

5. The MMPA provides for civil and criminal penalties. Note that neither is restricted to acts specifically prohibited. For example, section 1375(b) makes criminal every knowing violation of "any provision" of the act or of any regulation issued pursuant to its authority. Civil penalties may be assessed by the Secretary without regard to actual or constructive knowledge, intent, or even negligence. 16 U.S.C. § 1375(a). But to collect such a penalty, the Secretary must request the Department of Justice to bring a civil action at which the defendant may obtain a *de novo* review of the assessment. Under the Endangered Species Act, 16 U.S.C. § 1540(a), such review is on the basis of substantial evidence.

Difficult issues of enforcement have arisen in connection with prosecution of U.S. citizens who take marine mammals in the territorial waters of a foreign country, *United States v. Mitchell*, 553 F.2d 996 (5th Cir. 1977), *annotated*, 43 A.L.R. Fed. 585 (1979), *noted*, 16 Urb. L. Ann. 375 (1979) (act held not to apply), and use of U.S. airspace to transport captured marine mammals, *Marine Wonderland & Animal Park, Ltd., v. Kreps*, 610 F.2d 947 (D.C. Cir. 1979) (refusal to enjoin administrative proceedings against use of U.S. airspace to transport dolphins from Mexico to Canada). *See also Barcelo v. Brown*, 478 F. Supp. 646, 691 (D.P.R. 1979) (naval bombing held not to be a prohibited marine mammal taking), *remanded on other grounds*, 16 ERC 1593 (1st Cir. 1981), *rev'd on other grounds*, _____ U.S. _____ (April 27, 1982).

6. For commentary on the tuna–porpoise controversy, *see* Anderson, Anderson & Searles, *The Tuna–Porpoise Dilemma: Is Conflict Resolution Attainable?*, 18 Nat. Res. Law. 505 (1978); Erdheim, *The Immediate Goal Test of the Marine Mammal Protection Act and the Tuna/Porpoise Controversy,* 9 Envt'l L. 283 (1979); Nafziger, *The Management of Marine Mammals After the FCMA*, 14 Willamette L. Rev. 169 (1978); Nafziger & Armstrong, *The Porpoise–Tuna Controversy: Management of Marine Resources After Committee for Humane Legislation v. Richardson*, 7 Envt'l L. 223 (1977); Note, *Dolphin Controversy in the Tuna Industry: The United States' Role in an International Problem,* 16 San Diego L. Rev. 665 (1969).

For an excellent analysis of the MMPA, *see* Coggins, *Legal Protection for Marine Mammals: An Overview of Innovative Resource Conservation Legislation,* 6 Envt'l L. 1 (1975). *See also Animal Welfare Institute v. Kreps,* 561 F.2d 1002 (D.C. Cir.), *cert. denied,* 434 U.S. 1013 (1977) (baby fur seal import regulations invalidated); Annotation, *Construction and Application of Marine Mammal Protection Act . . . ,* 43 A.L.R. Fed. 599 (1979); Armstrong, *The California Sea Otter: Emerging Conflicts in Resources Management,* 16 San Diego L. Rev. 249 (1979); *Fouke Co. v. Mandell,* 386 F. Supp. 1341 (D. Md. 1974), *noted,* 47 Colo. L. Rev. 261 (1976) (Maryland statute prohibiting importation of sealskins held preempted); Gaines & Schmidt, *Wildlife Population Management Under the Marine Mammal Protection Act of 1972,* 6 Envt'l L. Rep. 50096 (1976); K. Hammond, *Fisheries Management Under the Fishery Conservation and Management Act, The Marine Mammal Protection Act, and the Endangered Species Act* (1980); Scarff, *The International Management of Whales, Dolphins and Porpoises: An Inter-disciplinary Assessment (Part One),* 6 Ecology L.Q. 323 (1977); Travalio & Clement, *International Protection of Marine Mammals,* 5 Colum. J. Envt'l L. 199 (1979). In addition, the U.S. Department of Commerce annually publishes a report on the administration of the MMPA. *See, e.g.,* U.S. Dept. of Commerce, Annual Report: The Marine Mammal Protection Act of 1972 (1980).

Subsistence Hunting of Marine Mammals

Subsistence hunting of the endangered bowhead whale by Alaskan Eskimos raises several important issues in marine mammal management including state versus federal versus international management of marine mammals.

REEVES, "THE BOWHEAD WHALE CONTROVERSY: A CRISIS FOR U.S. WHALE POLICY," OCEAN LAW MEMO ISSUE NO. 16 (Ocean Resources Law Program, University of Oregon School of Law, November 1979)

In June, 1977, the International Whaling Commission (IWC) voted to delete from its Schedule of Regulations the exemption for subsistence killing of bowhead whales by native peoples. Hardest hit by this deletion were Alaskan Eskimos who have historically hunted these whales for subsistence. The bowhead, whose habitat is the northern Pacific arctic and subarctic waters, is crucial to the Eskimo culture. The Eskimos' dependence on these animals and the hunt itself is far-reaching, providing villages with food, social order, cultural identity and some measure of economic independence. In the words of an Inupiat Eskimo, "without the whale, there is no Eskimo."

Since June of 1977, the Inupiat Eskimos have attempted to resist deletion of the bowhead exemption and subsequent IWC action in U.S. courts. The Eskimos' situation, and the litigation they initiated, raised a complex of issues having legal, international, political and environmental significance which have yet to be fully resolved. At stake is a species threatened with extinction, and a culture totally dependent on that species for survival.

The IWC

The IWC was established under the 1946 International Convention (treaty) for the Regulation of Whaling to provide for the conservation, development and optimum utilization of whale resources. The IWC meets at least yearly, and currently is composed of 20 contracting governments. It establishes in its schedule of regulations proper whaling procedures and whale-take quotas which are reviewed and, depending on current information, amended annually.

Until recent years, the IWC has not taken a conservationist stance. By all accounts, it rather juggled conflicting economic interests to produce immediate gain for whaling nations, until many whale species were dangerously depleted. The Scientific Committee of the IWC, originally composed of biologists who were natural historians, became increasingly concerned as whale populations declined. The Committee needed more quantitative data on whale populations, specifically statistics describing a species' ability to respond to the commercial harvest, and established a subcommittee of population dynamicists in 1961. A trend placing more emphasis on quantitative information continues within the Committee to the present day. The Committee is composed of scientists from whaling and non-whaling nations. Although each member nation may send scientists, not all nations are represented. In recent years, the IWC has attempted to make its decisions more objective and less susceptible to political trade-offs by relying on Scientific Committee recommendations in formulating IWC regulations.

IWC efforts at conservation have been further weakened by the terms of the treaty itself. Any member nation objecting to an IWC regulation is not bound by it. Hence, the IWC's only method of enforcement is publication of objections by member nations, and of violations of its regulations by members and non-members. Until 1973, whaling nations made liberal use of the objection provision.

The Controversy

The IWC regulations prohibit the general taking of bowheads but, until 1977, contained an exemption allowing hunting for subsistence use. In 1973, the Scientific Committee began requesting the U.S. to report the Eskimo kill of bowheads, and to make the native hunt more efficient, specifically by reducing the number of whales struck by the Eskimos, but not landed. The Committee's concern centered on the small size of the bowhead population, and the threat presented not only by the subsistence hunt, but also by the threat of potential harm caused by oil development in the North American Arctic. The U.S. did not comply with the Scientific Committee's requests. The Committee repeated these requests yearly through 1976, but the government neither responded nor informed the Eskimos of the Committee's position. Finally, in June of 1977, the Scientific Committee recommended deletion of the subsistence exemption and the IWC adopted its recommendation 16–0, with only the U.S. abstaining.

The IWC decision placed the government in a precarious position. The U.S. is required by the Marine Mammal Protection Act of 1972 (MMPA) to facilitate effective conservation and protection of whales on a global scale. Within the IWC, the U.S. was an aggressive conservationist force, and had consistently urged strict reliance on recommendations of the Scientific Committee in formulating regulations, stressing the need for objectivity in IWC decisions. The U.S. had strongly urged other countries to withhold objections in spite of any adverse domestic impact, and no objection to an IWC regulation had been filed by any nation since 1973. The symbolic international impact of the U.S. being the first to break this pattern could be grave, and could precipitate objections to other regulations by whaling nations.

But the U.S. also has a trust obligation to its native citizens, the Eskimo whalers severely affected by the deletion of the bowhead exemption. This long-recognized obligation requires the government to meet a high standard of protection of Eskimo interests. The Eskimos view the exemptions for native Alaskan subsistence hunting in the MMPA and the Endangered Species Act of 1973 (ESA) as implicit recognition of the trust obligation. An international body was denying the Eskimos the domestically recognized right to hunt for subsistence. Did the government's trust obligation therefore require that the U.S. object to the IWC regulation? Acting Secretary of the Interior James Joseph believed it did, and so indicated in a letter to Secretary of State Cyrus Vance. But because of the serious threat to U.S. credibility as a leader in whale protection, and the fear of resulting setbacks to IWC efforts at conservation, the government decided otherwise. On October 20, 1977, four days before expiration of the 90 day objection deadline, the Secretary announced that the U.S. would not object, but would instead attempt to work out a compromise at the upcoming December, 1977, meeting of the IWC. The next day, in an effort to gain additional time to challenge the government's decision, the Eskimos brought suit in U.S. District Court in Washington, D.C., seeking a temporary order directing the government to object.

Adams v. Vance [570 F.2d 950 (D.C. Cir. 1977)]

District Court Judge John Sirica balanced the harm to the Eskimos if the objection was not filed against harm to the government if it was. He concluded that, since failure to object foreclosed any opportunity for the Eskimos to argue the merits of their claims, and since the U.S. could withdraw its objection at any time, the scales tipped in the Eskimos' favor. Judge Sirica ordered the Secretary to object.

The government immediately appealed this order. On Oct. 24, 1977, the last day to file an objection with the IWC, the Court of Appeals reversed the District Court, and the U.S. Supreme Court refused to review that decision. The Court of Appeals assumed, without deciding, that the "political question doctrine," which denies courts jurisdiction to rule on matters which are committed by the Constitution to another branch of government, did not preclude review in this case. Because even a temporary order to object would intrude substantially into the concerns of the Executive branch, the court required the Eskimos to make extraordinary showing of the need for such an order. Although the Eskimos had raised serious questions of law on the trust obligation issue, they had not proved with certainty that irreparable harm would ensue, particularly since the government planned to propose a compromise at the December IWC meeting. The crux of the decision, however, rested on the severe harm to U.S. efforts at maintaining an effective international whale conservation program through the IWC. The Court of Appeals found clearly erroneous Judge Sirica's finding that an objection, even one that could be subsequently withdrawn, did not cause substantial harm to the U.S. On balance, the harm to U.S. foreign policy outweighed the harm to the Eskimos.

In compliance with the Court of Appeals decision, the Secretary did not file an objection and the U.S. was bound by the IWC regulation.

Subsequent IWC Action

At the IWC meeting in December, 1977, the U.S. negotiated a compromise between the nations advocating a ban on bowhead whaling and those advocating controlled, but continuing, subsistence hunting. The IWC, despite the Scientific Committee's recommendation of a complete moratorium, set a 1978 quota at 18 whales struck or 12 landed, whichever occurred first. The Eskimos were outraged by what they considered to be a low quota, and initially announced they would not comply. They later decided, in a show of good faith, to stay within the 1978 quota for the spring hunt.

In response to the IWC's actions, the United States, in cooperation with the Eskimos, developed a research program implemented by the National Marine Fisheries Service (NMFS), under the auspices of the National Oceanic and Atmospheric Administration (NOAA) of the Department of Commerce. The program was aimed at increasing knowledge of the bowhead, most immediately by obtaining a more accurate population estimate upon which to base quotas. . . .

At the June, 1978 IWC meeting, the U.S. presented its newly calculated "best estimate" of 2,264 whales migrating past Eskimo hunting grounds, compared with an estimate of 1,300 previously used by the Scientific Committee. Based on this new estimate, the U.S. recommended a maximum take of 2 percent of the best estimate of the population size, or 45 whales for 1979. Along with this recommendation, the U.S. agreed to maintain a research effort to detect any detrimental effect on the population and reduce the quota accordingly. The U.S. was supported in this proposal by the Alaska Eskimo Whaling Commission (AEWC), a group of Eskimo whalers formed in September, 1977, to protect Eskimo interests on the bowhead issue.

The Scientific Committee again recommended a zero take. The IWC did not adopt either proposal, but set a 1979 quota of 18 whales landed or 27 struck, and increased the 1978 quota for the fall hunt by 2.

The AEWC representatives demonstrated their disgust with the IWC actions by walking out of the meeting. The group later issued a statement of intent to remove itself from IWC jurisdiction, and to ignore IWC quotas. Although the AEWC has maintained this stance, no confrontation has occurred with NMFS which enforces IWC regulations domestically. At the close of the 1979 hunt, the Eskimo take was just within the IWC quota. (The quota had been reduced to 18/26 at the June, 1979 meeting, again over the Scientific Committee recommendation of a zero take.)

. . . .

NOTE

In *Hopson v. Kreps*, 462 F. Supp. 1374 (D. Alas. 1979), *rev'd and remanded*, 622 F.2d 1375 (9th Cir. 1980), the court was asked to determine whether the convention establishing the IWC was intended to cover subsistence hunting and whether the legislation implementing the convention delegates authority over Eskimo subsistence whaling to the Secretary of Commerce. In addition, the Eskimos alleged that Secretary Kreps ignored procedural requirements of the MMPA and the ESA and violated the U.S. trust responsibility to Eskimos. The government contended that interpretation of the Convention would involve foreign policy considerations, thus impinging on executive discretion. The district court agreed with the government and also accepted the view, shared by many government experts, that a decision favoring the Eskimos could seriously damage U.S. foreign policy in international whale conservation. The court thus limited its inquiry to the question of treaty interpretation and held this issue to be a nonjusticiable political question.

Despite the district court ruling in *Hopson*, the Eskimos continued to deny IWC jurisdiction over their activities and set a maximum take of 45 whales for the 1979 season, more than twice the IWC quota. Poor ice breakup and bad weather severely restricted the 1979 spring hunt and poor weather ended the fall hunt just as the IWC limit was reached. Possible quota violations during the 1980 bowhead whaling season led the Justice Department to bring the matter before a federal grand jury. But the Ninth Circuit Court of Appeals reversed and remanded the district court ruling in *Hopson*, holding that justiciable questions were presented as to whether the International Whaling Commission exceeded its jurisdiction under the International Whaling Convention when it eliminated the native subsistence whaling exemption and whether the Department of Commerce was authorized to implement the Commission's decision. 622 F.2d at 1382.

The 1981 amendments to Marine Mammal Protection Act providing for state management of marine mammals contained special provisions concerning subsistence hunting by Alaskan Eskimos. These provisions overrule effectively *People of Togiak*, 470 F. Supp. 123 (D.D.C. 1979), which invalidated Department of Interior regulations purporting to transfer authority over subsistence hunting to the State of Alaska, and authorize transfer of management authority to Alaska so long as priority to subsistence hunting is assured. *See* 16 U.S.C. §§ 1371(b); 1379(d), (e)(2)(B), (f). *See also* U.S. Dept. of Commerce, Laws and Treaties of the United States Relevant to Marine Mammal Protection Policy (1978).

The Endangered Species Act and Marine Mammals

Compare the MMPA moratorium provisions with the following language from section 7 of the Endangered Species Act of 1973 (ESA):

All Federal departments and agencies shall, in consultation with and the assistance of the Secretary, utilize their authorities in furtherance of the purposes of this chapter by . . . taking such action necessary to insure that actions authorized, funded or carried out do not jeopardize the continued existence of such endangered species or result in the destruction or modification of habitat of such species. . . .

16 U.S.C. § 1536.

With respect to marine mammals, many of which are listed as endangered, the ESA appears to afford great protection. Not only must the Secretary of the Interior enforce the moratorium on taking, he or she must also "insure" that the continued existence of endangered species is not threatened by government action.

It was suggested that under section 7, "an agency must always avoid the proscribed impacts on protected species regardless of cost, and may not balance other benefits against possible injury to a protected population in deciding whether to undertake a particular action." *See* Comment, *Obligations of Federal Agencies Under Section 7 of the Endangered Species Act of 1973*, 28 Stan. L. Rev. 1247 (1976).

This interpretation of section 7 found support in two cases which considered its operation. In *National Wildlife Federation v. Coleman*, 529 F.2d 359 (5th Cir. 1976), *cert. denied sub. nom. Boteler v. National Wildlife Federation*, 429 U.S. 979 (1976), the court reversed a lower court dismissal of a conservation group's action to enjoin the construction of a portion of I-10 in Mississippi. The NWF argued that insufficient consideration had been given to the highway's impact on the habitat of the Mississippi sandhill crane, an endangered species.

In agreeing with the conservationists, the court noted that although the project's final environmental impact statement "recognized and considered the danger the highway poses to the crane," the government had failed to take necessary steps to "insure" that the highway will not jeopardize the crane or modify its habitat.

Another important consideration, the court said, was the impact from the probable indirect effects of the project, traffic, commercial development, and increased construction in surrounding areas. *See also Palila v. Hawaii Dept. Nat. Resources*, 15 E.R.C. 1741 (9th Cir. 1981).

Then in *Tennessee Valley Authority v. Hill*, 98 S. Ct. 2279 (1978), the Supreme Court permanently enjoined operation of the completed $119 million Tellico Dam on the ground that opening the dam's floodgates would destroy critical habitat of the endangered 3-inch-long snail darter fish. Congress subsequently exempted the Tellico Dam from the ESA's restrictions and established a seven-member committee to rule on future exemptions; otherwise, the ESA's strong preservation mandates enforced in *Hill* remained intact.

The ESA's restrictions on the importation of endangered and threatened species, 16 U.S.C. § 1538, can affect living resource exploitation in foreign and international waters. *See*, e.g., *Cayman Turtle Farm, Ltd. v. Andrus*, 478 F. Supp. 125 (1979), upholding an Interior Department regulation prohibiting importation of all green sea turtle products produced in foreign mariculture operations. Here enforcement of the ESA is coordinated with U.S. implementation of the Convention on International Trade in Endangered Species of Wild Fauna and Flora. *See* 16 U.S.C. § 1538(c)(1).

Several concepts were borrowed from the MMPA when Congress in 1973 strengthened the protection of endangered species under the ESA. Among them were (1) the notion that a species might be considered depleted, and therefore eligible for special protection, even before it became endangered; (2) the protection of endangered populations of otherwise healthy species; and (3) federal limitations on the taking of protected species. *See* M. Bean, The Evolution of Federal Wildlife Law 386–417 (Council on Environmental Quality 1977).

Marine mammals protected under the ESA as well as the MMPA include several species of whales, and the manatee, dugong, and Mediterranean monk seal, which have been listed as endangered throughout all or a part of their ranges. *See* 5 Marine Mammal News No. 5 at 8 (May 1979). In cases of apparent conflict between the mandate of the ESA and the MMPA, section 17 of the ESA, 16 U.S.C. § 1543, states that, except as otherwise provided in the ESA, no provision of the ESA shall take precedence over any more restrictive conflicting provision of the MMPA.

See generally Coggins, *Federal Wildlife Law Achieves Adolescence: Developments in the 1970's*, 1978 Duke L.J. 753; Comment, *Implementing § 7 of the Endangered Species Act of 1973. First Notices from the Courts*, 6 ELR 10120 (1976); Lachenmeier, *The Endangered Species Act of 1973: Preservation or Pandemonium*, 5 Envt'l L. 29 (1974); Note, *Obligations of Federal Agencies Under Section 7 of the Endangered Species Act of 1973*, 28 Stan. L. Rev. 1247 (1976); Wood, *Section 7 of the Endangered Species Act of 1973: A Significant Restriction for All Federal Activities*, 5 Envt'l L. Rep. 50189 (1975).

Nonliving Resource Management

SECTION A: DEEP SEABED MINING

"DEEP SEA MINING ACT," 6 Environmental Law and Policy 134 (1980)

The Deep Seabed Hard Mineral Resources Act was signed by President Carter on June 28. The act established an interim regulatory procedure for ocean mining activities conducted by U.S nationals that will be superseded when a Law of the Sea Treaty enters into force for the United States.

. . . .

The legislation was originally introduced in 1971, but has been continuously revised since then. The Act is intended to serve three purposes: Firstly, to ensure that when a Law of the Sea treaty is implemented, there will be, in fact, a viable ocean mining industry. Secondly, it will subject ocean mining operations conducted in the interim to stringent domestic regulation to ensure protection of the marine environment, safety of life and property at sea, prevention of unreasonable interference with other uses of the high seas, and conservation of mineral resources. Thirdly, it will encourage nations that embark on ocean mining ventures before the treaty is in force to manage the activities of their nations in a similar fashion and to respect licenses and permits issued under this and other national legislation.

. . . It recognizes that the resources of the seabed are the common heritage of mankind, and requires that revenues from commercial production be set aside for developing countries. No sovereign jurisdiction is asserted over areas of the international seabed. No license will be issued for exploration to be conducted before July 1, 1981. More importantly, no permit for commercial recovery will be effective earlier than January 1, 1988.

It is felt that under this timetable the Law of the Sea Conference will have sufficient time to complete its work and to prepare for implementation of the treaty before commercial recovery under American law would actually take place. While, at the same time, potential ocean miners are assured that they may continue the orderly progress of their work without fear that delays in the international process could cause unforseen and costly interruptions in their development programmes.

The Act authorizes reciprocal agreements with any foreign nation that regulates the conduct of its citizens in a manner compatible with this legislation and recognizes the licenses, permits and priorities of right granted under it, and provides an interim framework for ocean mining that respects other nations' freedom of the high seas.

"DEEP SEABED MINERAL RESOURCE ACT," 20 Natural Resources Journal 164–166 (1980)

Licensing

Under the . . . act, the Administrator of the National Oceanic and Atmospheric Administration (NOAA) will regulate the mining activities and issue licenses to engage in exploration for the hard mineral resources. He would also issue permits for the commercial recovery of the mineral nodules. Each applicant must first prove to be financially responsible, have the necessary technical capability, and submit a work plan that meets the bill's requirements for environmental safeguards before the Administrator can certify issuance of a license or a permit. The Administrator also is required to determine whether the proposed exploration or commercial recovery will (1) unreasonably interfere with the freedoms of the high seas of other states, (2) conflict with any international obligations of the United States, (3) breach international peace and security, (4) have a significantly adverse effect on the quality of the environment or (5) pose an inordinate threat to the safety of life and property at sea. A valid license then entitles the holder to a permit, which allows him to "recover, own, take away, use and sell the hard mineral resources." The Administrator may modify or revise the terms of the permit to prevent any of the above and, after notice, may deny issuance, suspend, or revoke any license or permit if the holder fails to meet the requirements of the proposed act.

Regulation

Provisions of the act would be enforced by the Administrator. Licensees and permittees would have to allow federal officials on board ship to monitor exploratory and commercial recovery operations to assure stated goals were met. Authorized enforcement officers, under the control and supervision of the U.S. Coast Guard, could board, inspect and search a vessel if there were reasonable cause to believe a violation had been committed. The officers could seize the vessel with everything on board, including any recovered mineral resources, and arrest the persons involved. United States district courts would have exclusive jurisdiction over cases or controversies arising under the act and could adjudicate a civil forfeiture proceeding of any property seized. The other major civil penalty would be a maximum $25,000 fine for each violation. Criminal penalties are also included in the bill for willful and knowing violations of the act.

The act would also impose a tax of .75 percent on mining revenues. A Deep Seabed Fund would be established in the United States Treasury with funds matching those collected for mining. This fund will be available for purposes decided by Congress, which may include paying any financial obligations assumed by the United States pursuant to a ratified law of the sea deep seabed treaty.

Environmental Aspects

The act would regulate miners' effects on the environment by specifically requiring an Environmental Impact Statement (EIS) prior to issuance of a license or permit. There would be terms within each license or permit to limit the conduct of the holder concerning exploration or commercial recovery, thereby promoting safety of life and property at sea. The use of the best available technology for protection of safety, health and environment would be required. Included in the act are terms regarding the prevention of waste and providing for the future recovery of any remaining mineral nodules.

NOTES

1. The legislative history of the Deep Seabed Hard Mineral Resources Act, 30 U.S.C. §§ 1401–73, is summarized at U.S. Code Congressional & Administrative News, 96th Cong., 2d Sess. 3010 (1980).

2. Does the Deep Seabed Act as summarized in the excerpts above respond adequately to Frank's concerns about the environmental impacts of deep seabed mining expressed in Chapter 1, *supra*?

3. Why does the Deep Seabed Act not require the consent of adjacent coastal states to exploration licenses and commercial recovery permits issued under the Act like the Ocean Thermal Energy Conversion Act, 42 U.S.C. §§ 9101–67, and the Deepwater Port Act, *infra*? Is it because deep seabed mining will have only minimal impacts on the states' coastal zones? Consider section 102(c)(5) of the Deep Seabed Act, 30 U.S.C. § 1412(c)(5), which mandates, with very limited exceptions, that hard mineral resources recovered pursuant to the act shall be processed in the United States. Will the impacts of such processing be positive or negative?

Should nodule exploitation occur in the vicinity of Hawaii, a possibility which now seems quite likely, the public would benefit from the development of new industry. Once established, a nodule plant would provide some 2,400 permanent jobs and would increase the gross state product by $335 million. The state would continue to benefit by the taxes on gross revenues derived from sales of refined materials . . . . Such consequences may also be reasonably expected to inure to the benefit of other states with processing plants.

Arrow, *The Proposed Regime for the Unilateral Exploitation of Deep Seabed Mineral Resources*, 21 Harv. Int'l L.J. 337, 334 n.58 (1980).

4. Who owns manganese nodules resting on the ocean floor beyond the continental shelf of any coastal nation?

The legal premises of the Act are that, pursuant to customary international law, exploration for and recovery of seabed mineral resources beyond the limits of national jurisdiction is protected by the principle of freedom of the seas, that ownership of the resources involved would vest upon capture, and that no sovereign claim to the seabed itself is necessary to support a claim to harvest the resources thereon, any more than a sovereign claim to the seabed would be necessary to sustain a claim to mid-oceanic fishing rights.

Arrow, *The Proposed Regime for the Unilateral Exploitation of Deep Seabed Mineral Resources*, 21 Harv. Int'l L.J. 337–38 (1980). As described by Arrow, are the Act's legal premises correct? As a matter of property law? As a matter of international law? *See* Arrow, *The Customary Norm Process and the Deep Seabed,* 9 Ocean Dev. & Int'l L.J. 1 (1981).

5. For additional reading on deep seabed mining, *see* M. Ball, *Law of the Sea: Federal–State Relations* 71–73 (1978); Biggs, *Deep Seabed Mining and Unilateral Legislation*, 8 Ocean Dev. & Int'l L.J. 223 (1980); H. Dordrect, *Manganese Nodules: Dimensions and Perspectives* (1979); R. Frank, *Deepsea Mining and the Environment* (1976); Frank, *Environmental Aspects of Deepsea Mining*, 15 Va. J. Int'l L. 815 (1975); Miller & Delehant, *Deep Seabed Mining*, 11 J. Mar. L. & Com. 453 (1980); Note, *A New Combination to Davy Jones's Locker: Melee over Marine Minerals*, 9 Loyola-Chicago L. Rev. 935 (1978); Senate Commerce Committee, *Congress and the Nation's Oceans: Marine Affairs in the 94th Congress* 131–32 (1977).

6. Regarding the archaeological resources of the seabed, *see Treasure Salvors, Inc. v. Unidentified Wrecked and Abandoned Sailing Vessel*, 569 F.2d 330 (5th Cir. 1978). *See also* Note, *Marine Archaeology and International Law: Background and Some Suggestions*, 9 San Diego L. Rev. 668 (1972); Note, *Cultural Resource Preservation and Underwater Archaeology: Some Notes on the Current Legal Framework and a Model Underwater Antiquities Statute*, 15 San Diego L. Rev. 623 (1978).

SECTION B: OUTER CONTINENTAL SHELF OIL AND GAS

OCS Lands Act, 43 U.S.C. § 1331 *et seq.*

The consistent policy of the federal government since the fuel crisis of the early 1950s has been to expedite the exploration and development of oil and gas from the outer continental shelf (OCS). The presidential energy message of April 1979 reflected this policy by directing the Secretary of the Interior to add still more acreage to the already accelerated OCS oil and gas leasing schedule. In 1977, oil production from the outer continental shelf was estimated to be about 830,000 barrels per day, or roughly 5 percent of domestic oil consumption; gas production was estimated at about 3.7 trillion cubic feet, nearly 20 percent of

U.S. total supplies. Estimates by both government and industry suggest that 60 percent of the undiscovered oil and natural gas resources of the United States may be located in the OCS. The continental shelf will probably be the largest domestic source of oil and gas between now and the 1990s. As Senator Jackson, Chairman of the Senate Committee on Energy and Natural Resources, has said: "America's best hope for finding additional oil and gas resources and reducing our dependence on foreign oil" lies in the outer continental shelf. 124 Cong. Rec. §13,994 (daily ed., Aug. 22, 1978).

The controlling law for managing the outer continental shelf is the OCS Lands Act (43 U.S.C. § 1331 *et seq.*). Prior to 1978, this law gave the Secretary of the Interior broad discretionary powers over oil and gas leasing on the OCS, and the Secretary met this responsibility by issuing extensive and detailed regulations (30 C.F.R. § 250, 43 C.F.R. §§ 3301–3307 (1977)). The leasing program went forward under these regulations with little controversy from 1953 until 1969, when the Santa Barbara oil spill heightened public concern about the environmental risks of oil and gas development on the continental shelf.

The severe public reaction from this spectacular spill caused the Secretary of the Interior to suspend temporarily further exploration and development off the southern California coast—an action that promptly led to a lawsuit over the Secretary's authority to take such action. The public reaction was also significant in reinforcing the general environmental movement of the late 1960s and early 1970s, and helped persuade Congress that it should enact a series of environmental and wildlife protection laws that continue to impact OCS oil and gas development, including the National Environmental Policy Act (NEPA), federal Coastal Zone Management Act (CZMA), Marine Mammal Protection Act (MMPA), and Endangered Species Act (ESA).

The Santa Barbara spill and other similar, if less spectacular, incidents also served to warn state and local governments that accelerated development of outer continental shelf oil and gas, while benefiting the nation as a whole, threaten serious social, economic, and environmental problems for local onshore communities near where these resources are developed, and where they will be brought ashore.

The conflicts among the four principal participants—the oil companies, environmental groups, state and local governments, and the Department of the Interior—produced substantial controversy and litigation in the 1970s. By the mid-1970s, so much criticism had been raised about the leasing program under the act that in 1978 Congress massively overhauled the act and replaced it with a more comprehensive and detailed law. The extent of the 1978 revision is illustrated by the fact that the 1978 amendments take up 69 pages in the Statutes at Large, whereas the original act occupied only 10 pages.

Major provisions and reforms of the 1978 amendments include:

1. *Lease Sales–Bidding Systems:* The Department of the Interior and the Department of Energy were given the authority to investigate and use new bidding systems to determine the outcome on lease sales. Congress retained extensive oversight powers to assure adequate return and the effec-

tiveness of the new systems in promoting development. 43 U.S.C. § 1337 (Supp. II 1979).

2. *Competition Analysis:* The Department of the Interior was to give due consideration to the effect of any part of the leasing process on competition. The Attorney General in conjunction with the Federal Trade Commission was given discretionary authority to review any action prior to the lease award. The Secretary of the Interior is free to reject the Attorney General's recommendations by giving notice to all parties as to the reasons. 43 U.S.C. § 1337 (Supp. II 1979).

3. *Leasing Program:* The development, promulgation, and observance of a 5-year oil and gas leasing plan was required by the amendments. 43 U.S.C. § 1337 (Supp. II 1979).

4. *Safety and Environmental Protection:* The amendments provided for regulation of major health and safety problems which previously had not been tackled by the U.S. Coast Guard and the Occupational Health and Safety Administration because of uncertainties about jurisdiction. 43 U.S.C. § 1347 (Supp. II 1979). The environmental concerns were directly recognized by providing for suspension or cancellation of leases, clean air standards, and environmental review prior to sales. 43 U.S.C. § 1334 (Supp. II 1979).

5. *State and Local Government Involvement:* Onshore impacts are to be considered when preparing exploration, development, and production plans. The Secretary of Interior was to provide increased resource information to state and local governments to aid them in planning for onshore impacts. 43 U.S.C. § 1332 (Supp. II 1979).

6. *Litigation:* The amendments provide procedures for judicial review and a mechanism for citizen lawsuits to enforce the Act. Actions under other federal or state statutes were not precluded by these provisions, although the Congress hoped to encourage consolidation of all claims in one action. 43 U.S.C. § 1349 (Supp. II 1979).

7. *Oil Spills:* An oil pollution compensation fund was established to compensate for damages and cleanup costs from OCS oil spills. 43 U.S.C. § 1812 (Supp. II 1979).

8. *Due Diligence:* To forestall lessees from holding back on development, the amendments specify that a due diligence clause must be part of the lease terms. Lack of due diligence may cause cancellation of existing leases as well as the loss of future lease rights. 43 U.S.C. § 1337 (Supp. II 1979).

NOTE

For detailed discussions of the 1978 amendments, *see* Jones, Mead & Sorenson, *The Outer Continental Shelf Lands Act Amendment of 1978*, 19 Nat. Res. J. 886 (1979); Krueger & Singer, *An Analysis of the Outer Continental Lands Act Amendments of*

1978, 19 Nat. Res. J. 909 (1979); Comment, *The Outer Continental Shelf Lands Act Amendments of 1978: Balancing Energy Needs with Environmental Concerns,* 40 La. L. Rev. 177 (1979).

Sequence of Development

The OCS Lands Act and the extensive regulations promulgated thereunder describe and govern a process, a sequence of decisions and actions that starts with the development of a 5-year plan and ends with the termination or expiration of the lease for a particular tract.

The 5-year leasing plan is intended to govern the size, timing, and location of leasing activities by the federal government on the OCS. In developing the first 5-year plan to "best meet national energy needs for the five-year period following its approval," 43 U.S.C. § 1344 (Supp. II 1979), there was considerable controversy and debate. *See generally* Bureau of Land Management, U.S. Department of the Interior, Final Environmental Statement: Proposed Five Year OCS Oil and Gas Lease Sale Schedule March 1980 to February 1985 (1980); U.S. House of Representatives, Select Committee on the Outer Continental Shelf, Offshore Oil and Gas: The Five-Year Leasing Program and the Implementation of the Outer Continental Shelf Lands Act Amendments of 1978 (1980). In *California v. Watt*, 16 ERC 1561 (D.C. Cir. 1981), the court remanded the first five-year plan to the Secretary of Interior to correct violations of 43 U.S.C. § 1344(a) by: (1) evaluating different OCS areas according to their environmental sensitivity and marine productivity; (2) quantifying the potential damage to fishing, tourism, and similar activities caused by OCS activities, including oil spills; and (3) taking the foregoing factors into account in deciding upon a five-year plan.

The time needed to discover and identify a resource can vary from as little as 2 to as long as 7 years. The development phase during which the drilling and production platforms are installed and the pipelines are laid averages from 4 to 9 years. The production phase is dependent on the size of the resources and the optimum production rate. It can vary from 10 to 25 years, or even longer where there is a major resource. After production ceases, the shutdown phase lasts anywhere from 1 to 3 years, during which the platforms are dismantled and the wells sealed. Thus, the lease of a productive tract is the first step in a potentially long-term relationship between the federal government as lessor and regulator, and the oil company as lessee. *See generally* Swan, *Ocean Oil and Gas Drilling and the Law* (1979).

The following cases and materials illustrate the main themes of the controversies. The first section focuses on the rights, duties, and relationships of various parties under the OCS Lands Act, while the second section focuses on challenges to OCS development under other federal legislation such as NEPA. As you read the following materials, consider how these competing policy objectives might influence decision making on oil and gas development:

1. Maximizing domestic production of oil and gas
2. Maximizing revenues to the U.S. Treasury
3. Maintaining a competitive, free market system

4. Protecting marine resources
5. Protecting other environmental resources, e.g., air quality
6. Improving federal–state relations with respect to OCS development
7. Facilitating federal interagency cooperation

Suspension and Termination of Offshore Oil and Gas Leases

UNION OIL CO. OF CALIF. v. MORTON, 512 F.2d 743 (9th Cir. 1975)

CHOY, Circuit Judge:

Four major oil companies brought this action to set aside an order of the Secretary of the Interior denying them permission to construct a drilling platform in the Santa Barbara Channel which they allege is necessary for full exercise of their rights under a federal oil and gas lease. The companies also seek to enjoin the Secretary from further interference with enjoyment of their lease rights. The district court held that the Secretary's order was within his statutory authority and was not arbitrary, capricious, or an abuse of discretion, and dismissed the complaint. We vacate the decision of the district court and remand for further proceedings.

Factual Background

In February 1968, the four companies (hereinafter "Union") paid over $61 million for oil and gas rights on tract OSC–P 0241. The leased tract lies on the continental shelf in the Santa Barbara Channel, beyond the jurisdiction of the State of California. The Interior Department granted the lease under the authority of the Outer Continental Shelf Lands Act, 43 U.S.C. § 1331 et seq.

The lease gives Union the right to erect floating drilling platforms, subject to the provisions of the Act and to "reasonable regulations" not inconsistent with the lease issued by the Secretary. Two platforms, A and B, were installed, each supporting many productive wells. In September 1968, Union sought permission to install a third platform, C. The Secretary approved the application, and the Army Corps of Engineers issued the necessary permit. In January 1969, before platform C was installed, a blow-out occurred on one of the wells on platform A. The blowout caused the disastrous Santa Barbara oil spill which killed birds and marine organisms, damaged beaches and seafront properties, and restricted fishing and recreational activities in the area.

On February 7, 1969, the Secretary ordered all activities on this and certain other leases suspended pending further environmental studies. After these studies were completed, the Secretary announced on September 20, 1971, that Union would not be allowed to install platform C, because operation of that platform would be "incompatible with the concept of the Federal Sanctuary [which the Secretary had proposed to Congress]." He stated that all operations would remain suspended on certain other Channel leases, pending action by Congress cancelling the leases. *See* Gulf Oil Corp. v. Morton, 493 F.2d 141 (9th Cir. 1973).

The Department formally notified the companies the following month that the Secretary "has determined that the installation of Platform 'C' would be inconsistent with protection of the environment of the Santa Barbara Channel and has directed [the Regional Supervisor] to withdraw the approval of September 16, 1968." This suit resulted. On November 3, 1972, just prior to trial, the Secretary issued a statement further clarifying the environmental concerns contributing to his decision.

. . . .

We upheld the Secretary's suspension of the leases pending congressional action in *Gulf Oil, supra.* Because Congress had not acted within a reasonable time to cancel the leases in question, however, we declared the suspension invalid after October 18, 1972. 493 F.2d at 149. This appeal is limited to the validity of the order withdrawing permission for Union to install platform C.

The Act

The Outer Continental Shelf Act authorizes the Secretary to issue oil and gas leases on the outer continental shelf to the highest bidder. 43 U.S.C. § 1337(a). A lease issued under this Act, like a mineral lease granted under the Mineral Leasing Act of 1920, 30 U.S.C. § 181 et seq., does not convey title in the land, nor does it convey an unencumbered estate in the oil and gas. *See* Boesche v. Udall, 373 U.S. 472, 478, 83 S.Ct. 1373, 10 L.Ed.2d 491 (1963); McKenna v. Wallis, 344 F.2d 432, 440–41 (5th Cir. 1965), vacated, 384 U.S. 63, 86 S.Ct. 1301, 16 L.Ed.2d 369 (1966). The lease does convey a property interest enforceable against the Government, of course, but it is an interest lacking many of the attributes of private property. Oil and gas deposits beneath the continental shelf are precious resources belonging to the entire nation. Congress, although encouraging the extraction of these resources by private companies, provided safeguards to insure that their exploitation should inure to the benefit of all. These safeguards are not limited to those provided by covenants in the lease; Congress also authorized the Secretary to maintain extensive, continuing regulation of the oil companies' day to day drilling operations.

Careful study of the Act confirms that Congress intended to exercise both proprietary powers of a landowner and the police powers of a legislature in regulating leases of publicly owned resources. *Cf.* Forbes v. United States, 125 F.2d 404, 408 (9th Cir. 1942). The Secretary, to whom Congress has delegated these powers, may prescribe at any time those rules which he finds necessary for the conservation of natural resources. 43 U.S.C. § 1334(a)(1). Exercising its legislative power, Congress has provided criminal penalties for knowing violation of these rules. 43 U.S.C. § 1334(a)(2). In addition, those rules in effect at the time a lease is executed are incorporated statutorily into the terms of the lease. 43 U.S.C. § 1334(a)(2). The Secretary like a private property owner, may obtain cancellation of the lease if the lessee breaches such a rule. 43 U.S.C. § 1334(b)(1). Violation of rules issued after the lease has been executed does not enable the Secretary to cancel the lease, however. The property rights of the lessee are determined only by those rules in effect when the lease is executed. *See generally* Christopher, The Outer Continental Shelf Lands Act: Key to a New Frontier, 6 Stan.L.Rev. 23, 43–47 (1953).

. . . .

Suspension: Regulation or Taking?

Pursuant to 43 U.S.C. § 1334(a)(1), the Secretary issued a regulation on August 22, 1969, authorizing emergency suspension of any operation which "threatens immediate, serious, or irreparable harm or damage to life, including aquatic life, to property, to the leased deposits, to other valuable mineral deposits or to the environment. Such emergency suspension shall continue until in his judgment the threat or danger has terminated." 30 C.F.R. § 250.12. Refusal to allow installation of a previously approved platform could be justified only as a suspension of operations under this regulation.

The regulation properly provides for "conservation of the natural resources of the outer Continental Shelf," as we have construed that phrase. Nevertheless, Union points to the distinction between a suspension and a revocation, asserting that the Secretary did not in fact merely suspend operations, because a suspension by definition possesses a "temporary nature." United Air Lines, Inc. v. CAB, 198 F.2d 100, 108 (7th Cir. 1952); *see* Western Air Lines, Inc. v. CAB, 196 F.2d 933, 935–36 (9th Cir.), cert. denied, 344 U.S. 875, 73 S.Ct. 167, 97 L.Ed. 677 (1952). The structure of the Act demonstrates that Congress intended vested rights under the lease to be invulnerable to defeasance by subsequently issued regulations. Although 30 C.F.R. § 250.12 provides expressly that a "suspension" shall be limited in time only by the Secretary's judgment that the environmental threat has ended, and although 43 U.S.C. § 1334(a)(1) authorizes regulations providing not only for suspensions but for any other action affecting operations which the Secretary determines "necessary and proper" for "conservation of natural resources," Congress clearly did not intend to grant leases so tenuous in nature that the Secretary could terminate them, in whole or in part, at will.

Congress itself can order the leases forfeited even now, subject to payment of compensation. But without congressional authorization, the Secretary or the executive branch in general has no intrinsic powers of condemnation. Youngstown Sheet & Tube Co. v. Sawyer, 343 U.S. 579, 585, 588, 72 S.Ct. 863, 96 L.Ed. 1153 (1952); Hooe v. United States, 218 U.S. 322, 335, 336, 31 S.Ct. 85, 54 L.Ed. 1055 (1910). Congress' clear concern to distinguish police power regulation from invasion of property rights in these leases convinces us that Congress did not confer powers of condemnation upon the Secretary by implication.

The degree to which the Government may interfere with the enjoyment of private property by exercise of its police power without having to pay compensation is not a simple question. The courts, under a variety of tests, have recognized that regulation of private property can become so onerous that it amounts to a taking of that property. *See* Goldblatt v. Hempstead, 369 U.S. 590, 594, 82 S.Ct. 987, 8 L.Ed.2d 130 (1962); United States v. Central Eureka

Mining Co., 357 U.S. 155, 168, 78 S.Ct. 1097, 2 L.Ed.2d 1228 (1958); Pennsylvania Coal Co. v. Mahon, 260 U.S. 393, 415, 43 S.Ct. 158, 67 L.Ed. 322 (1922). If, as Union contends, platform C is a necessary means for the extraction of oil from a portion of the leased area, refusal to permit installation of that platform now or at any time in the future deprives Union of all benefit from the lease in that particular area. We therefore conclude that an open-ended suspension of the right granted Union to install a drilling platform would be a pro tanto cancellation of its lease.

Such a taking by interference with private property rights is within the constitutional power of Congress, subject to payment of compensation. *See* Dugan v. Rank, 372 U.S. 609, 83 S.Ct. 999, 10 L.Ed.2d 15 (1963). But Congress no more impliedly authorized the Secretary to take the leasehold by prohibiting its beneficial use than by condemnation proceeding. A suspension for which the fifth amendment would require compensation is therefore unauthorized and beyond the Secretary's power.

Whether the Secretary has taken Union's property depends on the conditions of the suspension. If operations are suspended indefinitely, property rights have been taken. To determine whether the suspension is indefinite, or, on the other hand, is a temporary suspension whose termination is conditioned by the occurrence of certain future events, we must examine the justifications which the Secretary has offered for the suspension. The Secretary explained the suspension most recently in his statement of November 3, 1972:

The following were the primary factors that led to my decision denying the platform applications:

(1) construction of the proposed platform and drilling wells would increase the risk of oil pollution in the Santa Barbara Channel by reason of:
   (a) the risks inherent in offshore oil drilling;
   (b) location of the Channel in an active seismic belt; and
   (c) with regard to Platform "C", the fact that the platform would be located on the damaged Dos Quadros [sic] structure;

(2) oil pollution in the Santa Barbara Channel would have adverse consequences, both short and longer term, because of the characteristics of the Channel environment; the following attributes of the Channel that would be affected by oil pollution were given particular consideration:
   (a) animal and plant marine life;
   (b) commercial and sport fisheries;
   (c) recreational use;
   (d) beaches and shore line of the Channel;
   (e) birds;

(3) the lack of systems and equipment which are completely effective in controlling and removing oil pollution under all weather and sea conditions;

(4) the suitability of the Dos Quadros [sic] structure (leases OCS–P 0241 and 0240) for unitization and the suitability of leases OCS–P 0240 and 0166 for unitization;

(5) additional platforms would increase interference with other uses of the Channel for recreational and commercial fishing;

(6) additional platforms would be aesthetically undesirable.

Factors 2, 4, 5, and 6 amount simply to a weighing of conflicting interests which the Secretary should have undertaken before the lease was granted. For the Secretary to offer these factors now to justify suspending Union's drilling activities asserts in effect that he can cancel the lease because he has changed his mind. These enumerated interests are not temporary concerns which the passage of time may eliminate.

Factors 1 and 3, however, suggest conditions which the development of new technology or further study may lessen as threats to the environment. Further study of seismic risks in the Channel, or of the geology of the Dos Cuadros structure, for example, may produce evidence of environmental risks unanticipated at the time the lease was executed. Knowledge of these newly-discovered risks might induce Congress to cancel the lease. A suspension also might provide time for an improved pollution control technology to be developed. A suspension whose termination was conditioned on the occurrence of events or the discovery of new knowledge which can be anticipated within a reasonable period of time would be a valid exercise of the Secretary's regulatory power, and not a fifth amendment taking.

The vague assertion of potential risks advanced in the Secretary's 1972 statement is totally inadequate to enable this court to decide whether such justifications for a suspension do exist, however, and whether they sufficiently restrict the duration of the suspension to avoid the need for compensation. The trial court decided without explanation that the suspension deprived Union of no property rights. We are uncertain as to the basis for this conclusion.

In view of the insufficient nature both of the Secretary's explanation for the suspension and the district court's justification of its judgment, we vacate the decision of the district court and remand the case to the district court for a determination whether the Secretary is taking property rights from Union. The court should allow the Secretary to prepare and present an amended statement of the grounds on which he bases the suspension. *See* Citizens to Preserve Overton Park, Inc. v. Volpe, 401 U.S. 402, 420, 91 S.Ct. 814, 28 L.Ed.2d 136 (1971); SEC v. Chenery Corp., 318 U.S. 80, 94–95, 63 S.Ct. 454, 87 L.Ed. 626 (1943). The court may, at its discretion, receive additional evidence and testimony in support of and in opposition to the Secretary's amended justification. The court should then determine whether each justification advanced by the Secretary is appropriate under 30 C.F.R. § 250.12, whether the Secretary has offered sufficient evidence to demonstrate that his decision was not arbitrary and capricious or an abuse of discretion, and whether the duration of a suspension based on the grounds offered is sufficiently conditioned on the occurrence of future events to avoid fifth amendment requirements of compensation.

If the trial court finds that the suspension, as limited by the Secretary's amended statement, complies with these requirements, Union's complaint should be dismissed. Otherwise, the order of suspension should be set aside as beyond the Secretary's statutory powers. 5 U.S.C. § 706(2)(C).

Because of the Secretary's continuing supervisory obligations, injunctive relief against further interference with Union's operations would be inappropriate.

Vacated and remanded.

NOTES

1. What exactly was the district court directed to determine? If a valid suspension order is one that is "sufficiently conditioned on the occurrence of future events," must it be certain that those events will in fact occur, or are only probable?

2. In *Sun Oil Co. v. United States*, 572 F.2d 786 (Ct. Cl. 1978), a court considered, as an explanation for a decision to disapprove a lessee's development plan, the same environmental factors offered in *Union Oil*, and found them unsupported by the evidence. The court held that the Secretary's denial of a development permit despite a favorable environmental impact statement "unreasonably interfered with and thereby breached plaintiff's lease right" to install a drilling platform and awarded "delay damages until such time as defendant allows plaintiffs to install Platform Henry or until such time as defendant justifies on conservation and/or environmental grounds" the refusal to allow the construction. *Id.* at 817. Does it make any difference whether the dispute is cast in terms of a breach of contract, as above, or in terms of a fifth amendment taking, as in *Union Oil*?

3. In *Pauley Petroleum Inc. v. United States*, 591 F.2d 1308 (Ct. Cl. 1979), a leaseholder filed suit shortly after the Santa Barbara blowout and the ensuing suspension of drilling by the Department of the Interior. The suit claimed that the Department's failure to act on the leaseholder's outstanding drilling permit and/or the change in oil spill liability regulations altered the contractual relationship between the parties. The court discussed but bypassed the leaseholder's claims of frustration, mutual mistake, total or partial breach or taking, because the leaseholder had not pursued potential administrative remedies for the problem. Is *Pauley* consistent with *Sun Oil*? Could contingency sales planned to compensate for lease sales held up by litigation or other circumstances alter the damages sustained by suspended lessees?

4. Congress attempted to clarify the rights of lessor and lessee in the OCS Lands Act Amendments of 1978. The section dealing with suspension and termination of leases provides in part (43 U.S.C. § 1334(a) (1978)):

The regulations prescribed by the Secretary under this subsection shall include, but not be limited to, provisions—

(1) for the suspension or temporary prohibition of any operation or activity, including production, pursuant to any lease or permit (A) at the request of a lessee, in the national interest, to facilitate proper development of a lease or to allow for the construction or negotiation for use of transportation facilities, or (B) if there is a threat of serious, irreparable, or immediate harm or damage to life (including fish and other aquatic life), to property, to any mineral deposits (in areas leased or not leased), or to the marine, coastal, or human environment, and for the extension of any permit or lease affected by suspension or prohibition under clause (A) or (B) by a period equivalent to the period of such suspension or prohibition, except that no permit or lease shall be so extended when such suspension or prohibition is the result of gross negligence or willful

violation of such lease or permit, or of regulations issued with respect to such lease or permit;

(2) with respect to cancellation of any lease or permit—

    (A) that such cancellation may occur at any time, if the Secretary determines, after a hearing, that—

        (i)   continued activity pursuant to such lease or permit would probably cause serious harm or damage to life (including fish and other aquatic life), to property, to any mineral (in areas leased or not leased), to the national security or defense, or to the marine, coastal, or human environment;

        (ii) the threat of harm or damage will not disappear or decrease to an acceptable extent within a reasonable period of time; and

        (iii) the advantages of cancellation outweigh the advantages of continuing such lease or permit in force;

    (B) that such cancellation shall not occur unless and until operations under such lease or permit shall have been under suspension, or temporary prohibition, by the Secretary, with due extension of any lease or permit term continuously for a period of five years, or for a lesser period upon request of the lessee;

    (C) that such cancellation shall entitle the lessee to receive such compensation as he shows to the Secretary as being equal to the lesser of (i) the fair value of the canceled rights as of the date of cancellation, taking account of both anticipated revenues from the lease and anticipated costs, including costs of compliance with all applicable regulations and operating orders, liability for cleanup costs or damages, or both, in the case of an oilspill, and all other costs reasonably anticipated on the lease, or (ii) the excess, if any, over the lessee's revenues, from the lease (plus interest thereon from the date of receipt to date of reimbursement) of all consideration paid for the lease and all direct expenditures made by the lessee after the date of issuance of such lease and in connection with exploration or development, or both, pursuant to the lease (plus interest on such consideration and such expenditures from date of payment to date of reimbursement).

(a) Note also that under 43 U.S.C. §§ 1334(c), (d) a lease is subject to cancellation for violation of any regulation no matter when the regulation was issued, not, as under the original act, only for violations of regulations "in force and in effect on the date of the issuance of the lease." Is it constitutional for Congress to avoid paying compensation for a canceled lease by putting a lessee on notice that his lease may be canceled for violation of subsequently issued regulations? In practice, would a court cancel a producing lease for a negligent violation or a trivial violation? Is cancellation in such circumstances required by the terms of the Act if requested by the Secretary and the violation is proven?

(b) What proprietary rights, if any, does a lessee retain under the section above? Has the leasehold become so tenuous as to discourage new ventures by industry? Alternative bidding systems could lessen the impact of cancellation. The Secretary of Interior is required to lease at least 20 percent of the area offered for lease each year by a bidding system other than the bonus bid/fixed royalty method, which had been the usual method. The lessees under this alternative bidding system would not be required to make such a high initial capital outlay as under the bonus bid system, so would not have as much at stake in the advent of a suspension or termination without compensation.

(c) Even if a lessee complies with all regulations and lease terms, the lease is subject to cancellation if the Secretary determines that the three conditions of 43 U.S.C. § 1334(a)(2)(A) above exist. Given the "arbitrary and capricious" standard of judicial review of such a determination, how much discretion will the Secretary have? Note that the required 5-year suspension period that must precede cancellation could mean that different presidential administrations would have to concur in a decision that a lease be canceled on environmental grounds.

(d) Leases may also be effectively canceled by disapproval of a development plan under section 25(h). And under section 25(h)(2)(C), a lease *must* be canceled if the Secretary finds that the lessee has failed to submit a development plan expeditiously and in good faith. See 43 U.S.C. § 1351 (1978).

Department of Interior regulations regarding OCS lease suspension or cancellation if operations present a threat to the environment are codified at 30 C.F.R. 250.34 (1980). *See also* Note, *Winter-Only Drilling Restriction Is Not a Suspension of Operations*, 20 Nat. Res. J. 363 (1980).

5. For additional litigation arising out of the Santa Barbara oil spill, *see County of Santa Barbara v. Hickel*, 426 F.2d 164 (9th Cir. 1974) (right to a hearing prior to resumption of drilling); *Union Oil Co. v. Miner*, 437 F.2d 408 (9th Cir. 1970) (state prosecution for criminal nuisance enjoined); *Oppen v. Aetna*, 485 F.2d 252 (9th Cir. 1973) (pleasure boat owners may recover for physical damage but not loss of navigation); *Union Oil Co. v. Oppen*, 501 F.2d 558 (9th Cir. 1974) (commercial fishers may recover lost profits).

6. The ability of the Secretary of the Interior to exercise continuing control over production activities has figured prominently in challenges to OCS activity under the National Environmental Policy Act (NEPA) and related federal environmental protection laws. As you read the following materials, consider how the Secretary's powers under the amended act will affect future NEPA and related challenges to OCS oil and gas drilling.

Challenges to OCS Oil and Gas Development Under the National Environmental Policy Act and Other Federal Laws Relating to Ocean and Coastal Resource Use

The National Environmental Policy Act (NEPA)
42 U.S.C. § 4321 *et seq.*

NEPA was enacted in December 1969. At the time, few people thought this novel environmental law would be the basis of significant environmental litigation. Virtually nothing was said in the hearings or floor debates about judicial enforcement of the Act. Its sponsors thought that its main impact would be internal to the federal agencies.

What happened in the courts surprised everyone. Abetted by judicial relaxation of the standing requirement, NEPA litigation literally poured into the courts. In its Tenth Annual Report, the Council on Environmental Quality reported that during the 9 years from 1969 to 1978, 1,052 NEPA lawsuits were filed raising challenges to slightly less than 10 percent of the 11,000 Environmental Impact Statements filed by the federal agencies during that period. Courts issued injunctions related to NEPA matters in 217 or about 20 percent of these cases. Since 1975 there has been a leveling off of NEPA lawsuits, although in 1978 there were still 114 lawsuits challenging federal actions under the act.

The bulk of the NEPA litigation in the early years was initiated by environmental groups and individuals. In recent years, state and local governments, and commercial and industrial firms have initiated a relatively higher percentage of these suits.

The most frequent complaint in NEPA lawsuits in 1978, comprising some 57 percent of the allegations, was that the federal agencies should have prepared an EIS but failed to do so. The second most common allegation, 30 percent of the total, was that the EIS was inadequate. This distribution has remained fairly constant over recent years.

Much of the litigation has been over section 102(2)(C) of NEPA, 42 U.S.C. § 4332(2)(C), which provides:

> The Congress authorizes and directs that, to the fullest extent possible: . . . all agencies of the Federal Government shall—
> . . . .
>
> (C) include in every recommendation or report on proposals for legislation and other major Federal actions significantly affecting the quality of the human environment, a detailed statement by the responsible official on—
>   (i) the environmental impact of the proposed action,
>   (ii) any adverse environmental effects which cannot be avoided should the proposal be implemented,
>   (iii) alternatives to the proposed action,
>   (iv) the relationship between local short-term uses of man's environment and the maintenance and enhancement of long-term productivity, and
>   (v) any irreversible and irretrievable commitments of resources which would be involved in the proposed action should it be implemented.

Four principal issues have arisen under section 102(c)(2):

1. When must an EIS be prepared?

2. What must an adequate EIS contain?

3. What is the proper standard of judicial review?

4. What effect does (or should) and EIS have on agency decision making?

See C. Meyers & D. Tarlock, *Water Resource Management* 538–590 (1971); Note, *The NEPA Model for the Protection of Coastal Aesthetics*, 28 Buf. L. Rev. 817 (1979); W. Rodgers, *Environmental Law* 697–834 (1977).

Some of the leading cases interpreting NEPA have arisen from court challenges to OCS exploration and development activities.

1. The agency itself makes the decision whether a contemplated action requires an EIS, a decision subject only to an "arbitrary and capricious" standard of judicial review. *See* Baum, Canary, Reeve & Scott, *Negative NEPA: The Decision Not to File*, 6 Envt'l L. 309 (1977). There are several stages along the OCS development path where an EIS may be required. The Interior Department prepared a programmatic EIS (PEIS) on the effects of the expansion of OCS oil and gas leasing initiated in the 1970s, and relied on that statement for preparation of the new 5-year leasing program mandated by the amended act.

   In *California ex rel. Younger v. Morton*, 404 F. Supp. 26 (C.D. Cal. 1975), plaintiff argued that the Secretary of the Interior should be compelled to prepare an EIS before recommending lease acceleration to the President, before identifying any offshore area as a possible target of exploration, and before applying to Congress for funds to finance a leasing program. The court rejected such a step-by-step approach to NEPA compliance, stating that such a requirement would "unduly fetter early investigative stages of DOI aimed only at testing possible feasibility of the program" and that "it was in appropriate compliance with [NEPA] for the Secretary to time the completion of a final statement so as just to precede his final decision whether there should be a sale." *Id.* at 31. On appeal, the Ninth Circuit Court of Appeals in *People of the State of California ex rel. Younger v. Andrus*, 608 F.2d 1247 (1979), raised the issue of California's standing to challenge the PEIS. Because California has assented to "injury" the court vacated the District Court's earlier opinion and remanded the case for further consideration.

   A similar statement is found in *County of San Diego v. Andrus*, 7 Envt'l L. Rep. 20,754 (S.D. Cal., Aug. 17, 1977): "Before a meaningful EIS can be prepared the agency must first formulate a proposal of sufficient definiteness upon which the EIS can be based." *Id.* Plaintiff contended that an EIS should have been prepared before the Secretary's call for nominations for tracts to be included in a base sale off southern California. But if an agency must spend considerable time and effort formulating a proposal, is there not a danger that their vested interest in the project will prevent them from making a disinterested evaluation of the EIS data? Whether the agency actually uses the EIS as a decision-making aid, or merely as a post hoc rationalization of a decision already made, is a question of fact for the trial court to resolve.

2. When is the point of no return reached in the so-called "easily divisible" project? Certainly not after a lease sale has been held. The act only authorizes, not directs, the Secretary to grant leases, and if after comparison of bonus bids with U.S. Geological Survey estimates of tract values, he or she decides that it would not be in the public interest to grant the leases, he or she may reject all bids. The Secretary's power to do so was upheld in *Kerr-McGee Corp. v. Morton*, 527 F.2d 838 (D.C. Cir. 1975). Must the Secretary make a reviewable finding that the bids are not in the public interest, or can he or she simply change his mind? *See Chevron Oil Co. v. Andrus*, 588 F.2d 1383, 1389–91 (5th Cir. 1979).

3. *Get Oil Out, Inc. v. Andrus*, 477 F. Supp. 40 (C.D. Cal. 1979), accords the Secretary of the Interior considerable discretion as to whether to prepare an EIS in connection with the approval or disapproval of an exploration or development plan, or any construction pursuant to such plans. Also, in *Village of Kaktovik v. Corps of Engineers*, 9 Envt'l L. Rep. 20117 (D. Alas., Dec. 29, 1978), the Army Corps of Engineers issued a permit to a holder of a state offshore oil and gas lease for construction of a gravel drilling pad for exploratory drilling, without first preparing an EIS. The court, noting that although the Corps had not pre-

Changed slightly by #3 OCS Admendments

pared an EIS as such, it had engaged in a study of the environmental impact of exploratory and development activity in the same area, refused to enjoin the construction:

[P]laintiffs have raised questions suggesting that a more thorough site-specific study should have been undertaken before the permit was issued. Although Exxon's plans incorporated protections against storms and ice movement, the data upon which the design was based was gathered over a limited five-year period from areas other than Duck Island. Furthermore, plaintiffs argue that the placement of the island at the mouth of the Sagavanirktok River poses special dangers from flooding. However, the Exxon plan does provide for protection against unusual ice conditions through its emergency half-hour shutdown procedure. In addition, since all structures and equipment will be removed prior to spring breakup of the Sagavanirktok River, spring flooding should not pose a substantial danger to the operation.

Plaintiffs also raise the issue of whether the Corps should have prepared an EIS on the cumulative effects of exploratory activity in the Beaufort Sea. In granting Exxon's permit, Corps' approval was limited to the construction of one gravel island in the Duck Island area. When the Corps is faced with permit applications for the construction of additional gravel islands, it will be required to consider the cumulative effect of gravel islands on the environment of the area. See *Kleppe v. Sierra Club*, 427 U.S. 390, 410 n.20 [6 ELR 20532, 20537 n.20] (1976). Thus, until presented with the proposed activity, the Corps should not be required to prepare an EIS on its effects.

. . . .

4. Was the Failure to Prepare an EIS on Production Activity a Violation of NEPA?

The next question to be considered under NEPA is whether the Corps of Engineers erred in failing to consider the environmental effects of future production activity from the island when issuing the permit to Exxon for the exploratory drilling stage without an EIS. Factors to be considered include the independence of the proposed activity, the known dimension of the activity, and whether the commitment of resources to exploratory drilling is so significant that approval for production activity will be difficult to deny once the exploratory activity has been completed.

Exxon maintains that it has no production plan for the well and concedes that it could not proceed into production from the island without additional Corps of Engineers approval together with the necessary environmental review. At the hearing, an Exxon official testified that it was highly unlikely that the Duck Island exploratory well would be converted to production activity. In any event, the plan of operations requires that the well be abandoned in May 1979 whether or not reserves are discovered in commercial quantities.

Based on these factors, I conclude that analysis by the Corps of environmental effects of production activity should be made when and if a production plan is proposed for agency approval because the exploratory activity is sufficiently independent from possible future production to be considered separately in the agency review process.

In regard to Exxon's commitment of resources to the exploratory well, Exxon maintains that despite the anticipated $11 million investment in drilling the Duck Island well, Exxon is not irretrievably committed to production. Compared to a cost of $8–20 million for an exploratory well in the Arctic, a company must invest approximately 50 times that amount, roughly $400 million to $1 billion, to obtain production from such a well. Industry figures indicate that less than one percent of the exploratory wells drilled on the North Slope have resulted in production operations.

In light of these factors, I conclude that Exxon's commitment of resources, although a substantial investment, is not so great that approval for production activity will be difficult to deny once the exploratory stage has been completed. A purpose of such exploratory activity is to provide information as to whether production activity in an area would be justified. Environmental effects of production activity and the increased impacts on the environment from production and transport facilities may be considered when a specific production plan has been proposed. Thus, plaintiffs have not shown even a fair likelihood of success on the merits of this NEPA claim.

Does the Balance of Irreparable Harm Favor Plaintiffs?

Plaintiffs claim irreparable harm to their subsistence hunting and fishing and to their way of life if the preliminary injunction is not granted.

Defendant Exxon claims that over $7.0 million has been expended on the project to date and that daily drilling costs average $60,000. In addition, Exxon claims that if operations were suspended for 30 days or more, Exxon would not have sufficient time to evaluate the well prior to spring 1979 breakup and the fall 1979 expiration date for the Duck Island Unit lease. Exxon alleges that the nine leases comprising the Duck Island Unit were obtained at a cost in excess of $20 million. Failure to drill the exploratory well before the end of the primary term of the leases in September 1979 could result in the loss of these leases.

Plaintiffs claim of harm to the environment and to the wildlife upon which they depend for their way of life must be examined in terms of Exxon's exploratory project and not a more generalized concern about future oil and gas development and production activity in the Beaufort Sea.

Exxon's permit is clearly limited to exploratory drilling and to the conditions of its Plan of Operations approved by the State. It must stop all drilling activity by March 31, 1979 and remove the drilling rig, all facilities, equipment, and personnel prior to May 1, 1979, or spring breakup, whichever occurs first.

The permit requires additional authorization before production activity would be allowed. Thus, concerns expressed by plaintiffs in regard to production from the site would be properly addressed only in the event Exxon applies for authorization to engage in production activity.

After reviewing the testimony, exhibits, and affidavits in regard to the possibility of unusual ice movements, oil spills and cleanup, and the effect of the drilling activity on wildlife, I conclude that the balance of harm does not favor the plaintiffs in the context of this carefully designed exploratory well. Unless circumstances change to alter Exxon's plan of operations which calls for cessation of drilling by March 31, I conclude that the balance of equities favors the defendants.

The public interest favors both the plaintiffs and defendants in this case. NEPA and the Endangered Species Act reflect a strong public interest in environmental concerns. Exploration for additional oil and gas resources is also an important national interest. Because possible adverse environmental effects of this single exploratory well have been studied and carefully limited, I conclude that, in the specific factual framework of this motion, the public interests favors the denial of preliminary relief.

Id. at 20122–23.

4. It has been suggested that intermediate, regional EISs be prepared for OCS development, each covering the environmental impact on a section of coastline off of which several separate lease sales are to take place (each with their own site-specific EIS). For a non-OCS case discussing whether NEPA mandates regional EISs, *see Sierra Club v. Morton (Great Plains Coal)*, 514 F.2d 856 (D.C. Cir. 1975), *rev'd sub. nom. Kleppe v. Sierra Club*, 427 U.S. 390 (1976), *discussed in* Hildreth, *The Coast: Where Energy Meets the Environment*, 13 San Diego L. Rev. 253, 279–84 (1976).

5. *NRDC v. Morton*, 458 F.2d 827 (D.C. Cir. 1972) is the leading OCS case on the scope of alternatives that must be discussed in an EIS. For other cases on the alternatives issue, *see National Helium Corp. v. Morton*, 361 F. Supp. 78 (D. Kan. 1973); *NRDC v. Froehlke*, 473 F.2d 346 (8th Cir. 1972); and *NRDC v. Callaway*, 524 F.2d 79 (2d Cir. 1975).

   In July 1979, the Council on Environmental Quality promulgated new regulations designed to implement NEPA more effectively and bind all federal agencies. *See* 40 C.F.R. §§ 1500–08 (1980). These regulations provide that federal agencies shall vigorously explore all reasonable alternatives under NEPA, devoting "substantial equal treatment" to each, including the proposed action. The analysis of alternatives must be factual and detailed, not merely assertive. The treatment of alternatives is to be analytical rather than encyclopedic, and normally not more than 150 pages long. (This provision is to stop the "kitchen sink" approach.) The regulations require that the agency state in the record whether "all practicable means to avoid or minimize environmental harm have been adopted." 40 C.F.R. §1505.2. The agency preparing the EIS must identify the "environmentally preferable alternative" and if another alternative is selected, explain in its public "record of decision" the reasons why it chose an alternative other than the one involving the least environmental harm. *Id.* The agency must justify this selection in terms of overriding national policy considerations. *Id.* In *Sierra Club v. Andrus*, 440 U.S. 904 (1979), the Supreme Court broadly endorsed these new regulations, quoting from them extensively on the purpose of environmental impact statements, the timing of EIS preparation, the definition of an EIS, and the definition of a major federal action.

6. Would a court be justified in relying on U.S. Geological Survey regulations as a means of preventing pollution notwithstanding a history of weak enforcement? The court so held in *Sierra Club v. Morton,* 510 F.2d 813 (5th Cir. 1975). *See also* Note, *The Outer Continental Shelf Lands Act Amendments of 1978: Balancing Energy Needs with Environmental Concerns*, 40 La. L. Rev. 177, 186 (1979), for a discussion of the "checks and balances" approach to raising environmental concerns during the continuum of OCS development.

7. The judicial findings of whether an EIS is adequate are integrally related to the standard of review applied by the court. How deeply should the Court review the agency's findings and presumptions? What sort of deference should be given to the agency's conclusions if they followed the correct procedure to get there?

   There has been considerable argument both in and out of court as to whether NEPA grants substantive, as well as procedural, rights. *See EDF v. Corp.*, 470 F.2d 289 (8th Cir. 1972), *cert. denied*, 412 U.S. 931 (1973); Robie, *Recognition of Substantive Rights Under NEPA*, 7 Nat. Res. Law. 387 (1975). After a finding that an agency has complied with procedural requirements of NEPA in preparing an adequate EIS, the scope of a court's substantive review of the agency decision is limited. The U.S. Supreme Court has stated that

   neither the statute nor its legislative history contemplates that a court should substitute its judgement for that of the agency as to the environmental consequences of its actions. . . . The only role for a court is to ensure that the agency has taken a "hard look" at environmental consequences; it cannot "interject itself within the area of discretion of the executive as to the choice of the action to be taken.

Kleppe v. Sierra Club, 427 U.S. 390, 410 n.21 (1976), *quoting, NRDC v. Morton,* 458 F.2d 827, 838 (D.C. Cir. 1972).

If an agency action is enjoined by a court on grounds of an inadequate EIS, can the agency simply amend or supplement the EIS to meet the court's requirements, and then go ahead with the action? The delay produced does enable environmental groups to build political opposition to the agency action. But in OCS oil development, where the oil companies have made such large front-end investments, NEPA suits probably have negligible harassment value.

8. The evaluation of alternatives required by *NRDC v. Morton,* 458 F.2d 827 (D.C. Cir. 1972), is only one of the issues considered when judicially testing the adequacy of an EIS. Unknown or unquantifiable impacts are another considera- tion. In *Sierra Club v. Morton,* 510 F.2d 813 (5th Cir. 1975), the lack of baseline data on the existing environment was one basis for the challenge. In *Alaska v. Andrus,* 580 F.2d 465 (D.C. Cir. 1978), *vacated and remanded in part sub. nom. Western Oil & Gas Association v. Alaska,* 439 U.S. 922 (1979), the plaintiffs challenged a lease sale prior to the completion of a massive environmental and scientific study of the area. In April 1976, the Department of the Interior sched- uled a sale of OCS tracts in the northern Gulf of Alaska despite strong protests from EPA, NOAA, and the CEQ that the area was one of the extreme environ- mental risks, and that the Secretary possessed inadequate baseline information about the area which would enable him to design and implement technology to mitigate the environmental hazards. NOAA already had under way at the time of the sale a major environmental research program in the area which needed several more years before completion. Environmental risks of the area included a high incidence of earthquakes and storms, wave heights regularly reaching 80 feet, an important bird habitat and fishing grounds, and a pristine environment on surrounding lands. The court refused to enjoin the sale despite finding that Interior made no attempt to balance the costs of delaying the sale against the benefits of better environmental data. Was the court correct in assuming that exploratory drilling is less risky than production?

9. Data and information are critical to the selection of tracts both by the govern- ment and the oil companies. *See* 30 C.F.R. § 352; *Geophysical Corp. of Alaska v. Andrus,* 453 F. Supp. 361 (D. Alaska 1978).

10. What are the onshore impacts of offshore oil drilling? Are the effects positive or negative? What mechanisms are available to state and local governments for planning and controlling onshore impacts? NEPA? The public trust doctrine? *See Boone v. Kingsbury,* 206 Cal. 148, 273 p. 797 (1928), *cert. denied,* 280 U.S. 517 (1929), Chapter 3, Section B, *supra.* The state navigation servitude? State coastal zone management programs? *See* Comment, *Coastal Zone Impacts of Offshore and Oil and Gas Development: An Accommodation Through the California Coastal Act of 1976,* 8 Pac. L.J. 783 (1977). Local planning and zoning laws? Would *Ventura County v. Gulf Oil Corp.,* 601 F.2d 1080 (9th Cir. 1979), which held a local zoning ordinance inapplicable to federally owned land onshore leased for oil drilling under the federal Mineral Lands Leasing act, be controlling with respect to land onshore needed to support drilling offshore?

The court in *County of Suffolk v. Secretary of Interior,* 562 F.2d 1368 (2d Cir. 1977), *cert. denied,* 434 U.S. 1064 (1978), denied Suffolk County's request to enjoin an Atlantic OCS sale due to its adverse onshore effects and implied that coastal states are *required* to prepare coastal zone management programs under the federal Coastal Zone Management Act discussed in Chapter 11, *infra.* Was the court correct? The *Suffolk County* court also relied on the divisibility of offshore oil development in denying Suffolk County's request. Are the stages of OCS development truly divisible? *See* Kameron, *Offshore Oil Development and the Demise of NEPA*, 7 B.C. Envt'l L. Rev. 83 (1978).

11. The international application of NEPA was not made clear in NEPA, and was much debated in the years prior to 1979. However, on 4 January of that year President Carter issued Executive Order 12114, which clarified federal agency responsibilities with respect to the international application of NEPA. The executive order had two principal provisions: the first required that federal agencies must prepare EISs for major federal actions that have significant environmental effects on the global commons, e.g., the oceans and Antarctica; the second required that under certain circumstances agencies must prepare concise environmental reviews (or participate in bilateral/multilateral environmental studies) of the impacts of major federal actions on foreign countries. President Reagan revoked Executive Order 12114 soon after taking office.

MASSACHUSETTS v. ANDRUS, 594 F.2d 872
(1st Cir. 1979)

LEVIN H. CAMPBELL, Circuit Judge.

The Commonwealth of Massachusetts and various conservation groups filed suit in the district court on January 19, 1978, seeking to enjoin the Secretary of the Interior from proceeding with the proposed sale of leaseholds in the Outer Continental Shelf off the coast of New England, styled OCS Sale No. 42. The Secretary had scheduled the opening of bids to take place on January 31. At the end of the day on Saturday, January 28, 1978, after three days of hearings, the district court issued a preliminary injunction forbidding the Secretary from taking further steps to consummate the sale. The sale was, as a result, cancelled,[1] and the Secretary and various oil companies that had been permitted to intervene appealed.

Subsequent to argument of the appeal in this court last spring and, indeed, at about the time that our decision in this case would have been anticipated, Congress adopted major amendments to the Outer Continental Shelf Lands Act, Pub.L.No. 95–372, 92 Stat. 629 (*amending* 43 U.S.C. § 1331 *et seq.*). These complex amendments provided for an oil spill fund and other safeguards whose absence figured largely in the district court's decision to enjoin the sale. They also added considerably to the law under which the leasing activity is to take place. We accordingly withheld any decision premised on the prior law, and invited supplemental briefing addressed to the effects of the amendments on this appeal.

In this opinion we now deal with the preliminary injunction in a legal and factual context that is altogether different from that which existed when the injunction was first issued.

I. Background

This dispute concerns the first step toward the commencement of oil drilling in Georges Bank—a region described in the final environmental impact statement as "one of the most productive fishing grounds in the world." The

---

[1]After a hearing, a judge of this court denied the appellants' motion for a stay of the preliminary injunction on January 30, 1978. At that point the Secretary announced that he would postpone the sale pending resolution of this appeal. Stay was not sought in the Supreme Court.

offering of Georges Bank leaseholds is one of several similar transactions involving possible oil fields in the Outer Continental Shelf, each of which has produced its own history of litigation.[2] These sales received their impetus in 1974, when the President directed the Secretary of the Interior to increase the amount of acreage to be made available for oil and gas development as part of a national effort to reduce dependency on foreign energy sources. The Outer Continental Shelf Lands Act, 43 U.S.C. § 1331, *et seq.*, enacted in 1953, had earlier spelled out this nation's jurisdiction over offshore seabeds. Extending "[t]he Constitution and laws and civil and political jurisdiction of the United States . . . to the subsoil and seabed of the Outer Continental Shelf," § 1333(a)(1), the Act authorized the Secretary to grant oil and gas leases in the outer shelf by competitive bidding. § 1337. In response to the President's 1974 directive, the Secretary called for positive and negative nominations of tracts in the North Atlantic region. After receiving extensive comments and consulting with various interested parties, including officials of the states affected, the Secretary in January 1976 designated 206 tracts in the Georges Bank area for potential leasing.

A draft environmental impact statement covering this sale was published by the Secretary in October 1976. In December 1976, the Secretary withdrew 28 of the tracts from the proposed sale pending resolution of a boundary dispute with Canada. Discussion of the sale of the remaining 178 tracts focused on the conflict between oil drilling and fishing and on concerns about the possible impact of oil contamination on the aquatic and onshore environment. The Environmental Protection Agency, in its written response to the draft environmental statement, concluded,

> "The integration of petroleum development with the highly productive fishing industry of Georges Bank represents a critical balancing of the nation's immediate energy needs and its long term usage of the renewable living resources of this area. In order to successfully pursue the simultaneous exploitation of both these resources, it is essential that a full appraisal of the environmental consequences of the proposed action be made. The DEIS on the proposed sale fails to accomplish this purpose; despite the wealth of information presented, there are a number of important areas with unsupported conclusions regarding the actual environmental impacts of oil and gas development (both primary and secondary) on the specific resources of Georges Bank, and on the onshore environment. Therefore we have rated this environmental statement as Category 3—Inadequate."

Specific concerns of the EPA were the lack of integration of the statement's discussion of environmental hazards, which obscured the analysis of particular

[2]OCS Sale No. 40, involving the Baltimore Canyon Trough, was conducted on August 17, 1976, after a district court preliminary injunction was stayed by the Second Circuit. *County of Suffolk v. Secretary of Interior*, 562 F.2d 1368 (2d Cir. 1977), *cert. denied*, 434 U.S. 1064, 98 S.Ct. 1238, 55 L.Ed.2d 764 (1978). Sale No. 39, involving the Gulf of Alaska took place on April 13, 1976, although the environmental impact statement for the sale has since been found inadequate. *Alaska v. Andrus*, 188 U.S. App.D.C. 202, 580 F.2d 465 (1978). The environmental impact statement issued in connection with the decision to accelerate the leasing program has been sustained by a district court. *California ex rel. Younger v. Morton*, 404 F.Supp. 26 (C.D.Cal.1975), *appeal pending*, No. 76–1431 (9th Cir.).

risks, and the failure of the statement to follow through in its discussion of certain hazards, thereby not fully exposing the risks involved. The long-term consequences of the project, including pollution of estuaries used by support facilities and the increase of petroleum in the marine food supply over time, were not adequately addressed. In spite of these criticisms, however, the EPA did not find that the proposed sale was environmentally "unsatisfactory", a finding which would have triggered further review of the project by the Council on Environmental Quality. 42 U.S.C. § 1857h–7; *see Alaska v. Andrus*, 188 U.S.App.D.C. at 207–08, 580 F.2d at 470–71.

The Department of Commerce also had "serious reservations about the adequacy of the draft in some respects." Perhaps its most telling criticism concerned the statement's discussion of long-term effects on the marine population:

> "The statement is devoid of support conclusions regarding the probable impact of gas and oil development on the environment and resources of Georges Bank and adjacent waters. No acknowledgement is readily apparent regarding our limited capability for assessing catastrophic, lethal, or sublethal effects of petroleum hydrocarbons (refined/unrefined) on the four million metric tons of fish biomass estimated to inhabit the area. No quantitative estimate is given of the magnitude of the fish populations that could be affected by petroleum hydrocarbon spills."

Other comments touched on inadequate biological data and, in one instance, inaccurate information depreciating the danger of small quantities of petroleum to fish spawning.

Representatives of all of the states immediately affected by the sale responded to the draft statement; a substantial share of the comments and criticisms were made by the Commonwealth of Massachusetts. The Commonwealth recommended that 26 of the proposed tracts be removed from the sale because of their proximity to the coast and consequent increased danger to the shore from oil spills. It also recommended various lease stipulations and operating orders governing development operations to decrease the environmental risks from operating the wells. Among the measures recommended were a requirement of unitization where the number of structures would thereby be reduced, the burial of pipelines whenever technologically feasible, and a commitment to require another environmental impact statement before development of the fields, if marketable quantities of oil and gas were discovered. The Commonwealth also endorsed various measures suggested in the draft statement as possible steps to mitigate harmful consequences of drilling operations, including the establishment of a compensation fund for fishermen who suffer equipment loss as a result of offshore drilling activity. It criticized the draft statement for an inadequate discussion of the impact of oil spills on future fish supplies.

A. The Final Environmental Impact Statement

After the distribution of the draft statement, the conduct of four days of public hearings in Boston and Providence, the receipt of over 300 written comments, and the response to the same, the Secretary released a final environmental impact statement on OCS Sale No. 42 on August 29, 1977. The final statement incorporated many modifications in response to the above comments; other changes were held to be infeasible in light of a conceded lack of detailed scientific knowledge about the long-term effects of oil pollution on the marine environment. The final statement describes extensively the nature of the proposed drilling operations and their possible impact on the region.

The tracts involved range from 63 to 167 miles east southeast of Nantucket Island, with all but one located more than 85 miles away from the nearest land. Each tract contains approximately 5700 acres; total acreage of the sale as currently contemplated would amount to roughly 730,000 acres, or 1,140 square miles. Water depths vary from 120 to 690 feet. The estimates of available energy resources run from .15 to .53 billion barrels of oil and 1 to 3.5 trillion cubic feet of natural gas. The projected field life is twenty years, with production beginning as soon as six years after the sale. However, no oil actually has been discovered in this area, and the estimates about available resources are just that. One of the principal uncertainties in evaluating the environmental impact of this sale is the lack of knowledge about how much production actually will take place in these fields.

The adverse environmental impact, as the statement indicates, may be considerable. To begin with, drilling platforms unavoidably will reduce the area in which fishing can take place. If the field is successful, 113 square miles of present fishing ground could be displaced; the figure could run as high as 466 square miles if it becomes necessary to leave pipelines unburied. Mud from the drilling operations will be discharged back into the ocean, as will other wastes produced by the platforms. Onshore facilities will have to be built both to service the drilling operations and to handle the oil and gas that is mined from the tracts.

The overwhelming environmental concern, however, is the danger of oil spills. The area has been the site of substantial earthquakes, although the seismic risk of the field is not as great as parts of southern California and the Gulf of Alaska where offshore drilling has been approved. During the winter the region experiences extratropical cyclones (northeasters) which "are often intense and severe and are generally accompanied by strong, gusting winds and high seas." Hurricanes occasionally pass through the area during the summer and fall. The region exhibits some of the world's worst weather and sea conditions.[3] Nonetheless, the environmental statement indicates that properly designed drilling rigs and pipes would be capable of withstanding such conditions. Similar or even worse conditions exist in some other regions where drilling is now taking place or is authorized. Both the North Sea and the Gulf of Alaska are said to experience even greater sustained winds and wave height. Although confidence in these meteorological measurements is qualified by gaps in the data, it being

[3]The maritime historian, Samuel Eliot Morison, wrote,

"[A]nything might happen to you in the North Atlantic, even in summer, . . . [E]veryone but French fishermen avoided sailing in winter. Westerly gales hurled crested seas . . .; easterly gales drenched the sailors with chilling rain; fierce northerlies ripped their sails and cracked their masts."

The European Discovery of America: The Northern Voyages, A.D. 500–1600, at 3 (1971).

hardest to obtain accurate measurements during the worst weather, the threat of a storm or large waves damaging a drilling platform or pipeline and causing a major oil spill appears to be no greater than that faced in the North Sea and is, like earthquake risk, slightly less than that endangering operations off Alaska.

The final environmental statement estimates the probabilities of oil spills during each phase of operations in Georges Bank, based in part on the experience with offshore drilling in the Gulf of Mexico. During the exploration phase there is estimated to be a very low probability of a large spill. However, even with full safety measures, at least one large oil spill attributable to human error is projected during the development and production phases. At least one large spill is also predicted during the transportation of the oil. The use of pipelines might lessen the risk of a spill during transportation, but tankers will be used unless an unexpectedly large amount of oil is found. Spills during transportation would be offset, however, to the extent the oil and gas obtained from the North Atlantic replace imports that also are shipped by sea, and pose similar risks.[4]

As important as the likelihood of a spill is its location. As the environmental statement states, "[t]he Northwest Atlantic area, and in particular Georges Bank, is one of the most productive fishing grounds in the world."[5] The region is so important that its depletion by foreign fishing fleets was a major factor leading Congress to enact the Fishery Conservation and Management Act, 16 U.S.C. §§ 1801 *et seq.*, in order to put management of the fishery in American hands. *See generally Maine v. Kreps*, 563 F.2d 1043 (1st Cir. 1977). A primary aim of the Act is to rebuild the now diminished stocks of fish, allowing the

[4]The following chart, contained in the proposed decision option document presented to the Secretary and based on data considered in the impact statement, gives some idea of the possible incidence of oil spills if operations get under way:

ESTIMATED CHANGES IN EXPECTED NUMBER OF OIL SPILLS IN U.S. WATERS IF DOI PROCEEDS WITH OCS SALE #42

Spill size (range in bbls.)	Incremental increase in expected number of OCS oil spills		Incremental decrease in expected number of import tanker oil spills
	Pipeline	Tanker Oil	
0–2.4	919.48	699.45	62.99
2.4–23.8	65.62	56.48	21.21
23.8–238	11.81	8.00	5.47
238 –2381	2.25	1.47	.93
2381 –23810	.37	.56	.83
over 23810	.09	.13	.19
Expected total amount spilled (in bbls.)	9,150	16,401	23,671

[5]The plaintiffs originally asserted that the Georges Bank produced "as much as 15% of the world fish protein," and sought to contrast this with a "high find" on Georges Bank over a predicted 20 year life of the field of but 0.13% of annual world oil production and 0.099% of world gas production. Plaintiffs now appear to concede that 15% is too high a figure for Georges Bank fish, but nonetheless maintain, "Even utilizing intervenors' fishery figures, Georges Bank will produce a far larger percentage of world food fish than of world energy. Moreover, the fishery is perpetually renewable; the oil and gas would be withdrawn within 20 years."

domestic fishery to flourish. Estimates of the potential United States catch in this region for the period in which the wells would operate range from 500 to 750 million pounds.

The impact of an oil spill on this resource might be devastating. The oil would kill directly almost all planktonic fish eggs and larvae in its path, many benthic organisms residing on or near the ocean floor, and some portion of actively swimming fish, depending on the as yet undetermined ability of the last to avoid the contaminated area. Furthermore, among the species of fish whose spawning grounds are most exposed to the danger are those, such as haddock, already threatened by overfishing. A severe oil spill could destroy the New England haddock fishery by lowering the schools below the point of recruitment failure, or irreversible depletion. Even without this lethal long-term effect, which could remove from mankind's use for all time a resource of incalculable worth, the loss of even a particular year class of fish would cause substantial economic damage. The environmental statement estimated the value of an average year class of several important commercial species at the following values—haddock, $34.1 million; cod, $18.3 million; silver hake, $9.7 million; yellowtail flounder, $9.1 million; red hake, $3.0 million.

In addition, the indirect effect of oil pollution on the marine environment, although not fully understood, may give cause for alarm. Crude oil contains various heavy metals and hydrocarbons that are known carcinogens. Spilled oil can become mixed with sediments on the ocean floor, to be released slowly into the water over periods as long as a decade. As the environmental statement points out,

> "Synergistic effects of oil, heavy metals, and other pollutants are not understood very well. The biota of the North Atlantic contain relatively high concentrations of polychlorinated biphenyls. . . . The high levels of PCB may lower the tolerance of the biota to petroleum hydrocarbons and trace metals. The synergistic interaction may result in severe, adverse impacts on the marine ecosystem, and is an area that needs more research."

One result might be sublethal but extensive contamination of commercial fisheries creating a substantial hazard to human health.

An oil spill also could come ashore, fouling beaches and killing nearshore wildlife. A large portion of the shoreline facing the tracts and the proposed routes for transporting the oil is used for recreation, and an oil spill in these areas could both harm the local tourist industry and destroy unique and beautiful scenery. An oil spill of the size that would be necessary to come ashore is unlikely during the exploration phase of drilling, but would be possible during production and development and even more likely during transportation operations.[6]

The environmental statement considered various alternatives to the pro-

---

[6]The following chart gives the probability that an oil spill of an assumed size will affect particular resources, including onshore recreation areas. The tracts were divided into 11 production areas; all of the tracts in areas 1 through 4 and all but one of five tracts in area 5 have since been withdrawn from the sale. Transportation route A would be to New Jersey, B to Portland, and C to Rhode Island or southern Massachusetts. The table does not reflect the likelihood of a spill occurring

posed sale, including exclusion of particular tracts, substitution of tracts on the continental slope, delay until additional environmental data or more effective safety measures were available, and withdrawal of the sale in favor of developing other energy sources. All of the other energy sources considered, however, either were not yet developed enough to be realistic alternatives or involved environmental and other costs that exceeded those of the contemplated sale. On balance, the environmental statement concluded, going forward with the sale as planned, with stringent safeguards, appeared to be the best alternative.

B. The Secretary's Decision

After publication of the final statement, the staff of the Secretary of the Interior prepared a program decision option document, apparently a digest of the environmental statement along with a description of possible modifications in the sale. After reviewing this document, the Secretary on October 14, 1977, announced his tentative decision to proceed with the sale but deleted 12 of the 24 tracts nearest to shore from the sale. On November 7, the Governor of the Commonwealth wrote the Secretary expressing his general satisfaction with progress on the sale but noting three remaining areas of concern. First, the Governor strongly urged the removal of the remaining 12 tracts nearest to shore

---

at any particular point, and in fact the risk would vary depending on the amount of oil found and other factors.

PERCENT PROBABILITIES THAT AN OIL SPILL OCCURRING AT POTENTIAL PRODUCTION AREAS AND ALONG ANTICIPATED TRANSPORT ROUTES IN THE NORTH-ATLANTIC LEASE AREA WOULD IMPACT IMPORTANT BIOLOGICAL RESOURCES AND RECREATION AREAS

Resources group	Production areas											Transportation routes		
	1	2	3	4	5	6	7	8	9	10	11	A	B	C
Beaches and recreation areas	16	10	13	6	7	3	2	1	1	1	1	42	10	80
Wildlife sanctuaries & wintering areas	5	3	6	3	4	1	1	1	•	•	•	9	4	33
Coastal bird breeding areas	3	2	2	1	3	1	•	•	•	•	•	7	9	7
Pelagic bird nesting areas	•	•	•	•	•	•	•	•	•	•	•	•	1	•
Pelagic bird wintering area	17	10	17	12	10	5	3	2		1	2	21	10	51
Eagle and osprey nesting sites	3	2	2	1	1	1	•	•	•	•	•	14	1	14
Cod and haddock spawning areas	25	20	31	35	40	25	27	16	20	12	26	10	37	13
Silver and red hake spawning areas ..	24	33	17	24	12	24	25	43	36	46	22	9	4	3
Sea herring spawning areas	8	6	16	8	12	5	4	•	2	1	2	3	12	3
Atlantic salmon migration routes	•	•	•	•	•	•	•	•	•	•	•	•	•	•
Shortnose sturgeon areas	•	•	•	•	•	•	•	•	•	•	•	•	•	•
Shellfish areas	6	3	4	2	3	1	1	1	1	•	•	20	5	40
Harbor seal whelping areas	•	•	•	•	•	•	•	•	•	•	•	•	1	•
Grey seal whelping areas	1	1	•	•	•	•	•	•	•	•	•	2	•	7
Salt marshes	2	1	1	•	1	•	•	•	•	•	•	10	•	3
Eel grass beds	•	•	•	•	•	•	•	•	•	•	•	•	•	•
Kelp beds	•	•	•	•	•	•	•	•	•	•	•	•	•	•
OVERALL PROBABILITY ASHORE	23	17	23	14	21	8	6	4	4	3	4	44	40	79
RANK ORDERING (Oil Spill Impact Risk)	110	91	109	91	93	66	63	64	62	61	53			

*Less than 0.5 percent probability

**Obtained by combining percent probabilities in each resource category (assuming equal weight or value for each resource). The higher the total, the greater the risk anticipated.

from the sale. Second, he requested a commitment that another environmental impact statement would be prepared before the development phase of operations began. Finally, he recommended that the final notice of sale include as part of its specifications a mandatory personnel training program to help oil company employees coordinate their activities with commercial fishing operations; a requirement that offshore oil transport and storage structures be minimized; and a requirement that all equipment carried from platforms to shore be marked to enable identification if lost overboard. The governors of Maine, New Hampshire, Rhode Island, Connecticut and New York also responded to the tentative notice of sale and generally expressed their approval of the project.

Subsequent contacts between the Department of the Interior and the Commonwealth revealed that other differences remained. Massachusetts, disappointed by setbacks in Congress for legislation that would have affected the Secretary's power to regulate offshore drilling operations,[7] proposed that the Secretary implement some of the measures administratively. The Commonwealth specifically sought to have the Secretary create by regulation two funds, one to compensate fishermen who suffer economic loss because of drilling operations and the other to pay for damage caused by oil spills. The latter fund was seen also as a deterrent measure, with liability for compensation payments tied to responsibility for spills. The impact statement had referred to these funds as a means of enhancing the Secretary's power to mitigate the adverse environmental consequences of the sale, but it assumed both that the Secretary would have to await legislation before he could implement the funds and that in any event the legislation would apply to leases already sold.

The Environmental Protection Agency also registered its dissatisfaction with the proposed sale. After reviewing the final environmental impact statement, the EPA complained that the Department of the Interior had failed to develop the kind of integrated oil spill model careful analysis demanded, and that Interior's responses to EPA's earlier criticisms of the draft statement were in some cases superficial. The agency recommended that Interior delay the sale until either Congress enacted the legislation that would permit greater precautions or further environmental studies provided more data about risk to the environment. Interior responded to EPA's criticisms on December 2, 1977, pointing out that a regulation recently adopted by the Secretary provided for the suspension of drilling operations upon discovery of unforeseen environmental risks, thereby obviating need for the lease cancellation procedure contained in the proposed legislation which EPA regarded as critical. The response also argued that the more sophisticated risk model advocated by EPA could not be applied to the Georges Bank sale at this time because of a lack of data about the effects of spilled petroleum on the marine environment.

---

[7]A bill to amend the Outer Continental Shelf Lands Act to give the Secretary more definite authority with respect to management of these leases passed both houses of Congress in 1976, but the legislation died after a conference committee failed to work out differences between the House and Senate versions. In the next session the Senate passed S.9, containing similar provisions, and the House was considering this bill as the Secretary deliberated on whether to proceed with this sale. On February 2, 1978, after the district court had issued the preliminary injunction and the Secretary had postponed the sale, the House passed its version of the Senate bill. 124 Cong. Rec. H602-22 (Feb. 2, 1978). The legislation was finally enacted and signed by the President in September of 1978.

The final notice of sale was published on December 30, 1977, announcing that the Secretary would open bids on January 31, 1978. Many but not all of the Commonwealth's concerns were met in the final notice. Massachusetts had asked that the 12 tracts nearest to shore be deleted from the sale, and Maine had joined the request as to one of the 12 which was especially close to a major fishing ground. The Secretary's staff had contended that the tracts in question did not pose as substantial a hazard to fishing as the 12 tracts that had been deleted earlier from the sale, but conceded that the one tract that Maine had focused on was immediately adjacent to an area identified as important for fishing and, given the inaccuracy of available data, might also overlap with substantial fishing operations. The Secretary instead ordered the deletion of the 11 tracts that presented a lesser hazard but retained the one tract singled out by Maine. The Secretary also adopted a regulation requiring preparation of another environmental impact statement before production of any consequence could begin and stipulated that oil company personnel must receive environmental training. He also added lease stipulations to reduce the number of offshore support structures and to require marking of equipment that might be lost overboard. The Secretary continued to maintain that he lacked legal authority to implement an oil spill liability fund or a fishermen's gear compensation fund and therefore took no action on these proposals. He recognized the importance of these funds and on several occasions during this period expressed a strong desire for Congress to pass the authorizing legislation, but he also continued to believe that the legislation, when enacted, could be applied to leases already entered into by the government.[8]

C. The case

1. The district court's decision   Less than two weeks before the sale was to take place, Massachusetts and other plaintiffs filed this suit.[9] They argued that the Secretary's decision to go ahead with the sale in spite of his apparent lack of authority to implement what he conceded to be desirable environmental safeguards violated a legal duty established by the Outer Continental Shelf Lands Act to protect the Georges Bank fishery, and was arbitrary and capricious. The complaints also charged that the sale would illegally interfere with implementation of the Fishery Conservation and Management Act and the Massachusetts Coastal Zone Management Plan, and violated the National Environmental Policy Act, the Marine Sanctuaries Act, and the Endangered Species Act.

After three days of hearings and the submission of documentary evidence, the district court, acting under considerable time pressure, issued a preliminary injunction forbidding the Secretary from proceeding with the sale. In an opinion delivered orally from the bench, the district court ruled that plaintiffs would likely prevail on the merits, because the Secretary of the Interior had committed

[8]After the final notice of sale, the Secretary removed 27 more tracts from the sale because of a boundary dispute with Canada.

[9]Jurisdiction was asserted under several statutes: 28 U.S.C. § 1331; 43 U.S.C. § 1333(b) (Outer Continental Shelf Lands Act); 16 U.S.C. § 1861(d) (Fishery Conservation and Management Act); 42 U.S.C. § 4321 (National Environmental Policy Act); 5 U.S.C. §§ 701–06 (APA); 28 U.S.C. § 1361 (Mandamus). The Secretary does not dispute the jurisdiction of the district court.

several statutory violations. The court found that the Secretary had violated the Outer Continental Shelf Lands Act by not meeting "the affirmative duty of taking all steps reasonably possible" to preserve the fishery resources of Georges Bank. The court noted that the Fishery Conservation and Management Act, 16 U.S.C. §§ 1801 *et seq.* and the Coastal Zone Management Act, 16 U.S.C. §§ 1451 *et seq.*, although not directly applicable, further underscored the "duty of the Secretary to be especially concerned and to be the guardian in a sense of fishing in the Outer Continental Shelf waters. . . ." The court found a violation of this duty in the Secretary's permitting of sales to take place before enactment of the legislation that would authorize several important safeguards designed to protect fishing. These safeguards were an oil spill liability fund, a fishermen's gear compensation fund, and a procedure for compensating lessees whose drilling operations are suspended because of unforeseen environmental hazards.[10] The court felt that the Secretary did not then have the authority to create these safeguards by administrative action, and that prior passage of the pending legislation was essential if the Secretary was to protect the fisheries. The court ruled further that the Secretary's decision to proceed with the sale before passage of the pending legislation was "arbitrary and capricious," and therefore subject to judicial reversal under the Administrative Procedure Act, 5 U.S.C. § 706(2)(A).

The court also found that the environmental impact statement and other studies relied upon by the Secretary, including the proposed decision option document, did not satisfy the standards of the National Environmental Policy Act, 42 U.S.C. §§ 4321 *et seq.* A principal deficiency of the impact statement, the court found, lay in its failure to discuss the environmental benefits to be gained by delaying the sale until Congress passed the above-mentioned legislation. In addition, the court regarded as deficiencies the absence of any reference to the possible use of the area as a marine sanctuary, and insufficient specific reference to the damage to beaches on Martha's Vineyard and Cape Cod that a major oil spill might cause. As a final deficiency the court noted the inadequacy of Interior's response to EPA's criticisms of the final environmental statement.

Having thus found it likely that plaintiffs would prevail on the merits of their claims, the court undertook to assess the relative harm to the different parties stemming from the grant of a preliminary injunction. The court felt that going ahead with the sale before Congress acted might forever foreclose application of the lease condemnation procedure and the compensation and liability funds to these leases. While delay would be costly to the oil companies, these increased costs could be reflected in the form of lower bids:

> "We are not talking here, and I think this is important to emphasize, about prohibiting leasing of oil and gas tracts in the Georges Bank area. None of the plaintiffs has contended that such exploration and exploitation be banned outright. The plaintiffs are looking for a delay of a relatively few months to preserve a resource that has taken millions of years to accrue, and which will be with us for better or worse for untold centuries to come."

[10]As already noted, the Outer Continental Shelf Lands Act Amendments, Pub.L.No. 95–372, 92 Stat. 926, enacted in the summer of 1978 after the district court had ruled, and after this appeal was argued, includes the three provisions the absence of which had so troubled the district court.

Believing the irreparable harm involved in immediate action to outweigh the costs of delay, the court granted the injunction and forbade the Secretary from taking further steps on the sale.

2. Contentions of the parties on appeal As we have pointed out, see note 10, *supra*, this appeal from the granting of a preliminary injunction was argued and briefed prior to the enactment of the 1978 amendments to the Outer Continental Shelf Lands Act. In their original arguments before us, the Government and the oil company intervenors[11] conceded that the Secretary had some authority, and perhaps even some duty, to take steps to protect the fisheries. But they minimized the extent of his obligations in this regard, and they strenuously denied that the district court had any right to hold up the sale of leases in Georges Bank until Congress beefed up the Secretary's powers to protect the fisheries. In their view, Congress intended the Secretary to act with whatever protective authority he had at the time, whether or not adequate. They felt the district court overemphasized the Secretary's legal responsibility to safeguard fishing and fishery interests. They also took issue with the district court's criticism of the environmental impact statement. The court, they felt, was relying too much upon its own appraisal of the merits or demerits of the leasing decision, rather than deferring to the Secretary's views, which should be reviewed under a restricted "rule of reason" standard.

The Commonwealth and the conservationist plaintiffs responded that the Secretary had violated fiduciary and statutory duties by proceeding with the Georges Bank sale. To have permitted leasing as planned was in their view premature and unwarranted. The Commonwealth did not oppose drilling operations in Georges Bank in principle, but argued that the lease sale must "be preceded by regulatory safeguards sufficient to protect the Massachusetts fishing and tourist industries, and adequate to fulfill the responsibilities imposed upon the Secretary. . . ." In particular the Commonwealth contended that the safeguards contained in the pending amendments to the Outer Continental Shelf Lands Act were essential to ensure the degree of protection of the marine environment which the Secretary of the Interior was charged with ensuring. The conservationist plaintiffs agreed with Massachusetts that drilling operations should not commence without further safeguards; and, going even further, they listed additional measures believed to be necessary. They also urged this court to uphold the district court's preliminary finding that the environmental impact statement was inadequate.

On September 18, 1978, the President signed the 1978 Outer Continental Shelf Lands Act Amendments embodying provisions for an oil spill fund, for fishermen's gear compensation, and for suspension of drilling, absence of which from the earlier law was cited by the district court as a major reason for its injunction. At our request, supplemental briefs were filed addressing the amend-

[11]In addition, the State of Rhode Island and the New England Legal Foundation, joined by the New England Council for Economic Development, the Boston Chamber of Commerce, the New Bedford Chamber of Commerce, and the Greater Providence Chamber of Commerce, have submitted briefs as *amici curiae* supporting generally the position of the Secretary and the oil company intervenors and arguing in particular that the district court improperly disregarded regional energy needs and national energy policy.

ments' impact on this appeal. In these, defendants have continued to oppose the injunction, and plaintiffs have continued to support it. The Government argues that the amendments divest the preliminary injunction of its "nuclei." The Government says that it will take "about seven months" after the injunction is lifted before a sale of leases can take place. Any need for equitable relief is thus far less apparent than in the period immediately before the scheduled sale, when the district court first acted. The intervenor oil companies endorse the Government's stand against the injunction, and insist as well that the 1978 amendments are at odds with the district court's belief that a sale would violate NEPA and the APA.

While the Government continues to stress the need for expedition in oil and gas development, and to deny any overriding duty to protect the fisheries, it concedes that the amendments require it to conduct the leasing program in such a way as to protect other resources, including the fisheries. The key word in the Secretary's reading of the amendments appears to be "balance"—balances must be struck, he says, between oil and gas development and protection of the other uses of the outer continental shelf and coastal environment. The Secretary says that he is at work promulgating the regulations the amendments require, and that there is no need for an injunction.

Massachusetts, on the other hand, urges that we uphold and continue the injunction. It argues that the amendments do not "moot" the case, because not being self-executing, they do not satisfy the Secretary's obligation to protect fisheries, and because they do not overcome the alleged inadequacies of the environmental impact statement. Both Massachusetts and the conservationist plaintiffs would like this court to rule on the issues that survive passage of the amendments—such as the adequacy of the environmental statement. They also believe that we should promulgate directions to the Secretary on how to interpret and carry out his duty under the amendments, maintaining the injunction in the meantime.

II. Appellate Review of the District Court's Opinion

We must emphasize the limited focus of this appeal. The appeal is from a preliminary injunction issued on the eve of a proposed sale of leases. This is not an appeal from a final judgment after a full hearing on the merits, nor can it take full account of the recent legislative revisions and the Secretary's actions thereunder. Prior to passage of the recent amendments to the Outer Continental Shelf Lands Act, the question would simply have been whether the district court abused its discretion in concluding that plaintiffs enjoyed a probability of success on the merits and that irreparable harm would occur without an injunction. Since passage of the amendments there has arisen the further question whether the original grounds for the injunction have not, in large measure, been mooted.

A. Mootness of the question of secretary's duty to await legislation

The reason for granting preliminary relief which the district court stressed above others was that it would be a breach of the Secretary of the Interior's duty to safeguard the fisheries to proceed with the sale without awaiting enactment of the protections embodied in legislation then pending. This reason was premised on certain suppositions, *see infra*, concerning the degree of responsibility imposed by the then-existing Outer Continental Shelf Lands Act upon the Secretary to safeguard fishery resources. Holding that the Secretary's legal duty of care was a high one, the district court pointed to statements of the Secretary himself regarding a need for the pending legislation, and concluded that the Secretary could not conscientiously proceed with the sale without awaiting congressional action on this vital legislation.

Whatever the legal merits of the district court's position—and much of the pre-amendments argument in this case was addressed to that issue—it is obvious that the issue is now moot. The legislation has in fact been enacted, and we now review the district court's injunction under the law as it presently is, not as it once was. *Bradley v. School Board*, 416 U.S. 696, 711, 94 S.Ct. 2006, 40 L.Ed.2d 476 (1974). To the extent the intended object of the injunction was to hold up the sale until Congress could enact legislation of this nature, that object has been achieved, and is no longer capable of furnishing support for injunctive relief.

B. The other grounds for the injunction

Since the need to await legislative safeguards is no longer a reason capable of supporting the injunction, it can now be sustained only if other grounds cited by the district court warrant continued equitable relief. These relate to possible deficiencies in the environmental impact statement, and we shall turn next to them.

. . . .

1. Pending legislation The district court deemed inadequate the environmental statement's cost-benefit analysis of the alternative of delaying the sale until Congress enacted legislation to define more clearly the Secretary's authority to implement the various conservation measures which have since been included in the amendments. This criticism of the environmental statement is obviously no longer pertinent, the legislation having passed. It furnishes no basis for continued injunctive relief.

2. Martha's Vineyard and Cape Cod Another flaw in the environmental statement found by the district court was its failure to calculate cost estimates for the fouling of beaches on Martha's Vineyard and Cape Cod as the result of a major oil spill. The court recognized that the environmental statement calculated the probability of these particular events occurring and generally recognized the recreational and aesthetic importance of these areas, and noted that the statement did include a quantitative estimate for damage to Long Island beaches, but held that the absence of a like calculation for Martha's Vineyard and Cape Cod constituted a fatal gap in the statement's weighing of the risks of the sale.

Although a more detailed analysis of the risks of the sale to these areas would have seemed desirable in view of their special recreational value and beauty, that an otherwise satisfactory analysis of the oil spill threat to onshore recreational activities did not single them out cannot be regarded as a violation of NEPA. The entire New England shoreline, much of which is beautiful and significant recreationally in an economic sense, would be exposed to some risk as a result of this sale. It would hardly be feasible to estimate the separate economic importance of each mile of shoreline in order to calculate with even greater precision the risks presented. The calculation of Long Island served as a model for suggesting what kind of damage could be expected by each of these recreationally significant areas, and no reason has been advanced to suggest that as a model it is inadequate. This is so, at least, under the Outer Continental Shelf Lands Act as it existed when the district court acted, and nothing has been called to our attention in the amendments that would change our analysis.

3. Use as a marine sanctuary Under the Marine Sanctuaries Act, 16 U.S.C. §§ 1431–34, the Secretary of Commerce can designate portions of the Outer Continental Shelf as marine sanctuaries, which would give the Secretary authority to issue and enforce "necessary and reasonable regulations to control any activities permitted within the designated marine sanctuary. . . ." 16 U.S.C. § 1432(f). The Secretary of Commerce could exercise this power to exclude all drilling operations and otherwise take steps to conserve and protect the natural resources of the region; alternatively, he could permit drilling operations to the same extent as the Secretary of the Interior acting under the Outer Continental Shelf Lands Act. The district court ruled that the absence of any reference to designation of Georges Bank as a marine sanctuary in the environmental impact statement constituted a breach of the Secretary's duty to discuss reasonable alternatives to the sale. The district court believed that this failure led the Secretary to disregard the positive benefits that could be achieved by cultivating the fishing industry in Georges Bank through the Sanctuaries Act.

In some respects this claim is similar to one raised and rejected in *Sierra Club v. Morton,* [510 F.2d 813]. There it was argued that the failure of an impact statement for an off-shore oil lease sale to discuss the alternative of exploratory drilling conducted by the federal government rather than by private companies constituted a violation of the Secretary's duties under NEPA. The Fifth Circuit ruled that federal exploration would present substantially the same environmental hazards as private operations, and "[a]n alternative which would result in similar or greater harm need not be discussed." 510 F.2d at 825. Here the environmental statement both considered in detail the alternative of not going ahead with the sale at all and recognized the likelihood that the Georges Bank fishing industry would increase in importance as a result of the Secretary of Commerce's authority under the Fishery Conservation and Management Act. The Secretary of Commerce already has substantial power under the Fishery Act to conserve and protect the Georges Bank fishing grounds from both foreign and domestic depredation, *see Maine v. Kreps, supra,* and the Secretary of the Interior has broad regulatory authority to promote conservation under the Outer Continental Shelf Lands Act, as amended in 1978, including the power not to authorize oil and gas leases that will constitute an unreasonable risk to the fishery resources, *infra.*

But while under the Marine Sanctuaries Act the land-use options of the Secretary of Commerce are much the same as those of the Secretary of the Interior under the Outer Continental Shelf Lands Act, the management objectives are different. It is thus possible that different environmental hazards would result depending on which program was invoked. Under the latter Act, the emphasis is upon exploitation of oil, gas and other minerals, with, to be sure, all necessary protective controls. Under the Sanctuaries Act, the prime management objectives are conservation, recreation, or ecological or esthetic values. 16 U.S.C. § 1432. Drilling and mining may be allowed, but the primary emphasis remains upon the other objects. The marked differences in priorities could lead to different administrative decisions as to whether particular parcels are suitable for oil and gas operations. And should there be particular areas of Georges Bank that are uniquely important to the fishery, for example, a key breeding area or the like, management by the Secretary of Commerce, the administrator of the Fishery Act, rather than by the Secretary of the Interior might be advantageous. At least the question seems worth exploring.

These considerations strongly suggest that the environmental impact statement should discuss the possible applicability of the Marine Sanctuaries Act. Such a discussion would focus additional attention upon the question of whether or not there are any portions of Georges Bank so uniquely valuable that they should be singled out for this special protective status. We cannot, however, be sure what impact the 1978 amendments may have upon this analysis. The amendments are extremely complex, and we hesitate at this juncture to foreclose argument on whether passage of the amendments reflects a congressional purpose to rule out applicability of the Marine Sanctuaries Act and similar provisions. There is the further question, also, as to whether plaintiffs' failure to seek a study of the possible application of the Marine Sanctuaries Act at some earlier date precludes the matter now. *Vermont Yankee Nuclear Power Corp.*, 435 U.S. at 553–54, 98 S.Ct. 1197. These issues were not before the district court at the hearing on the preliminary injunction nor were they argued initially before us. As an appellate court, we prefer not to rule on issues of this complexity without a lower court decision and without a more adequate presentation before us. There is time for them to be heard as the case continues in the district court. We therefore leave it open, for future ruling by the district court, whether the amendments provide any reason to modify what is our tentative decision, that the environmental impact statement should be extended to include a discussion of the marine sanctuary alternative. The court should also consider the issue in light of the Supreme Court's *Vermont Yankee* opinion.

Whatever the outcome, we do not see the lack of prior treatment of this subject in the environmental statement as a reason for maintaining the present injunction. The emergency that prompted the injunction—the threatened February 1978 sale of leases—has passed. There is presently ample time for inclusion of such a discussion in the environmental statement, if required, and for the Secretary to take account of it, prior to a leasing decision. We are confident that the Secretary will include such a statement either on his own initiative, if he so determines, or upon order of the district court if the matter remains disputed and if the district court rules against the Secretary. Injunctive relief is now premature. *See Rhode Island Minority Caucus, Inc. v. Baronian,* 590 F.2d 372, 374 (1st Cir. 1979).

4. **Response to EPA comments** The Environmental Protection Agency, in its comments on the final impact statement, criticized the oil spill risk model

employed as not sufficiently elaborate to give a satisfactory picture of the environmental costs of the sale. The Department of the Interior responded that although a more sophisticated model would be desirable, not enough scientific data was available to make the kind of model envisioned by EPA worthwhile. Even though EPA did not itself believe this flaw was sufficiently important to require delay of the sale for further study, the district court found that the criticism was telling and Interior's response inadequate. The court adopted the EPA comments as indicating another NEPA violation.

EPA generally had regarded Interior's actions concerning offshore oil leasing to be precipitate, and in some objective sense it may be correct. *See Alaska v. Andrus*, 188 U.S.App.D.C. 202, 580 F.2d 465; *County of Suffolk v. Secretary of Interior*, 562 F.2d 1368. We can only hope that the Department of the Interior is not moving faster than technology safely allows. The law is clear, however, that NEPA requires only that an agency respond adequately to EPA criticisms of a proposed action; the EPA view is not to be treated as controlling. *Id*. Here, Interior made a reasonable response not contradicted by the record or otherwise shown to be in bad faith, to a criticism that EPA itself did not regard as so important as by itself to require delay. Greater use of modern analytical techniques for calculating the possible consequences by agencies contemplating environmentally significant activities may be desirable, *see generally,* Maechling, *Systems Analysis and the Law*, 62 Va.L.Rev. 721 (1976), but within wide limits, the final decision as to how much analysis is necessary in view of the available data must be the agency's, subject to judicial review only for obviously incorrect results or methodology. Flaws of such magnitude have not been shown.

Ours is, of course, only a preliminary ruling based on the factual situation that existed when the district court ruled on the issuance of a preliminary injunction. Depending on the need for a supplemental environmental statement and on possible relevant requirements of the 1978 amendments—matters on which we do not pass, as they are not necessary to this decision—as well as on the availability of new studies and data, the question of what is or is not an acceptable environmental statement could take on new dimensions, although plaintiffs' burden to show error would at all times remain, *see* discussion *infra*. We do not mean to foreclose the district court from further inquiry which it believes to be justified by new circumstances.

In any event, however, for the same reasons stated regarding the marine sanctuary issue, we see no basis for continuing the present preliminary injunction.

5. Conclusion against continuing injunction   We conclude, therefore, that none of the criticisms of the environmental statement contained in the district court's injunctive ruling warrant continuing the preliminary injunction, although at least one of them—relating to the marine sanctuary designation—warrants further consideration. To the extent the environmental statement should go into the marine sanctuary alternative, this matter can be pursued in the time remaining before a fresh sale is attempted—an injunction is not currently needed to ward off any threatened irreparable harm. Should the government fail in this or other respects to do its duty, there will be time to obtain appropriate relief in the district court after further proceedings. With the threat of an imminent sale of

leases over, the court can proceed expeditiously to the merits, following any amendment of pleadings needed to take account of the 1978 amendments and present realities.

C. Propriety of our consideration of matters arising after enactment of 1978 amendments

The plaintiffs urge that the injunction be continued in order to prevent the Secretary from pushing ahead with the lease sale in a manner and for reasons that they fear would be improper. They point out that implementation of the 1978 Outer Continental Shelf Lands Act Amendments calls for the Secretary to promulgate regulations, that the effectiveness of the authorized protective measures depends on the quality of the regulations, that it may be that the Secretary will not fulfill his duty, and that it is, in effect, too early for anyone, including the fish, to relax. All of this may be true, but it affords no reason for continued injunctive relief at this point. The conservationist plaintiffs go too far when they urge that we instruct the district court to continue the injunction "until such time as the Secretary has complied with OCSLA, as amended, and NEPA and demonstrated unequivocally his good faith in proceeding with the Georges Bank leasing program." Citing to cases where federal courts have sought to overcome racial discrimination in local schools, or to force municipal officials to remedy unconstitutional conditions in jails, these plaintiffs urge us to place the Secretary of the Interior in virtual receivership to make certain that he does not subordinate the interests of the fisheries to the interests of those seeking to tap underseas oil and gas deposits.

There is no legal or constitutional precedent for our doing so. Federal courts are courts of limited jurisdiction, and, except for a possible range of exceptions not involved here, may exercise only the authority granted to them by Congress.

. . . . Congress has certainly given us no general authority to place prior restraints upon the Department of the Interior in order to force its decision-making into a particular mold. *Compare Vermont Yankee Nuclear Power Corp. v. NRDC*, 435 U.S. at 544–45, 98 S.Ct. 1197. Our usual authority is limited to reviewing the Secretary's actions as they emerge—as provided in 5 U.S.C. § 706, which, when there is no claim of constitutional or procedural violation, permits a court to set aside the decision only if it is "arbitrary, capricious, an abuse of discretion, or otherwise not in accordance with law. . . ." So long as the Secretary's determinations are within the law, are based upon consideration of the relevant factors, and do not involve clear errors of judgment, a court may not substitute its view. . . .

. . . .

If it appears the Secretary is not complying with the Outer Continental Shelf Lands Act as amended, that will be a matter of further action in the district court. Questions such as whether the amendments require a supplemental environmental impact statement and similar matters of this ilk cannot be settled in this appeal; their existence affords no basis for continuing an injunction issued for other reasons and in other circumstances.

D. Comments on the secretary's duty to protect fishing

While for reasons stated we decline to decide some of the questions that have been argued in the briefs and supplemental briefs, there are certain remaining issues, argued and briefed before us and of importance to the future conduct of the case, on which we can appropriately comment.

In their discussion of the Secretary's legal duty to protect fisheries, the parties have referred to former § 3(b) of the Outer Continental Shelf Lands Act, 43 U.S.C. § 1332(b), now §1332(2), which reads,

> "this subchapter shall be construed in such a manner that the character of the waters above the Outer Continental Shelf as high seas and the right to navigation and fishing therein shall not be affected."

Plaintiffs have argued that this imposes a duty on the Secretary to see that mining and drilling are conducted absolutely without harm to fisheries. However, it is clear that the clause was inserted with no such purpose in mind and we question its materiality to the issue at hand. The reference to "fishing" was inserted in the bill that eventually became the Outer Continental Shelf Lands Act to show that the United States' extension of its jurisdiction into the Outer Continental Shelf was limited to the subsoil and seabed. The Nation was not, by the Act, asserting control over the waters of the region. This message was believed necessary lest the Act give foreign nations an excuse for interfering with navigation and fishing in the high seas off their own coasts. See S.Rep.No. 411, 83d Cong., 1st Sess. 7 (1953); Hearing on S. 1901, 83d Cong., 1st Sess. 385, 393–94 (1953). The Convention on the Continental Shelf, signed in 1958, confirmed this Nation's continued willingness to observe the traditional three-mile limit notwithstanding its assertion of jurisdiction over mineral wealth farther offshore. 15 U.S.T. 471. Not until enactment of the Fishery Conservation and Management Act in 1976, 16 U.S.C. §§ 1801 *et seq.* did the United States undertake to regulate not only the seabed and subsoil of the Outer Continental Shelf but the fish and fishing activities in the waters above. This later, unrelated legislation reflected a federal policy for the conservation of fishery resources, but we are unable to see that it altered the meaning and purpose of § 3(b), which had been directed at the legal right to fish rather than at prohibiting physical impediments.

We leave open, for consideration with the merits, the significance, if any, of Congress's reenactment of § 3(b) in the 1978 amendments. Quite likely, the more explicit language in the amendments, indicating the Secretary's obligation to take affirmative measures to conserve the fishery and other resources, will reduce the importance of the section as a possible argument for the plaintiffs.

While § 3(b) seems to us of questionable significance here, we believe that both past and present versions of the Outer Continental Shelf Lands Act place the Secretary under a duty to see that gas and oil exploration and drilling is conducted without unreasonable risk to the fisheries. His duty includes the obligation not to go forward with a lease sale in a particular area if it would create unreasonable risks in spite of all feasible safeguards. As we see it, the question is not whether the Secretary's task is to put the interest of fishing "above" everything else, on the one hand, or whether, on the other, he is mindlessly to lease every square foot of seabottom at whatever risk to other resources. Both the previous and amended Outer Continental Shelf Lands Act seem to us to reflect Congress's underlying belief that mineral development can be so orchestrated with the development and preservation of renewable resources like fish as to do no irreparable harm to them. It is left to the Secretary to harmonize the interests of the various resources wherever they impinge upon one another. Congress nowhere simplified his difficult task by attaching overriding priority to the extraction of mineral wealth alone. We see no evidence that Congress sanctioned the destruction of a fishery as an acceptable price for oil and gas development. Some adverse effects on fishing and the coastal environs were doubtless anticipated, as the legislative establishment of oil spill and fishermen's gear funds indicates; but we think the underlying assumption was that both sets of interests—those concerned with the preservation of the fishery resource for future use by mankind, and those concerned with securing the extraction of oil and gas—can be served. Where the two sets of interests conflict, where particular mineral leases threaten particular fishing interests, the Secretary must determine which interests must give way, and to what degree, in order to achieve a proper balance. Thus in a case where a particular drilling operation poses too great a threat to a fishery, the Secretary must refuse to permit it. By the same token, if the threat is relatively small, and the damage posed to fishing of no major consequence, the Secretary may determine that leasing should proceed even if some harm may result. But the concept of balance rules out a policy based on sacrificing one interest to the other.

In arguments made under the Outer Continental Shelf Lands Act before the 1978 amendments, the Secretary conceded a "duty to consider fully the adverse impact of his activities under the Outer Continental Shelf Lands Act on the fisheries and to act with reasonable regard to those fisheries" but tended to be coy about admitting to any "affirmative duty on the Secretary to not affect fish in OCS oil and gas activities." He would not agree that the Act *commanded* that he regulate the oil and gas activities so as to maximize the harmony with fishing—rather he said merely he was *empowered* to do so. We would have ruled that the Secretary took too restricted a view of his duties even under the far from explicit standards of the unamended Act. Under § 5(a)(1) as then written, the Secretary's power to take measures to prevent waste and conserve natural resources was prefaced with the word "may," but we think the word as there used was not inconsistent with imposition of a duty. "Where a statute confers a power to be exercised for the benefit of the public or of a private person, the word 'may' is often treated as imposing a duty rather than conferring a discretion." *United States ex rel. Siegel v. Thoman*, 156 U.S. 353, 359, 15 S.Ct. 378, 380, 39 L.Ed. 450 (1895); *Supervisors v. United States*, 71 U.S. (4 Wall.) 435, 18 L.Ed. 419 (1867); *Mason v. Fearson*, 50 U.S. (9 How.) 248, 13 L.Ed. 125 (1850); *Thompson v. Clifford*, 132 U.S.App.D.C. 351, 355, 408 F.2d 154, 158 (1968).

In our view, by conferring powers upon the Secretary to provide for "the prevention of waste and conservation of the natural resources of the Outer Continental Shelf," Congress had indicated, even in the earlier legislation, a serious concern with balanced use of all resources in the area. To grant such powers indicated an expectation that reasonable use would be made of them for their intended purpose. Selection of the word "may" reflected Congress's recognition that because of the unforeseeability of the problems that would arise, the Secretary had to have broad discretion in the choice of means. But we feel the provision implied an underlying duty to exercise due diligence that the resources be in fact protected. *United States ex rel. Siegel v. Thoman, supra.* Such a duty would be in keeping with the longstanding view of the Secretary as "the guardian of the people of the United States," who is bound to see that "none of the public domain is wasted or is disposed of to a party not entitled to it." *Knight v. United States Land Association,* 142 U.S. 161, 181, 12 S.Ct. 258, 264, 35 L.Ed. 974 (1891); *see Hannifin v. Morton,* 444 F.2d 200, 202 (10th Cir. 1971); *Sierra Club v. Department of Interior,* 398 F.Supp. 284 (N.D.Cal.1975). It would be also consistent with the legislative history, which nowhere suggested that Congress expected or desired oil and gas leasing to go forward under conditions, or in particular locations, where serious and permanent damage to other important resources would result. The Act was never framed so as to mandate the singleminded exploitation of oil and gas resources at the expense of other important resources. Rather it couched the Secretary's power to enter into oil and gas leases in discretionary terms, 43 U.S.C. § 1337, leaving him free to withhold from leasing those areas where drilling operations would not be in the public interest, either because too dangerous to the marine environment or for some other reason. *Udall v. Tallman,* 380 U.S. 1, 85 S.Ct. 792, 13 L.Ed.2d 616 (1965). The Secretary could withhold specific lease areas in the interest of the proper management of all resources, just as he was empowered under § 5(a)(1) to condition leases on proper safeguards.

This interpretation of the unamended Act also drew sustenance from the enactment, in 1976, of the Fishery Conservation and Management Act. If the Outer Continental Shelf Lands Act were read as empowering the Secretary to give absolute priority to the extraction of oil and gas without paying heed to possible destructive effects upon the Georges Bank fishery, one federal statute would be read as countenancing the destruction of a resource which another, later statute was enacted to preserve. Common sense dictates that two statutes be read, insofar as possible, in harmony with one another.

> "Statutory interpretation requires more than concentration upon isolated words; rather, consideration must be given to the total corpus of pertinent law and the policies that inspired ostensibly inconsistent provisions." *Boys Markets v. Retail Clerks Local 770,* 398 U.S. 235, 250, 90 S.Ct. 1583, 1592, 26 L.Ed.2d 199 (1970).

The Fishery Conservation and Management Act was enacted in large part to protect the very resource here at stake, the Georges Bank fishery. Among the Act's purposes is "to promote domestic commercial and recreational fishing under sound conservation and management principles. . . ." 16 U.S.C. §

1801(b)(3).[12] The Fishery Act is thus no less an assertion of a federal interest in conserving the fishery resources in the waters of the Outer Continental Shelf than was the earlier Outer Continental Shelf Lands Act an assertion of a federal interest in developing the oil and gas wealth of the subsoil and seabed in the same area. To give effect to both policies, both Acts have to be construed in such a way as to minimize any conflict. A construction allowing oil and gas exploitation to take absolute priority over fishing would be to sanction a schizophrenic national policy, in which one hand was busily at work undoing what the other was seeking to accomplish.

For us to construe even the unamended Outer Continental Shelf Lands Act as requiring the Secretary to manage the resources committed to his care in such a way as to avoid serious harm to the fisheries was also consistent with policies laid down in the National Environmental Policy Act, 42 U.S.C. §§ 4321 et seq., which contains the following statement:

"The Congress, recognizing the profound impact of man's activity on the interrelations of all components of the natural environment, particularly the profound influences of population growth, high-density urbanization, industrial expansion, resource exploitation, and new and expanding technological advances and recognizing further the critical importance of restoring and maintaining environmental quality to the overall welfare and development of man, declares that it is the continuing policy of the Federal Government, in cooperation with State and local governments, and other concerned public and private organizations, to use all practicable means and measures, including financial and technical assistance, in a manner calculated to foster and promote the general welfare, to create and maintain conditions under which man and nature can exist in productive harmony, and fulfill the social, economic, and other requirements of present and future generations of Americans."

42 U.S.C. § 4331(a). This statute makes clear a national commitment to the intelligent use of all our natural wealth, which requires responsible federal officials to balance the benefits to be gained from the exploitation of one resource against the possible harm that may accrue to others.

Thus even prior to the 1978 amendments, we think it clear that the Secretary had a legal duty to avoid unreasonable risks to the fisheries in waters over the Outer Continental Shelf, even to the point of refusing to lease particular areas where risks would be unreasonable. We agree with plaintiffs that this duty has now been spelled out in the 1978 amendments, which contain numerous provisions indicating that the Secretary is required to minimize or eliminate any conflict associated with the exploitation of oil and gas resources. 43 U.S.C. § 1801(13); see also § 1332. To be sure, the amendments also reflect congressional desire to expedite the development of the oil and gas resources; but clearly Congress intends that this be done without serious damage to "the renewable

---

[12]Preservation of the offshore fisheries was of such importance that Congress was willing to take the major foreign policy risk of excluding foreign fishing fleets from the high seas over the Outer Continental Shelf; henceforth the fish there came under United States protection and management. If there had formerly been any doubt of the importance placed on the fisheries vis-a-vis other resources, enactment of the Fishery Conservation and Management Act dispelled that.

resources of the Outer Continental Shelf which are a continuing and increasingly important source of food and protein to the Nation and the world." 43 U.S.C. § 1801(14).

It is thus left to the Secretary to develop policies that will result in the extraction of oil and gas without unreasonable risks and damage to renewable resources such as fish. If it were 100% certain that particular precautions would obviate all danger, the task would be simple; but there is a large element of the unknown created by gaps in science, by possible human error, and by freak weather conditions. Thus, the Secretary must engage in an uneasy calculus akin to that described by Judge Learned Hand, weighing "the probability" of accident, "the gravity of the resulting injury" and "the burden of adequate precautions." *United States v. Carroll Towing Co.*, 159 F.2d 169, 173 (2d Cir. 1947). This task is committed to the Secretary, and so long as he carries it out rationally and in conformity to the law, the courts may not intervene. There can be no question, however, that his legal duty embraces a solemn responsibility to see that the great life systems of the ocean are not unreasonably jeopardized by activities undertaken to extract oil and gas from the seabed.

The preliminary injunction is vacated and the case remanded for further proceedings not inconsistent herewith.

NOTES

1. Was the goal of the state as plaintiff to stop oil development off its coast, or merely to ensure that proper environmental safeguards were used?

2. Is NEPA a dead letter as far as significantly affecting OCS development? Consider the results of *Suffolk* (Baltimore Canyon), *Massachusetts v. Andrus* (Georges Bank), and *California ex rel. Younger v. Morton* (Santa Barbara), cited in footnote 2.

3. *Massachusetts v. Andrus* illustrates an additional approach to OCS litigation. In addition to attacking the Department of the Interior's regulatory programs and the department's compliance with NEPA procedures, the plaintiffs utilized the mandates of specific resource protection statutes and comprehensive management programs. The conflict in federal agency mandates and priorities was argued to be a substantial barrier to OCS development. What benefits did the plaintiffs in *Massachusetts v. Andrus* gain from this new approach? Consider the following excerpt from Finn, *Interagency Relationships in Marine Resource Conflicts: Some Lessons from OCS Oil and Gas Leasing*, 4 Harv. Envt'l L. Rev. 359, 369–72 (1980):

Following the decision of the First Circuit, Interior prepared a supplemental environmental impact statement (EIS) specifically considering marine sanctuary alternatives and fisheries issues. But before the draft of this document (DSES) was circulated for public review and comment, one of the plaintiffs in the still pending litigation formally petitioned the Secretary of Commerce to designate Georges Bank as a marine sanctuary. The petition requested that the entire Georges Bank area be designated as a sanctuary and called for undefined but strict regulation of all potentially conflicting activities to make fisheries production and conservation the primary objectives of federal management of the area. After receiving the sanctuary nomination, NOAA, which had previously submitted critical comments on the proposed sale and accompanying environmental analyses, selected Georges Bank as an "active candidate" for designation as a marine sanctuary. It then provided its comments on the DSES to Interior, specifically directing Interior's attention to the sanctuary nomination and finding Interior's discussion of the marine sanctuary alternative inadequate.

NOAA then published an "issue paper" discussing the merits of designating Georges Bank as a marine sanctuary. This paper became the basis for a series of public workshops held to consider the nomination. The chief management alternative presented in the issue paper was to designate all of Georges Bank as a sanctuary. NOAA would allow oil and gas operations in areas included in Lease Sale No. 42, but would subject such operations to additional regulations, which would presumably be similar to the additional actions that NOAA had proposed Interior should take if a sanctuary were not designated.

In response to NOAA's actions on the marine sanctuary petition, Interior claimed that it had "exclusive authority" under the amended OCSLA to ensure that oil and gas activities would not unduly affect the marine resources of the area. Interior argued that any attempt by NOAA to designate Georges Bank as a sanctuary, before experience under lease indicated that such resources were actually being injured, would be an attempt to "preempt" Interior's primary regulatory authority. Interior pointed out that it already had a mandate under the amended OCSLA to ensure that "oil and gas exploration and development are conducted without unreasonable risk to the fisheries and the other resources . . ." and "to assure environmental protection."

. . . .

For several weeks, Interior and NOAA proceeded with their separate plans for management of Georges Bank while conducting negotiations toward a unified position. On September 21, 1979, the Departments of the Interior and Commerce announced an agreement under which Interior would adopt certain additional safeguards: NOAA would withdraw Georges Bank as an active candidate for marine sanctuary designation; and Interior, NOAA, and the Environmental Protection Agency (EPA) would draw up a memorandum of understanding for continued interagency coordination.

In most respects, the agreement between NOAA and Interior was a victory for Interior. In its comments on the DSES, NOAA had presented a strong case that there would be an unreasonable risk to commercial fishery resources and endangered whales if its recommendations were not followed. Under the agreement, however, few of NOAA's recommendations were adopted.

. . . .

The plaintiffs in the still pending litigation challenged both the substantive adequacy of the agreed measures and the procedural validity of the actions of Interior and NOAA. They claimed that both Interior and NOAA had failed to give proper consideration to the possible nomination of Georges Bank as a sanctuary. Indeed, the plaintiffs claimed that NOAA's failure to proceed further on the nomination petition itself was a "major federal action" requiring preparation of an EIS. Finally, the plaintiffs sought to prevent Interior from "interfering" further with NOAA's sanctuary designation process. They argued that these deficiencies rendered the lease sale proposal defective and should prevent the sale until Interior and NOAA had adequately discharged their responsibilities.

The plaintiffs were unsuccessful in asserting these claims in their motion for a new preliminary injunction delaying the sale then scheduled for November 6,

1979. The District Court concluded that Interior had adequately considered the marine sanctuary alternative, and that NOAA had acted within its discretion in concluding its agreement with Interior.

On appeal, the Circuit Court agreed that Interior had adequately discharged its responsibility to analyze the environmental aspects of the proposed sale, including the marine sanctuary alternative. The court also indicated that NOAA's actions regarding the sanctuary supported the proposition that the Secretary of Interior had had adequate opportunity to consider the marine sanctuary alternative.

Is there any reason to believe that the plaintiffs generally will be more successful in affecting lease sales by using resource protection statutes or comprehensive management programs? The marine sanctuaries program discussed further in Chapter 9 and the "consistency" clause of the federal Coastal Zone Management Act discussed in Chapter 11 are examples of such tools. *See* Moore, *Outer Continental Shelf Development and Recent Application of the Coastal Zone Management Act of 1971*, 15 Tulsa L.J. 443 (1980). *See generally* Breeden, *Federalism and the Development of the Outer Continental Shelf Mineral Resources*, 28 Stan. L. Rev. 1107 (1976).

4. On December 22, 1980, the district court accepted an agreement between the parties in *Massachusetts v. Andrus*:

Terms of Agreement

The settlement agreement gives the state and the conservation group access to federal studies already done, underway, or planned in the future on Georges Bank. "This allows us more convenient access to scientific work before it is formally released," according to Douglas Foy, executive director of the Conservation Law Foundation.

The agreement also commits the National Oceanic and Atmospheric Administration of the Commerce Department to re-evaluate the nomination of a proposed marine sanctuary for the area, with recommendations due by Dec. 1, 1981. The marine sanctuary proposal was dropped when Interior and Commerce agreed on the Georges Bank plan last year.

Under the settlement, the use of best available and safest technology will be required for all drilling operations on the Georges Bank. The agreement requires Interior to develop new standards defining best available and safest technology for drilling operations before such activities are approved.

Finally, the settlement requires Interior to make a "good faith consideration" for approval and funding of all future study recommendations by the Biological Task Force, which was set up to protect the rich fishery resources in the area. Interior must give the plaintiffs specific reasoning for its final determinations on Biological Task Force recommendations and must apprise the plaintiffs each time it decides whether to do an environmental impact statement on development and production plans.

Stephen Leonard, chief of the environmental protection division in the Massachusetts Attorney General's office, stated that 22 oil companies challenged the settlement in court because they wanted the lawsuit dismissed and did not want approval of the agreement.

"The challenge to legality of Lease Sale 42 is over," Leonard said, but the state and the conservation group will watch carefully and challenge, if necessary, the ocean discharge permits to be issued by the Environmental Protection Agency for drilling wastes, exploration plans to be approved by Interior, and endangered species findings to be submitted by NOAA.

Reactions to Settlement

"We feel we have accomplished what we set out to do when we filed this three years ago. We've made sure that at this predrilling stage a number of mechanisms are set up to protect Georges Bank from environmental damage," Foy said. However, "this is not the end of the battle over the quality of protection for fisheries on Georges Bank. This was the first round in an extended series of efforts to force adequate protection," he concluded.

Massachusetts Attorney General Francis X. Bellotti Dec. 22 said the agreement is the latest in a "long legal process by which we have assured that everything possible is being done to protect this extraordinary natural resource."

Interior Secretary Cecil Andrus said "I believe the agreement we have reached with the Commonwealth of Massachusetts and the other plaintiffs provides for a resolution of this litigation in the best interests of all concerned."

A petroleum industry spokesman Dec. 24 told BNA "It sounds like the Justice Department has given away the store in agreeing to this out-of-court settlement. The specifics of the settlement will certainly provide the Conservation Law Foundation with more opportunities for litigating the approval of exploration, development, and production plans."

Oil and gas exploration is to begin along the bank in 1981, but it will be years before oil actually flows from the area, according to Leonard.

15 Envt'l Rptr. 1347 (1981).[13] *See* Finn, *Georges Bank: The Legal Issues*, 23 Oceanus 30 (1980). In the end, what did the plaintiffs gain from their efforts to protect fishing on Georges Bank?

5. The procedural strategy of OCS opponents has been to enjoin the lease sales. Does the nature of the relief sought affect the nature of the litigation and the final outcome of these cases? *See* Note, *Stemming the Tide of Offshore Oil Development Through Preliminary Injunctive Relief—The Key to Effective Legal Challenges*, 7 Hofstra L. Rev. 499 (1979).

6. Should federal agencies be allowed to resolve disputes over OCS development without interference from the courts?

Another issue raised by interagency relationships is the possibility of informal resolution of such conflicts within the executive branch, with no opportunity for public scrutiny or participation. In the Georges Bank case, for example, NOAA's comments on Interior's FSES and statements made by its own Administrator indicated that the agency opposed the lease sale, believing that it would present an unreasonable risk to fisheries and a potential hazard to endangered whales. A marine sanctuary designation could have diminished these dangers; thus NOAA should have continued with the designation process. At the very least, preparation of a draft EIS on marine sanctuary alternatives would have put the agency in a better position to determine whether designation of a marine sanctuary was justified. There is some reason, therefore, to question whether NOAA performed its responsibility to implement the Marine Sanctuaries Act in good faith.

Finn, *Interagency Relationships in Marine Resource Conflicts: Some Lessons from OCS Oil and Gas Leasing*, 4 Harv. Envt'l L. Rev. 359, 377 (1980).

7. Should Congress intervene to protect especially sensitive offshore areas from the impacts of OCS oil and gas development? See the proposed Georges Bank

---

[13]Reprinted by special permission from Environmental Reporter, copyright 1981 by The Bureau of National Affairs, Inc., Washington D.C.

Protection Act, S. 2119, 96th Cong., 2d Sess. (1980), and H.R. 164, 97th Cong., 1st Sess. (1981), which would have created a National OCS Reserve off the coast of California in which only the President and Congress could authorize leasing.

8. Serious conflicts also arose over the impacts of OCS oil and gas development in the Beaufort Sea on Alaska native subsistence life-styles and the endangered bowhead whale:

. . .The Beaufort Sea is an area of harsh weather and sea conditions offshore artic Alaska. Several national environmental organizations and representatives of indigenous coastal communities feared that oil and gas development in this area would threaten endangered species, especially the bowhead whales which migrate through shallow coastal waters during the spring and fall. These groups challenged the proposed sale under NEPA and the ESA.

The District Court for the District of Columbia held that Interior's failure to prepare a satisfactory environmental analysis and NOAA's failure to furnish Interior with an adequate biological opinion rendered the proposed lease sale invalid under both NEPA and the ESA. The court found that Interior's environmental analysis did not satisfy NEPA because it did not adequately discuss the cumulative effects of expected arctic lease sales, available alternative mitigation measures, and the alternatives of management under other statutes such as the Marine Sanctuaries Act.

The court held that the proposed sale was also defective under the ESA because the interagency consultation requirement of the statute had not been fulfilled. Section 7(a)(2) of the ESA prohibits any federal action that would be likely to jeopardize the continued existence of any endangered species or adversely affect its critical habitat. It also requires that federal agencies undertaking, authorizing, or supporting activities which could affect an endangered species consult with the federal agency (the FWS or the NMFS) having jurisdiction over that species. Thus, if an agency's action might affect whales, it must consult with the NMFS. Under section 7(b), the consulting agency must, within ninety days after initiation of consultation, provide a "biological opinion" detailing the likely effects of the proposed action on the endangered species. The action agency then determines whether it can proceed with its proposed action while meeting its statutory responsibilities under section 7(a)(2).

The ESA scheme significantly constrains federal agencies contemplating actions that could affect endangered species. Once consultation is begun, the action agency may not undertake, or authorize its applicants to undertake, any irreversible or irretrievable commitments of resources which could foreclose alternatives to the proposed action until issuance of a biological opinion which resolves the endangered species issues one way or the other. If the biological opinion issued is unfavorable, any attempt by the agency to proceed with its proposed action would be politically and legally vulnerable. The agency can, however, obtain an exemption from the standard of section 7(a)(2) through action of the Endangered Species Committee, a Cabinet-level interagency standing committee.

In the Beaufort Sea case, the NMFS responded to Interior's request for consultation with two letters, the last stating that the information available to it was sufficient to enable the NMFS to determine whether the lease sale would be likely to jeopardize endangered whales. The court found that the letters provided by the NMFS were not an adequate biological opinion since they did not contain sufficient deliberative material to meet the requirements of section 7(b). The court held, however, that as long as it met the formal requirements of section 7(b), an opinion stating that there was "insufficient information" could still be considered an adequate biological opinion for certain preliminary actions. A final biological opinion based on sufficient information would be required only before Interior made irretrievable commitments of resources that might prejudice future decisions. Meanwhile, consultation under section 7(b) would continue.

Finn, *Interagency Relationships in Marine Resource Conflicts: Some Lessons from OCS Oil and Gas Leasing*, 4 Harv. Envt'l L. Rev. 359, 373–75 (1980). *See also* Geraci & St. Aubin, *Offshore Petroleum Resource Development and Marine Mammals: A Review and Research Recommendations*, 42 Marine Fisheries Rev. No. 11 at 1 (1980); Moore, *Outer Continental Shelf Development and Recent Applications of the Coastal Zone Management Act of 1971* [*sic*], 15 Tulsa L.J. 443, 455–58 (1980).

The district court opinion described in the excerpt above was reversed in *North Slope Borough v. Andrus*, 15 ERC. 1633 (D.C. Cir. 1980), *rev'g*, 486 F. Supp. 326 (D.D.C. 1979). In *Conservation Law Foundation v. Andrus*, 623 F.2d 712, 715 (1st Cir. 1979), the plaintiffs' challenge to the Georges Bank sale based on threats to the endangered right and humpback whales was rejected.

9. Regarding air pollution from offshore operations, *see* 43 U.S.C. § 1334; 30 C.F.R. § 250.57; *California v. Kleppe*, 604 F.2d 1187 (9th Cir. 1979); Kirwin, *Application of the Clean Air Act to Petroleum Operations on the Outer Continental Shelf*, 13 Nat. Res. Law. 411 (1980); Note, *California v. Kleppe: Who Regulates Air Quality over the Outer Continental Shelf?*, 29 Cath. U. L. Rev. 461 (1980); Note, *Clean Air Act Provisions Extended to Outer Continental Shelf*, 18 Nat. Res. J. 903 (1978).

10. For additional reading on OCS oil and gas development, *see*, Council on Environmental Quality, Oil and Gas in Coastal Waters (1977); Hildreth, *The Coast: Where Energy Meets the Environment*, 13 San Diego L. Rev. 253 (1976); Lee, *Decision to Lease Outer Continental Shelf Lands,* 2 Coastal Zone Mgmt. J. 31 (1975); Mead & Sorenson, *The Outer Continental Shelf Lands Act Amendments of 1978*, 19 Nat. Res. J. 885 (1979); Note, *Onshore Impacts of Offshore Drilling: The Police Power Alternative,* 8 Sw. U. L. Rev. 967 (1976); A. Reitze, *Environmental Planning: Law of Land and Resources*, ch. 20 at 3–8 (1974); Rubin, *The Role of CZM in Development of Oil and Gas*, 8 Nat. Res. Law. 399 (1975); Shaffer, *OCS Development and the Consistency Provisions of the Coastal Zone Management Act*, 40 Ohio N. L. Rev. 595 (1977); Senate Commerce Committee, Congress and the Nation's Oceans: Marine Affairs in the 94th Congress 109–12 (1977); T. Stoel, *Energy in Federal Environmental Law* 937–40 (1974); U.S. Office of Coastal Zone Management, Coastal Management Aspects of OCS Oil and Gas Developments (1975); Wilman, *OCS Development and Commercial and Recreational Fishing*, 5 Coastal Zone Mgmt. J. 211 (1979).

Oil Spills

In 1967, the tanker *Torrey Canyon* went aground on Seven Stones Reef off Cornwell, England. Although almost 19,000,000 gallons of oil spilled into the sea, some good did result from this maritime catastrophe—national and international attention began to focus on the problems inherent in the marine transport of oil. Congress finally began to consider measures for the prevention of oil spills, cleanup of spills, liability for spillers, and compensation for oil pollution damages. Three years after the *Torrey Canyon* grounding, the Water Quality Improvement Act of 1970, Pub. L. No. 91–224, amending the Federal Water Pollution Control Act (FWPCA), emerged from Congress. Although its oil liability provisions were later integrated into section 311 of the FWPCA amendments of 1972, Pub. L. No. 92–500, 33 U.S.C. § 1321, the wording remained virtually the same. Section 311 of what is now known as the Clean Water Act (CWA) is the primary federal statute governing oil spills in coastal and ocean waters out to 200 miles. *See* M. Ball, *Law of the Sea: Federal–State Relations* 16 n.69 (1978); Environmental Law Institute, *Air and Water Pollution Control Law: 1980* at 433 n.2 (1980).

There is no doubt of our need for oil to maintain and enhance economic growth. The crucial dilemma lies in striking a balance between development of oil resources with the commensurate costs of pollution damage to the ocean and coastal environment. A host of federal statutes introduced within address the problems of maritime oil transport, tanker regulation, facility siting, and liability for oil pollution damage. This chapter also addresses common law liability for spills, constitutional considerations relevant to overlapping state and federal regulation of oil pollution, and finally, federal legislation concerning deep-water ports for the transhipment of oil.

For an excellent overview of oil spill law, *see* W. Rodgers, *Environmental Law* 499–524 (1977). *See also* Council on Environmental Quality, Oil and Gas in Coastal Waters 39–41 (1977); Senate Commerce Committee, Congress and the Nation's Oceans 214–18 (1977).

SECTION A: SPILL LIABILITY

Liability at Common Law

BURGESS v. M/V TAMANO, 370 F. Supp. 247 (D. Me. 1973),
aff'd per curiam, 559 F.2d 1200 (1st Cir. 1977)

GIGNOUX, District Judge

Plaintiffs in these class actions seek to recover damages incurred as a result of the discharge into the waters of Casco Bay of approximately 100,000 gallons of Bunker C oil from the tanker M/V TAMANO early on the morning of July 22, 1972, when she struck an outcropping of "Soldier Ledge" while passing through Hussey Sound en route to the port of Portland. Variously named as defendants or third-party defendants are the TAMANO, her owners, her captain, her pilot and the local pilots' association, her charterer, Texaco, Inc., the State of Maine, and the United States of America. Liability is asserted on theories of negligence, unseaworthiness, trespass and nuisance, as well as under Section 13 of the Rivers and Harbors Act of 1899, 33 U.S.C. § 407, and Section 11(b)(2) of the Water Quality Improvement Act of 1970, 33 U.S.C. § 1161(b)(2). The admiralty and maritime jurisdiction of the federal courts is invoked pursuant to 28 U.S.C. § 1333(1) and 46 U.S.C. § 740.

Presently before the Court are defendants' motions to dismiss the claims of three of the plaintiff classes: the commercial fishermen in Nos. 13–111 and 13–156; the commercial clam diggers in No. 13–120; and, in No. 13–115, the owners of motels, trailer parks, camp grounds, restaurants, grocery stores, and similar establishments in Old Orchard Beach, whose businesses are dependent on tourist trade. Principally relying on Smedberg v. Moxie Dam Co., 148 Me. 302, 92 A.2d 606 (1952), defendants contend that the economic interests (loss of profits and impairment of earning capacity) which these classes of plaintiffs assert to have been damaged by the oil spill are not legally cognizable because none of the classes had any property interest in the coastal waters and marine life or shores claimed to have been injured by the spill. For reasons to be briefly stated, the Court holds that the motions to dismiss the claims of the commercial fishermen and clam diggers must be denied, but that the motions to dismiss the claims of the Old Orchard Beach businessmen, other than those who owned shore property physically injured by the spill, must be granted.

The parties agree that, as alleged in the complaints in these actions, an oil spill occurring in Maine's coastal waters constitutes a maritime tort and is within the admiralty jurisdiction of this Court. Maryland v. Amerada Hess Corp., 350

F.Supp. 1060, 1063–1065 (D.Md.1972); California v. S.S. Bournemouth, 307 F.Supp. 922, 926–928 (C.D. Cal.1969).

. . . .

[T]he view which this Court takes of the case makes it unnecessary to determine whether the general maritime law or the law of Maine is controlling.

First, as to the claims of the commercial fishermen and clam diggers, it is not disputed that title to its coastal waters and marine life, including the seabeds and the beds of all tidal waters, is vested in the State of Maine and that individual citizens have no separate property interest therein.

. . . .

See also McCready v. Virginia, 94 U.S. 391, 394, 24 L.Ed. 248 (1876); Toomer v. Witsell, 334 U.S. 385, 402 (1948); *id.* at 408, 68 S.Ct. 1156, 92 L.Ed. 1460 (Frankfurter, J., concurring). It is also uncontroverted that the right to fish or to harvest clams in Maine's coastal waters is not the private right of any individual, but is a public right held by the State "in trust for the common benefit of the people." Moulton v. Libbey, 37 Me. 472, 488 (1854); State v. Leavitt, *supra* 105 Me. at 78–79, 75 A. 875. *See also* Martin v. Waddell, 41 U.S. (16 Pet.) 367, 413, 10 L.Ed. 997 (1842). Since the fishermen and clam diggers have no individual property rights with respect to the waters and marine life allegedly harmed by the oil spill, their right to recover in the present action depends upon whether they may maintain private actions for damages based upon the alleged tortious invasion of public rights which are held by the State of Maine in trust for the common benefit of all the people.[1] As to this issue, the long standing rule of law is that a private individual can recover in tort for invasion of a public right only if he has suffered damage particular to him—that is, damage different in kind, rather than simply in degree, from that sustained by the public generally. Prosner, Law of Torts § 88 at 586–87 (4th ed. 1971); Prosser, Private Action for Public Nuisance, 52 Va.L.Rev. 997, 1004–11 (1966); Restatement (Second) of Torts § 821C(1) (Tent.Draft No. 17, 1971). Concededly, the line between damages different in kind and those different only in degree from those suffered by the public at large has been difficult to draw. *See generally* Prosner, Law of Torts, *supra*, § 88 at 589–91. But the Court is persuaded that the commercial fishermen and clam diggers have sufficiently alleged "particular" damage to support their private actions.

The commercial fishermen and clam diggers in the present cases clearly have a special interest, quite apart from that of the public generally, to take fish and harvest clams from the coastal waters of the State of Maine. The injury of which they complain has resulted from defendants' alleged interference with *their* direct exercise of the public right to fish and to dig clams. It would be an incongruous result for the Court to say that a man engaged in commercial fishing or clamming, and dependent thereon for his livelihood, who may have had his business destroyed by the tortious act of another, should be denied any right to

---

[1]Plaintiffs' principal claims sound in nuisance, and, although they also assert claims based on negligence, unseaworthiness, trespass and statutory violations, it is not suggested that their right to recover damages for pecuniary losses sustained by them as a result of the oil spill may differ according to the theory upon which they predicate defendant's liability.

recover for his pecuniary loss on the ground that his injury is no different in kind from that sustained by the general public. Indeed, in substantially all of those cases in which commercial fishermen using public waters have sought damages for the pollution or other tortious invasion of those waters, they have been permitted to recover. . . .

These cases are no more than applications of the more general principle that pecuniary loss to the plaintiff will be regarded as different in kind "where the plaintiff has an established business making a commercial use of the public right with which the defendant interferes . . . ." Prosser, Law of Torts, *supra*, § 88 at 590. *See also* Restatement (Second) of Torts, *supra*, § 821C, comment h and illustration 11. In the view of this Court, to the extent their pecuniary losses can be established, the commercial fishermen and clam diggers should be entitled to recover for the same.

Unlike the commercial fishermen and clam diggers, the Old Orchard Beach businessmen do not assert any interference with *their* direct exercise of a public right. They complain only of loss of customers indirectly resulting from alleged pollution of the coastal waters and beaches in which they do not have a property interest. Although in some instances their damage may be greater in degree, the injury of which they complain, which is derivative from that of the public at large, is common to all businesses and residents of the Old Orchard Beach area. In such circumstances, the line is drawn and the courts have consistently denied recovery. . . .

. . . .

In accordance with the foregoing, it is ordered as follows:

(1) In Nos. 13–111 and 13–156 (consolidated), defendants' motions to dismiss the claims of the commercial fishermen are denied;

(2) In No. 13–120, defendants' motions to dismiss the claims of the commercial clam diggers are denied;

(3) In No. 13–115, defendants' motions to dismiss the claims of the Old Orchard Beach businessmen who are not the owners of real or personal property claimed to have been damaged by the oil spill are granted, and said claims are dismissed.

NOTE

See *Bowman v. Helser,* 143 Wash. 397, 255 P. 146 (1927); *Captain Kevin Corp. v. Bay Drilling Corp.,* 380 So. 2d 639 (La. Ct. App. 1979) (plaintiff state oyster bed lessees entitled to recover damages for defendant's negligence in drilling oil well); *Jurisch v. Louisiana Southern Oil and Gas Co.,* 284 So. 2d 173 (1973) (mineral lessee is not liable to an oyster lessee of coextensive property for damage resulting from necessary and prudent activities incident to the mineral lease); *Pure Oil v. Renton,* 207 Okla. 151, 248 P.2d 580 (1952); *Skansi v. Signal Petroleum,* 375 So. 2d 965 (La. Ct. App. 1979) (oyster bed lessee entitled to recover damages for oil pollution causing oily taste.)

MAINE v. M/V TAMANO, 357 F. Supp. 1097
(S.D. Me. 1973)

GIGNOUX, District Judge

The State of Maine and the Board of Environmental Protection, an agency of the State, have brought this suit to recover damages incurred as a result of the discharge into the waters of Casco Bay of approximately 100,000 gallons of Bunker C oil from the tanker M/V TAMANO early on the morning of July 22, 1972, when she struck an outcropping of "Soldier Ledge" while passing through Hussey Sound en route to the port of Portland. Plaintiffs seek to recover damages in three distinct categories: (1) the State in its proprietary capacity seeks to recover for damage to property, such as state parks, which the State itself owns, including the land under the waters of the marginal seas of the State; (2) the Board, by virtue of the authority granted it by the Maine Oil Discharge Prevention and Pollution Control Act, 38 M.R.S.A. § 541 *et seq.* (1972 Supp.) sues to recover all sums expended or to be expended by it in payment of third-party damage claims and clean-up costs;[2] and (3) the State in its *parens patriae* capacity "as owner and/or trustee for the citizens of the State of Maine of all of the natural resources lying in, on, over, under and adjacent to" its coastal waters seeks to recover for damage to such waters and the marine life therein. Defendants concede that plaintiffs have valid causes of action with respect to the first two categories, but they contest that the State has stated a viable claim as to the third, and have moved to dismiss the complaint to that extent. Their assertion is essentially that the State has no sufficiently independent interest in its coastal waters and their marine life to permit it to sue as *parens patriae* on behalf of its citizens. The Court disagrees.

Suits by a State, *parens patriae*, have long been recognized. Thus the Supreme Court has entertained suits *parens patriae* to enjoin the discharge of sewage into the Mississippi River; to restrain the diversion of water from an interstate stream; to prevent a copper company from discharging noxious fumes across a state border; to enjoin the discharge of sewage into New York harbor; to preclude restraints on the commercial flow of natural gas; to restrain drainage changes increasing the flow of water in an interstate stream; and to enjoin alleged discriminatory freight rates charged by railroad companies to the State and its citizens.

These cases establish that the right of a State to sue as *parens patriae* is not limited to suits to protect only its proprietary interests; a State also may

[2] The Maine Oil Discharge Prevention and Control Act was enacted by the Maine Legislature in 1970 in an attempt to establish a comprehensive scheme for the prevention and control of oil pollution of Maine's coastal waters. Laws of Maine of 1970, ch. 572 (1970). The Act creates the Maine Coastal Protection Fund, to be financed by license fees paid by the oil industry, and provides for the payment from the Fund by the Board of Environmental Protection of the claims of persons suffering damage from the discharge of oil and the costs involved in the abatement of pollution resulting from the discharge of oil. The Act imposes unlimited liability without fault upon offending vessels and terminal facilities, and directs the Board to recover all sums expended from the Fund from the person responsible for the discharge.

. . . .

maintain an action *parens patriae* on behalf of its citizens to protect its so-called "quasi-sovereign" interests. A quasi-sovereign interest must be an interest of the State "independent of and behind the titles of its citizens," that is, in order to maintain a *parens patriae* suit, the State "must show a direct interest of its own and not merely seek recovery for the benefit of individuals who are the real parties in interest."

It is clear that Maine has an independent interest in the quality and condition of her coastal waters. It has long been established by decisions of the Supreme Court, and of the Supreme Judicial Court of Maine, that a State has sovereign interests in its coastal waters and marine life, as well as in its other natural resources, which interests are separate and distinct from the interests of its individual citizens. In *McCready v. Virginia*, 94 U.S. 391, 24 L. Ed. 248 (1876), the Supreme Court stated:

> The principle has long been settled in this court, that each State owns the beds of all tide-waters within its jurisdiction, unless they have been granted away. In like manner, the States own the tide-waters themselves, and the fish in them, so far as they are capable of ownership while running. For this purpose the State represents its people, and the ownership is that of the people in their united sovereignty. *Id.* at 394.

More recently, in *Toomer v. Witsell*, 334 U.S. 385, 68 S. Ct. 1156, 92 L. Ed. 1460 (1948), Mr. Justice Frankfurter, joined by Mr. Justice Jackson, concurring, reaffirmed the continued vitality of *McCready* and described the foundation of the State's power to protect its natural resources as follows:

> A State may care for its own in utilizing the bounties of nature within her borders because it has technical ownership of such bounties or, when ownership is in no one, because the State may for the common good exercise all the authority that technical ownership ordinarily confers. *Id.* at 408, 68 S. Ct. at 1168.

Similarly, the Maine Court has repeatedly declared the sovereign interests of the State in its coastal waters. . . .

Defendants further urge that in order to maintain a *parens patriae* action, the State must also show that the damage to its coastal waters has an adverse effect upon a substantial part of its citizens. Whether or not this is a requirement, it is plainly met here. The conclusion is inescapable that if injury to Maine's coastal waters and marine life has occurred as a result of this spill, the environment of the State and the recreational opportunities and welfare of all her citizens have seriously suffered. In the words of *Georgia v. Pennsylvania R. Co.* [324 U.S. 439, 451, 65 S. Ct. 716, 723, 89 L. Ed. 1051, 1059 (1945)], "[t]hese are matters of grave public concern in which [Maine] has an interest apart from that of particular individuals who may be affected. [Maine's] interest is not remote; it is immediate."

Defendants argue finally that the State cannot maintain a *parens patriae* suit for damages. They correctly observe that all but two of the Supreme Court *parens patriae* cases were actions for solely injunctive relief. And it is true that in both of its *parens patriae* damage suits, the Supreme Court denied recovery. . . . But the plain implication to be drawn from both cases is that, absent some substantive bar, the Court was willing to allow damages to a State suing as *parens patriae*.

Defendants point out that there is a risk of double damages when a State's quasi-sovereign interests are asserted. They also argue that any injury to the State's interests is too speculative to be reduced to money damages. The latter is a problem of proof to be met at trial. Nor does permitting the State to sue *parens patriae* "necessarily lead to double recovery. Since [Maine] is by definition asserting claims 'independent of and behind the titles of its citizens,' there may be excluded from its recovery any monetary damages that might be claimed by her citizens individually or as part of a properly constituted class. That problem, like uncertainty of damages, is better answered after trial than on the pleadings."

In sum, this Court agrees with the District Court in the *Standard Oil* case that "[t]here is no merit in defendants' claim that there can never be a *parens patriae* suit for damages." 301 F. Supp. at 987. Indeed, two lower federal courts, in cases substantially indentical to the instant one, have recently permitted a State to bring a damage claim in a *parens patriae* capacity for injury to its waters and marine life allegedly resulting from marine oil spills. *Maryland v. Amerada Hess Corp.*, 350 F. Supp. 1060 (D. Md. 1972); *California v. S.S. Bournemouth*, 307 F. Supp. 922 and 318 F. Supp. 839 (C.D. Cal. 1970). . . .

If Maine can establish damage to her quasi-sovereign interests in her coastal waters and marine life, independent of whatever individual damages may have been sustained by her citizens, there is no apparent reason why the present action to recover such damage cannot be maintained. In the view of this Court, the complaint states a viable *parens patriae* cause of action, which cannot be dismissed at this stage.

Defendants' motion to dismiss is denied.

It is so ordered.

COMMONWEALTH OF PUERTO RICO v. SS ZOE COLOCOTRONI, 628 F. 2d 652 (1st Cir. 1980), cert. denied, 15 ERC. 1697 (1981)

LEVIN H. CAMPBELL, Circuit Judge.

In the early morning hours of March 18, 1973, the SS ZOE COLO-COTRONI, a tramp oil tanker, ran aground on a reef three and a half miles off the south coast of Puerto Rico. To refloat the vessel, the captain ordered the dumping of more than 5,000 tons of crude oil into the surrounding waters. An oil slick four miles long, and a tenth of a mile wide, floated towards the coast and came ashore at an isolated peninsula on the southwestern tip of the island—a place called Bahia Sucia. The present appeal concerns an action in admiralty brought by the Commonwealth of Puerto Rico and the local Environmental Quality Board (EQB) to recover damages for harm done to the coastal environment by the spilled oil.

Defendants have raised numerous objections to the district court's judgment awarding plaintiffs $6,164,192.09 in damages for cleanup costs and environmental harm. The primary objections are that the district court: . . . (4) erred in finding plaintiffs had standing to sue for environmental damages; . . . . The facts and circumstances of the oil spill and its aftermath are set forth in detail in the district court's opinion, *Commonwealth of Puerto Rico v. SS Zoe Colotroni*, 456 F. Supp. 1327 (D.P.R. 1978). After a brief review of these facts and of the trial testimony, we will address defendant's contentions in turn.

The following facts found by the district court are not in serious dispute. On March 15, 1973, the ZOE COLOCOTRONI departed La Salina, Venezuela, carrying 187,670 barrels of crude oil en route to Guayanilla, Puerto Rico. For the first two days of the voyage, the vessel proceeded by celestial navigation. The last star fix, however, was taken at 1859 hours on March 17. For the next eight hours, the ship proceeded by dead reckoning. As the vessel approached the south coast of Puerto Rico, it was, the district court stated, "hopelessly lost." At 0300 hours on March 18, the ship grounded on a reef. Efforts to free the tanker by alternately running engines in forward and reverse were unsuccessful. After ten minutes, the captain ordered the crew to lighten ship by emptying the cargo of crude oil into the sea.[3] By the time the vessel refloated, some 1.5 million gallons of crude oil—5,170.1 tons—had poured into the surrounding waters. . . .

. . . .

The oil floated westward from the site of the spill throughout the daylight hours of March 18, and began coming ashore after nightfall. Bahia Sucia is a crescent-shaped bay facing southeastward from the Cabo Rojo peninsula, which forms the southwest tip of Puerto Rico. The Oil entered Bahia Sucia, washed onto the beaches, and penetrated the mangrove forests that line the western edge of the bay. . . .

. . . .

The Commonwealth of Puerto Rico and the EQB instituted the present action on March 19, 1973, invoking the admiralty jurisdiction of the district court. A six-week trial, addressed solely to damages commenced on November 7, 1977. . . .

. . . .

We turn first to the issue of plaintiffs' right to bring this lawsuit. The district court held that the Commonwealth had "standing" to recover for damages to natural resources, namely the mangrove trees and the various species of marine creatures living in and around them, on the theory that the Commonwealth was the "trustee of the public trust in these resources" and had an interest in them as *parens patriae*. 456 F. Supp. at 1337; *See Maryland v. Amerada Hess Corp.*, 350 F. Supp. 1060 (D. Md. 1972); *Maine v. M/V Tamano*, 357 F. Supp. 1097 (D. Me. 1973); *In re Steuart Transportation Co.*, 495 F. Supp. 38, No. 76–697–N (E.D. Va. 1980). The court also ruled that the Environmental Quality Board had standing to proceed as co-plaintiff seeking similar relief under a state statute authorizing the EQB to bring damages actions for environmental injuries. 456 F. Supp. at 1337; 12 L.P.R.A. § 1131(29).

While the parties and the district court speak in terms of "standing," we

---

[3]The captain was ultimately tried and convicted on a charge of violating 33 U.S.C. § 1321 (b) (5) in connection with the dumping of oil. 456 F. Supp. at 1333 n.9.

think the question is more properly whether plaintiffs have stated a cognizable cause of action.[4] Defendants concede that Puerto Rico, as owner of the real property primarily affected by the oil spill, *see* 48 U.S.C. § 749, would, like any private landowner, have a cause of action in admiralty to recover whatever damages it could prove under conventional principles for its private economic loss as measured by diminution of market value in the coastal land. *See* 46 U.S.C. § 740. The Commonwealth made no attempt to show such damages, however. It seeks relief instead under an asserted right to recover as a governmental entity on behalf of its people for the loss of living natural resources on the land such as trees and animals.[5]

Defendants contend that Puerto Rico's assertion of a recoverable interest in wildlife and other living natural resources is undercut by a line of Supreme Court cases culminating in *Hughes v. Oklahoma,* 441 U.S. 322, 99 S. Ct. 1727, 60 L. Ed. 2d 250 (1979). *See also Douglas v. Seacoast Products, Inc.*, 431 U.S. 265, 284, 97S.Ct. 1740, 1751, 52 L. Ed. 2d 304 (1977); *Toomer v. Witsell*, 334 U.S. 385, 402 & n.37, 68 S. Ct. 1156, 1165 & n.37, 92 L. Ed. 1460 (1948); *Missouri v. Holland*, 252 U.S. 416, 434, 40 S. Ct. 382, 383, 64 L. Ed. 641 (1920); *cf. Geer v. Connecticut*, 161 U.S. 519, 16 S. Ct. 600, 40 L. Ed. 793 (1896). In *Hughes*, the Court formally overruled *Geer v. Connecticut*, invalidating on Commerce Clause grounds a state ban on interstate transportation of wildlife lawfully caught in the state and completing the long erosion of *Geer's* theory of state ownership of wildlife. The court recognized, however, that states retain an important interest in the regulation and conservation of wildlife and natural resources. "[T]he general rule we adopt in this case makes ample allowance for preserving, in ways not inconsistent with the Commerce Clause, the legitimate state concerns for conservation and protection of wild animals underlying the 19th Century legal fiction of state ownership." 441 U.S. at 335–36, 99 S. Ct. at 1736. Later, the Court said, "We consider the States' interests in conservation and protection of wild animals as legitimate local purposes similar to the States' interests in protecting the health and safety of their citizens." *Id.* at 337, 99 S. Ct. at 1737.

[4]Plaintiffs' Article III standing is not challenged here, since, assuming plaintiffs have a valid cause of action, they clearly are the proper parties to raise it. *See Davis v. Passman*, 442 U.S. 228, 239 & n.18, 99 S.Ct. 2264, 2273–4 & n.18, 60 L.Ed.2d 846 (1979).

[5]We note at this point several questions which are not presented in this case, and on which we express no opinion. First, since the lands in question were all owned by Puerto Rico, we need not decide whether or in what circumstances a state might have a cause of action for environmental harm to privately owned land. Second, since the living natural resources in issue here were all attached more or less permanently to the land, we also do not decide whether any cause of action would accrue, and if so what remedies would be available, where more transitory forms of wildlife such as birds or fish were damaged. Third, this case does not present the issue of overlapping state and federal causes of action. While the Federal Clean Water Act of 1977 specifically stated that it did not preempt the imposition of a state of "any requirement or liability with respect to the discharge of oil or hazardous substance into any waters within such State," 33 U.S.C. § 1321 (*o*) (2), a problem of double recovery might be raised under some circumstances. Here, however, the United States made no claim for environmental damage (at the time this case arose there was no federal statute authorizing such an action) and asserted no legal interest in the affected lands. The interplay of the state cause of action asserted here with the federal remedial legislation discussed *infra* is an issue we therefore leave for another day.

Plaintiffs argue that a state regulatory interest in wildlife and other living resources, expressed metaphorically in the states' status as "public trustee" of its natural resources is sufficient in itself to support an action for damages to those resources. *See, e.g., Maryland v. Amerada Hess Corp.*, 350 F. Supp. 1060, 1066–67 (D. Md. 1972). Defendants reply that, absent a proprietary interest in the resource actually damaged, a state's unexercised regulatory authority over wildlife will not support a proper cause of action. *See e.g., Commonwealth v. Agway, Inc.*, 210 Pa. Super. 150, 232, A.2d 69 (1967). We see no need to decide this difficult question in the present case. Here the Commonwealth of Puerto Rico, exercising its undisputed authority to protect and conserve its natural environment, has by statute authorized one of its agencies to maintain actions of this sort. Under the statute, 12 L.P.R.A. § 1131(29), co-plaintiff Environmental Quality Board has, among others, the following duties, powers and functions:

> "(29) To bring, represented by the Secretary of Justice, by the Board's attorneys, or by a private attorney contracted for such purpose, civil actions for damages in any court of Puerto Rico or the United States of America to recover the total value of the damages caused to the environment and/or natural resources upon committing any violation of this chapter and its regulations. The amount of any judgment collected to such effect shall be covered into the Special Account of the Board on Environmental Quality."

We read this statute both as creating a cause of action of the type described by its terms and as designating the EQB as the proper party to bring such an action. We see nothing in *Hughes v. Oklahoma* or in the federal Constitution to prohibit such legislation. Whatever might be the case in the absence of such a local statute, we think that where the Commonwealth of Puerto Rico has thus legislatively authorized the bringing of suits for environmental damages, and has earmarked funds so recovered to a special fund, such an action must be construed as taking the place of any implied common law action the Commonwealth as trustee, might have brought. Any other construction would invite the risk of double recovery and lead to confusion as to the rights of the two state plaintiffs in their identical or nearly identical actions. It is unnecessary, therefore, for us to consider whether, had the legislature of Puerto Rico not delegated to the EQB the right to maintain such suits, the Commonwealth would have an inherent right to bring them itself.

Defendants assert, as a sort of last ditch rebuttal to this line of argument, that the present action is not authorized under section 1131(29), because plaintiff EQB failed to allege in the complaint "any violation of this chapter and its regulations." This assertion is erroneous. In the third amended complaint, plaintiff specifically alleged a violation of 24 L.P.R.A. § 595, which provides:

> "It shall be unlawful for any person, directly or indirectly, to throw, discharge, pour, or dump, or permit to be thrown, discharged, poured or dumped into the waters, any organic or inorganic matter capable of polluting or of leading to the pollution of said waters in such manner as to place them out of the minimum standards of purity that the Secretary of Health may establish under section 599 of this title."

This statute is explictly made a part of Title 12, chapter 121 by 12 L.P.R.A. § 1132(b). The "minimum standards of purity" referred to in section 595 have been promulgated, and they make clear that any unauthorized discharge of petroleum into the waters–including the territorial waters—of Puerto Rico is considered unlawful. *See* P.R. Rules & Regulations, Title 24 § 589–5. Defendant's challenge to the right of the EQB to maintain this action is thus without merit.

. . . .

Affirmed in part, vacated in part, and remanded for further proceedings consistent with this opinion.

NOTES

1. The owners of private pleasure boats that contact an oil spill bring an action against the oil company seeking to recover for physical damages to their boats and for loss of navigation rights in the channel and harbor. In light of the principal cases, are these damages recoverable? *See Oppen v. Aetna Insurance Co.*, 485 F. 2d 252 (9th Cir. 1973), a case arising out of the 1969 Santa Barbara oil spill.

2. Another case arising from the Santa Barbara spill was *Union Oil Co. v. Oppen*, 501 F. 2d 558 (9th Cir. 1974). There the court said that under maritime law and the law of California the oil companies were under a duty to commercial fishers to conduct their offshore drilling and production in a "reasonably prudent manner" so as to avoid "negligent diminution of aquatic life." 501 F. 2d at 570. Is this ruling consistent with *Burgess v. M/V Tamano*? *See Louisiana v. The M/V TESTBANK*, 16 ERC 1724 (E.D. La. 1981).

3. *U.S. v. Ira S. Bushey & Sons, Inc.*, 363 F. Supp. 110 (D. Vt.), *aff'd*, 487 F. 2d 1393 (2d Cir. 1973), *cert. denied*, 417 U.S. 976 (1974), involved an oil barge transportation company responsible for five large spills over a 3-year period. Injunctive relief was granted on nuisance grounds, claiming unreasonable interference with the public's rights in navigable waters.

4. In *Commonwealth of Puerto Rico v. SS Zoe Colocotroni*, the court noted a trilogy of issues which it did not address. The first was whether or in what circumstances a state might have a cause of action for environmental harm from oil spills to privately owned land (the lands in question in the *Zoe Colocotroni* were owned by Puerto Rico). The second issue was whether any state or federal cause of action would accrue for damage from oil spills to transitory forms of wildlife. This issue involves the question of proprietary interest and, in the *Zoe Colocotroni*, the damaged natural resources were "all attached more or less permanently to the land." But the court in *In re Steuart Transportation Co.*, 495 F. Supp. 38 (E.D. Va. 1980), held that the United States and affected states have a cause of action for loss of waterfowl from oil spills under the public trust doctrine and the doctrine of parens patriae. This right of recovery was not dependent on the establishment of an ownership interest in the migratory waterfowl. The third issue involved the potential overlap of state and federal causes of action and the problem of double recovery under some circumstances. This possibility will be discussed in the following material on the Federal Clean Water Act of 1977, 33 U.S.C. § 1321(a)(2).

   The *Zoe Colocotroni* decision is also remarkable and controversial with respect to the court's valuation and assessment of natural resource damages.

See DuBey & Fidell, *The Assessment of Pollution Damage to Aquatic Resources: Alternatives to the Trial Model*, 19 Santa Clara L. Rev. 641, 644 (1979).

5. The failure of traditional legal remedies to adequately assess oil pollution damage, compensate victims of oil pollution damage, and to penalize the parties responsible has been the subject of several law review articles. *See* DuBey & Fidell, *The Assessment of Pollution Damage to Aquatic Resources: Alternatives to the Trial Model*, 19 Santa Clara L. Rev. 641 (1979); Maloof, *Oil Pollution: Cleaning Up the Legal Mess*, 43 Ins. Counsel J. 605 (1976); Mattson, *Compensating States and the Federal Government for Damages to Natural Resources from Oil Spills*, 5 Coastal Zone Mgmt. J. 307 (1979); Post, *A Solution to the Problem of Private Compensation in Oil Discharge Situations*, 28 U. Miami L. Rev. 524 (1974); Roady, *Remedies in Admiralty for Oil Pollution*, 5 Fla. St. L. Rev. 361 (1977); Swan, *International and National Approaches to Oil Pollution Responsibility: An Emerging Regime for a Global Problem*, 50 Or. L. Rev. 506 (1971); Wood, *Requiring Polluters to Pay to Aquatic Natural Resources Destroyed by Oil Pollution*, 8 Nat. Res. Law. 545 (1976); Note, *Assessment of Civil Monetary Penalties for Water Pollution: A Proposal for Shifting the Burden of Proof Regarding Damages*, 30 Hastings, L.J. 651 (1979).

Statutory Liability

The Clean Water Act, 33 U.S.C. § 1321 (FWPCA § 311)

The Federal Water Pollution Control Act, as amended by the Clean Water Act (the "CWA"), is the primary federal law governing spills of oil and other hazardous substances into navigable waters. The broad policy of the act is that "there should be no discharge of oil or hazardous substances into or upon the navigable waters of the United States. . . ." 33 U.S.C. § 1321(b)(1) (1976 Supp. III 1979), and "[t]he discharge of oil or hazardous substances . . . into or upon the navigable waters of the United States . . . in harmful quantities as determined by the President . . . is prohibited." *Id*. § 1321(b)(3) (1976 Supp. III 1979). In the event of a discharge, the act provides a comprehensive plan for cleanup and assessment of liability for cleanup costs.

Unlawful discharges of oil are subject to a $5,000 civil penalty for each offense. The penalty is levied against any spill source "owner, operator, or person in charge," 33 U.S.C. § 1321(b)(6) (1976 Supp. III 1979). Failure to report a spill results in a fine of up to $10,000 or imprisonment up to 1 year. *Id*. § 1321(b)(5) (1976 Supp. III 1979).

Federal agencies are authorized to clean up oil spills if the party responsible does nor or cannot be identified. To encourage rapid mobilization of cleanup efforts, the CWA establishes a $35 million fund which is available for financing state and federal cleanup costs. 33 U.S.C. § 1321(k) (1976 Supp. III 1979).

The CWA also provides that liability for damages resulting from a discharge or from the removal of oil or hazardous substances is not affected or modified in any way. (Damages should be contrasted with the removal costs and civil penalty provided for in the CWA). Further, the CWA does not preempt state or local authorities from imposing liability for discharges, nor does it affect or modify existent federal law regulating onshore or offshore facilities. 33 U.S.C. § 1321(o)(1)–(3) (1976 Supp. III 1980).

Finally, the CWA establishes a "National Oil and Hazardous Substances Pollution Contingency Plan." *See* 33 U.S.C. § 1321(c)(2) (1976); 40 C.F.R. Part 1510 (1980). The purposes of this plan, prepared by the Council on Environmental Quality, are to do the following: designate federal agencies to work in coordination with state and local agencies (the designated agencies are the Coast Guard and the Environmental Protection Agency); establish regional "strike forces" to respond immediately to oil spills (these have been created within the Coast Guard); and establish methods of containing, dispersing, and removing spills.

The liability provisions of the CWA provide an additional source of compensation for cleanup costs. Under these provisions, owners or operators of vessels from which oil is discharged are liable for (1) the greater of $125 per gross ton or $125,000 for inland barges; (2) the greater of $150 per gross ton or $150,000 for other tank vessels; and (3) $150 per gross ton for all other vessels. Owners and operators of both onshore and offshore facilities are liable for the cost of removal up to $50 million. However, where it can be proven that the discharge was the result of "willful negligence or willful misconduct" within the party's "privity and knowledge," the amount of liability is unlimited. 33 U.S.C. § 1321(f)(1)–(3) (1976 Supp. III 1979). To ensure that potential dischargers will be able to cover liability assessment, the CWA requires oil tankers and barges over 300 gross tons utilizing U.S. waters to show proof of financial responsibility. *Id.* § 1321(p) (1976 Supp. III 1979).

Liability can be avoided where a discharge of oil is proven to be the result of "(A) an act of God, (B) an act of war, (C) negligence on the part of the United States government, or (D) an act or omission of a third party without regard to whether any such act or omission was or was not negligent." 33 U.S.C. § 1321(f)(1)–(3) (1976 Supp. III 1979).

NOTES

1. Section 1321(a)(7) of the CWA provides that a "person," for the purposes of the Act, "includes an individual, firm, corporation, association, and a partnership . . . ." Is a state, or political subdivision thereof, such as a municipality, a "person" within the meaning of § 1321(a)(7), and thus subject to civil penalties assessed under the CWA for causing oil spills into navigable waters? *See U.S. v. Massachusetts Bay Transportation Authority*, 614 F. 2d 27 (1st Cir. 1980); *U.S. v. City of New York*, 463 F. Supp. 604 (S.D.N.Y. 1979).

2. In *U.S. v. Ward*, 100 S. Ct. 2636 (1980), a $500 civil penalty was assessed under section 1321(b)(6) where an oil discharge from a drilling site had been reported after cleanup. The Court held that Congress intended the penalty for oil spills to be a civil rather than criminal sanction, and further, that the penalty was not so punitive in purpose or effect as to negate this intention. Thus, the reporting

requirement of the act did not violate the fifth amendment privilege against self-incrimination.

3. For a discussion and application of the no-fault provision of the act, *see U.S. v. Texas Pipe Line Co.*, 611 F. 2d 345 (10th Cir. 1979), where a $2,500 civil penalty against a company was upheld even though the company was not at fault and even though the company took prompt action to clean up the spill. *See also U.S. v. Beatty, Inc.,* 401 F. Supp. 1040 (W.D. Ky. 1975) ($2,000 fine upheld for a spill of 5 to 15 gallons of oil); Note, *Spilling Oil May Be Hazardous to Your Wealth*, 19 Nat. Res. J. 735 (1979).

4. Is the CWA the exclusive federal remedy for the recovery of costs incurred in oil spill removal and cleanup? Or may the government pursue additional statutory and nonstatutory remedies to recover cleanup costs? In *U.S. v. Dixie Carriers, Inc.,* 627 F. 2d 736 (5th Cir. 1980), the court addressed issues of statutory construction, and the interplay between section 1321(f)(1), which limits the recovery based upon strict liability, and section 1321(b)(1)–(2), which does not limit public and private actions for property damage. The court held section 1321(f)(1) to be the exclusive federal remedy. The court denied alternative statutory remedies under the Refuse Act, 33 U.S.C. § 407 *et seq.*, the Clean Water Act, 33 U.S.C. § 1251 *et seq.*, and nonstatutory alternatives under negligence or public nuisance theories. *Accord, In re Oswego Barge Corp.,* 16 ERC 1777, (1st Cir. 1981). But *see* Comment, *Oil Spills and Cleanup Bills: Federal Recovery of Oil Spills Cleanup Costs,* 93 Harv. L. Rev. 1761 (1980), suggesting that the CWA does not exclude additional recovery under maritime tort or public nuisance theories.

5. Towage agreements often place oil barges in the control of third-party independent operators. Section 1321(f)(1)(D) of the CWA provides an affirmative defense to oil spill liability "where the discharge was caused solely by an act or omission of a third party without regard to whether such an act or omission was or was not negligent." Would a barge owner's liability depend on the degree of control exercised over a third party during towing in the event of a spill? *See U.S. v. Hollywood Marine, Inc.,* 487 F. Supp. 1211 (S.D. Texas 1980).

6. Section 1321(f)(4) provides that federal costs incurred in the restoration or replacement of natural resources damaged or destroyed by oil spills are part of the removal costs recoverable by the federal government. Under section 1321(f)(5), the President, or an authorized state representative, is empowered "to act on behalf of the public as trustee of the natural resources to recover for the costs of replacing or restoring such resources." How do sections (f)(4) and (f)(5) of section 1321 relate to *Maine v. M/V Tamano?* DuBey & Fidell, *The Assessment of Pollution Damage to Aquatic Resources: Alternatives to the Trial Model*, 19 Santa Clara L. Rev. 641, 673 (1979), suggests that "it is unclear whether the trustee of the natural resources must first assess or expend moneys to restore or replace the natural resource damage caused by the spill before the trustee may add these costs to the overall government claim for costs of removal assessed against the spiller." Do sections 1321(f)(4) and (f)(5) implicitly cover pollution damage assessment studies as part of the costs of removal, restoration, or replacement to be borne by parties liable under the act?

7. Authority for administration of the oil and hazardous substance provisions of the CWA has been divided between the U.S. Coast Guard and the Environmental Protection Agency. These agencies have been delegated the task of determining the meaning of "harmful" discharges and formulating programs to eliminate them. The Coast Guard regulations can be found at 33 C.F.R. §§ 151.01–153.419 (1979), and the EPA regulations at 40 C.F.R. §§ 112.1–112.7 (1979). *See United States v. Chevron Oil Co.,* 583 F. 2d 1357 (5th Cir. 1978) ("sheen test" for determining harmful discharges held valid.)

Other Federal Statutes

In addition to the CWA, there are several other federal statutes which affect liability for oil pollution. Many of their provisions are similar to the CWA and the coverage may overlap.

The Trans-Alaska Pipeline Authorization Act (TAPS), 43 U.S.C. § 1651 et seq.

TAPS is the first federal statute to address specifically the problem of property damage that results when a vessel discharges oil. However, the liability provisions of TAPS are limited in their application. Only oil that has been transported through the trans-Alaska pipeline and loaded on vessels at the pipeline's terminal facilities is governed by TAPS. Furthermore, the vessel responsible for the discharge must be engaged in transportation between the pipeline's terminal facilities and ports under U.S. jurisdiction; once the Alaskan oil is brought ashore at one of these ports, liability under TAPS ends.

Unlike the FWPCA, which applies only to cleanup costs, TAPS expands liability to cover *all damages* (including cleanup costs). Vessel owners and operators are strictly liable without regard to fault for damages suffered by any person or entity (public or private), including Canadian residents; however, liability may be avoided under certain circumstances.

For any one incident, TAPS imposes a $100,000,000 liability ceiling; owners and operators are responsible for the first $14,000,000 of damages. The remainder is covered by the Trans-Alaska Pipeline Liability Fund. Should the damages exceed the liability ceiling, they will be reduced proportionately. Recovery of the unpaid portions may be pursued under other applicable federal or state laws.

The Liability Fund is the most innovative provision of TAPS. When a barrel of oil is loaded on a vessel, the owner of the oil pays a 5-cent fee. Fee collection ceases when the Fund reaches $100,000,000 and resumes when the Fund falls below that figure.

Included in TAPS is a provision (similar to one in the FWPCA) which declares that the field of strict liability is not preempted nor is a state precluded from imposing additional requirements.

In *Alyeska Pipeline Service Co. v. U.S.*, 16 ERC 1812 (Ct. Clms. 1981), the court held that TAPS section 204(b) which makes Alyeska solely liable for the cost of oil spill removal prevails over CWA section 311(i) which allows cleanup cost recovery from the U.S. government where the discharge is caused by a third party.

The Deepwater Port Act of 1974 (DWPA), 33 U.S.C. § 1501 et seq.

The Deepwater Port Act, as amended by the Port and Tanker Safety Act of 1978, is best described as a synthesis of its predecessors. It takes only a cursory reading to ascertain those provisions of the act which have their origins in the

Federal Water Pollution Control Act and those which have their roots in the Trans-Alaska Pipeline Authorization Act.

The DWPA is limited to discharges occurring at a deepwater port, discharges within a deepwater port's safety zone, and discharges from a vessel that has received oil from another vessel at a deepwater port.

Liability is imposed without regard to fault for cleanup costs *and* damages. For the owners and operators of a vessel that discharges oil in a safety zone or of a vessel that has received oil from another vessel at the deepwater port, liability is not to exceed the lesser of $150 per gross ton of the vessel or $20,000,000. For the licensee of a deepwater port, a $50,000,000 liability ceiling is imposed when oil is discharged from the deepwater port or from a vessel moored at the deepwater port. If the discharge is the result of gross negligence or willful misconduct within the privity and knowledge of the licensee or the vessel's owners or operators, liability is unlimited. Like the FWPCA and TAPS, the DWPA relieves a discharger of liability under certain circumstances.

To compensate injured parties when damages from a spill exceed the liability limits or when a discharger is exonerated from liability, the act creates a Deepwater Port Liability Fund. The Fund is provisioned by a 2-cents-per-barrel fee collected from the owner of the oil when it is loaded or unloaded at the deepwater port. (Oil for a vessel's use and oil transported through the Trans-Alaska pipeline are not subject to the fee.) The Fund is to contain $100,000,000, but when damages exceed that amount, the Fund is to borrow the remainder from the U.S. Treasury.

Contained in the act is a novel provision which allows the Attorney General to bring a class action on behalf of those damaged citizens who would be more adequately represented as a class; if he does not act, any member of that group may maintain a class action. Another unique provision allows the Secretary of Transportation to act on behalf of the public as trustee of the natural resources of the marine environment. Any compensation he recovers for damages to the natural resources is to be used for their rehabilitation and restoration.

Like its predecessors, the DWPA does not expressly preempt the field of liability nor preclude a state from imposing additional requirements or liability for any discharge of oil from a deepwater port or a vessel within a deepwater port's safety zone.

Other significant aspects of the DWPA are its comprehensive definitions of "damages" and "cleanup costs." Damages are defined as

> all damages (except cleanup costs) suffered by any person, or involving real or personal property, the natural resources of the marine environment, or the coastal environment of any nation, including damages without regard to ownership of any effects lands, structures, fish, wildlife, or biotic or natural resources. . . .

33 U.S.C. § 1517(m) (1976). Cleanup costs are defined as

> all actual costs, including but not limited to costs of the Federal Government or of any State or local government, of other nations or of their contractors or subcontractors incurred in the . . . removing or attempting to remove or . . . taking

other measures to reduce or mitigate damages from, any oil discharged into the marine environment. . . .

Id.

Outer Continental Shelf Lands Act (OCSLA), 43 U.S.C. § 1801 *et seq.*

The Outer Continental Shelf Lands Act (as amended in 1978) governs liability for oil spills from any offshore facility or vessel operating in conjunction with an OCS lease. Under this act, owners and operators of offshore facilities and vessels have unlimited liability for the costs of oil spill clean up. Liability for other damages is up to $35 million for offshore facilities and $300 per gross ton or $25,000 for vessels. There is no liability for damages where the spill is caused by an act of war, an unavoidable natural disaster, or a third party. Liability is unlimited when a spill is caused by willful misconduct or gross negligence.

The OCSLA also provides for civil penalties of up to $10,000 per day for failure to comply with the act or with the terms of a lease. The Secretary of Interior can suspend or cancel a lease for failure to comply and is directed to do so if a particular operation "would probably cause serious harm or damage to life (including fish and other aquatic life), to property . . . or to the marine, coastal or human environment." 43 U.S.C.A. § 1344 (1976 Supp. II 1978). The act also permits any person having a legal interest that may be adversely affected to file suit against any person or governmental agency for violations of the act or a lease.

An important provision of the OCSLA is the establishment of a $200 million Offshore Oil Pollution Compensation Fund supported by a per barrel fee imposed on OCS oil. Claims for damages from OCS oil spills can be made directly to the fund. The fund then acquires the claimant's rights to sue the spiller. In addition to cleanup costs, claims for damages may include loss or injury of property and natural resources and loss of earnings.

The OCSLA also establishes a Fishermen's Contingency Fund of $1 million with regional accounts of $100,000. This fund is designed to aid commercial fishers whose livelihood is jeopardized by OCS activities. The fund provides compensation for damaged equipment, such as fishing nets torn by underwater pipelines or boats coated with oil.

Superfund Proposals

Congress has for several years considered oil spill "superfund" proposals to compensate for inadequacies in pollution damage assessment and to resolve problems caused by overlapping federal and state oil spill liability laws. In many ways, these proposals are similar to the federal statutes described above. They have generally provided for a large compensation fund supported by a per barrel fee available for cleanup costs and damages; imposition of strict, though not unlimited, liability; and establishment of enforcement mechanisms.

The issues that blocked passage of the proposed oil spill superfund bills included (1) whether the law should cover other hazardous substances in addition to oil, and (2) whether state oil spill liability laws should be preempted by the new federal law. *See, e.g.*, Cong. Q. Weekly Rep. 2075 (Aug. 5, 1978). *See also* S.B. 684, 96th Cong., 2d Sess. (1980). With the passage of a superfund law covering chemical spills other than oil in 1980, Congress turned its attention to various separate oil spill superfund proposals.

Limitation of Liability Act, 46 U.S.C. § 181 *et seq.*

A major obstacle to recovery for oil spill damages from tanker-source pollution has been the Limited Liability Act of 1851. Section 183(a) of this Act allows the owners of vessels involved in maritime accidents to limit their liability to the value of the vessel as determined at the termination of the voyage during which the damaging incident occurred. Thus claimants for an oil spill are unable to recover from the owners of the vessel if the discharging vessel sinks or is otherwise destroyed and rendered worthless. This limitation requires a showing that the incident that caused the damage was outside the "privity or knowledge" of the vessel owner. *Id.*

The effect of this ancient law has been modified to a substantial degree by the federal compensation statutes described above. For example, *In re Hokkaido Fisheries Co.*, 506 F. Supp. 631 (D. Alaska 1981), held that the United States may recover oil spill cleanup costs under CWA section 311(f)(1) independently of the shipowner's limitation of liability under the Limitation of Liability Act. The Act, however, may affect private damage suits or actions brought by the federal government under doctrines of maritime tort or the federal common law of nuisance. *See* G. Gilmore & C. Black, *The Law of Admiralty*, ch. 10 (1975); Note, *The Role of Privity and Knowledge in the Shipowner's Limitation of Liability Act*, 23 Loy. L. Rev. 480 (1977); Volk & Cobbs, *Limitation of Liability*, 51 Tul. L. Rev. 953 (1977).

NOTES

1. Section 1653(c)(7) of the Trans-Alaska Pipeline Authorization Act provides that "Strict liability under this subsection shall cease when the oil has first been brought ashore at a port under the jurisdiction of the United States." At what point in transit would oil be considered "brought ashore?" Could this mean passage through the initial line valve, or deposit in an onshore storage facility?

2. How does the *Zoe Colocotroni* decision above affect the interpretation of section 1517(i)(3) of the DWPA, which provides that the Secretary of Transportation "may act on behalf of the public as trustee of the natural resources of the marine environment" to recover for damages to such resources under the act? Is the *Zoe Colocotroni* decision consistent with this statutory provision?

3. The Outer Continental Shelf Lands Act contains a novel provision requiring the Secretary of the Interior, subsequent to leasing and development of any area, to conduct studies of the area as he deems necessary for environmental information. 43 U.S.C. § 1346(b) (1976 Supp. II 1978). This "monitoring" requirement is

designed to provide data that can be used to identify "significant" changes in the quality and productivity of the environment, to establish trends in the areas studied and monitored, and to design experiments to identify the causes of such changes." *Id.*

4. An administrative rule-making procedure for valuation and pollution damage assessment has been suggested as an alternative to the complexities of the case-by-case approach. Administrative valuation and damage assessment may provide more procedural fairness, greater understanding of economic resource valuation, greater national uniformity, and reduce the costs and uncertainty of environmental litigation. *See* DuBey & Fidell, *The Assessment of Pollution Damage to Aquatic Resources: Alternatives to the Trial Model*, 19 Santa Clara L. Rev. 641 (1979).

5. Does the federal Coastal Zone Management Act, Chapter 11, *infra*, provide any means for a state to combat oil pollution? *See* Comment, *The Coastal Zone Management Act Amendments of 1976: Tailoring Coastal Zone Protection to Expanded Offshore Oil Production*, 6 Envt'l L. Rep. 10193 (1976).

State Liability Statutes

ASKEW v. AMERICAN WATERWAYS OPERATORS, INC., 411 U.S. 325, 93 S. Ct. 1590, 36 L. Ed. 2d 280 (1973)

Mr. Justice Douglas delivered the opinion of the Court.

This action was brought by merchant shipowners and operators, world shipping associations, members of the Florida coastal barge and towing industry, and owners and operators of oil terminal facilities and heavy industries located in Florida, to enjoin application of the Florida Oil Spill Prevention and Pollution Control Act, Fla. Laws 1970, c. 70–244, Fla. Stat. Ann. §376.011 *et seq.* (Supp. 1973) (hereinafter referred to as the Florida Act). Officials responsible for enforcing the Florida Act were named as defendants, but the State of Florida intervened as a party defendant, asserting that its interests were much broader than those of the named defendants. A three-judge court was convened pursuant to 28 U.S.C. §2281.

The Florida Act imposes strict liability for any damage incurred by the State or private persons as a result of an oil spill in the State's territorial waters from any waterfront facility used for drilling for oil or handling the transfer or storage of oil (terminal facility) and from any ship destined for or leaving such facility. Each owner or operator of a terminal facility or ship subject to the Act must establish evidence of financial responsibility by insurance or a surety bond. In addition, the Florida Act provides for regulation by the State Department of Natural Resources with respect to containment gear and other equipment which must be maintained by ships and terminal facilities for the prevention of oil spills.

Several months prior to the enactment of the Florida Act, Congress enacted the Water Quality Improvement Act of 1970, 84 Stat. 91, 33 U.S.C. §1161 *et seq.* (hereinafter referred to as the Federal Act). This Act subjects shipowners and terminal facilities to liability without fault up to $14,000,000 and

$8,000,000, respectively, for cleanup costs incurred by the Federal Government as a result of oil spills. It also authorizes the President to promulgate regulations requiring ships and terminal facilities to maintain equipment for the prevention of oil spills. It is around that Act and the federally protected tenets of maritime law evidenced by *Southern Pacific Co. v. Jensen*, 224 U.S. 205 [37 S. Ct. 524, 61 L. Ed. 1086 (1917)], and its progeny that the controversy turns. The District Court held that the Florida Act is an unconstitutional intrusion into the federal maritime domain. It declared the Florida Act null and void and enjoined its enforcement. 335 F. Supp. 1241.

The case is here on direct appeal. We reverse. We find no constitutional or statutory impediment to permitting Florida, in the present setting of this case, to establish any "requirement or liability" concerning the impact of oil spillages on Florida's interests or concerns. To rule as the District Court has done is to allow federal admiralty jurisdiction to swallow most of the police power of the States over oil spillage—an insidious form of pollution of vast concern to every coastal city or port and to all the estuaries on which the life of the ocean and the lives of the coastal people are greatly dependent.

I.

It is clear at the outset that the Federal Act does not preclude, but in fact allows, state regulation. Section 1161(o) provides that:

(1) Nothing in this section shall affect or modify in any way the obligations of any owner or operator of any vessel, or of any owner or operator of any onshore facility or offshore facility to any person or agency *under any provision of law for damages to any publicly owned or privately owned property* resulting from a discharge of any oil or from the removal of any such oil.

(2) Nothing in this section shall be construed as preempting any State or political subdivision thereof from imposing *any requirement or liability* with respect to the discharge of oil into any waters within such State.

(3) Nothing in this section shall be construed . . . to affect any State or local law not in conflict with this section. (Emphasis added.)

According to the Conference Report, "any State would be free to provide requirements and penalties similar to those imposed by this section or *additional requirements and penalties.* These, however, would be separate and independent from those imposed by this section and would be enforced by the States through its courts." (Emphasis added.) The Florida Act covers a wide range of "pollutants," §3(7), and a restricted definition of pollution. §3(8). We have here, however, no question concerning any pollutant except oil.

The Federal Act, to be sure, contains a pervasive system of federal control over discharges of oil "into or upon the navigable waters of the United States, adjoining shorelines, or into or upon the waters of the contiguous zone." §1161(b)(1). So far as liability is concerned, an owner or operator of a vessel is liable to the United States for actual costs incurred for the removal of oil discharged in violation of §1161(b)(2) in an amount "not to exceed $100 per gross ton of such vessel or $14,000,000, whichever is lesser," §1161(f)(1), except for discharges caused solely by an act of God, act of war, negligence of the United States, or act or omission of another party. With like exceptions the owner or operator of an onshore or offshore facility is liable to the United States for the actual costs incurred by the United States in an amount not to exceed $8,000,000. §1161(f)(2)–(3). But in each case the owner or operator is liable to the United States for the full amount of the costs where the United States can show that the discharge of oil was "the result of willful negligence or willful misconduct within the privity and knowledge of the owner." Comparable provisions of liability spell out the obligations of "a third party" to the United States for its actual costs incurred in the removal of the oil. §1161(g).

So far as vessels are concerned the federal Limited Liability Act, 46 U.S.C. §§181–189, extends to damages caused by oil spills even where the injury is to the shore. That Act limits the liabilities of the owners of vessels to the "value of such vessels and freight pending." 46 U.S.C. §189.

Section 12 of the Florida Act makes all licensees[6] of terminal facilities "liable to the state for all costs of cleanup or other damage incurred by the state and for damages resulting from injury to others," it not being necessary for the State to plead or prove negligence.[7] There is no conflict between §12 of the Florida Act and §1161 of the Federal Act when it comes to damages to property interests, for the Federal Act reaches only costs of cleaning up. As respects damages, §14 of the Florida Act requires evidence of financial responsibility of a terminal facility or vessel—a provision which does not conflict with the Federal Act.

The Solicitor General says that while the Limited Liability Act, *so far as vessels are concerned,* would override §12 of the Florida Act by reason of the Supremacy Clause, the Limited Liability Act has no bearing on "facilities" regulated by the Florida Act. Moreover, §12 has not yet been construed by the Florida courts and it is susceptible of an interpretation *so far as vessels are concerned* which would be in harmony with the Federal Act. Section 12 does not *in terms* provide for unlimited liability.

Moreover, while the Federal Act determines damages measured by the cost to the United States for cleaning up oil spills, the damages specified in the Florida Act relate in part to the cost to the State of Florida in cleaning up the spillage. Those two sections are harmonious parts of an integrated whole. Section 1161(c)(2) directs the President to prepare a National Contingency Plan for the containment, dispersal, and removal of oil. The plan must provide that federal agencies "shall" act "in coordination with State and local agencies." Cooperative action with the States is also contemplated by §1161(e), which provides that "[i]n addition to any other action taken by a State or local

---

[6]Those required to obtain a license are those who operate a terminal facility. §6(1). *But licenses to terminal facilities include "vessels used to transport oil, petroleum products, their by-products, and other pollutants between the facility and vessels within state waters." §6(4).* [Emphasis added.]

[7]Section 12 also provides that the pilot or the master of any vessel or person in charge of any licensee's terminal facility who fails "to give immediate notification of a discharge to the port manager and the nearest coast guard station" may be imprisoned for not more than two years or fined not more than $10,000.

government" the President may, when there is an imminent and substantial threat to the public health or welfare, direct the United States Attorney of the district in question to bring suit to abate the threat. The reason for the provision in §1161(o)(2), stating that nothing in 1161 pre-empts any State "from imposing any requirement or liability with respect to the discharge of oil into any waters within such State," is that the scheme of the Act is one which allows—though it does not require—cooperation of the federal regime with a state regime.

If Florida wants to take the lead in cleaning up oil spillage in her waters, she can use §12 of the Florida Act and recoup her costs from those who did the damage. Whether the amount of costs she could recover from a wrongdoer is limited to those specified in the Federal Act and whether in turn this new Federal Act removes the pre-existing limitations of the liability in the Limited Liability Act are questions we need not reach here. Any opinion on them is premature. It is sufficient for this day to hold that there is room for state action in cleaning up the waters of a State and recouping, at least within federal limits, so far as vessels are concerned her costs.

Beyond that is the potential claim under §12 of the Florida Act for "other damage incurred by the state and for damages resulting from injury to others." The Federal Act in no way touches those areas. A State may have public beaches ruined by oil spills. Shrimp may be destroyed, and clam, oyster, and scallop beds ruined and the livelihood of fishermen imperiled. The Federal Act takes no cognizance of those claims but only of costs to the Federal Government, if it does the cleaning up.

We held in *Skiriotes v. Florida*, 313 U.S. 69 [61 S. Ct. 924, 85 L. Ed. 1193 (1941)], that while Congress had regulated the size of commercial sponges taken in Florida waters, it had not dealt with any diving apparatus that might be used. Florida had such a law and was allowed to enforce it against one of its citizens. Mr. Chief Justice Hughes, speaking for the Court, said: "It is also clear that Florida has an interest in the proper maintenance of the sponge fishery and that the statute so far as applied to conduct within the territorial waters of Florida, in the absence of conflicting federal legislation, is within the police power of the State." *Id.*, at 75 [61 S. Ct. at 928, 85 L. Ed. at 1199].

Similarly in *Manchester v. Massachusetts*, 139 U.S. 240, 266 [11 S. Ct. 559, 565, 35 L. Ed. 159, 167 (1891)], we stated that if Congress fails to assume control of the fisheries in a bay, "the right to control such fisheries must remain with the State which contains such bays."

Florida in her brief accurately states that no remedy under Federal Act exists for state or private property owners damaged by a massive oil slick such as hit England and France in 1967 and the *Torrey Canyon* disaster. The *Torrey Canyon* carried 880,000 barrels of crude oil. Today not only is more oil being moved by sea each year but the tankers are much larger.

The average tanker used during World War II had a capacity of 16,000 tons, but by 1965 that average had risen to 27,000 tons, and new tankers delivered in 1966 average about 76,000 tons. A Japanese company has launched a 276,000-ton tanker, and other Japanese yards have orders for tankers as large as 312,000 tons. More than sixty tankers of 150,000 tons or more are on order throughout the world, tankers of 500,000 to 800,000 tons are on the drawing boards, and those of more than one million tons are thought to be feasible. On the new 1,010 foot British tanker 'Esso Mercia' two officers have been issued bicycles to help patrol the decks of the 166,890 ton vessel.

The size of the tanker fleet itself is growing at a rate that rivals the growth in average size of new tankers. In 1955 the world tanker fleet numbered about 2,500 vessels. By 1965 it had increased to 3,500, and in 1968 it numbered some 4,300 ships. At the present time nearly one ship out of every five in the world merchant fleet is engaged in transporting oil, and nearly the entire fleet is powered by oil. [10 Harvard Int'l L.J. at 317–318].

Our Coast Guard reports that while in 1970 there were 3,711 oil spills in our waters, in 1971 there were 8,736. The damage to state interests already caused by oil spills, the increase in the number of oil spills, and the risk of ever-increasing damage by reason of the size of modern tankers underlie the concern of coastal states.

While the Federal Act is concerned only with actual cleanup costs incurred by the Federal Government, the State of Florida is concerned with its own cleanup costs. Hence there need be no collision between the Federal Act and the Florida Act because, as noted, the Federal Act presupposes a coordinated effort with the States, and any federal limitation of liability runs to "vessels," not to shore "facilities." That is one of the reasons why the Congress decided that the Federal Act does not pre-empt the States from establishing either *"any requirement or liability"* respecting oil spills.

Moreover, since Congress dealt only with "cleanup" costs, it left the States free to impose "liability" in damages for losses suffered both by the States and by private interests. The Florida Act imposes liability without fault. So far as liability without fault for damages to state and private interests is concerned, the police power has been held adequate for that purpose. State statutes imposing absolute liability on railroads for *all* property lost through fires caused by sparks emitted from locomotive engines have been sustained. The Federal Act, however, while restricted to cleanup costs incurred by the United States, imposes limited liability for those costs and provides certain exceptions, unless willfullness is established. Where liability is imposed by §§1161(f)–(g), previously summarized, the United States may recover the full amount of the costs where the oil spillage was the result of "willful negligence or willful misconduct." If the coordinated federal plan in actual operation leaves the State of Florida to do the cleanup work, there might be financial burdens imposed greater than would have been imposed had the Federal Government done the cleanup work. But it will be time to resolve any such conflict between federal and state regimes when it arises.

Nor can we say at this point that regulations of the Florida Department of Natural Resources requiring "containment gear" pursuant to §7(2)(a) of the Florida Act would be *per se* invalid because the subject to be regulated requires uniform federal regulation. Resolution of this question, as well as the question whether such regulations will conflict with Coast Guard regulations promulgated on December 21, 1972, pursuant to §1161(j)(1) of the Federal Act, 37 Fed. Reg. 28250, should wait a concrete dispute under applicable Florida regulations. Finally, the provision of the Florida Act requiring the licensing of terminal facilities, a traditional state concern, creates no conflict *per se* with federal legislation. Section 1171(b)(1) of the Federal Act provides that federal permits will not be issued to terminal facility operators or owners unless the applicant first supplies a certificate from the State that his operation "will be conducted in a manner which will not violate applicable water quality standards." And Tit. I, §102(b), of the recently enacted Ports and Waterways Safety Act of 1972, Pub. L. 92–340, 86 Stat. 426, 33 U.S.C. §1222(b) (1970 ed., Supp. II), provides that the Act does not prevent "a state or political subdivision thereof from prescribing for structures only higher safety equipment requirements or safety standards than those which may be prescribed pursuant to this title."

II

And so, in the absence of federal pre-emption and any fatal conflict between the statutory scheme, the issue comes down to whether a State constitutionally may exercise its police power respecting maritime activities concurrently with the Federal Government.

The main barriers found by the District Court to the Florida Act are *Southern Pacific Co. v. Jensen*, 244 U.S. 205 [37 S. Ct. 524, 61 L. Ed. 1086 (1917)], and its progeny. *Jensen* held that a maritime worker on a vessel in navigable waters could not constitutionally receive an award under New York's workmen's compensation law, because the remedy in admiralty was exclusive. Later, in *Knickerbocker Ice Co. v. Stewart*, 253 U.S. 149 [40 S. Ct. 438, 64 L. Ed. 834 (1920)], after Congress expressly allowed the States in such cases to grant a remedy, the Court held that Congress had no such power.

But those decisions have been limited by subsequent holdings of this Court. As stated by Mr. Justice Frankfurter in *Romero v. International Terminal Co.*, 358 U.S. 354, 373 [79 S. Ct. 468, 480, 3 L. Ed. 2d 368, 382 (1959)], Jensen and its progeny mark isolated instances where "state law must yield to the needs of a uniform federal maritime law when this Court finds inroads on a harmonious system." Mr. Justice Frankfurter added, however:

> But this limitation still leaves the States a wide scope. State-created liens are enforced in admiralty. State remedies for wrongful death and state statutes providing for the survival of actions, both historically absent from the relief offered by the admiralty, have been upheld when applied to maritime causes of action. Federal courts have enforced these statutes. State rules for the partition and sale of ships, state laws governing the specific performance of arbitration agreements, state laws regulating the effect of a breach of warranty under contracts of maritime insurance—all these laws and others have been accepted as rules of decision in admiralty cases, even, at times, when they conflicted with a rule of maritime law which did not require uniformity. [79 S. Ct. at 480–481, 3 L. Ed. 2d at 382–383].

Moreover, in *Just v. Chambers*, 312 U.S. 383 [61 S. Ct. 687, 85 L. Ed. 903 (1941)], we gave our approval to *The City of Norwalk*, 55 F. 98[1893], written by Judge Addison Brown, holding that a State may modify or supplement maritime law even by creating a liability which a court of admiralty would recognize and enforce, provided the state action is not hostile "to the characteristic features of the maritime law or inconsistent with federal legislation," 312

U.S., at 388 [61 S. Ct. at 691, 85 L. Ed. at 907]. Mr. Chief Justice Hughes after citing *Steamboat Co. v. Chase*, 16 Wall. 522 [21 L. Ed. 369 (1873)], and *Sherlock v. Alling*, 93 U.S. 99 [23 L. Ed. 819 (1876)], went on to hold that, while no suit for wrongful death would lie in the federal courts under general maritime law, state statutes giving damages in such cases were valid. He said,

> The grounds of objection to the admiralty jurisdiction in enforcing liability for wrongful death were similar to those urged here; that is, that the Constitution presupposes a body of maritime law, that this law, as a matter of interstate and international concern, requires harmony in its administration and cannot be subject to defeat or impairment by the diverse legislation of the States, and hence that Congress alone can make any needed changes in the general rules of the maritime law. But these contentions proved unavailing and the principle was maintained that a State, in the exercise of its police power, may establish rules applicable on land and water within its limits, even though these rules incidentally affect maritime affairs, provided that the state action 'does not contravene any acts of Congress, nor work any prejudice to the characteristic features of the maritime law, nor interfere with its proper harmony and uniformity in its international and interstate relations.' It was decided that the state legislation encountered none of these objections. The many instances in which state action had created new rights, recognized and enforced in admiralty, were set forth in *The City of Norwalk*, and reference was also made to the numerous local regulations under state authority concerning the navigation of rivers and harbors. There was the further pertinent observation that the maritime law was not a complete and perfect system and that in all maritime countries there is a considerable body of municipal law that underlies that maritime law as the basis of its administration. These views find abundant support in the history of the maritime law and in the decisions of this Court. 312 U.S. at 389–390 [61 S. Ct. at 692 85 L. Ed. at 907–908].

Mr. Chief Justice Hughes added that our decisions as of 1941, the date of *Just v. Chambers*, gave broad "recognition of the authority of the States to create rights and liabilities with respect to conduct within their borders, when the state action does not run counter to federal laws or the essential features of an exclusive federal jurisdiction." *Id.*, at 391[61 S. Ct. at 693, 85 L. Ed. at 908].

Historically damages to the shore or to shore facilities were not cognizable in admiralty. Mr. Justice Story wrote in 1813, "In regard to torts I have always understood, that the jurisdiction of the admiralty is exclusively dependent upon the locality of the act. The admiralty has not, and never (I believe) deliberately claimed to have any jurisdiction over torts, except such are maritime torts, that is, such as are committed on the high seas, or on waters within the ebb and flow of the tide." *Thomas v. Lane*, 23 F. Cas. 957, 960 (No. 13,902) (CC Me.).

On June 19, 1948, Congress enacted the Admiralty Extension Act, 46 U.S.C. §740.[8] The Court considered the Act in *Victory Carriers, Inc. v. Law*, 404 U.S. 202 [92 S. Ct. 418, 30 L. Ed. 2d 383 (1971)]. In that case, the Court held that the Admiralty Extension Act did not apply to a longshoreman performing loading and unloading services on the dock. The longshoreman was relegated to his remedy under the state workmen's compensation law. *Id.*, at 215 [92 S.

---

[8]It provides in relevant part: "The admiralty and maritime jurisdiction of the United States shall extend to and include all cases of damage or injury, to person or property, caused by a vessel on navigable water, notwithstanding that such damage or injury be done or consummated on land."

Ct. at 426, 30 L. Ed. 2d at 393]. The Court said, "At least in the absence of explicit congressional authorization, we shall not extend the historic boundaries of the maritime law." *Id.*, at 214 [92 S. Ct. at 426, 30 L. Ed. 2d at 392–393].

The Admiralty Extension Act has survived constitutional attack in the lower federal courts and was applied without question by this Court in *Gutierrez v. Waterman S.S. Corp.*, 373 U.S. 206 [83 S. Ct. 1185, 10 L. Ed. 2d 297 (1963)]. The Court recognized in *Victory Carriers*, however, that the Act may "intrude on an area that has heretofore been reserved for State Law." *Id.* at 212 [92 S. Ct. at 425, 30 L. Ed. 2d at 391]. It cautioned that under these circumstances, "we should proceed with caution in construing constitutional and statutory provisions dealing with the jurisdiction of the federal courts." *Ibid.* While Congress has extended admiralty jurisdiction beyond the boundaries contemplated by the Framers, it hardly follows from the constitutionality of that extension that we must sanctify the federal courts with exclusive jurisdiction to the exclusion of powers traditionally within the competence of the States. One can read the history of the Admiralty Extension Act without finding any clear indication that Congress intended that sea-to-shore injuries be exclusively triable in the federal courts.

Even though Congress has acted in the admiralty area, state regulation is permissible, absent a clear conflict with the federal law. Thus in *Kelly v. Washington*, 302 U.S. 1 [58 S. Ct. 87, 82 L. Ed. 3 (1937)], it appeared that, while Congress had provided a comprehensive system of inspection of vessels on navigable waters, *Id.*, at 4 [58 S. Ct. at 89, 82 L. Ed. at 7], the State of Washington also had a comprehensive code of inspection. Some of those state standards conflicted with the federal requirements, *Id.*, at 14–15 [58 S. Ct. at 94, 82 L. Ed. at 13]; but those provisions of the Washington law relating to safety and seaworthiness were not in conflict with the federal law. So the question was whether the absence of congressional action and the need for uniformity of regulation barred state action. Mr. Chief Justice Hughes, writing for the Court, ruled in the negative, saying:

> A vessel which is actually unsafe and unseaworthy in the primary and commonly understood sense is not within the protection of that principle. The State may treat it as it may treat a diseased animal or unwholesome food. In such a matter, the State may protect its people without waiting for federal action providing the state action does not come into conflict with federal rules. If, however, the State goes farther and attempts to impose particular standards as to structure, design, equipment and operation which in the judgment of its authorities may be desirable but pass beyond what is plainly essential to safety and seaworthiness, the State will encounter the principle that such requirements, if imposed at all, must be through the action of Congress which can establish a uniform rule. Whether the State in a particular matter goes too far must be left to be determined when the precise question arises.

Id., at 15 [58 S. Ct. at 94, 83 L. Ed. at 13–14].

That decision was rendered before the Admiralty Extension Act was passed.

Huron Cement Co. v. Detroit, 362 U.S. 440 [80 S. Ct. 813, 4 L. Ed. 2d 852 (1960)], however, arose after that Act became effective. Ships cruising navigable waters and inspected and licensed under federal acts were charged with violating Detroit's Smoke Abatement Code. The company and its agents were, indeed, criminally charged with violating that Code. The Court in sustaining the state prosecution said:

> The ordinance was enacted for the manifest purpose of promoting the health and welfare of the city's inhabitants. Legislation designed to free from pollution the very air that people breathe clearly falls within the exercise of even the most traditional concept of what is compendiously known as the police power. In the exercise of that power, the states and their instrumentalities may act, in many areas of interstate commerce and maritime activities, concurrently with the federal government.

Id., at 442 [80 S. Ct. at 815, 4 L. Ed. 2d at 855].

The Court reasoned that there was room for local control since federal inspection was "limited to affording protection from the perils of maritime navigation," while the Detroit ordinance was aimed at "the elimination of air pollution to protect the health and enhance the cleanliness of the local community." *Id.*, at 445 [80 S. Ct. at 817, 4 L. Ed. 2d at 857]. The Court, in reviewing prior decisions, noted that a federally licensed vessel was not exempt (1) "from local pilotage laws"; (2) "local quarantine laws"; (3) "local safety inspections"; or (4) "local regulation of wharves and docks." *Id.*, at 447 [80 S. Ct. at 818; 4 L. Ed. 2d at 858].

It follows, *a fortiori* that sea-to-shore pollution—historically within the reach of the police power of the States—is not silently taken away from the States by the Admiralty Extension Act, which does not purport to supply the exclusive remedy.

As discussed above, we cannot say with certainty at this stage that the Florida Act conflicts with any federal Act. We have only the question whether the waiver of pre-emption by Congress in §1161(o)(2) concerning the imposition by the State of "any requirement of liability" is valid.

It is valid unless the rule of *Jensen* and *Knickerbocker Ice* is to engulf everything that Congress chose to call "admiralty," pre-empting state action. *Jensen* and *Knickerbocker Ice* have been confined to their facts, *viz.*, to suits relating to the relationship of vessels, plying the high seas and our navigable waters, and to their crews. The fact that a whole system of liabilities was established on the basis of those two cases, led us years ago to establish the "twilight zone" where state regulation was permissible. Where there was a hearing by a federal agency and a conclusion by that agency that the case fell within the federal jurisdiction, we made its findings final. Where there were no such findings, we presumed state law, in terms applicable, was constitutional. That is the way the "twilight zone" has been defined.

Jensen thus has vitality left. But we decline to move the *Jensen* line of cases shoreward to oust state law from situations involving shoreside injuries by ships on navigable waters. The Admiralty Extension Act does not pre-empt state law in those situations.

The judgment below is

Reversed.

1. The treaty power of article 2, section 2, and the admiralty power of article 3, section 2, are other constitutional grants of authority to the federal government which affect state and national marine environmental policies.

   In regard to the admiralty power, Paul Kauper noted in *Constitutional Law, Cases and Materials* 239–40 (1980) that "[a]lthough the commerce clause appears to be an adequate basis for federal legislation relating to admiralty matters, it appears to be accepted that the grant of admiralty jurisdiction to the federal courts implies a legislative authority of Congress to deal with the subject matter." He also observed that "[t]he power of the federal courts to adjudicate admiralty matters and the power of Congress to legislate in this area do not completely preclude state legislation and jurisdiction over admiralty matters." *Id.*, at 444.

2. Can a state impose damages above the maximum of the FWPCA and the Limited Liability Act? Can a state regulate oil terminals inconsistently with federal regulations? Does the *Askew* decision give a firm answer to these questions? *See Steuart Transportation Co. v. Allied Towing Corp.*, 596 F. 2d 609 (4th Cir. 1979) (spill provisions do not preempt state statute imposing unlimited strict liability for state cleanup costs.)

3. In *Portland Pipeline Corp. v. Environmental Improvement Commission*, 307 A. 2d 1 (Me. 1973), the Supreme Court of Maine was faced with a laundry list of constitutional challenges to that state's oil pollution statute. The plaintiffs alleged, *inter alia*, violations of the due process clause, the equal protection clause, the import–export clause, the commerce clause, and the admiralty clause. Your defense? Citing *Askew* and other decisions, the court upheld the law against each challenge. *See also* Comment, *Maine Coastal Conveyance of Oil Act: Jurisdictional Considerations*, 24 Me. L. Rev. 299 (1972); Comment, *The Port of Oakland Decision: California Oil Legislation Gets Watered Down*, 7 Golden Gate U. L. Rev. 499 (1977).

4. Does the *Askew* decision indicate how much control a state may have over the operation of tankers in its waters? *See* DuBey, *Control of Oil Transport in the Coastal Zone: A Look at Puget Sound*, 56 Or. L. Rev. 593 (1977), and Section B following.

5. For further discussion of the *Askew* case, *see* Barett & Warren, *History of Florida Oil Spill Legislation*, 5 Fla. St. L. Rev. 337 (1977); Katz, *Private Compensation for Oil Pollution: Florida's Practical Solution,* 27 U. Fla. L. Rev. 546 (1975); Swan, *American Waterways: Florida Oil Pollution Legislation Makes It Over The First Hurdle*, 5 J. of Mar. Law & Com. 77 (1973).

SECTION B: TANKER OPERATIONS

The Ports and Waterways Safety Act (PWSA), 33 U.S.C. § 1221 *et seq.*; 46 U.S.C. § 391a

The imposition of liability under the FWPCA is an indirect method of grappling with the problems of oil in the marine environment. Congress's next action, the PWSA, as amended by the Port and Tanker Safety Act of 1978, confronted the issue of how to prevent oil pollution: It was a call for updated standards in ship design, construction, and operation and a grant of authority to the Coast Guard to control ship movements.

Vessel Construction

Title II of the act, which amended the Tank Vessel Act, 46 U.S.C. § 391a, addresses bulk cargo vessels that carry oil, hazardous substances, or inflammable or combustible liquids. The Secretary of Transportation (in whose department the Coast Guard operates) is directed to establish additional rules and regulations for vessel design, construction, alteration, repair, maintenance, and operation. These categories reach such areas as hulls, places for stowing and carrying cargo, equipment and appliances for the prevention of mitigation of damage to the marine environment, vessel inspections, and crew qualifications.

The Secretary was also given a special and immediate mandate ("as soon as practicable") to begin promulgating regulations for ship design, construction, alteration, and repair with the express purpose of protecting the marine environment. These regulations are to cover vessel maneuvering and stopping abilities, lowering the possibilities of collisions and groundings, reducing cargo losses after accidents, and such normal vessel operations as ballasting and cargo handling. These special, environmental regulations are to apply to both foreign vessels and U.S. flag vessels operating in the foreign trade.

Title II has been implemented through regulations found at 33 C.F.R. § 157 (1978).

Traffic Control

Under Title I (33 U.S.C. § 1221 *et seq.*) the Coast Guard is given broad powers to control the movements of vessels in ports and areas where hazardous conditions exist. The Coast Guard may establish vessel traffic control systems, require compliance with those systems, and control vessel movements in hazardous areas or at times of adverse weather, reduced visibility, or congested traffic. Traffic controls include establishing vessel routing plans; setting vessel size, speed limits, and operating conditions; and restricting vessel operation in hazardous areas to vessels that have particular characteristics and capabilities necessary for safe operation.

The Coast Guard regulations adopted pursuant to Title I are found at 33 C.F.R. §§ 160–64 (1978).

The PWSA was amended by the Port and Tanker Safety Act of 1978, Pub. L. No. 95–474, 92 Stat. 1471. The Coast Guard's Title I authority to regulate vessel movement was generally expanded, such as allowing for the reservation of port access routes through outer continental shelf oil and gas equipment. The Coast Guard was also authorized to deny entry into U.S. ports to vessels with histories of accidents or pollution incidents, vessels that failed to comply with vessel traffic systems or design specifications, and vessels with inadequately trained crews. In addition, the Federal Water Pollution Control Act authorizes the Coast Guard to deny entry into port to those vessels that cannot produce proof of financial responsibility. 33 U.S.C. § 1321 (Supp. I 1977).

Title II of the PWSA was strengthened with more stringent and specific design, construction, and alteration standards for new and existing tankers, improved crew training requirements, increased inspection programs, a marine safety information system, and other protective measures. The Secretary was specifically authorized to set stricter standards for vessels engaged in domestic trade.

The following materials give some indication of the interaction of local, state, federal, and international tanker regulatory programs. As you review them, consider these questions: Which level of control is most likely to succeed in preventing tanker pollution? What factors, political, economic, and legal, work against effective regulation at each level?

RAY v. ATLANTIC RICHFIELD CO., 435 U.S. 151 (1978)

MR. JUSTICE WHITE delivered the opinion of the Court.

Pursuant to the Ports and Waterways Safety Act of 1972 (PWSA), 86 Stat. 424, 33 U.S.C. § 1221 *et seq.* (1970 ed., Supp. V) and 46 U.S.C. § 391a (1970 ed., Supp. V), navigation in Puget Sound, a body of inland water lying along the northwest coast of the State of Washington, is controlled in major respects by federal law. The PWSA also subjects to federal rule the design and operating characteristics of oil tankers.

This case arose when ch. 125, 1975 Wash. Laws, 1st Extr. Sess., Wash. Rev. Code § 88.16.170 *et seq.* (Supp. 1975) (Tanker Law), was adopted with the aim of regulating in particular respects the design, size, and movement of oil tankers in Puget Sound. In response to the constitutional challenge to the law brought by the appellees herein, the District Court held that under the Supremacy Clause, Art. VI, cl. 2, of the Constitution, which declares that the federal law "shall be the supreme Law of the Land," the Tanker Law could not coexist with the PWSA and was totally invalid. *Atlantic Richfield Co. v. Evans* [9 ERC 1879 (W.D. Wash. Sept. 24, 1976)].

I

Located adjacent to Puget Sound are six oil refineries having a total combined processing capacity of 359,500 barrels of oil per day. In 1971, appellee Atlantic Richfield Co. (ARCO) began operating an oil refinery at Cherry Point, situated in the northern part of the Sound. Since then, the crude oil processed at that refinery has been delivered principally by pipeline from Canada and by tankers from the Persian Gulf; tankers will also be used to transport oil there from the terminus of the Trans-Alaska Pipeline at Valdez, Alaska. Of the 105 tanker deliveries of crude oil to the Cherry Point refinery from 1972 through 1975, 95 were by means of tankers in excess of 40,000 deadweight tons (DWT),[9] and, prior to the effective date of the Tanker Law, 15 of them were by means of tankers in excess of 125,000 DWT. . . .

[9]The term "deadweight tons" is defined for purposes of the Tanker Law as the cargo-carrying capacity of a vessel, including necessary fuel oils, stores, and potable waters, as expressed in long tons (2,240 pounds per long ton).

II

The Court's prior cases indicate that when a State's exercise of its police power is challenged under the Supremacy Clause, "we start with the assumption that the historic police powers of the States were not to be superseded by the Federal Act unless that was the clear and manifest purpose of Congress."

. . . .

Under the relevant cases, one of the legitimate inquiries is whether Congress has either explicitly or implicitly declared that the States are prohibited from regulating the various aspects of oil-tanker operations and design with which the Tanker Law is concerned. . . .

. . . .

Even if Congress has not completely foreclosed state legislation in a particular area, a state statute is void to the extent that it actually conflicts with a valid federal statute. A conflict will be found "where compliance with both federal and state regulations is a physical impossibility . . . ." . . . , or where the state "law stands as an obstacle to the accomplishment and execution of the full purposes and objectives of Congress." . . .

III

With these principles in mind, we turn to an examination of each of the three operative provisions of the Tanker Law. We address first Wash. Rev. Code § 88.16.180 (Supp. 1975), which requires both enrolled and registered[10] oil tankers of at least 50,000 DWT to take on a pilot licensed by the State of Washington while navigating Puget Sound. The District Court held that insofar as the law required a tanker "enrolled in the coastwise trade" to have a local pilot on board, it was in direct conflict with 46 U.S.C. §§ 215, 364. We agree.

Section 364 provides that "every coastwise seagoing steam vessel subject to the navigation laws of the United States . . . not sailing under register, shall, when under way, . . . be under the control and direction of the pilots licensed by the Coast Guard." Section 215 adds that "[n]o State or municipal government shall impose upon pilots of steam vessels any obligation to procure a State or other license in addition to that issued by the United States. . . ." It goes on to explain that the statute shall not be construed to "affect any regulation established by the laws of any State, requiring vessels entering or leaving a port in any such State, *other than coastwise steam vessels,* to take a pilot duly licensed or authorized by the laws of such State. . . ." (Emphasis added.) The Court has long held that these two statutes read together give the Federal Government exclusive authority to regulate pilots on enrolled vessels and that they preclude a State from imposing its own pilotage requirements upon them. . . . Thus, to the extent that the Tanker Law requires enrolled tankers to take on state-licensed pilots, the District Court correctly concluded, as the State now concedes, that it was in conflict with federal law and was therefore invalid.

While the opinion of the court below indicated that the pilot provision of

---

[10]Enrolled vessels are those "engaged in domestic or coastwide trade or used for fishing," whereas registered vessels are those engaged in trade with foreign countries. *Douglas v. Seacoast Products, Inc.,* 431 U.S. 265, 272–273 (1977).

the Tanker Law was void only to the extent that it applied to tankers enrolled in the coastwise trade, the judgment itself declared the statute null and void in its entirety. No part of the statute was excepted from the scope of the injunctive relief. The judgment was overly broad, for just as it is clear that States may not regulate the pilots of enrolled vessels, it is equally clear that they are free to impose pilotage requirements on registered vessels entering and leaving their ports. Not only does 46 U.S.C. § 215 so provide, as was noted above, but so also does § 101(5) of the PWSA, 33 U.S.C. § 1221(5) (1970 ed., Supp. V), which authorizes the Secretary of Transportation to "require pilots on self-propelled vessels engaged in the foreign trades in areas and under circumstances where a pilot is not otherwise required by State law to be on board until the State having jurisdiction of an area involved establishes a requirement for a pilot in that area or under the circumstances involved. . . ." Accordingly, as appellees now agree, the State was free to require registered tankers in excess of 50,000 DWT to take on a state-licensed pilot upon entering Puget Sound.

IV

We next deal with § 88.16.190 (2) of the Tanker Law, which requires enrolled and registered oil tankers of from 40,000 to 125,000 DWT to possess all of the following "standard safety features":

> "(a) Shaft horsepower in the ratio of one horsepower to each two and one-half deadweight tons; and
> "(b) Twin screws; and
> "(c) Double bottoms, underneath all oil and liquid cargo compartments; and
> "(d) Two radars in working order and operating, one of which must be collision avoidance radar; and
> "(e) Such other navigational position location systems as may be prescribed from time to time by the board of pilotage commissioners. . . ."

This section contains a proviso, however, stating that if the "tanker is in ballast or is under escort of a tug or tugs with an aggregate shaft horsepower equivalent to five percent of the deadweight tons of that tanker . . . ," the design require-ments are not applicable. The District Court held invalid this alternative design/tug requirement of the Tanker Law. We agree insofar as we hold that the foregoing design requirements, standing alone, are invalid in the light of the PWSA and its regulatory implementation.

The PWSA contains two Titles representing somewhat overlapping provi-sions designed to insure vessel safety and the protection of the navigable waters, their resources, and shore areas from tanker cargo spillage. The focus of Title I, 33 U.S.C. §§ 1221–1227 (1979 ed., Supp. V), is traffic control at local ports; Title II's principal concern is tanker design and construction. . . .

. . . .

Title II also directs the Secretary to inspect tank vessels for compliance with the regulations which he is required to issue for the protection of the marine environment. § 391a (6). Compliance with these separate regulations, which must satisfy specified standards, and the consequent privilege of having on board the relevant cargo are evidenced by certificates of compliance issued by the

Secretary or by appropriate endorsements on the vessel's certificates of inspection. Certificates are valid for the period specified by the Secretary and are subject to revocation when it is found that the vessel does not comply with the conditions upon which the certificate was issued. In lieu of a certificate of compliance with his own environmental regulations relating to vessel design, construction, alteration, and repair, the Secretary may, but need not, accept valid certificates from foreign vessels evidencing compliance with rules and regulations issued under a treaty, convention, or agreement providing for reciprocity of recognition of certificates or similar documents. § 391a (7) (D).

This statutory pattern shows that Congress, insofar as design characteristics are concerned, has entrusted to the Secretary the duty of determining which oil tankers are sufficiently safe to be allowed to proceed in the navigable waters of the United States. This indicates to us that Congress intended uniform national standards for design and construction of tankers that would foreclose the imposition of different or more stringent state requirements. In particular, as we see it, Congress did not anticipate that a vessel found to be in compliance with the Secretary's design and construction regulations and holding a Secretary's permit, or its equivalent, to carry the relevant cargo would nevertheless be barred by state law from operating in the navigable waters of the United States on the ground that its design characteristics constitute an undue hazard.

We do not question in the slightest the prior cases holding that enrolled and registered vessels must conform to "reasonable, nondiscriminatory conservation and environmental protection measures . . ." imposed by a State. *Douglas v. Seacoast Products, Inc.,* 431 U.S. 265, 277 (1977), citing *Smith v. Maryland,* 18 How. 71 (1855); *Manchester v. Massachusetts,* 139 U.S. 240 (1891); and *Huron Portland Cement Co. v. Detroit,* 362 U.S. 440 (1960). Similarly, the mere fact that a vessel has been inspected and found to comply with the Secretary's vessel safety regulations does not prevent a State or city from enforcing local laws having other purposes, such as a local smoke abatement law. *Ibid.* But in none of the relevant cases sustaining the application of state laws to federally licensed or inspected vessels did the federal licensing or inspection procedure implement a substantive rule of federal law addressed to the object also sought to be achieved by the challenged state regulation. *Huron Portland Cement Co. v. Detroit,* for example, made it plain that there was "no overlap between the scope of the federal ship inspection laws and that of the municipal ordinance . . ." there involved. *Id.,* at 446. The purpose of the "federal inspection statutes [was] to insure the seagoing safety of vessels . . . to affor[d] protection from the perils of maritime navigation," while "[b]y contrast, the sole aim of the Detroit ordinance [was] the elimination of air pollution to protect the health and enhance the cleanliness of the local community." *Id.,* at 445.

Here, we have the very situation that *Huron Portland Cement Co. v. Detroit . . .* put aside. Title II aims at insuring vessel safety and protecting the marine environment; and the Secretary must issue all design and construction regulations that he deems necessary for these ends, after considering the specified statutory standards. The federal scheme thus aims precisely at the same ends as does § 88.16.190 (2) of the Tanker Law. Furthermore, under the PWSA, after considering the statutory standards and issuing all design requirements that in his judgment are necessary, the Secretary inspects and certifies each vessel as sufficiently safe to protect the marine environment and issues a permit or its equivalent to carry tank-vessel cargoes. Refusing to accept the federal judgment, however, the State now seeks to exclude from Puget Sound vessels certified by the Secretary as having acceptable design characteristics, unless they satisfy the different and higher design requirements imposed by state law. The Supremacy Clause dictates that the federal judgment that a vessel is safe to navigate United States waters prevail over the contrary state judgment.

Enforcement of the state requirements would at least frustrate what seems to us to be the evident congressional intention to establish a uniform federal regime controlling the design of oil tankers. The original Tank Vessel Act, amended by Title II, sought to effect a "reasonable and uniform set of rules and regulations concerning ship construction . . . ," H.R. Rep. No. 2962, 74th Cong., 2d Sess., 2 (1936); and far from evincing a different purpose, the Title II amendments strongly indicate that insofar as tanker design is concerned, Congress anticipated the enforcement of federal standards that would pre-empt state efforts to mandate different or higher design requirements.

That the Nation was to speak with one voice with respect to tanker-design standards is supported by the legislative history of Title II, particularly as it reveals a decided congressional preference for arriving at international standards for building tank vessels. The Senate Report recognizes that vessel design "has traditionally been an area for international rather than national action," and that "international solutions in this area are preferable since the problem of marine pollution is world-wide." Senate Report 23. Congress did provide that the Secretary's safety regulations would not apply to foreign ship holding compliance certificates under regulations arrived at by international agreement; but, in the end, the environmental protection regulations were made applicable to foreign as well as to American vessels since it was thought to be necessary for the achievement of the Act's purposes.[11]

. . . .

Congress expressed a preference for international action and expressly anticipated that foreign vessels would or could be considered sufficiently safe for certification by the Secretary if they satisfied the requirements arrived at by treaty or convention; it is therefore clear that Title II leaves no room for the States to impose different or stricter design requirements than those which Congress has enacted with the hope of having them internationally adopted or has accepted as the result of international accord. A state law in this area, such as the first part of § 88.16.190 (2), would frustrate the congressional desire of achieving uniform, international standards and is thus at odds with "the object sought to be obtained by [Title II] and the character of obligations imposed by it . . . ." *Rice v. Santa Fe Elevator Corp.*, 331 U.S., at 230. In this respect, the District Court was quite correct.

[11]The Senate Report notes that eliminating foreign vessels from Title II would be "ineffective, and possibly self-defeating," because approximately 85% of the vessels in the navigable waters of the United States are of foreign registry. *Id.*, at 22. The Report adds that making the Secretary's regulations applicable only to American ships would put them at a competitive disadvantage with foreign-flag ships. *Ibid.*

V

Of course, that a tanker is certified under federal law as a safe vessel insofar as its design and construction characteristics are concerned does not mean that it is free to ignore otherwise valid state or federal rules or regulations that do not constitute design or construction specifications. Registered vessels, for example, as we have already indicated, must observe Washington's pilotage requirement. In our view, both enrolled and registered vessels must also comply with the provision of the Tanker Law that requires tug escorts for tankers over 40,000 DWT that do not satisfy the design provisions specified in § 88.16.190 (2). This conclusion requires analysis of Title I of the PWSA, 33 U.S.C. §§ 1221–1227 (1970 ed., Supp. V).

A

In order to prevent damage to vessels, structures, and shore areas, as well as environmental harm to navigable waters and the resources therein that might result from vessel or structure damage, Title I authorizes the Secretary to establish and operate "vessel traffic services and systems" for ports subject to congested traffic, as well as to require ships to comply with the systems and to have the equipment necessary to do so. §§ 1221 (1) and (2). The Secretary may "control vessel traffic" under various hazardous conditions by specifying the times for vessel movement, by establishing size and speed limitations and vessel operating conditions, and by restricting vessel operation to those vessels having the particular operating characteristics which he considers necessary for safe operation under the circumstances. § 1221 (3). In addition, the Secretary may require vessels engaged in foreign trade to carry pilots until the State having jurisdiction establishes a pilot requirement, § 1221 (5); he may establish minimum safety equipment requirements for shore structures, § 1221 (7); and he may establish waterfront safety zones or other measures for limited, controlled, or conditional access when necessary for the protection of vessels, structures, waters, or shore areas, § 1221 (8).

In carrying out his responsibilities under the Act, the Secretary may issue rules and regulations. § 1224. In doing so, he is directed to consider a wide variety of interests that might affect the exercise of his authority, such as possible environmental impact, the scope and degree of the hazards involved, and "vessel traffic characteristics including minimum interference with the flow of commercial traffic, traffic volume, the sizes and types of vessels, the usual nature of local cargoes, and similar factors." § 1222 (e). Section 1222 (b) provides that nothing in Title I is to "prevent a State or political subdivision thereof from prescribing for structures only higher safety equipment requirements or safety standards than those which may be prescribed pursuant to this chapter."

Exercising this authority, the Secretary, through his delegate, the Coast Guard, has issued Navigation Safety Regulations, 33 CFR Part 164 (adopted at 42 Fed. Reg. 5956 (1977)). Of particular importance to this case, he has promulgated the Puget Sound Vessel Traffic System containing general rules, communication rules, vessel movement reporting requirements, a traffic separation scheme, special rules for ship movement in Rosario Strait, descriptions and geographic coordinates of the separation zones and traffic lanes, and a specification for precautionary areas and reporting points. 33 CFR Part 161, Subpart B (1976), as amended, 42 Fed. Reg. 29480 (1977). There is also delegated to Coast Guard district commanders and captains of ports the authority to exercise the Secretary's powers under § 1221 (3) to direct the anchoring, mooring, and movements of vessels; temporarily to establish traffic routing schemes; and to specify vessel size and speed limitations and operating conditions. 33 CFR § 160.35 (1976). Traffic in Rosario Strait is subject to a local Coast Guard rule prohibiting "the passage of more than one 70,000 DWT vessel through Rosario Strait in either direction at any given time." During the periods of bad weather, the size limitation is reduced to approximately 40,000 DWT. . . .

B

A tug escort provision is not a design requirement, such as is promulgated under Title II. It is more akin to an operating rule arising from the peculiarities of local waters that call for special precautionary measures, and, as such, is a safety measure clearly within the reach of the Secretary's authority under §§ 1221 (3)(iii) and (iv) to establish "vessel size and speed limitations and vessel operating conditions" and to restrict vessel operation to those with "particular operating characteristics and capabilities . . . ." Title I, however, merely authorizes and does not require the Secretary to issue regulations to implement the provisions of the Title; and assuming that § 1222 (b) prevents a State from issuing "higher safety equipment requirements or safety standards,". . . it does so only with respect to those requirements or standards "which may be prescribed pursuant to this chapter."

The relevant inquiry under Title I with respect to the State's power to impose a tug-escort rule is thus whether the Secretary has either promulgated his own tug requirement for Puget Sound tanker navigation or has decided that no such requirement should be imposed at all. It does not appear to us that he has yet taken either course. He has, however, issued an advance notice of proposed rulemaking, 41 Fed. Reg. 18770 (1976), to amend his Navigation Safety Regulations issued under Title I, 33 CFR Part 164 (1977), so as to require tug escorts for certain vessels operating in confined waters. The notice says that these rules, if adopted, "are intended to provide uniform guidance for the maritime industry and Captains of the Port." 41 Fed. Reg. 18771 (1976). It may be that rules will be forthcoming that will pre-empt the State's present tug-escort rule, but until that occurs, the State's requirement need not give way under the Supremacy Clause.

Nor for constitutional purposes does it make substantial difference that under the Tanker Law those vessels that satisfy the State's design requirements are in effect exempted from the tug-escort requirement.[12] Given the validity of a general rule prescribing tug escorts for all tankers, Washington is also privileged, insofar as the Supremacy Clause is concerned, to waive the rule for tankers

[12]In fact, at the time of trial all tankers entering Puget Sound were required to have a tug escort, for no tanker then afloat had all of the design features required by the Tanker Law. App. 66.

having specified design characteristics.[13] For this reason, we conclude that the District Court erred in holding that the alternative tug requirement of § 88.16.190 (2) was invalid because of its conflict with the PWSA.

VI

We cannot arrive at the same conclusion with respect to the remaining provision of the Tanker Law at issue here. Section 88.16.190 (1) excludes from Puget Sound under any circumstances any tanker in excess of 125,000 DWT. In our view, this provision is invalid in light of Title I and the Secretary's actions taken thereunder.

We begin with the premise that the Secretary has the authority to establish "vessel size and speed limitations," § 1221 (3) (iii), and that local Coast Guard officers have been authorized to exercise this power on his behalf. Furthermore, § 1222 (b), by permitting the State to impose higher equipment or safety standards "for structures only," impliedly forbids higher state standards for vessels. The implication is strongly supported by the legislative history of the PWSA. The House Report explains that the original wording of the bill did "not make it absolutely clear that the Coast Guard regulation of vessels preempts state action in this field" and says that § 1222 (b) was amended to provide "a positive statement retaining State jurisdiction over structures and making clear that State regulation of vessels is not contemplated." House Report 15.

Relying on the legislative history, the appellants argue that the preclusive effect of § 1222 (b) is restricted to vessel equipment requirements. The statute, however, belies this argument, for it expressly reaches vessel "safety standards" as well as equipment. A limitation on vessel size would seem to fall squarely within the category of safety standards, since the Secretary's authority to impose size limits on vessels navigating Puget Sound is designed to prevent damage to vessels and to the navigable waters and is couched in terms of controlling vessel traffic in areas "which he determines to be especially hazardous."

The pertinent inquiry at this point thus becomes whether the Secretary, through his delegate, has addressed and acted upon the question of size limitations. Appellees and the United States insist that he has done so by his local navigation rule with respect to Rosario Strait: The rule prohibits the passage of

---

[13]We do not agree with appellees' assertion that the tug-escort provision, which is an alternative to the design requirements of the Tanker Law, will exert pressure on tanker owners to comply with the design standards and hence is an indirect method of achieving what they submit is beyond state power under Title II. The cost of tug escorts for all of appellee ARCO's tankers in Puget Sound is estimated at $277,500 per year. While not a negligible amount, it is only a fraction of the estimated cost of outfitting a single tanker with the safety features required by § 88.16.190 (2). The Office of Technology Assessment of Congress has estimated that constructing a new tanker with a double bottom and twin screws, just two of the required features, would add roughly $8.8 million to the cost of a 150,000 DWT tanker. Thus, contrary to the appellees' contention, it is very doubtful that the provision will pressure tanker operators into complying with the design standards specified in § 86.16.190 (2). While the tug provision may be viewed as a penalty for noncompliance with the State's design requirements, it does not "stan[d] as an obstacle to the accomplishment and execution of the full purposes and objectives of Congress." Hines v. Davidowitz, 312 U. S. 52, 67 (1941). The overall effect of § 88.16.190 (2) is to require tankers of over 40,000 DWT to have a tug escort while they navigate Puget Sound, a result in no way inconsistent with the PWSA as it is currently being implemented.

more than one 70,000 DWT vessel through Rosario Strait in either direction at any given time, and in periods of bad weather, the "size limitation" is reduced to approximately 40,000 DWT. On the record before us, it appears sufficiently clear that federal authorities have indeed dealt with the issue of size and have determined whether and in what circumstances tanker size is to limit navigation in Puget Sound. The Tanker Law purports to impose a general ban on large tankers, but the Secretary's response has been a much more limited one. Because under § 1222 (b) the State may not impose higher safety standards than those prescribed by the Secretary under Title I, the size limitation of § 88.16.190 (1) may not be enforced.

There is also force to the position of appellees and the United States that the size regulation imposed by the Tanker Law, if not pre-empted under Title I, is similar to or indistinguishable from a design requirement which Title II reserves to the federal regime. This may be true if the size limit represents a state judgment that as a matter of safety and environmental protection generally, tankers should not exceed 125,000 DWT. In that event, the State should not be permitted to prevail over a contrary design judgment made by federal authorities in pursuit of uniform national and international goals. On the other hand, if Washington's exclusion of large tankers from Puget Sound is in reality based on water depth in Puget Sound or on other local peculiarities, the Tanker Law in this respect would appear to be within the scope of Title I, in which event also state and federal law would represent contrary judgments, and the state limitation would have to give way.

Our conclusion as to the State's ban on large tankers is consistent with the legislative history of Title I. In exercising his authority under the Title, the Secretary is directed to consult with other agencies in order "to assure consistency of regulations . . . ," § 1222 (c), and also to "consider fully the wide variety of interests which may be affected . . . ." § 1222 (e). These twin themes—consistency of regulation and thoroughness of consideration—reflect the substance of the Committee Reports. The House Report indicates that a good number of the witnesses who testified before the House subcommittee stated that one of the strong points of Title I was "the imposition of federal control in the areas envisioned by the bill which will insure regulatory and enforcement uniformity throughout all the covered areas." House Report 8.[14] . . .

. . . .

We read these statements by Congress as indicating that it desired someone with an overview of all the possible ramifications of the regulation of oil tankers

[14]During the hearings in the House, for example, Representative Keith expressed concern that States might on their own enact regulations restricting the size of vessels, noting that Delaware had already done so. He stated that "[w]e do not want the States to resort to individual actions that adversely affect our national interest." Hearings on H. R. 867, H. R. 3635, H. R. 8140 before the Subcommittee on Coast Guard, Coast and Geodetic Survey, and Navigation of the House Committee on Merchant Marine and Fisheries, 92d Cong., 1st Sess., 30 (1971). The Commandant of the Coast Guard, Admiral Bender, responded that the Coast Guard "believe[s] it is preferable for the approach to the problem of the giant tankers in particular to be resolved on an international basis." Ibid.

A representative of the Sierra Club testified before the Senate committee considering the PWSA and suggested the advisability of regulations limiting the size of vessels. Hearings on S. 2074 before the Senate Committee on Commerce, 92d Cong., 1st Sess., 78 (1971). In response to this suggestion, Senator Inouye questioned whether the necessary result of such a regulation would not be

to promulgate limitations on tanker size and that he should act only after balancing all of the competing interests. While it was not anticipated that the final product of this deliberation would be the promulgation of traffic safety systems applicable across the board to all United States ports, it was anticipated that there would be a single decisionmaker, rather than a different one in each State.

Against this background, we think the pre-emptive impact of § 1222 (b) is an understandable expression of congressional intent. Furthermore, even without § 1222 (b), we would be reluctant to sustain the Tanker Law's absolute ban on tankers larger than 125,000 DWT. The Court has previously recognized that "where failure of . . . federal officials affirmatively to exercise their full authority takes on the character of a ruling that no such regulation is appropriate or approved pursuant to the policy of the statute," States are not permitted to use their police power to enact such a regulation. . . . We think that in this case the Secretary's failure to promulgate a ban on the operations of oil tankers in excess of 125,000 DWT in Puget Sound takes on such a character. As noted above, a clear policy of the statute is that the Secretary shall carefully consider "the wide variety of interests which may be affected by the exercise of his authority," § 1222 (e), and that he shall restrict the application of vessel size limitations to those areas where they are particularly necessary. In the case of Puget Sound, the Secretary has exercised his authority in accordance with the statutory directives and has promulgated a vessel-traffic-control system which contains only a narrow limitation on the operation of supertankers. This being the case, we conclude that Washington is precluded from enforcing the size limitation contained in the Tanker Law.[15]

VII

We also reject appellees' additional constitutional challenges to the State's tug-escort requirement for vessels not satisfying its design standards. Appellees contend that this provision, even if not pre-empted by the PWSA, violates the Commerce Clause because it is an indirect attempt to regulate the design and equipment of tankers, an area of regulation that appellees contend necessitates a

---

an increase in the number of tankers, so as to meet the Nation's requirements for oil. The Sierra Club witness acknowledged that there was "some controversy even among the oil company people as to which would be the most hazardous, more smaller ships or fewer bigger ships." *Id.*, at 81. This statement is consistent with the stipulation of facts, App. 84, which states:

"Experts differ and there is good faith dispute as to whether the movement of oil by a smaller number of tankers in excess of 125,000 DWT in Puget Sound poses an increased risk of oil spillage compared to the risk from movement of a similar amount of oil by a larger number of smaller tankers in Puget Sound."

[15]We find no support for the appellants' position in the other federal environmental legislation they cite, *i.e.*, the Federal Water Pollution Control Act Amendments of 1972, 86 Stat. 816, 33 U. S. C. § 1251 *et seq.* (1970 ed., Supp. V); the Coastal Zone Management Act of 1972, 86 Stat. 1280, 16 U. S. C. § 1451 *et seq.* (1976 ed.); and the Deepwater Port Act of 1974, 88 Stat. 2126, 33 U. S. C. § 1501 *et seq.* (1970 ed., Supp. V). While those statutes contemplate cooperative state-federal regulatory efforts, they expressly state that intent, in contrast to the PWSA. Furthermore, none of them concerns the regulation of the design or size of oil tankers, an area in which there is a compelling need for uniformity of decisionmaking.

uniform national rule. We have previously rejected this claim, concluding that the provision may be viewed as simply a tug-escort requirement since it does not have the effect of forcing compliance with the design specifications set forth in the provision. See n.25, *supra*. So viewed, it becomes apparent that the Commerce Clause does not prevent a State from enacting a regulation of this type. Similar in its nature to a local pilotage requirement, a requirement that a vessel take on a tug escort when entering a particular body of water is not the type of regulation that demands a uniform national rule. See *Cooley v. Board of Wardens*, 12 How. 299 (1852). Nor does it appear from the record that the requirement impedes the free and efficient flow of interstate and foreign commerce, for the cost of tug escort for a 120,000 DWT tanker is less than one cent per barrel of oil and the amount of oil processed at Puget Sound refineries has not declined as a result of the provision's enforcement. . . . Accordingly, we hold that § 88.16.190 (2) of the Tanker Law is not invalid under the Commerce Clause.

Similarly, we cannot agree with the additional claim that the tug-escort provision interferes with the Federal Government's authority to conduct foreign affairs. Again, appellees' argument is based on the contention that the overall effect of § 88.16.190 (2) is to coerce tanker owners into outfitting their vessels with the specified design requirements. Were that so, we might agree that the provision constituted an invalid interference with the Federal Government's attempt to achieve international agreement on the regulation of tanker design. The provision as we view it, however, does no more than require the use of tug escorts within Puget Sound, a requirement with insignificant international consequences. We, therefore, decline to declare § 88.16.190 (2) invalid for either of the additional reasons urged by appellees.

Accordingly, the judgment of the three-judge District Court is affirmed in part and reversed in part, and the case is remanded for further proceedings consistent with this opinion.

. . . .

MR. JUSTICE MARSHALL, with whom MR. JUSTICE BRENNAN and MR. JUSTICE REHNQUIST join, concurring in part and dissenting in part.

. . . .

I also cannot agree with the Court's conclusion in Part VI of its opinion that the size limitation contained in the Tanker Law is invalid under the Supremacy Clause. To reach this conclusion, the Court relies primarily on an analysis of Title I of the PWSA and the Secretary of Transportation's actions thereunder. I agree with the Court that the Secretary has authority to establish vessel size limitations based on the characteristics of particular waters, and that a State is not free to impose more stringent requirements once the Secretary has exercised that authority or has decided, after balancing all of the relevant factors, that a size limitation would not be appropriate. On the other hand, Title I does not by its own force pre-empt all state regulation of vessel size, since it "merely authorizes and does not require the Secretary to issue regulations to implement the provisions of the Title." . . . Thus, as the Court notes, "[t]he pertinent inquiry at this point . . . [is] whether the Secretary, through his delegate, has addressed and acted upon the question of size limitations." . . .

The Court concludes that the Secretary's delegate, the Coast Guard, has in fact considered the issue of size limitations for Puget Sound and reached a judgment contrary to the one embodied in the Tanker Law. Under well-established principles, however, state law should be displaced "'only to the extent necessary to protect the achievement of the aims of'" federal law; whenever possible, we should "reconcile 'the operation of both statutory schemes with one another rather than holding [the state scheme] completely ousted.'" . . . Viewed in light of these principles, the record simply does not support the Court's finding of conflict between state and federal law.

The Coast Guard's unwritten "local navigation rule," which prohibits passage of more than one 70,000 DWT vessel through Rosario Strait at any given time, is the sole evidence cited by the Court to show that size limitations for Puget Sound have been considered by federal authorities. . . . On this record, however, the rule cannot be said to reflect a determination that the size limitations set forth in the Tanker Law are inappropriate or unnecessary. First, there is no indication that in establishing the vessel traffic rule for Rosario Strait the Coast Guard considered the need for promulgating size limitations for the entire Sound.[16] Second, even assuming that the Rosario Strait rule resulted from consideration of the size issue with respect to the entire area, appellees have not demonstrated that the rule evinces a judgment contrary to the provisions of the Tanker Law. Under the express terms of the PWSA, the existence of local vessel-traffic-control schemes must be weighed in the balance in determining whether, and to what extent, federal size limitations should be imposed.[17] There is no evidence in the record that the Rosario Strait "size limitation" was in existence or even under consideration prior to passage of the Tanker Law. Thus appellees have left unrebutted the inference that the Coast Guard's own limited rule was built upon, and is therefore entirely consistent with, the framework already created by the Tanker Law's restrictions.

Perhaps in recognition of the tenuousness of its finding of conflict with federal regulation under Title I, the Court suggests that the size limitation imposed by the Tanker Law might also be pre-empted under Title II of the

---

[16]The Rosario Strait "size limitation" in not contained in any written rule or regulation, and the record does not indicate how it came into existence. The only reference in the record is the following statement in the stipulation of facts:

"The Coast Guard prohibits the passage of more than one 70,000 DWT vessel through Rosario Strait in either direction at any given time. During periods of bad weather, the size limitation is reduced to approximately 40,000 DWT." App. 65.

The Puget Sound Vessel Traffic System, 33 CFR Part 161, Subpart B (1976), as amended, 42 Fed. Reg. 29480 (1977), does not contain any size limitation, and the necessity for such a limitation apparently was never considered during the rulemaking process. See 38 Fed. Reg. 21228 (1973) (notice of proposed rulemaking); 39 Fed. Reg. 25430 (1974) (summary of comments received during rulemaking).

[17]Title I provides in relevant part:

"In determining the need for, and the substance of, any rule or regulation or the exercise of other authority hereunder the Secretary shall, among other things, consider—

"(6) existing vessel traffic control systems, services, and schemes; and
"(7) local practices and customs . . . ." 33 U. S. C. § 1222 (e) (1970 ed., Supp. V).

PWSA. . . . In particular, the Court theorizes that the state rule might be preempted if it "represents a state judgment that, as a matter of safety and environmental protection *generally,* tankers should not exceed 125,000 DWT." . . . (Emphasis added.) It is clear, however, that the Tanker Law was not merely a reaction to the problems arising out of tanker operations in general, but instead was a measure tailored to respond to unique local conditions—in particular, the unusual susceptibility of Puget Sound to damage from large oil spills and the peculiar navigational problems associated with tanker operations in the Sound. Thus, there is no basis for preemption under Title II.

For similar reasons, I would hold that Washington's size regulation does not violate the Commerce Clause. Since water depth and other navigational conditions vary from port to port, local regulation of tanker access—like pilotage and tug requirements, and other harbor and river regulation—is certainly appropriate, and perhaps even necessary, in the absence of determinative federal action. See, *e.g., Cooley v. Board of Wardens,* 12 How. 299, 319 (1852); *Packet Co. v. Catlettsburg,* 105 U.S. 559, 562–563 (1882). Appellees have not demonstrated that the Tanker Law's size limit is an irrational or ineffective means of promoting safety and environmental protection, nor have they shown that the provision imposes any substantial burden on interstate or foreign commerce. Consequently, it is clear that appellees have not carried their burden of showing that the provision's impact on interstate or foreign commerce "is clearly excessive in relation to the putative local benefits." *Pike v. Bruce Church, Inc.,* 397 U.S. 137, 142 (1970).

I do not find any of appellees' other arguments persuasive. I would therefore sustain the size limitation imposed by the Tanker Law.

[The opinion of Mr. Justice Stevens, with whom Mr. Justice Powell joins, concurring in part and dissenting in part, is omitted.]

NOTES

1. Is Justice White's analysis of the Coast Guard preemption of vessel size limitations convincing? Could not, as Justice Marshall argues, the Coast Guard Rosario Strait rule and the Washington Tanker Law stand together? Compare the analysis of the local rules regarding size limitations and tugboat requirements. Immediately following the decision in *Ray v. ARCO,* Secretary of Transportation Adams issued a regulation closing Puget Sound to tankers greater than 125,000 DWT. 43 Fed. Reg. 12257 (1978), extended, 44 Fed. Reg. 36174 (June 21, 1979). Congress had restricted tanker traffic in Puget Sound even before the court's decision. *See* 33 U.S.C. § 476 (Supp. I 1977).

2. Of what practical significance is the state authority to require pilots on registered vessels in light of the Jones Act, section 27 of the Merchant Marine Act of 1920, 46 U.S.C. § 883 (1976), requiring that goods shipped between American ports be carried on American vessels? All coastwise or enrolled tankers will carry federally licensed pilots pursuant to Coast Guard rules adopted under 46 U.S.C. § 364 (1976).

3. How relevant was the cost of tug service to the Court's decision? As the Court stated, Washington's tug requirement could stand only until the Coast Guard decided whether to impose such a rule. The State of Alaska's attempt to require

tug assistance was held to be preempted by the Coast Guard's Prince William Sound Vessel Traffic System. *See Chevron v. Hammond,* No. A77-195 Civil (D. Alas. 1978). *See generally* Note, *Oil Tanker Regulation: A State or Federal Area?* 19 Nat. Res. J. 701 (1979).

4. Puget Sound and Prince William Sound are among the few areas of the country where maritime traffic is governed by a Vessel Traffic System (VTS). In an area where no VTS exists and where no negative declaration regarding its necessity has been made by the Coast Guard, could a state or local government implement its own VTS? Could a local vessel size limitation operate as a valid traffic control measure in the absence of a federal VTS?

5. As noted before, the PWSA was significantly strengthened by the Port and Tanker Safety Act of 1978, Pub. L. No. 95–474, 92 Stat. 1471. Although not as stringent as some believe necessary (*see,* e.g., President Carter's statement calling for, among other design standards, double bottoms on all new tankers, 13 Weekly Comp. of Pres. Doc. 408 (1977)), the new regulations offer definite improvements in tanker design and operational standards. The amendments do not appear to affect the state–federal regulatory balance as defined in *Ray v. ARCO.*

6. As recognized in *Ray v. ARCO,* the ultimate solution to pollution problems presented by oil tanker operations must be applied on an international scale to be truly effective. International standards for tanker operations and design have been promulgated by the Inter-Governmental Maritime Consultive Organization, IMCO, an agency operating under the auspices of the United Nations. Criticism of IMCO focuses on the often conflicting organizational goals of encouraging maritime commerce and protecting the marine environment. *See* Greenberg, *IMCO: An Environmentalist's Perspective,* 8 Case Western Reserve J. Int'L Law 131 (1976) and Juda, *IMCO and the Regulation of Ocean Pollution from Ships,* 26 Int'l & Comp. L.Q. 558 (1977).

The primary, currently effective, international agreement regarding tankers is the 1954 International Convention for the Prevention of Pollution of the Sea by Oil, 1 M.S.T. 2989, T.I.A.S. 4900, *as amended,* 2 M.S.T. 1523, T.I.A.S. 6109. *See* 9 Int'l Legal Materials 1 (1970). This agreement offers minimal protection from pollution, being limited to lenient operational standards with no specific design requirements, and is considered ineffective in controlling oil pollution. Only those ships whose flag nations have accepted the Convention are covered. Enforcement remains at the discretion of the flag nation and has generally been less than vigorous. Also, the lack of port facilities to receive oily residues has provided tanker operators with an excuse for discharging at sea.

The 1954 Convention is to be replaced by the 1973 International Convention for the Prevention of Pollution from Ships when the 1973 Convention becomes effective. *See* 12 Int'l Legal Materials 1319 (1973). Although it is hoped that the 1973 Convention will enter into force in the early 1980s, some doubt has been expressed that enough nations will ever accept or ratify the agreement for it to become enforceable. Along with more stringent discharge standards, the most significant improvements contained in the 1973 Convention are the provisions for limited port–state enforcement and selected design and structural requirements.

In response to continuing demands for more protection from oil pollution, President Carter's call for unilateral adoption of strict safety standards (see note 5 above), and pending U.S. legislation, a February 1978 IMCO Conference adopted vastly improved tanker design and operational standards. *See* 43 Fed. Reg. 16886 (1978). Congress, however, was not satisfied with the protection offered by the 1978 IMCO standards. The 1978 amendments to the PWSA thus exceed the international standards in several important respects. The U.S. Coast Guard has long held the view that the wisest course for U.S. tanker regulation would be to maintain standards equal to those adopted on the international level. What political and economic consequences are likely to flow from U.S. adoption of stricter standards?

7. For an overview of the oil tanker pollution problem, *see* Council on Environmental Quality, Oil and Gas in Coastal Waters 48–53 (1977); Senate Commerce Committee, Congress and the Nation's Oceans 183–85 (1977); U.S. Congress, Office of Technology Assessment, Oil Transportation by Tankers: An Analysis of Marine Pollution and Safety Measures (1975).

   Some commentators believe that strict structural standards are unnecessary and wasteful and that they should be replaced by more stringent liability rules. It is conversely argued that even the toughest standards would add but a cent or two to the cost of a gallon of gasoline. *Compare* Cummins, Logue, Tollison & Willett, *Oil Tanker Pollution Control: Design Criteria vs. Effective Liability Assessment,* 7 J. Mar. L. & Com. 169 (1975) with Pedrick, *Tankship Design Regulation and Its Economic Effect on Oil Consumers,* 9 J. Mar. L. & Com. 377 (1978). Should such a choice be based solely on economic grounds? Would the imposition of costly structural standards for new tankers encourage the retention and use of older tankers beyond their normal life expectancies? What problems could such a trend produce? Another alternative would be to set performance standards without limiting the methods of achieving them.

8. In discussions of tanker operations, air pollution traditionally did not receive much attention. Yet pollution from tanker loading and unloading and oil spills can seriously affect the marine and coastal environment. *See* U.S. Environmental Protection Agency, The Alaskan Oil Disposition Study: Potential Air Quality Impact of a Major Off-Loading Terminal in the Pacific Northwest (1977). The problem is not addressed by the PWSA, but recall that *Huron Portland Cement Co. v. Detroit,* 362 U.S. 440 (1960), discussed in *Askew* and *Ray, supra,* upheld enforcement of the Detroit Smoke Abatement Code against federally licensed vessels. Is there any limit to the states' ability to regulate air pollution from oil tankers? Typical commerce clause objections to such state regulations appear to have been overcome by the passage of the Clean Air Act, 42 U.S.C. §§ 7401–7642 (Supp. I 1977). The Clean Air Act evinces congressional intent to allow states to restrict certain sources of air pollution as stringently as they choose. Clean Air Act § 116, 42 U.S.C. § 7416 (Supp. I 1977). *See Union Electric Co. v. E.P.A.,* 427 U.S. 246 (1976). But do oil tankers fit within that category of air pollution sources over which states may exercise complete control?

9. Certain tanker operations which are performed solely for safety purposes also produce significant amounts of air pollution. Can states restrict such activities? The federal Environmental Protection Agency (EPA) has promulgated but never enforced hydrocarbon emission limitations for tanker operations. *State of Texas v. EPA,* 499 F. 2d 289, 316 (5th Cir. 1974). In general, states have even greater authority in this area than does EPA. Clean Air Act § 116, 42 U.S.C. § 7416 (Supp. I 1977). Suppose that the U.S. Coast Guard promulgated regulations requiring such operations for safety purposes—could a state air pollution program be designed so as to avoid conflict with the Coast Guard regulations?

10. Another affirmative grant of state authority allows state pilot requirements for vessels engaged in foreign trade. 46 U.S.C. §§ 211, 215, 364 (1976). The extent of state authority in this field was clearly defined in *Warner v. Dunlap,* 532 F. 2d 767 (1st Cir. 1976).

11. Some state regulation of oil tanker operations can be accomplished indirectly through the regulation of shore facilities or the use of liability programs. What other indirect methods are available for a state seeking to protect its environment from tanker source pollution? *See,* for example, § 9(b)(1) of the Deepwater Port Act of 1974, 33 U.S.C. § 1508(b)(1) (1976), discussed in the following section.

12. Does the federal Coastal Zone Management Act, 16 U.S.C. §§ 1451–1464 (1976), provide yet another opportunity for indirect state regulation of oil tankers? *See* Du Bey, *Control of Oil Transport in the Coastal Zone: A Look at Puget Sound*, 56 Or. L. Rev. 593, 630 (1977).

SECTION C: DEEPWATER PORTS

MELTZ, "THE DEEPWATER PORTS ACT OF 1974: HALF SPEED AHEAD," 5 Environmental Law Reporter 50043 (1975) Reprinted with permission

On January 3, 1975, the Deepwater Ports Act of 1974 was signed into law, and the United States thereby prepared to join the sizeable fraternity of nations already using this type of facility. . . . The legislation, . . . , gives primary responsibility for licensing and regulating deepwater ports beyond the 3-mile limit to the Secretary of Transportation and contains strong environmental safeguards. The immediate effect of the Act, therefore, is to extend federal jurisdiction to facilities beyond the territorial waters of the United States, and thereby fill the regulatory void which has so far deterred deepwater port development.

Background

Proponents of deepwater ports advance a simple, and seemingly irrefutable, argument[18] based on three premises. First, the inability of domestic oil production to meet domestic oil consumption, which began about 1971, promises to continue and in fact increase for the foreseeable future. Neither Project Independence (by increasing production) nor high oil import tariffs (by decreasing consumption) can eliminate this shortfall, so that oil importation in substantial amounts will be necessary for some time to come. Second, the most economically and environmentally sound way of transporting large amounts of oil over long distances, as from the Persian Gulf, is by supertanker. Supertankers, or "Very Large Crude Carriers," range up to 1200 feet in length and have carrying capacities of 200,000 to 500,000 deadweight tons (dwt), as much as twelve times the capacity of conventional tankers currently using United States ports. Thus, the argument goes, use of supertankers will result in a substantial reduction of per-barrel shipping costs. At the same time, supertankers will bring environmental benefits by reducing port congestion and hence the number of vessel collisions and groundings. Third, deepwater ports located as much as 20 to 30 miles offshore will be necessary to accommodate supertankers, since existing inshore ports are too shallow to take their 60 to 90 foot drafts.[19]

[18]*See, e.g.,* Staff of Senate Comm. on Interior and Insular Affairs, 93d Cong. 2d Sess., *Deepwater Port Policy Issues,* 1 (Comm. Print 1974).

[19]The deepest United States ports have vessel size capacities as follows: Long Beach, Cal.— 100,000 dwt; Los Angeles, Cal.—100,000 dwt; Portland, Me.—80,000 dwt; Beaumont, Tex.— 80,000 dwt; and Nisiki, Alaska—60,000 dwt. Petroleum Publishing Institute, *International Petroleum Encyclopedia* 407 (1972).

Indeed, the Gulf of Mexico ports, where most supertanker-imported oil will probably arrive, are currently restricted to ships of 50,000 dwt or less.

This, then, is the rationale for superports, and while numerous cautionary qualifications will be discussed throughout this Note, its logic is basically sound. At least two other factors, however, played significant roles in the enactment of the Deepwater Ports Act. The first was the unbridled enthusiasm of the Gulf Coast states, with the exception of Florida, for deepwater port development off their shores. This has been in marked contrast to the hesitation—in some cases even staunch opposition—of East Coast and West Coast states. Louisiana and Texas have been separately laying the groundwork for superport development since 1971.[20] Alabama and Mississippi have been proceeding jointly since 1972.[21] Costly studies have been done at both state and industry expense, enabling legislation has been enacted,[22] superport authorities created, and statewide public relations campaigns conducted. For Texas and Louisiana, the stakes are particularly high. The heavily oil-dependent economies of these states are today facing the prospect of prolonged economic decline as oil production within their borders drops off, seemingly irreversibly. In Texas, 25 percent of public school funds and 18 percent of state tax revenues are derived from the oil industry. Under such circumstances the federal government is unlikely to ignore altogether the desires of these states.

. . . .

The Environmental Threats

The environmental provisions of the Deepwater Ports Act are responses to the specific environmental threats posed by superports and supertankers. Hence, some familiarity with superport procedures is indispensible to an understanding of the Act.

Since U.S. planners favor the floating "monobuoy" type of deepwater port over the large artificial sea island, the main environmental threats appear to lie in the operation, rather than construction, phase. . . . Needless to say, the huge size of supertankers drastically reduces the margin for error in all these operations, and greatly increases the consequences of any mishap. The effects of major oil spills have been extensively documented elsewhere; suffice it here to say that the damage wrought by a major spill off the East Coast could run in the billions of dollars. The technology of oil spill containment is still in its infancy.

Landside impacts of port-induced industrial growth present another distinct

---

[20]The Louisiana Offshore Oil Port proposal, or LOOP, would be sited some 20 miles off Bayou Lafourche. Its onshore terminal would be connected with CAPLINE, a major overland pipeline supplying Mid-West refineries. The Texas proposal, SEADOCK, would be 25–30 miles off Freeport, near Texas refinery centers.

Both proposals would be initially constructed as a two- or three-monobuoy cluster, more monobuoys to be added at a later date. Both would be entirely financed by oil company consortia. LOOP and SEADOCK are the most advanced deepwater port proposals.

[21]Their proposal, Ameraport, would be operated by a state-owned corporation. Its viability depends on attracting considerable new refinery capacity to the area.

[22]34 La. Rev. Stat. §§3101 *et seq.*

set of problems. According to the Draft Environmental Impact Statement on Deepwater Ports, such landside effects "could have a more significant environmental impact than any other component of a deepwater port system over a long period of time." . . .

Provisions of the Act

The regulatory scheme set forth by the Deepwater Ports Act begins at the beginning. Preconstruction testing of potential port sites is limited where the environment could be adversely affected. Thereafter, no person may construct, operate, or own a deepwater port except in accordance with a license issued by the Secretary of Transportation. The license may contain any appropriate conditions, and may be issued only if the Secretary determines, *inter alia*, that the applicant is financially responsible (important for oil spill liability, *infra*); that the deepwater port will be in the "national interest" and consistent with United States energy and environmental goals; and that the port will utilize the "best available technology" to minimize adverse environmental impacts. The Secretary is directed to establish environmental review criteria consistent with NEPA for use in evaluating proposed ports. A separate NEPA impact statement is mandated for each local area in which applications are being considered. Further provisions require the Secretary to establish procedures with respect to vessel movement, loading and unloading, and equipment necessary to prevent or clean up discharged pollutants, or minimize other environmental effects.

The EPA Administrator has both binding and advisory functions under the Act. His determination that the proposed port will not conform with the Clean Air Act or the Federal Water Pollution Control Act bars the issuance of a license. (Deepwater ports are defined as "new sources" for the purposes of these statutes.) On the other hand, EPA's role in developing the environmental review criteria is purely one of recommendation. Since the Act makes all federal laws applicable to deepwater ports, other statutory responsibilities of EPA will undoubtedly come into play.

Other aspects of the Act's regulatory scheme address primarily the landside impacts. First and foremost is the state veto: all adjacent states must approve the issuance of a deepwater port license. "Adjacent state" is liberally defined to include the pipeline-connected state, any state within 15 miles of the port, or any state threatened with environmental impacts equal to or greater than the pipeline-connected state. Secondly, a license may not issue unless the pipeline-connected state is making "reasonable progress" in developing its coastal zone management plan under the Coastal Zone Management Act of 1972. Lastly, the laws of the nearest adjacent coastal state are declared applicable to superports as federal law.

The remedies and liability sections of the Act include a large arsenal of enforcement techniques. Any failure by the port licensee to comply may result in suspension or revocation of the license. When an "imminent and substantial" threat to the environment is involved, suspension is immediate. More stringent remedies for failure of compliance include civil monetary penalties, criminal fines for willful violations, specific equitable relief, and *in rem* liability of vessels used in violations of the Act. The oil spill liability provisions are patterned after the Federal Water Pollution Control Act, and are especially strict.

Any discharge of oil, from either vessel or port, leads to civil fines—and vessel and port operators are required to report all such discharges. Most important, strict liability for clean-up costs and damages resulting from escaped oil is imposed on owners and operators of vessels, and on port licensees. Liability ceilings of $20 million[23] and $50 million, respectively, are set. Damages and cleanup costs beyond these ceilings may be recovered from a Deepwater Port Liability Fund,[24] which is financed by a 2 cent per barrel port fee and is liable without fault or limit for the remainder. The Attorney General may bring class actions on behalf of any group of damaged citizens; otherwise, the group may sue on its own. Should there be damage to the public lands, the Secretary of Transportation may act on behalf of the public as "trustee of the natural resources of the marine environment" to recover for damage to such resources. Citizen suits to compel compliance are also authorized, with provision for recovery of attorneys' fees. States are not pre-empted and may impose additional requirements or liabilities.[25]

Strengths

As is apparent, the Deepwater Ports Act displays an environmental concern one could well wish were evident in all energy legislation. A wide spectrum of environmental issues is addressed—oil spillage, cleanup side effects, land-based development, oceanographic effects, and human health and welfare. The interests of virtually all directly affected third parties are considered—nearby states (the veto), alternate users of the ocean (in the environmental review criteria), shore dwellers (unlimited strict liability for polluters), and recreational users of the public shorelands (suits by the Secretary as trustee of the marine environment). The licensing process for each port is exhaustive, emphatically recognizing the importance of planning in the early stages of development.

Liabilities incurred for oil spill damage are harsh, but no harsher than necessary considering the possible dimensions of supertanker oil spills. Deterrence was an express congressional objective. On the other hand, the liability limits set for port licensees and vessels using deepwater ports are no higher than the insurance available to them, so as not to impair competition for deepwater port licenses. Recovery without limit, through the Deepwater Port Liability Fund, ensures that no person suffering oil spill damage will be barred from full compensation. The element of strict liability provides injured parties with easily reachable defendants and shifts the evidentiary burden of determining the negligent party to the polluter. Individually and jointly, the liability provisions accomplish another important shift by placing a portion of the risk burden on the consuming public who ultimately benefit from the use of deepwater ports and supertankers.

[23]For smaller tankers, the liability limit is $150/gross ton.

[24]Patterned after the Trans-Alaskan Pipeline Liability Fund established by the Trans-Alaskan Pipeline Authorization Act (86 Stat. 862).

[25]The power of a state to set oil spill liability limits higher than the federal limits was accepted in Askew v. American Waterways Operators, 3 ELR 20362 (U.S. 1973). The Act's provision merely ensures that power with regard to deepwater ports.

Weaknesses

The many strengths of the Deepwater Ports Act ought not obscure its weaknesses, which, although not damning, are troublesome. Pre-eminent among these is the failure of the Act to impose a nationwide limit on the number of superports that may be built. This is no academic issue, as there are currently at least nine active proposals.[26] All the Act requires is that each deepwater port licensed must be "in the national interest," but in a nation which has no coordinated port policy, this phrase can have little meaning. . . .

Another area of omission is the failure of the Act to cover deepwater ports within the 3-mile limit, the extent of state jurisdiction. Again, the issue is more than hypothetical—as the Act now stands, both the Estero Bay, California proposal (2.6 miles out) and the Eastport, Maine proposal (immediately offshore) would be exempt. The argument for non-coverage has been that port licensees within territorial waters would still be required to obtain authorization from state or local governments, as well as a federal permit under the 1899 Rivers and Harbors Act. However, it is the close-in sites where supertanker collisions and groundings are most likely, and where spilled oil is surest to reach shore. The Maine proposal, in particular, ignores treacherous navigation conditions in order to utilize naturally occurring deep water close to land. Subjecting ports far off shore to an extensive regulatory apparatus while relegating the most potentially harmful ports to the limited resources of local enforcement seems at best unjustifiable.

At any distance from shore, the basic problem with superports is, quite simply, supertankers. To what extent, then, should the Deepwater Ports Act have required that supertankers using licensed deepwater ports employ the full panoply of structural safeguards—in particular, double hulls and segregated ballast? A bitter, longstanding controversy swirls around these features. It is no small matter, since the cost of a double hull/segregated ballast system may add 17 to 23 percent to the construction cost of a vessel. Even a single hull/segregated ballast system adds 4 to 10 percent. Much as these structural features may be environmentally desirable, therefore, the fact that they have substantial economic consequences suggests that imposing them as merely an ancillary matter in deepwater ports legislation would be inappropriate. A more suitable route would seem to be through separate legislation. Certainly there is little likelihood that a full complement of structural safeguards will be required in forthcoming Coast Guard regulations under the Ports and Waterways Safety Act. . . .

Other deficiencies of the Act are less significant than the foregoing, but still bear watching as the regulatory process unfolds in the months ahead. Potentially troublesome is the requirement that the Secretary consider, as an alternative to any offshore port, pre-existing plans for dredging a nearby harbor to supertanker depths. Though generalizations are difficult due to varying site conditions, the dredging alternative must result in at least three environmental impacts: direct loss of bottom habitat, effects of particle suspension in the water

---

[26]These are: Puget Sound, Wash.; Estero Bay, Calif.; Harbor Island, Texas; Freeport, Texas (SEADOCK); Bayou Lafourche, La. (LOOP); Alabama–Mississippi (Ameraport); Stone Beach, Del.; Newburyport, Mass. (MASSPORT); and Eastport, Me.

(on filter-feeding animal life in particular), and effects of deposition of suspended matter and dredging spoils (further loss of habitat, and estuary damage). Annual redredging may also be required, and the poor maneuverability of supertankers leaves the goundings and collisions problems unresolved. . . .

The massive landside industrialization which a superport would induce has led the Sierra Club to favor a ban on superport licensing pending actual approval of the adjacent state's coastal zone management program. . . .

Assuming that at least a small number of superports should be built, the Deepwater Ports Act of 1974 marks an environmentally sound beginning. In creating numerous channels for local input, the Act assures that coastal interests will not be sacrificed to satisfy the oil appetite of consumers a thousand miles inland. And the administrative sequence established for superport licensing follows an unequivocal "plan first" approach. As always, the evolving regulatory process may bring its surprises, but at this time the Deepwater Ports Act seems a reasonable legislative response to a complex problem.

NOTES

1. One of the effects of the DWPA was to extend federal jurisdiction to facilities beyond the territorial waters of the United States. Compare this move with the extensions of jurisdiction under the Outer Continental Shelf Lands Act of 1953, the Fisheries Conservation Management Act of 1976, and the Ocean Thermal Energy Conversion and Deep Seabed Hard Mineral Resources acts of 1980. For further discussion of the DWPA and deepwater port *see* L. Bragaw, *The Challenge of Deepwater Terminals* (1975); Comment, *Territorial Status of Deepwater Ports*, 15 San Diego L. Rev. 603 (1978); Council on Environmental Quality, Oil and Gas in Coastal Waters 42–48 (1978); Krueger, Nordquist & Wessely, *New Technology and International Law*, 17 Va. J. Int'l L. 597 (1977); Note, *Deepwater Port Act of 1974: Some International and Environmental Impacts*, 6 Ga. J. Int'l & Comp. L. 535 (1976); U.S. Congress, Office of Technology Assessment, Coastal Effects of Offshore Energy Systems 21–23 (1977).

2. As the Meltz article points out, coastal areas landward of deepwater ports will experience extensive and rapid change because of construction of related facilities such as pipelines, refineries, and service industries. These impacts are of the type normally dealt with in a state's coastal zone management program. However, the DWPA does not require an adjacent coastal state to have an approved CZM program prior to deepwater port development. Instead, it requires that adjacent states make "reasonable" progress in developing such a program. 33 U.S.C. § 1503 (1976).

3. Meltz concludes his article by noting that one of the strengths of the Deepwater Port Act is that it assures that the environmental interests of coastal states will not be sacrificed to the oil appetite of inland states. On the other hand, it could be argued that one of the weaknesses of the Act is that it allows the economic interests of inland states to be defeated by a coastal state's veto of a deepwater port. No more crude—no more food? Consider the next note.

4. Section 1508 of the Deepwater Port Act (DWPA) vests in "adjacent coastal states" a power amounting to a veto over licensing decisions:

> . . . The Secretary shall not issue a license [to own, construct, or operate a deepwater port facility] without the approval of the Governor of each adjacent coastal state . . . .

33 U.S.C. § 1508 (1976). There are two ways a state achieves designation as an "adjacent coastal state": (a) automatically, by being directly connected by pipeline to the facility or being within 15 miles of the facility; or (b) by approval of the Secretary of Transportation on submission of a request for adjacent coastal state status. It is the second method that has caused some controversy.

One year after the enactment of the DWPA, two private corporations, Louisiana Offshore Project (LOOP), Inc., and SEADOCK, Inc., submitted applications for licenses. They sought to construct and operate deepwater ports in federal waters off the coasts of Louisiana and Texas. The proposed facilities would be capable of handling "supertankers."

Shortly after these applications were submitted, the Governor of Florida wrote the Secretary of Transportation requesting adjacent coastal state status for Florida as to both projects. The request pointed to Florida's beaches, fisheries, and estuaries as vital to the state's tourist and fishing economies. It asserted that oil spills or discharges from tankers in transit to and from the proposed deepwater ports would constitute a major threat to these resources.

The Secretary of Transportation did not dispute the basic validity of this assertion, but nevertheless decided against designating Florida as an adjacent state. The Secretary's decision concluded that the dangers arising from tankers in transit to and from the facilities were beyond the scope of the risk calculations required under the Act. In addition, the decision said the risks were not changed as a result of merely switching operations from existing harbors to deepwater ports unless there was an increase in the total shipping tonnage.

The Secretary's decision set two noteworthy precedents. First, in assessing the potential hazards resulting from a deepwater port, the risks to be evaluated are only those proximate to the port and its pipelines. Second, the risks of oil spills are viewed as not likely to be increased unless there is an increase in the amount of oil transported in the area.

The practical effect of the Secretary's decision was to leave Florida with merely an opportunity to be heard on the licensing decision rather than having a veto power.

Query: Does the Secretary's decision not overlook the fact that the supertankers that will use deepwater ports have less maneuverability than other tankers as a result of their size? Will this lack of maneuverability not increase the potential hazards of oil spills in congested navigation areas such as the Straits of Florida?

For further discussion, see Barkley, *The Deepwater Port Act of 1974: The Definition of Adjacent Coastal States*, 29 Baylor L. Rev. 1051 (1976); Comment, *Florida Denied Adjacent Coastal State Status in Gulf Deepwater Ports Decision*, 6 Envt'l L. Rep. 10123 (1976).

5. As of January 1, 1981, only one deepwater port, the Louisiana LOOP project, had been licensed under the DWPA. Does this indicate that Congress should repeal the DWPA as unneeded legislation?

Disposal
of Wastes
in the Ocean

SECTION A: OCEAN DUMPING

The capacity of the world's oceans to assimilate industrial and municipal wastes has already been reached in some coastal areas, and surpassed in others. In 1972, a group of nations became sufficiently concerned about this ocean pollution problem that they negotiated the Convention on Prevention of Marine Pollution by Dumping of Wastes and Other Matters (Ocean Dumping Convention). The treaty came into force in 1975. By October 1979, it had been ratified or acceded to by 43 nations, including the United States.

Although the oceans off the U.S. coasts have been used as a disposal site for many years, until recently only relatively small amounts of material were dumped. The annual amount of material (industrial wastes, sewage sludge, solid wastes, and construction and demolition debris) dumped in the early 1950s was approximately 1.7 million tons. By the mid-1960s, this figure rose to 7.4 million tons per year—a 335 percent increase. These figures do not include the amount of dredge spoil disposed; this is generally estimated to be four times, by weight, that of all other materials. Congressional Research Service, Library of Congress, Ocean Dumping Regulations: An Appraisal of Implementation 1 (1976). Today, sources of waste material are identified as dredged material (680 million metric tons per year nationally, with 25 percent of it dumped into the ocean); sewage sludge (5.9 million wet metric tons were ocean dumped in 1979, and 2.8 million wet metric tons were discharged through the Los Angeles and Boston outfalls); industrial waste (2.6 million tons were ocean dumped in 1979); solid waste (570 million tons); nonpoint sources (vast amounts of wastes from urban runoff, mining wastes, and agriculture and silviculture runoff); and potential new sources (synfuel and other energy development could lead by the year 2000 to the additional production of 400 million tons of spent oil shale and 50 million tons of coal project wastes annually). 12 Nautilus Press, Coastal Zone Mgmt. Newsletter No. 6, Feb. 11, 1981, at 2–3.

Several probable causes of this drastic increase are identifiable:

1. There was a widely held perception, which to some degree continues today, that the ocean can serve as a vast ultimate sink for wastes. This view gave rise to the assumption that the ocean was a "safe" disposal site able to dilute and absorb otherwise harmful material.

2. Between 1930 and 1970 the population in coastal areas approximately doubled. This growth of population and associated land development led to the generation of tremendous amounts of solid waste. At the same time, this growth reduced the amount of land available for landfill disposal methods.

3. Since the late 1960s there have been growing numbers and types of controls upon air and water discharge. This has led to:
   (a) A transfer of waste disposal processes to coastal and ocean dumping, transferring pollution from one medium to another rather than eliminating it; and
   (b) Pollution controls have themselves expanded the amount of waste needing disposal. Sewage treatment has generated more sewage sludge, and stack scrubbers collect large amounts of fly ash. Both of these are bulky wastes that require some type of disposal.

4. Until 1972 there was no federal regulation of ocean dumping. In many instances this encouraged use of ocean dumping over other methods of waste disposal.

In response to this dramatic increase in ocean dumping, the President's Council on Environmental Quality took a deep look at the problem presented by unregulated ocean dumping. It recommended a "comprehensive national policy on ocean dumping of wastes to ban *unregulated* dumping of all materials and strictly *limit* ocean disposal of any materials harmful to the marine environment." Council on Environmental Quality, Ocean Dumping: A National Policy at v (1970) (emphasis added).

In response to the report's recommendations, Congress passed the Marine Protection, Research and Sanctuaries Act (MPRSA) of 1972. Titles I and II pertain to ocean dumping and are commonly referred to as the Ocean Dumping Act; Title III concerns marine sanctuaries and is discussed later.

Section 2 of the Ocean Dumping Act states:

(a) Unregulated dumping of material into ocean waters endangers human health, welfare, and amenities, and the marine environment, ecological systems, and economic potentialities.

(b) The Congress declares that it is the policy of the United States to regulate the dumping of all types of materials into ocean waters and to prevent or strictly limit the dumping into ocean waters of any material which would adversely affect human health, welfare, or amenities, or the marine environment, ecological systems, or economic potentialities.

33 U.S.C. §§ 1401(a), (b) (1976).

To carry out its purposes, the Act establishes a regulatory system for the transportation of materials for the purpose of dumping into ocean waters.

The Act prohibits the dumping of wastes into the oceans without a permit. The Environmental Protection Agency (EPA) is the permit agency for the transportation of all nondredged materials (industrial and municipal wastes) for the purpose of ocean dumping, while the Army Corps of Engineers (Corps) has permit authority for dredged materials using criteria established by the EPA. The EPA has the authority to veto any Corps permit. 33 U.S.C. § 1413 (1976).

The ocean dumping of radiological, chemical, and biological warfare agents and high-level radioactive waste is entirely prohibited. 33 U.S.C. § 1412(a) (1976). Several types of dumping are exempted from the Act, including discharges from ocean outfall structures subject to the regulatory provisions of other legislation discussed below, routine discharges from boat motors, and the construction of a fixed structure for purposes other than discharge (such as an offshore oil platform), if otherwise regulated by another federal or state program of law. The U.S. Coast Guard has surveillance responsibility for ocean dumping.

In 1977 Congress amended the Act to eliminate the ocean dumping of sewage sludge. In amending MPRSA, Congress provided in 33 U.S.C. 1412(a) that:

(a) The Administrator of the Environmental Protection Agency . . . shall end the dumping of sewage sludge into ocean waters . . . as soon as possible after November 4, 1977, but in no case may the Administrator issue any permit, or any renewal thereof [under Title I of MPRSA] which authorizes any such dumping after December 31, 1981.

(b) For purposes of this section, the term 'sewage sludge' means any solid, semisolid, or liquid waste generated by a municipal wastewater treatment plant the ocean dumping of which may unreasonably degrade or endanger human health, welfare, amenities, or the marine environment, ecological systems, or economic potentialities.

In *City of New York v. EPA*, 15 ERC 1965 (S.D.N.Y. 1981), the City of New York challenged EPA's refusal to consider certain factors in its decision not to extend the City's ocean sewage sludge dumping permit beyond the December 31, 1981, deadline. The City had developed a short-term land-based alternative plan for disposal of its sewage sludge. As the deadline neared for cut-off of its ocean dumping, however, the City urged the EPA to consider drawbacks of the land-based alternative in its decision as to whether the City's ocean dumping permit should be extended. The EPA refused, arguing primarily that the 1977 amendment to the Marine Protection, Research and Sanctuaries Act (MPRSA) set an absolute deadline for ocean dumping of sewage sludge. Judge Sofaer agreed with the City that the EPA must consider the impacts of the land-based alternative before ocean dumping can be denied, and that the 1977 amendment did not establish an absolute deadline. In reaching his decision, Judge Sofaer engaged in a lengthy but cogent analysis of the 1972 version of the MPRSA, the EPA regulations and practices thereunder, and the 1977 amendments.

The opinion begins by explaining that the 1972 Act only prohibited ocean dumping that "unreasonably" degraded the marine environment. In making that decision in individual cases the EPA must consider statutory criteria, specifically including "land based alternatives and the probable impact of requiring use of such alternative locations or methods upon considerations affecting the public interest." Despite this rather explicit expression of congressional intent that the only dumping to be permitted was that which, based on a balancing of the relevant statutory criteria, does not "unreasonably degrade the marine environment," the EPA developed rules which permitted *some* municipalities to continue dumping even when doing so was "unreasonable" within the meaning of the statute. That exception was to permit continued dumping by jurisdictions which in "good faith" had attempted to obtain financing to develop alternatives but had not yet succeeded, thereby elevating financial considerations to a preeminent position. In the opinion of Judge Sofaer, upon a convincing show of legislative history, it was this lenient practice of the EPA that Congress sought to remedy when it amended the MPRSA in 1977 by adding that the EPA "shall end the dumping of sewage sludge into ocean waters . . . as soon as possible after November 4, 1977, but in no case may the Administrator issue any permit . . . which authorizes any such dumping after December 31, 1981." It was at this juncture that the EPA and the City diverged. The EPA looked no further and argued that because of this language it was not authorized to extend the permit of the City. The City argued, and Judge Sofaer agreed, that the statutory definition of "sewage sludge" as municipal waste "the ocean dumping of which may *unreasonably* degrade . . . human health . . . or the marine environment . . . ," in conjunction with the 1977 amendment, provided for continued dumping of that sludge which does not unreasonably degrade, but that no dumping should be permitted based on fiscal considerations alone.

The result is that the EPA does have the authority to permit continued ocean sewage dumping, but only for dumping that does not unreasonably degrade, and the determination of reasonableness must be based on a balancing of the statutory criteria in the MPRSA, including the environmental dangers of land-based alternatives.

Relationship of Ocean Dumping Act to Other Laws

Sections 106(a) and (d) of the Ocean Dumping Act provide:

> (a) After the effective date of this subchapter, all licenses, permits, and authorizations other than those issued pursuant to this subchapter shall be void and of no legal effect, to the extent that they purport to authorize any activity regulated by this subchapter, and whether issued before or after the effective date of this subchapter. . . .
>
> . . . .
>
> (d) After the effective date of this subchapter, no State shall adopt or enforce any rule or regulation relating to any activity regulated by this subchapter. Any

State may, however, propose to the Administrator criteria relating to the dumping of materials into ocean waters within its jurisdiction, or into other ocean waters to the extent that such dumping may affect waters within the jurisdiction of such State, and if the Administrator determines, after notice and opportunity for hearing, that the proposed criteria are not inconsistent with the purposes of this subchapter, may adopt those criteria and may issue regulations to implement such criteria. Such determination shall be made by the Administrator within one hundred and twenty days of receipt of the proposed criteria. For the purposes of this subsection, the term "State" means any State, interstate or regional authority, Federal territory or Commonwealth or the District of Columbia.

33 U.S.C. § 1415(a), (d) (1976).

The Ocean Dumping Act relates to the Clean Water Act (CWA), 33 U.S.C. §§ 1251 et seq. (1976), in several respects. Under section 403 of the CWA, 33 U.S.C. § 1343 (1976), the Administrator of the Environmental Protection Agency is to promulgate guidelines "for determining the degradation of waters of the territorial seas, the contiguous zone, and the oceans." Criteria used in making this determination are substantially similar to those pertinent to the evaluation of permits under section 102(2) of the Ocean Dumping Act, 33 U.S.C. § 1412(a).[1] Section 403(c)(2) of the CWA is, however, more explicit that permits can be issued only if justified by adequate data: " . . . In any event where insufficient information exists on any proposed discharge to make a reasonable judgment on any of the guidelines . . . no permit shall be issued. . . ." 33 U.S.C. § 1343(c)(2) (1976).

An important distinction between the Ocean Dumping Act and the CWA concerns the role of states. Section 106(d) of the Ocean Dumping Act, quoted above, prohibits states from adopting or enforcing any rule relating to ocean dumping, although states can propose special criteria relating to dumping within state waters or waters that may affect state waters. The CWA, on the other hand, provides a mechanism for delegating permit authority to states which meet certain standards and specifically allows states to adopt water quality standards stricter than federal minimums. 33 U.S.C. §§ 1342, 1370 (1976).

Permit Program for Municipal and Industrial Wastes

The EPA Administrator is to establish and apply criteria for reviewing and evaluating permit applications for municipal and industrial wastes. In developing these criteria, he is to consider:

(A) The need for the proposed dumping.

(B) The effect of such dumping on human health and welfare, including economic, esthetic, and recreational values.

(C) The effect of such dumping on fisheries resources, plankton, fish, shellfish, wildlife, shorelines and beaches.

[1]In fact, the regulations originally promulgated pursuant to the Ocean Dumping Act (38 Fed. Reg. 28610 (1973)) also applied to ocean sewage outfalls. The final ocean dumping regulations (40 C.F.R. §§ 220–227 (1977)) apply only to ocean dumping. Final EPA guidelines on ocean discharge criteria were published on October 3, 1980 (45 Fed. Reg. 65942).

(D) The effect of such dumping on marine ecosystems, particularly with respect to—

  (i) the transfer, concentration, and dispersion of such material and its byproducts through biological, physical, and chemical processes,

  (ii) potential changes in marine ecosystem diversity, productivity, and stability, and

  (iii) species and community population dynamics.

(E) The persistence and permanences of the effects of the dumping.

(F) The effect of dumping particular volumes and concentrations of such materials.

(G) Appropriate locations and methods of disposal or recycling, including land-based alternatives and the probable impact of requiring use of such alternate locations or methods upon considerations affecting the public interest.

(H) The effect on alternate uses of oceans, such as scientific study, fishing, and other living resource exploitation, and non-living resource exploitation.

(I) In designating recommended sites, the Administrator shall utilize wherever feasible locations beyond the edge of the Continental Shelf.

33 U.S.C. § 1412(a) (1976).

NOTES

1. Interestingly, the major problems of ocean dumping are on the east, not the west coast. Since 1973, when the Ocean Dumping Act permit program went into effect, the Atlantic Ocean has received more than 90 percent of the total, and the Pacific Ocean almost none. U.S. Environmental Protection Agency, Annual Report to Congress (Jan.–Dec. 1979) on Administration of the Marine Protection, Research, and Sanctuaries Act of 1972, As Amended (P.L. 92–532) and Implementing the International Ocean Dumping Convention 6 (1980). In fact, municipal sewage sludge disposal has increased between 1973 and 1979 while industrial waste dumping has dropped by about 50 percent. Paradoxically, the rise in sewage sludge dumping is directly related to the national water cleanup effort. The Clean Water Act requires mandatory secondary treatment for all municipal wastewaters in an effort to "restore and maintain the chemical, physical, and biological integrity of our nation's waters." 33 U.S.C.A. § 1251(a). Secondary treatment necessarily creates more sewage sludge needing disposal, and cities and towns, especially along the Atlantic coast, have turned increasingly to ocean disposal.

2. Title II of the Ocean Dumping Act was adopted in response to the serious data and information gaps on the effects of ocean dumping emphasized in the Council on Environmental Quality's report. Title II requires the Secretary of Commerce, through the National Oceanic and Atmospheric Administration (NOAA) and in coordination with the U.S. Coast Guard to:

Initiate a comprehensive and continuing program of monitoring and research regarding the effects of the dumping of material into ocean waters or other coastal waters . . . and . . . report from time to time, not less frequently than annually, his findings (including an evaluation of the short-term ecological effects and the social and economic factors involved) to the Congress.

33 U.S.C. § 1441 (1976). *See also* The National Ocean Pollution Planning Act of 1978, 33 U.S.C. §§ 1701–1709 (1978), which requires the NOAA Administrator to

first develop a comprehensive plan for the overall federal effort in ocean pollution research and monitoring, and then revise this plan every two years.

In May 1980, the EPA announced that it planned to revise the ocean dumping criteria under the Ocean Dumping Act because new data indicates that the ocean can assimilate more than originally thought. This move is based on studies of some 45 dump sites. Another reason for the proposed revision is that the ocean dumping criteria under the Ocean Dumping Act are more stringent than those under section 403 of the Clean Water Act, and this inconsistency should be rationalized. 11 BNA Env. Rep. Current Dev. 146 (No. 5, May 30, 1980).

3. An important question is whether the long-range goal of the Ocean Dumping Act is to phase out all ocean dumping of wastes or to continue ocean dumping as a feasible disposal alternative under adequate regulation and control. Support for phasing out ocean dumping is provided in section 203 of the Act, which suggests that Title II's research and development program is intended for "determining means of minimizing or ending, as soon as possible after October 6, 1980, all dumping into ocean waters . . . of material which may unreasonably degrade or endanger human health . . . or the marine environment. . . ." 33 U.S.C. § 1443(a).

Does section 4(a) of the 1977 amendment to the Act, 33 U.S.C. § 1412a (1976), which states that the dumping of sewage sludge shall end as soon as possible, but in no case later than December 31, 1981, provide additional support? Could an argument be made that an extension beyond the 1981 deadline may be allowable if the sewage discharge in question would not "unreasonably degrade or endanger human health or the ocean environment"? See 33 U.S.C § 1443(b); Comment, *Ocean Dumping Revisited: New Statutory Deadline May Not Stop Sea Disposal of Sewage Sludge*, 7 Envt'l L. Rep. 10226 (1977).

Does the 1977 amendment affect EPA's practice of issuing interim permits for dumping sewage sludge? Consider also sections 2(a) and (b) of the Act, which discuss "unregulated dumping" and "the policy of the United States . . . to prevent or strictly limit the dumping into ocean waters of any material which would adversely affect human health, welfare, or amenities, or the marine environment, ecological systems, or economic potentialities." 33 U.S.C. §§ 1401(a), (b) (1976).

4. Note that the Ocean Dumping Act does not regulate ocean dumping per se, but rather "transportation" for the purpose of dumping. One explanation for this is that transportation of wastes was used as the basis for asserting jurisdiction beyond the 12-mile limit, to avoid potential international conflicts resulting from an attempt to regulate actual dumping on the high seas, particularly when foreign vessels are involved. Is the same approach still necessary in light of legislation like the Fishery Conservation and Management Act of 1976, 16 U.S.C. § 1811 *et seq.* (1976)? *See* Greenwald, *Pollution Control at the Maritime Frontier: The Limits of State Extraterritorial Power*, 19 Santa Clara L. Rev. 747 (1979).

The Convention on the Prevention of Marine Pollution by Dumping of Wastes and Other Matters was ratified by the United States in August 1973; the Convention entered into force on August 30, 1975. The Convention imposes on its signatories the duty to prohibit ocean dumping of high-level radioactive materials, oil, and highly toxic wastes, and to regulate strictly the dumping of heavy metals, pesticides, and other wastes. Convention on the Prevention of Marine Pollution by Dumping of Wastes and Other Matters, Art. IV(1), Annexes I, II. To meet this duty, the Ocean Dumping Act was amended in 1974 to require that the EPA apply the criteria of the Convention and its Annexes where the criteria are no less stringent than the restrictions established under the Act. 33 U.S.C. § 1412(a) (1976). The amendment also extended coverage of the act to U.S. ships transporting materials for dumping on the high seas from foreign ports. 33 U.S.C. § 1411(a)(2) (1976).

5. Some courts have found private causes of action under the Ocean Dumping Act

for parties allegedly injured by New York City's dumping. *See Township of Long Beach v. City of New York*, 445 F. Supp. 1203 (D.N.J. 1978) (suit over massive fish kill in New York bight not barred by sovereign immunity); *National Sea Clammer's Ass'n v. City of New York*, 616 F.2d 1222 (3d Cir. 1980), *rev'd*, 16 E.R.C. 1118 (June 26, 1981).

6. When is putting something in the water not "dumping" within the meaning of 33 U.S.C. § 1402(f)? *See Barcelo v. Brown*, 478 F. Supp. 646 (D.P.R. 1979), *remanded on other grounds*, 16 ERC 1593 (1st Cir. 1981), *rev'd on other grounds*, ___ U.S. ___ (April 27, 1982), (discharge of ordnance by the navy during ocean war games held not to require an ocean dumping permit).

7. For additional reading on ocean dumping, *see* Comment, *Ocean Dumping, the Revised EPA Criteria, and the National Soil Fertility Program*, 6 Envt'l L. Rep. 10144 (1976); Environmental Law Institute, *Air and Water Pollution Control Law: 1980* at 474–84 (1980); Lester, *Domestic Structure and International Technology Collaboration: Ocean Pollution Regulation*, 8 Ocean Dev. & Int'l L.J. 299 (1980); Lettow, *The Control of Marine Pollution*, in Environmental Law Institute, *Federal Environmental Law* 596 (1974); Lumsdaine, *Ocean Dumping Regulation: An Overview*, 5 Ecology L.J. 753 (1976); Miller, *Ocean Dumping—Prelude and Fugue*, 9 J. Mar. L. & Com. 51 (1973); National Advisory Committee on Oceans and Atmosphere, The Role of the Ocean in a Waste Management Strategy (1981); W. Rodgers, *Environmental Law* 409–15, 488–499 (1977); Senate Commerce Committee, Congress and the Nation's Oceans 204–07 (1977); U.S. Army Corps of Engineers, 1977 Report to Congress on Administration of Ocean Dumping Activities (1978); U.S. Congress, House Committee on Science & Technology, The Environmental Effects of Dumping in the Ocean and Great Lakes (1976); U.S. Environmental Protection Agency, Ocean Dumping in the United States—1977, Fifth Annual Report (1977); U.S. Environmental Protection Agency, Ocean Disposal of Barge-Delivered Liquid and Solid Wastes from U.S. Coastal Cities (1971); U.S. General Accounting Office, Some Communities May Not Be Able to Meet the December 31, 1981, Ocean Dumping Phaseout Deadline for Municipal Sewage Sludge (1979); Zener, *The Federal Law of Water Pollution Control*, in Environmental Law Institute, *Federal Environmental Law* 682, 738–41 (1974).

Permit Program for Dredged Material

Based on the EPA criteria, the Secretary of the Army (through the Corps) may issue permits

> . . . for the transportation of dredged material for the purpose of dumping it into ocean waters, where the Secretary determines that the dumping will not unreasonably degrade or endanger human health, welfare, or amenities, or the marine environment, ecological systems, or economic potentialities.

33 U.S.C. § 1413(a) (1976).

It is interesting to note that the amount of dredged spoil from Corps' projects is approximately 10 times the volume of spoil dumped by others. Library of Congress, Congressional Research Service, Ocean Dumping Regulation: An Appraisal of Implementation 31 (1976).

Although the EPA's criteria for determining whether to grant a permit must be applied to proposals to ocean dump dredge spoil, a waiver procedure is specified in the act if the Secretary of the Army determines that " . . . there is no economically feasible method or site available [other than a site which violates the criteria] he shall so certify and request a waiver from the Administrator of the specific requirements involved." 33 U.S.C. § 1413(a) (1976). The Administrator must grant the waiver within 30 days " . . . unless [he] finds that the dumping of the material will result in an unacceptably adverse impact on municipal water supplies, shell-fish beds, wildlife, fisheries (including spawning and breeding areas), or recreational areas." 33 U.S.C. § 1413(d) (1976).

The dredged spoil aspect of the ocean dumping program is particularly important because of the large quantities of material involved. For instance, in 1978, 34,620,000 cubic meters of dredged material were dumped, in comparison to a total of 8,101,173 tons of industrial (2,548,173) and municipal (5,535,000) nondredged wastes. U.S. Environmental Protection Agency, Annual Report to Congress (Jan.–Dec. 1979) on Administration of the Marine Protection, Research, and Sanctuaries Act of 1972, as Amended (P.L. 92–532) and Implementing the International Ocean Dumping Convention 10, 18 (1980). The disposal of dredged materials is thus approximately 75 percent of the total amount of material ocean dumped each year.

NOTES

1. Strong criticism continues to be leveled at the Corps' implementation of the act. Three specific aspects of the dredge spoil program have been questioned: (a) the adequacy of the criteria developed by EPA for dredged spoils dumping, (b) the failure of the Corps to strictly apply the EPA criteria in granting permits for ocean dumping of dredged spoils, and (c) the Corps' failure to follow the EPA criteria in its own dredge spoil dumping, which does not require a permit. Library of Congress, Congressional Research Service, Ocean Dumping Regulation: An Appraisal of Implementation 26 (1976). The conscientiousness with which the Corps carries out its own dredge disposal requirement in lieu of permits has been analogized to the "fox watching the henhouse"; that is, the Corps routinely approves its own dumping as consistent with the EPA ocean dumping criteria.

2. *National Wildlife Federation v. Benn*, 491 F. Supp. 1234 (S.D.N.Y. 1980) and *National Wildlife Federation v. Costle*, 629 F.2d 118 (D.C. Cir. 1980) are the result of 5 years of litigation between the National Wildlife Federation and EPA over ocean dumping regulation:

   There is little reason to expect that *Benn* and *Costle* will produce major changes in EPA's and the Corps' regulation of ocean dumping. Although the court in *Costle* vacated EPA's separate treatment of dredged and non-dredged materials it emphasized that the Ocean Dumping Act provides the Agency with ample authority to apply different criteria and remanded only for the purpose of requiring the Agency to justify its distinction in writing. The Corps of Engineers will almost certainly not be making any substantive changes in its procedures for implementing the Ocean Dumping Act as a result of the *Benn* decision, since the district court repeatedly deferred to the agency's expertise in implementing its responsibilities.

   If either of the opinions will have significant long term impacts, it will probably be the ruling in *Benn* that a programmatic EIS is required for the Corps' dumping program. It is hoped that such a document will contain a thorough assessment of dumping practices and their cumulative environmental impact. On the basis of the information, Congress and the agencies may wish to reappraise whether the current regulatory system is sufficiently strict.[2]

The fact is, however, that the existing system was not intended by either the signatories to the Convention or Congress to establish the kind of stringent regime that exists with respect to other environmental regulatory programs. For example, the 1972 Convention imposed few rigorous obligations on the signatories.[3] The Ocean Dumping Act is hardly more Draconian, as it gives the Corps the power to regulate itself and vests both it and EPA with wide discretion to permit dumping as they see fit. Thus, neither EPA nor the Corps can be condemned for failing to regulate, at least with respect to dredged wastes, as aggressively as some might wish. This implicit conclusion is the most striking aspect of *Benn* and *Costle*.

10 Envt'l L. Rep. 10181, 10182 (1980).

3. As noted above, section 106(d) of the Ocean Dumping Act provides that "no state shall adopt or enforce any rule or regulation relating to any activity regulated by this subchapter." 33 U.S.C. § 1416(d) (1976). In light of section 106(d), what role can state and local governments play in the regulation of ocean dumping? Can ocean dumping directly affect the coastal zone of a state? If so, must the Corps' issuance of an ocean dumping permit or Corps' dumping of its own dredge spoils be consistent with the state's federally approved coastal zone management program?

4. For a study of the pollution effects of dredge spoil dumping, *see* Thibodeaux, Benedict & Grimwood, *Ocean Dumping of Dredged Material–Gulf of Mexico*, 2 Coastal Zone '78 at 1113 (1978).

SECTION B: OCEAN DISCHARGES

The previous section examined the legal authority provided by the Marine Protection, Research and Sanctuaries Act (MPRSA) for the control of ocean dumping. This section examines the authority provided by section 403 of the Clean Water Act to control the discharge of pollutants into the waters of the territorial seas, the contiguous zone, and the oceans.

Section 403 calls for prevention of unreasonable degradation of the marine environment and authorizes the use of effluent limitations, including a prohibition of discharge, if necessary, to ensure this goal. Although section 403 of the CWA and section 102 of the MPRSA are similar, they are not identical. In essence, however, the MPRSA applies to dumping from vessels into ocean waters and does not apply to discharges from outfalls, which are subject to

[2]Congress may also wish to reevaluate dumping practices based on a comprehensive national survey of public opinion on environmental issues recently released by the Council on Environmental Quality, which reveals that 57 percent of the persons polled believe that the government should prohibit the disposal of hazardous chemical wastes in the ocean. Final Results of the Resources for the Future, National Environmental Survey for the President's Council on Environmental Quality, Question 38 (Aug. 1980) (Released Oct. 9, 1980).

[3]T.I.A.S. No. 8165, ELR STAT. & REG. 40329. The most rigorous requirement is the ban on the dumping of certain substances listed in Annex I of the Convention; however, dredged wastes may be dumped despite contamination with "trace" amounts of these substances. EPA's regulations do not clearly define what constitutes trace amounts.

control under the CWA. All discharges seaward of the inner boundary of the territorial seas are subject to section 403 requirements.

The administrative framework of the CWA differs fundamentally from that provided in the MPRSA. With certain exceptions, the CWA focuses on state pollution control programs which are federally reviewed and approved, thus giving states substantial regulatory authority over sources of pollution. The MPRSA is premised on a federally run program and explicitly preempts state regulatory activity.

Section 301 of the CWA makes unlawful "the discharge of any pollutant by any person" except in compliance with the terms of that and other specifically enumerated sections. In short, section 301 prohibits the discharge of untreated sewage. In addition, section 301(b)(1)(B) requires all publicly owned sewage treatment works to achieve secondary treatment as defined by EPA. See section 304(d)(1). Criteria developed pursuant to section 403 supplement section 301 requirements and are applicable to permit proceedings authorized by section 402 as well as to municipal marine discharges seeking a modification of the secondary treatment requirements as provided by section 301(h). It should be noted, however, that the ocean discharge guidelines promulgated by EPA on October 3, 1980 (45 Fed. Reg. 65942), *presume* that discharges in compliance with section 301(h) and state water quality standards will not cause unreasonable degradation of the marine environment.

Inconsistencies that exist between the regulations implementing the CWA and the MPRSA are the result of several factors. Ocean dumping criteria first promulgated by EPA in 1973 also served as ocean discharge criteria. The ocean dumping regulations were amended in 1977, but EPA did not promulgate new ocean discharge criteria until 1980. EPA has cautioned that "in addition to any statutory distinctions, differences in the manner of disposal and the types of pollutants discharged may warrant different regulatory approaches under these two statutes." 45 Fed. Reg. 65952–53 (Oct. 3, 1980).

NOTES

1. The regulations concerning the Modification of Secondary Treatment Requirements for Discharges into Marine Waters (301(h) regulations) were issued on June 15, 1979, 44 Fed. Reg. 34784 (1979), and are codified at 40 C.F.R. § 125.56–.67 (1980). The opportunity to obtain a modification of applicable secondary requirements is available only to publicly owned treatment works (POTW) which have an existing discharge into marine waters as of December 27, 1977. Additionally, the POTW must have submitted a preliminary application to EPA by September 24, 1978. 44 Fed. Reg. at 34785. The regulations, 40 C.F.R. § 125.59 (b)(7)(i) (1980), specified that modified discharges located within an area covered by an approved state coastal zone management program must be certified as consistent with that program pursuant to section 307(c) of the federal Coastal Zone Management Act, 16 U.S.C. § 1456(c) (1976). The regulations, 40 C.F.R. § 125.59 (b)(7)(iii) (1980), also provide that modified discharges are prohibited in designated marine or estuarine sanctuaries if not certified as consistent with sanctuary regulations adopted pursuant to Title III of the Marine Protection

Research and Sanctuaries Act, 16 U.S.C. § 1431 *et seq.* (1976), or the Coastal Zone Management Act, 16 U.S.C. § 1461 (1976).

EPA has adopted a special policy with respect to coastal native villages in Alaska and small communities in Puerto Rico and the U.S. territories in the Caribbean and Pacific. EPA will use its discretion in scheduling secondary treatment for these communities

where industrial toxic wastes are not a factor, in cases where such course of action is determined to be in the interest of providing basic public health protection, and where any such delays will not result in unreasonable adverse water quality impacts. In such cases, attention will be given to planning wastewater treatment facilities for these communities with the objective of assuring that inadequacies in sewage collection or treatment which result in public health problems are remedied, and to examining alternatives to traditional secondary treatment, including individual systems and BPWTT [best practicable water treatment technology] options (including land treatment). . . .

44 Fed. Reg. 34784, 34792 (1979).

EPA's 301(h) regulations were upheld with two exceptions in *Natural Resources Defense Council v. EPA*, 16 ERC 1417 (D.C. Cir. 1981).

2. In adding section 301(h) to the Clean Water Act, 33 U.S.C. § 1311(h) (Supp. 1, 1977), Congress recognized the difficulty in meeting federal water quality standards, as well as the ocean's ability to absorb a certain amount of waste materials. Is this shift in policy consistent with the policy in the 1977 amendment to the Ocean Dumping Act, 33 U.S.C. § 1421(a) (Supp. 1, 1977), mandating an end by 1982 of ocean dumping of sewage sludge? Consider again the issue of whether the metropolitan New York area can meet the 1981 ocean dumping deadline. Would a modification such as section 301(h) embodies be conceivable?

3. Ocean discharges under sections 403, 405, and 301 of the Clean Water Act must be consistent with federally approved state coastal zone management programs. In what situations would an ocean discharge be inconsistent with a state's coastal zone management program? Would EPA approval of a continued primary treatment discharge under section 301(h) be inconsistent with a state coastal zone management program requiring secondary treatment only if the amount discharged was increased? *See* 12 Nautilus Press, Coastal Zone Mgmt. Newsletter No. 5, Feb. 4, 1981 at 6.

4. In *Pacific Legal Foundation v. Costle,* 586 F.2d 650 (9th Cir. 1978), *rev'd in part*, 100 S. Ct. 1095 (1980), *reh. denied*, 100 S. Ct. 2170 (1980), the court held that an ocean discharge permit, issued in compliance with the then existing ocean discharge (section 403) guidelines, could be reissued at a time when the previous guidelines had been withdrawn for revision, but "at some point an 'extention' may become an original issuance rather than a reissuance." Would *modification* of the secondary treatment standards that an ocean discharge must meet constitute a new issuance or a reissuance?

5. In *Barcelo v. Brown*, 478 F. Supp. 646 (D.P.R. 1979), *remanded on other grounds*, 16 ERC 1593 (1st Cir. 1981), *rev'd on other grounds*, ____U.S.____(April 27, 1982), which found that navy bombing practice in nearshore waters was not "dumping" but concluded that the activity was a "discharge" under the Clean Water Act, the court stated that "it would be a strained construction of ambiguous language for the Court to interpret that the release or firing of ordnance from aircraft into the navigable waters of Vicques is not 'any addition of pollutant . . . from any point source' particularly in view of the broad rather than narrow interpretation given to this type of statute." 478 F. Supp. at 664. Was the court correct in requiring the navy to file for an NPDES permit to cover such activity?

6. The section 403 ocean discharge criteria also apply to discharges from offshore oil and gas facilities. *See* Nautilus Press, Coastal Zone Mgmt. Newsletter No. 40, Oct. 8, 1980 at 5. *See also API v. Costle*, 15 ERC. 1138 (W.D. Louisiana 1980).

7. For additional material on ocean discharges, *see City of North Miami v. Train*, 377 F. Supp. 1264 (S.D. Fla. 1974); Belvedere, Murphy, Van Weele & Gilbert, *Southwest Ocean Outfall: Coastal and Offshore Considerations*, 3 Coastal Zone '78 at 1845 (1978); Bendix & Sahm, *Environmental Review of a Coastal Sewerage Project*, 4 Coastal Zone '78 at 2911 (1978); Treadwell, Hervert, Otus, Gilbert & Plunkett, *Southwest Ocean Outfall: Geotechnical and Oceanographic Predesign Studies*, 3 Coastal Zone '78 at 1862 (1978); Williams, Meighan, Treadwell & Murphy, *Environmental Case History of an Ocean Outfall*, 1 Coastal Zone '80 at 703 (1980).

8. For efforts to decide how the Clean Water Act, the Rivers and Harbors Act, the Marine Protection, Research and Sanctuaries Act, the federal common law of nuisance, and the federal constitution relate to sewage discharges and other waste disposal practices which cause substantial fish and shellfish kills, *see Moore v. Hampton Roads Sanitation District Comm'n*, 557 F.2d 1030 (4th Cir. 1977); *National Sea Clammers Ass'n v. New York*, 616 F.2d 1222 (3d Cir. 1980), *rev'd*, 16 ERC 1118 (June 26, 1981); *Township of Long Beach v. City of New York*, 445 F. Supp. 1203 (D. New Jersey 1978). In *Columbia River Fisherman's Protective Union v. City of St. Helens*, 160 Or. 654, 87 P.2d 195 (1939), plaintiff commercial gillnet fishers were held to have a special interest distinct from the public in fishing their drift which entitled them to enjoin defendant city's sewage pollution, which destroyed their nets and interfered with their fishing. *See Hampton v. North Carolina Pulp Co.*, 27 S.E.2d 538 (1943). *But see Hampton v. North Carolina Pulp Co.*, 49 F. Supp. 625 (E.D. N.C. 1943) (lower riparian may not sue upper riparian whose pollution had destroyed the fish in the river).

SECTION C: THERMAL POLLUTION

BROGA, "THERMAL POLLUTION," in ENVIRONMENTAL LAW INSTITUTE, AIR AND WATER POLLUTION CONTROL LAW: 1980 at 466–469 (1980)

Thermal pollution, the alteration of natural water temperatures by man, is an extremely pervasive pollutant form[4] which can have subtle, but potentially devastating effects on aquatic life forms. An increase in water temperature can affect the development, the metabolism and even the birth rate of aquatic organisms. Further, a rise in water temperature decreases the quantity of dissolved oxygen in the water, while heightening the toxic effects of some harmful chemicals.

Heat, like other pollutants under the Federal Water Pollution Control Act, is regulated primarily by technology-based effluent standards. Although the general rule is that such standards should be uniformly applied, section 316 of the Act creates a unique exception for thermal discharges. This exception allows an individual discharger to demonstrate to the permit-issuing authority (either

[4]By one estimate, steam electric generating plants will require one half to three quarters of the average daily runoff in the U.S. in 1990. *See* S. Mathur, Waste Heat from Steam Electric Generating Plants and Its Control, 54 (published by the Federal Water Pollution Control Administration, 1968).

EPA or the state) that an effluent limit is "more stringent than necessary to assure the protection and propagation of a balanced indigenous population of shellfish, fish and wildlife. . . ."[5] If this showing is made, then the individual discharger may obtain a variance permitting emissions in excess of the effluent limitation.[6]

Briefly stated, the rationale for this exception is based upon the following considerations. Although it can have significant environmental consequences, heat dissipates over time. Thus, the consequences of allowing an excessive thermal discharge are felt to be less drastic than the consequences of mistakenly allowing the discharge of a more persistent pollutant. The second consideration supporting the section 316 exception is the belief that "the optimum method of control of any thermal discharge may be dependent upon local conditions, including the size and type of the receiving body of water."[7] Adjudications under section 316 are therefore made on a case-by-case basis.

Recent events affecting control of thermal pollution include further developments in the controversy surrounding the proposed construction of the Seabrook nuclear power generating plant in New Hampshire . . . .

NOTE

For litigation concerning thermal effluents from the Seabrook nuclear plant, *see Atomic Energy Seacoast Anti-Pollution League v. Costle*, 597 F.2d 306 (1st Cir. 1979); *In the Matter of Public Service Co. of New Hampshire, Administrator, Environmental Protection Agency*, No. 76–7, 7 Envt'l L. Rep. 30007 (1977), *rev'd and remanded sub. nom. Seacoast Anti-Pollution League v. Costle*, 572 F.2d 872 (1st Cir. 1978), *cert. denied*, 439 U.S. 824 (1978).

For other litigation involving thermally polluted effluents, *see Appalachian Power Co. v. Train*, 545 F.2d 1351 (4th Cir. 1976); *Sandusky Portland Cement Co. v. Dixon Pure Ice Co.*, 221 F. 200 (7th Cir. 1915) (riparian rights and nuisance); *State v. Jersey Central Power & Light Co.*, 69 N.J. 102, 351 A.2d 337 (1976); *United States v. Florida Power & Light Co.*, 311 F. Supp. 1391 (S.D. Fla. 1970) (hot water held to be "refuse" requiring permit under federal Refuse Act but preliminary injunction refused in absence of showing of irreparable harm to bay); *Weyerhaeuser Co. v. Costle*, 590 F.2d 1011 (D.C. Cir. 1978); *Wisconsin Electric Power Co. v. State Natural Resources Board*, 90 Wis. 2d 656, 280 N.W.2d 218 (1979) (Wisconsin thermal standards held invalid as exceeding federal effluent limitations).

For reading regarding thermal pollution, *see* Bloom, *Heat–A Growing Water Pollution Problem*, 1 BNA Envt'l Rep. Mon. No. 4 (1970); Comment, *Thermal Electric Power and Water Pollution: A Siting Approach*, 45 Ind. L.J. 61 (1970); Comment, *Thermal Pollution: "The Dishonorable Discharge"–New York's Criteria Governing Heated Liquids*, 34 Albany L. Rev. 539 (1970); Edwards, *Legal Control of Thermal Pollution*, 2 Nat. Res. Law. 1 (1969); Jost, *Cold Facts on Hot Water: Legal Aspects of Thermal Pollution*, 1969 Wis. L. Rev. 253 (1969); Maloney, *More Heat than Light: Thermal Pollution Versus Heat Energy Utilization*, 25 U. Fla. L. Rev. 693 (1972); Thomas, *Thermal Discharges: A Legal Problem*, 38 Tenn. L. Rev. 369 (1971); U.S. Environmental Protection Agency, Biologically Allowable Thermal Pollution Limits (1974).

[5]33 U.S.C. § 1326.

[6]EPA has issued regulations outlining the factors, criteria, and standards for establishment and imposition of alternative thermal effluent limitations under Section 316(a), 43 Fed. Reg. 37134 (August 21, 1978).

[7]H.R. 11896, 92d Cong., 2d Sess. § 316 (1972).

Comprehensive Ocean Management

SECTION A: MARINE SANCTUARIES

Title III of the Marine Protection, Research and Sanctuaries Act of 1972 (Act) authorizes the Secretary of Commerce, with presidential approval, to designate ocean waters as marine sanctuaries for the purpose of preserving or restoring their conservation, recreational, ecological, or esthetic values. Marine sanctuaries may be designated as far seaward as the outer edge of the continental shelf and in coastal waters where the tide ebbs and flows, or in the Great Lakes and their connecting waters. Marine sanctuaries are built around the existence of distinctive marine resources whose protection and beneficial use requires comprehensive geographically oriented planning and management. The National Oceanic and Atmospheric Administration (NOAA) administers the program through its Office of Coastal Zone Management (OCZM).

As of January 1981, six sanctuaries had been designated:

1. *Monitor Marine Sanctuary:* This sanctuary serves to protect the wreck of the Civil War ironclad, U.S.S. *Monitor.* It was designated in January 1975 and is an area 1 mile in diameter southeast of Cape Hatteras, North Carolina.

2. *Key Largo Coral Reef Marine Sanctuary*: This sanctuary, designated in December 1975, provides protective management of a 100-square-mile coral reef area south of Miami.

3. *Channel Islands National Marine Sanctuary:* This sanctuary, designated in September 1980, consists of an area of approximately 1,250 square nautical miles off the coast of California adjacent to the northern Channel

Islands and Santa Barbara Island. The sanctuary ensures that valuable habitats for marine mammals and seabirds are preserved.

4. *Looe Key National Marine Sanctuary:* The sanctuary consists of a 5-square-nautical-mile submerged section of the Florida reef tract southwest of Big Pine Key. The site includes a beautiful "spur and groove" coral formation supporting a diverse marine community and a wide variety of human uses.

5. *Gray's Reef National Marine Sanctuary*: The site is a submerged live bottom area located on the South Atlantic continental shelf due east of Sapelo Island, Georgia. The sanctuary, which encompasses about 17 square nautical miles, would protect a considerably productive and unusual habitat for a wide variety of species, including corals, tropical fish, and sea turtles.

6. *Point Reyes–Farallon Islands National Marine Sanctuary:* This 948-square-nautical-mile area off the California coast north of San Francisco contains a diverse array of marine mammals and marine birds, as well as fishery, plant, and benthic resources. The sanctuary ensures that the area receives long-term, comprehensive protection.

Several other locations from Puerto Rico and the Virgin Islands to Hawaii were under consideration for designation. *See* U.S. Office of Coastal Zone Management, CZM Information Exchange, January 1981 at 42–43. *See also* the final environmental impact statements published by OCZM in connection with the designation of each sanctuary; Curtis & Phillips, *Proposed Gray's Reef Marine Sanctuary: A Case Study,* 3 Coastal Zone '80 at 1969 (1980); and the following additional publications by OCZM: Hawaiian Humpback Whale Sanctuary Workshop (1979); Issue Paper on Possible California Marine Sanctuary Sites (1978); Key Largo Coral Reef Marine Sanctuary Management Plan (1979).

Section 302(a) of the Act provides that the Secretary of Commerce

> . . . after consultation with the Secretaries of State, Defense, the Interior, and Transportation, the Administrator [of the Environmental Protection Agency], and the heads of other interested Federal agencies, and with the approval of the President, may designate as marine sanctuaries those areas of the ocean waters, as far seaward as the Outer Continental Shelf . . . , of other coastal waters where the tide ebbs and flows, or of the Great Lakes and their connecting waters, which he determines necessary for the purpose of preserving or restoring such areas for their conservation, recreational, ecological, or esthetic values. The consultation shall include an opportunity to review and comment on a specific proposed designation.

16 U.S.C. § 1432(a) (1976). Other sections deal with consultation requirements, enforcement, and regulation of other marine activities. Any sanctuary located within the territorial waters of a state can be disapproved by the state's governor within 60 days of designation. 16 U.S.C. § 1432(b)(2)(A) (Supp. 1981).

Equally important is what is absent from the legislation. First, the designation of a marine sanctuary requires no congressional approval as does the establishment of a national seashore or wildlife refuge, although the act was amended in 1980 to provide for congressional disapproval by a concurrent resolution adopted within 60 session days after a designation. 16 U.S.C. § 1432(b)(2)(B) (Supp. 1981). Second, the Secretary of Commerce determines the activities allowed and prohibited within the sanctuary. Regulations must be issued to accompany each sanctuary as it is created, tailored to promote the purpose for which the sanctuary is established.

The program lay dormant, without funding or regulations, for 2 years after enactment. The first use of the program was to protect the wreck of the Civil War ironclad the U.S.S. *Monitor,* which lay 16 miles off Cape Hatteras, North Carolina. The regulations for the *Monitor* sanctuary describe the *Monitor* as a "source of historic, cultural, aesthetic and/or maritime information" and prohibit activities that might hinder orderly archaeological research. 15 C.F.R. § 924 (1980). The second sanctuary was established to protect a coral reef off Key Largo, Florida. Regulations prohibit destruction of the coral in any way, dredging or filling activities, construction of any kind, and discharge of pollutants within the sanctuary, but allow diving and sport and commercial fishing, including the taking of crab and lobster. Exceptions to the prohibited activities may be granted by the Administrator of NOAA if for the purpose of research or salvage of lost property. 15 C.F.R. § 929 (1980).

Environmentalists originally had grandiose plans for the sanctuary program. They read the flexibility provided the Secretary in defining a sanctuary, and the other provisions of the act, as a broad mandate from Congress to use the sanctuary system as a tool for comprehensively managing all marine activities within a designated area. Section 302(f) originally read as follows:

> After a marine sanctuary has been designated under this section, the Secretary, after consultation with other interested Federal agencies, shall issue necessary and reasonable regulations to control any activities permitted within the designated marine sanctuary, and no permit, license, or other authorization issued pursuant to any other authority shall be valid unless the Secretary shall certify that the permitted activity is consistent with the purposes of this title . . . and can be carried out within the regulations promulgated under this section.

16 U.S.C. § 1432(f) (1976).

In 1980, section 302(f) was amended to read in part as follows:

> (f) (1) The terms of the designation shall include the geographic area included within the sanctuary; the characteristics of the area that give it conservation, recreational, ecological or esthetic value; and the types of activities that will be subject to regulation by the Secretary in order to protect those characteristics. The terms of the designation may be modified only by the same procedures through which an original designation is made.
>
> (2) The Secretary, after consultation with other interested Federal and State agencies, shall issue necessary and reasonable regulations to implement the terms of the designation and control the activities described in it, except that all permits,

licenses, and other authorizations issued pursuant to any other authority shall be valid unless such regulations otherwise provide.

. . . .

16 U.S.C. § 1432(f) (Supp. 3 1980).

NOTES

1. If the designation for a sanctuary is silent on floating nuclear power plants, would the siting of such plants within the sanctuary be subject to regulation by the Secretary of Commerce?

2. Does authority to regulate activities occurring within a sanctuary include the power to meet threats from outside the sanctuary? For example, an oil spill from a source outside the sanctuary could drift across the sanctuary boundary. Ultimately, must the Secretary depend on the cooperation of other agencies to protect marine sanctuaries?

3. What values is the marine sanctuary program intended to protect? Should all ocean areas with any of the following resource values be considered for sanctuary designation?

   (1) Important habitat on which any of the following depend for one or more life cycle activity, including breeding, feeding, rearing young, staging, resting or migrating:
      (i) Rare, endangered or threatened species, or
      (ii) Species with limited geographic distribution, or
      (iii) Species rare in the waters to which the [Marine Sanctuaries] Act applies, or
      (iv) Commercially or recreationally valuable marine species.
   (2) A marine ecosystem of exceptional productivity indicated by an abundance and variety of marine species at the various trophic levels in the food web.
   (3) An area of exceptional recreational opportunity relating to its distinctive marine characteristics.
   (4) Historic or cultural remains of widespread public interest.
   (5) Distinctive or fragile ecological or geologic features of exceptional scientific research or education value.

   15 C.F.R. § 922.21(b) (1980). In addition to the values listed above, the Act states that preserving esthetic values is one reason for establishing marine sanctuaries. Could a marine sanctuary be used to protect some particularly pleasing ocean vista from the impact of visible drilling platforms?
      Could designation of a sanctuary ever result in restrictions on commercial and recreational fishing and diving activities?
      Which resource values should have priority in the designation of marine sanctuaries? Other factors taken into account in the designation of marine sanctuaries have included the potential threat to the resources of the area, the significance of the area for research, the value of the area in complementing other areas or programs with similar objectives, the beauty of the area, the economic value of the area which might have to be forgone if designated a sanctuary, and the economic benefit to be derived from protecting the area.

4. Should the marine sanctuaries program be used to resolve conflicts in ocean resource use and development? If so, how? Reread *Massachusetts v. Andrus* and

the accompanying notes in Chapter 6, Section B, and consider the following excerpt. *See also* U.S. Office of Coastal Zone Management, Georges Bank Marine Sanctuary Issue Paper (1979).

FINN, "INTERAGENCY RELATIONSHIPS IN MARINE RESOURCE CONFLICTS: SOME LESSONS FROM OCS OIL AND GAS LEASING,"
4 Harvard Environmental Law Review 359, 386–88 (1980)

The Georges Bank case demonstrates that significant institutional and legal difficulties can arise in cases where designation of a marine sanctuary could affect an action proposed by another agency. This potential for conflict is inherent in the Marine Sanctuaries Act, since once a sanctuary is designated, the Department of Commerce may regulate any activities within that area. Interagency conflict has been aggravated when NOAA, acting on behalf of Commerce, has begun the sanctuary designation process in response to actions proposed by other agencies.

NOAA should therefore develop a systematic process for designating marine sanctuaries, to limit the wide discretion it has under current regulations. The agency should develop a set of concrete management objectives under which potential sites would be classified. It should also establish a definite schedule for consideration of potential marine sanctuaries, perhaps in connection with foreseeable actions of other agencies, such as Interior's five-year oil and gas leasing program. Although NOAA could remain free to propose new designations outside the framework of such a schedule, it should try to avoid initiation of the consideration process in reaction to proposed actions of other federal agencies.

Second, NOAA should amend its regulations to clarify the Act's requirement that other federal agencies' actions be certified as consistent with the purposes of the statute. NOAA should also explain the relationship of this requirement to the regulations that are to be adopted for each sanctuary, and determine whether the consistency requirement extends to activities outside the sanctuary that could affect resources and activities within it.

Third, the present Act or the regulations should be amended to avoid one source of potential interagency conflict—NOAA's authority to adopt additional substantive regulations concerning activities in a sanctuary. The present Act states that "necessary and reasonable" regulations should be adopted after designation of a sanctuary. These provisions appear to be consistent with a much more limited approach to marine sanctuary management. Instead of adopting additional regulations for activities within a sanctuary, NOAA could establish specific policies for the sanctuary. NOAA would remain free to veto proposed actions of other federal agencies, as states do under the CZMA, by refusing to certify them as consistent with these policies. NOAA could also adopt regulations to simplify sanctuary administration.

The interests of applicants for federal authorizations would not be infringed by such a procedure, since designation of a sanctuary would be made only after extensive consultation within the executive branch and participation by the public and prospective applicants in the designation process, including review of the EIS on the proposed sanctuary. NOAA should also provide for a hearing when there is controversy about a request for certification, and accompany any denial of certification with a statement of reasons. The prospect that NOAA might refuse to certify agencies' actions on the basis of policies adopted for a sanctuary would be less likely to arouse opposition by federal agencies during the designation process than would adoption of a new, preemptive set of regulations to govern activities already regulated by other agencies.

If NOAA did not promulgate substantive regulations for marine sanctuaries, and established a coherent program for future consideration and designation, the legal and institutional difficulties evident in the Georges Bank case would virtually disappear. Proposed actions of other federal agencies could not be challenged on the grounds that NOAA was considering additional regulations applicable to them, and consideration of the marine sanctuary alternative to proposed actions would become more manageable.

NOTE

For additional reading on marine sanctuaries, *See* Blum & Blumstein, *The Marine Sanctuaries Program: A Framework for Critical Areas Management in the Sea,* 8 Envt'l L. Rep. 50016 (1978); Lettow, *The Control of Marine Pollution,* in Environmental Law Institute, Federal Environmental Law Institute, *Federal Environmental Law* 676–77 (1974); M. Lynch, B. Laird & T. Smolen, *Marine and Estuarine Sanctuaries* (1974); O'Sullivan, *Marine Sanctuary Institutional Analysis,* 3 Coastal Zone '80 at 1979 (1980); Senate Commerce Committee, Coastal Zone Management and Marine Sanctuaries Reauthorization, 96th Cong., 1st Sess., Serial No. 96–31 at 14–16, 38–43 (Apr. 11, 1979); Kifer, *NOAA's Marine Sanctuary Program,* 2 Coastal Zone Mgmt. J. 177 (1975).

SECTION B: ALTERNATIVE MANAGEMENT REGIMES

Given that the marine sanctuaries program provides only a limited foundation for comprehensive ocean management, what other approaches are possible? Should the multiple-use, sustained-yield approach to public lands management onshore be extended offshore to the ocean waters and seabeds subject to United States jurisdiction? Should ocean waters be managed separately from seabed resources? Should the legal regime governing the territorial sea simply be extended seaward? Or should the present outer continental shelf lands management regime merely be broadened to make it more comprehensive? Where should the balance between development and preservation be struck? How should the interests of national security and private industry be accounted for? How much management responsibility should each level of government—federal, state, and local—exercise? These are but a few of the important questions to be answered in discussing ocean management. In formulating your responses to them, reread the excerpts from Epting and Laist in Chapter 1, Section A, *supra,* and consider the following excerpt:

FINN, "INTERAGENCY RELATIONSHIPS
IN MARINE RESOURCE CONFLICTS,"
4 Harvard Environmental Law Review 360–66, 381–82 (1980)

Although the resources of the OCS have been subject to federal jurisdiction since 1945, the federal effort to manage marine resources has evolved incrementally, largely in response to the development of new or expanded maritime activities. Three major approaches have emerged. In general, early statutes applicable in marine areas established *regulatory* programs which applied to specific activities of concern, such as the regulation of OCS oil and gas activities. Agencies administering regulatory programs are commonly accorded broad discretion to regulate the activities within their jurisdiction in order to achieve enumerated statutory goals. These goals generally include both objectives for development of regulated activity and more general mandates to protect other values, including resource values.

Although most federal programs relating to marine areas are regulatory in nature, in the last decade Congress has recognized that the regulation of specific activities may not adequately protect valuable marine resources. As a result Congress has established a number of *resource protection* programs, in the Departments of Commerce and the Interior, concerning endangered species, fishery resources, and marine mammals. Agencies administering resource protection programs are generally authorized to protect the resource through direct regulation of activities which could injure the resource, review of actions of other agencies which could affect the resource, and affirmative programs of study, planning, and management.

Congress has also enacted programs for the *comprehensive management* of activities and resources within specially identified marine areas. The coastal zones of states with federally-approved coastal zone management (CZM) programs and marine sanctuaries designated by the Secretary of Commerce are governed by such programs. Certain actions of federal agencies must be consistent with the management plans for these areas.

Resource protection and comprehensive management statutes impose additional responsibilities on the action agencies with primary authority to regulate specific activities. The courts have required that such agencies consider the objectives of resource protection statutes and specific management alternatives that would be available under comprehensive management programs. Action agencies must also comply with various procedural mechanisms created by statute or executive directive to coordinate their actions with mission agencies. The National Environmental Policy Act (NEPA), for example, subjects agency actions to formal environmental analysis and interagency and public review. Similarly, the Fish and Wildlife Coordination Act (FWCA) requires action agencies to consult formally with the Fish and Wildlife Service (FWS) of Interior, the National Marine Fisheries Service (NMFS) of the National Oceanic and Atmospheric Administration (NOAA), and state wildlife agencies, in order to ensure that the action agency gives "equal consideration" to wildlife values when undertaking certain actions. The Endangered Species Act (ESA) establishes a highly structured consultation procedure, requiring the preparation of a "biological opinion" by the consulting agency (either the FWS or the NMFS) to guide the action agency in interpreting its duties under the Act. The strongest coordinating mechanism is the requirement that certain federal actions be certified as "consistent" with applicable comprehensive management programs, such as the marine sanctuaries program and approved state coastal zone management programs.

. . . .

Because of the fragmentation of federal authority offshore among programs with potentially conflicting objectives, federal agencies have with increasing frequency clashed over resource protection matters. These disagreements typically occur when a regulatory agency proposes to authorize an activity that other agencies dispute on the grounds that it could harm valuable resources or impede effective overall management of the area. The responses of these agencies create interagency relationships that are of great importance to the success of the federal effort to manage marine resources.

. . . .

The first benefit offered by interagency relationships is that they tend to broaden the perspective applied to regulatory actions. Through the establishment of specific coordinating mechanisms, action agencies may be forced to consider competing statutory objectives, the views of mission agencies regarding resource protection matters, and practical resource management alternatives.

Second, interagency relationships bring the expertise of resource-oriented agencies to bear on proposed regulatory actions. Regulatory decisions with great significance for marine resources are often entrusted to agencies whose primary missions are not concerned with those resources. Although agencies conducting regulatory programs are often required to weigh factors apart from their primary missions, their consideration of such factors will inevitably be from their own institutional viewpoints, and thus may be insensitive to complex resource considerations.

Finally, interagency relationships could contribute to a public sense of the legitimacy of regulatory decisions. If such decisions were made in the context of lively interactions among agencies with contrasting missions, the public might not feel that regulatory agencies had been "captured" by their constituents.

These advantages suggest that interagency relationships should be encouraged in marine resources management, and perhaps in other fields as well. . . .

NOTES

1. What would be the role of state and local governments in the process envisioned by Finn? What should be the role of state and local governments in ocean management? *See* U.S. Department of Commerce, *Ocean Management: Seeking a New Perspective* 41–45, 56 (1980).

2. For an interesting attempt to assess management and research needs in the Atlantic offshore area comprehensively, *see* Delaware Sea Grant Program, Atlan-

tic Offshore Users Workshop (1977). *See also*, J. Armstrong and & P. Ryner, *Coastal Waters: A Management Analysis* (1978); Beltrami & Carroll, *A Land-Use Planning Model for Coastal Zone Management,* 4 Coastal Zone Mgmt. J. 83 (1978); Breaux, *Coastal and Ocean Management: Perspectives for the Future,* 4 Coastal Zone '78 at 2459 (1978); Brown, *Ocean Uses and Coastal Planning,* 4 Coastal Zone '78 at 2587 (1978); Delogu, *Land Use Control Principles Applied to Offshore Coastal Waters,* 59 K. L.J. 606 (1971); Island County, Washington, Shoreline Management Act Master Program (1978); Ryner & Armstrong, *Coastal Waters: A Management Issue*, 1 Coastal Zone '78 at 285 (1978); P. Ryner, *The Management of Surface Activities on Lakes, Streams, Rivers and Bays* (1973).

10

Alteration of Coastal Waterways and Wetlands

The federal government's first effort at curbing water pollution was the Rivers and Harbors Appropriation Act of 1899, 30 Stat. 1151, 33 U.S.C. § 401 *et seq.*, whose most noteworthy provisions were sections 10 and 13. Section 10 (discussed later in this subsection) required Corps of Engineers' permits for dredging and filling operations and construction in navigable waters. Section 13, commonly referred to as the Refuse Act, prohibited the dumping of refuse ("other than that flowing from streets and sewers and passing therefrom in a liquid state") into navigable waters. Dumping was allowed with a permit issued by the Corps, but only after a determination that the refuse would not injure anchorage

The Refuse Act was an ineffective weapon against water pollution. For almost 50 years after its enactment, polluters continued to degrade the nation's waters while the federal government sat idly by. With the passage of the Federal Water Pollution Control Act (FWPCA), 62 Stat. 1155, in 1948 came greater congressional recognition of the pollution problems plaguing our waters. But under the 1948 act, the federal government appeared only to be testing the waters—its role was limited to providing technical assistance and funds to bolster state and local pollution control programs.

In 1965, the federal government assumed a stronger role in establishing water quality standards. The Water Quality Act of 1965, Pub. L. No. 89–234 (amending the FWPCA), gave states the opportunity to establish water quality standards for interstate waters; in the absence of state action, the federal government would formulate standards. The standards were to emphasize the maintenance of the quality of the receiving waters rather than to deal with the treatment of discharged substances.

Meanwhile, the Refuse Act received some attention from the U.S. Supreme Court. Although the Act had long been interpreted as applying only to those discharges that obstructed or impeded navigation, the Supreme Court ruled otherwise in the 1966 case of *United States v. Standard Oil Company,* 384 U.S. 224, 86 S. Ct. 1427, 16 L. Ed. 2d 492 (1966). The Court declared that "refuse" encompassed all foreign substances and pollutants except those expressly excluded and that the Act reached not only navigational menaces but pollution. However, it was not until 1970, amid a growing clamor for "zero discharge" of pollutants, that enforcement of the Refuse Act began in earnest.

Two years later, after Congress overrode President Nixon's veto of the Federal Water Pollution Control Amendments of 1972, Pub. L. No. 92–500, the federal government was given primary responsibility for directing the cleanup of the nation's waters.

With respect to construction activities such as dredging and filling, permits are required under both section 10 of the Rivers and Harbors Act of 1899 and section 404 of the Federal Water Pollution Control Act Amendments of 1972. The extent of federal control of dredge and fill activities in wetlands was a key issue in the congressional debate over the Clean Water Act of 1977. This act, which amended the FWPCA, was the next step in the transformation of the Corps jurisdiction. The CWA also provides for the transfer of some federal dredge and fill permit-issuing authority to states that submit a program meeting the Act's requirements. 33 U.S.C. § 1344(g),(h),(i) (1978). The state programs are approved and monitored by the Corps of Engineers and the Environmental Protection Agency. *See* 40 C.F.R. § 1261 (1980).

When reading the cases and materials in this chapter, consider how they reflect the evolution of the Corps' jurisdiction. Also note the difference between the Corps' jurisdiction under the Rivers and Harbors Act and its jurisdiction under the FWPCA.

SECTION A: THE CORPS' REGULATORY ROLE

The Army Corps of Engineers is one of the most powerful and visible of the many federal agencies having jurisdiction in the coastal zone. Through its involvement in the construction and maintenance of civil works projects and its regulation of dredging and filling, the Corps has substantial influence over the use of coastal resources.

Initially, the regulatory role of the Corps consisted merely of the general authority to establish lines beyond which piers and wharves could not be built and fill deposits could not be made. This power evolved into the current Corps program, which requires the issuance of a permit as a prerequisite to any dredge or fill activity in navigable waters. Permits are issued by the Secretary of the Army acting through the regional chief of engineers.

The original authority for the Corps' regulation of dredging and filling was a series of annual rivers and harbors acts, which culminated in the Rivers and Harbors Act of 1899, 33 U.S.C. §§ 401–418 (1976). Jurisdiction under these acts was based on the necessity of maintaining the navigability of the nation's waterways. Jurisdiction was limited to those waterways that were "navigable in fact." A waterway was "navigable in fact" if it was (1) capable of being used in interstate commerce, or (2) had the capability of such use by means of "reasonable improvements." *See The Daniel Ball,* 77 U.S. 557 (1870); *U.S. v. Appalachian Electric,* 311 U.S. 377 (1940).

As long as the Corps' only responsibility over the nations's waterways was to protect and enhance their navigability, this narrow definition of jurisdiction created no difficulties. Increasing concern with environmental protection, however, led to an expansion of the Corps' regulatory powers.

The first step in this expansion came with the landmark case of *Zabel v. Tabb,* 430 F.2d 199 (5th Cir. 1970), *cert. denied,* 401 U.S. 910 (1971). In that case, the plaintiff-landowners sought to compel the Corps to issue a permit to dredge and fill a portion of a Florida bay for the construction of a trailer park. The Corps conceded from the outset that the proposed project would not have an adverse effect on navigation but claimed the power to deny the permit on the grounds the work would result in a "distinctly harmful effect" on fish and wildlife in the bay. The court sided with the Corps and held that they were authorized to consider ecological and environmental factors in determining whether or not to grant a permit. The court also held that a permit could be denied on the basis of such factors alone, in the absence of any adverse effect on navigability. Along with the Rivers and Harbors Act, the court relied on the Fish and Wildlife Coordination Act, 16 U.S.C. §§ 662–667 (1976), and the National Environmental Policy Act, 42 U.S.C. §§ 4331–4374 (1976).

The second step in the transformation of the Corps' jurisdiction came with the passage of the Federal Water Pollution Control Act of 1972 (FWPCA). Recognizing that the actual destruction or removal of a waterway could be as environmentally disruptive as the polluting of a waterway, Congress included control over dredging and filling with the FWPCA. The Act specifically gave to the Corps the authority to administer the permit system controlling these activities. The extent of the Corps' jurisdiction under the act was not so specific, however. The act said that it applied only to "navigable waters," but the term was broadly defined as "waters of the United States, including the territorial seas." 33 U.S.C. § 1362(7) (1976). Thus, the exact scope of this definition was left to the courts upon review of the agency regulations.

An often cited case construing this definition is *U.S. v. Holland,* 373 F. Supp. 665 (M.D. Fla. 1974). That case involved the filling in of *nonnavigable* canals and wetlands without a Corps permit. The court reasoned that in passing the FWPCA, Congress intended to reach the source of water pollution, even if this necessitated breaching the traditional "navigability" limitation. The court concluded that the artificial canals were covered by the FWPCA since they emptied into a navigable body of water, and the wetlands were within the Act's scope since "fill activities on land periodically inundated by tidal waters constituted discharges entering 'waters of the United States.'" 373 F. Supp. at 676.

One year after the decision in *Holland,* The U.S. District Court for the District of Columbia in *Natural Resources Defense Council, Inc. v. Callaway,* 392 F. Supp. 685 (D.D.C. 1975), declared that in the FWPCA, Congress intended to assert federal jurisdiction over the nation's waters to the maximum extent permissible under the Commerce Clause. The court held that the Corps of

Engineers had acted unlawfully by adopting, in its regulations, a narrower definition of the waters to be protected than that mandated by the FWPCA. The Corps was ordered to revise its regulations to reflect properly the scope of its statutory mandate. They did so in July 1977 (42 Fed. Reg. 37122). Several months later the regulations were unsuccessfully challenged by the State of Wyoming. *See State of Wyoming v. Hoffman,* 437 F. Supp. 114 (D. Wyo. 1977).

New regulations were then promulgated by both the Corps of Engineers and the Environmental Protection Agency following the issuance of an Attorney General Opinion, 45 Op. Att'y Gen. No. 15 (Sept. 5, 1979) to the effect that EPA, not the Corps, had the administrative authority under the FWPCA to construe "navigable waters" and to define the exemptions authorized by 33 U.S.C. § 1344(f). The two agencies signed a Memorandum of Understanding as to the jurisdiction of each over the dredge-and-fill program, 45 Fed. Reg. 45018 (July 2, 1980). The EPA guidelines are codified in 40 C.F.R. § 230 (1981). Proposed Corps rules were issued as part of a massive revision of the Corp's regulatory program. 45 Fed. Reg. 62732 (September 19, 1980).

Also relevant to the dredge-and-fill permitting process are Presidential Executive Order 11988, 3 C.F.R. § 117 (1978), dealing with wetlands protection, and Executive Order 11990, 3 C.F.R. § 121 (1978), restricting federal construction and licensing of development in floodplains. *See generally* Barker, *Sections 9 and 10 of the Rivers and Harbors Act of 1899: Potent Tools for Environmental Protection,* 6 Ecology L.Q. 109 (1976); Chastain, *The Corps of Engineers Permit Program,* 1 Coastal Zone '78 at 539 (1978); Comment, *Sections 9 and 10 of the Rivers & Harbors Act of 1899: The Erosion of Administrative Control by Environmental Suits,* 1980 Duke L.J. 170 (1980); J. Kusler, *Emerging Issues in Wetland/Floodplain Management* (1979); W. Rodgers, *Environmental Law* 387–409 (1977); U.S. Environmental Protection Agency, A Guide to the Dredge or Fill Regulatory Program (1979).

SECTION B: CONSTRUCTION IN NAVIGABLE WATERS

HART & MILLER ISLANDS v. CORPS OF ENGINEERS
621 F.2d 1281 (4th Cir. 1980), *cert. denied,* 49 U.S.L.W. 3372
(1980)

WIDENER, Circuit Judge:

The State of Maryland applied to the U.S. Army Corps of Engineers (the Corps), in 1972, for a permit pursuant to Section 10 of the Rivers and Harbors Act of 1899, 33 U.S.C. § 403, to construct a diked disposal area for dredged material on and adjacent to Hart and Miller Islands in Chesapeake Bay. The purpose of the project is to provide a site for dumping material dredged from the bottom of Baltimore Harbor and its approach channels. This material will include spoil from maintenance dredging and spoil produced by the Baltimore

Harbor Channel Project, which is a Corps project designed to increase the depth of Baltimore Harbor.

The Corps held a public hearing on the proposal in August 1972 and completed a draft environmental impact statement in February 1973. Action on the Maryland application was delayed in order to comply with Section 404 of the Federal Water Pollution Control Act of 1972, Pub. L. 92–500, 86 Stat. 816, 884, 33 U.S.C. § 1344. A second public hearing was held in May 1975, see 459 F. Supp. 279, 281–282, and additional written comments were received in response to circulation of the draft environmental impact statement. The Corps issued a final environmental impact statement in February 1976. The Secretary of the Army, in November 1976, acting through the Corps, issued a permit to the State of Maryland, under Section 10 of the Rivers and Harbors Act of 1899 and Section 404 of the Federal Water Pollution Control Act of 1972, authorizing construction of the diked disposal facility.

Two environmental groups and a number of individuals commenced this action against the Corps in June 1977, seeking declaratory and injunctive relief voiding the permit. The complaint alleges that the Corps lacks the authority to issue the permit under Section 10 of the Rivers and Harbors Act because the barrier to surround the fill constitutes a "dike" which requires Congressional approval under Section 9 of that act, 33 U.S.C. § 401. The State of Maryland and the Steamship Trade Association of Baltimore intervened as defendants. All parties filed cross-motions for summary judgment in May 1978. 459 F.Supp. 280.

The district court granted the plaintiffs' motion for summary judgment and denied the motions filed by the defendants. *Hart and Miller Islands Area Environmental Group, Inc. v. Corps of Engineers,* 459 F. Supp. 279 (D. Md. 1978). The court held that the Corps could not authorize construction of the disposal facility because it was a dike within the meaning of Section 9 of the Rivers and Harbors Act of 1899 and therefore required Congressional approval.

Section 9 of that statute requires the consent of Congress for the construction of "any bridge, dam, dike, or causeway over or in" any navigable water of the United States. Under Section 10 of the same act the authorization of the Secretary of the Army is sufficient for the construction of "any wharf, pier, dolphin, boom, weir, breakwater, bulkhead, jetty, or other structures." The sole issue decided in this appeal is whether the Hart and Miller Islands diked disposal area is subject to Section 9 or Section 10 of the Rivers and Harbors Act. We hold that the structure is not a dike within the meaning of Section 9 and is governed by Section 10 of the statute. Therefore, it does not require Congressional approval. We thus approve the issuance of the permit by the Corps and reverse the district court.

Baltimore Harbor and its nearby navigation channels have been dredged many times in the past. Dredging will continue, both to maintain existing channels and to increase the depth of the harbor and channels.[1] An estimated 100 million cubic yards of bottom sediment will be dredged from Baltimore Harbor

---

[1]In 1970, Congress authorized funds for the Baltimore Harbor Channel project, which will deepen the Harbor and its approach channels to a depth of fifty feet. The present depth is from thirty-nine to forty-two feet. Rivers and Harbors Act of 1970, Pub.L. 91–611, § 101, 84 Stat. 1818.

and nearby channels in the next twenty years. Historically, the dredged material has been dumped in the open waters of Chesapeake Bay. Such open water dumping causes pollution in the vicinity of the disposal site since the dredged bottom sediment contains toxic chemicals, heavy metals, oil, grease, and other substances. The spoil material deposited by open water dumping, of course, may also damage bottom dwelling fauna.[2] The disposal area is designed to improve the water quality of Upper Chesapeake Bay by the elimination of open water dumping.

Hart and Miller Islands are privately owned, contain no permanent structures, and are used by a limited number of boaters for recreation (without the owner's permission). There are beaches and wetlands on both islands, and part of Hart Island is forested. Both islands have a serious erosion problem which has decreased the area of Hart Island from 150 acres in 1933 to 120 acres in 1967, and decreased the area of Miller Island from 50 acres in 1933 to 33 acres in 1967. The maximum elevation of either island is 5.5 feet.

The disposal area will be 1,100 acres, approximately 12,430 feet by 4,700 feet, and will contain 52 million cubic yards of sediment when filled to its capacity of 18 feet above mean low water. About 52 percent of Miller Island (18.4 acres) and 11.5 percent of Hart Island (10.9 acres) will be covered by the facility. The dike will be constructed from sand deposits adjacent to and underlying the enclosure, and the face toward the bay will be riprapped with stone. Three sluice gates will be provided to prevent overtopping and washout of the dike. The islands are approximately one mile from the nearest point on the mainland, the western side of the bay. The containment area will be located on the eastern or bay side of the islands. The dike will extend from Hart and Miller Islands no more than 4,700 feet into the Bay in an area where the Bay is about 7 miles wide. Essentially the area is made by connecting Hart and Miller Islands with a wall, and, using the islands as two corners, then extending other walls into the Bay at right angles to the connecting wall between the islands, the ends of the walls extended into the Bay then being connected by another wall.

The dredged material will be retained in the disposal area for months or years. Sediment will settle and water will slowly percolate through the bottom of the dike until a water-level equilibrium is reached. All particulate matter will be retained in the containment area. While the Harbor spoil can be expected to contain substances that exert a biochemical oxygen demand, the slow filtration through the dike walls will eliminate the oxygen demand before the filtrate reaches the Bay. Sedimentation and filtration, coupled with the long retention period, will effectively remove and destroy any pathogenic bacteria that might be present in the Harbor mud.

The Army Corps of Engineers processed the permit application under Section 10 of the Rivers and Harbors Act. Since the adoption of that statute, the

[2]Open-water dumping has been the subject of continuous criticism. As a consequence, the State tells us without contradiction that in 1969 the Maryland legislature authorized the expenditure of $13,000,000 for the design and construction of one or more containment areas to act as a receptacle for spoil dredged from Baltimore Harbor and the approach channels. Recognizing the deleterious environment effects of open water dumping. In 1975 Maryland prohibited the discharge of spoil from Baltimore Harbor unless it was deposited in containment facilities. Md. Natural Resources Code, Sec. 8–1602.

Corps has consistently interpreted Section 9 as requiring Congressional approval only for structures which completely span a navigable waterway. Under Section 10, the Corps has administratively authorized structures which do not extend entirely across a waterway, no matter how large and whether or not called dikes. See *infra* at 1289. The Corps argues that the statute is ambiguous and therefore the paucity of case law emphasizes the significance of the relevant legislative history and administrative practice and interpretation. . . .

> The true intent of the Act of Congress was that unreasonable obstructions to navigation and navigable capacity were to be prohibited, and in the cases described in the second and third clauses of Section 10, the Secretary of War, acting on the recommendation of the Chief of Engineers, was authorized to determine what in the particular cases constituted an unreasonable obstruction.
>
> This construction of Section 10 is sustained by the uniform practice of the War Department for nearly thirty years. Nothing is more convincing in interpretation of a doubtful or ambiguous statute.
>
> . . . .
>
> The practice is shown by the opinion of the Acting Attorney General, transmitted to the Secretary of War, 34 Op. Attys. Gen. 410, 416. The Secretary of War acted on this view on May 8, 1899, about two months after the passage of the Act. . . .The fact that the Secretary of War acted on this view was made known to Congress by many reports.

278 U.S. 367, 412–414, 49 S. Ct. at 170 (Citations omitted).

Plaintiffs claim that the language contained in the Rivers and Harbors Act is clear, and that its plain meaning should control without reference to legislative history or administrative practice. The few decided cases do not support this argument. . . .

As stated, the issue in the present case is whether the Hart and Miller Islands disposal area is governed by the second clause of Section 10 or the first clause of Section 9 of the 1899 Act. The second clause of present Section 10 (33 U.S.C. § 403) derives from the first clause of Section 7 of the 1890 Act. The only significant change is that dam is not among the structures listed in the present Section 10. The first clause of Section 9 (33 U.S.C. § 401) derives from the second clause of Section 7 of the 1890 Act, which referred to works authorized by State legislatures.

The Corps of Engineers, the agency that wrote the statute and is charged with its execution, has interpreted Section 9 as applying only "to that class of structures such as bridges and dams which extend entirely across a waterway." . . .

In construing Sections 9 and 10, we are guided by the "venerable principle that the construction of a statute by those charged with its execution should be followed unless there are compelling indications that it is wrong." *Red Lion Broadcasting Co. v. F.C.C.*, 395 U.S. 367, 381, 89 S.Ct. 1794, 1802, 23 L. Ed.2d 371 (1969).

The legislative history of the Federal Water Pollution Control Act Amendments of 1972 demonstrates that Congress was not only aware of, but approved and encouraged the Corps' practice of issuing permits for diked disposal areas, without specific Congressional approval. . . .

Congress, when it authorized the Baltimore Harbor Channel Project in 1970, gave an indication of its understanding that its further approval was not needed for diked disposal facilities. That Congress expected the dredged spoil to be placed behind retaining structures such as the dike at issue here is shown in the House Report. . . .

For most of this century at least, Congress has been aware of the Corps' interpretation of the Act. . . .

Sections 9 and 10 of the Rivers and Harbors Act of 1899 must be construed together in a logical and consistent manner in order to best effectuate the intent of Congress. A logical distinction between those structures listed in Section 9 (which require Congressional approval) and those listed in Section 10 (which do not) is that the former class of structures completely span a waterway, while the latter do not. Section 9 structures are capable of completely blocking a navigable waterway, while Section 10 structures merely protrude into a waterway and require only a rerouting of waterborne traffic. Since Section 9 structures usually necessarily destroy navigation, they require Congressional approval. Since Section 10 structures do not usually or necessarily destroy, but merely obstruct, navigation, they require only Corps approval.

Finally, . . . the expansive reading of Section 9 put forward by the plaintiffs could render Section 10 meaningless, since structures such as jetties, breakwaters, and fills would be covered by Section 9 although they are literally within Section 10. Limiting Section 9 to waterway-spanning structures as the Corps has done, provides a clear, convenient, and workable distinction between Section 9 and Section 10. This construction is reasonable and is supported by the legislative history of the statute.

We hold that the Corps of Engineers acted correctly in processing the application for the Hart and Miller Islands diked disposal facility under Section 10 of the Rivers and Harbors Act of 1899, 33 U.S.C. § 403. Accordingly the judgment appealed from is

REVERSED.

NOTES

1. In *Hart & Miller*, does the Corps of Engineers' dual role as regulatory agency and harbor dredger pose any problems? *See* Power, *The Fox in the Chicken Coop: The Regulatory Program of the U.S. Army Corps of Engineers*, 63 Va. L. Rev. 547 (1977). In addition to beach erosion control and harbor maintenance, the Corps has responsibility for other civil works projects in the coastal zone. These include projects for storm protection, recreation development, and dredging of navigable waterways. Inland projects of the Corps, such as dam construction, may also affect coastal resources. *See,* Power, *The Federal Role in Coastal Development,* in Environmental Law Institute, *Federal Environmental Law* 796 (1974); W. Rosenbaum, *The Politics of Environmental Concern* 168–89 (1973).

2. Corps civil works projects must comply with federal laws such as the National Environmental Policy Act and the Federal Water Pollution Control Act. The Corps of Engineers generally is required to comply with NEPA for the initial construction of a civil works project. The Corps also may have to file an EIS in conjunction with the maintenance of these projects. In *Sierra Club v. Mason,* 351 F.

Supp. 419 (D. Conn. 1972), the court enjoined the redredging of New Haven Harbor and required the Corps to file an EIS. The court said that in view of the magnitude of the potential environmental damage the project could not be considered "ongoing maintenance" but had a "life of its own." 351 F. Supp. at 425; *accord, Save Crystal Beach Ass'n v. Calloway,* 8 ERC 1641 (D. Fla. 1975); *Wisconsin v. Callaway,* 371 F. Supp. 807 (W. D. Wis. 1974).

Must the Corps also comply with state environmental laws such as a state statute requiring a state permit for dredging in navigable waters within the state's boundaries? *Minnesota v. Hoffman,* 543 F.2d 1198 (8th Cir. 1976), *cert. denied,* 430 U.S. 977 (1977), held "no." Is the potential impact of *Minnesota v. Hoffman* mitigated by the consistency requirements of the federal Coastal Zone Management Act, 16 U.S.C. § 1456(c) (1976)? Under those provisions federal agencies conducting or supporting activities directly affecting a state's coastal zone or undertaking development in the state's coastal zone are required to do so consistent with the state's federally approved coastal zone management program. What is the effect of Federal Water Pollution Control Act section 404(t) enacted after *Minnesota v. Hoffman* and quoted below?

Nothing in this section shall preclude or deny the right of any State or interstate agency to control the discharge of dredged or fill material in any portion of the navigable waters within the jurisdiction of such State, including any activity of any Federal agency, and each such agency shall comply with such State or interstate requirements both substantive and procedural to control the discharge of dredged or fill material to the same extent that any person is subject to such requirements. This section shall not be construed as affecting or impairing the authority of the Secretary to maintain navigation.

33 U.S.C. § 1344(t) (1978). Compare section 404(r), 33 U.S.C. § 1344(r) (1978), which exempts from regulation under the FWPCA the discharge of dredged or fill material as part of the construction of a federal project if information on the effects of the discharge has been provided to Congress in an environmental impact statement.

3. The federal Fish and Wildlife Coordination Act provides in part:

. . . [w]henever the waters of any stream or other body of water are proposed or authorized to be impounded, diverted, the channel deepened, or the stream or other body of water otherwise controlled or modified for any purpose whatever, including navigation and drainage, by any department or agency of the United States, or by any public or private agency under Federal permit or license, such department or agency first shall consult with the United States Fish and Wildlife Service, Department of the Interior, and with the head of the agency exercising administration over the wildlife resources of the particular State wherein the impoundment, diversion, or other control facility is to be constructed, with a view to the conservation of wildlife resources by preventing loss of and damage to such resources as well as providing for the development and improvement thereof in connection with such water-resource development.

16 U.S.C. § 662(a) (1976). What are the Corps' obligations under the act with respect to (a) public works projects carried out by the Corps, and (b) permits issued by the Corps under the Rivers and Harbors Act and the FWPCA?

In *Zabel v. Tabb,* 430 F.2d 199 (5th Cir. 1970), the court stated:

The Fish and Wildlife Coordination Act clearly requires the dredging and filling agency (under a governmental permit), whether public or private, to consult with the Fish and Wildlife Service, with a view of conservation of wildlife resources. If there be any question as to whether the statute directs the licensing agency (the

Corps) to so consult it can quickly be dispelled. Common sense and reason dictate that it would be incongruous for Congress in light of the fact that it intends conservation to be considered in private dredge and fill operations (as evidenced by the clear wording of the statute), not to direct the only federal agency concerned with licensing such projects both to consult and to take such factors into account.

The second proof that the Secretary is directed and authorized by the Fish and Wildlife Coordination Act to consider conservation is found in the legislative history. The Senate Report on the Fish and Wildlife Coordination Act states:

> Finally, the nursery and feeding grounds of valuable crustaceans, such as shrimp, as well as the young of valuable marine fishes, may be affected by dredging, filling, and diking operations often carried out to improve navigation and provide new industrial or residential land.
>
> . . . .
>
> Existing law has questionable application to projects of the Corps of Engineers for the dredging of bays and estuaries for navigation and filling purposes. More seriously, existing law has no application whatsoever to the dredging and filling of bays and estuaries by private interests or other non-Federal entities in navigable waters under permit from the Corps of Engineers. This is a particularly serious deficiency from the standpoint of commercial fishing interests. The dredging of these bays and estuaries along the coastlines to aid navigation and also to provide land fills for real estate and similar developments, both by Federal agencies or other agencies under permit from the Corps of Engineers, has increased tremendously in the last 5 years. Obviously, dredging activity of this sort has a profound disturbing effect on aquatic life, including shrimp and other species of tremendous significance to the commercial fishing industry. The bays, estuaries, and related marsh areas are highly important as spawning and nursery grounds for many commercial species of fish and shellfish. 430 F.2d at 209.

This Report clearly shows that Congress intended the Chief of Engineers and Secretary of the Army to consult with the Fish and Wildlife Service before issuing a permit for a private dredge and fill operation.

This interpretation was judicially accepted in *Udall v. FPC:*

> Section 2(a), 16 U.S.C. § 662(a) provides that an agency evaluating a license under which 'the waters of any stream or other body of water are proposed . . . to be impounded first shall consult with the United States Fish and Wildlife Service, Department of the Interior . . . with a view to the conservation of wildlife resources by preventing loss of and damage to such resources . . . .' Certainly the wildlife conservation aspect of the project must be explored and evaluated. [387 U.S. 428, 443–444, 87 S. Ct. 1712, 1720, 18 L. Ed. 2d 869, 879 (1967)]

The meaning and application of the Act are also reflected by the actions of the Executive that show the statute authorizes and directs the Secretary to consult with the Fish and Wildlife Service in deciding whether to grant a dredge and fill permit.

More recently, the effect of the Fish and Wildlife Coordination Act was explored in *Sierra Club v. Alexander,* 484 F. Supp. 455, 469 (1980):

Pursuant to the Fish and Wildlife Coordination Act, §§ 661 *et seq.,* the Army Corps of Engineers is obligated to consult with the Fish and Wildlife Service concerning the impact on fish and wildlife resources of issuance of a Section 404 permit. See *Zabel v. Tabb*, 430 F.2d 199, 209 (5th Cir. 1970). Plaintiff contends that the Corps failed to comply with the Act in issuance of the permit to Pyramid.

There is no question but that Fish and Wildlife Service officials were opposed to issuance of the permit to Pyramid, without certain modification of the project proposed by the Service. The proposed modifications involved changes which would dispense with the need for the rechannelization of Mud Creek. Pyramid, given the opportunity to respond to the Fish and Wildlife Service position as required under 33 C.F.R. § 325.2(a)(3), found the proposed modifications economically unfeasible. Regulation which required it to give "great weight" to the views of the Fish and Wildlife Service concerning fish and wildlife conservation.

Plaintiff fails to recognize, however, that the final decision rested with the Corps, which had to base its determination not only on the impact of the project on fish and wildlife but on a "careful weighing of all those factors which become relevant in each particular case . . . . The benefit which reasonably may be expected to accrue from the proposal must be balanced against its reasonably foreseeable detriments." 33 C.F.R. § 320.4(a)(1).

The Fish and Wildlife Coordination Act does not require that the Corps decision always correspond to the views of the Fish and Wildlife Service. Rather the Act requires that the views be given serious consideration, and there is nothing in the Corps record which shows that the Corps failed to do so.

See *Environmental Defense Fund v. Andrus,* 596 F.2d 848 (9th Cir. 1979); Shipley, *The Fish & Wildlife Coordination Act's Application to Wetlands,* in A. Reitze, *Environmental Planning: Law of Land and Resources* at two 49–59 (1974).

4. Corps civil works projects may adversely affect adjacent property, for example: Dredge spoil disposal may interrupt the littoral drift of a waterway, causing shore erosion; construction of a jetty may cause interference with a littoral landowner's access to a navigable waterway; or the dredging of a channel may injure or destroy oyster beds. What causes of action if any do injured parties have? Are their rights affected by the federal navigation servitude discussed previously? If so, how?

In *Hoe v. Alexander,* 483 F. Supp. 746 (D. Hawaii 1980), the plaintiffs tried to enjoin local officials and the Corps from proceeding with a beach erosion stabilization project partially funded under 33 U.S.C. § 426(g) which authorizes the Corps to undertake construction of small beach restoration projects costing less than $1 million. The National Historic Preservation Act, 16 U.S.C. § 470 (1976), also was involved in *Hoe* because the beach erosion was taking place near Anaupua's of Kualoa, which is listed in the National Register of Historic Places.

In *Save the Dunes Council v. Alexander,* 584 F.2d 158 (7th Cir. 1978), the plaintiffs unsuccessfully tried to force the Corps to mitigate the erosion impacts of the harbor it had constructed at Michigan City, Indiana, under 33 U.S.C. § 426(i), which authorizes the Corps to mitigate shore damage caused by federal navigation works.

In *Lewis Blue Point Oyster Cultivation Co. v. Briggs,* 229 U.S. 82, 57 L. Ed. 1083 (1913), Congress had authorized the dredging of a navigation channel that would do substantial damage to an oyster bed. Although the oyster beds were privately owned under the laws of the state, no compensation was awarded for their destruction. However, in *Bay State Lobster Co. v. Perini Corporation,* 355 Mass. 794, 245 N.E.2d 759 (1969), the court awarded damages for tank-raised lobsters smothered by silt negligently caused by defendant's dredging performed under a contract with the U.S. Coast Guard. *Compare Texas Oyster Growers Association v. Odom,* 385 S.W.2d 899 (Tex. Ct. Civ. App. 1965), where state sovereign immunity and the lack of vested property rights were used to defeat a suit to overturn state-issued permits for dredging which threatened shell reefs fished by the plaintiff commercial oyster fishers.

What are the rights if any of fishers aggrieved by dredging activities? In *Bordelon v. T. L. James & Co.,* 380 So. 2d 226 (La. Ct. App. 1980), fishers brought an action against a dredging company for damage to their nets. The court found that the dredging company had breached no duty owed to the fishers. Furthermore, the court held that the nets when used in a manner impairing navigation were an illegal obstruction of navigation under the federal Rivers and Harbors Act and that the paramount policy favoring free and open navigation of U.S. waters precluded recovery. *Accord, Anderson v. Columbia Contract Co.,* 94 Or. 171, 184 P. 240, 185 P. 231 (1919); *cf. Kuramo v. Hamada,* 30 Hawaii 841 (1929) (public right to navigate in sampans and row boats upheld even though a private fishing right was disturbed); *Taylor Sands Fishing Co. v. State Land Board,* 56 Or. 157, 108 P. 126 (1910) (seining of sand bars purchased from the state is subject to the paramount right of public navigation).

5. Does a valid state or local permit authorizing construction in navigable waters obviate the need for Corps approval under section 9 or 10 of the Rivers and Harbors Act? *See U.S. v. Ferrer,* 613 F.2d 1188 (1st Cir. 1980) (wooden house on stilts constructed in navigable waters pursuant to local permit).

6. Do private parties injured by violations of the Rivers and Harbors Act have a cause of action based on the act? The Supreme Court held "no" in *California v. Sierra Club,* 15 ERC 1929 (U.S. Sup. Ct. 1981), *rev'g, Sierra Club v. Andrus,* 610 F.2d 581 (9th Cir. 1979). *See also City of Milwaukee v. Illinois,* 15 ERC 1908 (U.S. Sup. Ct. 1981) (Federal Water Pollution Control Act precludes federal common law of nuisance action against city's sewage discharges); *City of Evansville v. Kentucky Liquid Recycling, Inc.,* 604 F.2d 1008 (7th Cir. 1979) (no private cause of action created by Federal Water Pollution Control Act for damages caused by illegal discharges).

7. Section 15 of the Rivers and Harbors Act, 33 U.S.C. § 409 (1976), requires the owners of vessels sunk in navigable channels to remove them and authorizes federal removal if the owner fails to. *See, e.g., U.S. v. City of Redwood,* 15 ERC 1699 (9th Cir. 1981); *U.S. v. Ohio Barge Lines, Inc.,* 607 F.2d 624 (3d Cir. 1979).

8. Can an action approved by the Corps under the Rivers and Harbors Act significantly affect land and water uses in a state's coastal zone? If so, the state must determine that the action is consistent with the state's federally approved coastal zone management program before the action is approved by the Corps. *See* 16 U.S.C. § 1456(c) (1976), discussed in Chapter 11, *infra.*

SECTION C: SCOPE OF CORPS JURISDICTION

Tidelands

LESLIE SALT CO. v. FROEHLKE
578 F.2d 742
(9th Cir. 1978)

SNEED, Circuit Judge:

These appeals deal with the scope of the regulatory jurisdiction of the U.S. Army Corps of Engineers ("Corps") over "navigable waters of the United States" as that term is used, first, in the Rivers and Harbors Act of 1899, 33

U.S.C. § 401 et seq., and, second, in the Federal Water Pollution Control Act of 1972, 33 U.S.C. § 1251, et seq.

Suit was initiated on March 29, 1972, by the Sierra Club against Leslie Salt Co. ("Leslie"), seeking a declaratory judgment that Leslie's diked evaporation ponds in and around Bair Island in San Francisco Bay were built in violation of the Rivers and Harbors Act of 1899 because Leslie had failed to seek or obtain permits from the Corps. The action also sought a permanent injunction ordering removal of the dikes or, in the alternative, prohibiting further construction or maintenance of dikes at Bair Island. Leslie then sued the Corps on December 20, 1973, seeking a declaration that the regulatory jurisdiction of the Corps over tidal marshlands in San Francisco Bay under both the Rivers and Harbors Act of 1899 and the Federal Water Pollution Control Act of 1972 ("FWPCA") is delimited by the line of mean high water ("MHW"). The Sierra Club was permitted to intervene in this action.

. . . .

I. Facts.

Leslie owns some 35,000 acres of property along the shores of south San Francisco Bay. Appellant Mobil Oil Estates Ltd. (Bair Island Investments) is the owner of a 3,000-acre parcel in San Mateo County known as "Bair Island." The subject lands were originally conveyed by the United States to the State of California pursuant to the Arkansas Swamp Act of 1850, 43 U.S.C. § 981 et seq., and then patented by the state to Leslie's predecessors in interest. In its natural condition, the property was marshland subject to the ebb and flow of the tide. Commencing in 1860, the land was diked and reclaimed and has since that time been used primarily for salt production by means of solar evaporation of Bay waters introduced into Leslie's salt ponds. These dikes were completed, for the most part, in 1927, although some work continued through 1969. Because of these dikes, the land in question has not been subject to tidal action on a regular basis, although most of it is periodically inundated by Bay waters for salt production. The Bair Island property was removed from salt production in 1965; because of the continued maintenance of dikes on the island, it has become dry land.

In 1971 and 1972, the San Francisco District of the Corps published two Public Notices (No. 71–22 on June 11, 1971, and No. 71–22(a) on January 18, 1972), stating that the Corps had changed its policy and would henceforth require permits for all "new work" on unfilled marshland property within the line of "former mean higher high water," whether or not the property was presently diked off from the ebb and flow of the tides.

In these Public Notices the Corps purported simply to redefine the scope of its regulatory authority within the ambit of the Rivers and Harbors Act of 1899, sections 9 and 10 of which prohibit filling or the construction of any "dam," "dike," "obstruction," or "other structures" within the "navigable water of the United States," without the prior authorization of the Corps of Engineers. 33 U.S.C. §§ 401, 403.

An understanding of the technical tide line terminology is critical to this case. Every 24.8 hours, both the Pacific and Atlantic coasts of the United States experience two complete tidal cycles, each including a high and a low tide. The Gulf coast tides, known as diurnal, have but one high and one low tide each lunar day. On the Atlantic coast, the difference between the two daily tidal cycles, known as semi-diurnal tides, is relatively slight. Accordingly, there is in most instances little difference between the two high tides or between the two low tides in a given day on the east coast. The two daily Pacific coast tidal cycles (known as "mixed type" tides), however, in most locations are substantially unequal in size, with one high tide significantly higher than the other. The mean high water line is the average of both of the daily high tides over a period of 18.6 years; the mean higher high water line is the average of only the higher of the two tides for the same period of time. Thus, on the Atlantic coast the difference between the MHW and the MHHW is relatively small, while on the Pacific coast generally it is relatively large. *Sierra Club v. Leslie Salt, supra,* 412 F.Supp. at 1098–99.

We shall first discuss Leslie's suit and then turn to that of the Sierra Club.

II. Leslie's Suit.

A. Summary Judgment in Leslie's Suit.

A threshold question is raised by Leslie as to whether summary judgment was improperly granted. We find that the district court did not err in deciding that there were no genuine issues of material fact. The issues to be decided in Leslie's suit were purely legal. As framed by Leslie, the action was for a declaratory judgment that the regulatory jurisdiction of the Corps under both the Rivers and Harbors Act and the FWPCA extended only to the MHW line, and an injunction restraining the Corps from requiring permits for properties located above the MHW line. The suit did not involve action or inaction by the Corps on any particular application by Leslie for a permit under the Rivers and Harbors Act or the FWPCA, since Leslie has refused to apply for any permits. Thus, the particular circumstances and characteristics of Leslie's property in this case were not material to the questions raised on the motions for summary judgment.

B. Scope of Corps's Jurisdiction Under Rivers and Harbors Act.

Analysis of the Rivers and Harbors Act must begin by acknowledging that it does not define the terms "navigable water of the United States" or "waters of the United States." Pertinent regulations defining these terms have recently been adopted by the Corps. On July 25, 1975, after the San Francisco District of the Corps issued the two Public Notices dealing with the use of the MHHW line as the limit of its jurisdication, the Corps promulgated the following definition of "navigable waters of the United States":

> The term, "navigable waters of the United States," is administratively defined to mean waters that have been used in the past, are now used, or are susceptible to use as a means to transport interstate commerce landward to their ordinary high water mark and up to the head of navigation as determined by the Chief of Engineers, and also waters that are subject to the ebb and flow of the tides shoreward to their mean high water mark (*mean higher high water mark on the*

Pacific coast). See 33 C.F.R. 209.260 (ER 1165–2–302) for a more definitive explanation of this term.

33 C.F.R. § 209.120(d)(1) (emphasis added). Regulation 209.260, adopted September 9, 1972, provides in most pertinent part, as follows:

> *Shoreward limit of jurisdiction.* Regulatory jurisdiction in coastal areas extends to the line on the shore reached by the plane of the mean (average) high water. *However, on the Pacific coast, the line reached by the mean of the higher high waters is used.*

33 C.F.R. § 209.260(k)(1)(ii) (emphasis added).

Prior to these amendments the Regulation did not address itself to the shoreward limit of its jurisdiction and deferentially set forth its views regarding what constitutes navigable water as merely "the views of the Department since the jurisdiction of the United States can be conclusively determined only through judicial proceedings." 33 C.F.R. § 209.260(a) (1971).

Leslie contends that the district court's ruling upholding the Corps's regulations is contrary to every reported decision defining the boundaries of tidal water bodies. Conceding that Congress may in theory have the power under the Commerce Clause to legislate with respect to land between the MHW and the MHHW line, Leslie argues that the "navigable waters of the United States" within the meaning of the Rivers and Harbors Act have consistently been judicially extended only to the MHW line. In response, the Corps and the Sierra Club argue that the extent of Rivers and Harbors Act jurisdiction on the Pacific coast is an issue of first impression for any appellate court, and has arisen in only two previous court cases.[3] They urge that the Corps's use of the MHHW line on the Pacific coast is a logical and reasonable attempt to "harmonize" its regulatory program throughout the country. Inasmuch as Leslie accurately describes the state of the authorities, the Corps and Sierra Club in effect invite us to read the Act differently than in the past to accommodate the desire of the Corps to extend its jurisdiction on the Pacific coast. We decline the invitation because we believe it is misdirected. It should be addressed to Congress rather than the Judiciary.

Turning to the authorities, the Supreme Court in 1915 held that federal regulatory jurisdiction over navigable tidal waters extends to the MHW line. *Willink v. United States,* 240 U.S. 572, 580, 36 S.Ct. 422, 60 L.Ed. 808 (1916). While *Willink* was concerned with the boundaries of the tidal waters on the Atlantic coast, the case is significant because it deals directly with the relationship between the federal navigational servitude and the Corps's regulation of "navigable waters of the United States." The servitude, which reaches to the limits of "navigable water," permits the removal of an obstruction to navigable capacity without compensation. *See* 33 U.S.C. § 403. Accordingly, an expansion of "navigable water" shoreward diminishes the protection of the Fifth

___

[3]One of these is unreported, *United States v. Freethy,* No. 73–1470 (N.D.Cal. Feb. 24, 1975); the other makes only passing mention of the use of the MHHW line as the Corps's limit of jurisdiction, *United States v. Kaiser Aetna,* 408 F.Supp. 42, 50 n.18 (D.Hawaii 1976), *appeal docketed,* No. 76–1968 (9th Cir. May 3, 1976).

Amendment. We think an interpretation of the Act which accomplishes this, first advanced seventy-two years after its enactment, should be viewed with skepticism to say the least.

. . . .

Consistent with *Willink,* however, is the leading case defining the extent of tidal water bodies on the Pacific coast. *Borax Consolidated, Ltd. v. City of Los Angeles,* 296 U.S. 10, 56 S.Ct. 23, 80 L.Ed. 9 (1935) originated in a property dispute brought by Los Angeles to quiet title to land on an island in Los Angeles harbor. At issue was the proper boundary between *tidelands* as to which the State possessed original title upon admittance to the Union, and *uplands,* which became public lands of the United States at the time of their acquisition from Mexico. . . .

The Supreme Court, affirming a decision of this court, held that the tideland extends to the MHW mark as technically defined by the United States Coast and Geodetic Survey: that is, "the average height of *all* the high waters" at a given place over a period of 18.6 years. *Id.* at 26–27, 56 S.Ct. at 31 (emphasis added).

. . . .

The district court below distinguishes *Borax* on the grounds that the Supreme Court was dealing with an issue of *title* and "made no reference to the federal navigational servitude under the Rivers and Harbors Act or to the distinction of MHHW and MHW." *Sierra Club v. Leslie Salt Co., supra,* 412 F.Supp. at 1101. However, *Borax* cannot be brushed aside so easily. The considerations involved in the regulation of navigable waters under the commerce power are intimately connected to the question of title to tidelands. The term "navigable waters" was been judicially defined to cover: (1) nontidal waters which were navigable in the past or which could be made navigable in fact by "reasonable improvements." *United States v. Appalachian Electric Power Co.,* 311 U.S. 377, 61 S.Ct. 291, 85 L.Ed. 243 (1940); . . . and (2) waters within the ebb and flow of the tide. *The Propeller Genesee Chief v. Fitzhugh,* 53 U.S. (12 How.) 443, 13 L.Ed. 1058 (1851); . . . . Tideland, by definition, is the soil underlying tidal waters. To fix the shoreward boundary of tideland there must be fixed the shoreward limit of tidal water which, in turn, should fix the shoreward limit of "navigable waters" in the absence of a contrary intent on the part of Congress. To fix the limit of "navigable water," for the purposes of the Rivers and Harbors Act, further shoreward than *Borax* fixed the limit of "tidal water" assumes the existence of an intent of Congress at the time of the Act's enactment of which we have no evidence.

. . . .

This long-standing recognition that, for the purpose of fixing a shoreward limit, the terms tide water and navigable water are interchangeable strongly suggests that in *Borax* the Supreme Court, in the course of settling a title dispute, also fixed the shoreward boundary of navigable water on the Pacific coast. This is buttressed by the fact that since *Borax* and *Willink,* the MHW line has been routinely cited as the boundary of federal regulatory jurisdiction over tidal waters by every court to consider the question, with the two recent exceptions upon which the Corps and Sierra Club rely. *United States v. Stoeco Homes, Inc., supra,* 498 F.2d 597 (3d Cir. 1974), *cert. denied,* 420 U.S. 927,

95 S.Ct. 1124, 43 L.Ed.2d 397 (1975); *United States v. Holland,* 373 F.Supp. 665 (M.D.Fla.1974); *United States v. Cannon,* 363 F.Supp. 1045 (D.Del.1973); *United States v. Pot–Nets,* 363 F. Supp. 812 (D.Del.1973); *United States v. Lewis,* 355 F.Supp. 1132 (S.D.Ga.1973). . . . Although these cases all arose on the Atlantic or Gulf coasts, each implicitly accepts *Borax,* a Pacific coast case, as enunciating a rule applicable to all coasts of the United States. Taken together, they indicate the extent to which the MHW line has been consistently accepted as the boundary of "navigable waters of the United States." . . .

Moreover, we have already indicated that more is involved than simply an expansion of the Corps's regulatory authority. As stated by the Supreme Court in *United States v. Virginia Electric Co.,* 365 U.S. 624, 81 S.Ct. 784, 5 L.Ed.2d 838 (1961):

> This navigational servitude—sometimes referred to as a "dominant servitude," . . . or a "superior navigation easement," . . . —is the privilege to appropriate without compensation *which attaches to the exercise of the "power of the government to control and regulate navigable waters in the interest of commerce." United States v. Commodore Park,* 324 U.S. 386, 390, 65 S.Ct. 803, 89 L.Ed. 1017.

United States v. Virginia Electric, 365 U.S. at 627–28, 81 S.Ct. at 787 (emphasis added). The navigational servitude reaches to the shoreward limit of navigable waters. To extend the servitude on the basis of a recently formulated administrative policy is to impose an additional burden of unknown magnitude on all private property that abuts on the Pacific coast.

We wish to point out, however, that our interpretation of the Rivers and Harbors Act is not governed by a belief that the Act represents the full exertion by Congress of its authority under the Commerce Clause. . . .

We hold that in tidal areas, "navigable waters of the United States," as used in the Rivers and Harbors Act, extend to all places covered by the ebb and flow of the tide to the mean high water (MHW) mark in its unobstructed, natural state. Accordingly, we reverse the district court's decision insofar as it found that the Corps's jurisdiction under the Rivers and Harbors Act includes all areas within the former line of MHHW in its unobstructed, natural state.

Our holding that the MHW line is to be fixed in accordance with its natural, unobstructed state is dictated by the principle recognized in *Willink, supra,* that one who develops areas below the MHW line does so at his peril. We recognize that under this holding issues of whether the Government's power may be surrendered or its exercise estopped, and if so, under what circumstances and to what extent, may arise. Leslie, for example, may contend that there has been a surrender by the Corps of its power under the Rivers and Harbors Act with respect to certain land below the MHW line. Such contentions, however, are not presently before us in this case. Therefore, at this time it is not necessary for us to pass on issues such as were before the court in *Stoeco, supra.*

C. Scope of Corps's Jurisdiction Under FWPCA.

The scope of regulatory authority under the FWPCA presents a substantially different issue. The district court's holding that the Corps's regulatory jurisdiction under the FWPCA is "coterminous" with that under the Rivers and

Harbors Act, extending to "the former line of MHHW of the bay in its unobstructed, natural state," is faulty. *Sierra Club v. Leslie Salt, supra,* 412 F.Supp. at 1102–03. In its opening brief in this appeal, Leslie properly concedes that:

> . . . the Corps' jurisdiction under Section 404 of the FWPCA is broader than its jurisdiction under the Rivers and Harbors Act in that it encompasses existing marshlands located above as well as below the lines of mean high water and mean higher high water which are currently subject to tidal inundation.

Brief for Appellant Leslie Salt Co. at 60.[4] Leslie contends, however, that the use of the *former* unobstructed, natural MHHW line "extends the Corps' regulatory authority significantly further than is authorized by the FWPCA," because it results in the possibility that the Corps would be able to regulate discharges onto dry lands under an Act whose purpose is to control pollution of the nation's waters. *Id.*

This contention presents a false issue. Neither the Corps nor the Sierra Club argues for the result envisioned by Leslie. Instead, they contend that under the FWPCA, the case law interpreting it, and the Corps's own regulations, neither the MHW nor the MHHW line marks the full limit of the Corps's jurisdiction to regulate the pollution of the *waters* of the United States. The appellees, however, agree with appellant Leslie that, as stated in the Sierra Club's brief,

> [i]f any portions of Leslie's property were in fact dry, solid upland as of the date of the passage of the FWPCA, therefore, not subject to being returned to their former natural condition of periodic tidal inundation should the artificial obstructions be abated, that property would fall outside the Corps' Section 404 jurisdiction.
>
> . . . .

Brief for Appellee Sierra Club at 84.

Where the parties differ is on the question of whether the Corps's jurisdic-

---

[4]Leslie's concession is well taken, since the case law clearly supports an expansive reading of the term "navigable waters" as used in the FWPCA, 33 U.S.C. § 1251, et seq. In *United States v. Holland*, 373 F.Supp. 665 (M.D.Fla. 1974), the district court, in an excellent analysis, held that the discharge of "sand, dirt and dredged soil on land which, although above the mean high water line, was periodically inundated with the waters of Papy's Bayou" was within the reach of the FWPCA, since Congress intended to control the discharge of pollutants into waters at the *source* of the discharge, regardless of its location vis-a-vis the MHW or MHHW lines. The court stated that:

> . . . the mean high water line is no limit to federal authority under the FWPCA. While the line remains a valid demarcation for other purposes, it has no rational connection to the aquatic ecosystems which the FWPCA is intended to protect. Congress has wisely determined that federal authority over water pollution properly rests on the Commerce Clause and not on past interpretations of an act designed to protect navigation. And the Commerce Clause gives Congress ample authority to reach activities above the mean high water line that pollute the waters of the United States.
>
> The defendants' filling activities on land periodically inundated by tidal waters constituted discharges entering "waters of the United States" and, since done without a permit, were thus in violation of 33 U.S.C. § 1311(a).

Holland, supra, 373 F.Supp. at 676.
The legislative history of the FWPCA reviewed by the *Holland* court amply supports its conclusion.

tion covers waters which are no longer subject to tidal inundation because of man-made obstructions such as Leslie's dikes. These are the waters which the district court apparently wanted to include under the aegis of the FWPCA through the use of the historic MHHW line "in its unobstructed, natural state."

There are at least two problems with the district court's solution to the issue of Corps authority over Leslie's salt ponds. First, it goes beyond the necessities of this case. Although the appellees insist that the court did not mean to include "fast land," or "improved solid upland" within the ambit of its decision, its order is in fact ambiguous. It simply states that:

> Pursuant to the FWPCA the Corps may require permits for the discharge of dredged or fill material up to the line of MHHW in its unobstructed natural state, as defined in effect in the Corps' Public Notices 71–22 and 71–22(a) . . . .

Sierra Club v. Leslie Salt Co., supra, 412 F.Supp. at 1104.

. . . .

Second, and much more important, the court below actually placed undue limits on the FWPCA when it stated that "the geographical extent of the Corps' jurisdiction under the Rivers and Harbors Act is coterminous with that under FWPCA." *Sierra Club v. Leslie Salt Co., supra,* 412 F.Supp. at 1102. It is clear from the legistative history of the FWPCA that for the purposes of that Act, Congress intended to expand the narrow definition of the term "navigable waters," as used in the Rivers and Harbors Act. This court has indicated that the term "navigable waters" within the meaning of the FWPCA is to be given the broadest possible constitutional interpretation under the Commerce Clause. *California v. Environmental Protection Agency,* 511 F.2d 963, 964 n.1 (9th Cir. 1975), *rev'd on other grounds sub nom. Environmental Protection Agency v. State Water Resources Control Board,* 426 U.S. 200, 96 S.Ct 2022, 48 L.Ed.2d 578 (1976) ("Congress clearly meant to extend the Act's jurisdiction to the constitutional limit. . . ."). *See United States v. Phelps Dodge Corp.,* 391 F.Supp. 1181 (D.Ariz. 1975); *United States v. Holland, supra,* 373 F.Supp. 665 (M.D.Fla.1974). . . .

The water in Leslie's salt ponds, even though not subject to tidal action, comes from the San Francisco Bay to the extent of eight to nine billion gallons a year. We see no reason to suggest that the United States may protect these waters from pollution while they are outside of Leslie's tide gates, but may no longer do so once they have passed through these gates into Leslie's ponds. Moreover, there can be no question that activities within Leslie's salt ponds affect interstate commerce, since Leslie is a major supplier of salt for industrial, agricultural, and domestic use in the western United States. Much of the salt which Leslie harvests from the Bay's waters at the rate of about one million tons annually enters interstate and foreign commerce.

Our suggestion that the full extent of the Corps's FWPCA jurisdiction over the "waters of the United States" is in some instances not limited to the MHW or the MHHW line is reinforced by regulations published by the Corps on July 19, 1977 and found at 33 C.F.R. § 323.2, as published at 42 Fed.Reg. 37144–37145.

Without determining the exact limits of the scope of federal regulatory jurisdiction under the FWPCA, we find that the regulations at 33 C.F.R. § 323.2 are reasonable, consistent with the intent of Congress, and not contrary to the Constitution. We therefore hold that the Corps's jurisdiction under the FWPCA extends at least to waters which are no longer subject to tidal inundation because of Leslie's dikes without regard to the location of historic tidal water lines in their unobstructed, natural state. We express no opinion on the outer limits to which the Corps's jurisdiction under the FWPCA might extend.

Our holdings with respect to the Rivers and Harbors Act of 1899 and the FWPCA dispose of the declaratory judgment sought by Leslie in its case. Any claims by Leslie, which may be engendered by these holdings, and which are not also involved in Sierra Club's case, whether based on equitable considerations, estoppel, or surrender, must be made and considered in a separate and independent proceeding.

III. Sierra Club's Suit.

The district court applied its ruling in Leslie's case against the Corps to the Sierra Club's suit as well. In an order filed June 30, 1976, the court ruled that "there are no issues remaining to be tried in action No. C–72–561 WTS," and dismissed the Sierra Club's complaint in that case. On appeal, the Sierra Club has contended that genuine issues of material fact remain to be tried in the *Bair Island* case which preclude summary dismissal of its complaint in that action. In oral argument before this Court, Leslie conceded that the Sierra Club's action does involve unresolved issues not properly determined on summary judgment. We agree, and therefore remand case No. 76–2696 for trial.

. . . .

The decision of the district court with respect to the Rivers and Harbors Act of 1899 is reversed. The decision of the district court with respect to the FWPCA is reversed in part and modified in part. The action of the Sierra Club against Leslie Salt is remanded for further proceedings not inconsistent with this opinion.

Reversed in part, Modified in part, and Remanded in part.

NOTES

1. How would you summarize the relationship between FWPCA section 404 and sections 10 and 13 of the Rivers and Harbors Act? Consider the following:

   Acknowledging the "established role" of the U.S. Army Corps of Engineers in the dredging and maintenance of navigable channels and ports, Section 404 of the 1972 Amendments ordains a separate permit program for the discharge of dredged or fill material. Those qualifying for section 404 permits are exempted from the NPDES permit system. Some confusing overlap exists between the reach of the Corps-administered section 404 and EPA's ocean dumping permit program. But there is no difficulty reconciling the key features of the Rivers and Harbors Act with section 404: section 13 discharges not approved by a section 404 permit are disallowed. The section 10 permit program, addressing obstructions to navigation and channel alterations, differs from section 404 in coverage but is administered under exactly the same procedures, even to the extent of using the same forms. The principal difference is that section 404 reaches only discharges while section 10 applies to activities modifying channels without regard to whether there has been a discharge.

The scope of section 404 is measured chiefly by (1) the meaning of dredged or fill material; (2) the definition of navigable waters; (3) available remedies and (4) criteria for site selection and permit issuance. Also pertinent are (5) the activities of the Corps of Engineers itself and (6) related federal and state laws regulating wetland development.

W. Rodgers, *Environmental Law* 399–400 (© West Publishing 1977). *See* Blumm, *The Clean Water Act's Section 404 Permit Program Enters Its Adolescence: An Institutional and Programmatic Perspective,* 8 Ecology L.Q. 410 (1980); Caplin, *Is Congress Protecting Our Water? The Controversy over Section 404, Federal Water Pollution Act Amendments of 1972, 31 Miami L. Rev. 445 (1977);* Hall, *The Clean Water Act of 1977,* 11 Nat. Res. Law. 343 (1978); Note, *The Clean Water Act of 1977: Midcourse Corrections in the Section 404 Program,* 57 Neb. L. Rev. 1092 (1978).

2. Why is navigability still an important question under the Rivers and Harbor Act but not under FWPCA section 404? *Compare Minnehaha Creek Watershed District v. Hoffman, 449 F. Supp. 876, aff'd in part, rev'd in part, 597 F.2d 617 (8th Cir. 1979), with U.S. v. Earth Sciences, Inc., 599 F.2d 368 (7th Cir. 1979). See* Finnell, *Navigability: The Changing Legal Perspective,* 3 Coastal Zone '78 at 2036 (1978).

3. How workable is the mean high-tide line as the upland limit of Corps Rivers and Harbor Act jurisdiction? Is the line fixed or ambulatory? Recall the boundary determination discussion in Chapter 2, *supra. See* Teleky, *Are the Cries of Hermes Being Heard in the Wetlands?,* 3 Coastal Zone '78 at 2026 (1978).

Wetlands

AVOYELLES SPORTMEN'S LEAGUE v. ALEXANDER
473 F. Supp. 523 (D. La. 1979)

NAUMAN S. SCOTT, Chief Judge.

Plaintiffs[5] brought this declaratory and injunctive action alleging that land-clearing operations being carried on by the private defendants[6] have and will: alter and modify the course, condition and capacity of the navigable waters of the United States in violation of § 10 of the Rivers and Harbors Act of 1899, 33 U.S.C.A. § 403; result in the discharge of dredged and fill material into the waters of the United States in violation of § 404 of the Federal Water Pollution Control Act (hereinafter FWPCA), 33 U.S.C.A. § 1344; result in the discharge of pollutants into the waters of the United States in violation of § 402 of the FWPCA, 33 U.S.C.A. § 1342; and violate Louisiana State law under Louisiana Civil Code arts. 667 and 857. The plaintiffs requested that we compel the

---

[5]The Avoyelles Sportsmen's League, Inc., Point Basse Hunting Club, Inc., Avoyelles Bass Runners, Inc., Ira J. Marcotte, Avoyelles Natural Guard, Inc., The Environmental Defense Fund, Inc., and The National Wildlife Federation.

[6]Albert Prevot, H. P. Lambright and Elder Realty Co., Inc.

federal defendants to regulate the land-clearing activities and enjoin the land-clearing activities until the extent of the federal defendants' jurisdiction has been determined and permits applied for under 33 U.S.C.A. §§ 403, 1342 and 1344.

The land subject to this proceeding and being cleared is an approximately 20,000 acre tract (hereinafter referred to as the Lake Long Tract) situated in Avoyelles Parish, Louisiana between the Grassy Lake State Management Area and the Spring Bayou State Management Area. It lies within the Bayou Natchitoches basin which, along with the Ouachita, Black and Tensas river basins, makes up the Red River backwater area. The Bayou Natchitoches basin itself is an area comprised of approximately 140,000 acres. Much of this basin has been cleared of forest but before the private defendants' land clearing operations commenced, approximately 80,000 acres of this area still was forested. Consequently, prior to the commencement of the private defendants' land-clearing operations, the Lake Long tract represented one-quarter of the remaining forested acreage in the Bayou Natchitoches basin.

The Bayou Natchitoches basin serves as a major overflow or backwater area for the Red River. Backwater flooding occurs in the Bayou Natchitoches basin when the Red River rises to a point where its waters cannot flow downstream efficiently and instead flow west into Bayou Natchitoches, then into Bayou Jeansonne, over the Lake Long tract and further westward into the Spring Bayou State Management area. Generally, during the recession of backwater floods, the flood waters on the Lake Long tract drain in an easterly direction back into the Red River.

More than half of the tract, i.e., everything at or below 45.8 feet MSL, is subject to the average annual flood. Virtually all of the tract, i.e., everything at or below 49.6 feet MSL is subject to the average bi-annual flood.

The clearing of the Lake Long Tract began in June of 1978. Sometime prior to that loggers had harvested much of the commercially valuable hardwoods with chainsaws. Thereafter, the private defendants took various steps to remove all the remaining trees and vegetation from the tract so that it could be put to agricultural use and specifically into soybean production.

Initially, bulldozers outfitted with shearing blades cut the timber and vegetation at or just above ground level. The shearing blades were v-shaped, had a serrated edge and flat bottom and were approximately 18–20 feet in length. The blades were adjusted to be free floating so that they would ride along the top surface of the ground. Occasionally, however, the blades would gouge the surface of the ground. Although the blades were adjusted to ride on the ground's surface, they did scrape the leaf litter and humus that overlaid the soil as they moved from tree to tree.

After the shearing was completed in a section, bulldozers outfitted with rake blades pushed the felled trees into wind rows. The upper portion of the raking blade was solid whereas the lower portion had tines that permitted soil to pass through the openings. The raking blades were also outfitted so that they generally operated on top of the soil. However, in the process of windrowing the trees and debris, soil and leaf litter was also scraped into the windrows. It is not clear whether the blades themselves or the broom-like action of the trees and brush that they were pushing actually scraped the soil and the overlying leaf litter. In any event the photographic evidence clearly demonstrated that soil and leaf litter was piled up during the windrowing process—this movement filled in low areas and along with the discing which followed, had a levelling effect on the surface of the land.

The trees and other vegetation that had been windrowed were then burned. The remaining ashes were later disced into and across the tract. Some of the felled trees and other debris would not burn. This material was buried in four or five pits, each approximately 50 feet long and 6 feet deep that had been dug with backhoes by the private defendants.

Tractors pulling chunk rakes would go over the areas that had been sheared and windrowed and rake together any remaining debris. Basically, the chunk rakes were sets of tines that were outfitted on cultivators that had had their blades removed. The chunk rakes gathered the small debris into piles where it was presumably burned. These ashes were also disced into the soil.

After the shearing, windrowing and chunk raking the land was disced to prepare it for soybean cultivation. A disc is a bowl-shaped blade that cuts into the ground and fluffs the soil up. The disc's used on this tract were 24 inches in diameter and would cut into the ground approximately 9 inches. During discing, some soil would ride in front of the disc and would be redeposited in other areas of the tract, resulting in substantial displacement and redepositing of the soil itself.

Defendants also dug a drainage ditch that was approximately three-quarters of a mile long. The earth excavated from the ditch was piled alongside the ditch and was to be spread over the adjacent area. Construction of at least four or five miles of additional ditches were contemplated for soybean cultivation.

On November 7, 1978 we granted a temporary restraining order whereby the private defendants were prohibited from engaging in any further landclearing activity. More specifically, they were prohibited from conducting ditch excavation, altering the surface of the land, logging, except by chainsaw, destroying vegetation, plowing, discing, or discharging any biologic material or pollutants onto the land. They were permitted to clean up debris already on the ground.

On January 17, 1979 it was ordered that the federal defendants prepare a final wetland determination within sixty days. The private defendants were permitted to engage in normal cultivation, plowing and seeding without obtaining a permit on the land already cleared, approximately 10,000 acres. The private defendants were ordered to and agreed under protest, to apply for permits under § 404 for any ditching, levee construction and drainage work construction on the land already cleared. As to the uncleared land, the prohibitions of the temporary restraining order remained unchanged.

On March 26, 1979 the federal defendants filed their final wetland determination which designated certain portions of the tract, including substantial portions of the cleared lands, to be wetlands. Thereafter the private defendants filed objections to this determination.

. . . .

. . . Consequently, the only issue now before us is whether the type of activities allowed in the government's statement, such as the shearing of trees to convert forested wetlands to other purposes, require permits under the FWPCA and § 10 of the Rivers and Harbors Act of 1899. We hold that permits are required under § 404 of the FWPCA.

. . . .

Since "navigable waters" includes wetlands, 33 C.F.R. § 323.2(a), it is clear that the following issues must be resolved in determining whether any or all of the private defendants' landclearing activities require a permit under § 404: (1) are there any point sources of pollution? (2) if so, is there a discharge of dredged or fill material? (3) if so, does the activity constitute normal farming or silviculture activities which are exempted from the permit program under § 404(f)(1)(A) and (4) if so, will the activities result in a change in the use of the land so that the flow or circulation of the waters may be impaired or that reach of the waters may be reduced thereby making the exemption unavailable under § 404(f)(2)?

(1) Are there any point sources of pollution? § 502(14) of the FWPCA defines a point source as:

"any discernable, confined and discrete conveyance, including but not limited to any . . . ditch, channel . . . discrete fissure, container, rolling stock . . . from which pollutants are or may be discharged. . . . "

We determine that defendants' landclearing equipment (bulldozers fitted with V-blades, bulldozers fitted with raking blades, and the tractor-pulled rakes), ditch excavation equipment (the backhoe used to excavate the three-quarter mile drainage ditch as well as any equipment used to excavate the proposed drainage ditches) and discing equipment, (unless used in connection with "normal farming"), are point sources. The general definition of point source and the illustrative examples connote that a point source is an isolable, identifiable activity that conveys a pollutant, dredged or fill material. The operation of defendants' equipment was certainly an identifiable and isolable activity. It also conveyed dredged or fill material since it collected, gathered and transported the sheared trees and vegetation, leaf litter and soil across the wetland which, for reasons set out below, we determine to be dredged material. It is clear beyond cavil that any machinery used in ditch excavation is a point source since such machinery excavates the wetland soil and then discharges this soil back into the wetland.

This determination is buttressed by the cases of *U.S. v. Fleming Plantations*, 12 E.R.C 1705 (E.D.La.1978), and *U.S. v. Holland*, 373 F. Supp. 665 (M.D.Fla.1974). In the former case it was determined that marsh buggies and draglines were point sources. In the latter case it was determined that dump trucks, draglines and bulldozers were point sources.

(2) Is there a discharge of dredged or fill material? As just indicated above, we have determined that the sheared trees and vegetation and scraped soil and leaf litter constitute dredged or fill material. We will deal first with the sheared trees and vegetation. To reinterate 33 C.F.C. § 323.2(k) defines dredged material as "material that is excavated or dredged from waters of the United States." This essentially means that excavated material is the removal of some part of the waters of the United States. When dealing with a traditional water body such as a lake or a river, this would involve digging up the bottom or floor of the water

body. However, herein we are not dealing with such traditional water bodies. Rather the area in dispute has been determined to be a wetland. The term "wetlands" is defined as:

> "those areas that are inundated or saturated by surface or ground water at a frequency and duration sufficient to support, and that under normal circumstances do support, *a prevalence of vegetation typically adopted for life in saturated soil conditions*. Wetlands generally include swamps, marshes, bogs and similar areas." 33 C.F.R. 323.2(c). (Emphasis supplied)

The above quoted definition makes it clear that wetlands include the vegetation that grows thereon. Such lands in the absence of vegetation can supply hardly any of the purposes of the Act. Consequently, in determining what constitutes dredged material in a wetland area, the inquiry does not end at the surface of the earth or water. Rather, any such inquiry must also consider vegetation, the very thing that defines a wetland. Accordingly, we determine that clearing the land of trees and vegetation, which are parts of the waters of the United States under 33 C.F.R. § 323.2(a) and (c) constitutes the discharge of dredged material.

Our determination that the soil and detritus was scraped up and conveyed across the tract is buttressed by the fact that many of the small sloughs were filled and the larger ones were partially filled in the landclearing process. The process had a levelling effect which also qualified the material moved as fill material.

. . . .

The evidence demonstrated that the Lake Long wetland area performed the functions mentioned in 33 C.F.R. § 320.4(b)(2)(i), (iii), (v) and (vii). Aside from the flood storage capacity function recognized in 33 C.F.R. § 320.4(b)(2)(v) which will not be affected by the removal of the wetland vegetation, the evidence disclosed that the other wetland functions performed by the Lake Long tract will be seriously impaired, if not destroyed, by permanent removal of the wetland's vegetation since the vegetation on the land, not the land itself, makes these functions possible.

Functions identified in 33 C.F.R. § 320.–4(e)(2)(i): Forested wetland provides habitat for many animals such as deer, otter, beaver and nutria. Of course, cleared agricultural land does not provide food and shelter for these animals.

The permanent removal of the trees and vegetation will also result in a loss of detritus—an important link in the aquatic food chain. Detritus, a particulate organic material formed when bacteria, insects and other small organisms feed on the fallen leaves that have accumulated on the forest floor (referred to as leaf litter), is an important source of food energy for the fish and shellfish of the Natchitoches Basin and Red River. Fish and shellfish that are carried into the backwater area feed heavily on detritus. The receding flood waters carry out detrital material into the Red River where it is used as food.

Clearing of the wetland's vegetation will also seriously impair fish spawning. Fish that inhabit the Red River and its basins spawn in the backwater areas. Many of these fish are broadcast spawners—they spew their eggs out into the water which attach to vegetation by means of an adhesive material that covers them. The eggs will have no vegetation on which to attach after clearing, and as a result the eggs will fall to the bottom where they will be covered with silt resulting in suffocation of the embryo.

Fish nursery grounds will also be adversely affected by the clearing. Many fish larvae use the backwater area as a nursery where they feed on detritus and seek out vegetated areas for protection from predators. This will no longer be possible if the wetlands are cleared.

Functions identified in 33 C.F.R. § 320.—4(b)(2)(iii): Sedimentation patterns will be adversely affected by clearing since there would be a drastic increase in the amount of sedimentation produced by the wetland. Forested wetland produces only three-quarters of a ton of sediment per acre yearly whereas agricultural land produces substantially more than five tons of sediment per acre yearly.

In addition, there will be an increase in the rate of erosion if the land is cleared. The forest overstory tends to break the momentum of precipitation and thereby decrease the impact of the precipitation on the soil lying below. The leaf litter and humus which covers the forest floor also protects the underlying soil from the impact of precipitation. If cleared, the soil would be subject to the full impact of the rain and will erode at a quicker rate than it would if it remained forested. Of course, this increased erosion helps explain why sedimentation will be greatly increased after clearing.

The wetland's natural drainage characteristics will also be affected by clearing since precipitation runs off agricultural land much quicker than it does from forested land. On forested land, leaf litter and humus lying on the forest floor absorbs much of the precipitation and thereby slows down the rate of drainage. Additionally, tree roots slow down the rate of drainage since they trap and hold precipitation. Needless to say, the rate of drainage will be further increased by any ditching activities.

Function identified in 33 C.F.R. § 320.—4(b)(2)(vii): As precipitation slowly drains off a forested area it percolates through the leaf litter and humus which tends to purify it. If there is no leaf litter and humus to act as a filtration system, needless to say, this purification process will be seriously impaired if not destroyed.

The FWPCA would be emasculated insofar as wetlands are concerned were we to conclude that the permanent removal of the wetland's vegetation in the process of converting it to agricultural land was not subject to the § 404 permit program. As the above discussion makes evident, wetlands are important to the public interest because of the various functions they perform. If one destroys a wetland's ability to perform these functions, he has in effect destroyed the wetland insofar as the public interest is concerned. Many of the functions that wetlands perform are dependent on the presence of vegetation. Obviously, if a wetland area is cleared of its vegetation it would no longer functionally exist in many respects and the public interest would be seriously affected. Common sense dictates that an activity that results in the effective destruction of a wetland resource should be subject to regulation under an Act that has as its purpose the restoration and maintenance of the "chemical, physical and biological integrity" of our nation's wetlands.

(3) Does the activity of the private defendants constitute normal farming or silviculture so as to be exempt from the § 404 permit program by §

404(f)(1)(A)? We note at the outset that the legislative history to the Clean Water Act indicates that the exemptions to the § 404 permit program should be narrowly construed.

. . . .

Although clear-cutting may be part of a normal silviculture operation under other circumstances, it is clear that the private defendants' clear-cutting was not part of a normal silviculture operation herein since no regeneration of the timber is contemplated.

(4) Finally we are buttressed in our conclusion that the defendants' land conversion activities are not exempt under 404(f)(1)(A) by the fact that 404(f)(2) specifically takes away the exemption for activities that involve converting the use of the land. Even assuming arguendo that the clearing activities were normal farming or silviculture, the evidence demonstrated that these activities would fall within the technical terms of the 404(f)(2) limitation. Under that provision activities that would be exempted under 404(f)(1)(A) are denied exempt status if they are incidental to an activity which will convert a wetlands area to another use where the reach of the water may be reduced or the flow or circulation of the water may be impaired.

Private defendant's clearing of the land so that it could be used for soybean production was definitely a change in use. . . .

. . . .

Since we have determined that defendants' land-clearing activities are subject to the § 404 permit program, we find it unnecessary to decide whether there was any violation of § 10 of the Rivers and Harbors Act of 1899 and § 402 of the FWPCA. *U.S. v. Fleming Plantations,* 12 E.R.C. § 1704 (E.D.La.1978).

Up to this point in the opinion we have been concerned with the uncleared wetlands on the Lake Long Tract, as the Government determination of March 26, 1979 has defined "wetlands". We now are concerned with the cleared wetlands on that tract. If the private defendants' clearing activities were not exempt under the provisions of § 404(f)(1)(A) as we have now determined then perhaps the private defendants should be ordered to restore the forested wetlands, *U.S. v. Fleming Plantation, supra.* But in our final injunction and order dated May 4, 1979, the private defendants were permitted to engage in normal farming operations on all wetlands that were cleared prior to the issuance of the temporary restraining order. This decision was based on the following equitable considerations: Defendants' land-clearing operations began in the summer of 1978. They had cleared several thousand areas when the Corps issued a cease and desist order so that it could determine what areas of the tract were wetlands and thus subject to its jurisdiction under the § 404 program. The private defendants stopped their landclearing activities in compliance with the cease and desist order. Subsequently the Corps surveyed the tract and made a determination of what areas it considered to be wetlands. Thereafter the private defendants commenced their land-clearing operations and cleared several thousands acres that the Corps had determined not to be wetlands. On November 7, 1978 this court granted a temporary restraining order that prohibited all land-clearing and ditching activities on the tract. The defendants have not engaged in any land-clearing activities or ditching activities since the TRO was granted. Unfortunately, the final wetland determination filed on March 26, 1979 by the federal defendants differed from the determination that had been made at the time of the cease and desist order by the Corps. As a result, the private defendants cleared some areas of the tract that had initially been determined not to be wetlands and which were subsequently determined to be wetlands in the March 26, 1979 wetland determination. There has been no evidence of any bad faith on the part of the defendants who at all times have acted in full compliance with the directives of the Corps and this court. Under such circumstances, we feel that the private defendants should be permitted to conduct normal farming operations on the land already cleared with the exception that no ditching will be conducted without § 404 permits on any of the wetland area including those areas that had already been cleared.

NOTES

1. Section 404(f)(1), 33 U.S.C. § 1344(f)(1) (1978), discussed by the court in *Avoyelles,* creates a number of specific exemptions to dredge-and-fill regulation. What are the policy reasons behind these exemptions? *See* Blumm, *The Clean Water Act's Section 404 Permit Program Enters Its Adolescence: An Institutional and Programmatic Perspective,* 8 Ecology L.Q. 409, 419–28 (1980). Are the exempted activities still subject to state dredge-and-fill regulations? *See Bartell v. State,* 284 N.W.2d 834 (Minn. 1979); *Saxon v. Division of State Lands, 31 Or. App. 511, 570 P.2d 1197 (1977);* Jones & Lynch, *Local Environmental Management–Can It Work? A Case Study of the Virginia Wetlands Act,* 4 Coastal Zone Mgmt. J. 127 (1978).

2. Other cases upholding Corps jurisdiction over nonnavigable wetlands under FWPCA section 404 include *American Dredging Co. v. Dutchyshyn,* 480 F. Supp. 957 (D. Pa. 1979); *Parkview Corp. v. Corps of Engineers,* 455 F. Supp. 1350 (D. Wis. 1978), 469 F. Supp. 247 (1979), 85 F.R.D. 145 (1980), 490 F. Supp. 1278 (1980); *United States v. Byrd,* 9 Envt'l L. Rep. 20757 (7th Cir. 1979); *United States v. Fleming Plantations,* 9 Envt'l L. Rep. 20103 (E.D. La. 1978); *USI Properties Corp. v. EPA,* 16 ERC 1408 (D.P.R. 1981). *See* Emmer, *Upstream Limits of Section 404 Federal Jurisdiction,* 3 Coastal Zone '78 at 2013 (1978); Note, *Federal Control over Wetland Areas: The Corps of Engineers Expands Its Jurisdiction,* 28 U. Fla. L. Rev. 787 (1976); Note, *The Wetlands Controversy: A Coastal Concern Washes Inland,* 52 Notre Dame Law. 1015 (1977); Note, *Wetlands' Reluctant Champion: The Corps Takes a Fresh Look at Navigable Waters,* 6 Envt'l Law. 217 (1975).

3. On the role of wetlands in the coastal ecology, recall the Clark excerpt in Chapter 1, Section B, *supra,* and *see* Greeson, Clark & Clark, Wetland Functions and Values: The State of Our Understanding (American Water Resources Assoc. 1978); Jensen & Tyrawski, *Wetlands and Water Quality,* 2 Coastal Zone '78 at 1145 (1978); Kockelman & Blanchfield, *Protecting Suisun Marsh–85,000 Acres of Habitat,* 2 Coastal Zone '80 at 1138 (1980); Odum, *The Importance of Tidal Freshwater Wetlands in Coastal Zone Management,* 2 Coastal Zone '78 at 1196 (1978); Sears, *Perceiving the Unseen Value of Coastal Wetlands,* 1 Coastal Zone '80 at 484 (1980); Shabman & Batie, *Economic Value of Natural Coastal Wetlands: A Critique,* 4 Coastal Zone Mgmt. J. 231 (1978); Walker, *Wetlands Preservation and Management on Chesapeake Bay: The Role of Science in Natural Resources Policy,* 1 Coastal Zone Mgmt. J. 75 (1973); Wilen & Nye, *National Wetlands Inventory,* 3 Coastal Zone '80 at 1847 (1980).

4. Was the court in *Avoyelles* correct in not ordering restoration of the wetlands cleared without the required permit? Consider the saga of *U.S. v. Joseph G. Moretti, Inc.* Moretti was a mobile-home park developer who filled in a portion of

a Florida bay without a Corps permit and also destroyed a mangrove wetland area. The district court ordered the removal of the fill and the replanting of the mangroves. 331 F. Supp. 151 (S.D. Fla. 1971).

On appeal, the Fifth Circuit vacated the district court's decision since it found that the administrative processing of the defendant's application for an after-the-fact permit had not been completed. 478 F.2d 418 (5th Cir. 1973).

After the Corps of Engineers had denied Moretti's application for an after-the-fact permit, the district court again granted an injunction and required the defendant to restore the area to "its original condition." 387 F. Supp. 1404 (S.D. Fla. 1974).

On appeal of this decision the Fifth Circuit noted that the district court had authority to order the restoration, but reversed and remanded the decision for an evidentiary hearing on the manner of restoration to be performed. The court said that the defendant must be afforded an opportunity to present objections to the feasibility and environmental advisability of the restoration plan. 526 F.2d 1306 (5th Cir. 1976).

Back in the district court, after a full factual hearing the injunction and the restoration plan were upheld. The court said the plan was designed to confer "maximum environmental benefits" while being tempered with a "touch of equity" and was within the resources of the defendant. The plan, along with a map, are included in the published opinion. 423 F. Supp. 1197, 1201 (S.D. Fla. 1976).

On March 27, 1979, the Fifth Circuit, without opinion, vacated and remanded the district court's decision. 592 F.2d 1189 (5th Cir. 1979). What is the end result of ordering restoration if protracted litigation results in the bankruptcy of the developer? Should the court impose a judicial lien securing restoration? Should restoration be ordered as a matter of course? Considering the difficulties of enforcing court-ordered restoration, are there any alternative remedies available? Would they be as effective in discouraging permit requirement violations as ordering restoration? *See* Haagenson, *Restoration as a Federal Remedy for Illegal Dredging and Filling Operations,* 32 U. Miami L. Rev. 105 (1977).

Other cases in which the courts have ordered restoration include *Parkview Corp. v. Corps of Engineers,* 490 F. Supp. 1278 (D. Wis. 1980); *State v. Davidson Industries,* 620 P.2d 942 (Or. Ct. App. 1980); *United States v. De Felice,* 15 ERC. 1896 (5th Cir. 1981); *United States v. Kirkland,* 16 ERC 1465 (S.D. Fla. 1981); *United States v. Sexton Cove Estates, Inc.,* 389 F. Supp. 602 (S.D. Fla. 1974), *rev'd in part,* 526 F.2d 1293 (5th Cir. 1976), *noted,* 31 U. Miami L. Rev. 697 (1977); *United States v. Sunset Cove, Inc.* 3 Envt'l L. Rep. 20,371 (D. Ore., Feb. 13, 1973), *modified in part,* 514 F.2d 1089 (9th Cir. 1975), *cert. denied,* 423 U.S. 865 (1975); *United States v. Weisman,* 489 F. Supp. 1331 (M.D. Fla. 1980); *Weiszmann v. Dist. Eng. U.S. Corps of Eng.,* 526 F.2d 1306 (5th Cir. 1976).

5. The foregoing cases have a great deal to say about the extent of Corps jurisdiction but offer relatively little guidance on how the Corps should rule on applicants' requests for permits. Under what circumstances should the Corps allow dredging and filling in navigable waterways and wetlands? Should filling be allowed only for water-dependent uses? *See* 40 C.F.R. pt. 230 (1980) (EPA FWPCA section 404(b) fill discharge guidelines). Is an airport runway a water-dependent use? *See Morse v. Division of State Lands,* 30 Or. App. 516, 581 P.2d 520 (1978), *aff'd on different grounds,* 285 Or. 197, 590 P.2d 709 (1979). Is a shopping center a water-dependent use? *See Sierra Club v. Alexander,* 484 F. Supp. 455 (D.N.Y. 1980). Are residential and commercial facilities connected with a marina water-dependent uses? *See* Christensen & Snyder, *Establishment of Residential Waterfront Property by Construction of Canal Systems in Coastal Wetlands: Problems and Solutions,* 2 Coastal Zone '78 at 1301 (1978); Power, *Watergate Village: A Case Study of a Permit Application for a Marina Submitted to the U.S. Army Corps of Engineers,* 2 Coastal Zone Mgmt. J. 103 (1975).

6. Should applicants granted permission to fill be required to mitigate the impacts of their fills by restoring equivalent degraded areas? *See Morse v. Division of State Lands, supra;* Balco, *Evaluating Wetlands: Status and Needs,* 1 Coastal Zone '80 at 494 (1980); Banta & Nauman, *Mitigation in Federal Dredge and Fill Permits,* 2 Coastal Zone '78 at 1316 (1978); Beeman & Benkendorf, *Productive Land Use of Dredged Material Areas,* 2 Coastal Zone '78 at 721 (1978); Emmer, *The Evolution of Mitigation in a Highway System,* 2 Coastal Zone '80 at 1119 (1980); Hershman & Ruotsala, *Implementing Environmental Mitigation Policies,* 2 Coastal Zone '78 at 1333 (1978); Reimold, *Coastal Alternative Dredged Material Rehabilitation,* 2 Coastal Zone '78 at 736 (1978); Smith, *Habitat Development: An Alternative Method of Dredged Material Disposal,* 2 Coastal Zone '78 at 795 (1978); Snyder, *Is There Life Beyond Mitigation?,* 1 Coastal Zone '80 at 470 (1980); Walsh, Patin, & Malkasian, *Land Use of Dredged Material Containment Areas,* 2 Coastal Zone '78 at 804 (1978).

   See generally Converse & Shapiro, *Wetlands Reviews—A California Experience,* 3 Coastal Zone '80 at 1829 (1980); Guste & Ellis, *Louisiana Tidelands Past and Future,* 21 Loy. L. Rev. 817 (1975); Mumphrey & Brooks, *Guidelines for Urban Development in Louisiana's Coastal Wetlands,* 4 Coastal Zone Mgmt. J. 165 (1978); Odu & Skjei, *The Issue of Wetlands Preservation and Management: A Second View,* 1 Coastal Zone Mgmt. J. 151 (1974); Onuf, *Science and Plans: California Coastal Wetlands,* 3 Coastal Zone '80 at 1858 (1980); U.S. Dept. of the Interior, Proceedings of the National Wetland Protection Symposium, Reston, Va. (1977).

7. Based on the materials in this chapter, in what ways do you think the Corps' regulatory program could be improved to protect better the nation's coastal waterways and wetlands? *See* U.S. Comptroller General, Improvements Needed in the Corps of Engineers' Regulatory Program for Protecting the Nation's Waters (1977).

8. Can the activities approved in a Corps dredge-and-fill permit affect land and water uses in a state's coastal zone? If so, the state must determine that they are consistent with the state's federally approved coastal zone management program before the permit may be issued. *See* 16 U.S.C. § 1456(c) (1976), discussed in Chapter 12, *infra.*

   What if a federally approved state coastal zone program allows filling of the particular wetland in question—is the Corps obligated by the consistency requirement to *issue* a fill permit? *See* Blumm, *Wetlands Protection and Coastal Planning: Avoiding the Perils of Positive Consistency,* 5 Colum. J. Envt'l L. 69 (1978). With regard to this positive consistency problem, note that FWPCA section 404(c), 33 U.S.C. § 1344(c) (1978) authorizes the administrator of the federal Environmental Protection Agency to prevent dredge spoil disposal in any specified area if the administrator determines that the discharge will have an unacceptable adverse effect on municipal water supplies, shellfish beds and fishery areas, or wildlife and recreational areas. *See* J. Cole, *Evaluation of Laws and Regulations Impacting the Land Use of Dredged Material Containment Areas* (1978).

9. Can denial by the Corps of a fill permit constitute a taking of private property requiring just compensation? *See Deltona Corporation v. United States,* 16 ERC 1482 (Ct. Clms. 1981); *Jentgen v. United States,* 16 ERC 1474 (Ct. Clms. 1981); *Kaiser–Aetna v. United States,* Chap. III, Section B, *supra.*

11

The Federal Coastal Zone Management Act

Congress passed the Coastal Zone Management Act (CZMA) in 1972 with the stated goal of furthering "a national interest in the effective management, beneficial use, protection, and development of the coastal zone." 16 U.S.C. § 1451(a) (1976). The CZMA has been amended three times since 1972, first in 1976, then again in 1978, and most recently in 1980. Before 1972, a few coastal states had enacted or were preparing comprehensive coastal plans, while many others had passed legislation regulating specific uses of the coastal zone. Most coastal states had delegated substantial authority to local governments. The result was a variety of state mechanisms for managing the coastal zone, with overall responsibility shared with the federal controls discussed in the preceding chapters.

Substantively, the act was limited to encouraging states to adopt more rational resource allocation procedures, and furthering intergovernmental coordination. Analytically, however, the act provides a useful framework for examining state management of the coastal zone. State management programs developed under the act's guidelines highlight the differing approaches available to states in managing the coast, each with advantages and disadvantages. The act raises special problem areas that confront coastal states, such as energy facility siting, shoreline access, and regional planning. Once state management programs have been developed and approved under the CZMA, the central issue becomes one of implementation. How are abstract goals and policies translated into concrete rules and decisions consistent with the program? The challenge of implementation typically revolves around two subissues: coordination of federal and state authorities, and coordination of state and local authorities. The CZMA seeks to facilitate both interactions.

See generally, Comment, *Toward Better Use of Coastal Resources: Coor-dinated State and Federal Planning Under the Coastal Zone Management Act*, 5 Geo. L.J. 1057 (1977); Hollings, *Congress and Coastal Zone Management*, 1 Coastal Zone Mgmt. J. 115 (1973); Knecht, *Coastal Zone Management—A Federal Perspective*, 1 Coastal Zone Mgmt. J. 123 (1973); D. Mandelker, *Environmental and Land Controls Legislation* 223–46 (1976 & 1980 Supp.); Mandelker & Sherry, *The National Coastal Zone Management Act of 1972*, 7 Urb. L. Ann. 119 (1974); Symposium, *Implementation of the Coastal Zone Management Act of 1972*, 16 Wm. & Mary L. Rev. No. 4 (1975); Yahner, *The Coastal Zone Management Act Amendments of 1976*, 1 Harv. Envt'l L. Rev. 259 (1976); Zile, *A Legislative Political History of the Coastal Zone Management Act of 1972*, 1 Coastal Zone Mgmt. J. 235 (1972).

SECTION A: STATE PROGRAM DEVELOPMENT AND APPROVAL

The most important judicial consideration of the act is *American Petroleum Institute v. Knecht*, 456 F. Supp. 889 (C.D. Cal. 1978), *aff'd*, 609 F.2d 1306 (9th Cir. 1979) which follows. At issue was the California coastal management program which was approved by NOAA in 1977. Increased interest in potential oil and gas deposits off the California coast, especially on the federal outer continental shelf, led to inclusion of a substantial oil and gas element in the California program, part of which is quoted here:

Oil and Gas Development

The [California] Coastal Act includes the following policies on oil and gas development:

Oil and gas development shall be permitted in accordance with Section 30260, if the following considerations are met:

(a) The development is performed safely and consistent with the geologic conditions of the well site.

(b) New or expanded facilities related to such development are consolidated, to the maximum extent feasible and legally permissible, unless consolidation will have adverse environmental consequences and will not significantly reduce the number of producing wells, support facilities, or sites required to produce the reservoir economically and with minimal environmental impacts.

(c) Environmentally safe and feasible subsea completions are used when drilling platforms or islands would substantially degrade coastal visual qualities unless use of such structures will result in substantially less environmental risks.

(d) Platforms or islands will not be sited where a substantial hazard to vessel traffic might result from the facility or related operations, determined in consultation with the United States Coast Guard and the Army Corps of Engineers.

(e) Such development will not cause or contribute to subsidence hazards unless it is determined that adequate measures will be undertaken to prevent damage from subsidence.

(f) With respect to new facilities, all oilfield brines are reinjected into oil-producing zones unless the Division of Oil and Gas of the Department of Conservation determines to do so would adversely affect production of the reservoirs and unless injection into other subsurface zones will reduce environmental risks. Exceptions to reinjections will be granted consistent with the Ocean Waters Discharge Plan of the State Water Resources Control Board and where adequate provision is made for the elimination of petroleum odors and water quality problems.

Where appropriate, monitoring programs to record land surface and near-shore ocean floor movements shall be initiated in locations of new large-scale fluid extraction on land or near-shore before operations begin and shall continue until surface conditions have stabilized. Costs of monitoring and mitigation programs shall be borne by liquid and gas extraction operators. (Section 30262)

In considering permits for and in planning related to oil and gas development, the Commission coordinates with the appropriate Federal and State agencies including the California Division of Oil and Gas, State Lands Commission, and the U.S. Department of the Interior. In considering the public welfare aspects of any such proposed developments, the Commission utilizes legislation and policy statements and reports of appropriate State and Federal agencies, including the Office of the President, Interior Department, Federal Energy Administration, the Energy Commission, Governor's Office of Planning and Research, and others.

Refineries and Petrochemical Facilities

The Coastal Act includes the following policies on refineries and petrochemical facilities:

(a) New or expanded refineries or petrochemical facilities not otherwise consistent with the provisions of this division shall be permitted if (1) alternative locations are not feasible or are more environmentally damaging; (2) adverse environmental effects are mitigated to the maximum extent feasible; (3) it is found that not permitting such development would adversely affect the public welfare; (4) the facility is not located in a highly scenic or seismically hazardous area, on any of the Channel Islands, or within or contiguous to environmentally sensitive areas, and (5) the facility is sited so as to provide a sufficient buffer area to minimize adverse impacts on surrounding property.

(b) In addition to meeting all applicable air quality standards, new or expanded refineries or petrochemical facilities shall be permitted in areas designated as air quality maintenance areas by the State Air Resources Board and in areas where coastal resources would be adversely affected only if the negative impacts of the project upon air quality are offset by reductions in gaseous emissions in the area by the users of the fuels, or, in the case of an expansion of an existing site, total site emission levels, and site levels for each emission type for which national or State ambient air quality standards have been established, do not increase.

(c) New or expanded refineries or petrochemical facilities shall minimize the need for once-through cooling by using air cooling to the maximum extent feasible and by using treated waste waters from inplant processes where feasible. (Section 30263)

In considering the public welfare aspects of such facilities, the Commission utilizes policy statements and reports from appropriate State and Federal agencies, including the Energy Commission, Federal Energy Administration, Governor's Office of Planning and Research, and the Office of the President.

U.S. Department of Commerce, State of California Coastal Management Program and Final Environmental Impact Statement 68–69 (1977).

AMERICAN PETROLEUM INSTITUTE v. KNECHT, 456 F. Supp. 889 (C.D. Cal. 1978), aff'd, 609 F.2d 1306 (9th Cir. 1979)

KELLEHER, District Judge,

Plaintiffs American Petroleum Institute, Western Oil and Gas Association, and certain oil company members of the aforesaid Institute and Association brought this action against three federal officials ("the federal defendants") in their official capacities as Secretary of Commerce, Administrator of the National Oceanic and Atmospheric Administration ("NOAA"), and Acting Associate Administrator of the Office of Coastal Zone Management ("OCZM"), seeking declaratory and injunctive relief against defendants' imminent grant of "final approval" of the California Coastal Zone Management Program ("CZMP") pursuant to § 306 of the Coastal Zone Management Act of 1972, as amended ("CZMA") (16 U.S.C. §§ 1451 et seq.) and seeking further relief in the nature of mandamus directing the federal defendants to grant "preliminary approval" to the CZMP pursuant to § 305(d) of the Act.

In brief, plaintiffs contend that the California Program cannot lawfully be approved by the federal defendants under § 306 of the CZMA, principally for two reasons. First, the CZMP is not a "management program" within the meaning of § 304(11) of the Act in that (a) it fails to satisfy the requirements of §§ 305(b) and 306(c), (d), and (e), and regulations promulgated thereunder, as regards content specificity; and (b) it has not been "adopted by the state" within the meaning of § 306(c)(1). Second, the procedures by which the CZMP has reached the present state of development violate the CZMA, the National Environmental Policy Act ("NEPA") (42 U.S.C. §§ 4321 et seq.), and California statutes in that the final environmental impact statement, which differs substantially from both the draft and revised draft environmental impact statements, was not subject to formal notice and hearings, yet purports to contain one of five "elements" of the CZMP.

. . . The order further provided, however, that pending entry of final judgment in this Court, any such approval under § 306 by the federal defendants would be deemed ineffective to trigger the "consistency" provisions of § 307(c) and (d). The CZMP was given final approval by Acting Associate Administrator

Knecht, to whom the duty of approving or disapproving management programs submitted under § 306 had been and continues to be delegated, on November 7, 1977. His findings were issued at that time.

For reasons set forth below, the Court affirms the federal defendants' § 306 approval of the CZMP and grants judgment for defendants and against plaintiffs.

Facts

The following facts appear to be before the Court without dispute:

1. Plaintiff American Petroleum Institute ("API"), a corporation organized under the District of Columbia nonprofit corporation laws, is a national trade association of approximately 350 companies and 7,000 individuals engaged in the petroleum industry. Its members include companies and individuals actively engaged in exploration, production, refining and marketing of petroleum products in the United States, including the State of California and the Outer Continental Shelf off the coast of California.

2. Plaintiff Western Oil and Gas Association ("WOGA"), a corporation organized under the California nonprofit corporation laws, is a regional trade assocation of over 75 member companies and individuals engaged in the petroleum industry. Its members include companies and individuals responsible for in excess of 65 percent of the production of petroleum, in excess of 90 percent of the refining of petroleum, and in excess of 90 percent of the marketing of petroleum in the southern western states of the United States, including California and the Outer Continental Shelf off the coast of California.

3. Plaintiffs Champlin Petroleum Company; Chevron U.S.A., Inc.; Continental Oil Company; Exxon Corporation; Getty Oil Company; Gulf Oil Corporation; Mobil Oil Corporation; Reserve Oil & Gas Company; Shell Oil Company; Texaco, Inc.; and Union Oil Company of California ("the oil company plaintiffs") are each corporations organized under the laws of the various states and are members of API or WOGA. The oil company plaintiffs, among other activities, are engaged in the business of exploration for and production of oil and natural gas both within the state of California and on the Outer Continental Shelf ("OCS") off the California coast. Some of the oil company plaintiffs own interests in OCS leases purchased in federal lease sales under the provisions of the Outer Continental Shelf Lands Act (43 U.S.C. §§ 1331 et seq.). The remaining plaintiffs have interests in the coastal zone of California and/or are oil and gas consumers engaged in business in California.

4. Defendant Juanita Kreps, sued herein in her official capacity, is Secretary of the United States Department of Commerce ("Secretary") and is charged with administering the CZMA, which includes approval or disapproval of coastal zone management programs submitted by the coastal states, of which California is one. NOAA exists within the Department of Commerce. By administrative directive dated October 13, 1976, the Secretary delegated, inter alia, the CZMA approval function to the Administra-

tor of NOAA and expressly reserved other powers under the Act. Defendant Richard Frank is the Administrator of NOAA and is sued herein in his official capacity. Within NOAA there exists the Office of Coastal Zone Management ("OCZM"). Defendant Robert W. Knecht is the Acting Associate Administrator ("Acting Administrator") for coastal zone management and is sued herein in his official capacity. By administrative directive dated October 20, 1976, the Administrator of NOAA delegated to the Associate Administrator for Coastal Zone Management the authority to exercise all functions under the CZMA not expressly reserved to either the Secretary or the Administrator of NOAA.

5. The defendant-in-intervention, California Coastal Commission, is an agency of the State of California created pursuant to the California Coastal Act of 1976 (Cal.Pub.Res.Code §§ 30000, et seq.). The Coastal Commission is the successor in interest to the California Coastal Zone Conservation Commision created pursuant to Proposition 20 (Cal.Pub.Res.Code §§ 27000, et seq.), which expired on December 31, 1976. The California Coastal Act became effective on January 1, 1977.

6. Defendants-in-intervention, Natural Resources Defense Council, Inc., and the Sierra Club ("NRDC") are associations whose members claim an interest in coastal zone management.

7. On March 31, 1976, the California Coastal Zone Conservation Commission submitted to the federal defendants a coastal zone management program for approval under the provisions of CZMA § 306.

8. In September of 1976 the federal defendants issued a Draft Environmental Impact Statement ("DEIS") wherein they announced their tentative decision to approve the California Coastal Zone Management Program submitted in March. Thereafter, the State of California enacted the Coastal Act of 1976, which declared itself to be "California's coastal zone management program within the coastal zone for purposes of the Federal Coastal Zone Management Act of 1972 . . . ." (Cal.Pub.Res.Code § 30008.)

9. On October 20, 1976, the DEIS was withdrawn and the public hearings to be held thereon were cancelled. On April 12, 1977, the federal defendants issued a Revised Draft Environmental Impact Statement ("RDEIS") and announced their tentative decision to approve the revised coastal zone management program submitted by the Coastal Commission. At this time the CZMP was described as consisting of the California Coastal Act of 1976, the Coastal Conservancy Act (Cal.Pub.Res.Code §§ 31000 et seq.), and the Urban and Coastal Park Bond Act (Cal.Pub.Res.Code §§ 5096.111 et seq.). Public hearings were held on the RDEIS and the CZMP as therein described on May 19, 1977, in Los Angeles, California. Plaintiffs appeared and (by oral testimony and written comments submitted before the hearing and additional comments submitted thereafter) recommended that the CZMP not be approved and that a new environmental impact statement be prepared.

10. On August 16, 1977, the federal defendants issued their Final Environmen-

tal Impact Statement ("FEIS"), together with Attachment K, containing written statements from parties commenting on the CZMP. In the FEIS, the CZMP was described as consisting of five elements: the Coastal Act of 1976, the Coastal Conservancy Act, the Urban and Coastal Park Bond Act, the Coastal Commission's final regulations (Cal.Admin.Code, Title 14, §§ 13000 to 14000), Part II (Introduction and Chapters 1–14) ("the Program Description") of the FEIS. On September 1, 1977, plaintiffs submitted to the federal defendants written comments objecting to approval of the CZMP as defendants proposed in the FEIS. Defendants replied by letter dated September 8, 1977, from Acting Administrator Knecht to plaintiffs' counsel, by which letter defendants indicated that they intended to proceed with approval of the CZMP. As noted previously, final approval, accompanied by a recital of findings, occurred on November 7.

The Court has before it for determination both preliminary and for ultimate disposition questions of the highest importance, greatest complexity, and highest urgency. They arise as the result of high legislative purpose, low bureaucratic bungling, and present inherent difficulty in judicial determination. In other words, for the high purpose of improving and maintaining felicitous conditions in the coastal areas of the United States, the Congress has undertaken a legislative solution, the application of which is so complex as to make it almost wholly unmanageable. In the course of the legislative process, there obviously came into conflict many competing interests which, in typical fashion, the Congress sought to accommodate, only to create thereby a morass of problems between the private sector, the public sector, the federal bureaucracy, the state legislature, the state bureaucracy, and all of the administrative agencies appurtenant thereto. Because the action taken gives rise to claims public and private which must be adjudicated, this matter is now involved in the judicial process.

In whatever technical form the questions and issues are here presented, they resolve themselves into the familiar situation in which a court must sit in some form of judicial review of administrative action—and it isn't easy.

We deal here with a hybrid kind of record and consequent hybrid form of review. As will appear from the extensive discussion below, the several approaches to and differing views of the proper scope and kind of judicial review are here brought under consideration.

We have questions of whether review is proper or timely and, if so, of what proper scope and result. We treat each *seriatim*.

Standing

This issue need not detain us long. While defendants originally urged that plaintiffs in this case lack standing to litigate speculative harms, during oral argument counsel for the NRDC, to whom the task of pressing defendants' standing and ripeness contentions was apparently assigned, conceded that what had previously been designated an issue of standing was more properly characterized as a ripeness problem. The Court nevertheless briefly examines the standing of plaintiffs to maintain the present action before addressing the ripeness issue.

The Supreme Court has liberalized the law of standing so that, while injury in fact is always required, *Sierra Club v. Morton*, 405 U.S. 727, 740, 92 S.Ct. 1361, 31 L.Ed.2d 636 (1972), "an identifiable trifle is enough."

. . . .

In the present case plaintiffs, whose activities will be regulated by the CZMP to the extent that their activities in exploring for and developing oil and gas resources on the OCS must be consistent therewith, have alleged and shown injury in fact. For upon approval by the federal defendants of the CZMP under § 306 of the CZMA, the consistency provisions of § 307 are triggered. Thereafter, before federal agencies may approve certain activities of plaintiffs relating to exploration and development of OCS resources, plaintiffs must certify that the proposed activity is consistent with the CZMP. Although the state is afforded six months to certify to the federal agency whether or not a proposed activity is consistent, the initial burden of determining consistency falls to the applicant. The gravamen of the complaint is that the submitted CZMP as approved by the federal defendants lacks the requisite specificity under CZMA and consequently may not be approved under § 306. If approved, plaintiffs claim immediate and substantial harm by compulsion to expend large sums of money to determine if their proposed activities are consistent. Moreover, plaintiffs allege that this lack of specificity increases their burden and makes it impossible to discharge, since they cannot with any reasonable assuredness certify that any activity subject to § 307 is in fact consistent with the CZMP. The undeniable interest of plaintiffs in the areas subject to the CZMP, the fact that once § 306 approval is given, their activities are subject to regulation under it, and the fact that an immediate consequence is to compel plaintiffs to expend financial resources in an effort to satisfy the requirements of § 307, combined with their claim that this burden is substantially increased by virtue of the very defects which they assert make approval improper, provide the necessary injury in fact to give plaintiffs standing to challenge the federal defendants' action in approving the CZMP under § 306.

Accordingly, the Court finds that the plaintiffs have standing to litigate the issues presented.[1]

Legislative History of The CZMA

A seemingly unbridgeable gulf between the parties concerning the proper construction of the CZMA establishes the cutting edge of this action. First, noted at the outset of this memorandum of decision, plaintiffs complain that the California Program fails to qualify for final approval under § 306 because it lacks the requisite specificity Congress intended management programs to embody, especially with respect to the substantive requirements of §§ 305(b) and 306(c), (d), and (e), so as to enable private users in the coastal zone subject to an approved program to be able to predict with reasonable certainty whether or not their proposed activities will be found to be "consistent" with the program

---

[1]In another case bearing the same name, plaintiffs challenged NOAA's approval of the Massachusetts and Wisconsin CMPs. Again, the allegation was the application of the consistency provisions would cause them serious harm. But here the court granted summary judgment for defendants, based on standing. The court held that due to the "speculative" nature of the asserted harms, plaintiffs had not shown "any legally cognizable injury providing standing." American Petroleum Institute v. Knecht, (1978) 8 Env. L. Rep. 20886 (D.D.C., Sept. 6, 1978).

under § 307(c). Second, plaintiffs contend that a proper understanding of § 306(c)(8), particularly in light of the 1976 Amendments, compels the conclusion that in requiring "adequate consideration" Congress intended that an approvable program affirmatively accommodate the national interest in planning for and siting energy facilities and that the CZMP fails so to do. The Court here addresses each of these contentions.

A. The definition of "management program."

Any attempt to resolve this underlying dispute, out of which most of the issues in this lawsuit arise, must begin with Congress' definition of a "management program" in § 304(11) of the Act:

> The term "management program" includes, but is not limited to, a comprehensive statement in words, maps, illustrations, and other media of communication, prepared and adopted by the state in accordance with the provisions of this title, setting forth *objectives, policies* and *standards to guide public and private uses of lands and waters in the coastal zone.*

(Emphasis supplied.) This definition is exactly as originally contained in the Senate version of the CZMA (S.3507). In its report on S.3507, the Committee on Commerce stated:

> "Management program" is the term to refer to the *process* by which a coastal State . . . proposes . . . to manage land and water uses in the coastal zone so as to reduce or minimize a direct, significant, and adverse effect upon those waters, including the development of criteria and of the governmental structure capable of implementing such a program. In adopting the term "Management program" the Committee seeks to convey the importance of a *dynamic* quality to the planning undertaken in this Act that permits adjustments as more knowledge is gained, as new technology develops, and as social aspirations are more clearly defined. The Committee does *not* intend to provide for management programs that are *static* but rather to create a *mechanism for continuing review* of coastal zone programs on a regular basis and to provide a framework for the allocation of resources that are available to carry out these programs.

S.Rep.No.92–753, 92d Cong., 2d Sess. (1972), U.S.Code Cong. & Admin.News 1972, pp. 4776, 4784, reprinted in Senate Committee on Commerce, Legislative History of the CZMA 201–02 (Comm. Print 1976) ("Legislative History") (emphasis supplied). The House version (H.R. 14146) did not contain a definition of "management program" and the Conference Report (H.Rep. No.92–1544, 92d Cong., 2d Sess. [1972] [Legislative History at 443]) failed to add anything further to the above explanation.

The Court agrees with defendants that Congress never intended that to be approvable under § 306 a management program must provide a "zoning map" which would inflexibly commit the state in advance of receiving specific proposals to permitting particular activities in specific areas. Nor did Congress intend by using the language of "objectives, policies, and standards" to require that such programs establish such detailed criteria that private users be able to rely on them as predictive devices for determining the fate of projects without interaction between the relevant state agencies and the user. To satisfy the definition in the Act, a program need only contain standards of sufficient specificity "to guide public and private uses."

The CZMA was enacted primarily with a view to encouraging the coastal states to plan for the management, development, preservation, and restoration of their coastal zones by establishing rational processes by which to regulate uses therein. Although sensitive to balancing competing interests, it was first and foremost a statute directed to and solicitous of environmental concerns. See §§ 302 and 303. "The key to more effective use of the coastal zone in the future is introduction of management systems permitting conscious and informed choices among the various alternatives. The aim of this legislation is to assist in this very critical goal." S.Rep.No.92–753, U.S. Code Cong. & Admin.News 1972, p. 4781 (Legislative History at 198) See H.Rep.No. 92–1049, 92d Cong., 2d Sess. (1972) (Legislative History at 313 and 315).

The Amendments of 1976 made clear the national interest in the planning for, and siting of, energy facilities (to be discussed *infra*). Apparently neither the Act nor the Amendments thereto altered the primary focus of the legislation: the need for a rational planning process to enable the state, not private users of the coastal zone, to be able to make "hard choices." "If those choices are to be rational and devised in such a way as to preserve future options, the program must be established to provide guidelines which will enable the selection of those choices." H.Rep.No. 92–1049 (Legislative History at 315). The 1976 amendments do not require increased specificity with regard to the standards and objectives contained in a management program: (Specificity as it relates to § 306(c)(8) will be discussed *infra*.)

In conclusion, to the extent plaintiffs' more specific challenges to the Acting Administrator's § 306 approval are premised on an interpretation of congressional intent to require that such programs include detailed criteria establishing a sufficiently high degree of predictability to enable a private user of the coastal zone to say with certainty that a given project must be deemed "consistent" therewith, the Court rejects plaintiffs' contention.

Section 306(a)(1) requires the Secretary, prior to approval of a management program under § 306, find that it contains that which § 305(b) specifies. Plaintiffs have focused their attack in large measure on what they charge is the CZMP's failure to include those items which § 305(b) mandates, especially those required by paragraphs (2), (3), and (5) thereof. The attack is premised not on any alleged invalidity of or ambiguity in NOAA's regulations (15 C.F.R. Parts 920 and 923)—although plaintiffs insist the proposed (now interim final) program approval regulations (Part 923), rather than the then-existing regulations, should have been utilized in evaluating the California Program—but rather on the alleged failure of the Acting Administrator properly to apply the regulations to the CZMP.

The Court has reviewed the Acting Administrator's findings, the CZMA, and the regulations (both then-existing, proposed, and now interim final), and concludes that the Acting Administrator's finding that the Program satisfies the requirements of § 305(b) (as required by § 306(a)(1)) was not arbitrary or capricious, and further, that his application of the then-existing regulations (published January 9, 1975) was not an abuse of discretion or otherwise not in accordance with law. 5 U.S.C. § 706(2)(A).

The Court has reviewed in great detail Attachment J to the FEIS, wherein the OCZM summarizes and responds to comments received both from other governmental agencies (state and federal) and from private interests addressed to the draft management program and EIS. Attachment J includes OCZM's responses to similar concerns voiced by a number of reviewers (FEIS at J–1 through J–12) and its responses to comments received from individual reviewers (FEIS at J–13 through J–48), including plaintiffs (FEIS at J–29 through J–41) and various federal agencies (such as the Federal Energy Administration, the Federal Power Commission, and the Department of the Interior) whom plaintiffs have characterized as opposing § 306 approval (FEIS at J–17 through J–22).

In their comments the various parties have raised most of the issues which plaintiffs have raised in this action. The Court finds additional support for the Acting Administrator's decision in the thoughtfulness and reasonableness with which OCZM has addressed the views of the various reviewers. The Acting Administrator had these comments and responses before him at the time of his approval of the CZMP and they lend further support to the nonarbitrary character of his decision.

The Court notes that while the interaction between the state (Coastal Commission) and various interested and affected federal agencies during the review process was substantially less than ideal in this instance, a situation of which the Acting Administrator was painfully aware, nevertheless the requirement of § 307(b) that "the views of Federal agencies principally affected by such program have been adequately considered" before § 306 approval may be granted has been satisfied.

Without belaboring the point or embarking on a needless point-by-point analysis and refutation of plaintiffs' assertions regarding the Acting Administrator's findings under § 305(b), the Court, consistent with the previously-expressed view of the specificity which the Act requires, finds the "performance standards" approach embodied in the California Program to be permissible. The CZMA, as noted earlier, does not speak to this issue beyond defining "management program" in § 304(11).

The requirements of §§ 305(b) and 306(c), (d), and (e) do not constrain the state in the manner in which it meets them; nor does it constrain the Secretary or NOAA in establishing through regulations that which it will require of a management program in this regard. Congress has granted the Secretary and Acting Administrator considerable discretion. They have exercised it in promulgating approval regulations. The Court's review of these indicates that rule-making itself has been an open process and has involved ongoing interaction between NOAA and interested parties.

As noted previously, the Court, cognizant of Congress' expression of approval for the manner in which NOAA and OCZM (and particularly Mr. Knecht) have carried out its mandate (see S.Rep.No.94–277, 94th Cong., 1st Sess. 30 (1975) U.S.Code Cong. & Admin.News 1976, p. 1768 (Legislative History at 756)), and further cognizant of Congress' resolving its original uncertainty over whether the CZMA should be administered by the Department of the Interior or the Department of Commerce in favor of the latter largely because of the "requisite oceanic, coastal ecosystem, and coastal land use expertise" found in NOAA (*see* S.Rep. No.94–277 at 7 n.5 (Legislative History at 733)), concludes that considerable deference is due NOAA's interpretation of its own regulations. In short, the Acting Administrator's findings and Attachment J of the FEIS, when viewed in the context of the legislative history of the Act and of the statutory language itself, satisfy the Court that approval of the California Program has not been arbitrary, capricious, an abuse of discretion, or otherwise not in accordance with law.

B. Adequate consideration of the national interest

Plaintiffs' fundamental grievance with the California Program stems from its assertion that the Program fails to satisfy the mandate of § 306(c)(8)—that before the Secretary grant approval to a management program, under § 306 she find that it

> provides for adequate consideration of the national interest involved in planning for, and in the siting of, facilities (including energy facilities in, or which significantly affect, such state's coastal zone) which are necessary to meet requirements which are other than local in nature.

Plaintiffs urge that the CZMA, particularly in light of the 1976 Amendments, requires an "affirmative commitment" on the part of the state before § 306 approval is proper. The California Program allegedly fails adequately to make that commitment in that its general lack of specificity, coupled with what plaintiffs characterize as California's overall antipathy to energy development (as embodied in the policies and practices of its Coastal Commission), combine to give the Coastal Commission a "blank check" effectively to veto any or all exploration and development activities subject to § 307(c)(3) simply by finding such activity not to be "consistent" with the CZMP.

Defendants, beyond taking issue with plaintiffs' characterization of California's energy posture, assert first, that plaintiffs premise that the Act requires an affirmative commitment is incorrect as a matter of law and second, that the Program contains adequate consideration of national energy interests. Defendants contend that the CZMP contains "performance standards and criteria" more than adequate to satisfy the requirements of the CZMA and serve as a guide to plaintiffs in planning their activities in the coastal zone. Implicit in the various provisions of the Coastal Act (and in particular those in §§ 30001.2 and 30260–64) and in Chapter 11 of the Program Description is a wholly adequate consideration of the national energy interest.

Plaintiffs apparently focus on language in H.Rep.No.92–1049 (which accompanied H.R. 14146) to the effect that, "if the program as developed is to be approved and thereby enable the State to receive funding assistance under this title, the State *must take into account and must accommodate* its program to the specific requirements of various Federal laws which are applicable to its coastal zone." Legislative History at 321. The report continues:

To the extent that a State program does not recognize these overall national interests, as well as the specific national interest in the generation and distribution of electric energy . . . or is construed as conflicting with any applicable statute, the Secretary may not approve the State program until it is amended to recognize those Federal rights, powers, and interests.

Id. at 322.

It is to be noted that the reference in the House Report to the state's need to "accommodate" its program is to "the specific requirements of various [applicable] Federal laws." It is not a requirement that the state program expressly "accommodate" energy interests. In the program approval regulations published on January 9, 1975 (40 Fed.Reg. 1683), NOAA stated that:

A management program which integrates . . . the siting of facilities meeting requirements which are of greater than local concern into the determination of uses and areas of Statewide concern will meet the requirements of Section 306(c)(8).

15 C.F.R. § 923.15(a). In subsection (b) NOAA amplified on the above requirement.

. . . The requirement should not be construed as compelling the States to propose a program which accommodates certain types of facilities, but to assure that such national concerns are included at an early stage in the State's planning activities and that such facilities not be arbitrarily excluded or unreasonably restricted in the management program without good and sufficient reasons. . . . No separate national interest "test" need be applied and submitted other than evidence that the listed national interest facilities have been considered in a manner similar to all other uses, and that appropriate consultation with the Federal agencies listed has been conducted.

The Coastal Zone Management Act Amendments of 1976, Pub L. 94–370 ("1976 Amendments"), while largely prompted by the 1973 Arab oil embargo and while expressly recognizing the national interest in the planning for and siting of energy facilities, nevertheless did not alter the requirement of "adequate consideration" in § 306(c)(8) or make any changes in the degree of specificity required under the Act. Rather, recognizing that coastal states like California were currently burdened by the onshore impacts of Federal offshore (OCS) activities and likely to be burdened further by the plans for increased leases on the OCS, Congress sought to encourage or induce the affected states to step up their plans *vis-á-vis* such facilities.

The primary means chosen to accomplish this result was the Coastal Energy Impact Program ("CEIP") contained in new § 308. As the Conferees explained, the purpose of the 1976 Amendments was

to coordinate and further the objectives of national energy policy by directing the Secretary of Commerce to administer and coordinate, as part of the [CZMA], a coastal energy impact program.
. . .The conference substitute follows both the Senate bill and the House amendment in amending the 1972 Act to encourage new or expanded oil and natural gas production in an orderly manner from the Nation's outer Continental

Shelf (OCS) by providing for financial assistance to meet state and local needs resulting from specified new or expanded energy activity in or affecting the coastal zone.

H.Rep.No.94–1298, 94th Cong., 2d Sess. 23 (1976), U.S.Code Cong. & Admin.News 1976, pp. 1820, 1821 (Legislative History at 1073.) The formula Congress provided for calculating a state's share of the Coastal Energy Impact Fund ("the Fund") established to carry out the CEIP's purposes is itself further evidence of the congressional intention to provide "built-in incentives for coastal states to assist in achieving the underlying national objective of increased domestic oil and gas production." H.Rep.No.94–1298 at 25, U.S.Code Cong. & Admin.News, p. 1822. (Legislative History at 1075).

> The formula, as so constructed, provides incentives to coastal states (if they are interested in increasing their share of the funds appropriated for this purpose) to encourage and facilitate achievement of the basic national objective of increasing domestic energy production. This provision would be in harmony with sound coastal zone management principles because Federal aid would be available only for states acting in accord with such principles. For example, since the grant is based on new leasings, production, first landings, and new employment, it is to the state's interest to apply the "consistency" provisions and related processes to the issuance of oil exploration, development and production plans, licenses, and permits as quickly as possible rather than to postpone decision-making for the statutory 6-month period.

Id. The Congress was particularly careful to circumscribe the role of the federal government in particular siting decisions. Thus, § 308(i) provides:

> The Secretary shall not intercede in any land use or water use decision of any coastal state with respect to the siting of any energy facility or public facility by making siting in a particular location a prerequisite to, or a condition of, financial assistance under this section.

This provision is consistent with the approach of the CZMA as a whole to leave the development of, and decisions under, a management program to the state, subject to the Act's more specific concern that the development and decision-making process occur in a context of cooperative interaction, coordination, and sharing of information among affected agencies, both local, state, regional, and federal. This last, especially as regards energy facility planning, is the policy behind the Energy Facility Planning Process ("EFPP") of § 305(b)(8) and the Interstate Grants provision of new § 309 (which encourages the coastal states to give high priority to coordinating coastal zone planning utilizing "interstate agreements or compacts"). It should be noted that the only amendment to the national interest requirement of § 306(c)(8) effectuated by the 1976 Amendments is the additional requirement that in fulfilling its obligation to provide "adequate consideration of the national interest" in the case of energy facilities, the state also give such consideration "to any applicable interstate energy plan or program" established under § 309.

The Court rejects plaintiffs' argument that affirmitive accommodation of energy facilities was made a *quid pro quo* for approval under § 306 by the 1976 Amendments. In addition to the above, the Court notes that Congress itself did not assume that such siting was automatically to be deemed necessary in all instances. For instance, in its report on H.R. 3981, the Committee on Merchant Marine and Fisheries stated that the addition of the EFPP in § 305(b)(8)

> reflects the Committee's finding that increasing involvement of coastal areas in providing energy for the nation is likely, as can be seen in the need to expand the Outer Continental Shelf petroleum development. State coastal zone programs should, therefore, specifically address how major energy facilities are to be located in the coastal zone if such siting is necessary. Second, the program shall include methods of handling the anticipated impacts of such facilities. The Committee in no way wishes to accelerate the location of energy facilities in the coasts; on the contrary, it feels a disproportionate share are there now. . . . There is no intent here whatever to involve the Secretary of Commerce in specific siting decisions.

H.Rep.No.94–878 at 45–46 (Legislative History at 931–32) (emphasis supplied). The concern that the CEIP not encourage the siting in the coastal zone of energy facilities which could be located elsewhere is embodied in § 308. *See* H.Rep.No.94–878 at 15 and 26 (Legislative History at 900 and 912).

The Senate Committee on Commerce, in reporting S. 586 to the full Senate, stated:

> The Secretary of Commerce (through NOAA) should provide guidance and assistance to States under this section 305(b)(8), and under section 306, to enable them to know what constitutes "adequate consideration of the national interest" in the siting of facilities necessary to meet requirements other than local in nature. The Committee wishes to emphasize, consistent with the overall intent of the Act, that this new paragraph (8) requires a State to develop, and maintain a planning process, but does not imply intercession in specific siting decisions. The *Secretary of Commerce (through NOAA), in determining whether a coastal State has met the requirements, is restricted to evaluating the adequacy of that process.*

S.Rep.No.94–277 at 34, U.S.Code Cong. & Admin. News 1976, p. 1801 (Legislative History at 760) (emphasis supplied).

Consistent with this mandate, NOAA has promulgated revised program approval regulations (43 Fed.Reg. 8378, March 1, 1978). These interim final rules follow the submission of comments on the proposed rules published on August 29, 1977 (42 Fed.Reg. 43552). The Court looks to the revised regulations because they reflect NOAA's interpretation of any changes wrought by the 1976 Amendments, the former regulations against which the California Program was tested having been promulgated after the Arab oil embargo but before the 1976 Amendments.

In its response to several reviewers' suggestions that § 306(c)(8) be interpreted to require that facilities be accommodated in a State's coastal zone, the agency reiterated the position it has maintained since the inception of the CZMA that the purpose of "adequate consideration" is to achieve the act's "spirit of equitable balance between State and national interests." As such, consideration of facilities in which there may be a national interest must be undertaken within the context of the act's broader finding of a "national interest in the . . . beneficial use, protection, and development of the coastal zone" (Section 302(a)). Subsection 302(g) of the Act gives "high priority" to the protection of natural systems. Accordingly, while the primary focus of subsection 306(c)(8) is on the planning for and siting of facilities, adequate consideration of the national interest in these facilities must be based on a balancing of these interests relative to the wise use, protection and other development of the coastal zone. As the Department of Energy noted in its comments on the proposed regulations:

> The Act presumes a balancing of the national interest in energy self-sufficiency with State and local concerns involving adverse economic, social, or environmental impacts.

43 Fed.Reg. 8379.

Section 306(c)(8) is treated at length in 15 C.F.R. § 923.52. After generally noting that one "need not conclude that any and all such facilities proposed for the coastal zone need be sited therein," the regulation proceeds to set forth requirements which must be met by the management program in order to satisfy § 306(c)(8). While these are considerably more detailed than those contained in its predecessor (15 C.F.R. § 923.15, January 9, 1975), they do not change the basic tenor of the rule as interpreted by NOAA. Having previously determined that the Acting Administrator's utilization of the then-existing regulations was proper—indeed, to have applied proposed regulations arguably would have been improper—and having determined that it was not abuse of discretion to proceed with approval of the California Program rather than await promulgation of final revised approval regulations, given the fact that the proposed regulations effected no fundamental change of philosophy, but merely a "shift in emphasis" (42 Fed.Reg. 43552), the Court concludes that the Acting Administrator's finding that the CZMP satisfied § 306(c)(8) is neither arbitrary nor capricious.

The Court notes further in this regard that the standards established by the Coastal Act (and in particular §§ 30260–64 and 30413) for making energy facilities siting decisions, in the words of the Coastal Commission staff, "establish the general findings that must be made to authorize coastal dependent industrial facilities, liquefied natural gas terminals, oil and gas developments, refineries, petrochemical facilities and electric power plants." FEIS, Part II (Chapter 9) at 66. The key to the California approach, and one which the Acting Administrator and this Court find acceptable under the CZMA, is that the standards require that "findings" be made upon which specific siting decisions ensue. For instance, in dealing with the siting of oil tanker facilities, § 30261(a) requires that

> . . . [t]anker facilities shall be designed to (1) minimize the total volume of oil spilled, (2) minimize the risk of collision from movement of other vessels, (3) have ready access to the most effective feasible containment and recovery equipment for oil spills, and (4) have onshore deballasting facilities to receive any fouled ballast water from tankers where operationally or legally required.

As can readily be seen from these provisions, whether a particular tanker facility siting proposal will be deemed "consistent" with these requirements of the California Program will turn on specific findings of a factual nature. The California Program sensibly does not attempt to map out in advance precisely what type or size tanker facilities will be found to meet these requirements in particular areas of its almost 1,000-mile coastline. Rather, by its very nature, the Coastal Act encourages plaintiffs with a particular facility in mind to address themselves to the standards set forth in the Coastal Act and to plan such a facility in cooperation and communication with the Coastal Commission from the inception. This approach seems consonant with the overall approach of the CZMA itself. In this regard it is noteworthy that the Senate Committee on Commerce, in summarizing the "key findings" of a number of reports made under the aegis of the committee-created National Ocean Policy Study, stated that "coastal States often have been criticized unfairly for delaying the siting of energy facilities when such action often is the result of lack of information and planning." S.Rep.No.94–277 at 3, U.S.Code Cong. & Admin.News 1976, p. 1770 (Legislative History at 729). The CZMP takes an approach which has received the congressional blessing. To the extent plaintiffs seek not guidance with respect to the way in which coastal resources will be managed but instead a "zoning map" which would implicitly avoid the need to consult with the state regarding planned activities in or affecting its coastal zone, the Court rejects their position. While wholly sympathetic to the legitimate concerns of corporate officers and planners who must conform their activities to the standards of CZMP, the Court nevertheless concludes that the Acting Administrator's finding that the Program satisifies § 306(c)(8) is supportable and hence not arbitrary or capricious. It proceeds from a correct interpretation of the CZMA.

Finally, the Court notes that both the California Program and the CZMA contain safeguards to protect plaintiffs from arbitrary exercise by the Coastal Commission of its § 307 consistency powers. First, plaintiffs under the Coastal Act may seek judicial review of a decision of the Coastal Commission finding a specific proposed activity of plaintiffs to be inconsistent with the CZMP. Such review certainly may encompass a challenge to the Commission's interpretation of the California Program as well as a challenge to specific findings upon which the determination presumably would be based. Second, with respect to an adverse consistency determination regarding any proposed activity for which a federal license or permit is required or which involves an OCS plan, the party against whose activity such a determination has been made may seek review by the Secretary of Commerce (who could also undertake review on her own initiative) on the grounds that "the activity is consistent with the objectives of this title or is otherwise necessary in the interest of national security." § 307(c)(3)(A) and (B). Third, under § 312(a) the Secretary is obliged to conduct "a continuing review of (1) the management programs of the coastal states and the performance of the such states with respect to coastal zone management; and (2) the coastal energy impact program provided for under section 308." Subsection (b) provides:

> The Secretary shall have the authority to terminate any financial assistance extended under section 306 . . . if (1) [s]he determines that the state is failing to adhere to and is not justified in deviating from the program approved by the Secretary . . . .

In short, both as regards specific determinations of inconsistency and as regards general trends in and manner of issuance of such determinations, plaintiffs are amply protected by and have various forms of recourse under the California Program itself and §§ 307 and 312 of the CZMA.

Approval By The Federal Defendants

Plaintiffs have charged that the procedures followed by the state in developing and adopting, and by the federal defendants in approving, the California Program violated both the CZMA and NEPA.

Section 306(c)(1) requires the Secretary to find that

> [t]he state has developed and adopted a management program for its coastal zone in accordance with rules and regulations promulgated by the Secretary, after notice, and *with the opportunity of full participation* by relevant Federal agencies, state agencies, local governments, regional organizations, port authorities, and other interested parties, public and private, *which is adequate to carry out the purposes of this title* and is consistent with the policy declared in section 303 of this title.

(Emphasis supplied.) The Acting Administrator has so found. Findings at 13–14 (and references to the FEIS contained therein). Section 306(c)(3) amplifies the requirement of § 306(c)(1) by demanding a finding be made that "[t]he state has held public hearings in the development of the management program." This too has been found. Findings at 16 (and references to the FEIS contained therein).

Plaintiffs' claims of invalid adoption by the state having been discussed previously, the Court merely adds that the process of developing a coastal zone management program for the state of California has been ongoing since the enactment of Proposition 20 (the California Coastal Zone Conservation Act of 1972) and that the Acting Administrator's finding that that process has been open within the meaning of § 306(c)(1) and (3) is supported by the record. Under the arbitrary and capricious standard applicable to such findings, they must be sustained.

Plaintiffs mount an assault on the review process undertaken by the federal defendants in approving the CZMP under § 306, focusing on the purported inadequacies of the environmental review process culminating in the FEIS. As noted earlier, a challenge under NEPA invites broader-ranging evidentiary review (not limited to the administrative record) and requires application of the observance of procedure standard of review. 5 U.S.C. § 706(2)(D); *Cady v. Morton, supra,* 527 F.2d at 793, citing *Trout Unlimited v. Morton, supra,* 509 F.2d at 1282, and *Lathan v. Brinegar, supra,* 506 F.2d 677; *Ethyl Corp. v. EPA, supra,* 176 U.S.App.D.C. at 406 n.71, 541 F.2d at 34 n.71. Having done so, the Court concludes that the environmental review process here followed and the FEIS produced thereby are adequate under § 102(2)(C) of NEPA (42 U.S.C. § 4332(2)(C).

Section 102(2)(C) mandates that an EIS address:

> (i) the environmental impact of the proposed action;
> (ii) any adverse environmental effects which cannot be avoided should the proposal be implemented;
> (iii) alternatives to the proposed action;

(iv) the relationship between local short-term uses of man's environment and the maintenance and enhancement of long-term productivity; and

(v) any irreversible and irretrievable commitments of resources which would be involved in the proposed action should it be implemented.

Plaintiffs contend first, that the federal defendants utilized the environmental review process not to conduct a *bona fide* environmental review but to advocate a prior decision to grant final approval to the CZMP; second, that the FEIS is deficient because the Program discussed therein differs substantially from that disclosed in the RDEIS; third, that it fails to adequately discuss possible alternatives to § 306 approval; fourth, that it fails to consider all available relevant information; and fifth, that it fails to discuss potential and unavoidable adverse impacts of approving and implementing the CZMP.

The Court discusses these claims in order.

First, the Court finds nothing improper in the federal defendants' informing the public and other organs of government of its tentative conclusion that the California Program meets the requirements of § 306 so as to qualify for final approval. The nature of the cooperative interaction between the state and federal governments envisioned by the CZMA in the development of a management program makes it wholly unrealistic to assume that the federal agency charged with reviewing that program will entertain no preliminary conclusions as to its adequacy under the Act.

With respect to plaintiffs' second claim—that the RDEIS and FEIS differ substantially in their description of the elements of the California Program—the Court concludes that such claim lacks merit. First, the two statutory elements of the Program other than the Coastal Act both were noted in the RDEIS (at 8, 12, and 77). Neither establishes standards in the sense that the Coastal Act does; rather, these companion statutes provide a portion of the implementation authority required by § 306(c)(6), (7), (d) of the CZMA. Second, the RDEIS contains the original version of the Program Description found in the FEIS. As discussed at length in another section of this memorandum, Chapter 11 of the Program Description has been formally adopted by the Coastal Commission; and the remaining chapters, being of an essentially descriptive nature, were not required to be. The procedures followed may have been sloppy, but the Court cannot say that the failure expressly to designate Part II of the RDEIS and "element" of the CZMP was fatal—particularly in light of the Court's conclusions regarding the legal status of the Program Description. Finally, the Court notes that the revisions made in the Program Description were largely prompted by comments received on the original Program Description, including those received from plaintiffs.

Plaintiffs' third argument—that the FEIS fails adequately to discuss alternatives to § 306 approval—is premised on plaintiffs' insistence that the federal defendants should have denied final approval and instead granted the CZMP preliminary approval under § 305(d), particularly in light of the fact that the local coastal programs required by the Coastal Act (not due until 1980) will add the requisite degree of specificity to enable the Program to qualify for § 306 approval. While there is support for plaintiffs' position in the legislative history surrounding the addition of "preliminary approval" to § 305 effected by the 1976

Amendments (H.Rep.No.94–878, 94th Cong., 2d Sess. 48 (1976) (Legislative History at 934)), nevertheless the FEIS discusses this alternative to § 306 approval and rejects it on the basis of a reasonable construction of §§ 306(e)(1) (dealing with permissible implementation techniques for control of land and water uses) and 305(d), the NOAA regulations relevant thereto (15 C.F.R. § 923.26), the pertinent legislative history, and the application of the above to the provisions of the CZMP. FEIS at 184–85. The federal defendants' conclusion— that "if a state has the necessary authorities in place and will employ acceptable implementation techniques, the 'preliminary approval' option is inappropriate" (FEIS at 184)—is reasonable in order to give harmonious and full effect to §§ 305(d) and 306(e)(1). Again, while the Court, if faced with the choice, might have opted for preliminary approval, we may not substitute our judgment for that of the Acting Administrator. It is sufficient for present purposes to note that, contrary to plaintiffs' contention, the FEIS does adequately discuss this alternative.

Plaintiffs' final two claims are premised on the alleged failure of the FEIS to discuss the adverse impact nationwide should California utilize its § 307 consistency powers to retard or preclude OCS and related energy development. Plaintiffs also assert that the FEIS fails adequately to discuss the impact of the CZMP on the "socio-economic" environment (e.g. impact on "urban sprawl"). The Court rejects this argument.

As this Circuit has stated:

> . . . [A]n EIS is in compliance with NEPA when its form, content, and preparation substantially (1) provide decision-makers with an environmental disclosure sufficiently detailed to aid in the substantive decision whether to proceed with the project in the light of its environmental consequences, and (2) make available to the public, information of the proposed project's environmental impact and encourage public participation in the development of that information.

Trout Unlimited v. Morton, supra, 509 F.2d at 1283. "An EIS need not discuss remote or highly speculative consequences. . . . [The] adequacy of the content of the EIS should be determined through use of a rule of reason." *Id.* In elaborating on this "rule of reason" the Second Circuit has observed that

> an EIS need not be exhaustive to the point of discussing all possible details bearing on the proposed action but will be upheld as adequate if it has been compiled in good faith and sets forth sufficient information to enable the decision-maker to consider fully the environmental factors involved and to make a reasoned decision after balancing the risks of harm to the environment against the benefits to be derived from the proposed action, as well as to make a reasoned choice between alternatives. [Citations omitted.]

County of Suffolk v. Secretary of the Interior, supra, 562 F.2d at 1375.

In this instance, the inadequacies raised by plaintiffs rest on the highly speculative assumption that in implementing its management program California will abuse its § 307 consistency powers, the California courts will acquiesce therein, and, further, the Secretary of Commerce will fail to discharge her duties under §§ 307(c)(3) and 312. As stated during our discussion of the ripeness issue, the Court declines to make such an assumption—nor must the federal defendants in preparing the FEIS engage in such speculation.

The Court views the situation with which it is here presented as not unlike that presented in *Life of the Land v. Brinegar,* 485 F.2d 460 (9th Cir. 1973). In that case an action was brought by environmental groups to enjoin construction of a new seaward runaway at Honolulu International Airport. The defendants in preparing the EIS determined that it was unnecessary to undertake air pollution studies because of the very nature and location of the proposed project. In rejecting plaintiff-appellants' claim that such omission was fatal to the adequacy of the EIS, this Circuit remarked:

> The Reef Runway will relocate aircraft takeoffs, the major source of aircraft air pollution, 6,700 feet seaward, and away from the populated areas of Honolulu. The essence of this project, therefore, involves moving the sources of the air pollution away from people. The federal and state officials concluded that detailed air pollution studies were unnecessary, on the premise that at the very least, the project was extremely unlikely to worsen the air quality in any relevant sense.

Id. at 470.

Similarly, the "essence" of the CZMP, in accordance with §§ 302 and 303 of the CZMA, is sensitivity to environmental concerns in establishing standards for utilization of the coastal zone; consequently, fewer and less detailed environmental studies would be expected because the Program emphasizes environmental preservation.

Finally, the Court notes that the act of approving the California Program in itself does not result in the undertaking of any specific project by the state or federal governments or any private user(s) of the coastal zone. The concerns raised by plaintiffs—in particular, the alleged omission in the FEIS of an adequate discussion of the significance of permitting OCS development to go forward and the impact of precluding such development—will be addressed in connection with the preparation and dissemination of environmental impact statements for specific proposed activities. The environmental review here undertaken resembles that frequently utilized where a "multistage" project is involved; consequently, the failure of the FEIS to discuss such possibilities is justified on this alternative ground. The Second Circuit addressed this issue in *County of Suffolk, supra.* That case involved preparation of an EIS in connection with the proposed lease-sale by the Department of the Interior of federal lands on the OCS to petroleum companies. There, in reversing the district court's finding that that EIS was inadequate in its failure to explore the possibility that state and local governments affected by such lease-sale might bar the landing of pipelines on their shores and thereby in necessitating the use of tankers increase the hazards of oil pollution, the Court reasoned:

> . . . [T]he extent to which treatment of a subject in an EIS, for a multistage project may be deferred, depends on two factors: (1) whether obtaining more detailed

useful information on the topic of transportation is "meaningfully possible" at the time when the EIS for an earlier stage is prepared, *see Natural Resources Defense Council v. Morton*, [148 U.S.App.D.C. 5, at 15,] 458 F.2d [827] at 837, and (2) how important it is to have the additional information at an earlier stage in determining whether or not to proceed with the project, *see National Resources Defense Council v. Callaway*, 524 F.2d at 88.

If the additional information would at best amount to speculation as to future event or events, it obviously would not be of much use as input in deciding whether to proceed. As we said in *Callaway, supra,* referring to *Morton, supra:*

> "NEPA does not require a 'crystal ball' inquiry . . . An EIS is required to furnish only such information as appears to be reasonably necessary under the circumstances for evaluation of the project rather than to be so all-encompassing in scope that the task of preparing it would become either fruitless or well nigh impossible, *Indian Lookout Alliance v. Volpe*, 484 F.2d 11 (8th Cir. 1973). A government agency cannot be expected to wait until a perfect solution of environmental consequences of proposed action is devised before preparing and circulating an EIS." 524 F.2d at 88.

Where the major federal action under consideration, once authorized, cannot be modified or changed, it may be essential to obtain such information as is available, speculative or not, for whatever it may be worth in deciding whether to make the crystallized commitment (*e.g.,* the construction of a bridge of a specified type between two precise points). But *where a multistage project can be modified or changed in the future to minimize or eliminate environmental hazards disclosed as the result of information that will not become available until the future, and the Government reserves the power to make such a modification or change after the information is available and incorporated in a further EIS, it cannot be said that deferment violates the "rule of reason." Indeed, in considering a project of such flexibility, it might be both unwise and unfair not to postpone the decision regarding the next stage until more accurate data is at hand.*

562 F.2d at 1378 (emphasis supplied). The court concluded that "projection of specific pipeline routes was neither 'meaningfully possible,' nor 'reasonably necessary under the circumstances.'" *Id.* at 1382. This factor of multistage projects whose various stages are "substantially independent" of one another similarly has been considered by this Circuit in assessing the adequacy of an EIS. *See, e.g., Cady v. Morton, supra.* 527 F.2d at 794 n.7; *Trout Unlimited v. Morton, supra,* 509 F.2d at 1285.

The Court concludes that this action presents an analogous situation to which this reasoning applies. Approval and implementation of the CZMP no more indicates which of potentially dozens of projects will be certified as consistent (and undertaken subject to what conditions) than the decision of the Department of the Interior to proceed with the lease-sale of a large tract of federal OCS lands indicated which of potentially dozens of exploration and development projects would be permitted (and under what conditions).

The Court concludes, as did the court in *Cady v. Morton supra,* that "although the EIS could be 'improved by hindsight,' it has satisfied the intent of the statute. *National Forest Preservation Group v. Butz,* 485 F.2d 408, 412 (9th Cir. 1973)." 527 F.2d at 797.

The length, complexity and convolutions of this memorandum and of the findings and conclusions set forth herein speak louder and much more eloquently than the words themselves. The message is as clear as it is repugnant: under our so-called federal system, the Congress is constitutionally empowered to launch programs, the scope, impact, consequences and workability of which are largely unknown, at least to the Congress, at the time of enactment; the federal bureaucracy is legally permitted to execute the congressional mandate with a high degree of befuddlement as long as it acts no more befuddled than the Congress must reasonably have anticipated; if ultimate execution of the congressional mandate requires interaction between federal and state bureaucracy, the resultant maze is one of the prices required under the system.

The foregoing shall constitute the Court's findings of fact and conclusions of law.

The administrative action is affirmed; the petition is denied, each side to bear its costs.

NOTES

1. In a section of the opinion not included above, the court considered the standard of review appropriate to the administrative decision in dispute:

   That deference is due an agency's interpretation of its own regulations and the statute it is charged with administering is indisputable. . . . The principle of deference itself is premised on the twin notions of agency expertise and congressional acquiescence in that interpretation.

   456 F. Supp. at 906. The court ultimately found both factors important in its decision to give "considerable deference" to the interpretations made by the federal defendants of their regulations:

   . . . Congress placed responsibility for administering the CZMA in the Department of Commerce with the clear expectation that such responsibility ultimately would be delegated to NOAA, an agency favored by Congress expressly because of its technical expertise in matters relating to the Nation's coasts. Moreover, during enactment of the 1976 Amendments, Congress applauded NOAA's administration of the Act and directed it to promulgate regulations further clarifying the requirements of the Act.

   Id. at 908. What other factors might lead the reviewing court to defer to NOAA's construction of both the act and regulations accompanying it? Should it be relevant that in amending the CZMA in 1976, Congress limited NOAA discretion in determining how the act would be implemented?

   What result would you predict if the Secretary of Commerce had disapproved the California program and California challenged the Secretary's disapproval? Or what if the Secretary later withdrew approval of the California program under section 312(d), 16 U.S.C. § 1458 (1980 Supp.), based on oil industry complaints?

2. According to Judge Kelleher:
   (a) Was the original environmental preservation orientation of the 1972 act

changed by the 1976 amendments? *See* Ditton, Symour & Swanson, *Historical Aspects of Managing Coastal Resources* 78 (1977).

(b) Are state coastal programs required to accommodate particular energy facilities by CZMA section 306(c)(8), 16 U.S.C. § 1455(c)(8) (1980 Supp.), which requires state programs to provide for "adequate consideration of the national interest involved in . . . the siting of . . . energy facilities"? *See* Privett, *The Coastal Zone Management Act and Its Potential Impact on Coastal Dependent Energy Development*, 8 Nat. Res. Law. 455 (1979). If so, how is a coastal state's "fair share" of energy facilities needed in the national interest to be determined? *See* Hildreth, *The Coast: Where Energy Meets the Environment*, 13 San Diego L. Rev. 253, 296–97 (1976). *See generally* Ducsik, *Integrating Coastal Zone and Electric Facility Planning: Weak Links in the Institutional Chain*, 8 Coastal Zone Mgmt. J. 263 (1980). If not, what is "adequate consideration"? *See* 16 U.S.C. § 1454 (1980 Supp.) (state programs required to have a "planning process" for energy facilities); 45 Fed. Reg. 85770 (Dec. 30, 1980).

(c) More generally, are state programs required to commit portions of the state's coastal zone to particular uses before they may be federally approved?

(d) How may project applicants obtain review of state determinations that their federally licensed activities are inconsistent with the state's federally approved coastal program?

3. How important was NOAA's compliance with the environmental impact statement requirements of the National Environmental Policy Act (NEPA), 42 U.S.C. § 4321 *et seq.* (1978), to Judge Kelleher's decision upholding approval of the California program? How well did NOAA comply with NEPA? *See generally* Cameron, *NEPA and the CZMA: The Environmental Impact Statement and Section 306 Guidelines*, 16 Wm. & Mary L. Rev. 773 (1975).

4. Based on *API v. Knecht*, compare the level and quality of participation by federal agencies other than NOAA in development of the California coastal program with the level of public participation generally. What are the purposes of sections 306(c)(1), 16 U.S.C. § 1455(c)(1) (1980 Supp.), and 307(b), 16 U.S.C. § 1456(b) (1980 Supp.), requiring states to provide federal agencies "full participation" in state program development and to "adequately consider" the views of federal agencies? *See* Hershman, *Achieving Federal–State Coordination in Coastal Resources Managment*, 16 Wm. & Mary L. Rev. 747 (1975); Hershman & Folkenroth, *Coastal Zone Management and Intergovernmental Cooperation*, 54 Or. L. Rev. 13 (1975). *See also* 16 U.S.C. § 1456(a) (1980 Supp.) (Secretary of Commerce required to consult with other interested federal agencies). Were those purposes achieved in the development of the California program?

5. As *API v. Knecht* illustrates, questions frequently arise about the enforceability of certain elements of a state coastal zone program. In Washington State the problem took the form of a gubernatorial policy statement:

State policy favoring the siting of an oil tanker superport outside of Puget Sound has been deleted from the state coastal zone management program. The deletion request, made by Governor Ray in 1977 shortly after taking office, was approved by the federal government on December 31, 1979.

The issue stems from 1976 when then-Governor Daniel Evans included the policy in the coastal zone program being finalized for approval by the Office of Coastal Zone Management. It read, "The State of Washington, as a matter of overriding policy, positively supports the concept of a single, major crude petroleum receiving and transfer facility at or west of Port Angeles."

The federal decision to approve deletion was based on an environmental impact statement issued by the Office of Coastal Zone Management. It said, in part, that the policy was unenforceable under state law and of limited influence under federal law.

Furthermore, because of other laws now in effect, deletion of the policy will not significantly decrease protection of the valuable resources of greater Puget Sound. The most salient other law is the Magnuson amendment to the Marine Mammal Protection Act. In effect, it prohibits any dock construction east of Port Angeles which would result in the handling of increased volumes of petroleum for other than consumption in this state.

4 Washington Department of Ecology, Shoreline/Coastal Zone Management 2 (January 1980).

Two issues are at the bottom of the state law question: (1) the power of the state executive to issue and to rescind policy statements or executive orders, and (2) the effect of such a statement or order. The resolution of those two points will depend on the variations in individual state constitutions and legislation. The issues are highlighted because of the "networking" approach to CZM planning adopted by many states. The networking approach consists of piecing together existing legislation and regulations with the glue of an executive policy statement or order, in constrast to the more comprehensive approach utilized in California. *See* Bradley, *The Networking Approach to Coastal Zone Management*, 2 Coastal Zone '80 at 1504 (1980); Wingo & Fawcett, *Coastal Zone Integration of State and Local Plans*, 3 Coastal Zone '80 at 2052 (1980).

6. Once the state's management plan has been approved, what must the state do to amend it? The regulatory scheme distinguishes between proposed changes according to their effect: (a) routine program implementation, (b) amendments that will not change the status of an approved program, and (c) amendments that will change the program such that it would no longer be acceptable under CZMA section 306. *See* 15 CFR § 923.80–.84 (1980).

7. For purposes of the CZMA, the "coastal zone" is defined as extending seaward to the outer limit of the U.S. territorial sea, and inland "only to the extent necessary to control shorelands, the uses of which have a direct and significant impact on the coastal waters. Excluded from the coastal zone are lands the use of which is by law subject solely to the discretion of or which is held in trust by the Federal Government, its officers or agents." 16 U.S.C. § 1453(1) (1980 Supp.). How far inland can state coastal zone management programs reach? How far inland should they reach? *See* Woodruff, Langley & Reed, *Inland Boundary Determinations for Coastal Management Purposes,* 4 Coastal Zone Mgmt. J. 189 (1978).

Are all federally owned lands excluded from the coastal zone? *See* Letter Opinion of Antonin Scalia, Assistant Attorney General Office of Legal Counsel, Department of Justice, to William C. Brewer, Jr., General Counsel, National Oceanic and Atmospheric Administration (Aug. 10, 1976). If so, what difficulties does the federal lands exclusion pose for state coastal zone management? *See* Landstrom, *State and Local Governmental Regulation of Private Land Using Activities on Federal Lands*, 7 Nat. Res. Law. 77 (1974); Note, *Coastal Zone Management and Excluded Federal Lands: The Viability of Continued Federalism in the Management of Federal Coastlands*, 7 Ecology L.Q. 1101 (1979); Williamson, *Federal Lands and Consistency: An Intergovernmental Planning Proposal for the Coastal Zone*, 4 Coastal Zone Mgmt. J. 435 (1978). If the territorial sea is expanded from 3 to 12 miles by international action, should the seaward limit of the "coastal zone" for CZMA purposes also be changed to 12 miles?

8. Is participation by the states in coastal zone management mandatory or voluntary under the CZMA? What incentives to participate does the CZMA offer the states? What problems are likely to result from leaving the management of the coastal zones under state and local control?

9. For what purposes are the states to manage their coastal zones under the act?

The following excerpt from an OCZM report details the differing expectations for the federal coastal zone management program:

For those concerned with our diminishing supply of natural resources and their environmental degradation, coastal zone management means protection or restoration of wetlands, beaches, dunes, and barrier islands.

For those who make a living from fishing or indulge in it as a sport, coastal zone management means protection of the habitats in which fish spawn, breed and congregate. . . .

The developer feels that coastal zone management should mean freedom from protracted government procedures and unnecessary or duplicative permitting requirements.

For the tourist, coastal zone management means easy access to unspoiled beaches and parks, and the preservation of scenic coastal vistas. It means a ready supply of recreational facilities, hotels, and restaurants to service their needs.

The energy industry believes that coastal zone management should mean siting for major energy facilities that serve the nation's energy needs located where they can take advantage of coastal locations and resources. . . .

For those who seek a wilderness experience, free from outside intrusion and away from the pressures of everyday life, coastal zone management means that portions of the nation's coastline will remain forever in their natural state, permanently protected from alteration or destruction.

Office of Coastal Zone Management, The First Five Years of Coastal Zone Management: An Initial Assessment 1–2 (1979).

Given these conflicting expectations, how likely is it that any state program approved under the act will satisfy everyone with a stake in the allocation of coastal resources? The OCZM report notes:

Managing the coastal zone would be easier if only a single objective were involved. But CZM is meant to address multiple objectives and not to serve any one to the exclusion of all others. Even so, every objective cannot be met fully nor can every option be preserved indefinitely. Therefore, coastal zone management generally means making rational choices among competing objectives. If this is achieved, the cumulative effect of our decisions and choices will be the preservation, protection, development, and where possible, the restoration and enhancement of this nation's coastal resources, which is the goal Congress intended when the CZMA was passed in 1972.

Id. at 3. Does the foregoing adequately explain the lack of substance in the CZMA's requirements for state program approval?

10. How important in determining state program compliance are the policy declarations of the act and the congressional findings upon which these policies are based? The declaration of policy section was substantially revised by the 1980 amendments to add nine national goals for coastal zone management:

(a) Protect natural resources, e.g., estuaries, barrier islands, coral reefs, and fish and wildlife and their habitat;

(b) Manage coastal development to minimize loss of life and property from flooding, erosion, etc.;

(c) Give priority to coastal dependent facilities, e.g., energy, fisheries, etc.;

(d) Increase public access to the coast for recreation;

(e) Redevelop urban waterfronts and ports;

(f) Promote coordination and simplification of coastal management procedures;

(g) Have state and local governments given adequate consideration to federal agency views;

(h) Increase opportunities for public and local government participation in coastal zone management;

(i) Support comprehensive management of living marine resources for pollution control and aquaculture facilities in the coastal zone.

See 16 U.S.C. § 1452(2) (1981 Supp.). What effect should these newly articulated policies have on already approved state programs? *See* 16 U.S.C. § 1458(c) (1981 Supp.) providing for a 30 percent maximum reduction in program administration funding for coastal states that fail to make significant improvement in achieving the nine objectives listed above; Cong. Rec. at S14096 (Sept. 30, 1980) (states with approved programs can only have funds if significant improvements are being made). *See generally* Coastal Zone Management Advisory Committee, Public Support for Coastal Zone Management Programs (1978); Englander, Feldman & Hershman, *Coastal Zone Problems: A Basis for Evaluation,* 3 Coastal Zone Mgmt. J. 217 (1977); Feldman & McCrea, *Evaluating the Effectiveness of CZM Programs,* 1 Coastal Zone '78 at 117 (1978); General Accounting Office, The Coastal Zone Management Program: An Uncertain Future (1976); General Accounting Office, Problems Continue in the Federal Management of the Coastal Zone Program (1980); Kermond, *Coastal Zone Management Evaluation: Some Alternatives,* 1 Coastal Zone '80 at 412 (1980); Lowry & Okamura, *Evaluation and Inter-Governmental Relations in CZM,* 1 Coastal Zone '80 at 429 (1980); Noble, Epting, Blumm & Blumstein, *Evaluating State Coastal Plans: Questions to Ask,* 1 Coastal Zone '78 at 101 (1978); Reimold, *Effectiveness of Assessments of Coastal Management,* 1 Coastal Zone '80 at 444 (1980); Travis, *CZM Evaluation from a State Perspective,* 1 Coastal Zone '80 at 451 (1980); Wang & Wang, *An Approach for Evaluation of Coastal Zone Management,* 1 Coastal Zone '78 at 129 (1978).

11. CZMA section 315(1), 16 U.S.C. § 1461(1) (1981 Supp.) authorizes the Secretary of Commerce to grant coastal states up to 50 percent of the costs of acquiring and operating estuarine sanctuaries. As of January 1981, nine estuarine sanctuaries from Hawaii (Waimanu) through Ohio (Old Woman Creek) to Rhode Island (Narragansett Bay) had been established. *See* Dennis, Browning & Bissell, *Elkhorn Slough: The Making of an Estuarine Sanctuary,* 3 Coastal Zone '80 at 1939 (1980); Hanselman & Vogel, *Old Woman Creek, Ohio: The Designation of a Freshwater Estuarine Sanctuary,* 4 Coastal Zone Mgmt. J. 329 (1978); Ross & Hepp, *Estuarine Sanctuaries—The Oregon Experience,* 1 Coastal Zone Mgmt. J. 433 (1974); Young, *Duplin River Estuarine Sanctuary—A Description,* 4 Coastal Zone Mgmt. J. 223 (1978).

   What are some possible differences in purpose and scope between the marine sanctuary program discussed in Chapter 10 and the estuarine sanctuary program? *See* M. Lynch, B. Laird & T. Smolen, *Marine and Estuarine Sanctuaries* (1974). What are some alternative mechanisms for comprehensively managing sensitive estuarine areas? *See e.g.,* 16 U.S.C. § 1452(3) (special area management plans encouraged by the 1980 CZMA amendments); Davis, *Principles and Techniques for Special Area Management—The Grays Harbor and Coos Bay Experience,* 1 Coastal Zone '80 at 761 (1980); Evans, *Conflict Resolution: Lessons from Grays Harbor,* 1 Coastal Zone '80 at 776 (1980). What about placing them in national parks or national seashores? *See, e.g.,* 16 U.S.C. §§ 410, 459 (1981 Supp.). *See also* The Estuary Protection Act of 1968, 16 U.S.C. 1221 *et seq.*.

12. The case law dealing with the CZMA in addition to *API v. Knecht* and *Ray v. ARCO* is not extensive; the following points have been discussed by the courts:

   (a) In *City and County of San Francisco v. United States,* 615 F.2d 498 (9th Cir.

1980) the court rejected the plaintiff's argument "that although the [San Francisco Bay Conservation and Development] Commission's plan was not formally approved, the Secretary of Commerce had 'tacitly' approved the plan prior to the effective date of the lease and the Navy was fully informed of the plan's provisions," on the grounds that "it was unlikely that 'tacit' approval would be sufficient to trigger the statute [CZMA]," and that practically, the agency had had the draft plan less than a week when the lease decision was made. 615 F.2d at 504.

(b) In *Barcelo v. Brown,* 478 F. Supp. 646, 681 (D.P.R. 1979), *remanded on other grounds*, 16 ERC 1593 (1st Cir. 1981), *rev'd on other grounds*, ___U.S.___ (April 27, 1982), the court discussed the definition and operation of the terms "coastal zone" and "federal lands" under the act.

(c) In *Hoe v. Alexander,* 483 F. Supp. 746, 749 (D. Hawaii 1980) the plaintiff asserted that "the project violates state law and hence cannot possibly meet the CZMA consistency requirements." The court's conclusion was: "Were the question of the applicability of this statute to the Lualoa project before the court, it would abstain because as stated heretofore, the interpretation of state statutes is a matter for the courts of the state of Hawaii and this statute remains unconstrued by them."

(d) In *Town of North Hempstead v. Village of North Hills,* 482 F. Supp. 900 (E.D.N.Y. 1979), the court held that the CZMA is neither a jurisdictional grant nor a basis for stating a claim upon which relief can be granted. Given the ocean and coastal resources involved, why has there been relatively little litigation under the CZMA? Are potential litigants awaiting the application of state coastal management programs to specific resource allocation questions that affect them before initiating legal action? Consider the cases in the following chapter concerning legal issues in state coastal zone management.

(e) Deferring consideration of the *North Hempstead* holding, the court in *Save Lake Washington v. Frank,* 641 F.2d 1330 (9th Cir. 1981), held that NOAA had complied sufficiently with federal and state consistency procedures in finding that the mooring of NOAA ocean-going research vessels on Lake Washington was consistent with the Washington coastal program. *See also Northwest Environmental Defense Fund v. Bratton,* 16 ERC 1097, 1688 (D. Ore. 1981).

13. In contrast to the case law, the literature concerning coastal zone management is voluminous. Some works of general interest not cited elsewhere in this book include: Beltrami & Carroll, *A Land-Use Planning Model for Coastal Zone Management,* 4 Coastal Zone Mgmt. J. 83 (1978); J. Devanney, G. Ashe & B. Parkhurst, *Parable Beach: A Primer in Coastal Zone Economics* (1976); R. Ditton, J. Seymour & G. Swanson, *Coastal Resources Management: Beyond Bureaucracy and the Market* (1977); Finnell, *The Federal Regulatory Role in Coastal Land Management,* 1978 A.B.F. Res. J. 173; R. Healy, *Protecting the Golden Shore: Lessons from the California Coastal Commissions* (1978); J. Heikoff, *Coastal Resources Management* (1977); M. Hershman & J. Feldman, *Coastal Management: Readings and Notes* (1979); J. Hite & J. Stepp, *Coastal Zone Resource Management* (1971); H. Odum, B. Copeland & E. McMahan, *Coastal Ecological Systems of the U.S.* (1977); Rettig, *Some Economic Aspects of Conflicts over Land Use in the Coastal Zone,* 1 Coastal Zone Mgmt. J. 292 (1974); Rosener, *Intergovernmental Tension in Coastal Zone Managemet,* 7 Coastal Zone Mgmt. J. 95 (1980); Russell & Kneese, *Establishing the Scientific, Technical, and Economic Basis for Coastal Zone Management,* 1 Coastal Zone Mgmt. J. 47 (1973); Schoenbaum & Silliman, *Coastal Planning: The Designation and Management of Areas of Critical Concern,* 13 Urb. Law Ann. 23 (1977); S. Scott, *Governing California's Coast* (1971); Stanford Environmental Law Society, Coastal Futures: Legal Issues Affecting Development of the California Coast (1979); Swanson, Seymour & Ditton, *An Alternative Perspective on Common Property Resource Allocation*

Decisions in the Coastal Zone, 4 Coastal Zone Mgmt. J. 25 (1978); Symposium, *Urban Coastal Management,* 6 Coastal Zone Mgmt. J. Nos. 2–3 (1979); U.S. Dept. of Commerce, *Who's Minding the Shore? A Citizens Guide to Coastal Management* (1976); Zile, *Some Legal Issues in the Coastal Zone Management Act: Grant-in-Aid Aspects,* 3 Coastal Zone Mgmt. J. 39, 151 (1976 & 1977); Zwicky & Clark, *Environmental Protection Motivation in Coastal Zone Land-Use Legislation,* 1 Coastal Zone Mgmt. J. 103 (1973).

A growing body of literature in English concerning coastal zone management in other countries also exists. *See e.g.,* Center for Ocean Management Studies, Comparative Marine Policy 45–86 (1981); Harrison & Sewell, *Shoreline Managment: The French Approach,* 5 Coastal Zone Mgmt. J. 161 (1979); Hildreth, *Coastal Land Use Control in Sweden,* 2 Coastal Zone Mgmt. J. 1 (1975); McCombs, *Coastal Management and Planning in New Zealand,* 3 Coastal Zone '78 at 1712 (1978); E. Miles & J. Gamble, *Law of the Sea: Conference Outcomes and Problems of Implementation* 61–88 (1977); Mobarek & Goodman, *Coastal Development at the Nile Mediterranean Outlets,* 1 Coastal Zone '80 at 724 (1980); Morgan & Secter, *Managing Shore Development in British Columbia,* 1 Coastal Zone '80 at 715 (1980); Shapiro, *Two Approaches to Coastal Area Planning in Japan,* 1 Coastal Zone '80 at 741 (1980); Steers, *Saving the Coast: The British Experience,* 4 Coastal Zone Mgmt. J. 7 (1978); Vaidyaraman, Brahme, Gokhale & Vaze, *Coastal Zone Management–East Coast of India,* 3 Coastal Zone '78 at 1752 (1978).

14. Why were the plaintiffs in *API v. Knecht* so concerned about the secretary's approval of the California program? Was potential application of the CZMA federal consistency requirements to federal OCS oil and gas leasing off California an important factor in their decision to sue? Why?

SECTION B: FEDERAL CONSISTENCY WITH APPROVED STATE PROGRAMS

As the court noted in *API v. Knecht,* once a state coastal program has been approved by the Secretary of Commerce, the federal consistency provisions of CZMA sections 307(c) and (d), 16 U.S.C. §§ 1456(c), (d) (1981 Supp.), require that federal agency actions "directly affecting" the state's coastal zone be consistent with the state's program "to the maximum extent practicable." The federal consistency obligation extends to (1) activities conducted or supported by federal agencies; (2) federal development projects in the state's coastal zone (remember, however, that certain federal lands are by definition excluded from the state's coastal zone); (3) federal licenses, permits, and OCS oil and gas exploration and development· plan approvals authorizing private and public activities affecting land or water uses in the coastal zone; and (4) projects approved as part of federal assistance grants to state and local governments. With respect to (3) and (4) only, the Secretary of Commerce may override a state finding of inconsistency by finding that the proposed action is consistent with CZMA's objectives or otherwise necessary in the interests of national security.

NOTES

1. Under what circumstances does a federal action ·"directly affect" a state's coastal zone such that the federal consistency obligation applies? *See* Cong. Rec. at H10111 (Sept. 30, 1980) (whether a federal action directly affects a state's coastal

zone essentially is a question of fact); 44 Fed. Reg. 37142 (June 25, 1979) (same).

For example, can activities, such as tract selection prior to an OCS oil and gas lease sale, "directly affect" a state's coastal zone? In *California v. Watt*, 16 ERC 1729 (C.D. Cal. 1981), the court held that prelease activities connected with OCS Lease Sale No. 53 "directly affected" the California coastal zone because they define the basic parameters for subsequent development and production. According to the court, the Department of Interior must consider approved state coastal programs in its decisions with respect to tract size and location, special lease stipulations, and sale timing. *See* Linsley, *Federal Consistency and Outer Continental Shelf Oil and Gas Leasing: The Application of the "Directly Affecting" Test to Pre-Lease Sale Activities*, 9 Envt'l Affairs 429 (1981). *See also California v. Watt*, 16 ERC 1561 (D.C. Cir. 1981) (Interior's 5 year leasing program held to violate 1978 OCS Lands Act amendments); Behr, *Implementing Federal Consistency Under the Coastal Zone Management Act of 1972*, 3 N.Y. Sea Grant L. & Policy J. 3 (1980); Schoenbaum & Parker, *Federalism in the Coastal Zone: Three Models of State Jurisdiction*, 57 N.C. L. Rev. 231 (1979).

2. How important an incentive to state CZMA participation are the consistency provisions? Consider the treatment the consistency obligation received from the courts in *Ray v. ARCO*, 435 U.S. 151 (1978), Chapter 7 *supra*. The Washington state coastal program became the first statewide program to be approved in the spring of 1976. Shortly thereafter the case of *ARCO v. Evans* was argued in the trial court. Recall from Chapter 7 that the issue was whether the federal Ports and Waterways Safety Act had preempted the Washington Tanker Safety Law. The state argued that because the Tanker Safety Law was part of the state's federally approved coastal program, the Coast Guard was bound to implement the federal act consistent with this state law. At the least, argued the state, the CZMA consistency obligation was a persuasive congressional statement that other federal laws

and the authority of federal agencies thereunder, must be interpreted consistently with the purposes of the Coastal Zone Management Act and its intention that the federal and state regulatory efforts be harmonized to the fullest extent possible. In the instant case, given the absence of a clear expression of congressional intent to preempt, federal approval of the State Program provides a . . . reason to hold that [the Tanker Safety Law is not preempted].

Jurisidictional Brief of Appellants Evans and Others Before United States Supreme Court 20–21. The trial court rejected Washington's argument as follows:

[T]he State of Washington asserts that the Commerce Department's approval of its coastal management plan (to which the Tanker Law is related) somehow waives federal preemption of the area. The Secretary of Commerce can approve a state's coastal management plan . . . only if "the view of Federal agencies principally affected by such program have been adequately considered." 16 U.S.C. Section 1456(b) (1970). The Secretary may or may not have "considered" the views of the Coast Guard. The Secretary may or may not have noticed the preemptive effect of the PWSA on Washington's Tanker Law. That is not before us. We cannot read the Secretary's approval of a coastal management plan, to which the Tanker Law is only collaterally related, as foreclosing our inquiry into the federal preemption of oil tanker regulation.

The U.S. Supreme Court similarly rejected the state's arguments, with even less discussion. *See Ray v. ARCO*, 435 U.S. 151, 178 n.28 (1978). If the *Ray v. ARCO* approach is followed, how significant an incentive to the states is the consistency requirement? *See generally* Blumm & Noble *The Promise of Federal Consistency Under § 307 of the Coastal Zone Management Act*, 6 Envt'l L. Rep. 50047 (1976); Brewer, *Federal Consistency and State Expectations*, 2 Coastal

Zone Mgmt. J. 315 (1976); D. Hagman, *Urban Planning and Land Development Control Law* 585 (1975 Supp.); Lawyer, *Federal Consistency—Is It Working? A Perspective from the Northwest*, 3 Coastal Zone '80 at 2123 (1980).

3. How should ambiguities in the meaning of the consistency provisions be clarified? By judicial interpretation as in *Ray v. ARCO, supra*? Through administrative regulations? *See* 15 C.F.R. pt. 930 (1980) (NOAA consistency regulations); Senate Bill 96–783, 96th Cong., 2d Sess. at 11 (1980) (hope expressed that through the rule-making process "future areas of disagreement over the application of federal consistency will be substantially reduced"). Through the secretarial mediation process created by section 307(h), 16 U.S.C. § 1456(h) (1981 Supp.)?

In 1980, the dispute between the state of California and various federal agencies over OCS development off California was submitted to mediation in an effort to define "directly affecting" under section 307(c). All parties deemed the effort unsuccessful. *See* Appendix A06 of H.R. 96–1012, 96th Cong. 2d Sess. (1980), for the text of the letters exchanged by the parties involved and 11 BNA Environment Reporter Current Developments 449 (June 9, 1980) for Secretary Andrus's response to Senator Cranston's questions on the matter. *See also* 11 Nautilus Press, Coastal Zone Mgmt. Newsletter No. 10 at 1–2 (Mar. 5, 1980), No. 11 at 2–3 (Oct. 29, 1980). Is it fair to assume that the parties ultimately will meet in court in situations involving serious consistency disagreements? *See* Deller, *Federalism and Offshore Oil and Gas Leasing: Must Federal Tract Selections and Lease Stipulations Be Consistent with State Coastal Zone Management Programs*, 14 U.C. Davis L. Rev. 105 (1980); DuBey, Koshuta & Steinborn, *Striking the Balance in Energy Project Siting*, 3 Coastal Zone '80 at 2135 (1980); Karp, *Consistency Review of OCS Activities Off California*, 3 Coastal Zone '80 at 2103 (1980); Moore, *Outer Continental Shelf Development and Recent Applications of the Coastal Zone Management Act of 1971* [*sic*], 15 Tulsa L.J. 443, 445–49, 458–64 (1980).

4. How could the consistency process be improved? Consider the following from Finn, *Interagency Relationships in Marine Resources Conflicts: Some Lessons from OCS Oil and Gas Leasing*, 4 Harv. Envt'l L. Rev. 359, 389 (1980):

The CZM consistency requirement has caused significant intergovernmental conflict over OCS oil and gas activities. Although no state has yet challeneged an OCS lease sale in court as inconsistent with its CZM program, states have used the policies contained in CZM programs to impose additional requirements on OCS exploration, development, and production activities. This approach has caused considerable difficulties, since the policies contained in CZM programs are often not only extremely general, but also inapplicable on their face to activities on the OCS, which are outside the state's jurisdiction.

Although a state can use the consistency requirement to veto a private applicant's proposed activity, it need not, under NOAA regulations, provide the applicant with a hearing, or even a written statement of findings. An applicant may appeal to the Department of Commerce, but only on the grounds that the proposed activity is consistent with the federal CZMA or necessary in the interest of national security. Furthermore, such an appeal is available only after the final state objection, which may take up to six months. Although hearings may be required by some states, securing these hearing rights in the state system may be costly and time-consuming for federal permit applicants.

To remedy these potential sources of unfairness, the federal CZM regulations should require a state to provide a hearing whenever it objects to a consistency certification. States should accompany their consistency concurrences and objections with a statement of reasons, allowing effective judicial review and public scrutiny of these actions. Finally, the regulations should provide better guidance as to the meaning of the terms "consistent with state CZM programs" and "actions that affect the coastal zone," in order to provide more predictable implementation of the consistency requirement.

5. What is the relationship between the consistency provisions and section 307(e), 16 U.S.C. § 1456(e) (1981 Supp.), which provides that nothing in the CZMA shall be construed "to diminish either Federal or state . . . control of water resources, submerged lands, or navigable waters" or as "modifying . . . existing laws applicable to the various federal agencies"? Cf. 42 U.S.C. §§ 4231(c), 4332 (1976); *EPA v. California*, 426 U.S 200 (1976); *Hancock v. Train*, 426 U.S. 167 (1976).

   Section 307(f), 16 U.S.C. § 1456(f) (1981 Supp.), provides that federal, state, and local requirements established under the federal Clean Air and Clean Water Acts shall be the air and water pollution control requirements applicable to state coastal management programs. *See generally* Andrews, *EPA Authority Under the Coastal Zone Management Act of 1972*, 10 Nat. Res. Law. 249 (1977); Comment, *The EPA and CZM: Striking a Federal–State Balance of Power in Land Use Management*, 11 Houston L. Rev. 1152 (1974). Are state and local governments prevented by section 307(f) from adopting special, more stringent coastal air pollution regulations as part of an approved state coastal program? Not as long as the CZMA's intergovernmental coordination requirements are met, because both the federal Clean Air and Clean Water Acts allow state and local governments to impose air and water pollution standards stricter than those promulgated by the federal Environmental Protection Agency. *See* 33 U.S.C. § 1370 (1981 Supp.); 42 U.S.C. § 7416 (1981 Supp.); Hildreth, *The Operation of the Federal Coastal Zone Management Act as Amended*, 10 Nat. Res. Law. 211, 215 n.25 (1977).

SECTION C: FAST-TRACK LEGISLATION AND THE COASTAL ZONE

It is important to remember that all of the federal, as well as state, laws, regulations, and permit requirements that affect the coastal zone are either the direct product of congressional action (i.e., Ocean Dumping Act, OCS Lands Act, Marine Mammal Protection Act) or are allowed to continue by the acquiescence of Congress, either through delegation to the states, i.e., under the CZMA, or by the congressional choice not to exercise federal preemptive powers. Congress has very broad powers to alter these federal and state requirements. Several times in recent years, Congress has concluded that national security, economic welfare, or some other national interest requires that a specific project or action be speeded up and that the normal permit process be circumvented or accelerated. Examples of three ways Congress may do so are discussed further: (1) so-called "fast-track" legislation, expediting the regulatory process and limiting judicial review of certain types of projects; (2) greater legislative oversight of areas usually left to executive and administrative action through devices such as the legislative veto; and (3) special legislation designed to expedite a particular project.

Public Utility Regulatory Policies Act of 1978 (PURPA)[2]

Northern tier states have traditionally received a large portion of their crude oil supplies from western Canadian sources, delivered by pipeline to Washington, Montana, North Dakota, and Minnesota. A shortage of crude oil may occur in the northern tier states during the next 20 years as a result of three factors: the eventual curtailment of all Canadian imports, the lack of adequate delivery systems to bring in replacement crude supplies to these states, and declining oil production in the northern tier, Rocky Mountain, and Midwest regions.

At the same time, an excess of Alaskan North Slope (ANS) crude oil has developed in west coast states because most refineries there are not designed to process large amounts of the low-gravity, high-sulfur ("sour") ANS crude. This excess may increase by 1985, when North Slope deliveries to the port of Valdez, Alaska, are expected to reach 1.6 to 2 million barrels per day.

Among the proposed options for distributing Alaskan crude to states where it will be needed are the following: (1) various pipeline routes; (2) shipment by supertankers around Cape Horn or transfer to smaller tankers for passage through the Panama Canal; (3) overland transport by unit trains; and (4) arctic marine transportation systems that would pass through the Northwest Passage to the eastern United States. Of these, only a direct pipeline system from the west coast to the northern tier states assures those states of receiving a crude supply to offset the Canadian curtailment.

Title 5 of the Public Utilities Regulatory Policies Act of 1978 (PURPA), Pub. L. No. 95–617, 43 U.S.C. § 2001 *et seq.* (Supp. II, 1978), seeks to accomplish three goals: (1) to provide a means of selecting systems that will deliver crude oil to northern tier and inland states so as to resolve the west coast surplus and the northern tier shortage; (2) to provide an alternative federal permitting procedure to expedite the construction and operation of any delivery system that receives the requisite "Title 5 approval"; and (3) to assure that federal decisions concerning crude oil transportation systems are coordinated with state decisions "to the maximum extent practicable." Pub. L. No. 95–617, § 502. Title 5 is based on findings by Congress that a west-to-east crude oil delivery system is necessary to reduce the projected west coast crude surplus and alleviate a potentially severe shortage of crude oil in the northern tier states. Pub. L. No. 95–617, § 501. National security is cited as another reason for such a crude oil delivery system. *Id.*

If PURPA did not exist, each of the contending proposals would have to go through the complex process of complying fully with all federal (as well as state) permitting processes. At the federal level this would include compliance with most of the federal laws discussed in this book, including the Rivers and Harbors Act of 1899, the Clean Water Act, the Marine Protection, Research and Sanctuaries Act (Ocean Dumping Act), the Ports and Waterways Safety Act, the Clean Air Act, and the Coastal Zone Management Act.

---

[2]The authors wish to acknowledge the work of Mr. T. Beuttler. A seminar paper written while he was an LL.M. candidate at the University of Washington was used in drafting this subsection.

PURPA changes much of this. Specifically, under the act the first step is submitting the application for Title 5 eligibility to the Department of Interior, the lead agency under the act (§ 504). The Secretary of Interior ensures that an applicant provides all information necessary for review of the proposal by appropriate federal agencies. After the heads of such agencies have reviewed the proposed transportation system, they submit their recommendations to the Secretary. After providing a period for comments from the governor and officials of any state as well as from the public, the Secretary forwards all federal agency recommendations and subsequent comments to the President (§ 505).

The President must then review all of the information submitted to him concerning the proposed crude oil transportation systems that are eligible for Title 5 consideration. After consulting with the Secretaries of Energy, the Interior, and Transportation, the President decides which, if any, of the proposed systems will receive expedited processing and exemption from designated federal regulatory laws (§ 507(a)(1)). Presumably, the CZMA federal consistency provisions are waivable under this section. The President's decision must be based on a list of criteria specified in the act as well as on a determination that the construction and operation of the approved system is in the national interest (§§ 507(a), (b)(1)). Any law is deemed waived only upon enactment of a joint resolution of Congress (§ 508(a)). Once a transportation system has been approved by the President, all federal officials and agencies must "expedite, to the maximum extent practicable," their actions involved in the authorization, construction, and operation of the systems (§ 509(a)). Judicial review of federal actions taken pursuant to Title 5 is restricted (§§ 511(b),(c)).

PURPA has been used only once to date. In 1980, President Carter designated the Northern Tier Pipeline with a marine terminal in Washington State as the system to be expedited under PURPA. 16 Weekly Comp. of Pres. Doc. 99 (January 17, 1980). But PURPA affects only federal laws and regulations. It says nothing about state processes. This left intact Washington State's authority to determine where a marine oil terminal shall be sited, or whether in fact it should be sited within the state at all. In 1979, and again in 1980, bills were introduced in Congress to amend PURPA to expedite state as well as federal procedures. *See e.g.*, H.R. 3243, 96th Cong., 2nd Sess. (1980).

Energy Mobilization Board

President Carter proposed the creation of an Energy Mobilization Board (EMB) during a presidential address on July 15, 1979. The key element of the proposal was the creation of a board with extensive, delegated powers to (1) designate priority energy producing projects, (2) establish a master project decision schedule that would govern the various agencies, (3) usurp the decision-making power of a tardy agency, and (4) waive the application of new laws and the ability to recommend to the President and Congress that existing laws be waived in regard to a given project. Limited judicial review would occur in the Temporary

Emergency Court of Appeals. Unlike PURPA discussed above, the EMB also could affect state and local decision-making processes.

NOTES

1. Are PURPA and the EMB appropriate mechanisms for ensuring that coastal states do not obstruct coastal energy facilities felt to be in the national interest? *See* Knouse, *Achieving Federalism in the Regulation of Coastal Energy Facility Siting*, 8 Ecology L.J. 533 (1980). Or does the CZMA provide the preferable process? *See* Hildreth, *The Coast: Where Energy Meets the Environment*, 13 San Diego L. Rev. 253, 305 (1976).

2. Does *National League of Cities v. Usery*, 426 U.S. 823 (1976), pose a serious obstacle to federal preemption of state and local land use planning and facility siting functions? Consider Justice Rehnquist's two-step test of whether a federal law unconstitutionally interferes with state and local integral governmental functions: (a) "whether these determinations are functions essential to separate and independent existence . . . so that Congress may not abrogate the States' otherwise plenary authority to make them." 426 U.S. at 845 (1976); and (b) the congressional interference must not impose a substantial financial burden or "substantially restructure traditional ways in which the local government arranged its affairs." 426 U.S. at 846 (1976). *See* Cheit, *The Energy Mobilization Board*, 8 Ecology L.J. 727 (1980).

3. For discussion of energy facility siting problems in the absence of federal preemption, *see* M. Baram, *Environmental Law and the Siting of Facilities* (1976); D. Deal, *The Durham Controversy: Energy Facility Siting and the Land Use Planning and Control Process*, 8 Nat. Res. Law. 437 (1975); Hershman & Fontenot, *Local Regulation of Pipeline Sitings and the Doctrines of Federal Preemption and Supremacy* 1975–76 La. L. Rev. 929; Peters, *Durham, New Hampshire: A Victory for Home Rule?*, 5 Ecology L.Q. 53 (1973).

Greater Legislative Oversight

Section 12 of the Coastal Zone Management Act Amendments of 1980, 16 U.S.C. § 1463 (Supp. 1981), provides for a congressional veto of implementing regulations issued by the Secretary of Commerce. Previously considered in Chapter 10, Section A, was the 1980 amendment to the Marine Sanctuaries Act providing for congressional disapproval of marine sanctuaries designated by the President. 16 U.S.C. § 1432(b)(2)(B) (Supp. 1981). President Carter made the following comment when signing the 1980 amendments to the Marine Sanctuaries Act:

> Nevertheless, I am signing S. 1140 reluctantly, as I have serious reservations about the constitutionality of its legislative veto provision. Section 2, which purports to confer authority on Congress to disapprove—by concurrent resolutions not to be presented to the President—certain designations of marine sanctuaries, violates the presentation clauses of the Constitution, Art. I, Section 7, cls. 2 and 3, and violates the separation of powers doctrine by interfering with the discretion of the

executive branch in the administration of an ongoing program. Pursuant to my message to Congress dated July 21, 1978, I will treat the legislative veto provision as a "report-and-wait" provision. If Congress adopts a resolution under its authority, the resolution will be given serious consideration but, under my reading of the Constitution, will not be considered binding.

16 Weekly Comp. of Pres. Doc. 1592 (Aug. 29, 1980). What merit is there to President Carter's argument? *See* Bruff & Gellhorn, *Congressional Control of Administrative Regulation: A Study of Legislative Vetoes*, 90 Harv. L. Rev. 1369 (1977).

Legislation Expediting a Particular Project

A classic example of federal legislation expediting a particular project is the Trans-Alaska Pipeline Authorization Act, 43 U.S.C. §§ 1651–55 (1978), which limited administrative and judicial review of the Trans-Alaska Pipeline.

See generally, Kenney, *Port Permitting Problems*, 1 Coastal Zone '80 at 791 (1980); Layton & Buck, *Expediting the Coastal Approval Process*, 3 Coastal Zone '80 at 1998 (1980).

NOTE

Major coastal and ocean energy development projects often have stressed state and local coastal zone managment decision-making processes severely. *See Public Interest Research Group of New Jersey, Inc. v. State*, 152 N.J. Super. 191, 377 A.2d 915, *cert. denied*, 75 N.J. 538, 384 A.2d 517 (1977); Harms and Gutshall, *Potential Coastal Zone Impacts of Alternative Ocean Energy Systems*, 2 Coastal Zone '80 at 947 (1980); Hildreth, *The Coast: Where Energy Meets the Environment*, 13 San Diego L. Rev. 253 (1976); Peters, *Durham, New Hampshire: A Victory for Home Rule?*, 5 Ecology L.Q. 53 (1973). Recall *American Petroleum Institute v. Knecht, supra,* involving the effect of the California coastal program on offshore oil and gas development. *See* Ahern, *Energy Facilities and the California Coast*, 1 Coastal Zone '80 at 379 (1980).

The Delaware Coastal Zone Act, upon which Delaware's federally approved program is based, bans new heavy industry, including refineries, within 2 miles of the coast. Del. Code Ann. tit. 7, ch. 70, § 7003 (1974); *see Kreshtool v. Delmarva Power & Light Co.*, 310 A.2d 649 (Del. 1973); Comment, *Land-Use Management in Delaware's Coastal Zone*, 6 U. Mich. J. L. Reform 251 (1972); 118 Cong. Rec. 14173–75 (1972); Note, 21 Buffalo L. Rev. 481 (1972); Pedrick, *Land Use Control in the Coastal Zone: The Delaware Example*, 2 Coastal Zone Mgmt. J. 345 (1976). The Washington Shoreline Management Act of 1971 prohibits surface drilling for oil and gas in Puget Sound and the Strait of Juan de Fuca and on land within 1,000 feet of those waters. Wash. Rev. Code Ann. § 90.58.160 (1974); *see* Crooks, The Washington Shoreline Management Act, 54 Or. L. Rev. 35, 58 (1975). Recall that in *Ray v. Atlantic Richfield Co., supra,* major portions of the Washington Tanker Law controlling oil tanker traffic in Puget Sound were held preempted by federal law.

Georgia and Virginia, two states without federally approved coastal programs, have taken more sympathetic stances with respect to coastal energy development,

Georgia with respect to oil and gas development on the federal outer continental shelf, and Virginia with respect to construction of facilities for increased coal exports. *See* Nautilus Press, Coastal Zone Mgmt. Newsletter, Dec. 17, 1980 at 1–2; Phillips & Barber, *Balancing Fish and Fuel on Georgia's OCS*, 2 Coastal Zone '80 at 1098 (1980). Do states with federally approved coastal programs, such as California, New Jersey, North Carolina, and Washington, have any advantages in dealing with the impacts of coastal energy development?

12

Legal Issues in State Coastal Zone Management

The key to more effective protection and use of the land and water resources of the coastal zone is to encourage the states to exercise their full authority over the lands and waters in the coastal zone by assisting the states, in cooperation with Federal and local governments and other vitally affected interests, in developing land and water use programs for the coastal zone, including unified policies, criteria, standards, methods, and processes for dealing with land and water use decisions of more than local significance. [Section 302(h) of the Federal Coastal Zone Management Act of 1972]

In responding to Congress' "clarion call," coastal states have followed a variety of paths. Some have used existing statutes, such as wetland protection laws, as the framework for their management programs; others have enacted comprehensive coastal zone management legislation.

D. MANDELKER, ENVIRONMENTAL AND LAND CONTROLS LEGISLATION 247 (Bobbs-Merrill, 1976)

Three general issues pervade the coastal legislation that has been adopted so far: whether the statute should be narrowly based on protectionist objectives within narrow coastal areas or whether it should have broader land development control objectives; whether the coastal control system should be overlaid on existing local regulatory programs or be integrated with them; and whether coastal controls should be limited to permit approval systems or attempt more comprehensive land development control programs. At one extreme, the legislation may single out endangered wetlands for statutory protection and authorize a supplementary state permit system applicable solely to dredging and filling activities. A decision to approve or disapprove a dredge and fill permit will then be determined by whether or not the proposed activity, if allowed, would endanger the wetlands area. At the other extreme the legislation might be broadly applicable to all coastal areas and to all development within such areas, require state approval and modification of local plans and land development regulations within these areas, and contain comprehensive standards for the approval of developments subject to the coastal legislation. . . .

The first state considered, North Carolina, is an example of the comprehensive approach.

SECTION A: NORTH CAROLINA

Legislative Delegation of Comprehensive
Management Authority

ADAMS v. NORTH CAROLINA DEPARTMENT OF NATURAL AND ECONOMIC RESOURCES, 249 S.E.2d 402 (1978)

Plaintiffs Jack Adams, et al., instituted their action on 5 November 1976. Plaintiffs Alphious K. Everett, Sr., et al., instituted their action on 24 March 1977. Upon joint motion of plaintiffs and defendants these actions were consolidated for trial on 29 August 1977.

In this consolidated action, brought under the Declaratory Judgment Act, plaintiffs attack the constitutionality of the Coastal Area Management Act of 1974, G.S. 113A–100, et seq., hereinafter referred to as the Act. Plaintiffs allege in pertinent part:

1. That the Act is a prohibited local act under Article II, section 24 of the North Carolina Constitution.

2. That the Act delegates authority to the Coastal Resources Commission (hereinafter referred to as CRC) to develop and adopt "State Guidelines" for the coastal area without providing adequate standards to govern the exercise of the power delegated in violation of Article I, section 6 and Article II, section 1 of the North Carolina Constitution.

3. That the provisions of the Act, and the State guidelines adopted by the CRC, deprive them of their property without due process of law in violation of the Fifth and Fourteenth Amendments and in violation of Article I, section 19 of the North Carolina Constitution.

4. That Section 113A–126 of the Act authorizes warrantless searches by the CRC which are repugnant to the Fourth Amendment of the United States Constitution and Article I, section 20 of the North Carolina Constituion.

5. That the guidelines for the coastal area promulgated by the CRC exceed the powers delegated by the Act and are impermissibly inconsistent with the goals of the Act as set forth in Section 113A–102.

The Coastal Area Management Act of 1974 is a "cooperative program of coastal area management between local and State governments." (G.S. 113A–101). Its basic objective is to "establish a comprehensive plan for the protection, preservation, orderly development, and management of the coastal area of North Carolina." (G.S. 113A–102(a)).

Primary responsibility for implementing the Act is given to a fifteen-member citizen panel, the CRC, all but three of whom must have expertise in a specific phase of coastal activity such as commercial fishing, coastal engineering, coastal agriculture or coastal land development, or in local government in the twenty-county coastal area. Twelve of the fifteen are nominees of local government; all are appointed by the Governor. (G.S. 113A–104).

The CRC is assisted by the Coastal Resources Advisory Council (CRAC), composed of representatives appointed by each of the twenty coastal counties, plus four from coastal multi-county planning groups and eight from coastal towns and cities, as well as marine scientists and representatives of State agencies involved in coastal programs (G.S. 113A–105(b)).

The coastal area is generally defined as including all counties bordering the Atlantic Ocean or one of the coastal sounds. G.S. 113A–103(2).

A number of activities, including certain agricultural activities, are exempted from coverage of the Act by G.S. 113A–103(5)(b).

Four basic mechanisms are utilized by the Act to accomplish its objectives:

I. State Guidelines For The Coastal Area Are To Be Promulgated By The CRC. G.S. 113A–106 through 108.

The CRC is to develop state guidelines for the coastal area, specifying objectives, policies and standards to be followed in public and private use of land and water in the coastal area. These guidelines are to give particular attention to the nature of development which shall be appropriate within the various types of area of environmental concern designated by the CRC. (See Part III, infra.) G.S. 113A–107. The State guidelines have a threefold effect. All county land use plans (see Part II, infra) must be consistent with the guidelines. All development permits granted (see Part IV, infra) must be consistent with the guidelines. Finally, all land policies of the State relating to acquisition, use, disposition, and classification of coastal land shall be consistent with the guidelines. G.S. 113A–108.

II. Land Use Plans Are To Be Adopted By Each County Within The Coastal Area. G.S. 113A–109 through 112.

A land use plan is to "consist of statements of objectives, policies, and standards to be followed in public and private use of land within the county" which shall be supplemented by maps showing the appropriate location of particular types of land or water use in particular areas. The plan shall give special attention to the protection and appropriate development of areas of environmental concern designated by the CRC. G.S. 113A–110(a). If a coastal county fails to adopt a land use plan the CRC shall promptly prepare such a plan. G.S. 113A–109. The land use plans are to be consistent with the State guidelines promulgated by the CRC. G.S. 113A–110(a). No land use plan shall become effective until it is approved by the CRC. G.S. 113A–110(f). The county land use plans have a twofold effect. No development permit shall be issued under Part IV (infra) which is inconsistent with the approved land use plan for the county in which the development is proposed. G.S. 113A–111. No local ordinance or regulation shall be adopted within an area of environmental concern (see Part III, infra) which is inconsistent with the land use plan of the county in which said ordinance or regulation is effected. *Id.*

III. Designation Of Areas Of Environmental Concern By The CRC Through Rule Making. G.S. 113A–113 through 115.

"The [CRC] shall by rule designate geographic areas of the coastal area as areas of environmental concern and specify the boundaries thereof . . . ." G.S. 113A–113(a). In specifying areas of environmental concern (AEC) the CRC is to consider the criteria listed in G.S. 113A–113(b). "Prior to adopting any rule permanently designating any [AEC] the Secretary and the [CRC] shall hold a public hearing in each county in which lands to be affected are located, at which public and private parties shall have the opportunity to present comment and views." G.S. 113A–115(a). The CRC shall review the designated AEC's at least biennially. New AEC's may be added and others deleted in accordance with the procedures outlined above.

IV. Permits Must Be Obtained For Development Within AEC's G.S. 113A–116 through 125.

Every person before undertaking any development in any AEC must obtain a permit. G.S. 113A–118(a). Permits for major developments are obtained from the CRC and permits for minor developments are obtained in the first instance from the county in which the development is to take place. Permits for major development are obtained through a formal, quasi-judicial proceeding. G.S. 113A–122. All permit applicants for major development are entitled to a hearing in which evidence is taken and the rules of procedure applicable to civil actions are followed insofar as practicable. A transcript of this hearing is forwarded to the CRC which renders a decision supported by findings of fact and conclusions of law. *Id.* Any person directly affected by any final decision or order of the CRC may appeal to the superior court for judicial review. G.S. 113A–123. Permits for minor development are procured from the designated local official pursuant to an expedited system of review. These expedited procedures are formulated at the local level. G.S. 113A–121. Any person directly affected by a decision of the designated local official may request a hearing before the CRC.

Id. The procedure followed at this hearing is identical to that followed at hearings for major development permits. G.S. 113A–122.

The trial court upheld in all respects the constitutionality of the Act and the State guidelines promulgated by the CRC. Plaintiffs appealed to the Court of Appeals, and we allowed motion to bypass that court to the end that initial appellate review be had in the Supreme Court.

. . . .

HUSKINS, Justice:

Plaintiffs challenge the constitutionality of the Act on two grounds: (1) The Act constitutes local legislation prohibited by Article II, section 24 of the North Carolina Constitution; and (2) The Act unconstitutionally delegates authority to the Coastal Resources Commission (CRC) to develop and adopt "State guidelines" for the coastal area.

. . . .

Plaintiffs make a two-part argument in support of their position that the Act constitutes a prohibited local act. First they contend the General Assembly may not reasonably distinguish between the coast and the remainder of the State when enacting environmental legislation; and next, that even if the coast is sufficiently unique to justify separate environmental legislation, the twenty counties covered by the Act do not embrace the entire area necessary for the purposes of the legislation. We will address these arguments *seriatim*.

In support of the first contention plaintiffs argue that the natural resources and environmental needs of the coastal counties are not sufficiently unique to warrant special legislative treatment in the form of "a comprehensive plan for the protection, preservation, orderly development, and management of the coastal area of North Carolina." G.S. 113A–102(a). We disagree. The legislative findings on their face highlight the importance of the unique and exceptionally fragile coastal ecosystem:

"§ 113A–102. *Legislative findings and goals.*—(a) Findings.—It is hereby determined and declared as a matter of legislative finding that among North Carolina's most valuable resources are its coastal lands and waters. The coastal area, and in particular the estuaries, are among the most biologically productive regions of this State and of the nation. Coastal and estuarine waters and marshlands provide almost ninety percent (90%) of the most productive sport fisheries on the east coast of the United States. North Carolina's coastal area has an extremely high recreational and esthetic value which should be preserved and enhanced.

In recent years the coastal area has been subjected to increasing pressures which are the result of the often-conflicting needs of a society expanding in industrial development, in population, and in the recreational aspirations of its citizens. Unless these pressures are controlled by coordinated management, the very features of the coast which make it economically, esthetically, and ecologically rich will be destroyed. The General Assembly therefore finds that an immediate and pressing need exists to establish a comprehensive plan for the protection, preservation, orderly development, and management of the coastal area of North Carolina."

The following passages from 46 N.C.L.Rev. 779 and 49 N.C.L.Rev. 889–90 help to convey the exceptional qualities of the coastal zone which make it so important to this State and the nation:

> "The vast estuarine areas of North Carolina—'those coastal complexes where fresh water from the land meets the salt water of the sea with a daily tidal flux'—are exceeded in total area only by those of Alaska and Louisiana. Estuarine areas include bays, sounds, harbors, lagoons, tidal or salt marshes, coasts, and inshore waters in which the salt waters of the ocean meet and are diluted by the fresh waters of the inland rivers. In North Carolina, this encompasses extensive coastal sounds, salt marshes, and broad river mouths exceeding 2,200,000 acres. These areas are one of North Carolina's most valuable resources.
>
> . . . .
>
> This vast array of land and water combines to provide one of the largest relatively unspoiled natural areas on the eastern coast of the United States. . . . This massive ecosystem provides food, cover, nesting and spawning areas for countless finfish, shellfish, waterfowl, and fur and game animals."

The above cited legislative findings are confirmed by the trial record and indicate that the unique, fragile and irreplaceable nature of the coastal zone and its significance to the public welfare amply justify the reasonableness of special legislative treatment. We conclude that the coastal counties constitute a valid legislative class for the purpose of addressing the special and urgent environmental problems found in the coastal zone. *Accord, Toms River Affiliates v. Department of Environmental Protection*, 140 N.J.Super. 135, 355 A.2d 679 (1976); *Meadowlands Regional Development Agency v. State*, 112 N.J.Super. 89, 270 A.2d 418 (1970), aff'd. 63 N.J. 35, 304 A.2d 545 (1973). *See generally, Turnpike Authority v. Pine Island*, 265 N.C. 109, 143 S.E.2d 319 (1965).

Plaintiffs' contention that the environmental problems of the mountains and piedmont are equally deserving of legislative attention is not a valid constitutional objection to the Act in light of our finding that the coastal area is sufficiently unique to warrant special legislative attention.

. . . .

In the second part of their argument plaintiffs contend the General Assembly did not properly define the inland limits of the coastal sounds in G.S. 113A–103(3) and hence unreasonably excluded from the coverage of the Act counties which were coastal in nature. It should be noted that the inland limits of the coastal sounds in effect constitute the western boundaries of the coastal zone for purposes of the Act.

Plaintiffs' argument requires us to consider whether the General Assembly, in defining the inland limits of the coastal sound, drew boundary lines which were reasonably related to the purposes of the Act.

. . . .

To evaluate the legislative definition of the inland limits of the coastal sounds in its proper context, we must first examine the definition of coastal area in G.S. 113A–103(2). The coastal area is defined as those counties "that (in whole or in part) are adjacent to, adjoining, intersected by or bounded by the

Atlantic Ocean . . . or any coastal sound." This statutory definition of coastal area accurately reflects the unique geography of our coastal area. Some coastal counties are bounded by the Atlantic Ocean while others are bounded not by the ocean but by shallow, swampy, fertile coastal sounds which lie to the landward side of our extensive system of barrier islands known as the Outer Banks. The coastal sounds, of course, are the heart of the coastal area. *See generally*, Note, 49 N.C.L.Rev. 888–92 (1971).

These saltwater coastal sounds are in turn fed by the fresh water coastal rivers. One of the unique features of the North Carolina coastal zone is that its salty coastal sounds are contiguous with the fresh water coastal rivers. In fact, the sounds represent the mouths of the coastal rivers. *See generally,* G.S. 113A–103(3) for the names of the coastal sounds and rivers. Thus, in order to determine the inland limits of the coastal sounds and hence the western boundary of the coastal areas the Generaly Assembly had to decide where the salty, marshy, coastal sounds ended, and the fresh water coastal rivers began.

It is evident from the record that the boundaries of the coastal area could not be formulated with mathematical exactness. Affected by a number of varying conditions, the reaches of saltwater intrusion and tidal influence vary markedly from time to time and are thus incapable of exact determination. The criterion ultimately chosen by the General Assembly to distinguish the salty coastal sounds from the fresh water coastal rivers which fed into the sounds was "the limit of seawater encroachment" on a given coastal river under normal conditions. G.S. 113A–103(3). In effect, the limits of the coastal sounds were defined as those points on the coastal rivers where the salt content of the water measured below a scientifically determined amount.

The General Assembly added two refinements to the seawater encroachment criterion. The limits of seawater encroachment were legislatively established as the confluence of a given coastal river with an easily identifiable tributary near to but not always at the points indicated as the farthest inland reach of seawater encroachment. G.S. 113A–103(3). Given the difficulty of determining the precise location of the inland extent of seawater encroachment, we think the points of confluence provided a convenient method of implementing the seawater encroachment criterion. The General Assembly also excluded from the coverage of the Act all counties which adjoined a point of confluence and lay entirely west of said point. *Id.* Two counties—Jones and Pitt—were excluded from the coverage of the Act as a result of this exemptive clause. The record shows that these counties were not coastal in nature and contained insignificant quantities of coastal wetlands. We agree with the conclusion of the trial court that the slight extent of seawater encroachment into these two counties was of no significance to an accurate and reasonable definition of the coastal area.

We conclude that the western boundary of the coastal zone as determined by use of the seawater encroachment criterion is reasonably related to the purpose of the Act. The Record shows, and a look at any map of eastern North Carolina will confirm, that the twenty counties included within the purview of the Act under the statutory definition of coastal area are the counties which are substantially bounded by the large open bodies of water which may be logically, scientifically, or otherwise, considered to be coastal sounds. The coastal area as defined includes all those counties which intimately affect the quality of North Carolina's valuable estuarine waters. We thus hold that the Act is a general law which the General Assembly had power to enact.

Since we hold that the Act is a general law we need not determine whether it relates to or regulates one of the subjects as to which the Constitution prohibits local legislation. *See* N.C.Const., art. II, § 24.

The second issue for determination is whether the Act unconstitutionally delegates authority to the CRC to develop, adopt and amend "State guidelines" for the coastal area. *See* G.S. 113A-107.

Article I, section 6 of the North Carolina Constitution provides that the legislative, executive and judicial branches of government "shall be forever separate and distinct from each other." Legislative power is vested in the General Assembly by Article II, section 1 of the Constitution. From these constitutional provisions we glean the bedrock principle "that the legislature may not abdicate its power to make laws or delegate its *supreme* legislative power to any coordinate branch or to any agency which it may create." *Turnpike Authority v. Pine Island, supra.* It is obvious that if interpreted literally the Constitution would absolutely preclude any delegation of legislative power. However, it has long been recognized by this Court that the problems which a modern legislature must confront are of such complexity that strict adherence to ideal notions of the nondelegation doctrine would unduly hamper the General Assembly in the exercise of its constitutionally vested powers. *See, e.g., Turnpike Authority v. Pine Island, supra; Coastal Highway v. Turnpike Authority,* 237 N.C. 52, 74 S.E.2d 310 (1953). A modern legislature must be able to delegate—in proper instances—"a *limited* portion of its legislative powers" to administrative bodies which are equipped to adapt legislation "to complex conditions involving numerous details with which the Legislature cannot deal directly." . . . Thus, we have repeatedly held that the constitutional inhibition against delegating legislative authority does not preclude the legislature from transferring adjudicative and rule-making powers to administrative bodies provided such transfers are accompanied by adequate guiding standards to govern the exercise of the delegated powers. *See e.g., Hospital v. Davis,* 292 N.C. 147, 232 S.E.2d 698 (1977); *Guthrie v. Taylor,* 279 N.C. 703, 185 S.E.2d 193 (1971), *cert. denied,* 406 U.S. 920, 92 S.Ct. 1774, 32 L.Ed.2d 119 (1972), and cases sited therein.

The task of determining whether a particular delegation is accompanied by *adequate guiding standards* is not a simple one. The difficulties involved in making that determination were succinctly summarized by Justice Sharp, now Chief Justice, in *Jernigan v. State,* 279 N.C. 556, 184 S.E.2d 259 (1971): "The inherent conflict between the need to place discretion in capable persons and the requirement that discretion be in some manner directed cannot be satifactorily resolved." In her commentary the Chief Justice clearly perceives that the purpose of the adequate guiding standards test is to reconcile the legislative need to delegate authority with the constitutional mandate that the legislature retain in its own hands the supreme legislative power. . . .

In applying this test we must recognize that if the General Assembly is to legislate effectively it must have the capacity in proper instances to delegate authority to administrative bodies. On the other hand, it is our duty to insure that all such delegations are indeed necessary and do not constitute a total abdication by the General Assembly. We concur in the observation that "[t]he key to an intelligent application of this [test] is an understanding that, while delegations of power to administrative agencies are necessary, such transfers of power should be closely monitored to insure that the decision-making by the agency is not arbitrary and unreasoned and that the agency is not asked to make important policy choices which might just as easily be made by the elected representatives in the legislature." Glenn, The Coastal Management Act in the Courts: A Preliminary Analysis, 53 N.C.L.Rev. 303, 315 (1974).

In the search for adequate guiding standards the primary sources of legislative guidance are declarations by the General Assembly of the legislative goals and policies which an agency is to apply when exercising its delegated powers. We have noted that such declarations need be only "as specific as the circumstances permit."

. . . .

When there is an obvious need for expertise in the achievement of legislative goals the General Assembly is not required to lay down a detailed agenda covering every conceivable problem which might arise in the implementation of the legislation. It is enough if general policies and standards have been articulated which are sufficient to provide direction to an administrative body possessing the expertise to adapt the legislative goals to varying circumstances.

Additionally, in determining whether a particular delegation of authority is supported by adequate guiding standards it is permissible to consider whether the authority vested in the agency is subject to procedural safeguards. A key purpose of the adequate guiding standards test is to "insure that the decision-making by the agency is not arbitrary and unreasoned." . . . Procedural safeguards tend to encourage adherence to legislative standards by the agency to which power has been delegated. We thus join the growing trend of authority which recognizes that the presence or absence of procedural safeguards is relevant to the broader question of whether a delegation of authority is accompanied by adequate guiding standards. *See* K. Davis, 1 Administrative Law Treatise, § 3.15 at p. 210 (2d ed. 1978).

Applying these principles to the case *sub judice* we conclude that the Act properly delegates authority to the CRC to develop, adopt and amend State guidelines for the coastal area.

The State guidelines are designed to facilitate state and local government compliance with the planning and permit-letting aspects of the Act. G.S. 113A–108. Land use plans adopted by the coastal counties must be consistent with the guidelines. No permit for development within the AEC's shall be granted which is inconsistent with the guidelines. Finally, State land policies governing the acquisition, use, and disposition of land by State departments and agencies and any State land classification system must be consistent with the guidelines.

The Act states that "State guidelines for the coastal area shall consist of statements of objectives, policies, and standards to be followed in public and private use of land and water areas within the coastal area." G.S. 113A–107(a).

The Act then provides: "Such guidelines shall be consistent with the goals of the coastal area management system as set forth in G.S. 113A–102." These legislative goals are spelled out as follows in subsection (b) of G.S. 113A–102:

"(b) Goals.—The goals of the coastal area managment system to be created pursuant to this Article are as follows:

(1) To provide a managment system capable of preserving and managing the natural ecological conditions of the estuarine systems, the barrier dune system, and the beaches, so as to safeguard and perpetuate their natural productivity and their biological, economic and esthetic values;

(2) To insure that the development or preservation of the land and water resources of the coastal area proceeds in a manner consistent with the capability of the land and water for development, use, or preservation based on ecological considerations;

(3) To insure the orderly and balanced use and preservation of our coastal resources on behalf of the people of North Carolina and the nation;

(4) To establish policies, guidelines and standards for:

a. Protection, preservation, and conservation of natural resources including but not limited to water use, scenic vistas, and fish and wildlife; and management of transitional or intensely developed areas and areas especially suited to intensive use or development, as well as areas of significant natural value;

b. The economic development of the coastal area, including but not limited to construction, location and design of industries, port facilities, commercial establishments and other developments;

c. Recreation and tourist facilities and parklands;

d. Transportation and circulation patterns for the coastal area including major thoroughfares, transportation routes, navigation channels and harbors, and other public utilities and facilities;

e. Preservation and enhancement of the historic, cultural, and scientific aspects of the coastal area;

f. Protection of present common-law and statutory public rights in the lands and waters of the coastal area;

g. Any other purposes deemed necessary or appropriate to effectuate the policy of this Article."

We also note that the legislative findings in G.S. 113A–102(a) and the criteria for designating AEC's in G.S. 113A–113 provide further specific standards to aid the CRC in the formulation of State guidelines.

In our view the declarations of legislative findings and goals, articulated in G.S. 113A–102 and the criteria for designating AEC's in G.S. 113A–113 are "as specific as the circumstances permit." . . .

In reaching this conclusion we note that the process of developing and adopting detailed land use guidelines for the complex ecosystem of the coastal area is an undertaking that requires much expertise. Legislative recognition of this need is reflected in the composition of the CRC, which is to consist of fifteen members—twelve of whom are required to have expertise in different facets of coastal problems. G.S. 113A–104. The goals, policies and criteria outlined in G.S. 113A–102 and G.S. 113A–113 provide the members of the CRC with an adequate notion of the legislative parameters within which they are to operate in the exercise of their delegated powers.

In addition to providing the CRC with a comprehensive set of legislative standards, the General Assembly has subjected the actions of the CRC to an extensive system of procedural safeguards. In effect, the General Assembly has furnished both the standards which are to guide the CRC in the exercise of its delegated powers and a procedural framework which insures that the CRC will perform its duties fairly and in a manner consistent with legislative intent.

There are four sources of procedural safeguards: (1) those provided by the Act, (2) those contained in the North Carolina Administrative Procedure Act (APA), (3) the Administrative Rules Review Committee created by G.S. 120–30.26 and (4) the "Sunset" legislation enacted by the 1977 General Assembly, G.S. 143–34.10, *et seq.*

Initially, section 113A–107 of the Act sets forth in detail the procedures to be followed by the CRC in the adoption and amendment of the State guidelines. These include submission of the proposed guidelines for review and comment to the public, to cities, counties, and lead regional organizations, to all State, private, federal regional and local agencies which have special expertise with respect to environmental, social, economic, esthetic, cultural, or historical aspects of coastal development. Copies of the adopted guidelines must be filed with both Houses of the Legislature and the Attorney General. The CRC is also to mail copies of the adopted guidelines to all cities, counties, lead regional organizations, and to appropriate citizens and agencies. These broad provisions for input and review by groups representing all levels and types of agencies and interests provide a substantial curb against arbitrary and unreasoned action by the CRC. Additionally, the guidelines must be reviewed by the CRC every five years, although they may be reviewed from time to time as necessary. G.S. 113A–107(f). Any proposed amendments must follow these same procedures for public scrutiny before they can be adopted. Certified copies of any amendments must be filed with the Legislature.

Secondly, amendments to the State guidelines by the CRC are considered administrative rule-making under G.S. 150A–10 and thus subject to the comprehensive additional safeguards contained in the Administrative Procedure Act. G.S. 150A–1 *et seq.* The APA sets forth specific and mandatory guidelines for rule-making, including requirements for public hearings and publication of all agency rules. The mandatory provisions of the APA must now be read as complementing the procedural safeguards in the Act itself. *See* G.S. 150A–9 through 17.

Thirdly, pursuant to G.S. 120–30.24 *et seq.,* all rules adopted by the CRC are subject to review by a permanent committee of the Legislative Research Commission known as the Administrative Rules Committee. The purpose of this legislative scrutiny is to determine whether the agency whose rules are under review "acted within its statutory authority in promulgating the rule." G.S. 120–30.28(a). An elaborate review procedure is established whereby the Administrative Rules Committee and the Legislative Research Committee lodge objections to a particular rule with the appropriate agency. If the agency does not act upon the recommendations of the Commission, the Commission "may submit a report to the next regular session of the General Assembly recommending legislative action." G.S. 120–30.33.

Finally, under the "Sunset" legislation, entitled "Periodic Review of Certain State Agencies," G.S. 143–34.10 *et seq.*, the CRC is subjected to review by the Governmental Evaluations Commission, G.S. 143–34.16 and .17; to public hearings held by the Governmental Evaluations Commission, G.S. 143–34.18; and to hearings and recommendations of legislative committees. G.S. 143–34.19. The Act will stand repealed effective 1 July 1981 unless revived by legislative action. G.S. 143–34.12.

We conclude that the authority delegated to the CRC is accompanied by adequate guiding standards in the form of legislative declarations of goals and policies, and procedural safeguards. We therefore hold that the General Assembly properly delegated to the CRC the authority to prepare and adopt State guidelines for the coastal area.

At the trial of this case plaintiffs contended the Act effected an unconstitutional taking of their land and that the Act authorized warrantless searches violative of the Fourth Amendment. At the close of plaintiffs' evidence, the trial judge ruled that no genuine and justiciable controversy existed as to these issues and granted defendants' motion to dismiss on these issues. Plaintiffs assign this ruling as *error*.

. . . .

The gist of plaintiffs' contention on the taking issue is that designation of their land as an "interim" area of environmental concern by the CRC, G.S. 113A–114, and as a "conservation area" by the local land-use plans, in practical effect determines that their property will be formally designated eventually as an AEC under G.S. 113A–115 and that all applications for development permits will be denied on the ground that all development is inconsistent with the classification of their property as a conservation area. *See* G.S. 113A–120(a)(7).

We think it apparent that there has been no "taking" of plaintiffs' property which gives rise to a justiciable controversy at this time. Plaintiffs' assertion that their property has been "taken" by the Act rests on *speculative* assumptions concerning which a declaratory judgment will not be rendered. "It is no part of the function of the courts, in the exercise of the judicial power vested in them by the Constitution, to give advisory opinions, or to answer moot questions, or to maintain a legal bureau for those who may chance to be interested, for the time being, in the pursuit of some academic matter." *Poore v. Poore*, 201 N.C. 791, 161 S.E. 532 (1931).

A brief examination of relevant provisions of the Act demonstrates that plaintiffs' apprehension of diminished land value is premature and hence not justiciable.

At the outset we note that permits must be sought to develop land which falls within an AEC. G.S. 113A–118. It is further noted that the designation of land as an interim AEC under G.S. 113A–114 "does not subject development to a permit requirement; it merely requires the developer to give the state sixty days notice before undertaking the proposed activity." Schoenbaum, The Management of Land and Water Use in the Coastal Zone: A New Law is Enacted in North Carolina, 53 N.C.L.Rev. 275, 290 (1974). Before an area can be designated as an AEC the CRC must engage in full-blown administrative rule-making with public participation and consideration of factors enumerated in G.S. 113A–113.

Before a permit request can be granted or denied the CRC must hold a quasi-judicial hearing and make written findings of fact and conclusions of law. G.S. 113A–122. An applicant may appeal the decision of the CRC to the superior court and then to the Court of Appeals as a matter of right. G.S. 113A–123; G.S. 7A–27(b). Significantly, the Act also provides that in his appeal of a permit denial the applicant may also litigate the question whether denial of a permit constitutes a taking without just compensation. G.S. 113A–123(b). Moreoover, the Act exempts certain activities from its coverage, G.S. 113A–103(5)b, and also permits landowners to request a variance from the CRC. G.S. 113A–120(c).

It is evident that plaintiffs are in no position at this point to obtain a declaratory judgment determining whether the provisions of the Act have impermissibly impaired the usefulness and value of their land. At the time this case was tried few determinations which could lead to a genuine controversy over the taking of plaintiffs' land had been made. Although some land had been designated as an AEC, no development permits were required until 1 March 1978, the "permit changeover date" designated by the Secretary of the Department of Natural and Economic Resources pursuant to G.S. 113A–125. See G.S. 113A–118(a). The remainder of plaintiffs' land was designated as an "interim" AEC and was not subject to a permit requirement. Thus, at the time this case was tried plaintiffs had no occasion to seek development permits, variances, or exemptions from coverage. Hence, they could only speculate as to the effect the Act would have on the usefulness and value of their specific plots of land. A "suspicion" that all development permits within AEC's will be denied does not constitute a controversy within the meaning of our cases. . . .

Accordingly, we affirm the ruling of the trial judge that there is no justiciable controversy on the taking issue entitling plaintiffs to relief under the Declaratory Judgment Act.

For similar reasons we conclude that plaintiffs do not allege an actual or presently existing controversy with respect to the "search" issue. G.S. 113A–126(d)(1)c permits the CRC to assess a civil penalty of not more than one thousand dollars against any person who refuses entry to premises—"not including any occupied dwelling house or curtilage"—to an official of the CRC who is conducting an investigation authorized by the Act. Plaintiffs contend this provision authorizes warrantless searches in violation of the Fourth Amendment. However, plaintiffs did not allege that they had been subjected to actual searches or that they had been fined for refusing access to investigators. Since plaintiffs failed to allege a controversy as to an actual search it follows that the trial court was without jurisdiction to pass upon the constitutionality of this provision.

Plaintiffs contend the State guidelines adopted by CRC dealing with land-use planning in the coastal area, 15 NCAC 7B, exceed the authority granted by the Act and therefore the guidelines so adopted are void. Plaintiffs' argument on this issue, however, is couched in generalities which make it difficult for us to pinpoint where and in what manner that State guidelines adopted by CRC allegedly exceed the authority granted to it. Cf. State v, Kirby, 276 N.C. 123, 171 S.E.2d 416 (1970). Nonetheless, we have examined the guidelines in light of the arguments and find the arguments unpersuasive. Further discussion will serve no useful purpose. This assignment is overruled.

For the reasons stated the judgment appealed from are

AFFIRMED

BRITT, J., took no part in the consideration or decision of this case.

COPELAND, Justice, dissenting.

Article II, Section 24 of the North Carolina Constitution declares that "[t]he General Assembly shall not enact any local, private or special act or resolution" which falls within certain designated categories. Thus, there must be a two-prong analysis to determine whether a law is a prohibited local act or a valid general one.

First, the act in question must be local, which means,

"primary at least, a law that in fact, if not in form, is confined within territorial limits other than that of the whole state, . . . or [applies] to the property and persons of a limited portion of the state, . . . or is directed to a specific locality or spot, as distinguished from a law which operates generally throughout the state." McIntyre v. Clarkson, 254 N.C. 510, 518, 119 S.E.2d 888, 893 (1961).

An examination of the Coastal Area Management Act (the Act) itself warrants the conclusion that this piece of legislation is nothing more than a device enabling the implementation of conservation and land-use management. G.S. 113A–102(b) sets forth the goals of the Act, which include insuring the development and preservation of the land, water and natural resources and setting guidelines for economic development recreation facilities, historical and cultural enhancement and transportation in the coastal area. While these results are unquestionably desirable, no one would seriously contest that they can and should apply to all of North Carolina.

It is important to note that the Act merely lays out these broad policies and sets up the system by which the goals are to be reached, specifically through a Coastal Resources Commission and a Coastal Resources Advisory Council working with local governments. I do not doubt that economic, conservation and environmental problems differ significantly among various areas throughout the State. However, these problems are specifically dealt with outside the Act by the bodies set up for that purpose.

The trial court overlooked this fact when it found that "[a] comprehensive management plan of the type envisioned by the CAMA would be beneficial in dealing with problems in other regions of North Carolina, however, the uniqueness of the problems in the coastal area provided a rational basis for inclusion of the counties covered by the Act." In fact, the legislation in question does not even attempt to deal with these "unique" problems. Furthermore, a comprehensive statewide land-use management act is possible, viable and reasonable. *See,* e.g., Land Policy Act of 1974, N.C.G.S. §§ 113A–150 *et seq.*

The majority of this Court cites the legislative findings and goals in G.S. 113A–102 as signifying the importance and uniqueness of our coastal area, such that it can be singled out for this special treatment. The Mountain Area Management Act, Senate Bill 973, 1973 Session, which was introduced the same time as the Coastal Area Management Act but was not enacted, states its legislative goals in proposed § 113A–137.

"It is hereby determined and declared as a matter of legislative finding that the mountain area including its land and water resources is one of the most valuable areas of North Carolina. The forest and mineral resources of the region are of major importance to the economy of the State and nation. The clear and unpolluted streams, the vast forests, and the scenic vistas of the mountain region make it one of the most esthetically pleasing regions of the State and nation. Because of these features the mountain area of North Carolina has an extremely high recreational and esthetic value which should be preserved and enhanced.

The mountain area in recent years has been subjected to increasing pressures which are the result of the often conflicting needs of a society expanding in industrial development, in population, and in the recreational aspirations of its citizens. Unless these pressures are controlled by coordinated management, the very features of the mountain area which make it economically, esthetically and ecologically rich will be destroyed. The General Assembly, therefore, finds that an immediate and pressing need exists to establish a comprehensive plan for the protection, preservation, orderly development, and management of the mountain area of North Carolina."

This language is virtually identical in all possible respects to G.S. 113A–102, quoted above in the majority opinion.

The second question which must be answered to determine if a law is a prohibited local act is whether it falls within one of the subject matters listed in N.C.Const. art. 2, § 24. The trial court found that the Act "relates to health, sanitation and the abatement of nuisances and to non-navigable streams and CAMA regulates labor, trade, mining and manufacturing." It thus determined that the Act comes within three of the categories listed in our Constitution.

Although defendants except to this finding, I feel that their argument is without merit. For instance, G.S. 113A–102 dictates that guidelines must be set as to "economic development of the coastal area, including but not limited to construction, location and design of industries, port facilities, commercial establishments and other developments." Clearly these relate to the regulation of trade. Moreover, the same section of the Act states that "water resources shall be managed in order to preserve and enhance water quality." Again, I do not see how water pollution does not relate to "health, sanitation, and the abatement of nuisances." *See also* Glenn, *The Coastal Area Management Act in the Courts: A Preliminary Analysis*, 53 N.C.L.Rev. 303, 306–07 (1974).

In summary, the North Carolina Constitution forbids the Legislature to enact local laws that deal with certain topics. It was determined that concern over these subject matters embrace the entire State. The Coastal Area Management Act is such a prohibited local law; therefore, it is unconstitutional.

For the foregoing reason, I respectfully dissent.

NOTES

1. The court in *Adams* dealt with the issue of whether the Coastal Area Management Act (CAMA) violated the North Carolina constitutional prohibition against local acts. Are coastal areas sufficiently unique to be reasonably singled out as a

class deserving special legislative protection? The majority evidently thinks so and quotes in support the findings of the legislature as stated in CAMA.

What was the basis of the dissent's criticism of the majority opinion? Was the dissent objecting to any form of specialized legislative treatment of coastal matters or only with this particular attempt to implement comprehensive conservation and land use management over the coast while excluding other areas of the state? The dissent states:

I do not doubt that economic, conservation and environmental problems differ significantly among various areas throughout the state. However, these problems are specifically dealt with outside the Act by the bodies set up for that purpose.

249 S.E.2d at 416.

2. Is there an alternative approach more narrowly focused or limited in scope which would satisfy the dissent as well as meet the federal Coastal Zone Management Act's requirements for approvable state coastal zone management programs? Does the definition of coastal area in North Carolina's CAMA meet the CZMA requirement that the coastal zone to be managed extends inland "only to the extent necessary to control shorelands, the uses of which have a direct and significant impact on the coastal waters"? 16 U.S.C. § 1453(1) (1976).

3. Under the statutory scheme of North Carolina's CAMA, the Coastal Resources Commission (CRC) appointed by the Governor is delegated the power to develop state guidelines for implementing the coastal plan. These CRC guidelines are to serve as the basis for the creation by each coastal county of its own land use management plan. Decisions by the CRC and local governments regarding permits for development within a designated Area of Environmental Concern (AEC) are to be "consistent" with the guidelines. What does "consistent" mean in this context? CRC guidelines also are to guide the state in formulating all state land policies relating to acquisition, use, disposition, and classification of coastal lands. Should the legislature delegate such a significant function to a body such as the CRC? What reasons are there for letting the CRC flesh out the details of the state coastal guidelines? Is the legislature capable of fashioning the details of such a comprehensive system of planning and regulation?

4. In *Adams* the court ruled that a valid delegation of power by the legislature must be accompanied by "adequate guiding standards" to govern the exercise of the delegated powers. What were the sources of the adequate guiding standards providing in this case? Were they explicit enough to guide the CRC effectively in performing its duties, or do they give the agency too much discretion? The presence of procedural safeguards also played an important role in the court's upholding of the delegation. Do the procedural safeguards mentioned in the case adequately protect the public from arbitrary agency actions and ensure that the CRC will follow the legislature's intent?

5. Courts in other states have confronted the issue of whether an agency's powers over coastal or wetland areas have been properly delegated by the state legislature. In *CEEED v. California Coastal Zone Conservation Commission*, 43 Cal. App. 3d 306, 118 Cal. Rptr. 315 (1974), a California appellate court "took a liberal view" on the delegation issue in upholding the constitutionality of the California Coastal Zone Conservation Act of 1972. This view holds that legislatures are not always equipped to deal with the specifics of complex problems and therefore allows delegations of power to agencies when accompanied by general legislative standards and sufficient procedural safeguards. The agency is considered the proper body to promulgate more specific rules to govern the exercise of the

delegated powers. In *J.M. Mills, Inc. v. Murphy*, 116 R.I. 54, 352 A.2d 661 (1976), the constitutionality of the Rhode Island Freshwater Wetlands Act was upheld in the face of a challenge that broad statutory language provided inadequate standards for guidance of agency development permit decisions. However, in *Askew v. Cross Key Waterways*, 372 So. 2d 913 (1978), the Florida Supreme Court invalidated sections of Florida's Environmental Land and Water Management Act of 1972 on the ground that the legislature had improperly delegated legislative power to the executive branch.

6. The *Adams* opinion quotes the goals of the coastal area management system established under CAMA. Do the goals adequately address the coastal issues of concern?

    Barrier islands are a key feature of the North Carolina coast. Among other things, they moderate storm damage to the mainland. How adequate is the protection afforded barrier islands by the North Carolina coastal management program?

7. Are the procedures for regulating land use in the coastal area established by CAMA fair to affected property owners? Upon whom is the burden of proof with respect to a proposed development's compliance with the program? Are there potential loopholes in the coastal land use regulation program? How would you assess the opportunities for public participation in the development and administration of the North Carolina program?

8. North Carolina's CAMA contained a provision for the act's automatic repeal effective July 1, 1981, unless the act was revived by legislative action. The court in *Adams* viewed this "sunset" provision as a procedural safeguard supporting the constitutionality of the act's delegation of power to the CRC. As a federally approved state coastal managment program, the North Carolina program also is subject to periodic federal review under section 312 of the CZMA, 16 U.S.C. § 1458 (1976). The following is one commentator's assessment of administration of the North Carolina program to date:

The North Carolina coastal management program was approved in 1978. The Coastal Area Management Act is the primary basis for the program, although the governor has issued an executive order requiring state agency consistency with program goals and policies. State guidelines for critical areas have been adopted and local plans approved, although many of the local plans are too general to be useful in decision-making on permit applications. A large number of major and minor development permits in critical areas have been issued, both by the CRC and local governments; two-thirds of the minor permits were for residences. The state coastal agency does not actively monitor local permits, and there has been a great deal of inconsistency and variability in the permits issued at the local level.

At the state level, the state coastal office has not exercised as much leadership as the program contemplated. The governor, for example, announced support of a major oil refinery in the coastal zone without adequately considering the consistency of the project with the state coastal program.

D. Mandelker, *Environmental and Land Controls Legislation* 117 (Supp. Bobbs-Merrill 1980). What results would you predict for "sunset" review by the North Carolina legislature? For section 312 review by the federal Office of Coastal Zone Management? *See* M. Heath, The Coastal Area Management Act: A Progress Report (University of North Carolina, Institute of Government 1980); North Carolina Marine Science Council, North Carolina and the Sea: A Planning Report for the Development of North Carolina's Coastal Resources (1980).

Networking of Existing Controls

FINNELL, "COASTAL LAND MANAGEMENT IN FLORIDA," 1980
American Bar Foundation Research Journal 307

During the 1970s, the Florida legislature enacted some of the nation's most innovative and comprehensive state and local land-planning and regulatory programs. The Environmental Land and Water Management Act of 1972 adopted large parts of an early draft of article 7 of the ALI Model Land Development Code, *thereby asserting a state regulatory role in areas of critical state concern and for developments of regional impact; Florida's Local Government Comprehensive Planning Act of 1975 introduced planning and regulatory innovations that, if ever fully implemented, could place Florida in the vanguard of land regulatory reform at the local governmental level. . . .*

Although Florida can claim some limited successes in program implementation, its land management systems are still not adequately integrated and coordinated, and they have not been implemented as successfully as their proponents thought possible. For example, the state has several alternatives for complying with the federal requirements for an approved management program under the Federal Coastal Zone Management Act of 1972–the comprehensive land management system examined in this study being only one of the available ones. Yet Florida still has been unable to obtain federal approval, and if it ever does, will be one of the last of the major coastal states to do so. Much of Florida's difficulty in forging a well-integrated coastal land management process is attributable to substantial disagreements on two basic propositions; because of Florida's unique ecological characteristics, coastal land management should not be divorced from comprehensive land management for other purposes; and because of substantial regional diversities within the state, coastal land management in Florida should include a significant planning and regulatory role for local governments as well as for regional and state agencies.

Florida, which has one of the nation's longest coastlines and some innovative and effective land and water use management systems, still does not have a well-coordinated, comprehensive coastal planning and regulatory program. Probably since 1972, and certainly since 1975, Florida has had statutory law suitable not only for meeting the federal requirements for an approved coastal management program but also for designing a program as effective as California's. Good legislation, though, is but part of the solution; other forces can combine to expand, or contract, a program from its originally intended scope.

. . . .

One fundamental problem for Florida is that the entire state—certainly most of the peninsular Florida—arguably is in the "coastal zone," that ecologically unique area where sea and land meet and strongly influence each other. This partially explains why comprehensive coastal land management is considerably more difficult to achieve in Florida than elsewhere. California's legislature, in contrast, could realistically conclude that a basic 1,000-yard-wide land regulatory zone (smaller in urban areas and never more than five miles inland even for the most sensitive resource areas) was adequate because of the much different characteristics of the California coast.

Florida's need for comprehensive geographic coverage partially explains the legislature's decision, beginning with the 1972 session, to undertake not just reform of its coastal regulatory systems but development of statewide comprehensive land and water use management arrangements. . . . To accomplish effective coastal land management, Florida must have a comprehensive statewide approach closely relating land and water management. Development decisions in Florida must be made with understanding of the proposed development's effects on the state's water resources, particularly with a view to protecting Florida's vital wetlands. It was a 1971 water crisis in South Florida that was the impetus for Florida's recent move toward land and water use regulatory reform.

. . . .

There was more coastal protection legislation in 1970: a coastal construction setback-line program; the creation of a Coastal Coordinating Council, which was instructed to prepare a coastal plan; and an important constitutional amendment, submitted to and approved by the voters, to prohibit the sale of state-owned submerged lands except "when in the public interest." This reversed the language of the 1968 constitution allowing such sales if they were "not contrary to the public interest."

Florida's regulatory reform reached its peak in 1972 with the passage of the Environmental Land and Water Management Act, the State Comprehensive Planning Act, the Land Conservation Act, and the Florida Water Resources Act. In the years immediately following 1972, the environmental crisis was overshadowed by new crisis—in energy, the economy, and administration—while a housing shortage for low- and moderate-income persons looms large on the 1980s horizon. Although subsequent legislative sessions have been characterized by less attention to environmental protection issues and more attention to administrative reorganization and improvement of administrative procedures, the potentially far-reaching Local Government Comprehensive Planning Act of 1975 and the 1979 amendments to the area-of-critical-state-concern section of the Environmental Land and Water Management Act are significant indications that strict land and water use regulation still has a strong political constituency in Florida.

. . . .

I. Florida's Planning Framework

A. State comprehensive planning

. . . .

On August 28, 1978, Governor Askew, as chief planning officer of the state, adopted by executive order a state comprehensive plan to guide the preparation of more detailed planning documents and related planning activities undertaken by executive agencies. The 1978 amendments make the plan "advisory only," without the "force or effect of law," except as specifically authorized by law. The distinction between cases in which the plan will be "advisory only" and those in which it will have the "force or effect of law" is elusive. By the term "advisory only," the legislature probably meant that, unless otherwise specifically provided by statute, the state comprehensive plan was not entitled to legal observance and acceptance by anyone (although, practically, it most likely will be followed by anyone answerable to the governor, assuming that the extant plan indeed reflects the current governor's goals and objectives for the state). To illustrate the probable effect of a coastal management plan under the amended law, consider the following scenario.

Florida's state comprehensive plan is to be a statement of "goals, objectives, and policies," and the "policies" and "goals" of any state coastal zone management plan are required to be a part of the state comprehensive plan. If the governor, as chief planning officer, issued an executive order adopting coastal resources planning and management policies and goals similar to the public access, recreation, marine environment, land resource, development, and industrial development policies included in the California Coastal Act of 1976, would these policies and goals have the "force and effect of law" or be "advisory only"? It would depend on the circumstances. For example, the ELA requires a local government, when hearing an application for a permit to undertake a development of regional impact, to consider, among other things, whether the "development unreasonably interferes with the achievement of the objectives of an adopted state land development plan applicable to the area." In these circumstances, the coastal policies would seem to have the force and effect of law.

There are several statutory provisions that apparently would give any comprehensive plan accepted by the governor the effect of law. Most notable for coastal land management purposes are the requirement in the Local Government Comprehensive Planning Act of 1975 that the state comprehensive plan be used as a basis for reviewing and commenting on local comprehensive plans; the Electrical Power Plant Siting Act's requirement that ten-year site plans for electrical generating facilities and site certification requests for specific power plants be reviewed for consistency with the state plan; the ELA's requirement that the state comprehensive plan be considered by local governments when they decide whether permission should be granted to undertake development of regional impact; and the Florida Water Resources Act's requirement of interagency coordination and cooperation in the preparation of a Florida water use plan, which, when completed, is to be included in the state comprehensive plan. The post-1978 state planning act also continues to require the state land-planning agency to coordinate certain other planning functions, including planning that occurs pursuant to several important federal planning programs. Except where, as here, some other Florida statute thus expressly requires observance and acceptance of the state comprehensive plan, however, the coastal policies would be "advisory only" and not legally enforceable.

. . . .

B. Local comprehensive planning

Florida's Local Government Comprehensive Planning Act of 1975 (LGCPA) could make Florida the nation's leader in reform of the anachronistic local land regulatory process that exists throughout most of the country. . . .

The LGCPA required all local governments—incorporated municipalities, counties, and certain other units—to prepare and adopt local comprehensive plans by July 1, 1979, with extensions to be allowed on a showing of cause and good faith efforts. With some notable exceptions, such as the city of Sanibel Island, . . . Florida's cities and counties, as of late 1979, are not responding expeditiously and effectively to that requirement. Only 88 cities out of 390 and 13 counties out of 67 met the 1979 deadline. If a municipality refuses to adopt a plan, the act requires the county in which it is located to prepare one; if the county refuses, the state shall prepare and adopt one. An optimistic prediction is that local comprehensive plans are not likely to be fully completed until two or three years after the 1979 deadline.

. . . .

C. Regional planning

Most regional land and water use planning is performed by regional planning councils and water management districts. . . .

Florida's water management districts, which have planning and regulatory duties under the Florida Water Resources Act of 1972, also perform functions such as preparing the state's water resources plan and coordinating it with the state comprehensive plan. The state's Department of Environmental Regulation (DER), although mainly charged with regulatory responsibilities, also performs a limited planning function in conjunction with rule formulation and, through its district offices, has some influence on regional policies.

. . . .

Florida uses different regional boundaries for the five water management districts, the 11 regional planning councils, and the DER district offices. There are some problems inherent in not making these three sets of boundaries coterminous. Boundaries for the water management districts and DER district offices, at least, should be drawn along natural divisions, such as between Florida's watersheds. Drawing appropriate boundaries for the regional planning councils, which determine the regional impacts of major land developments, presents more complex problems. The greater Orlando area, for example, lies within several natural watersheds, and major developments in the Orlando area have significant and complex social and economic as well as environmental effects that might not be evaluated properly by a regional agency concerned mostly with the environmental consequences within one of the regional watersheds. The complexity of this problem—which requires, for instance, weighing the social or economic benefits of a regional development against detriments to the environment—can better be appreciated by considering Florida's experience with the Environmental Land and Water Management Act of 1972, particularly its development-of-regional-impact process.

II. The Florida Environmental Land And Water Management Act of 1972

A. History and overview

. . . .

The ELA was the product of the recommendations of the gubernatorial Task Force on Resource Management (1972 task force), which had been immediately charged with following up on the recommendations of the water management conference. The 1972 task force considered numerous options for solving Florida's land and water problems.

. . . .

At least five major policies were emphasized by the 1972 task force: that land regulation should remain as close to those affected as possible; that a large, centralized bureaucracy should be avoided; that the decision-making process should provide for a balanced consideration of all the competing environmental, economic, and social factors; that the state should have a potential regulatory capacity both geographically, in critical areas, and functionally, such as in construction of major public facilities; and that the decision-making process should provide for expeditious decisions on development applications within an institutional framework guaranteeing maximum protection against arbitrary action.

The model finally selected as best implementing these policies was article 7 of the third tentative draft of the ALI code . . .: "establishing standards (and authorizing a state agency to establish standards) with which certain of the more important local decisions must comply, and by authorizing appeal of these decisions to a state board."

The Florida ELA (and its companion legislation) has been described as "one of the strongest sets of land and water management laws yet to clear a state legislature." It includes mechanisms for defining certain critical areas and major development activities and provides for decision-making procedures that allow (1) consideration of the total extent and nature of the impact and (2) better representation of the total citizenry affected by the decision to permit or deny a proposed development.

The Environmental Land Act was only one component of a comprehensive land-planning and regulatory system that also included the Florida State Comprehensive Planning Act of 1972, the Land Conservation Act of 1972, and the Florida Water Resources Act of 1972. All but the last were products of the 1972 task force. The most significant complementary legislation subsequently passed was the Local Government Comprehensive Planning Act of 1975.

Some 1972 task force recommendations were not followed. One would have assigned quasi-legislative functions, for example, designating areas of critical state concern (critical areas) and adopting standards and guidelines for developments of regional impact (DRI), to the state land-planning agency, and quasi-judicial functions to a five-member adjudicatory commission, to be appointed by the governor, which would have heard appeals from local government development orders in areas of critical state concern and for the DRIs. Instead the legislation assigned both duties to the governor and independently elected cabinet members. The governor and cabinet, when performing their quasi-legislative function, are referred to as the administration commission; when performing their adjudicatory duties, they are designated the Florida Land and Water Adjudicatory Commission.

The legislative judgment to substitute the governor and cabinet now seems, at least for quasi-legislative decisions, to have been wise. True, the designation of critical areas and amendment of the DRI regulations have been slowed as a result, because the governor-and-cabinet unit is a politically sensitive body. I believe nevertheless that "quasi-legislative" decisions having substantial regional effects should be made by bodies composed of generalists who are reasonably accountable politically. It is more difficult, however, to support the decision to assign adjudicatory functions to this political body, except during the early years of a program. The Florida legislature should reconsider the governor and cabinet's adjudicatory role.

Another compromise decision, a legislative effort to check administrative discretion, was placement of a 5 percent (of all land in the state) acreage maximum on the amount of land that could be subject to critical area designation at any one time. Many supporters of the act thought this would be a severe limitation. Yet in 1973 the legislature itself designated the Big Cypress Swamp as a critical area and exempted the acreage from the 5 percent limitation. The governor and cabinet, in designating the Green Swamp and the Florida Keys as critical areas, have used only 22.2 percent of the 5 percent maximum. Given the suitability of many sensitive coastal areas for critical area designation, Florida's administrative response seems sluggish.

. . . .

B. Designation of areas of critical state concern

Designation of areas of critical state concern (critical areas) is one of Florida's main techniques for state participation in land development regulation, although the technique has been used in Florida only in the Big Cypress Swamp, the Green Swamp, and the Florida Keys. . . . The administration commission (governor and cabinet) designates a discrete geographical area as a critical area, specifies standards with which each affected local government's land development regulations must comply, and adopts, if local government fails to submit adequate regulations, suitable land development regulations to be administered by local government. The 1979 amendments to the ELA, passed in response to *Askew v. Cross Key Waterways,* also ensure strong legislative oversight: the administration commission's rule designating the area "critical" must be submitted to the legislature for "review," and land development regulations adopted within the critical area become effective only upon such review. The designation is then subject to a three-year "sunset" provision, further ensuring continued, close legislative scrutiny.

A developer proposing development within the critical area applies for a development permit to the relevant local government, which conducts an initial hearing on the application and issues its development order, granting or denying the permit. The order is final unless appealed to the Florida Land and Water Adjudicatory Commission (also the governor and cabinet).

The critical area technique provides incentives for local government to adopt and administer land development regulations that will protect the environmental or other values of state or regional importance that led to the designation of the area as critical. The appeals process, the continuing jurisdiction over amendments to the approved regulations, and an expeditious means for redesignation of an area after the designation is "lifted" provide the state with adequate means of assuring that local government will comply.

The legislature empowered the administration commission, by rule, to designate a critical area and specify standards to guide and control local government action, pursuant to specific legislative standards and strict procedural requirements. The rule designating the critical area is based on recommendations made by the state land-planning agency after giving notice to all relevant local governments and regional planning agencies and any other notice required by the Florida Administrative Procedure Act (APA).

The rule designating a critical area must adopt and specify "principles," or standards, to guide the formulation of land development regulations for the area. These regulations become effective, however, only after legislative review.

The 1979 amendments gave institutional status to an informal, cooperative process that the state land-planning agency had used successfully during the previous five years. A group called the resource planning and management committee (resource committee) must be appointed by the governor prior to recommending the designation of a critical area. The objective of the resource committee (whose membership must include, but is not limited to, elected officials from the local governments within the area under study and other enumerated state and regional agency officials) is to seek resolution, through voluntary and cooperative means, of the problems that may endanger the resources, facilities, and areas potentially subject to critical area designation.

If the state subsequently undertakes formal designation of a critical area, the state land-planning agency's recommendations to the administration commission must include any report or recommendation of the resource committee. Later, when the legislature reviews any designation of a critical area, "[t]he Legislature may . . . consider, among other factors, whether a resource planning and management committee established a program."

The state land-planning agency is justifiably pleased with the success of its two pilot programs: the Apalachicola river and bay area (the predominantly rural ecosystem in the Florida panhandle west of Tallahassee) and the Charlotte Harbor area (the environmentally sensitive area south of Sarasota, including Sanibel Island . . . that is currently threatened by large population increases and uncontrolled development). Although both areas were studied for possible critical area designations, the state has decided that, for the time being, informal cooperation of state agencies may be sufficient. The formal designation of the areas may never be required, although the process remains available, of course, if local resource management is later deemed inadequate.

1. Adoption of and changes in regulations within a critical area If the process functions at its best, designation of a critical area should provide incentive for local government to adopt land development regulations that will both achieve the state's purposes and be consistent with local objectives. An affected local government has 180 days after designation to transmit land development regulations to the state land-planning agency for approval. The local government will already have learned what the state believes is needed through the voluntary, cooperative resource committee work that is a precondition to designation of a critical area. In addition, the state land-planning agency and the applicable regional planning agency must provide technical assistance.

If the submitted regulations comply with the principles enumerated in the rule designating the critical area, the state land-planning agency must approve them within 60 days; if none are submitted or if they do not comply with the rule and "with the provisions of an adopted local government comprehensive plan," the state land-planning agency must submit recommended regulations to the administration commission. Land development regulations imposed by the state are not effective prior to legislative "review" of the original rule designating the area (although the legislature does not review the specific regulations). If the final regulations are not approved within 12 months of the rule designating the critical area, the designation terminates and the area may not be recommended for redesignation for 12 months.

. . . .

2. The decision-making process   If a proposed development is located within a critical area, the developer applies to local government for a development permit. Local government then proceeds much as it would have prior to enactment of the ELA. The changes (e.g., improved procedures and broadened categories of the parties who have standing to appeal) are designed to protect the state or regional interest. The development order of local government is final unless a party with standing stays the order by a timely and effective appeal.

3. Experience with the area-of-critical-state-concern process   *a) Big Cypress Swamp* □□ only three areas have been designated critical areas—the Big Cypress Swamp, the Green Swamp, and the Florida Keys, including all of the city of Key West. The administratively designated Green Swamp and Keys amount to only 392,000 acres, or approximately a fifth of the 5 percent of the state's 37 to 38 million acres that can be designated as critical areas. The 1973 legislature designated the Big Cypress Swamp, exempting it from the 5 percent acreage restriction and providing for direct state preparation and adoption of land development regulations. The areas were chosen principally because of the need to protect the environment and as areas around a "major public facility or other area of major public investment."

. . . .

C. Coordination and integration of coastal land management with governmental planning for other purposes

Florida has experienced unusual difficulty in developing a coastal management program that meets the requirements for section 306 funding under the Federal Coastal Zone Management Act of 1972; indeed, an administrator in the federal Office of Coastal Zone Management considered their experience in Florida to be their "least satisfactory" experience. The inherent difficulty, I believe, can be traced to two fundamental characteristics that distinguish Florida from many other coastal states: (1) because of Florida's unique ecological characteristics, coastal land management should not be divorced from comprehensive land management for other purposes; and (2) because of substantial regional diversities within the state, coastal land management in Florida should include a significant planning and regulatory role for local governments, as well as for regional and state agencies. Instituting a management system for achieving a few limited goals within a small geographic area near the coastline is considerably easier than developing a statewide comprehensive land and water management system for a large, diverse state with Florida's delicate ecological characteristics.

. . . .

Coastal land management in Florida should be coordinated and integrated with statewide comprehensive planning for other purposes. Without adequate integration and coordination, more than beaches and dunes may be lost; equally at risk are adequate clean drinking water, irreplaceable prime agricultural lands and fisheries, and, for increasing numbers of Floridians, adequate housing reasonably accessible to employment opportunities.

. . . .

NOTES

1. In *Askew v. Cross Key Waterways*, 372 So. 2d 913 (1978), the Florida Supreme Court held unconstitutional the provisions of Florida's Environmental Land and Water Management Act of 1972 which dealt with designation of areas of critical state concern. Is it clear that the legislative responses to *Askew* discussed by Finnell have removed the nondelegation doctrine as a barrier to further critical area designations? The legislature did not provide any priorities to guide the designation process, nor did it require affirmative legislation ratification, only legislative review. Assuming that the designation process will pass judicial scrutiny, does the nondelegation doctrine present any other barriers to Florida's attempt to deal with complex coastal and land use issues? Compare the Florida court's approach with that taken by the North Carolina court in *Adams, supra*. What are the advantages and disadvantages of the different ways of allocating power between coastal management agencies and the legislature?

2. Do you agree with Finnell that only a comprehensive state-wide plan of management will provide Florida with adequate coastal land management? Finnell mentions that some of Florida's coastal planning could be implemented locally on a voluntary basis. For an example of such local management involving Sanibel Island, a developing barrier island, *see* J. Clark, The Sanibel Report: Formulation of a Comprehensive Plan Based on Natural Systems (1976); Finnell, *Coastal Land Management in Florida*, 1980 A.B.F. Res. J. 307, 323–334.

3. For a general and historical discussion of development in Florida, *see* L.J. Carter, The Florida Experience: Land and Water Policy in a Growth State (1974). *See also* Pelham, *Regulating Areas of Critical Concern: Florida and the Model Code*, 1980 Urb. L. Ann. 3; T. Pelham, *State Land Use Planning and Regulation: Florida, The Model Code and Beyond* (1979).

4. Other Gulf Coast states have been slow in developing coastal programs for federal approval. Louisiana's coastal program was approved in 1980. The pressure on Louisiana's coastal resources is severe, as witnessed by the fact that the state contains one-third of the nation's coastal wetlands, accounts for one-third of its oil production, and one-third of the nation's fish landings.

SECTION C: GEORGIA *see Supp,*

Coastal Natural Hazards

ROLLESTON v. STATE, 266 S.E.2d 189 (Ga. Sup. Ct. 1980)

UNDERCOFLER, Chief Justice.

This case presents our first review of the Shore Assistance Act of 1979. Code Ann. § 43–3001 et seq., Ga.L.1979, p. 1636, eff. April 25, 1979. The constitutionality of the Act and the jurisdiction it establishes are among the questions raised.

Sea Island has been experiencing erosion of its beaches over the past decade. During the past year it has become increasingly severe. Efforts to arrest the erosion near 35th and 36th streets resulted in the building of a rock wall in that area in early 1979. The Shore Assistance Act became effective April 25, 1979, and, after that date, a state permit was required for further erosion control. In July, Rolleston made the first application under the Act, for permission to build a vertical steel interlocking bulkhead with a concrete cap similar to that built by the Navy during World War II in front of the King and Prince Hotel on St. Simons Island. Rolleston intended to put his wall on his own property.

Sea Island Properties, Inc., also applied to build a thirty foot wide sloping rock revetment from 4th to 31st streets, along the escarpment formed by the waves, part of which would be below the high water mark and, thus, on state property. *State v. Ashmore*, 236 Ga. 401, 224 S.E.2d 334 (1976). Some of the property owners did not want to build walls in front of their property. Mrs. Charles Nunnally also requested permission to build a bulkhead behind an existing rock revetment, which also required repairs.

In August, the Department of Natural Resources Shore Assistance Committee, Code Ann. § 43 3009 (Supp.1979), denied Rolleston's application and granted Mrs. Nunnally's and Sea Island's on condition that continuous walls be constructed from 4th to 18th streets and from 18th to 31st streets. Therefore, individual owners, except Mrs. Nunnally, could not build their own walls without the agreement of the others. Rolleston appealed under the Act Code Ann. § 43–3012 (Supp.1979), resulting in a supersedeas of Mrs. Nunnally's and Sea Island Properties' permits. Rule 391–2–2–.05(6)(a).

Hurricane David and higher-than-normal tides predicted for September and October prompted the Department of Natural Resources to promulgate an emergency rule suspending the supersedeas of the permits pending Rolleston's appeal, so that seawall construction could begin. Rule 391–2–2–.12. The individual lot owners desiring walls applied for permits to protect themselves, without the need for continuous walls. These permits were granted by the Shore Assistance Committee in September.

Rolleston then filed this action for injunctive relief. An interlocutory injunction was denied and Rolleston appeals. We affirm Case No. 36068.

As part of the proceedings below, the trial court fixed the Committee's jurisdiction under the Act by defining the "tree line." The state also appeals the trial court's ruling on this point in Case No. 36069, which we reverse.

1. Rolleston contends that the Shore Assistance Act of 1979 is unconstitutionally vague because the jurisdiction established under the Act is difficult to apply. He cites the record, containing the conflicting views of the Department of Natural Resources, Sea Island's landscape directors, and the engineers employed by Sea Island, as well as the trial court's own interpretation of the location of the tree line, to support his claim.

"The area of jurisdiction of [the Act] shall be: (a) The dynamic dune fields on the barrier islands of this State; and (b) the submerged shoreline lands of this State from the seaward limit of this State's jurisdiction landward to the dynamic dune fields . . ." Code Ann. § 43–3004 (Supp. 1979). " 'Dynamic dune field' means the dynamic ocean-facing area of beach and sand dunes, varying in height and width, the ocean boundary of which extends to the ordinary high-water mark and the *landward boundary of which is the first occurrence of either live native trees 20 feet in height or greater,* or coastal marshlands. . ., or an existing structure." Code Ann. § 43–3003(i) (Supp.1979). (Emphasis supplied.) It is the location of the tree line, the western boundary of the Act's jurisdiction, that Rolleston claims renders the Act too vague to be constitutional. We disagree.

The Act is clear and unambiguous. The tree line is determined by locating the easternmost 20 foot tall live native trees along the beach. We construe "native tree" to mean any tree, indigenous to the area, whether it sprang up naturally or was planted. We note that this was the method employed by the Department of Natural Resources in establishing its jurisdiction. See *Bentley v. Chastain*, 242 Ga. 348, 249 S.E.2d 38 (1978). In doing so, the department employees actually measured and mapped the 20 foot or taller trees along the beach and the existing structures, and sought points that were not an unreasonable distance apart. This produced a zigzag line along the shore forming the western jurisdictional boundary of the Act.

We find this method rationally related to the purpose of the Act, which is to protect a vital, but unstable, natural resource of this state. A native tree at least 20 feet tall marks an area that has been stable for a reasonable period of time. It is, however, a moving line; the testimony in this case is that some of the trees used on September 9, 1979, to mark this line have since fallen into the ocean.[1] Thus an area, stable for a long time, is now becoming unstable. As such trees fall into the ocean, the line must be moved back to the next qualifying tree. Thus, the newly unstable area remains under the jurisdiction of the Act so that the erosion problem may be treated as a whole. We hold, therefore, that the Shore Assistance Act of 1979 is not unconstitutionally vague.

This ruling also decides the issue on cross-appeal raised by the state in Case No. 36069. The trial court erred in holding that the tree line should be

---

[1] We note further that this line is not subject to manipulation because clearing vegetation and landscaping within the Act's jurisdiction require permits. Code Ann. §§ 43–3005(a), 43–3003(r).

determined in a manner different than that used by the Department of Natural Resources.

2. Rolleston also urges that the Shore Assistance Act of 1979 is unconstitutional because it constitutes a taking of property without just compensation, citing *Pennsylvania Coal Co. v. Mahon*, 260 U.S. 393, 43 S.Ct. 158, 67 L.Ed. 322 (1922). Rolleston, however, is not entirely deprived of the value and practical use of his property as in the *Mahon* case. On the contrary, the Act is a valid land use regulation well within the ambit of legislative authority. . . .

3. Rolleston next argues that the Act was unconstitutionally applied in granting the other permits and denying his. Basically, he claims it's his property and he should have the right to erect whatever type of seawall, if any, he desires. This is clearly not so. The necessity of regulation by the state stems from the fact that the sand, both on and off shore, constitutes an interacting network, which can be affected by even slight changes anywhere in the system. Code Ann. § 43–3002 (Supp.1979). Rolleston's permit application was denied because the type wall he wished to build does not protect the beach as much as possible by diffusing the wave energy.[2] We find this reason comports with the Act[3] and DNR regulations, and is well supported by the evidence in the record. We hold that the denial of Rolleston's permit, while granting the others, is not arbitrary or discriminatory, and does not amount to unconstitutional action by the Shore Assistance Committee.

The Committee's requirement that there be continuous walls is rendered moot by the subsequent emergency rule eliminating this requirement. . . . The Shore Assistance Committee did not abuse its discretion in granting the other permits and in denying Rolleston's, and the trial court did not err in so holding.

4. The Department of Natural Resources emergency rule is challenged by Rolleston as denying him due process of law. We disagree. By resolution, DNR superseded its rule granting an automatic stay of its permits pending Rolleston's administrative appeal, because of the dire situation on Sea Island in September, 1979, after Hurricane David. Rolleston claims that a retroactive application of the resolution to him denies him due process. Rolleston's attacks have been entertained here and resolved against him. The due process complaint is therefore moot.

5. Rolleston argues that the state has no right to issue revocable licenses. The state owns the foreshore to the high water mark. *State v. Ashmore*, supra.

---

[2]The Committee's minutes reflect that "previous revelations to the Committee of scientific data [show] that a bulkhead is most destructive of beach areas if used alone—that has been accepted by the Committee, . . ."

[3]Code Ann. § 43–3007(c)(3)(E): "In the event that shoreline stabilization is necessary, either low-sloping porous granite structures or other techniques which maximize the absorption of wave energy and minimize shoreline erosion shall be used; . . ."

Permission from all affected property owners is required by the Act as part of an application. Code Ann. § 43–3006(d) (Supp. 1979). Under Code Ann. § 91–402, "[t]he Governor shall have general supervision over all property of the State, with power to make all necessary regulations for the protection thereof, when not otherwise provided for. . . ." Pursuant to this authority, revocable licenses[4] were issued. In addition, the General Assembly clearly contemplated that under the Act, the Shore Assistance Committee could issue permits involving the state's property. E.g., Code Ann. §§ 43–3003(r), 43–3005, 43–3009(b) (Supp.1979). As we have already held, the permitting power has been validly exercised by the Shore Assistance Committee. . . .

6. Rolleston's final argument is that the federal law has pre-empted any regulation of the beaches to the high water mark. Since he has raised this issue for the first time on appeal, we decline to rule on its merits. . . .

. . . .

All the Justices concur, except BOWLES, J., who concurs in the judgments only.

NOTES

1. Is the court on firm ground in its statements concerning ownership above and below the high-water mark? How does erosion affect the ownership boundary? Recall the cases and materials in Chapter 2 on this question. How revocable in fact is a "revocable license" granted by the state to shoreline property owners to construct a 27-block-long, 30-foot-wide, sloping rock revetment partly on state property below the high-water mark? How is public shoreline access affected by the construction of such a revetment?

2. Was the court correct in giving such short shrift to Rolleston's claim that the state had taken his property by denying him a permit to build a bulkhead protecting it from erosion? Is it fair for the state to grant development permits in hazardous coastal areas and then deny permits to build protective works when the development is threatened with destruction? If allowed, who should pay the costs of constructing protective works, the public or the property owner? Why should protective works be avoided where possible? How can the need for protective works be avoided? *See generally* Hildreth, *Coastal Natural Hazards Management*, 59 Or. L. Rev. 201 (1980); W. Kaufman & O. Pilkey, *The Beaches Are Moving: The Drowning of American's Shoreline* (1979).

3. The court did not rule on Rolleston's contention that federal law has "pre-empted any regulation of the beaches to the high water mark" by the state. To which side of the high-water mark does the argument refer? Does it make any difference? What federal laws potentially are preemptive of state regulation of shoreline protective works? Is such state regulation preempted?

[4]Governors Carter and Busbee have designated James B. Talley, an official of the Department of Natural Resources, to issue revocable licenses regarding the state's beach property, which convey no fee interest, but grant "mere personal privileges," "revocable at any time."

4. Is your analysis of the federal preemption question changed by the fact that Georgia does not have a federally approved coastal zone management program? More generally, how does the lack of an approved program affect management of coastal resources in Georgia?

SECTION D: CALIFORNIA

Cumulative Impacts

BILLINGS v. CALIFORNIA COASTAL COMM'N, 103 Cal. App. 3d 329, 163 Cal. Rptr. 288 (1980)

TAYLOR, Presiding Justice.

The California Coastal Zone Conservation Commission and Central Coast Regional Commission (Commission) appeal from a judgment in two proceedings granting the petition of Billings. . . . As to one proceeding, the court concluded that the owners had a vested right to exemption from the permit requirements of the California Coastal Act of 1976 (1976 Coastal Act); as to the other, the court concluded that the Commission's action in denying the owners a permit for their minor subdivision was not supported by law, and directed issuance of the permit. For the reasons set forth below, we have concluded that the owners were not exempt but are entitled to a permit.

We turn first to the exemption proceeding. The pertinent facts, as found by the trial court, are as follows: In 1976, petitioners Billings acquired 118 acres of land in San Mateo County. The property is not adjacent to the beach or to the ocean, but is located on Stage Road, two or three miles inland from the coast, about one mile north of Pescadero and four miles south of San Gregorio. The property is rolling hill land with a rural character.

In 1976, the San Mateo County Planning Department approved a minor land division to create three parcels of 25, 26, and 67 acres, respectively, on the property in question.[5] A written permit was issued on December 30, 1976, subject to four conditions; final approval was granted without material change in May 1977, after the conditions had been duly completed.[*] The conditions were purely routine and ministerial and approval of the minor division was substantially completed when the initial permit issued in 1976. County authorities recognized that this permit constituted the final discretionary approval which the county had to give.

The 1976 Coastal Act became effective on January 1, 1977. Public Resources Code section 30608 states, so far as pertinent: "(a) No person who has

---

[5]Petitioners Billings contracted to sell the 25-acre parcel to petitioners Doppelt, and the 26-acre parcel to petitioners Killitz.

[*]Editor's footnote: The four conditions were dedication of a right-of-way, submission of plans and profiles for access to the proposed building site, submission of a soils and geology report, and submission of a parcel map. 103 Cal. App. 3d at 736 n.6, 163 Cal. Rptr. at 292 n.6.

obtained a vested right *in a development*[6] prior to the effective date of this division . . . ." (Emphasis added.)

The above statutory exemption is written in broader language than its predecessor, Public Resources Code section 27404, set forth below.[7] The question presented is whether, by virtue of the county's tentative approval of the subdivision map on December 30, 1976, the owners acquired a vested right to subdivide their land.

. . . .

The doctrine of vested rights protects property owners from changes in zoning or other land use regulations which occur before the completion of the owner's development project. (*Russian Hill Improvement Assn. v. Board of Permit Appeals,* 66 Cal.2d 34, 39, 56 Cal.Rptr. 672, 423 P.2d 824). A vested right to complete the project arises only after the property owner has performed substantial work, incurred substantial liability and shown good faith reliance upon a governmental permit (*Avco Community Developers, Inc. v. South Coast Regional Com.,* 17 Cal.3d 785, 132 Cal.Rptr. 386, 553 P.2d 546). The vested rights rule is neither a common law rule nor a constitutional principle, but a manifestation of equitable estoppel (*Raley v. California Tahoe Regional Planning Agency,* 68 Cal.App.3d 965, 137 Cal.Rptr. 699). "Where an owner of property, in good faith reliance upon a governmental representation that construction is fully approved, has suffered substantial detriment by proceeding with development, the government is estopped from prohibiting the project by a subsequent change in law. [Citations.] 'Where no such permit has been issued, it is difficut to conceive of any basis for such estoppel.' [Citations.] '[U]nless the owner possesses *all* the necessary permits, the mere expenditure of funds or commencement of construction does not vest any rights in the development.' [Citation]; italics added.)

> "It may be true that '[a]lthough the cases speak of vested rights in terms of reliance upon a *building permit* [citations omitted] . . . a building permit may no longer be a *sine qua non* of a vested right. . . . [U]nder modern land development practices various governmental approvals are required before the issuance of a building permit, each approval pertaining to different aspects of the project, and . . . a vested right might arise before the issuance of a building permit if the preliminary permits approve a specific project and contain all final discretionary approvals required for completion of the project.' [Citations.]"

[6]Public Resources Code section 30106 provides, so far as pertinent: "'Development' means . . . change in the density or intensity of use of land, including, but not limited to, subdivision pursuant to the Subdivision Map Act . . . ."

[7]"If, prior to November 8, 1972, any city or county has issued a building permit, no person who has obtained a vested right thereunder shall be required to secure a permit from the regional commission; providing that no substantial changes may be made in any such development, except in accordance with the provisions of this division. Any such person shall be deemed to have such vested rights if, prior to November 8, 1972, he has in good faith and in reliance upon the building permit diligently commenced construction and performed substantial work on the development and incurred substantial liabilities for work and materials necessary therefor. Expenses incurred in obtaining the enactment of an ordinance in relation to the particular development or the issuance of a permit shall not be deemed liabilities for work or material."

(Patterson v. Central Coast Regional Com., supra, 58 Cal.App.3d, p. 844, 130 Cal.Rptr., p. 175.)

The record here indicates no "good faith reliance" by the owners on the tentative permit issued on December 30, 1976. Prior to the permit, they spent about $520 for the cost of the survey; all other expenses relating to the subdivision were incurred after the January 1, 1977, effective date of the 1976 Coastal Act. These facts distinguish the instant matter from *Pardee Construction Co. v. California Coastal Com.,* 95 Cal.App.3d 471, 481, 157 Cal.Rptr. 184).

We conclude that the trial court erred as a matter of law in concluding that the owners had acquired a vested right to subdivide before the effective date of the 1976 Coastal Act.

We turn, therefore, to the permit proceeding, in which the trial court was limited to the substantial evidence. Our function is identical to that of the trial court and we review the administrative record to determine whether the Commission's denial of the permit was supported by substantial evidence (*Bixby v. Pierno,* 4 Cal.3d 130, 143, fn. 22, p. 149, 93 Cal.Rptr. 234, 481 P.2d 242).

As indicated above, the property here in issue was of marginal agricultural quality. All of the owners are natural persons and none is a real estate developer. In addition to the existing barn and farmhouse on the 67-acre parcel, the owners want to build one farmhouse and one barn on each of the two smaller parcels. The owners have offered to execute binding covenants running with the land to guarantee that this will be the limit of their "development" and that there will be no further division of the land. They will not convert the land to non-agricultural purposes, but will maintain the maximum feasible amount of prime and non-prime land in agricultural use. They have developed a workable plan to farm most of the land in common, as a unit, in a manner which would cover their costs and yield a moderate profit. This plan would put as much of the land as is feasible into productive agricultural use.

The major contentions on appeal pertain to the interpretation of Public Resources Code section 30250, subdivision (a), which then read as follows:

> *"New development,* except as otherwise provided in this division, *shall be located* within, contiguous with, or in close proximity to, existing developed areas able to accommodate it *or, where such areas are not able to accommodate it, in other areas with adequate public services and where it will no* [sic] *have significant adverse effects, either individually or cumulatively,* on coastal resources. In addition, *land divisions,* other than leases for agricultural uses, *outside existing developed areas shall be permitted only where 50 percent of the usable parcels in the area have been developed and the created parcels would be no smaller than the average size of surrounding parcels"* (emphasis added).

Also pertinent are Public Resources Code sections 30241 and 30242, which are set forth below.[8]

[8]Section 30241:

"The maximum amount of prime agricultural land shall be maintained in agricultural production to assure the protection of the areas' agricultural economy, and conflicts shall be minimized between agricultural and urban land uses through all of the following:

As each of the above provisions is a new one added by the 1976 Coastal Act, a brief look at its legislative history is useful. In attempting to divine the legislative purpose of the 1976 Coastal Act, a wide variety of factors may illuminate the legislative design, including the history of the times and of legislation on the same subject. . . .

The predecessor of the 1976 Coastal Act, the California Coastal Zone Conservation Act of 1972 (Pub. Resources Code § 27000, et seq.) specifically directed the preparation of a comprehensive, coordinated and enforceable plan for the coast (Coastal Plan) (Pub. Resources Code, § 27001, subd.(b)). The Coastal Plan was completed in December 1975, sent to the Governor, and a bill enacting its provisions introduced by Senator Beilenson (S.B. 1579). The Legislature, however, rejected the Beilenson bill after many amendments and subsequently enacted Senate Bill 1277 (Stats.1976, ch. 1330). As to the Coastal Plan, the Legislature did not incorporate it by reference but found and declared that some of the plan's recommendations are appropriate for immediate implementation as provided for in the 1976 Coastal Act, while others require additional review (Pub. Resources Code. § 30002).

Particularly helpful is an August 6, 1976, letter the Speaker of the Assembly sent to all members of that body prior to the final vote on Senate Bill 1277 in that house. As the letter summarizes the Legislature's discussion and events prior to the final passage of the 1976 Coastal Act, we may properly consider it as part of the legislative history. . . .

The Speaker's letter indicated that Senate Bill 1277 incorporated the major provisions of the Beilenson bill, referred to the many revisions, negotiations and compromises that led to the final version, detailed the final 22 major revisions, of which only two are pertinent here:

(a) By establishing stable boundaries separating urban and rural areas, including, where necessary, clearly defined buffer areas to minimize conflicts between agricultural and urban land uses.

(b) By limiting conversions of agricultural lands around the periphery of urban areas to the lands where the viability of existing agricultural use is already severely limited by conflicts with urban uses and where the conversion of the lands would complete a logical and viable neighborhood and contribute to the establishment of a stable limit to urban development.

(c) By developing available lands not suited for agriculture prior to the conversion of agricultural lands.

(d) By assuring that public service and facility expansions and nonagricultural development do not impair agricultural viability, either through increased assessment costs or degraded air and water quality.

(e) By assuring that all divisions of prime agricultural lands, except those conversions approved pursuant to subdivision (b) of this section, and all development adjacent to prime agricultural land shall not diminish the productivity of such prime agricultural lands." (Emphasis added.)

Section 30242: "*All other lands suitable for agricultural use shall not be converted to nonagricultural uses unless* (1) continued or renewed agricultural use is not feasible, or (2) *such conversion would preserve prime* agricultural land or *concentrate development consistent with Section 30250.* Any such permitted conversion shall be compatible with continued agricultural use on surrounding lands." (Emphasis added.)

"1. Amendments to make it clear the bill does *not* incorporate by reference the Coastal Plan and that the policies set forth in the bill constitute California's coastal program. (Asked for by most opponents)"

"8. Added language to balance social and economic needs of the people with the need to protect coastal resources. Modified many policies that were absolute by adding terms such as 'where feasible'. (CCEEB; developers; labor; utilities; oil companies; and others)"

The letter concluded that "A balance has been achieved . . . between the need to protect essential coastal resources . . . and the need to assure continued economic growth and properly sited development in California's Coastal Zone."

This concern with balance is reflected in the basic goals of the 1976 Coastal Act, set forth below,[9] and represents a departure from the 1972 Coastal Act.[10] Thus, the Legislature expressly recognized that conflicts may arise between the different policies of the legislation and specified that "*such conflicts be resolved* in a manner which *on balance* is most protective of *significant coastal resources*" (Pub. Resources Code, § 3007.5; emphasis added).

In the light of the above, we turn to the Commission's specific findings.

The Commission found that the owners' proposed development would not be consistent with Public Resources Code sections 30241 and 30242 "which require that the maximum amount of prime and nonprime agricultural lands remain agriculturally productive." This finding is an inaccurate summary of the two sections quoted above at footnote 7 on page 293. Section 30241 requires *only* that prime agricultural land (defined by § 30113) be maintained in agricultural production.

We note that one of the rejected provisions of the Beilenson bill, proposed

[9]Section 30001.5:
The Legislature further finds and declares that the basic goals of the state for the coastal zone are to:
(a) Protect, maintain, and, where feasible, enhance and restore the overall quality of the coastal zone environment and its natural and manmade resources.
(b) *Assure orderly balanced utilization and conservation of coastal zone resources taking into account the social and economic needs of the people of the state.*
(c) Maximize public access to and along the coast and maximize public recreational opportunities in the coastal zone consistent with sound resources conservation principles and constitutionally protected rights of private property owners.
(d) Assure priority for coastal-dependent development over other development on the coast.
(e) Encourage state and local initiatives and cooperation in preparing procedures to implement coordinated planning and development for mutually beneficial uses, including educational uses, in the coastal zone." (Emphasis added.)

[10] Section 27001:
"The people of the State of California hereby find and declare that the California coastal zone is a distinct and valuable natural resource belonging to all the people and existing as a delicately balanced ecosystem; *that the permanent protection of the remaining natural and scenic resources of the coastal zone is a paramount concern* to present and future residents of the state and nation; that in order to promote the public safety, health, and welfare, and to protect public and private property, wildlife, marine fisheries, and other ocean resources, and the natural environment, *it is necessary to preserve the ecological balance of the coastal zone and prevent its further deterioration and destruction*; that it is the policy of the state to preserve, protect, and, where possible, to restore the resources of the coastal zone for the enjoyment of the current and succeeding generations; . . . ." (Emphasis added.)

section 30215 (to effect policies 30c, 33a(2) and 36 of the Coastal Plan) required that *both* prime and non-prime land be maintained in agricultural use. As only 10–15 percent of the owners' land is "prime agricultural land," the pertinent provision is section 30242, which provides that other lands suitable for agriculture *shall not be converted* to non-agricultural use *unless such conversion would concentrate development* consistent with section 30250.

This language is substantially different from the rejected portions of the Beilenson bill: proposed section 30218 provided that non-prime agricultural land should not be converted from agricultural use, even in part, if that would "increase tax assessments on *nearby* agricultural parcels"; proposed section 30220 which stated that land divisions "shall not be permitted to reduce agricultural parcels to a size that could be uneconomic or impractical for continued agricultural production on the parcels in question *or on adjoining parcels*"; and proposed section 30221 which would not have allowed land *adjacent* to agricultural land to be divided if that would "have an adverse economic effect on the long-term preservation of agricultural lands" (emphases added).

The Legislature in rejecting the above provisions and adopting section 30242 chose the more limited approach of permitting the conversion of non-prime agricultural land to non-agricultural use where such conversion would *concentrate development consistent with section 30250*. Here, in view of the owners' affidavits indicating that they would dedicate the land to agricultural use, there is no evidence of any conversion of the land to a non-agricultural use.

Section 30250 . . . first requires that a new development shall not be located in a previously undeveloped area[11] unless there are adequate public services and the development "will not have *significant adverse effects, either individually or cumulatively,* on coastal resources."

The Commission did not find that the owners' minor subdivision would have a *significant adverse effect*. Rather, the Commission's finding as to sections 30241, 30242 and 30250 focused on its future adverse effect, as it "would encourage similar divisions of other large parcels" and threaten the continued viability of the mainly low intensive agriculture economy of the area. The Commission thus erroneously relied on the precedential impact of the owners' proposed minor subdivision and the difficulty of rejecting other future requests for similar minor subdivisions. Further, the Commission could not base its refusal of the permit on such a speculative future contingency. The Commission clearly has the authority to prohibit any future development whose cumulative effect is both significant and adverse.

The Commission urges that its reference to "significant effect" is sufficient, and points to its reliance on section 21083,[12] a part of the California

[11]Although the owners argued below that they were "in close proximity" to an existing developed area, one mile from the town of Pescadero, no evidence was introduced on this issue and the Commission did not proceed on this basis.

[12]Section 21083, so far as here pertinent, indicates that a project may have a "'significant effect on the environment' . . . if any of the following conditions exist: . . . [¶] The possible effects of a project are individually limited but *cumulatively considerable*" (emphasis added). *Cumulatively*

Environmental Quality Act (CEQA). We note that the particular language of this CEQA provision has been construed to include favorable as well as unfavorable effects on the environment (*Wildlife Alive v. Chickering,* 18 Cal.3d 190, 206, 132 Cal.Rptr. 377, 553 P.2d 537). As the Legislature did not repeat CEQA's elaborate definition of cumulatively in section 30250, and specifically used the narrower term "*significant adverse effect,*" we do not think "probable future projects" can or should be read into the term "cumulatively," as used in section 30250. Thus, the term should be given its everyday common sense definition. We conclude that the Commission erred in considering the precedential effect of the owners' minor subdivision.

The evidence does not and cannot support a finding of a significant adverse effect. The addition of two residences and two barns on the two smaller parcels, the increase in water use and additional traffic, while it may be significant, is not adverse. The Commission's finding is not supported by the evidence and does not meet the statutory requirement.

We turn next to the second requirement of section 30250, namely, that land divisions shall be permitted only where 50 percent of the usable parcels in the area have been developed[13] and "*the created parcels would be no smaller than the average size of surrounding parcels*" (emphasis added).

To ascertain the "surrounding parcels," the Commission applied its interpretative guideline of the parcels within one-fourth of a mile of the property; thus, the Commission considered eight parcels. As these eight parcels range in size from five to 750 acres, and five are over 100 acres, the average (mean) size is 286 acres. While the use of the one-fourth mile guideline may not be unreasonable, per se, or in other cases, we think the Commission's use of this guideline in the instant case was arbitrary. The record indicates that at the Regional Commission proceedings, the Regional Commission and the owners had agreed that the "surrounding area" was comprised of the 32 parcels along Stage Road between Pescadero and San Gregorio. This area has a distinctive rural and agricultural character, and is similar to the owners' property. Of these 32 parcels, 22 have already been developed; 10 have not. Fifteen of the 32 parcels are under 16 acres in size;[14] four are about 40 acres or more[15] and 13 are over 100 acres or more.[16]

The record indicates that the Commission also determined that "average" meant the arithmetic mean, computed by adding the total acreage of the eight parcels within the quarter-mile radius and dividing this figure by the number of parcels. The result was the mean of 286 acres, which the Commission then determined made the proposed new parcels of 25 and 26 acres smaller then 50

---

considerable is then defined to mean incremental effects when viewed in connection with past projects, other current projects and *probable future projects.*

[13]This criterion is not in issue here.

[14]These 15 range from .4 acres to 16 acres.

[15]These four range from 38 to 49 acres.

[16]These 13 range from 102 to 756 acres.

percent of the "average" in the surrounding area. The Commission also reasoned that it was required to use an arithmetic definition of average in order to have an objective standard and to carry out the legislative intent of preventing "leap frog" development. The Commission's approach ignores the fact that since some of the surrounding parcels are so large, the arithmetic mean is necessarily "skewed," even when properly computed on the basis of 32 parcels. Using this mean figure of 137, over two thirds of the parcels (22 of 32) are "below average" and 40 percent of the parcels (13 of 32) are about one-tenth as large as the "average," an absurd result.

The owners urge that if an arithmetic figure is appropriate, the arithmetic median (half above and half below) is more appropriate as it produces an average of 40 acres, the average (mean) size of the three new parcels to be created by their proposed minor subdivision.

The Legislature's use of the term "average," of course, is ambiguous. In an arithmetic sense, the term could describe either the mean, the median or the mode (the most frequently met figure).

While we can understand the Commission's search for a readily ascertainable and objective arithmetic standard, both in terms of the one-quarter mile guideline, and the arithmetic mean, we do not think that the Legislature intended such a standard. As no particular definition for "average" was provided, we can only conclude that the Legislature used "average" in its everyday sense of the term, to mean typical or representative. Applying this definition to the 32 parcels in the surrounding area, the record indicates that the 25 and 26-acre size of the two parcels to be created is no smaller than the average size of the 32 surrounding parcels.

We conclude that the Commission also abused its discretion and acted arbitrarily in applying its one-quarter mile guideline and construing "average" as the arithmetic mean. It follows that the record does not support the Commission's finding that the owners' proposed minor subdivision was contrary to section 30250.

The Commission also found that because of the increase in traffic on Highway 1 and in water use, the owners' proposed minor subdivision was prohibited by section 30254, set forth below.[17] The record indicates that this finding also was predicated on the precedential nature of the development and future traffic and water problems rather than the additional burden of the two additional residences and related farm buildings.

Specifically, the Commission found that as the instant subdivision could

---

[17] "New or expanded public works facilities shall be designed and limited to accommodate needs generated by development or uses permitted consistent with the provisions of this division; provided, however, that it is the intent of the Legislature that State Highway Route 1 in rural areas of the coastal zone remain a scenic two-lane road. Special districts shall not be formed or expanded except where assessment for, and provision of, the service would not induce new development inconsistent with this division. *Where existing or planned public works facilities can accommodate only a limited amount of new development, services to coastal dependent land use, essential public services and basic industries vital to the economic health of the region, state, or nation, public recreation, commercial recreation, and visitor-serving land uses shall not be precluded by other development"* (emphasis added).

not be distinguished from many similar parcels, it would conflict with the requirement that *limited public services be reserved for coastal dependent and visitor serving uses.* Section 30254, however, requires that the new development, because of its effect on limited existing services, would *preclude* coastal dependent and other preferred uses. No evidence in the record in the instant case support such a conclusion. There is no indication of the location of the owners' proposed minor subdivision in relation to existing preferred uses. Thus, the Commission's finding was not supported by the record and provides no basis for the denial of the permit to the owners.

Finally, the Commission found that approval of the owners' minor subdivision would prejudice the ability of local agencies to prepare an appropriate local coastal plan pursuant to section 30604, set forth, so far as pertinent below.[18] This finding also was based, in part, on the precedential nature of the instant minor subdivision and the result that "a pattern of land division would be committed." The Commission's finding also referred to the conflict between San Mateo's innovative RM zoning and certain policies of the act, and the necessity for smoothly meshing the coastal planning of adjacent Santa Cruz County, which was "attempting" to implement a policy of keeping large parcels of land intact. The statute requires that new development not *prejudice the ability* of a local government to prepare a local program.

We do not think, however, that the Legislature intended the local coastal programs to require a moratorium on all developments until each local program is completed. As indicated in our above summary of the legislative history and purposes of the 1976 Coastal Act (as distinct from its predecessor), the Legislature was concerned with balancing protection of coastal resources with development.

The proceeding in question indicates that the Commission was not sufficiently aware of its admittedly difficult and complex case-by-case balancing responsibilities. We note that the instant case, unlike most, involves landowners in good faith seeking a minor subdivision three miles from the coast. No significant natural or scenic coastal resources or other areas designated for special protection, preservation or restoration are threatened. We conclude that the instant record does not support the Commission's denial of the permit. However, the matter must be remanded to the Commission to permit the exercise of its proper discretion in imposing reasonable and appropriate conditions. . . .

The judgment is affirmed, and the cause remanded to the Commission to proceed in accordance with this opinion.

ROUSE and MILLER, JJ., concur.

Hearing denied; BIRD, C.J., and NEWMAN, J., dissenting.

[18] "(a) Prior to certification of the local coastal program, a coastal development permit shall be issued if the issuing agency, or the commission on appeal, finds that the proposed development is in conformity with the provisions of Chapter 3 (commencing with Section 30200) of this division and that the permitted development will not prejudice the ability of the local government to prepare a local coastal program that is in conformity with the provisions of Chapter 3 (commencing with Section 30200). A denial of a coastal development permit on grounds it would prejudice the ability of the local government to prepare a local coastal program that is in conformity with the provisions

1. The first portion of the *Billings* opinion deals with the vested rights problem. Why did the California legislature exempt from the 1976 California Coastal Act's development restrictions persons who had obtained a vested right in a development prior to the act's effective date? Why did the court reject Billings' claim to a vested right to subdivide the property?

2. Resolution of vested rights claims posed significant problems under the California Coastal Zone Conservation Act of 1972 enacted by popular vote November 8, 1972. *See Oceanic California, Inc., v. North Central Coastal Regional Comm'n*, 63 Cal. App. 3d 57, 133 Cal. Rptr. 664 (1976), *appeal dismissed*, 97 S. Ct. 2668 (1977), and authorities cited therein. Former California Public Resources Code section 27404 quoted in footnote 5 of the Billings opinion recognized vested rights to develop under certain conditions. Suppose that the coastal commission grants a developer a vested rights exemption for construction of a 231-unit condominium project commenced prior to November 8, 1972, based on a building permit, but due to economic conditions the developer completes only 152 units before the building permit expires. Does the developer still have a vested right to complete the 79 units? *See Pardee Construction Co. v. California Coastal Comm'n*, 95 Cal. App. 3d 471, 157 Cal. Rptr. 183 (1979). What other issues are raised by former section 27404? Would you recommend including a vested rights provision in a proposed statute regulating coastal development? Why or why not? How would you draft a provision recognizing vested rights? *See* Finnell, *Coastal Land Management in California,* 1978 A.B.F. Res. J. 647, 681–83.

3. Policy 36 of the 1975 California Coastal Plan referred to by the *Billings* court provided in part that "subdivisions and lot splits shall not be permitted to reduce agricultural parcels to a size that could be uneconomic or impractical for continued agricultural production on the parcel in question or on adjoining parcels. . . . Where divisions of agricultural lands are allowed for agricultural purposes . . . , the approval of such divisions shall be conditioned on the recording of appropriate restrictions precluding the future division of the parcels and limiting the use of the parcels to agricultural activities. . . ." California Coastal Zone Conservation Comm'ns, California Coastal Plan 61 (1975). What result if Policy 36 applied to Billings' subdivision request? Are the policies of the 1975 California Coastal Plan enforceable under the 1976 California Coastal Act? What other means are available for preserving prime coastal agricultural lands in agricultural production? Are there positive incentives that may be used as well as negative restrictions on conversion of prime agricultural lands? Are there any bases for distinguishing coastal agricultural lands from inland agricultural lands with respect to the preservation policies applied to them?

4. Does *Billings* hold (a) that the California Coastal Act of 1976 requires a case-by-case balancing of the need to protect coastal resources and the need to assure continued economic growth? If so, what are the criteria for such case-by-case balancing? Who does the balancing: the coastal commissions, the courts, or both? (b) that the California Coastal Commission may not disapprove a development to avoid setting a precedent for further development in the area? If so, how is the commission to avoid the adverse cumulative impacts of growth and

---

of Chapter 3 (commencing with Section 30200) shall be accompanied by a specific finding which sets forth the basis for such conclusion."

development in sensitive coastal resource areas? *See* D. Mandelker, *Environmental and Land Controls Legislation* 263 n.149 (Supp. 1980).

5. Compare with *Billings* the court's approach to the coastal commission's attempts to avoid adverse cumulative impacts in *Coastal Southwest Development Corp. v. California Coastal Zone Conservation Comm'n,* 55 Cal. App. 3d 525, 127 Cal. Rptr. 775 (1976), decided under the 1972 California coastal act. In that case the court upheld the commission's denial of a motel project based principally on the impacts on coastal wetland and scenic resources that would result if the development trends represented by the proposed project and similar projects already under construction were to continue, rather than the proposed project's particular effects. The commission found that the proposed project represented "the loss of yet another significant area for viewing the harbor and ocean front" and that the site was "the best remaining parcel for a public viewing area." 55 Cal. App. 3d at 532, 127 Cal. Rptr. at 778. In upholding the commission's denial, the court stated that "under the Act creating the Commission . . . it may be just that last outpost that will . . . hold onto some of the values the preservation of which is the stated purpose of the Act. That is consistent with the concept that a site which represents a diminishing coastal resource is to be preserved and gives a stronger reason for its preservation as such resource." 55 Cal. App. 3d at 538, 127 Cal. Rptr. at 782. How can *Billings* be reconciled with *Coastal Southwest?* *See* Boyd, *Cumulative Impact Assessment—California Coastal Law*, 3 Coastal Zone '80 at 1334–35 (1980). *See also Sea Ranch Association v. California Coastal Commission,* 16 ERC 1897 (N.D. Cal. 1981) (permit conditions to protect public access, views, highway capacity, and water supply from cumulative impacts of development upheld), *vacated for possible mootness*, 16 ERC 1952 (U.S. Sup. Ct. 1981) (see Cal. Pub. Res. Code § 30610.6); *Stanson v. San Diego Coast Regional Commission,* 101 Cal. App. 3d 38, 161 Cal. Rptr. 392 (1980) (coastal commission did not err when it took into account cumulative effect of future restaurant developments in denying restaurant project); T. Dickert, J. Sorenson, R. Hyman & J. Burke, 2 *Collaborative Land-Use Planning for the Coastal Zone* (1976) (sets forth a methodology for cumulative impact assessment). In response to *Billings,* the California legislature enacted Cal. Pub. Res. Code § 30105.5, which defines cumulative effect to mean that "the incremental effects of an individual project shall be reviewed in connection with the effect of past projects, . . . current projects, and . . . probable future projects." Could the development permit sought in *Billings* be denied based on section 30105.5?

6. In addition to the California Coastal Act of 1976, the other important component of California's federally approved coastal zone management program is the San Francisco Bay Conservation and Development Commission (BCDC).

The San Francisco Bay Conservation and Development Commission

Conceived in the early 1960s as a means of resolving conflicts between those who saw San Francisco Bay as a natural resource to be preserved and those who perceived the Bay as an area to be developed, the San Francisco Bay Conservation and Development Commission (BCDC) is one of the most comprehensive coastal management schemes that has been developed.

The residents of the Bay area have not been the only recipients of the

BCDC's actions—the State of California relied heavily on the experiences of the BCDC when it formulated its state-wide coastal zone management program.

BAUM, "SAN FRANCISCO BAY CONSERVATION AND DEVELOPMENT COMMISSION," 5 Lincoln Law Review 98, 99–117 (1970)

History: The Alliance of Citizens, Scientists, Publicists and Politicians

In the beginning was the Bay

To many San Francisco Bay has always represented "the most valuable single natural resource of an entire region, a resource that gives special character to the bay area. . . ." Conservationists, yachtsmen, weekend fishermen, water sports enthusiasts, scientists, and aesthetes have always viewed the Bay as a magnificent asset to be preserved. However, ever since California first became a state in 1850, the Bay has had another importance to other people—an importance which for 110 years seemed to predominate over all other concerns. "To attorneys, developers, title insurance companies, land companies, manufacturers of salt and cement, and innumerable government officials, members of the state legislature, and many others it is some of the most valuable real estate in California." In most cases, this value could not be realized unless the Bay were diked or filled. Thus, until the 1960's San Francisco Bay was disappearing at the average rate of three and one-half square miles a year.

The pressures to fill showed no signs of abating and every indication of accelerating. The population of the nine-county Bay Area, at 4.5 million in 1968, was estimated to grow to 7.5 million by 1990 and almost 11 million by 2020. Developers wanted the profits to be gained from fill to accommodate some of this growth. Cities and counties wanted the added tax revenues. A clash between those who saw the Bay as a valuable natural resource or amenity and those who saw it as real estate was inevitable. And when this clash came, it produced one of the most truly popular and heated political issues in the state's history. It was out of this confrontation of interests that there emerged in 1965 by action of the state legislature the San Francisco Bay Conservation and Development Commission.

But the story of BCDC began some years earlier, when the initial mobilization of citizen interest in the Bay occurred. . . .

. . . .

[Baum then outlines the formation of the Save San Francisco Bay Association (Save-The-Bay) in the early 1960's.]

. . .[T]he citizens group [Save-The-Bay] sought to publicize the issues and make people all around the Bay as aware of the problem and the dangers as they were. Wisely, they interested a prospective author to write a book concerning this problem. The author was Mel Scott. His book, *The Future of San Francisco Bay*, was published in an inexpensive paperbound format by the University of California (Institute of Government Studies) in 1963. This book played a major role in the events that followed because it was written for laymen, was well-researched, and gave ample ammunition for the first legislative battles.

It was found that beginning as early as 1851 the state legislature had granted vast tracts of Bay lands—including submerged lands, tidelands, and marshlands—to both local entities and private interests, sometimes for as little as a dollar an acre. By 1880 when a state consitutional amendment became effective prohibiting all sales of tidelands within certain distances of incorporated cities to private interests, thousands of acres of tidelands and submerged areas had been sold into private ownership. However, sale of Bay lands beyond the two mile limit continued until 1909 throughout the Bay Area. When expectations of great developments following upon the opening of the Panama Canal abounded, the legislature granted large sections of the Bay to cities for the purpose of port and related maritime development, stipulating that while the land could not be sold to private interests it could be so leased for long periods. These grants for harbor, and more recently, airport development continued into the 1950's. As of 1968 private interests claimed ownership of about 22% of the Bay (title in many areas is disputed), and much of this was concentrated in the hands of four large owners. Significantly, most of the privately claimed parts of the Bay are in the most critical and valuable areas adjacent to the shoreline, thus also shallow and easily filled. Cities and counties hold about 23% of the Bay, much of it also close to shore. Five per cent is owned by the Federal government. The State only owns about 50% of the Bay, including the majority of San Pablo and Suisun Bays, but less than half of San Francisco Bay proper.

Some of the state-granted land was filled and built upon, though much more is still submerged or subject to tidal action and held with an eye to filling and development. In portions of the Bay, such as at Candlestick Point or in Richardson Bay, large areas which are still tidal or wholly submerged have already been platted with block numbers affixed and street names chosen. Still larger areas were diked off for use as saltponds for production of salt through solar evaporation of sea water. In 1850 the surface of San Francisco Bay covered 680 square miles. By 1960 only 430 square miles of open water remained, though most of the loss was not from filling but the diking off of saltponds or managed wetlands. And the marshes which constitute one of the essential, perhaps the most essential, link in the chain of life that depends on San Francisco Bay were reduced from 304 to 78 square miles in that same 110 year period. Even more disquieting is the fact that the remainder of the Bay throughout much of its area is so shallow it invites filling. Seventy per cent is less than 18 feet at low tide and fifty per cent less than 6 feet. The U.S. Army Corps of Engineers estimates that almost 248 square miles of tide and submerged land are "susceptible of reclamation."

The next step for the citizens group was to make the Bay a political issue and to gather sponsorship from politicians and government officials of sufficient strength to push through the legislation then thought to be needed. They badgered legislators in Sacramento to stop piecemeal filling. In 1964 Oakland Assemblyman Nicholas Petris . . . introduced a bill that would have halted Bay filling while a plan for the Bay was prepared. The bill found little support.

Finally the citizens were able to secure the support of the late Senator J. Eugene McAteer of San Francisco who was one of the most powerful men in the State Senate and in the State Legislature. He was a lawmaker with a reputation for getting things done, but had not been previously known as an ardent conservationist. Senator McAteer recognized that here was an important issue, and a politically popular one. He devised a strategy which proved to be quite successful for "saving" San Francisco Bay, and which probably has application to other controversial environmental problems.

The Three-Step Procedure: Study, Temporary Commission and Permanent Agency

First step: study commission

McAteer believed that the first priority was to make the Legislature aware of the threat to the Bay so that a strong bill could be passed in a later year. He secured passage in 1964 of a one-year study commission (of which he became chairman) to analyze the issues affecting San Francisco Bay and report back with specific recommendations. The membership of the commission, representing most of the varied interests concerned with the Bay and appointed in part by the Governor and in part by the two houses of the Legislature, included conservationists, local officials, and developers. After a whirlwind series of public hearings held all around the Bay, the commission issued its report six months later with a definite recommendation: (1) establish a successor commission to make a more detailed study of the Bay; (2) use the results to prepare a plan for the intelligent conservation and development of the Bay; and (3) protect the Bay from further piecemeal filling during the interim study period.

Second step: temporary commission (BCDC)

In the next session of the Legislature, McAteer introduced legislation to implement the recommendations of his study commission. He was joined by Assemblyman Petris. The bill which they proposed was strongly opposed by various powerful interests who saw it as a threat to the Bay's vast potential for profitable development. However, the bill was passed, largely as the result of one of the largest letter-writing and Sacramento-visiting campaigns that has ever been launched. Citizens groups, such as the Save-The-Bay Association, kept up the pressure on wavering legislators. Carloads of Bay Area residents descended upon the Capitol whenever hearings were to be held on the bill. Telegrams and letters by the sackful arrived on the desks of surprised legislators, more mail than was sent on any other subject in the 1965 Legislature. And those legislators who were thought to be hostile to the McAteer bill received little sacks of sand that carried notes reading, "You'll wonder where the water went if you fill the Bay with sediment." The Legislators in Sacramento came to realize that the save-the-bay movement was more than a fleeting conservationist crusade. The issue somehow struck a previously undiscovered nerve among a large number of citizens on the nine-county Bay area. It was what some politicians would call an issue with "sex appeal." When the bill finally carried in Sacramento, it was due in large part to a realization of the breadth, depth, and emotional strength of the save-the-bay movement.

September 17, 1965 marked the effective date of the McAteer-Petris Act [Stats. 1965 Ch. 1162] creating the San Francisco Bay Conservation and Development Commission. The goals of the McAteer-Petris Act were set forth in the words of the California Supreme Court "with remarkable clarity." The Legislature acknowledged the public interest in San Francisco Bay "as the most valuable single natural resource of an entire region." It found that the Bay operates as a "delicate physical mechanism in which changes that affect one part of the bay may also affect all other parts." The Legislature further declared that "the present uncoordinated, haphazard manner in which the San Francisco Bay is being filled threatens the bay itself and is therefore inimical to the welfare of both present and future residents of the area. . . ." It noted that "no governmental mechanism exists for evaluating individual projects as to their effect on the entire bay . . . (and) a new regional approach is necessary." The Legislature concluded, "It is in the public interest to create a politically-responsible, democratic process by which the San Francisco Bay and its shoreline can be analyzed, planned and regulated as a unit."

The Commission itself was large, consisting of 27 members drawn from all levels of government and from the public at large. . . .

Some, including some professional political scientists, said that 27 members too large a body to function efficiently, particularly if it were going to operate without committees (this latter decision was in part due to the difficulty of assemblying the Commissioners who may have to come from as far away as Sacramento to the usual meeting place in San Francisco). McAteer had made the policy decision that wide representation in planning was more important than the presumed efficiency of a smaller agency. The 27 members were chosen to represent the many and often conflicting interests in the Bay, which McAteer believed had to be brought together for common decision making if the Commission were to prove successful. McAteer's theory has proved correct, for the varied composition has been a boon for the operation of the Commission. The varied membership has proven to be a tremendous asset for liaison purposes, for obtaining information and dealing cooperatively with other agencies of government. Secondly, the variety of geographic locations, backgrounds, and interests of the Commissioners has contributed to the quality of their deliberations and their decisions. Many observers have noted that the Commission has maintained a balance between the two parts of its name—between conservation and development—without forming blocs. This can be traced partially to the composition.

BCDC operated under this second stage from September 17, 1965, to November 10, 1969. During that period the Commission was given two tasks by the Legislature. First, it was to prepare and report back to the Legislature in early 1969 with a "comprehensive and enforceable plan for the conservation of the waters of San Francisco Bay and the development of its shoreline." Secondly, and perhaps most importantly, the Legislature gave BCDC some potent muscle during the interim study and planning period. It authorized BCDC to "protect the present shoreline and body of the San Francisco Bay to the maximum extent possible" by exercising regulatory control through a permit and dredging *in the Bay*. A permit could be granted only if a project was (1) "necessary to the health, safety or welfare of the public in the entire bay area," or (2) "of such a nature that it will be consistent with the provisions of the title and with the provisions of the San Francisco Bay Plan then in effect." BCDC was empowered to put the brakes on piecemeal filling.

Planning method   It is likely that the method by which the Commission did its planning had much to do with the way in which its plan was later accepted by the public and the Legislature. The Commission adopted two important approaches. First, the *whole Commission* made the planning decisions. The Commission did not send its staff or consultants off to prepare a plan and report back to the Commission for adoption or rejection. Neither did the body divide into Committees which could easily become groups of specialists fighting for particular interests. The Commission hammered out its policy decisions as a whole, commissioners concerned with development hearing the arguments of ecologists and conservation-minded members hearing the needs for development. All Commissioners were involved in planning from the outset.

This was made possible (and public comprehension and support increased) by the way in which the planning assignment, the subject to be covered, was divided into manageable pieces. The Commission at separate meetings heard reports on 27 aspects of Bay planning, from Tidal Movement to Oil and Gas Production. For each of these subjects, two separate reports were prepared: a background or technical report (written either by the Commission staff or by consultants operating under very close staff supervision), and a brief, non-technical, popular version of the report (written by the staff but based on the technical report). Each of these reports came to the Commission accompanied by a mimeographed draft of brief conclusions that could be drawn from the report. The Commission did not vote on whether to approve each report in its entirety, some containing largely factual information and others often-controversial opinions. Rather the Commission, after public hearing, tentatively adopted the conclusions based upon the reports as they were submitted. The result was that, when the last 27 reports had been considered, the staff was able to compile the tentative conclusions into a coherent plan, to be brought back for further public hearing, discussion and approval. And when the day arrived for the final vote on the *San Francisco Bay Plan*, the BCDC Commissioners were able to vote with a unanimity on issues which would have seemed impossible three years earlier.

The second major aspect was that all planning was done "in a fishbowl." It was realized that the great public support which had been so instrumental in the formation of BCDC had to be maintained. The public had to be involved in the planning process as it progressed, so that the consensus of public opinion could be maintained and solidified. There was, of course, some difference between the report *preparation* stage and the report *review* stage. In the preparation stage, the Commission and its staff had the advantage of review by an advisory committee made up of various physical and social scientists and also representatives of the interest groups—public and private owners—that might have been critical of the Commission's operations. But once the reports have been reviewed for factual errors and prepared for distribution to the Commission, they were given wide distribution throughout the Bay Area and the Commission itself held public hearings which were well-attended and supplemented by written comments. The conclusions were revised repeatedly to take account of suggestions from outsiders when they had merit. The media carried excellent coverage. Representatives of various organizations and citizens at large continued to write letters, to appear at hearings and to make their views known, and this significantly influenced the Commission's work.

Third step: permanent agency

The original McAteer–Petris Act provided that BCDC should go out of existence on the 90th day after adjournment of the 1969 Regular Session of the Legislature. . . .

BCDC completed its *Bay Plan* in October 1968 and submitted it to the Governor and Legislature on schedule in January 1969. To implement its comprehensive plan, BCDC called for creation of a "multipurpose, limited regional government, concerned with other regional matters in addition to the Bay," in order to "avoid further fragmentation of regional responsibility by . . . proliferation of additional special purpose districts" and to be "able to consider the overall needs of the region as a whole . . . ." If that were not possible, it advocated a single-purpose regional agency concerned with the Bay. Significantly, the *Plan* recommended that the new Bay agency should have limited permit control over activities along the shoreline (which it had not had in the interim period), encompassing "enough shoreline land to make an effective use of each prime side" or at least for enough inland "to assure that no harmful uses are made of the shoreline." The Bay Plan advocated that the successor agency be able to "designate any reserve shoreline lands needed for priority (water-oriented) uses—ports, water-related industry, airports, wildlife areas, and water-related recreation,"—in a manner analogous to zoning and to be enforced through the permit system. All other shoreline areas could be used in any way that would not adversely affect enjoyment of the Bay.

The San Francisco Bay Plan submitted to the Legislature and the Governor by the Commission in January 1969 was a legislative program for 1969. Without it, of course the BCDC and all its powers would have expired at the end of the 1969 legislative session. Despite all that had been done, passage of a bill to continue meaningful regulation of conservation and development in San Francisco Bay was not a foregone conclusion. It required the same conjunction of a major legislative leader and of active and organized citizens' support that was required to get the original McAteer–Petris Bill through the Legislature in 1965. Fortunately the Bay found such a leader in Assemblyman Jack Knox of Richmond, Chairman of the Assembly Committee of Local Government. And it found citizens' support in the combination of the organizations which had been working for the Bay for years and new organization—groups of persons formed largely for the purpose of the 1969 Legislative campaign.

. . . .

[The campaign for the passage of the Knox Bill is detailed.]

Finally, after a stormy session Assemblyman Knox's Bill was finally enacted [Stats. 1969, Ch. 713(AB 2057)]. The bill amended the McAteer–Petris

Act (retaining its name) and embodied essentially all of the programs expressed in the San Francisco Bay Plan of January 1969. The bill became effective on November 10, 1969, and the Commission has been operating under it, with minor amendments in 1970, ever since.

Functions   As noted above, the Commission has had two major functions since its inception—planning and regulating activities affecting San Francisco Bay by a permit system. The fact that it has had both roles has been very important. It has insured that the Commission's *plans* are and will remain realistic and up-to-date and that its permit *decisions* are made with full consideration of the long-term consequences.

Planning   The Commission's *San Francisco Bay Plan* is a remarkable document. . . . It is important as a planning document for two reasons. It is a regional plan. The Bay Plan differs from the plans of cities and counties, even the *general* plans of counties. Both the geographic area and subject matter to which the plan applies are broader than the permit power of the Commission. Only in the areas of its permit jurisdiction (see below) does the Commission have the legislative power to control anything. But, as the Bay Plan notes, San Francisco Bay is part of a nine-county-wide region, the State of California, the west coast, and the entire United States. There are many activities and policies, both private and public, outside of the boundaries of permit jurisdiction which very much affect what happens in San Francisco Bay. . . . Recognizing this extra-territoriality of decisions and policies taken by others, the 1967 amendments to the McAteer–Petris Act gave the Commission the right to include in its Plan advisory provisions on functions and activities that are outside its jurisdiction but may have significant effects on the Bay.

Secondly, and perhaps most importantly, the *Plan* is a regulatory document. It is not merely a utopian or cosmetic projection of "how it ought to be X years from now." It is primarily a policies plan: the bulk of the document consists of policies for the guidance of the Commission's regulatory functions. The amended McAteer–Petris Act specified consistency with the policies of the San Francisco *Bay Plan* as one of the criteria in granting or denying permit applications. The *Plan* is roughly analogous to the standards applied to conditional uses under modern local zoning ordinances. All the policies derive from and amplify the Commission's stated objectives:

1. Protect the Bay as a great natural resource for the benefit of present and future generations.

2. Develop the Bay and its shoreline to their highest potential with a minimum of Bay filling.

A few examples of the policies are:

The surface area of the Bay and the total volume of water should be kept as large as possible in order to maximize active oxygen interchange, vigorous circulation, and effective tidal action. Filling and diking that reduce surface area and water volume should therefore be allowed only for purposes providing substantial public benefits and only if there is no reasonable alternative.

In addition to the public access to the Bay that will be provided by waterfront parks, beaches, marinas, and fishing piers, maximum feasible opportunity for pedestrian access to the waterfront should be included in every new development in the Bay or on the shoreline, whether it be for housing, industry, port, airport, public facility, or other use. If no such access can reasonably be provided, the development should not be allowed on the waterfront unless it must of necessity be there (i.e., unless it is an industry requiring access to deep water, a shipping terminal, etc.)

The *San Francisco Bay Plan* contains maps, in order to graphically apply the policies to the individual circumstances around the Bay. On the various maps certain areas along the shoreline of the Bay are colored blue (for ports or waterfront industry), green (for recreations or wildlife preserves), or gray (for salt ponds and managed wetlands); other shoreline areas are left white. The Commission judged that all the colored areas were particularly suited for these "water-oriented uses," and therefore as a matter of regional interest should be designated and reserved for that purpose in a manner analogous to zoning. The effect is to exclude all other uses, though the Commission's active power extends only to the first 100 feet inland from the shoreline. There was no regional need to reserve the white areas for any particular use, and therefore use control in the white areas was left to the exclusive jurisdiction of the local governments. The Commission projected in acres the future regional need for shoreline land for each type activity—water-related industry and recreation, ports, and wildlife areas. This projected need was provided for on the maps, thereby attempting to eliminate unnecessary pressures to fill the Bay in other areas. . . . The Commission's philosophy is that, "All desirable, high-priority uses of the bay and shoreline can be fully accommodated without substantial bay filling and without loss of large natural resource areas."

As to filling, the *Bay Plan* does not take an inflexible position that there may be no more filling of San Francisco Bay. "Some Bay filling may be justified for purposes providing substantial public benefits if these same benefits could not be achieved equally well without filling." However, filling will be approved only if it is the minimum amount necessary to achieve its purpose and it meets one of four conditions: (1) it is for one of the bay-related purposes for which the Bay Plan policies say fill may be needed (i.e., ports, water-related industry, and water-related recreation), and is shown as likely to be needed on the maps; or (2) it is for one of those purposes for which the *Bay Plan* policies say some fill may be needed if there is no other alternative (i.e., airports, roads and utility routes); or (3) it is a minor fill for improving shoreline appearance or public access; or (4) the filling would provide on privately owned property for Bay-oriented commercial recreation (i.e., restaurants, specialty shops, boatels, etc.).

Permits The Commission's planning functions are designed to mesh with its regulatory function. Permit decisions are made in part on the basis of *Plan* policies. The Commission operates very much like a local planning commission does when sitting in judgment upon conditional use applications; each application that comes before the BCDC is determined by applying criteria to the facts of the particular case; the criteria are found partly in the statute, partly and more extensively in the *San Francisco Bay Plan*. The criteria are by no means similar to rules contained in a traditional local zoning ordinance, which establishes exact limits on building, line, height, floor area, ratio, etc. In contrast, the application of criteria by BCDC to a particular case definitely requires the exercise of judgment and attention to precedents (i.e., previous exercises of judgment). It was partially for these reasons that the Commission was continued in existence by the 1969 Legislature to administer its own plan, rather then entrusting local governments to carry it out. Such decentralized administration of a highly technical plan would not have insured the statutory aim that "San Francisco Bay and its shoreline can be analyzed, planned, and regulated as a unit."

Any person or governmental agency wishing to place fill (including pilings), extract materials, or make "any substantial change in use of any water, land, or structure, within the area of the commission's jurisdiction," must secure a permit from the Commission, only to be issued or denied after public hearing. The permit jurisdiction of the Commission, as of November 1970, extends to the following:

1. The Bay, defined as all areas subject to tidal action including sloughs and marshlands;

2. A shoreline band, 100 feet wide, around the Bay (added in 1969 together with nos. 3 and 4);

3. Salt ponds;

4. Managed wetlands;

5. The tidal portions of several named creeks and tributaries which are particularly important to the Bay ecological system (added by amendment in 1970).

The Commission shares jurisdiction over any project with the affected local governments and with various federal and state agencies. In the shoreline areas designated for priority water-related uses on the *Bay Plan* maps and throughout the Bay in all areas subject to tidal action, the Commission *shares* with the local government control over the *use* to which the area is put. This is a shared or concurrent jurisdiction, or as it is sometimes called, a double veto system; no project can proceed in these areas without the permission of both the local government concerned and the BCDC. In the shoreline areas shown white on the maps, the Commission's only role is to insure that whatever use is put there with the approval of the local government, the project will provide maximum feasible public access to the shoreline consistent with the nature of the project. . . .

Although the nature of shared jurisdiction with local government is one to which most attention is given, it is well to point out that BCDC also shares jurisdiction with various federal agencies, such as the U.S. Army Corps of

Engineers which has to grant permits for any encroachment upon navigable waters; various state agencies, including the Regional Water Quality Control Board which sets requirements for any waste discharged into the Bay, and various other agencies, too.

The McAteer-Petris Act states that a permit shall not be granted by the Commission unless it finds that the project is "either (1) necessary to the health, safety or welfare of the public *in the entire bay area* (emphasis added), or (2) of such a nature that it will be consistent with the provisions of this title and with the provisions of the San Francisco Bay Plan then in effect." The first criteria has only been used twice in the Commission's history, one being a permit for portions of the Bay Area Rapid Transit trans-Bay tube. The Commission prefers to take a narrow reading of the regional public welfare. The contents of the Bay Plan policies which constitute the major criteria in permit decisions have been alluded to above. The major operative criteria within the McAteer-Petris Act are contained in one section and are as follows:

The Legislature further finds and declares:

(a) That further filling of San Francisco Bay should be authorized only when public benefits from fill clearly exceed public detriment from the loss of the water areas and should be limited to water-oriented uses (such as ports, water-related industry, airports, bridges, wildlife refuges, water-oriented recreation and public assembly, water intake and discharge lines for desalinization plants and power generating plants requiring large amounts of water for cooling purposes) or minor fill for improving shoreline appearance or public access to the bay.

(b) That fill in the bay for any purpose, should be authorized only when no alternative upland location is available for such purpose.

(c) That the water area authorized to be filled should be the minimum necessary to achieve the purpose of the fill.

(d) That the nature, location and extent of any fill should be such that it will minimize harmful effects to the bay area, such as, the reduction or impairment of the volume surface area or circulation of water, water quality, fertility of marshes or fish or wildlife resources.

(e) That public health, safety and welfare require that fill be constructed in accordance with sound safety standards which will afford reasonable protection to persons and property against the hazards of unstable geologic or soil conditions or of flood or storm waters.

(f) That fill should be authorized when the filling would, to the maximum extent feasible, establish a permanent shoreline.

(g) That fill should be authorized when the applicant has such valid title to the properties in question that he may fill them in the manner and for the uses to be approved.

In addition to simply granting or denying the permit, to effectuate the purposes of these criteria the Commission may grant the permit subject to reasonable terms and conditions.

. . . .

NOTES

1. The salt ponds referred to in the article are not natural bodies of brackish water which are diked off from the Bay, but are commercial salt ponds owned by the Leslie Salt Company. These salt ponds, comprising some 56,000 acres, are an important component of the Bay and form a large portion of its periphery. The original Bay Plan called for maintaining these ponds in commercial production for as long as practicable and then for public acquisition. Once the public acquired the ponds, the dikes were to be breached and the ponds were to be opened to the Bay. This was seen as very important, since it provided the only means by which the area of the Bay might be increased.

    Leslie Salt had other plans—once the ponds were withdrawn from production, Leslie wanted to fill them and build planned unit developments on the fill. The inclusion of the ponds in the BCDC jurisdiction was an important victory for the Commission.

2. For a more detailed analysis of the legislative and public relations skirmishes that preceded the permanent establishment of the BCDC, *see* Delezel & Warren, *Saving San Francisco Bay: A Case Study in Environmental Legislation*, 23 Stan. L. Rev. 349 (1971).

3. The BCDC's denial of a permit to fill a parcel of land submerged at high tide by the waters of the Bay was upheld in *Candlestick Properties, Inc. v. San Francisco Bay Conservation and Development Commission*, 11 Cal. App. 3d 557, 89 Cal. Rptr. 897 (1970), as a valid exercise of the police power. The Court of Appeal ruled that since the owner could not establish that the denial of the permit rendered its property useless, the owner had no cause of action to recover damages for the confiscation of its property without compensation.

4. The California Coastal Act of 1976 preserved BCDC's jurisdiction over the beds and shorelines of San Francisco Bay. *See* Cal. Pub. Res. Code § 30103(a). *See also* the Suisun Marsh Preservation Act of 1977, Cal. Pub. Res. Code §§ 29000–612.

SECTION E: WASHINGTON

Water Dependency

DEPARTMENT OF ECOLOGY v. BALLARD ELKS LODGE NO. 827, 84 Wn. 2d 551, 527 P.2d 1121 (1974)

HAMILTON, J.

This action and appeal stem from administrative procedures taken pursuant to the Shoreline Management Act of 1971, RCW 90.58. Appellant, the Ballard Elks Lodge No. 827, seeks review of a judgment of the Superior Court reversing a decision of the Shorelines Hearings Board which granted to appellant a substantial development permit allowing overwater construction of club facilities on Shilshole Bay in Seattle, Washington.

We reverse the judgment of the Superior Court and reinstate the order of the Shorelines Hearings Board.

In 1963, appellant, a fraternal order with a current membership of approximately 3,500, acquired a parcel of waterfront property situated upon Shilshole Bay. The property is 200 feet in width and is bounded on the east by Seaview Avenue Northwest and extends westerly to the northeast boundary of Salmon Bay Waterway, which connects Shilshole Bay to the Lake Washington Ship Canal. Areawise it contains approximately 157,000 square feet of which 57,000 square feet is tideland totally covered by water at mean high tide. Immediately northwesterly of appellant's property is an 8-story condominium and beyond that the Port of Seattle's Shilshole Bay Marina complex. Adjacent to and southerly from the property there are a boat sales and rental facility and various restaurants and cocktail lounges. The adjacent enterprises both to the north and south are in large part constructed on fills extending out and beyond what would otherwise be the line of mean high tide and to some extent out and beyond appellant's shoreline.

In years past, prior to appellant's acquisition, the property had been utilized as a shipyard. There is evidence that, for the use to which it had been put, it had been land filled seaward to the present line of mean high tide, which line had not been otherwise altered since the mid-1940s or early 1950s. After appellant acquired the property, it was cleared of extant buildings on the uplands, and an old ship grounded on the tidelands was burned and bulldozed.

In 1972, pursuant to RCW 90.58, appellant applied to the City of Seattle for a shorelines management substantial development permit to construct an over-the-water lodge building which would house such facilities as a restaurant, cocktail lounge, billiard room, gymnasium, lodge room, and similarly oriented accommodations for the membership and their guests. Appellant's first application projected a 38-foot to ultimately 48-foot landward high building constructed entirely on tideland fill westerly of the line of mean high tide, with the upland area being utilized for membership off-street vehicular parking. A second application altered the design of the proposed structure somewhat, reduced the ultimate landward height to 35 feet, provided an easement for public access to the water's edge, moved the building landward some 75 feet, and provided for the structure to be erected on pilings rather than fill, thus permitting the water to flow beneath and to the line of mean high tide.

The City of Seattle granted appellant a substantial development permit to erect the building on their property, conditioned, however, that construction not extend beyond the line of mean high tide and that shoreline stabilization be accomplished to minimize alteration thereof. Appellant sought review before the Shorelines Hearings Board pursuant to RCW 90.58.180(1). Review was appropriately certified, and the State Department of Ecology and Attorney General intervened in support of the permit as issued by the City of Seattle.

The Shorelines Hearings Board scheduled and conducted hearings, received testimony and documentary evidence, viewed the premises, and heard arguments of counsel. Thereafter, the board entered findings of fact, conclusions of law, and an order requiring the City of Seattle to issue a permit to appellant allowing construction of its proposed clubhouse over the water to a line approximately 30 feet easterly or landward of the position of the building proposed in appellant's second application for a substantial development permit.

The board's order was essentially based upon the theory that properties adjacent to and in the vicinity of appellant's property had been filled and developed westerly of appellant's shoreline prior to the adoption of RCW 90.58, and that to confine appellant's construction to "dry land" would be to ignore the realities of the situation and would unduly penalize appellant without serving any substantive public interest.

The Department of Ecology and the Attorney General petitioned the Superior Court for review of the board's order. The City of Seattle did not. The Superior Court reviewed the written record made before the board pursuant to RCW 34.04.130(5) and (6), reversed the board's order, and reinstated the conditional permit authorized by the City of Seattle upon the grounds that the board's order was "clearly erroneous in view of the entire record as submitted and the public policy contained in the act of the legislature authorizing the decision or order." RCW 34.04.130(6)(e). This appeal followed.

The Shorelines Hearings Board is a quasi-judicial body created by RCW 90.58.170, with authority to review the grant or denial of a shorelines management substantial development permit. Its proceedings are subject to pertinent provisions of the administrative procedure act (RCW 34.04), as is judicial review of its decisions. RCW 90.58.180(3).

The "clearly erroneous" test for judicial review of administrative action under RCW 34.04.130(6)(e) applies to both trial and appellate courts. Upon appeal from a superior court's application of the "clearly erroneous" standard, the appellate court applies the same standard directly to the administrative decision.

To reach a conclusion that a decision or order of an administrative tribunal, such as the Shorelines Hearings Board, is "clearly erroneous" within the purview of RCW 34.04.130(6)(e), the reviewing court must, based upon the record before it, be firmly convinced that a mistake has been committed, even though there be evidence supporting the decision or order. In the course of judicial review, due deference must be given to the specialized knowledge and expertise of the administrative agency. The reviewing court cannot simply substitute its judgment for that of the agency.

Our principal task, then, is to review the entire record before us to determine if the Shorelines Hearings Board order is "clearly erroneous" in view of the public policy enunciated in the Shoreline Management Act of 1971, RCW 90.58. If our evaluation of the record firmly convinces us that a mistake has been made, then the Superior Court correctly applied the "clearly erroneous" test. If not, the Superior Court did not.

The keynote policies of RCW 90.58 are well stated in the introductory section of the legislation. The legislation there states:

[I]t finds that ever increasing pressures of additional uses are being placed on the shorelines *necessitating increased coordination in the management and development of the shorelines of the state*. The legislature further finds that much of the shorelines of the state and the uplands adjacent thereto are in private ownership; that *unrestricted* construction on the privately owned or publicly owned shorelines of the state is not in the best public interest; and therefore, *coordinated planning is necessary* in order to protect the public interest associated with the shorelines of the state *while, at the same time, recognizing and protecting private property rights consistent with the public interest.* There is, therefore, a clear and urgent demand for a planned, rational, and concerted effort, jointly performed by federal, state, and local governments, to prevent the inherent harm in an uncoordinated and piecemeal development of the state's shorelines.

It is the policy of the state to provide for the management of the shorelines of the state *by planning for and fostering all reasonable and appropriate uses.* This policy is designed to insure the development of these shorelines in a manner which, while allowing for limited reduction of rights of the public in the navigable waters, will promote and enhance the public interest. This policy contemplates, protecting against adverse effects to the public health, the land and its vegetation and wildlife, and the waters of the state and their aquatic life, while protecting generally public rights of navigation and corollary rights incidental thereto.

. . . .

Permitted uses in the shorelines of the state shall be designed and conducted in a manner to minimize, insofar as practical, any resultant damage to the ecology and environment of the shoreline area and any interference with the public's use of the water. RCW 90.58.020 (Italics ours.)

From this statement of policy, it can readily be observed that it is within the contemplation of the legislation that there will, of necessity, be some future and additional development along shorelines in the state, including over-the-water construction, and it does not purport to totally prohibit such development. Rather, the enunciated policy stresses the need that such future development be carefully planned, managed, and coordinated in keeping with the public interest. In further recognition of the inevitability of future development, the introductory section states, in nonexclusive terms, those uses are to be preferred

which are consistent with control of pollution and prevention of damage to the natural environment, or are unique to or dependent upon use of the state's shoreline. Alterations of the natural condition of the shorelines of the state, *in those limited instances when authorized,* shall be given priority for single family residences, ports, shoreline recreational uses including *but not limited* to parks, marinas, piers, and other improvements facilitating public access to shorelines of the state, industrial and commercial developments which are particularly dependent on their location on or use of the shorelines of the state *and other development that will provide an opportunity for* substantial numbers of the people to enjoy the shorelines of the state. RCW 90.58.020. (Italics ours.)

Finally, the guidelines regarding commercial development which have been promulgated by the Department of Ecology pursuant to RCW 90.58 contemplate future developments akin to the one here involved. WAC [Washington Administrative Code] 173–16–060, entitled "The Use Activities," contains the following:

This section contains guidelines for the local regulation of use activities proposed for shorelines. Each topic, representing a specific use or group of uses, is broadly defined. . . .

. . . .

Finally, most of the guidelines are intentionally written in general terms to allow some latitude for local government to expand and elaborate on them as local conditions warrant. . . .

. . . .

(4) Commercial development. Commercial developments are those uses which are involved in wholesale and retail trade or business activities. Commercial developments range from small businesses within residences, to high-rise office buildings. Commercial developments are intensive users of space because of extensive floor areas and because of facilities, such as parking, necessary to service them. Guidelines:

    (a) Although many commercial developments benefit by a shoreline location, priority should be given to those commercial developments which are particularly dependent on their location and/or use of the shorelines of the state and *other development that will provide an opportunity for substantial numbers of the people to enjoy the shorelines of the state.*

    (b) *New commercial developments on shorelines should be encouraged to locate in those areas where current commercial uses exist.*

    (c) An assessment should be made of the effect a commercial structure will have on a scenic view significant to a given area or enjoyed by a significant number of people.

    (d) Parking facilities should be placed inland away from the immediate water's edge and recreational beaches. (Italics ours.)

Although appellant's proposed clubhouse is not, strictly speaking, a commercial development since patronage of its restaurant, cocktail lounge, billiard room, gymnasium, and swimming pool facilities will be limited to members and their guests, nevertheless all parties agree WAC 173–16–060(4) presents relevant guidelines.

Given these policies and guidelines, the Shorelines Hearings Board approached its decision concerning the development of appellant's property with a practical eye upon the densely developed portion of shoreline in the immediate vicinity of the subject property. In support of its decision, the board found, and the evidence sustains its findings, that: (1) many of the existing adjacent developments and structures are not water-dependent uses as defined in RCW 90.58; (2) navigation over appellant's tidelands was de minimus; (3) structural interference with view would be minor; (4) appellant's building over the water would not significantly affect public health, wild or aquatic life, shoreline environment, or public use of the water; (5) the proposed construction would provide an opportunity for substantial numbers of people to enjoy the shoreline; and (6) no public or local protest had been registered in opposition to the proposed structure. In addition, the board noted that to restrict appellant's structure to dry land would: (a) significantly and adversely diminish the area available for off-street vehicular parking; (b) preclude usage of a narrow spit of dry land extending seaward along the northern boundary of the property; and (c) inhibit the scenic view of patrons of the proposed clubhouse.

Given the unique factual situation here existing, we are satisfied the Shorelines Hearings Board, acting within the scope of its authority and expertise, appropriately considered the practical realities pertaining to the existing shoreline, the policy of RCW 90.58, and the relevant guidelines in arriving at its decision. We cannot, therefore, find its decision to be "clearly erroneous." The judgment of the Superior Court is accordingly reversed and the findings of fact, conclusions of law, and order of the board are reinstated.

HALE, C. J., and FINLEY, ROSELLINI, HUNTER, STAFFORD, WRIGHT, UTTER, and BRACHTENBACH JJ, concur.

NOTES

1. In *Ballard* the Washington Supreme Court based its decision in part on the policy statements in section 90.58.020 of the Washington Shoreline Management Act of 1971, Wash. Rev. Code § 90.58.010 *et seq.* Did the Supreme Court give sufficient weight to the preference expressed in section 90.58.020 for uses "which are particularly dependent on their location on or use of the shorelines of the state"? Did the Superior Court? Did the Shorelines Hearings Board? Did the City of Seattle? See Note, *Administrative Law–Shorelines Management–Judicial Review of Shorelines Hearings Board Decisions–Department of Ecology v. Ballard Elks Lodge No. 827*, 51 Wash. L. Rev. 405 (1976).

    In a shoreline development permit proceeding, which party should have the burden of proving compliance with the criteria governing shoreline development in the act and implementing regulations, the permit applicant or the regulating agency? Under the Washington Shoreline Management Act, initially the burden is on the applicant; upon review of a permit grant or denial, the burden of proof is on the person requesting review. Wash. Rev. Code § 90.58.140(6). In addition, if the permit requires a variance or conditional use, it shall be granted "only if extraordinary circumstances are shown and the public interest suffers no substantial detrimental effect," and local decisions granting such a variance or conditional use must be approved by the State Department of Ecology. Wash. Rev. Code § 90.58.140(11).

    Consider the following from *Hayes v. Yount,* 87 Wash. 2d 280, 552 P.2d 1038 (1976), decided by the Washington Supreme Court 2 years after *Ballard*:

    . . . The policy of preference for water-dependent uses reflects the legislature's careful attention to an important concept of environmentally sound land-use planning. Encouraging uses not dependent on the shoreline to locate in inland areas is an effective aid in the resolution of competing demands on our limited shorelines resources. The policy builds on the fundamental notions that the use of land should depend to a great extent on the suitability of a site for the particular use and that land may possess "intrinsic suitability" for certain uses. "In principle, only land uses that are inseparable from waterfront locations should occupy them; and even these should be limited to those which do not diminish the present or prospective value of surface water for supply, recreation or amenity." I. McHarg, *Design with Nature 58* (1969). This concept has been embodied in many plans for areas adjacent to water. The criterion of water dependency is included in other legislation and is applied by governmental agencies analogous to the Shorelines Hearings Board.

    . . . .

    . . . Logic and common sense suggest that numerous projects, each having no significant effect individually, may well have very significant effects when taken together. This concept of cumulative environmental harm has received legislative and judicial recognition. In the Shoreline Management Act of 1971 itself, the legislature and people of this state recognized the necessity of controlling the cumulative adverse effect of "piecemeal development of the state's shorelines" through "coordinated planning" of all development, not only "substantial development." RCW 90.58.020. *See* WAC 197–10–440(8)(c) (State Environmental Policy Act of 1971 guideline). The fact that respondent himself cannot control future filling in the Snohomish River estuary does not, in itself, render arbitrary and capricious the board's concern over the ultimate impact of such development in light of its statutory duties.

552 P.2d at 1047, 1043.

Is an Elks Lodge a water-dependent use of a shoreline? Is an Elks Lodge on pilings an appropriate use of publicly owned tidelands?

Is *Hayes* consistent with *Billings v. California Coastal Comm'n, supra* with respect to avoiding cumulative impacts and setting precedents? Are concerns about precedent setting different from concerns about cumulative impacts? Are they different from concerns about foreclosing planning options? If so, how? *See* e.g., *Tom Rivers Affiliates v. Department of Environmental Protection,* 140 N.J. Super, 135, 355 A.2d 679, *cert. denied,* 71 N.J. 435, 364 A.2d 1077 (1976).

2. Are eight residential houseboats a preferred, water-dependent use of a shoreline? If not preferred, are they allowable? Are the issues worth three amendments to the Seattle Shorelines Master Program, 7 days of hearings before the Washington Shorelines Hearings Board, a trial in the superior court, and an appeal to the Washington Supreme Court? Consider the following excerpts from *Portage Bay–Roanoke Park Community Council v. Shoreline Hearings Board,* 92 Wash. 2d 1, 593 P.2d 151, 152 (1979):

On May 21, 1973, Dr. David Hurlbut applied to the City of Seattle for a substantial development permit to construct a floating walk and service facilities for 12 floating homes (houseboats) and dryland parking for 12 cars. The city, on July 7, 1975, issued a substantial development permit to Dr. Hurlbut for the proposed project with two conditions imposed: the number of houseboats was reduced from 12 to 6, and the total development could extend no more than 350 feet northeast and normal to the centerline of vacated Fuhrman Avenue.

The Portage Bay-Roanoke Park Community Council (Council) and residents of the area appealed the issuance of the permit to the Board. The Council contended the permit should not have been issued because the project interferes with the view of property owners and restricts the public right of navigation and thus violates the Shoreline Management Act of 1971 (SMA), RCW 90.58. The Council also claims the city improperly failed to consider its own then-proposed Shorelines Master Program.

. . . .

After 7 days of hearings, the Board issued an order which modified the permit to allow construction of moorage and related improvements for 8 houseboats and ordered Dr. Hurlbut to execute an easement to ensure public access to the landscaped area of the project. . . .

. . . .

The contention that the permit is invalid because of a lack of public benefit is based on RCW 90.58.020. The Council points to the second paragraph which states:

It is the policy of the state to provide for the management of the shorelines of the state by planning for and fostering all reasonable and appropriate uses. This policy is designed to insure the development of these shorelines in a manner which, while allowing for limited reduction of rights of the public in the navigable waters, will promote and enhance the public interest. This policy contemplates protecting against adverse effects to the public health, the land and its vegetation and wildlife, and the waters of the state and their aquatic life, while protecting generally public rights of navigation and corollary rights incidental thereto.

As both Dr. Hurlbut and the Council observe, any common-law public benefit doctrine this state may have had prior to 1971 (*see Wilbour v. Gallagher*, 77 Wash.2d 306, 462 P.2d 232 (1969)), has been superseded and the SMA is the present declaration of that doctrine. Referring to the language in RCW 90.58.020, we said in *Department of Ecology v. Ballard Elks Lodge No. 827*, 84 Wash.2d 551, 557, 527 P.2d 1121, 1125 (1974):

[I]t is within the contemplation of the legislation that there will, of necessity, be some future and additional development along shorelines in the state, including over-the-water construction, and it does not purport to totally prohibit such development. Rather, the enunciated policy stresses the need that such future development be carefully planned, managed, and coordinated in keeping with the public interest.

The Council argues there must be a compensating or offsetting public benefit before the permit can be granted. This is not what RCW 90.58.020 requires. While it requires a recognition of public rights of navigation, it does not mandate a calculation of equal public benefits to be offset against private benefits. Rather, it declares public policy is to "[plan] for and [foster] all reasonable and appropriate uses . . . [allow] for limited reduction of rights of the public in the navigable waters" and "[protect] generally public rights of navigation and corollary rights incidental thereto." Both the Board and the trial court concluded that, when the resultant intensification of water uses by the houseboat occupants, their guests and others attracted to the area by the project was compared to the loss of some of the existing residential uses, the project was not prohibited by the SMA and was consistent with public residential rights. We agree. The position of the Board is neither arbitrary and capricious nor clearly erroneous.

The second attack by the Council under RCW 90.58.020 concerns view impairment and aesthetic considerations. The Board and the trial court specifically found no merit in the claim "view intrusion" would be created by the houseboats and held that "absent a refined master program which might address such consideration, the Shoreline Management Act cannot be read to preclude floating homes on esthetic grounds." The court and Board also found "Testimony was inconclusive that additional houseboats in the neighborhood would have a negative effect on property values."

To support its position, the Council cites *Department of Ecology v. Pacesetter Constr. Co.*, 89 Wash.2d 203, 571 P.2d 196 (1977). This case is inapposite on the question of compensation for view impairment. *Pacesetter* specifically found property values would be reduced by the buildings; here no such finding was made. While it is true we stated in *Pacesetter* at 211, 571 P.2d 196 that many cases have held protection of aesthetic values alone would justify the exercise of police power without payment, there was here neither a "refined master program" which addressed such matters and set aesthetic standards nor a violation of a specific aesthetic standard such as height limitation. *See* RCW 90.58.320. The Board did not err in refusing to vacate the permit on the grounds of aesthetics and view impairment.

On the question of the failure of the Board to apply the provisions of draft 4 of the Seattle Shorelines Master Program to the permit application, finding of fact 11 of the Board, affirmed by the trial court, says:

> On the date the application for the project was filed, May 21, 1973, Seattle had no draft master program. Draft Four of Seattle's Master Program which existed in published form when the permit for the project was issued on July 7, 1975 designated the subject site as an Urban Stable environment and deemed floating homes within such environment a conditional use. However, subsequent to the publication of Draft Four and *prior to* July 7, 1975, the Seattle City Council voted that floating homes in the Portage Bay area be a permitted, rather than a conditional use. Draft Five of the Seattle Master Program, published in November, 1975, continued to designate floating homes in the Portage Bay area as a permitted use. By the time this matter came to hearing in late December, 1975, the City Council had once again reversed it designations. The Portage Bay area was to be within the urban Residential environment and floating homes in Portage Bay were to be a conditional use. The final master plan adopted by the City Council on March 29, 1976 designated floating homes in the Portage Bay area as a permitted use although subsequent correspondence from Councilman Miller informed the Board that this was a drafting error and the use is in fact conditional.

. . . Conclusion of law 3 by the Board, adopted by the trial court, provides:

> Considering the uncertainty expressed by the City of Seattle with regard to the most desirable treatment of floating homes under its master program as documented in Finding of Fact XI, the Board concludes that, with regard to a use or environment designation for floating homes, *no ascertainable master program existed* for the City of Seattle at the time the permit was issued. Any attempt to either establish or limit property rights on the basis of decision making which has been demonstrably subject to such uncertainties would prompt serious constitutional concerns. Thus, the Board must rely in its review on the policies of the SMA enunciated in RCW 90.58.020. (Italics ours.)

RCW 90.58.140(2) provides:

(2) No substantial development shall be undertaken on shorelines of the state without first obtaining a permit from the government entity having administrative jurisdiction under this chapter.

A permit shall be granted:

(a) From June 1, 1971 until such time as an applicable master program has become effective, only when the development proposed is consistent with: (i) The policy of RCW 90.58.020; and (ii) after their adoption, the guidelines and regulations of the department; and (iii) *so far as can be ascertained,* the master program being developed for the area; (Italics ours.)

Could the master program be "ascertained"? The Board and the trial court concluded in view of the uncertainty experienced by the Seattle City Council spelled out in finding No. 11, no ascertainable master program existed. Adequate facts exist for this conclusion and we will not disturb it.

(a) In enacting the Shoreline Management Act of 1971, do you think the Washington legislature intended, as the court states in *Portage Bay*, to supersede "any common-law public benefit doctrine this state may have had prior to 1971"? Does the legislature have the power to "supersede" the public trust doctrine? Recall *Illinois Central Railroad v. Illinois, supra*, in Chapter 3. How did the Illinois legislature attempt to supersede the public trust doctrine in that case?

(b) Were the issues in *Portage Bay* correctly framed by the Community Council? By the Shorelines Hearings Board? By the Court? How would the issues be different if Dr. Hurlbut had proposed:

(1) Subdividing a previously undeveloped shoreline tract adjacent to Portage Bay into 12 single-family residential lots?

(2) Building a 12-unit condominium project on the tract adjacent to Portage Bay?

(3) Converting a 20-unit shoreline apartment building into 12 condominium units?

(4) Building a 12-unit condominium project on pilings over the waters of Portage Bay?

(5) Building an Elks Lodge on pilings over the waters of Portage Bay?

(6) Raising the level of his shoreline tract with solid waste as a sanitary landfill to create a marine industrial park on Portage Bay? *See Hayes v. Yount*, 87 Wash. 2d 280, 552 P.2d 1038 (1976).

(7) Placing dredge spoils on his tract in order to locate support facilities for his marine dredging business there? *See Skagit County v. State*, 613 P.2d 115 (1980).

3. How do you explain the different results in *Ballard* and *Skagit County v. State*, 613 P.2d 115 (1980), where on appeal to the Washington Supreme Court a shoreline development permit was granted to an Elks Lodge and denied to a company engaged primarily in water-dependent operations such as dredging and pile-driving whom the court acknowledged must be located on the shoreline to carry out its activities? How relevant to your explanation are each of the following factors?

(a) Local government denial of the applicant's request in *Ballard* and granting of the applicant's request in *Skagit County*.

(b) The urban location in *Ballard* as compared to the rural location in *Skagit County*.

(c) In *Skagit County* the sensitive nature of nearby Padilla Bay.

(d) The admission in Skagit County's and the permit applicant's brief that "some 30 unusual species of birds and/or wildlife may have used the site as a habitat."

(e) Expert testimony in *Skagit County* concerning the need to preserve the 7-acre portion of the site as a "buffer zone" protecting the waters and shores of Padilla Bay.

(f) The difference between the requested developments' precedential effects and possible cumulative impacts.

4. Should priority in use of remaining undeveloped shorelines be given to single-family residences as provided in section 90.58.020 of the Washington Shoreline Management Act quoted in *Ballard*? Is a single-family residence a water-dependent use? Why does the California Coastal Act favor water-dependent industry and water-dependent commercial recreation over private residential development? *See* Cal. Pub. Res. Code §§ 30001.5(d), 30222, 30255. How can residential development of a shoreline occur much more quickly than industrial or commercial development?

Section 90.58.030(3)(e)(vi) of the Washington Shoreline Management Act exempts from the shoreline development permit requirement construction on wetlands of a single-family residence for an owner's or lessee's own use, if its height does not exceed 35 feet above average grade level. Is this exemption consistent with other policies favoring preservation of wetlands in their natural state? For whose benefit was the single-family home exemption enacted? Wash. Rev. Code § 90.58.030(3)(e)(vii) also exempts private noncommercial pleasure craft docks costing under $2,500 and construction of normal protective bulkheads for single-family residences.

For whose benefit was the 35-foot-height limit enacted? *See* Wash. Rev. Code § 90.58.320, which provides that structures more than 35 feet above average grade level which "obstruct the view of a substantial number of residences" are to be permitted only "where a master program does not prohibit the same and then only when overriding considerations of the public interest will be served."

Should the Shoreline Management Act be used for private view preservation? For whose benefit was the Washington Shoreline Management Act enacted?

5. Why does section 90.58.230 authorize private persons to enforce the Shoreline Management Act? Who should have the primary burden of enforcing the act? Crooks, *The Washington Shoreline Management Act of 1971*, 49 Wash. L. Rev. 423, 453 (1974) summarizes the act's enforcement provisions:

Enforcement of the Act is primarily the responsibility of the Attorney General and the attorneys for local governments. Section 21 [Wash. Rev. Code § 90.58.210] authorized these officials to bring "injunctive, declaratory, or other actions" to insure compliance with the Act; Section 23 [Wash. Rev. Code § 90.58.230] enables them to bring suit for damages to public property, "including the cost of restoring the affected area to its condition prior to the violation [of the Act or a permit granted under it]." The latter section also provides for suits by private parties "on their own behalf and on the behalf of all persons similarly situated." The court may thus award damages for and require abatement of developments in violation of the Act; it also has discretion to award attorney's fees and costs to the prevailing party.

In addition to these civil sanctions, willful violators of the Act or the master programs adopted under it may be found guilty of a gross misdemeanor, punishable by fines of from $25 to $1,000 or 90 days in jail, with the fine escalated to $500 to $10,000 for the third such violation within a five-year period.

As one county prosecutor has suggested, effective enforcement will require local governments to develop an administrative inspection capacity, but will depend as well "on private persons to both bring possible violations to [local government's] attention and to bring suits enforcing the Act."

Given the significant restrictions placed on shoreline development by the Act and the tremendous pressures for such development, are the Act's enforcement provisions adequate? Who monitors developer compliance with conditions imposed in permits that are granted under the Act?

MERKEL v. PORT OF BROWNSVILLE, 8 Wn. App. 844, 509 P.2d 390 (1973)

PETRIE, J.

This is an action instituted by petitioners to enjoin respondent, Port of Brownsville, from proceeding with certain actions preliminary to the redevelopment of a small boat marina along Burke Bay. The Attorney General of the State of Washington and the Prosecuting Attorney of Kitsap County seek review of the trial court's refusal to grant a preliminary injunction prohibiting the port from cutting timber and clearing and grading the uplands portion of the project.

This case raises important issues under the State Environmental Policy Act of 1971 (SEPA) (RCW 43.21C), and the Shoreline Management Act of 1971 (SMA) (RCW 90.58). All parties agree that the provisions of these acts govern the disposition of this controversy, but do not agree to what degree they affect the present litigation.

The proposed project consists of constructing protected moorage facilities for recreational boats at Brownsville on Puget Sound. Brownsville is an unincorporated town on Burke Bay on the east side of the Kitsap Peninsula. In 1965 the Port of Brownsville contacted the Army Corps of Engineers and requested a survey report on the proposed marina expansion. After the survey was completed a detailed project report was prepared by the corps and finally approved in 1971. The comprehensive plan, with subsequent amendments, provides for the construction of a permanent breakwater, piers and floats which will more than double the present capacity, and for the installation of facilities for the sale and repair of boats, parking areas and other commercial services related to the project. The improvements encompass 12½ acres along Burke Bay and 10 acres of adjacent uplands at the mouth of the bay. At present this acreage is almost entirely undeveloped and remains heavily forested with Douglas fir trees.

Actual construction under the plan began with the cutting and clearing of timber in the upland portion of the property in September, 1972. After some 50 trees had been felled, petitioners commenced this action to enjoin any further activity by the port until it had obtained substantial development permits as required by the SMA. Petitioners further alleged that the provisions of SEPA required that an environmental impact statement be filed because the project contemplated by the port was a "major action having a substantial impact upon the environment."

On September 29, 1972, an ex parte restraining order was obtained by petitioners which temporarily restrained the port from proceeding further with excavation or construction on any portion of the project. Hearing on the order was held on October 6, 1972. The order was continued because the trial court found the impact statement filed by the port was deficient in that the port had failed to consult with and obtain comments from local, state and federal agencies having jurisdiction over any portion of the proposed project. The court also found that the uplands development constituted a major action significantly affecting the quality of the environment.

The port subsequently filed a revised statement. A hearing was held to determine its adequacy. The trial court again found that insufficient time had been given interested agencies to submit their comments to the port, and continued the restraining order in effect. On December 21, 1972, the port submitted the third version of its environmental impact statement. No challenge was made to the adequacy of that revised statement. The trial court modified the existing restraining order by limiting its application to the 200 feet "wetlands" only, and by removing the upland portion of the project from further restraint. Thereupon, petitioners instituted this action for a writ of review and stay of proceedings. Pursuant to CAROA 57(f)(4)(i) we granted the writ of certiorari and temporarily stayed the order of the trial court to the extent that it had dissolved the restraint in the area more than 200 feet inland from the level of ordinary high water.

Broadly stated, the central issue in this case is whether or not the development contemplated by the port, which is admittedly governed by the provisions of SEPA and SMA, is so interrelated and interdependent that no part of the project can proceed until all provisions of these acts have been fully complied with. Resolution of the issue necessitates an examination of these acts in some detail, as well as their application to the facts of the instant case.

The declared purpose of SEPA is to encourage productive and enjoyable harmony between man and his environment; to promote efforts which will prevent or eliminate damage to the environment; to stimulate the health and welfare of man; and to enrich the understanding of the ecological systems and natural resources important to the state and nation. RCW 43.21C.010. To achieve these goals, the act requires all state and local agencies, in performing their respective functions, to be cognizant of and responsive to possible environmental consequences in their actions. The act makes it the continuing responsibility of these agencies "to use all practicable means and measures," to carry out the policy of restoring and maintaining a quality environment. *See* RCW 43.21C.020. To assure that the substantive provisions of the act receive the attention they deserve, RCW 43.21C.030 prescribes certain procedural measures calculated to effectuate this policy. All branches of government in this state are required to:

> (a) Utilize a systematic, interdisciplinary approach which will insure the integrated use of the natural and social sciences and the environmental design arts in planning and in decision making which may have an impact on man's environment;
>
> (b) Identify and develop methods and procedures, in consultation with the department of ecology and the ecological commission, which will insure that presently unquantified environmental amenities and values will be given appropriate consideration in decision making along with economic and technical consideration; RCW 43.21C.030(2)(a), (b).

SEPA further requires these agencies to include an environmental impact statement within any proposal for a major activity which significantly affects the environment. The detailed statement must contain the environmental impact of the proposed action, any adverse effects by reason of such action, and any alternatives to the proposed action. RCW 43.21C.030(2)(c).

It is clear that the provisions of SEPA are innovative and place new and unusual responsibilities on governmental agencies. Environmental protection has become a mandate to every agency entrusted with its care. The statutory scheme contemplates that the goals of SEPA are realized by requiring these agencies to assess environmental consequences in formulating policies, and by compelling these agencies to follow SEPA procedures prior to initiating major activity. The court's function, minimally, is to insure that these procedures are followed.

The Shoreline Management Act of 1971 (SMA) (RCW 90.58), though dealing with a limited area of the environment, is as vigorous as SEPA in declaring a policy aimed at the preservation of our natural resources. "Shorelines", as that term applies to this case, includes those "wetlands" extending landward for 200 feet in all directions as measured on a horizontal plane from the ordinary high-water mark. RCW 90.58.030(2)(f).

This act is an acknowlegement that "the shorelines of the state are among the most valuable and fragile of its natural resources"; that unrestricted construction upon them is not in the best public interest; and, therefore, there is a need for coordinated planning to prevent the inherent harm occasioned by piecemeal development of the shorelines. RCW 90.58.020.

To assure the intelligent development of our shorelines the act establishes a permit system, with primary responsibility for its administration upon local government, for the control of such development. RCW 90.58.050 and RCW 90.58.140(2). The Department of Ecology and local governments are required to prepare and adopt master programs to aid in the coordination and systematic development of the shorelines and lands adjacent to them. RCW 90.58.340. RCW 90.58.100(2) provides that master programs shall include:

> (a) An economic development element for the location and design of industries, transportation facilities, port facilities, tourist facilities, commerce, and other developments that are particularly dependent on their location on or use of the shorelines of the state;
>
> . . . .
>
> (e) A use element which considers the proposed general distribution and general location and extent of the use on shorelines *and adjacent land areas* for housing, business, industry, transportation, agriculture, natural resources, recreation, education, public buildings and grounds, and other categories of public and private uses of the land; (Italics ours.)

At the very least, the legislative scheme of SMA contemplates a systematic and intelligent management of our shorelines. Emphasis is placed upon a cooperative and unified effort by all governmental agencies to achieve a use policy consistent with the provisions of the act. It is also clear that lands adjacent to shorelines must also be taken into consideration if the consistency stressed in the act is to be achieved.

Initially, we note that the Port of Brownsville has not to date obtained all of the permits required by the SMA. In fact, three permits [a conditional use permit and two SMA substantial development permits] must be acquired by the port in order to carry out the project as proposed.

With the foregoing discussion of the various provisions of SEPA and SMA as a backdrop, we now turn our attention to the case at bench. It is the position of the Port of Brownsville that SEPA governs the entire project and that, once having complied with its provisions, the port may proceed to cut the trees and clear the uplands without regard to whether or not the permits required by SMA have been issued. The port argues that because no objections have been raised to the revised environmental impact statement, there is nothing further for it to do. It is also the port's contention that references in SMA to lands adjacent to the shoreline constitute nothing more than an admonition to local government to adhere to the policies of the act in drafting guidelines for shorelines within their jurisdiction. Thus, the port concludes, no obstacles preclude clearing the uplands.

To accept the port's argument would require us to close our eyes to the obvious interrelation of this project upon the wetlands and adjacent uplands areas. There is nothing in the record before us to indicate that the contemplated construction has ever been anything but one project. The question, therefore, is whether the port may take a single project and divide it into segments for purposes of SEPA and SMA approval. The frustrating effect of such piecemeal administrative approvals upon the vitality of these acts compels us to answer in the negative. A brief look at the record lends credence to the soundness of this decision.

The supplemental environmental impact statement details at great length the impact this proposed project will have on the area. Among the changes are: the placement of boat buildings and other boat facilities on both the wetlands and uplands; the use of the uplands for dry storage; construction of parking facilities on the uplands to serve users of the marina; and use of the trees severed on the uplands portion in constructing floats for the marina expansion. Additionally, the present plan calls for the elimination of a large intertidal pool which lies on both the wetlands and uplands portions of the project.

The coercive effect the construction of one segment would have upon the other is obvious. If clearing and construction activity is allowed to continue in the uplands portion before the wetlands portion has been approved, it is obvious the entire area will be affected. The legislature, in extending the scope of SMA to consideration of the use of lands adjacent to shorelines, sought to prevent this type of coerced land use development.

To permit the piecemeal development urged upon us by the port would lower the environmental mandates of these acts to the status of mere admonitions. The result would be frustration rather than fulfillment of the legislative intent inherent in these acts. This project will have a significant effect upon the environment. It is to the public's benefit that any project significantly affecting the environment and shorelines of this state comply with the procedures established by SEPA and SMA to insure that the environmental aspects have been fully considered. Irreparable damage would flow from allowing any portion of this project to proceed without full compliance with the permit requirements of the SMA. We can appreciate the added expense the port must incur as a result of our holding but these inconveniences are far outweighed by the public's interest in attaining and maintaining an environment consistent with legislatively promulgated goals. It was, therefore, error to dissolve restraint in the area more than 200 feet inland from the level of ordinary high water. The injunction on the uplands as well as the wetlands should continue until all legal impediments imposed by the SMA have been removed.

Finally, petitioners argue that the port cannot legally sever any trees on this project until the comprehensive port plan is properly amended. They correctly state that the Brownsville Small Boat Basin Plan is an integrated project for which a comprehensive plan is required pursuant to the basic port district act as amended, RCW 53.20.010. This statute prohibits any improvements by a port district prior to official adoption of the plan by the port commission. The commission can only adopt the plan after a public hearing has been conducted following proper notice.

The record before us indicates that the port does have an officially adopted comprehensive plan, revised in September, 1972. This plan, however, does not reflect the changes in the project which have taken place since that time. The alterations from the officially adopted plan include the deletion and relocation of several buildings in the uplands area.

RCW 53.20.020 states:

> When such general plans shall have been adopted or approved, as aforesaid, *every improvement to be made by said commission shall be made substantially in accordance therewith unless and until such general plans shall have been officially changed by the port commission after a public hearing thereon,* of which at least ten days' notice shall be published in a newspaper in general circulation in such port district. (Italics ours.)

The clear intent of the legislature in enacting this law was to require a port commission, prior to entering into any improvement scheme, to place before the people an actual plan disclosing with reasonable definiteness the character of the improvements. Any amendment altering an officially adopted plan must also be preceded by a public hearing.

Because the port has not complied with RCW 53.20.020 in amending its comprehensive plan, it has no authority to make any improvements under the plan until the changes are officially adopted after public hearing in the manner prescribed by statute.

The writ is granted and the Superior Court for Kitsap County is directed to reinstate the restraints previously imposed upon the cutting of timber and the clearing and grading of the upland portions of this project.

PEARSON, C. J., and ARMSTRONG, J., concur.

NOTES

1. In *Sisley v. San Juan County,* 89 Wash. 2d 78, 69 P.2d 712 (1977), the Washington Supreme Court explained the relationship between Washington's State Environmental Policy Act (SEPA), Wash. Rev. Code § 43.21C.010 *et seq.,* and the Shoreline Management Act in the following way:

> A basic purpose of SEPA is to require local governmental agencies, including counties, to consider total environmental and ecological factors to the fullest extent when taking "major actions significantly affecting the quality of the environment." RCW 43.21C.030(2)(c). Such actions require preparation of an EIS. Where . . . the governmental action consists of issuing permits for a private project, we have employed a two-step analysis in determining whether there is a "major actions significantly affecting the quality of the environment." First, the nature or character of the "action" must be considered. Thereafter, the "significance" of the action's

impact must be examined to determine its effect on the quality of the environment. *Eastlake Com. Coun. v. Roanoke Assoc.*, 82 Wash.2d 475, 489–93, 513 P.2d 36 (1973).

In regard to the first step of this analysis, a governmental agency's approval of private projects by the granting of permits constitutes an "action" within the meaning of SEPA. *Eastlake Com. Coun. v. Roanoke Assoc., supra* at 489, 513 P.2d 36, see also WAC 197–10–040(2)(a), SEPA Guidelines, effective January 16, 1976.

. . . The fact that the private sector undertakes a project with governmental approval does not lessen the "major" impact of the governmental participation. *Eastlake* at 491, 513 P.2d 36.

The SMA, RCW 90.58, though dealing with a limited area of the environment, *i.e.,* the wetlands and adjacent uplands, is no less vigorous than SEPA in declaring a policy aimed at the preservation of our natural resources. In fact, the permit systems of the SMA is inextricably interrelated with and supplemented by the requirements of SEPA. *Merkel v. Port of Brownsville*, 8 Wash.App. 844, 850–1, 509 P.2d 390 (1973). The requirements of SEPA clearly overlay the whole SMA permit process. RCW 43.21C.060. Issuance of a substantial development permit under SMA will thus most often require an assessment of the environmental effects of the project. If an assessment leads to the conclusion that the project significantly affects the quality of the environment, an EIS must be prepared. *Juanita Bay Valley Com. v. Kirkland*, 9 Wash.App. 59, 73, 510 P.2d 1140 (1973).

. . . When a governmental agency makes this initial threshold determination, it must consider the various environmental factors even if it concludes that the action does not signficantly affect the environment and therefore does not require an EIS. *Juanita Bay* at 73, 510 P.2d 1140. We recently stressed the importance of this initial "threshold determination" in *Norway Hill v. King County Council*, 87 Wash.2d 267, at 273, 552 P.2d 674, at 678 (1976), where we stated: "The policy of the act, which is simply to insure via a 'detailed statement' the full disclosure of environmental information so that environmental matters can be given proper consideration during decision making, is thwarted whenever an incorrect 'threshold determination' is made." Therefore, according to *Eastlake* at 494 of 82 Wash.2d, 513 P.2d 36, if after considering the cumulative effects of the entire project, the government agency makes a determination of no significant impact under SEPA, *i.e.,* a "negative threshold determination," it must show "that environmental factors were considered in a manner sufficient to amount to prima facie compliance with the procedural requirements of SEPA." *Juanita Bay Valley Com. v. Kirkland, supra,* 9 Wash.App. at 73, 510 P.2d at 1149; *Narrowsview Preservation Ass'n v. Tacoma,* 84 Wash.2d 416, 422, 526 P.2d 897 (1974).

. . . .

. . . In considering whether "major actions" significantly affect the environment, we have held that an EIS is required "whenever more than a moderate effect on the quality of the environment is a reasonable probability," *Norway Hill* at 278 of 78 Wash.2d, at 680 of 552 P.2d.

. . . .

The most important aspect of SEPA is full consideration of environmental values, RCW 43.21C.030(2)(b) and this policy is carried out by the EIS procedure. However, the need for an EIS does not mean a proposed project cannot be built. It merely assures a full disclosure and consideration of environmental information prior to the construction of the project. *Norway Hill v. King County Council, supra* at 272, 552 P.2d 674. "It is an attempt by the people to shape their future environment by deliberation, not default." *Stempel v. Dept. of Water Resources,* 82 Wash.2d 109, 118, 508 P.2d 166, 172 (1973).

569 P.2d at 715–16, 716–17, 718. *See also State v. Lake Lawrence Public Lands Protection Ass'n*, 92 Wash. 2d 656, 601 P.2d 494 (1979).

Sisley involved a marina proposed for construction at Deer Harbor on Orcas Island in the San Juan Islands of Puget Sound:

Deer Harbor is a small, southerly-facing sheltered bay near the west tip of Orcas Island. It is approximately 4,000 feet in length and 2,000 feet at its widest point. A tidal lagoon is located at the northerly end of the harbor.

In October of 1972, defendant/respondent (respondent) Norman Carpenter applied for a substantial development permit under the Shoreline Management Act (SMA), RCW 90.58, to build a 94-slip marina at the head of Deer Harbor. The proposed project embraces 6½ acres, 3½ acres of state-owned aquatic land, managed by the State Department of Natural Resources, and 3 acres of tidelands and uplands. The planned structure would involve approximately 17,000 square feet of piling, finger piers, and docks and would extend 600 feet into the harbor. The channel entrance to the northerly lagoon area would be decreased to approximately 290 feet clearance between the proposed structure and the existing private moorage facility on the opposite shore. The contemplated upland support facilities include 27 parking spaces, a bathhouse-laundry, and a sewage dumping station with a 1500 foot sewer line and 1 acre drain field.

By May 1974, Mr. Carpenter had obtained the substantial development permit from defendant-respondent Board of County Commissioners of San Juan County (Board). In the next year he obtained a navigable water lease from the Department of Natural Resources, approval from the United States Army Corps of Engineers, and a building permit from respondent County with approval of the Department of Ecology to construct the upland support facilities. Although an EIS had not been prepared, respondent Carpenter began driving piling at the site of the proposed marina.

569 P.2d at 714.

The court found the record supporting the county board's decision not to prepare an EIS under SEPA on the proposed marina's environmental impacts inadequate:

. . . It is filled with many assertions, numerous unanswered questions and a paucity of information. Unfortunately the Board's conclusion, supported by a 2–1 vote, is accompanied by no reasoning, explanation or findings of fact, however informal. The minutes of the meeting and the so-called transcript of the public hearing add no clarification. However, one thing does appear from the record as a whole. In reaching the conclusion it did, in the manner it did, the Board misconceived its duty in making the negative threshold determination under the order of remand. This was evidenced at the public hearing, which was held as a direct result of the stipulation between the parties. A representative of the County Planning Department stated:

We've made this, we've pursued a study of the documents here, and did some findings, and a thorough reading of this chronology section reveals that considerable review of the proposed marina development was made at the State, Local, State and Federal levels prior to the approval of all the regulatory environmentally oriented permits were issued. And from this, it would seem administratively appropriate ↄo recommend that a negative declaration be made, and allow the project to . . . develop, to resume. This presumably would satisfy the procedural requirements of the State Environmental Policy Act.

The Summary Report of the Planning Department submitted to and apparently used by the Board makes it clear that although a number of federal and state agencies inquired into the environmental impact of the marina, as viewed from their own individual perspective, the Board made no attempt to synthesize or evaluate them, or the information or questions raised by them. Further, while the absence of a final report of the Board and a lack of findings of fact or reasons do not necessarily imply that the Board either ignored or adopted the views of these agencies, it does indicate that the public was denied an opportunity to understand or consider the Board's decision on the application. This lack of explanation in the record also makes it difficult for an appellate court to review the Board's action. . . .

569 P.2d at 717.

The court ordered the county commissioners to prepare an EIS because:

Having reviewed the entire Board record, in light of the public policy of SEPA, to determine whether "a mistake has been committed" in concluding that the marina's construction will have no signficant environmental impact on Deer Harbor we are firmly convinced that the decision of the Board was clearly erroneous.

For example, the legal notice published on March 21, 1974, by respondent Carpenter described the project as a major action significantly affecting the quality of the environment.

At the public hearing local residents expressed concern about water pollution and the flushing effect of the tidal action in Deer Harbor and the lagoon, shellfish and bird life, the impact of traffic and additional population, and the subject of aesthetics (view). These are all legitimate concerns to be considered by a governmental agency in making a threshold determination. However, the County Planning Department admitted it had conducted no field investigation and had no information concerning the proposed marina's impact in these areas. Rather, the County relied on the analyses of several federal and state agencies.

A letter from the Fish and Wildlife Service of the United States Department of Interior considers the upper end of Deer Harbor "biologically unique within the San Juan Islands and deserving a special consideration in any development considered for that vicinity." The agency was concerned about the cumulative effect of more marinas—massive boat parking lots—on the aquatic environment and stressed "we think this subject deserves careful examination and thus might appropriately be examined for planning purposes as a general shoreline management issue through the detailed and systematic approach supplied in the EIS procedure."

Some state agencies were in agreement with the Department of the Interior. The Department of Ecology urged that potentially significant environmental effects should be determined before the proposal was approved. The Department of Natural Resources Impact Analysis states the project "will create a considerable impact on the natural environment of the harbor by converting approximately 3 acres of unrestricted navigation use to marina use." This report places special emphasis on the fact that "[the] present scenic, natural view of the upper portion of Deer Harbor" would be replaced by a "man-made view of rows of moored pleasure craft."

A zoological consultant, professor emeritus from the University of Washington, informed the Planning Department by letter that the water and shore areas near the proposed marina were important to both sea and shore birds. He stressed the need to keep pollution to a minimum and expressed the view that too great an increase in boating and human activity would drive many of the birds away. This view raises some serious questions when considered in the light of a feasibility study for a Deer Harbor marina prepared by the United States Army Corps of Engineers. It referred to the harbor as being ideally located for a marina because it was "located in the heavy traffic flow area for boaters."

Further questions are raised by numerous photographs and blueprints found in the Planning Department report to the Board as well as the Department's own comments which state that (1) there are "other choices of action or alternatives available;" (2) the "action involve[s] substantial controversy originating from agencies or citizen groups;" (3) the action deals with "environmental conditions . . . that have been clearly recognized as being endangered; fragile; in severely short supply; or clearly approaching a precarious level of quality . . .;" (4) environmental effects would be both beneficial and adverse; (5) the environmental effects would be "long term 10–20 years."

. . . .

Reference to the foregoing examples alone makes it evident that under the stated public policy of SEPA there is a *reasonable probability* that the proposed marina will have *more than a moderate effect* on the quality of the Deer Harbor environment. Based on the entire record and the public policy evinced by SEPA, we are firmly convinced the Board's negative threshold determination was a mistake.

569 P.2d at 717–19.

Suppose that the county planning staff prepares an EIS incorporating the foregoing information and responding to the court's concerns. After considering the EIS at a public hearing, may the county commissioners then proceed to approve the proposed marina without fear of judicial reversal? Are there arguments in favor of expanding existing marinas such as Brownsville instead of constructing new marinas as was proposed in *Sisley? See Zittel's Marina, Inc. v. Thurston County*, 17 Wash. App. 774, 565 P.2d 1196 (1977).

2. As noted by the court in *Merkle*, the Port of Brownsville had not yet obtained the necessary shoreline development permits under Washington's Shoreline Management Act of 1971 (SMA) for its proposed expanded marina. Given the SMA's policies and requirements, should Kitsap County issue such permits to the Port of Brownsville? Would issuance by Kitsap County be upheld by the Shorelines Hearings Board and the courts upon appeal?

3. The California Environmental Quality Act (CEQA), Cal. Pub. Res. Code §§ 21000–176, is very similar to Washington's SEPA. *See* Hildreth, *Environmental Impacts Reports Under the California Environmental Quality Act: The New Legal Framework*, 17 Santa Clara L. Rev. 805 (1977). The federal National Environmental Policy Act (NEPA), 42 U.S.C. §§ 4321–47, discussed several places in this book, served as a model for both of them. Like EIS's prepared under NEPA and Washington's SEPA, environmental impact reports (EIR's) prepared under California's CEQA can play an important role in coastal zone management. For example, in *Coastal Southwest Development Corporation v. California Coastal Zone Conservation Commission*, 55 Cal. App. 3d 525, 127 Cal. Rptr. 775 (1976), the court upheld the coastal commission's rejection of a proposed nine-story motel adjacent to Oceanside Harbor, basing its decision on an EIR that disclosed significant cumulative adverse impacts of growth in Oceanside on the San Luis Rey River and Lagoon, on the wildlife and wildlife habitat in that area, on views of the harbor and oceanfront areas, and on surrounding lower intensity land uses that would be forced out by higher property taxes.

4. Section 90.58.030(2)(f) of the Washington Shoreline Management Act defines wetlands as

those lands extending landward for two hundred feet in all directions as measured on a horizontal plane from the ordinary high water mark; floodways and contiguous floodplain areas landward two hundred feet from such floodways; and all marshes, bogs, swamps, and river deltas associated with the streams, lakes, and tidal waters which are subject to the provisions of this [act] . . . .

Section 30121 of the California Coastal Act defines wetland for the purposes of state and local coastal management as "lands within the coastal zone which may be covered periodically or permanently with shallow water and include saltwater marshes, freshwater marshes, open or closed brackish water marshes, swamps, mudflats and fens." Is the California definition more workable than the Washington definition? If not, how about the following definition?

Wetlands are lands transitional between terrestrial and aquatic systems where the water table is usually at or near the surface or the land is covered by shallow water. For purposes of this classification, wetlands must have one or more of the following three attributes: (1) at least periodically, the land supports predominantly hydrophytes; (2) the substrate is predominantly undrained hydric soil; and (3) the substrate is nonsoil and is saturated with water or covered by shallow water at some time during the growing season of each year.

United States Fish and Wildlife Service, Mapping Conventions of the National Wetland Inventory (undated).

5. As interpreted in *Weyerhaeuser Co. v. King County*, 91 Wash. 2d 721, 592 P.2d 1108 (1980), Washington law requires a shoreline development permit for logging within shorelines but not for logging near shorelines. What about agricultural activities within and near shorelines? Should they be exempt from shoreline development permit requirements? What effects may such agricultural activities have on shorelines and coastal waters?

Section 30106 of the California Coastal Act defines "development" to include "the removal or harvesting of major vegetation other than for agricultural purposes . . . ." Interpreting this section, a California attorney general's opinion broadly defined "agricultural purposes" to include grading, tree cutting, and other major types of vegetation removal if conducted with the intent to begin, convert, or expand agricultural operations. Cal. A.G. Opinion No. 5077/39 I.L. (Apr. 6, 1978). The California Coastal Commission staff objected to this interpretation as overly broad and creating a loophole through which coastal agricultural lands ultimately could be converted to residential and other nonagricultural uses, with various adverse effects on the coastal environment. *See* Memorandum Regarding Jurisdiction to Require Coastal Permits for Removal of Major Vegetation, from Roy Gorman, Chief Counsel, to California Coastal Commission (Nov. 14, 1980).

Section 90.58.030(3)(e) of the Washington Shoreline Management Act of 1971 exempts from the act's shoreline development permit requirements:

. . . .

(iv) Construction and practices normal or necessary for farming, irrigation, and ranching activities, including *agricultural service roads* and utilities on wetlands, and the construction and maintenance of irrigation structures including but not limited to head gates, pumping facilities, and irrigation channels: . . .

. . . .

(viii) Operation, maintenance, or construction of canals, waterways, drains, *reservoirs,* or other facilities that now exist or are hereafter created or developed as a part of an *irrigation system* for the primary purpose of making use of system waters, including return flow and artificially stored ground water for the irrigation of lands. (Emphasis added.)

Is the exemption for agricultural roads and utilities on wetlands consistent with other policies favoring preservation of wetlands in their natural state?

Clallam County, Washington's 1973 Shoreline Management Ordinance did not exempt agricultural activities from its shoreline development permit requirements. Clallam County Ordinance No. 44–1973. The facts of *Ritchie v. Markley*, 23 Wash. App. 569, 597 P.2d 449 (1979) arose in Clallam County:

In January 1977, Markley bulldozed a 50 by 120 foot pit on his land about 200 feet from the Dungeness River. He intended to make the pit into a reservoir for an irrigation system. He hired a backhoe operator to dig it out to an average depth of about 5 feet, and the pit filled with water by natural percolation.

Markley hired a gravel pit operator to bring in rock-crushing equipment to the pond to make gravel out of the excavated rock. After crushing about 900 cubic yards of rock, the equipment broke down in mid-February 1977. During the breakdown the equipment operators spread about 350 cubic yards of gravel along Markley's private access road, and sold about 350 cubic yards to his own customers. The operator testified that the gravel was sold to meet previous commitments and that he had to use Markley's gravel because he could not move his disabled equipment to his own gravel pit. Markley received no money for the sale of the gravel, and in fact paid the operator for all work done on the property.

. . . .

. . . Markley testified that he always had intended his pond to be a reservoir for an irrigation system, and no evidence contradicted his claim. He had planted grass on the land he hoped to irrigate, and had grazed his horses on the land. The service road gave access to the pastureland, and equipment driven over the road had been used to clear stumps and underbrush from the pastureland. Markley paid the contractor for all work done and received no money from the sale of rock crushed on his land.

597 P.2d at 450, 451.

Clallam County filed suit to enjoin the rock-crushing operation until Markley obtained a county shoreline development permit. Should a shoreline development permit be required for activities like Markley's? Is a county shoreline development permit required? Is a state shoreline development permit required? If the state act exempts Markley from its permit requirements, may Clallam County still require a shoreline development permit under its ordinance? Do the state agricultural exemption provisions quoted above preempt local shoreline legislation requiring permits for activities like Markley's? Should they? *See* 597 P.2d at 451–52.

If the county's request for injunctive relief is denied, is *Markley* entitled to attorney's fees under section 90.58.230 of the Washington Shoreline Management Act, which provides:

If liability has been established for the cost of restoring an area affected by a violation the court shall make provision to assure that restoration will be accomplished within a reasonable time at the expense of the violator. In addition to such relief, including money damages, the court in its discretion may award attorney's fees and costs of the suit to the prevailing party.

See 597 P.2d at 453.

ENGLISH BAY ENTERPRISES, LTD. v. ISLAND COUNTY,
89 Wash. 2d 16, 568 P.2d 783 (1977)

DOLLIVER, Associate Justice.

The appellant is a Canadian corporation engaged in the business of clam harvesting on the tidelands near Camano Island. On April 5, 1974, appellant filed under protest a substantial development permit application with respondent Island County, seeking approval to harvest clams from all of its leased private tidelands in Livingston Bay and Port Susan Bay. Respondent's planning commission considered appellant's application at four public hearings and recommended approval of the application subject to certain conditions. The Board of County Commissioners then considered the matter and denied the application. The decision was appealed to the Shoreline Hearings Board (hereafter the Board) alleging that its operation was not subject to the Shoreline Management Act of 1971 (RCW 90.58) or, alternatively, that its project was consistent with the Shoreline Management Act. The Board's decision was appealed to the Superior Court for Thurston County and upheld by order dated August 2, 1975.

The appellant possesses a permit from the Department of Fisheries which allows clam harvesting. To comply with the State Environmental Policy Act (RCW 43.21C), the department issued a negative declaration with respect to an adjacent 80-acre parcel of tidelands for a predecessor permit which expired on December 31, 1974, concluding that clam harvesting under the terms of the permit was a minor action and the effects were not significant. No negative declaration was made in regard to the permit in effect after December 31, 1974.

The appellant harvests clams mechanically, using a self-propelled watercraft to which is attached a cutterhead with water nozzles and a steel mesh conveyor belt. A jet of water shoots through each nozzle and scours the ocean bed. The mechanism scoops the top 12 inches of bottom material onto a moving conveyor belt. The smaller matter falls through the mesh; the larger matter is sorted and the spoils are dumped into the water.

The Board made the following findings of fact: Much of the silt which is churned up does not fall into the trench but remains suspended in the water for a significant amount of time; after an area is harvested, the trench remains visible and may create a safety hazard; since appellant began its operations, the property owners have noticed an accumulation of silt and organic materials upon what were once clean sand and gravel beaches; the noise from appellant's motors disturbs the beach residents and may be heard day or night 7 days a week; appellant's operation imperils the aesthetics of the bay; plants (eelgrass, widgeon grass and bulrush) and the animals (snowgeese, Canadian geese and ducks), which feed on intertidal marine invertebrates and the plants, could be adversely affected by the operation.

The Board concluded: Clam harvesting, in the manner conducted by appellant, involves "dredging," "dumping," and "filling," and constitutes a "development" within the meaning of the Shoreline Management Act. RCW

90.58.030(3)(d). Such clam harvesting is a "substantial development" as described in RCW 90.58.030(3)(e), because the cost of the operation exceeds $1,000 and the clam harvesting "materially interferes with the normal public use of the water or shorelines of the state." RCW 90.58.030(2)(d). The State Environmental Policy Act is supplementary to and does not replace other statutory and regulatory obligations of appellant. RCW 43.21C.060. The Board has jurisdiction over the persons and subject matter in this proceeding. The Board further stated that its holding does *not* preclude all mechanical clam harvesting on shorelines of the state, but it does require that the Shoreline Management Act concerns be properly met.

The first issue before us is whether the Board erred in assuming jurisdiction over the appellant. In this regard, RCW 90.58.140(2) provides:

> No *substantial development* shall be undertaken on shorelines of the state without first obtaining a permit from the government entity having administrative jurisidiction under this chapter.

(Italics ours.) RCW 90.58.030(3) provides the following definitions:

> (d) "Development" means a use consisting of the construction or exterior alteration of structures; *dredging*; drilling; *dumping; filling;* removal of any sand, gravel or minerals; bulkheading; driving of piling; placing of obstructions; or any project of a permanent or temporary nature which interferes with the normal public use of the surface of the waters overlying lands subject to this chapter at any state of water level;
> (e) "Substantial development" shall mean any development of which the *total cost or fair market value exceeds one thousand dollars, or* any development which *materially interferes with the normal public use of the water or shorelines of the state;* except that the following shall not be considered substantial developments for the purpose of this chapter.
> . . . .

(Italics ours.)

The appellant contends that the statutory definition of "development" does not explicitly include clam harvesting. However, the Board found, and we find here, that it is not the goal of the appellant's activity which governs but rather it is the method employed. The appellant's operation involves the removal of earth from the bottom of the bay. In the plain and ordinary sense of the term, this procedure is "dredging." The Board found that this activity constitutes dredging; the interpretation of the Board is to be given great weight. *Hama Hama Co. v. Shorelines Hearings Bd.,* 85 Wash.2d 441, 536 P.2d 157 (1975). Furthermore, during the hearing before the Island County Planning Commission, the appellant's attorneys, the president of English Bay, an employee of English Bay, and an employee of the United States Fish and Wildlife Service all referred to appellant's machine as a "dredge."

The Shoreline Management Act is to be broadly construed in order to protect the state shorelines as fully as possible. *See* RCW 90.58.900. A liberal construction of the act is also mandated by the State Environmental Policy Act. *See* RCW 43.21C.030(1) and RCW 43.21C.020(3). The legislature expressly required that dredging operations obtain permits, and the plain and ordinary meaning of "dredging" encompasses English Bay's operation.

The appellant also contends that its operation is not a substantial development because it does not "materially interfere[s] with the normal public use of the water or shorelines. . . ." However, the record contains substantial evidence of a material interference. Additionally, the Board finding that the cost of the operation exceeds $1,000 remains unchallenged. Under RCW 90.58.030(3)(e), this alone would be sufficient to find a "substantial development."

. . . .

Finally, appellant raises the issue of whether the Department of Fisheries has the exclusive control over matters dealing with harvesting of shellfish. Appellant relies primarily upon *Simpson Timber Co. v. Olympic Air Pollution Control Authority*, 87 Wash.2d 35, 549 P.2d 5 (1976), in support of its contentions that the Department of Fisheries has exclusive control over its operation and that the Shoreline Hearings Board is without jurisdiction. That case turned on specific statutory language in the Washington Clean Air Act. RCW 70.94. There are no general principles established by this case regarding the exercise of concurrent jurisdiction by two or more state agencies. In *Simpson*, we found that the legislature intended the Department of Natural Resources to have exclusive control and authority over the types of burns listed in RCW 70.94.660 and thus preempted the area covered by that statute. This result was suggested not only by the language of RCW 70.94.660 which specifically assigns responsibility to the Department of Natural Resources for the burns listed therein, but also by the language of RCW 70.94.650(2), (3), which specifically excludes forest fires and the situations covered by RCW 70.94.660 from the responsibility of the Department of Ecology and air pollution control authorities. The Department of Fisheries' grant of authority (RCW Title 75) makes no similar grant of exclusive control over the harvesting of shellfish; the requirements of the Shoreline Management Act must be met by appellant.

We affirm the Shoreline Hearings Board and the Superior Court in all respects.

WRIGHT, C.J., and ROSELLINI, HAMILTON, STAFFORD, UTTER, BRACHTENBACH, HOROWITZ, and HICKS, JJ., concur.

NOTES

1. Is aquaculture a preferred use of Washington's shorelines? Is it a water-dependent use? *Should* aquaculture be a preferred use of Washington's shorelines?

2. Are the environmental impacts of mechanical clam harvesting cause for concern? Why did the Island County Board of Commissioners deny the Canadian corporation's application for a shoreline development permit?

3. Do aquaculture activities such as mechanical clam harvesting generally present more difficult issues of coastal management policy than marinas? If so, why? Does the Washington Shoreline Management Act provide an adequate basis for decision making about aquaculture? Why or why not?

4. The National Aquaculture Policy, Planning, and Development Act, 16 U.S.C. §§ 2801–10, called for a study of regulatory constraints on aquaculture. *See* 16 U.S.C. § 2808. Based on English Bay, would you cite the Washington Shoreline Management Act as a regulatory constraint on aquaculture? *See generally* G. Boden, *Coastal Aquaculture Law and Policy: A Case Study of California* (1980); L. Feldman, Effects of the Costs Imposed by the Regulatory Permit Process on California's Coastal Aquaculture Industry (1978); D. Hornstein, Salmon Ranching in Oregon: State and Federal Regulations (1980); T. Kane, *Aquaculture and the Law* (1970); McGlew & Brown, *Legal and Institutional Factors Affecting Mariculture in Texas*, 6 Coastal Zone Mgmt. J. 69 (1979); W. McNeil & J. Bailey, *Salmon Rancher's Manual* (1975).

5. For purposes of clam harvesting, English Bay Enterprises leased the beds of some Washington tidelands outside established harbor lines. But article XV of the Washington constitution provides that "the state shall never give, sell or lease to any private person, corporation or association any rights whatever in the waters beyond such harbor lines ...." Are the leases to English Bay valid? Consider the following excerpt from the Washington Harbor Line Commission et al., The 1972 Harbor Area Study: A Report to the 43rd Legislature of the State of Washington 31–32 (1972):

An argument can be made from the language that the remainder of Puget Sound, for example, "lies beyond" the harbor lines of Bellingham, Everett, Seattle, Tacoma and the other Sound ports where lines have been drawn. If so, then there are unconstitutional uses being made of any area of the bed of Puget Sound leased to private parties under the statutes allowing leases of the beds of navigable waters. Also railroads or other private organizations could not put a bridge pier in a navigable river beyond the outer harbor line nor could a gas company, power company, or telephone company lay cables or pipelines on the bed under a literal interpretation.

There are no cases construing the language cited above but it is clear that in practice a literal interpretation has not been given to the words. There are, of course, bridge piers beyond harbor lines and power and telephone lines are laid in many areas across the beds of navigable waters. There are also wharves built on leased areas of the beds of the state's navigable waters and aquaculture leases have been granted.

This problem has been considered in only one source, an Attorney General's Opinion [1963–64 AGO No. 46] on the legality of leasing the beds of navigable waters for oil exploration. The conclusion of the Attorney General was that such leasing was valid since the intent of the Constitution was to protect marine commerce and not to stifle other marine activities. A second reason given was that the Constitution speaks in terms of prohibiting the granting of rights in the waters beyond the harbor lines, not the beds. In other words the opinion drew a distinction between leasing the bed and the water column above it. This distinction should prove awkward now that there is a statute authorizing aquaculture projects and several of the projects in existence involve the use of the water column instead of the bed of the navigable waters.

Index